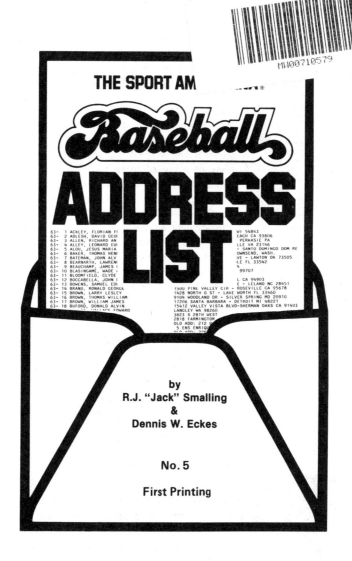

THE SPORT AM ...®

Baseball
ADDRESS
LIST

by
R.J. "Jack" Smalling
&
Dennis W. Eckes

No. 5

First Printing

ISBN 0937424-40-4

ABOUT THE AUTHORS

Jack Smalling has been an avid autograph collector for eighteen years and a card collector for more than thirty years. His collection of big league autographs is one of the best in the country. Reproductions of many of these signatures appear in this publication. He was educated at Iowa State University, obtaining a B.S. in Modern Languages and an M. Ed. in School Administration. His athletic activities have included officiating for twenty years—football, basketball and baseball. After a successful high school baseball career, he played thirteen years at the semi-pro level. A teaching and coaching career of fifteen years ended in 1979 when he joined the Compass Insurance Agency, Ltd., in Ames, IA, to sell commercial and personal lines of insurance. He and his wife, Marge, have four sons.

Denny Eckes has been an avid fan of baseball for as long as he can remember. In 1976, he founded Den's Collectors Den, one of the largest and most reputable sports memorabilia establishments in the country. Mr. Eckes holds a B.S. degree in chemistry and an M.B.A. degree in quantative methods, both from the University of Maryland. Before the establishment of Den's Collectors Den, he held positions as research chemist, information analyst, scheduling engineer, and program manager for a large engineering firm. Among his other published works are *The Sport Americana Baseball Card Price Guide, The Sport Americana Football, Hockey, Basketball and Boxing Card Price Guide, The Sport Americana Alphabetical Baseball Card Checklist, The Sport Americana Baseball Card Team Checklist, The Sport Americana Memorabilia and Autograph Price Guide,* and *The Sport Americana Price Guide to the Non-Sports Cards.* In all, Mr. Eckes has authored nearly 40 sucessful books.

THE SPORT AMERICANA
BASEBALL ADDRESS LIST
NO. 5

TABLE OF CONTENTS

PREFACE

This book concentrates on the personal signatures or autographs of baseball players. We attempt to provide the background, explanations, and wherewithal for a collector to begin or augment his collection. Many illustrations taken from what we believe are authenic signatures are presented for your observation. Some helpful hints are provided so that your autograph hunting pursuits may be simplified and fruitful.

When reading and using this book, please keep in mind the moral and legal rights of the ballplayers themselves. Some are more cooperative than others, some have more time to comply with your requests than others, but all are entitled to respect, privacy, and the right to affix or not affix his signature based on his own personal thoughts or moods.

There might be nothing more distinctive and personal that a person may do throughout his life than write his own name. This signature, how it changes from childhood to senility, its thin or broad stroke, its clarity, neatness, and readability is a reflexion of the character, mood, and personality of the signer. Perhaps for these reasons, a person's signature has become his universally accepted mark for identification, acknowledgement, and legal and contractual agreement.

As these addresses are under constant update because of the transient nature of the society in which we live, we should appreciate any information you can provide concerning the validity of the information and addresses contained herein. Please send all correspondence concerning address corrections, changes of address or death notices to:

R.J. "Jack" Smalling
2308 Van Buren Avenue
Ames, IA 50010

We hope this edition of the Sport Americana Baseball Address List provides a useful, interesting and enjoyable tool for your autograph and baseball historical pursuits.

Sincerely,

Jack Smalling
Denny Eckes

AUTHENTICITY

One of the enjoyable features of collecting autographs is knowing that one possesses an original mark made by another human being, a human being who for one reason or another has distinguished him or herself in the eyes of the collector. Facsimile autographs, autographs signed by someone other than the one whose name appears on the autograph, or photographs or copies of autographs do not comply with the definition of a true autograph; hence, they are of no value to the collector.

The only way one can be absolutely sure that an autograph is authentic is to personally witness the signer as he affixes his autograph. Practically speaking, were directly obtained autographs the only ones collected, logistic problems would prevent anyone from having but a modest collection. While authenticity can only be assured by directly obtaining autographs, many sources offer a high probability that an autograph is valid.

Knowing how a person's signature is supposed to look is a first step toward ascertaining authenticity. Facsimile autographs to compare with ones you are attempting to validate can be found on baseball cards, in books or magazines, or quite possibly, from the many facsimile autographs found in the text of this book. The reputation of the secondary source (dealer, friend, other collector) from whom you are obtaining the autograph is of utmost importance. Unfortunately, even the most reputable source may be unaware that he possesses a non-legitimate autograph.

Obtaining an autograph from a logical source increases the probability that an autograph is authentic. Other variables being equal, a resident of Boston is much more likely to have a valid autograph of a Red Sox player than is a resident of Butte, MT. A seventy-year old is much more likely to possess an autographed Babe Ruth ball than is a twelve-year old. Autographs obtained from the estate or from personal friends of the autographer are highly likely to be authentic. Autographs from financial or legal documents, such as cancelled checks or contracts, or any notarized communications can be considered authentic.

HOW TO OBTAIN AUTOGRAPHS

Although the text of this book is intended to provide the information necessary to obtain autographs through the mail, there are other ways to obtain autographs of ballplayers. There are basically two general categories by which you can obtain an autograph—first hand or directly, where you actually watch the ballplayer affix his signature, and second hand or indirectly, where you are not present at the time the ballplayer signs the autograph. As autograph collectors place such a high concern on authenticity, obtaining autographs first hand is preferential. Practically speaking, some autographs are impossible to obtain first hand, while many others are near impossible or at best very difficult to obtain first hand; hence, most collectors obtain a considerable portion of their collections via the indirect method.

OBTAINING AUTOGRAPHS FIRST HAND

The most obvious place to obtain a ballplayer's autograph is at the ballpark. The traditional crowd around the clubhouse awaiting the departure of their favorite players after the game, pens and papers in hands, is still perhaps the most viable means to obtain autographs. Many clubs provide special nights at the ballparks where, before the game, fans are encouraged to chat, photograph, and obtain autographs from the local team members who are available for these activities for the time periods specified.

Local merchants sometimes sponsor promotional activities at their establishments and feature a ballplayer as the guest celebrity. The ballplayer is normally available to sign autographs, and the merchants might well provide a medium (photo, postcard, etc.) for obtaining the autograph.

Other opportunities arise at hotels, airports, celebrity dinners or other public places where a ballplayer might chance to be during the course of his normal routine. However, we must emphasize again the necessity for patience and politeness when requesting an autograph in person from a ballplayer. Quite often time may allow only a few or no signatures to be signed before the ballplayer's schedule requires him to halt the autograph activities.

More and more over the past few years, the many sports collectibles conventions and shows held across the country have been featuring guest baseball players. These shows provide excellent opportunities for obtaining autographs from some of the most popular ballplayers.

Each year the Baseball Hall of Fame in Cooperstown, NY, holds induction ceremonies for newly elected members. Not only do the newly elected members attend, but also many of the members who have been previously elected are in attendance. There is probably no other time or place that occurs during the year when one can obtain, in person, as many living HOFer autographs as on induction day in Cooperstown.

OBTAINING AUTOGRAPHS INDIRECTLY

Most collectors, by necessity, obtain the bulk of their collections indirectly. Trading with other collectors, purchasing from dealers, purchasing from private parties, or bidding at auction from estate liquidations, hobby paper ads, or at sports collectibles conventions are the most prevalent methods which do not involve the sports personality himself. The most common way to obtain an autograph from the sports personality without the presence of the sports personality is through the mail. It is for this purpose that the SPORT AMERICANA BASEBALL ADDRESS LIST is most useful.

Autograph collecting is a reasonably popular hobby. It is not uncommon to find other collectors with autograph interests similar to yours. It is also not uncommon to find collectors who posses more than one autograph of the same player, a duplicate which they can be convinced to part with in exchange for an autograph which they desire but do not possess— one which you yourself may have in duplicate. These conditions form the basis for trade negotiations from which both parties can obtain satisfaction. Most trading is not quite this simple; however, the underlying motives of all tradings are to obtain something you do not posses and desire to have for something you have but do not place such a high value on as you do the item you desire to obtain.

3

Dealers in autographed material exist just as they do for any collectible. Many specialize in particular types of autographs. In any event, these dealers have acquired autograph material and are willing to sell it at a given price (a price which may or may not be negotiable). These dealers can be found at sports collectibles conventions, at local flea markets, and from advertisements in the hobby papers or autograph oriented periodicals (including this book).

A check of your local newspapers, particular the auction section of the Sunday editions, is an excellent way to become aware of estate and private party autograph sales and auctions. The auction method offers you the opportunity to obtain autographs you desire for amounts less than you might pay to a dealer. In fact, because of the scarcity of certain autographs, the auction method may be the only available way to obtain a particular autograph. In such cases a fair market value might not be known, and the auction offers a means to arrive at a price based on the value of the autograph to the collector.

OBTAINING AUTOGRAPHS THROUGH THE MAIL

A large number of active and retired baseball players honor autograph requests made through the mail. One of the prime purposes of compiling this book is to provide the collector with the wherewithal to obtain autographs he or she desires through the mails. The authors do not profess to know all players who will comply with your autograph requests nor those who will not comply. The authors also do not promote or sanction any harassment or excessive requests on your part of the ballplayers contacted through the addresses found in this Address List. To the contrary, we emphatically suggest a polite, patient and respectful course in obtaining autographs through the mail.

Ballplayers, particularly active players during the baseball season, have schedules much tighter and more regimented than the normal 9 to 5 worker. Mail they receive may not be opened for lengthy periods. Many schedule limited time periods that they devote to autograph requests. Quite possibly, dependent on the number of autograph requests a particular player receives, your autograph request might not be answered for a considerable period of time. Be patient. The authors know of cases where years have elapsed before an autograph request was returned.

Like everyone else, ballplayers are human beings and appreciate politeness. Words such as "please" and "thank you" are as pleasantly received and as revered by ballplayers as they are by parents of teenagers (fortunately, ballplayers hear them much more often). Excessive requests, imperative tones, and impoliteness are justifiably scorned.

Some ballplayers do not honor autograph requests, either in person or through the mail. Some do not even accept mail, and your letter may come back marked "refused." Some change their autographing philosophies over the years, becoming more liberal or conservative in their autographing habits. Whatever a player's thoughts or ideas are on accepting or rejecting autograph requests, they should be respected.

The mechanics of obtaining autographs through the mail are quite simple. Send the request, postpaid, to the ballplayer, including a politely written request outlining what you are asking of the ballplayer, any material that you wish to have autographed, and a SASE (self-addressed stamped envelope) large enough to contain the material you wish to be autographed and returned to you. Never send an autograph request postage due. To do so is presumptuous, in poor taste and completely uncalled for.

Do not send an unreasonable amount of material for autographing. A limit of three items per request has become the accepted practice of collectors. An exception to this limit is considered permissible if you have duplicates of the item you wish to have autographed, and you would like to give the ballplayer the opportunity to keep one of the duplicates for his own enjoyment. Ballplayers like most of us enjoy seeing and having interesting photos or other material concerning themselves, particularly if the item is novel or the ballplayer has never before seen it. Many collectors use this method, as a gesture of good faith and intent when requesting autographs through the mail. However, the limit of three items you wish to have signed and returned to you, exclusive of the items you wish to present to the ballplayer at his option to keep, is still the accepted standard.

It is not considered unreasonable to request a short personalization with an autograph; for example, "To John from...", or "Best Wishes to Gayle from...", etc. Requesting a two-page letter or an answer to a question that requires a dissertation is unreasonable. Do not do it.

Always include a SASE with sufficient postage to cover the material you expect might be returned to you. The SASE alleviates the need for the ballplayer to package and address your reply himself; it enables you to pay, as you should, for return postage; and it assures that the reply will be sent to the party requesting it (assuming you can competently write your own address on an envelope).

VALUES

The authors have purposely avoided any reference to price in the text of this book. Like other collectibles, there is a definite price structure for the autographs of ballplayers. Without printing prices for the autographs of specific ballplayers, we should like to present a discussion of values within a context of scarcity and desirability, which when all results are in, are the prime determinants of value for any collectible.

LIVING OR DECEASED

Like artists and martyrs, the values of whose accomplishments during their lifetimes is magnified and glorified after death, the value of a ballplayer's autograph increases considerable after his death. The deseased ballplayer can no longer, of course, sign autographs; hence, the supply of the autograph of this player ceases at this point in time. All autographs of deceased ball-players must be obtained second hand after his death, making authenticity questionable.

HALL OF FAME MEMBERS

The pinnacle of success for a ballplayer is election to baseball's Hall of Fame. This honor is limited to the most skillful and proficient players and those others who have made the most significant contributions to the game. The autographs of these men are among the most desireable and have, other factors being equal, the highest value to collectors.

POPULARITY AND NOTORIETY

While popularity can generally be measured by ballplaying skill, there are certainly exceptions. Many ballplayers whose skill on the field was limited, have achieved success and notoriety in other walks of life (William A. "Billy" Sunday, Joe Garagiola, Chuck Connors, Jim Thorpe to name but a few). The more popular the ballplayer, whether his popularity was derived by playing skill or by some other means, the higher the value placed on his autograph.

CONDITION AND TYPE OF AUTOGRAPH

Autographs, like other collectibles, exist in various physical conditions— from the weekest, broken pencil autograph to the boldest, unbroken indelable ink signature. The higher value is placed on the better condition autograph of the same person. Many types of media are available on which to obtain autographs. There are the relatively bland cuts and 3 X 5 varieties at one end of the spectrum and the most elaborate pieces of one of a kind items autographed by the player portrayed at the other end. In between there is a muriad of possible forms and designs that the autograph medium may take. The same autograph has a higher value based on the more interesting, enjoyable and attractive medium on which the autograph is written.

NEW IN THIS EDITION OF THE ADDRESS LIST

The Address List contains over 10,000 entries. The players new to the big leagues in 1986 and 1987 have been added with their corresponding debut years and numbers. Address corrections have been made, and obituary data has been supplied for those who have died since the last edition. In total, over 2,000 additions and corrections have been made.

SPORT AMERICANA PUBLICATIONS

The Number One Publisher of Reference Works for Sports Memorabilia and Trading Card Collectors

Baseball Card Price Guide No. 10 . . . .$ 12.95

Football, Hockey, Basketball & Boxing
    Card Price Guide No. 5 . . . .$ 12.95

Baseball Address List No. 5 (The Autograph
    Hunter's Best Friend) . . . .$ 10.95

Price Guide to the Non-Sports Cards No. 3, Part 2 . . .$ 12.95

Alphabetical Baseball Card Checklist No. 3 . . . .$ 9.95

Team Baseball Card Checklist No. 3 . . . .$ 9.95

Price Guide to Baseball Collectibles No. 2 . . . .$ 12.95

MAJOR LEAGUE TEAM ADDRESSES

BASEBALL COMMISSIONER'S OFFICE
Peter V. Ueberroth, Commissioner
350 Park Avenue
New York, NY 10022
(212) 371-2211

AMERICAN LEAGUE OFFICE
Robert W. Brown, President
350 Park Avenue
New York, NY 10022
(212) 371-7600

BALTIMORE ORIOLES
Edward Bennett Williams, Chairman, President
Memorial Stadium
Baltimore, MD 21218
(301) 243-9800

BOSTON RED SOX
Jean R. Yawkey, President
Fenway Park
4 Yawkey Way
Boston, MA 02215
(617) 267-9440

CALIFORNIA ANGELS
Gene Autry, Chairman, President
Anaheim Stadium
P.O. Box 2000
Anaheim, CA 92803
(714) 937-6700

CHICAGO WHITE SOX
Jerry Reinsdorf, Chairman
Eddie Einhorn, President
Comiskey Park
324 West 35th Street
Chicago, IL 60616
(312) 924-1000

CLEVELAND INDIANS
Richard E. Jacobs, Chairman
Hank Peters, President
Cleveland Stadium
Cleveland, OH 44114
(216) 861-1200

DETROIT TIGERS
John E. Fetzer, Chairman
James A. Campbell, President
Tiger Stadium
2121 Trumbull Avenue
Detroit, MI 48216
(313) 962-4000

KANSAS CITY ROYALS
Ewing Kauffman, Chairman
Joseph R. Burke, President
Royals Stadium
P.O. Box 419969
Kansas City, MO 64141
(816) 921-2200

MILWAUKEE BREWERS
Allan H. "Bud" Selig, President
Milwaukee County Stadium
201 South 46th Street
Milwaukee, WI 53214
(414) 933-7323

MINNESOTA TWINS
Carl R. Pohlad, Owner
Jerry Bell, Jr., President
Hubert H. Humphrey Metrodome
501 Chicago Avenue South
Minneapolis, Minnesota 55415
(612) 375-1366

NEW YORK YANKEES
George M. Steinbrenner, Principal Owner
Yankee Stadium
East 161st Street and River Avenue
Bronx, NY 10451
(212) 293-4300

OAKLAND A'S
Walter J. Haas, Jr., Owner
Oakland-Alameda County Coliseum
P.O. Box 2220
Oakland, CA 94621
(415) 638-4900

SEATTLE MARINERS
George R. Argyros, Chairman
Charles G. Armstrong, President
The Kingdome
P.O. Box 4100
Seattle, WA 98104
(206) 628-3555

TEXAS RANGERS
Eddie Chiles, Chairman
Michael H. Stone, President
Arlington Stadium
P.O. Box 1111
Arlington, TX 76010
(817) 273-5222

TORONTO BLUE JAYS
R. Howard Webster, Chairman
Exhibition Stadium
Box 7777, Adelaide Street P.O.
Toronto, Ontario, Canada M5C 2K7
(416) 595-0077

NATIONAL LEAGUE OFFICE
A. Bartlett Giamatti, President
350 Park Ave.
New York, NY 10022
(212) 371-7300

ATLANTA BRAVES
William C. Batholomay, Chairman
Stanley H. Kasten, President
Atlanta-Fulton County Stadium
P.O. Box 4064
Atlanta, GA 30312
(404) 522-7630

CHICAGO CUBS
John W. Madigan, Chairman
Wrigley Field
1060 West Addison Street
Chicago, IL 60613
(312) 281-5050

CINCINNATI REDS
Marge Schott, President
Riverfront Stadium
100 Riverfront Stadium
Cincinnati, OH 45202
(513) 421-4510

HOUSTON ASTROS
John J. McMullen, Chairman
The Astrodome
P.O. Box 288
Houston, TX 77001
(713) 799-9500

LOS ANGELES DODGERS
Peter O'Malley, President
Dodger Stadium
1000 Elysian Park Avenue
Los Angeles, CA 90012
(213) 224-1500

MONTREAL EXPOS
Charles R. Bronfman, Chairman
Claude R. Brochu, President
Olympic Stadium
P.O. Box 500, Station 'M'
Montreal, Quebec, Canada H1V 3P2
(514) 253-3434

NEW YORK METS
Nelson Doubleday, Chairman
Fred Wilpon, President
William A. Shea Stadium
126th Street & Roosevelt Avenue
Flushing, NY 11368
(212) 507-6387

PHILADELPHIA PHILLIES
William Y. Giles, President
Veterans Stadium
P.O. Box 7575
Philadelphia, PA 19101
(215) 463-6000

PITTSBURGH PIRATES
Douglas D. Danforth, Chairman
Carl F. Bargar, President
Three Rivers Stadium
P.O. Box 7000
Pittsburgh, PA 15212
(412) 323-5000

SAINT LOUIS CARDINALS
August A. Busch, Jr., Chairman, President
Busch Stadium
P.O. Box 8787
250 Stadium Plaza
St. Louis, MO 63102
(314) 421-4040

SAN DIEGO PADRES
Mrs. Joan Kroc, Chairwoman
Charles D. "Chub" Feeney, President
San Diego/Jack Murphy Stadium
P.O. Box 2000
San Diego, CA 92120
(619) 283-7294

SAN FRANCISCO GIANTS
Robert A. Lurie, Chairman
Al Rosen, President
Candlestick Park
San Francisco, CA 94124
(415) 468-3700

TRIPLE A LEAGUE TEAM ADDRESSES

AMERICAN ASSOCIATION
Ken Grandquist, President
P.O. Box 608
Grove City, OH 43123
(614) 871-0800

BUFFALO BISONS
Robert E. Rich, Jr., Chairman, President
Pilot Field
P.O. Box 538, Station "G"
Buffalo, NY 14213
(716) 878-8215

DENVER ZEPHYRS
Robert Howsam, Jr., President
Mile High Stadium
2850 West 20th Avenue
Denver, CO 80211
(303) 433-8645

INDIANAPOLIS INDIANS
Max B. Schumacher, President
Owen J. Bush Stadium
1501 West 16th Street
Indianapolis, IN 46202
(317) 632-5371

IOWA CUBS
Ken Grandquist, President
Sec Taylor Stadium
2nd & Riverside Drive
Des Moines, Iowa 50309
(515) 243-6111

LOUISVILLE REDBIRDS
Gene P. Gardner, President
Cardinal Stadium
P.O. Box 36407
Louisville, KY 40233
(502) 367-9121

NASHVILLE SOUNDS
Larry Schmittou, President
Herschel Greer Stadium
P.O. Box 23290
Nashville, TN 37202
(615) 242-4371

OKLAHOMA CITY 89ers
Allie Reynolds, Chairman
Patty Cox-Hampton, President
All Sports Stadium
P.O. Box 75089
Oklahoma City, OK 73147
405) 946-8989

OMAHA ROYALS
Irving Cherry, President
Rosenblatt Stadium
P.O. Box 3665
Omaha, NE 68103
(402) 734-2550

INTERNATIONAL LEAGUE
Harold Cooper, President
P.O. Box 608
Grove City, OH 43123
(614) 871-1300

COLUMBUS CLIPPERS
Donald A. Borror, President
Cooper Stadium
1155 West Mound Street
Columbus, OH 43223
(614) 462-5250

MAINE PHILLIES
John McGee, President
The Ballpark
P.O. Box 599
Old Orchard Beach, ME 04064
(207) 934-4561

PAWTUCKET RED SOX
Bernard G. Mondor, Chairman
Mike Tamburro, President
McCoy Stadium
P.O. Box 2365
Pawtucket, RI 02860
(401) 724-7300

RICHMOND BRAVES
William C. Batholomay, Chairman
Stanley H. Kasten, President
The Diamond
P.O. Box 6667
Richmond, VA 23220
(804) 359-4444

ROCHESTER RED WINGS
Anna B. Silver, Chairman
Fred Strauss, President
Silver Stadium
500 Norton Street
Rochester, NY 14621
(716) 467-3000

SYRACUSE CHIEFS
Royal O'Day, Chairman
Donald R. Waful, President
MacArthur Stadium
Syracuse, NY 13208
(315) 474-7833

TIDEWATER TIDES
Richard J. Davis, President
Met Park
P.O. Box 12111
Norfolk, VA 23502
(804) 461-5600

TOLEDO MUD HENS
Nel Skeldon, Chairman, President
Lucas County Recreation Center
2901 Key Street
Maumee, OH 43547
(419) 893-9483

PACIFIC COAST LEAGUE
William S. Cutler, President
2101 East Broadway, No. 35
Tempe, Arizona 85282
(602) 967-7679

ALBUQUERQUE DUKES
Robert Lozinak, Chairman
Pat McKernan, President
Albuquerque Sports Stadium
P.O. Box 26267
Albuquerque, NM 87125
(505) 243-1791

CALGARY CANNONS
Russel A. Parker, President
Foothills Stadium
P.O. Box 3690, Station B
Calgary, Alberta, Canada T2M 4M4
(403) 284-1111

COLORADO SPRINGS SKY SOX
David G. Elmore, Chairman
Fred Whitacre, President
Sand Creek Community Park
Colorado Springs, CO 80907
(303) 598-7656

EDMONTON TRAPPERS
Peter Pocklington, Owner
Mel Kowalchuk, President
John Ducey Park
10233 96th Avenue
Edmonton, Alberta, Canada T5K 0A5
(403) 429-2934

LAS VEGAS STARS
Larry Koentopp, Chairman, President
Cashman Field
850 Las Vegas Blvd. North
Las Vegas, NV 89101
(702) 386-7200

PHOENIX FIREBIRDS
Martin Stone, Chairman
Phoenix Municipal Stadium
5999 East Van Buren Street
Phoenix, AZ 85008
(602) 275-0500

PORTLAND BEAVERS
Joe Buzas, President
Portland Civic Stadium
1844 SW Morrison Avenue
Portland, OR 97207
(503) 233-2837

TACOMA TIGERS
Michael A. Tucci, Chairman
Stan Naccarato, President
Cheney Stadium
P.O. Box 11087
Tacoma, WA 98411
(206) 752-7707

TUCSON TOROS
William Yuill, Owner
Hi Corbett Field
P.O. Box 27045
Tucson, AZ 85726
(602) 215-2621

VANCOUVER CANADIANS
Norman Seagram, Chairman
Jack Beach, President
Nat Bailey Stadium
4601 Ontario Street
Vancouver, B.C., Canada V5V 3H4
(604) 872-5232

HOW TO USE THE SPORT AMERICANA BASEBALL ADDRESS LIST

The Address List is composed of four sections:

1. Players in the Baseball Hall of Fame
2. Players who debuted from 1910 to 1987
3. Umpires who debuted from 1910 to 1987
4. Coaches with no big league playing experience who debuted from 1910 to 1987

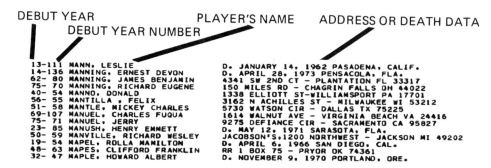

DEBUT YEAR   PLAYER'S NAME   ADDRESS OR DEATH DATA

      DEBUT YEAR NUMBER

```
13-111 MANN, LESLIE                    D. JANUARY 14, 1962 PASADENA, CALIF.
14-136 MANNING, ERNEST DEVON           D. APRIL 28, 1973 PENSACOLA, FLA.
62- 80 MANNING, JAMES BENJAMIN         4341 SW 2ND CT - PLANTATION FL 33317
75- 70 MANNING, RICHARD EUGENE         150 MILES RD - CHAGRIN FALLS OH 44022
40- 54 MANNO, DONALD                   1338 ELLIOTT ST-WILLIAMSPORT PA 17701
56- 55 MANTILLA , FELIX                3162 N ACHILLES ST - MILWAUKEE WI 53212
51- 58 MANTLE, MICKEY CHARLES          5730 WATSON CIR - DALLAS TX 75225
69-107 MANUEL, CHARLES FUQUA           1614 WALNUT AVE - VIRGINIA BEACH VA 24416
75- 71 MANUEL, JERRY                   9275 DEFIANCE CIR - SACRAMENTO CA 95827
23- 85 MANUSH, HENRY EMMETT            D. MAY 12, 1971 SARASOTA, FLA.
50- 59 MANVILLE, RICHARD WESLEY        JACOBSON'S,1200 NORTHWEST - JACKSON MI 49202
19- 54 MAPEL, ROLLA HAMILTON           D. APRIL 6, 1966 SAN DIEGO, CAL.
48- 63 MAPES, CLIFFORD FRANKLIN        RR 1 BOX 75 - PRYOR OK 74361
32- 47 MAPLE, HOWARD ALBERT            D. NOVEMBER 9, 1970 PORTLAND, ORE.
```

The address portion of the listing contains the known current address of the player if the player is now living or information as follows:

> ADDRESS NOT KNOWN—An old address is given for players for whom a current address is not known. In many cases, the year the address was last valid is shown in the data. Birth information is given if no other data is available. If no information is known about a player except his name, a blank space will appear in the address portion of the listing.

> DECEASED PLAYERS—The date and place of a player's death will be listed for deceased players. Incomplete death data is given for some players because complete information is not known. The abbreviation D. with no other information in the address portion of the listing indicates that a player is reportedly deceased, but that no other data is available.

PLEASE NOTE:
> Managers who never appeared in a big league game are listed with the year they first managed in the big leagues.
> Only those coaches who never appeared in a big league game are listed in the coaches section.
> The abbreviations used for states on addresses are standard U.S. Postal Service abbreviations.
> B. indicates born, D. indicates deceased, and other abbreviations are self-explanatory as they are used in normal written communications.

As this nation is known to be a nation of transients, one can expect that the addresses of a considerable number of the ballplayers listed will become invalid over the course of the next year or two.

BASEBALL HALL OF FAME MEMBERS

HOF177 AARON, HENRY LOUIS — 1611 ADAMS DR SW - ATLANTA GA 30311
HOF 14 ALEXANDER, GROVER CLEVELAND — D. NOVEMBER 4, 1950 ST. PAUL, NEB.
HOF181 ALSTON, WALTER EMMONS 'SMOKEY' — D. OCTOBER 1, 1984 OXFORD, OHIO
HOF 17 ANSON, ADRIAN CONSTANTINE 'CAP' — D. APRIL 14, 1922 CHICAGO, ILL.
HOF185 APARICIO, LUIS ERNEST — CALLE 67 #26-82 - MARACAIBO VENEZUELA S.A.
HOF 95 APPLING, LUCIUS BENJAMIN 'LUKE' — RR 7, BRAGG RD - CUMMINGS GA 30130
HOF147 AVERILL, HOWARD EARL — D. AUGUST 16, 1983 EVERETT, WASH.
HOF 74 BAKER, JOHN FRANKLIN 'HOME RUN' — D. JUNE 28, 1963 TRAPPE, MD.
HOF119 BANCROFT, DAVID JAMES — D. OCTOBER 9, 1972 SUPERIOR, WIS.
HOF158 BANKS, ERNEST — P.O. BOX 24302 - LOS ANGELES CA 90024
HOF 63 BARROW, EDWARD GRANT — D. DECEMBER 15, 1953 PORT CHESTER, N. Y.
HOF120 BECKLEY, JACOB PETER — D. JUNE 25, 1918 KANSAS CITY, MO.
HOF141 BELL, JAMES 'COOL PAPA' — 3034 JAMES COOL PAPA BELL AVE - ST. LOUIS MO 63106
HOF 64 BENDER, CHARLES ALBERT 'CHIEF' — D. MAY 22, 1954 PHILADELPHIA, PA.
HOF127 BERRA, LAWRENCE PETER 'YOGI' — 19 HIGHLAND AVE - MONTCLAIR NJ 07042
HOF142 BOTTOMLEY, JAMES LEROY — D. DECEMBER 11, 1959 SAINT LOUIS, MO.
HOF115 BOUDREAU, LOUIS — 15600 ELLIS AVENUE - DOLTON IL 60419
HOF 29 BRESNAHAN, ROGER PATRICK — D. DECEMBER 4, 1944 TOLEDO, O.
HOF190 BROCK, LOUIS CLARK — 12595 DURBIN DRIVE - SAINT LOUIS MO 63141
HOF 30 BROUTHERS, DENNIS 'DAN' — D. AUGUST 3, 1932 EAST ORANGE, N. J.
HOF 56 BROWN, MORDECAI PETER CENTENNIAL — D. FEBRUARY 14, 1948 TERRE HAUTE, IND.
HOF 6 BULKELEY, MORGAN G. — D. NOVEMBER 6, 1922 HARTFORD, CONN.
HOF 39 BURKETT, JESSE CAIL — D. MAY 27, 1953 WORCESTER, MASS.
HOF111 CAMPANELLA, ROY — 6213 CAPISTRANO - WOODLAND HILLS CA 91367
HOF 85 CAREY, MAX GEORGE — D. MAY 30, 1976 MIAMI, FLA.
HOF 15 CARTWRIGHT, ALEXANDER JOY — D. JULY 12, 1892 HONOLULU, HAWAII
HOF 16 CHADWICK, HENRY — D. APRIL 20, 1908 BROOKLYN, N. Y.
HOF 40 CHANCE, FRANK LEROY — D. SEPTEMBER 15, 1924 LOS ANGELES, CAL.
HOF178 CHANDLER, ALBERT BENJAMIN 'HAPPY' — 191 ELM STREET - VERSAILLES KY 40383
HOF152 CHARLESTON, OSCAR MCKINLEY — D. OCTOBER 11, 1954 PHILADELPHIA, PA.
HOF 41 CHESBRO, JOHN DWIGHT — D. NOVEMBER 6, 1931 CONWAY, MASS.
HOF 31 CLARKE, FRED CLIFFORD — D. AUGUST 14, 1960 WINFIELD, KAN.
HOF 91 CLARKSON, JOHN GIBSON — D. FEBRUARY 4, 1909 CAMBRIDGE, MASS.
HOF135 CLEMENTE, ROBERTO WALKER — D. DECEMBER 31,1972 SAN JUAN, P. R.
HOF 1 COBB, TYRUS RAYMOND — D. JULY 17, 1961 ATLANTA, GA.
HOF 50 COCHRANE, GORDON STANLEY 'MICKEY' — D. JUNE 2, 1962 LAKE FOREST, ILL.

HOF 18 COLLINS, EDWARD TROWBRIDGE SR. — D. MARCH 25, 1951 BOSTON, MASS.
HOF 32 COLLINS, JAMES JOSEPH — D. MARCH 6, 1943 BUFFALO, N. Y.
HOF116 COMBS, EARLE BRYAN — D. JULY 21, 1976 RICHMOND, KY.
HOF 19 COMISKEY, CHARLES ALBERT — D. OCTOBER 26, 1931 EAGLE RIVER, WIS.
HOF143 CONLAN, JOHN BERTRAND 'JOCKO' — 7810 EAST MARIPOSA DR - SCOTTSDALE AZ 85251
HOF153 CONNOLLY, THOMAS HENRY — D. APRIL 28, 1961 NATICK, MASS.
HOF 65 CONNOR, ROGER — D. JANUARY 4, 1931 WATERBURY, CONN.
HOF112 COVELESKI, STANLEY ANTHONY — D. MARCH 20, 1984 SOUTH BEND, IND.
HOF 82 CRAWFORD, SAMUEL EARL — D. JUNE 15, 1968 HOLLYWOOD, CALIF.
HOF 80 CRONIN, JOSEPH EDWARD — D. SEPTEMBER 7, 1984 OSTERVILLE, MASS.
HOF 20 CUMMINGS, WIILLIAM ARTHUR 'CANDY' — D. MAY 17, 1924 TOLEDO, O.
HOF108 CUYLER, HAZEN SHIRLEY 'KIKI' — D. FEBRUARY 11, 1950 ANN ARBOR, MICH.
HOF199 DANDRIDGE, RAYMOND — P.O. BOX 1139 - PALM BAY FL 32906
HOF 66 DEAN, JAY HANNA 'DIZZY' — D. JULY 17, 1974 RENO, NEV.
HOF 33 DELAHANTY, EDWARD JAMES — D. JULY 2, 1903 FORT ERIE, ONT.

HOF 71 DICKEY, WILLIAM MALCOLM
HOF159 DIHIGO, MARTIN
HOF 75 DIMAGGIO, JOSEPH PAUL
HOF194 DOERR, ROBERT PERSHING
HOF186 DRYSDALE, DONALD SCOTT
HOF 34 DUFFY, HUGH
HOF136 EVANS, WILLIAM GEORGE
HOF 42 EVERS, JOHN JOSEPH
HOF 21 EWING, WILLIAM BUCKINGHAM 'BUCK'

7611 CHOCTAW ROAD - LITTLE ROCK AR 72205
D. MAY 22, 1971 CIENFUEGOS, CUBA
2150 BEACH ST - SAN FRANCISCO CA 94123
33705 ILLAMO AGNESS RD - AGNESS OR 97406
2 LACERRA CIR - RANCHO MIRAGE CA 92270
D. OCTOBER 19, 1954 BOSTON, MASS.
D. JANUARY 23, 1956 MIAMI, FLA.
D. MARCH 28, 1947 ALBANY, N. Y.
D. OCTOBER 20, 1906 CINCINNATI, O.

HOF 96 FABER, URBAN CHARLES 'RED'
HOF 87 FELLER, ROBERT WILLIAM ANDREW
HOF187 FERRELL, RICHARD BENJAMIN 'RICK'
HOF 92 FLICK, ELMER HARRISON
HOF144 FORD, EDWARD CHARLES 'WHITEY'
HOF174 FOSTER, ANDREW "RUBE"
HOF 59 FOXX, JAMES EMORY
HOF117 FRICK, FORD CHRISTOPHER
HOF 51 FRISCH, FRANK FRANCIS
HOF102 GALVIN, JAMES F. 'PUD'
HOF 22 GEHRIG, HENRY LOUIS 'LOU'
HOF 57 GEHRINGER, CHARLES LEONARD
HOF128 GIBSON, JOSH
HOF175 GIBSON, ROBERT
HOF167 GILES, WARREN CHRISTOPHER
HOF129 GOMEZ, VERNON LOUIS 'LEFTY'
HOF109 GOSLIN, LEON ALLEN 'GOOSE'
HOF 81 GREENBERG, HENRY BENJAMIN
HOF 43 GRIFFITH, CLARK CALVIN

D. SEPTEMBER 25, 1976 CHICAGO, ILL.
BOX 157 - GATES MILLS OH 44040
2199 GOLFVIEW #203 - TROY MI 48084
D. JANUARY 9, 1971 BEDFORD, O.
38 SCHOOLHOUSE LANE - LAKE SUCCESS NY 11020
D. DECEMBER 9, 1930 KANKAKEE, ILL.
D. JULY 21, 1967 MIAMI, FLA.
D. APRIL 8, 1978 BRONXVILLE, N. Y.
D. MARCH 12, 1973 WILMINGTON, DEL.
D. MARCH 7, 1902 PITTSBURGH, PA.
D. JUNE 2, 1941 RIVERDALE, N. Y.
32301 LAHSER RD - BIRMINGHAM MI 48010
D. JANUARY 20, 1947 PITTSBURGH, PA.
215 BELLEVIEW BLVD SOUTH - BELLEVIEW NE 68005
D. FEBRUARY 7, 1979 CINCINNATI, O.
26 SAN BENITO WAY - NOVATO CA 94947
D. MAY 15, 1971 BRIDGETON, N. J.
D. SEPTEMBER 4, 1986 BEVERLY HILLS, CALIF.
D. OCTOBER 27, 1955 WASHINTON, D. C.

HOF 97 GRIMES, BURLEIGH ARLAND	D. DECEMBER 6, 1985 CLEAR LAKE, WIS.
HOF 52 GROVE, ROBERT MOSES 'LEFTY'	D. MAY 22, 1975 NORWALK, O.
HOF121 HAFEY, CHARLES JAMES 'CHICK'	D. JULY 2, 1973 CALISTOGA, CAL.
HOF118 HAINES, JESSE JOSEPH 'POP'	D. AUGUST 5, 1978 DAYTON, O.
HOF 86 HAMILTON, WILLIAM ROBERT	D. DECEMBER 16, 1940 WORCESTER, MASS.
HOF130 HARRIDGE, WILLIAM	D. APRIL 9, 1971 EVANSTON, ILL.
HOF148 HARRIS, STANLEY RAYMOND 'BUCKY'	D. NOVEMBER 8, 1977 BETHESDA, MD.
HOF 76 HARTNETT, CHARLES LEO 'GABBY'	D. DECEMBER 20, 1972 PARK RIDGE, ILL.
HOF 61 HEILMANN, HARRY EDWIN	D. JULY 9, 1951 DETROIT, MICH.
HOF149 HERMAN, WILLIAM JENNINGS BRYAN	3111 GARDEN EAST #33 - PALM BEACH GARDENS FL 33410
HOF122 HOOPER, HARRY BARTHOLOMEW	D. DECEMBER 18, 1974 SANTA CRUZ, CALIF.
HOF 27 HORNSBY, ROGERS	D. JANUARY 5, 1963 CHICAGO, ILL.
HOF113 HOYT, WAITE CHARLES	D. AUGUST 25, 1984 CINCINNATI, O.
HOF154 HUBBARD, ROBERT CAL	D. OCTOBER 16, 1977 ST PETERSBURG, FLA.
HOF 53 HUBBELL, CARL OWEN	SUNCREST APT #8,130 NORTH LESEUER #1 - MESA AZ 83205
HOF 98 HUGGINS, MILLER JAMES	D. SEPTEMBER 25, 1929 NEW YORK, N. Y.
HOF197 HUNTER, JAMES AUGUSTUS 'CATFISH'	RR 1 BOX 895 - HERTFORD NC 27944
HOF137 IRVIN, MONFORD MERRILL 'MONTE'	104 SYCAMORE CIRCLE - HOMOSASSA FL 32646
HOF179 JACKSON, TRAVIS CALVIN	D. JULY 27, 1987 WALDO, ARK.
HOF 35 JENNINGS, HUGH AMBROSE	D. FEBRUARY 1, 1928 SCRANTON, PA.
HOF 7 JOHNSON, BYRON BANCROFT 'BAN'	D. MARCH 28, 1931 ST. LOUIS, MO.
HOF 2 JOHNSON, WALTER PERRY	D. DECEMBER 10, 1946 WASHINGTON, D. C.
HOF150 JOHNSON, WILLIAM JULIUS 'JUDY'	3701 KIAMENSI - MARSHALLTON DE 19808
HOF164 JOSS, ADRIAN 'ADDIE'	D. APRIL 14, 1911 TOLEDO, O.
HOF170 KALINE, ALBERT WILLIAM	945 TIMBERLAKE DR - BLOOMFIELD HILLS MI 48013
HOF 99 KEEFE, TIMOTHY J.	D. APRIL 23, 1933 CAMBRIDGE, MASS.
HOF 23 KEELER, WILLIAM HENRY 'WEE WILLIE'	D. JANUARY 1, 1923 BROOKLYN, N. Y.
HOF182 KELL, GEORGE CLYDE	BOX 158 - SWIFTON AR 72471
HOF123 KELLEY, JOSEPH JAMES	D. AUGUST 14, 1943 BALTIMORE, MD.
HOF138 KELLY, GEORGE LANGE	D. OCTOBER 13, 1984 BURLINGAME, CALIF.
HOF 36 KELLY, MICHAEL JOSEPH	D. NOVEMBER 8, 1894 BOSTON, MASS.
HOF188 KILLEBREW, HARMON CLAYTON	BOX 626 - ONTARIO OR 97914
HOF151 KINER, RALPH MCPHERRAN	17 LEGRANDE AVENUE #17 - GREENWICH CT 06830
HOF171 KLEIN, CHARLES HERBERT	D. MARCH 28, 1958 INDIANAPOLIS, IND.
HOF 67 KLEM, WILLIAM J.	D. SEPTEMBER 16, 1951 MIAMI, FLA.
HOF131 KOUFAX, SANFORD 'SANDY'	1000 ELYSIAN PARK AVE - LOS ANGELES CA 90012
HOF 8 LAJOIE, NAPOLEON	D. FEBRUARY 7, 1959 DAYTONA BEACH, FLA.
HOF 28 LANDIS, KENESAW MOUNTAIN	D. NOVEMBER 25, 1944 CHICAGO, ILL.
HOF155 LEMON, ROBERT GRANVILLE	1141 CLAIBORNE DR-LONG BEACH CA 90807
HOF132 LEONARD, WALTER FENNER 'BUCK'	605 ATLANTIC AVE - ROCKY MOUNT NC 27801
HOF156 LINDSTROM, FRED CHARLES	D. OCTOBER 4, 1981 CHICAGO, ILL.

HOF160 LLOYD, JOHN HENRY	D. MARCH 19, 1964
HOF195 LOMBARDI, ERNEST NATALI	D. SEPTEMBER 26, 1977 SANTA CRUZ, CALIF.
HOF161 LOPEZ, ALFONSO RAMON	3601 BEACH DR - TAMPA FL 33609
HOF 77 LYONS, THEODORE AMAR	D. JULY 25, 1986 SULPHUR, LA.
HOF 9 MACK, CORNELIUS ALEXANDER 'CONNIE'	D. FEBRUARY 8, 1956 GERMANTOWN, PA.
HOF165 MACPHAIL, LELAND STANFORD 'LARRY'	D. OCTOBER 1, 1975 MIAMI, FLA.
HOF145 MANTLE, MICKEY CHARLES	5730 WATSON CIR - DALLAS TX 75225
HOF100 MANUSH, HENRY EMMETT 'HEINIE'	D. MAY 12, 1971 SARASOTA, FLA.
HOF 72 MARANVILLE, WALTER JAMES VINCENT	D. JANUARY 5, 1954 NEW YORK, N.Y.
HOF183 MARICHAL, JUAN ANTONIO SANCHEZ	3178 NW 19TH ST - MIAMI FL 33125

```
HOF124  MARQUARD, RICHARD WILLIAM 'RUBE'      D. JUNE 1, 1980 BALTIMORE, MD.
HOF166  MATHEWS, EDWIN LEE                    13744 RECUERDO DR - DEL MAR CA 92014
HOF  3  MATHEWSON, CHRISTOPHER                D. OCTOBER 7, 1925 SARANAC LAKE, N. Y.
HOF168  MAYS, WILLIE HOWARD                   51 MT VERNON LN - ATHERTON CA 94025
HOF 83  MCCARTHY, JOSEPH VINCENT              D. JANUARY 13, 1978 BUFFALO,N. Y.
HOF 44  MCCARTHY, THOMAS FRANCIS MICHAEL      D. AUGUST 5, 1922 BOSTON, MASS.
HOF196  MCCOVEY, WILLIE LEE                   P.O. BOX 620342 - WOODSIDE CA 94062
HOF 45  MCGINNITY, JOSEPH JEROME              D. NOVEMBER 14, 1929 BROOKLYN, N. Y.
HOF 10  MCGRAW, JOHN JOSEPH                   D. FEBRUARY 25, 1934 NEW ROCHELLE, N. Y.
HOF 88  MCKECHNIE, WILLIAM BOYD               D. OCTOBER 29, 1965 BRADENTON, FLA.
HOF110  MEDWICK, JOSEPH MICHAEL               D. MARCH 21, 1975 ST. PETERSBURG, FLA.
HOF176  MIZE, JOHN ROBERT                     BOX 112 - DEMOREST GA 30535
HOF114  MUSIAL, STANLEY FRANK                 85 TRENT DR - LADUE MO 63124
HOF 58  NICHOLS, CHARLES AUGUSTUS 'KID'       D. APRIL 11, 1953 KANSAS CITY, MO.
HOF 37  OROURKE, JAMES HENRY                  D. JANUARY 8, 1919 BRIDGEPORT, CONN.
HOF 60  OTT, MELVIN THOMAS                    D. NOVEMBER 21, 1958 NEW ORLEANS, LA.
HOF125  PAIGE, LEROY 'SATCHEL'                D. JUNE 8, 1982 KANSAS CITY, MO.
HOF 54  PENNOCK, HERBERT JEFFERIS             D. JANUARY 30, 1948 NEW YORK, N. Y.
'HOF 46  PLANK, EDWARD STEWART                D. FEBRUARY 24, 1926 GETTYSBURG, PA.
HOF 24  RADBOURN, CHARLES 'HOSS'              D. FEBRUARY 5, 1897 BLOOMINGTON, ILL.
HOF189  REESE, HAROLD HENRY 'PEE WEE'         3211 BEALS BRANCH RD - LOUISVILLE KY 40206
```

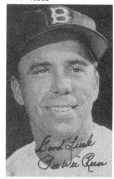

```
HOF 93  RICE, EDGAR CHARLES 'SAM'             D. OCTOBER 13, 1974 ROSSMOR, MD.
HOF105  RICKEY, WESLEY BRANCH                 D. DECEMBER 9, 1965 COLUMBIA, MO.
HOF 94  RIXEY, EPPA                           D. FEBRUARY 28, 1963 TERRACE PARK, O.
HOF157  ROBERTS, ROBIN EVAN                   504 TERRACE HILL DR - TEMPLE TERRACE FL 33617
HOF184  ROBINSON, BROOKS CALBERT              1506 SHERBROOK RD - LUTHERVILLE MD 21093
HOF180  ROBINSON, FRANK                       15557 AQUA VERDE DR - LOS ANGELES CA 90077
HOF 89  ROBINSON, JACK ROOSEVELT              D. OCTOBER 24, 1972 STAMFORD, CONN.
HOF 38  ROBINSON, WILBERT                     D. AUGUST 8, 1934 ATLANTA, GA.
HOF 90  ROUSH, EDD J                          D. MARCH 21, 1988 BRADENTON, FLA.
HOF106  RUFFING, CHARLES HERBERT 'RED'        D. FEBRUARY 17, 1986 MAYFIELD HEIGHTS, O.
HOF162  RUSIE, AMOS WILSON                    D. DECEMBER 6, 1942 SEATTLE, WASH.
HOF  4  RUTH, GEORGE HERMAN 'BABE'            D. AUGUST 16, 1948 NEW YORK, N.Y.
HOF 78  SCHALK, RAYMOND WILLIAM               D. MAY 19, 1970 CHICAGO, ILL.
HOF163  SEWELL, JOSEPH WHEELER                1618 DEARING PLACE - TUSCALOOSA AL 35401
HOF 68  SIMMONS, ALOYSIUS HARRY               D. MAY 26, 1956 MILWAUKEE, WIS.
HOF 25  SISLER, GEORGE HAROLD                 D. MARCH 26, 1973 ST. LOUIS, MO.
HOF191  SLAUGHTER, ENOS BRADSHER 'COUNTRY'    RURAL ROUTE 2 - ROXBOPO NC 27573
HOF172  SNIDER, EDWIN DONALD 'DUKE'           3037 LAKEMONT DR - FALLBROOK CA 92028
```

HOF139 SPAHN, WARREN EDWARD	RR 2 - HARTSHORNE OK 74547
HOF 26 SPALDING, ALBERT GOODWILL	D. SEPTEMBER 9, 1915 SAN DIEGO, CALIF.
HOF 11 SPEAKER, TRISTRAM E.	D. DECEMBER 8, 1958 LAKE WHITNEY, TEX.
HOF200 STARGELL, WILVER DORNEL	113 ASHLEY PLACE - STONE MOUNTAIN GA 30083
HOF103 STENGEL, CHARLES DILLON 'CASEY'	D. SEPTEMBER 29, 1975 GLENDALE, CAL.
HOF 73 TERRY, WILLIAM HAROLD	5598 FAIR LANE DRIVE - JACKSONVILLE FL 32244
HOF146 THOMPSON, SAMUEL L.	D. NOVEMBER 7, 1922 DETROIT, MICH.
HOF 47 TINKER, JOSEPH BERT	D. JULY 27, 1948 ORLANDO, FLA.
HOF 55 TRAYNOR, HAROLD JOSEPH 'PIE'	D. MARCH 16, 1972 PITTSBURGH, PA.
HOF 79 VANCE, CLARENCE ARTHUR 'DAZZY'	D. FEBRUARY 16, 1961 HOMOSASSA SPRINGS, FLA.
HOF192 VAUGHAN, JOSEPH FLOYD 'ARKY'	D. AUGUST 30, 1952 EAGLEVILLE, CALIF.

HOF 48 WADDELL, GEORGE EDWARD 'RUBE'	D. APRIL 1, 1914 SAN ANTONIO, TEX.
HOF 5 WAGNER, JOHN PETER 'HONUS'	D. DECEMBER 6, 1955 CARNEGIE, PA.
HOF 69 WALLACE, RHODERICK JOHN 'BOBBY'	D. NOVEMBER 3, 1960 TORRANCE, CAL.
HOF 49 WALSH, EDWARD AUGUSTIN	D. MAY 26, 1959 POMPANO BEACH, FLA.
HOF107 WANER, LLOYD JAMES	D. JULY 22, 1982 OKLAHOMA CITY, OKLA.
HOF 62 WANER, PAUL GLEE	D. AUGUST 29, 1965 SARASOTA, FLA.
HOF101 WARD, JOHN MONTGOMERY	D. MARCH 4, 1925 AUGUSTA, GA.
HOF126 WEISS, GEORGE MARTIN	D. AUGUST 13, 1972 GREENWICH, CONN.
HOF140 WELCH, MICHAEL FRANCIS 'MICKEY'	D. JULY 30, 1941 NASHUA, N. H.
HOF 84 WHEAT, ZACHARY DAVIS	D. MARCH 11, 1972 SEDALIA, MO.
HOF193 WILHELM, JAMES HOYT	BOX 2217 - SARASOTA FL 33578
HOF198 WILLIAMS, BILLY LEO	586 PRINCE EDWARD RD - GLEN ELLYN IL 60137
HOF104 WILLIAMS, THEODORE SAMUEL	P.O. BOX 5127 - CLEARWATER FL 34618
HOF169 WILSON, LEWIS ROBERT 'HACK'	D. NOVEMBER 23, 1948 BALTIMORE, MD.
HOF 12 WRIGHT, GEORGE	D. AUGUST 31, 1937 BOSTON, MASS.
HOF 70 WRIGHT, WILLIAM HENRY 'HARRY'	D. OCTOBER 3, 1895 ATLANTIC CITY, N. J.
HOF133 WYNN, EARLY	P.O. BOX 218 - NOKOMIS FL 34724
HOF173 YAWKEY, THOMAS AUSTIN	D. JULY 9, 1976 BOSTON, MASS.
HOF 13 YOUNG, DENTON TRUE	D. NOVEMBER 4, 1955 NEWCOMERSTOWN, O.
HOF134 YOUNGS, ROSS MIDDLEBROOK	D. OCTOBER 22, 1927 SAN ANTONIO, TEX.

PLAYERS DEBUTING FROM 1910 TO 1987

54-	1	AARON, HENRY LOUIS	1611 ADAMS DR SW - ATLANTA GA 30311
62-	1	AARON, TOMMIE LEE	D. AUGUST 16, 1984 ATLANTA, GA.
77-	1	AASE, DONALD WILLIAM	5055 VIA RICARDO - YORBA LINDA CA 92686
10-	1	ABBOTT, ODY CLEON	D. APRIL 13, 1933 WASHINGTON, D. C.
73-	1	ABBOTT, WILLIAM GLENN	4413 DAWSON - NORTH LITTLE ROCK AR 72116
50-	1	ABER, ALBERT JULIUS	7009 MEADOWBROOK AVE - CLEVELAND OH 44144
52-	1	ABERNATHIE, WILLIAM EDWARD	3395 SEPULVEDA - SAN BERNARDINO CA 92404
42-	1	ABERNATHY, TALMADGE LAFAYETTE	225 SPRING COURT - THOMASVILLE NC 27360
55-	1	ABERNATHY, THEODORE WADE	2211 ARMSTRONG PK RD - GASTONIA NC 28052
46-	1	ABERNATHY, VIRGIL WOODROW 'WOODY'	507 SOUTH KENTUCKY AVE - CHESNEE SC 29323
47-	1	ABERSON, CLIFFORD ALEXANDER	D. JUNE 23, 1973 VALLEJO, CAL.
87-	1	ABNER, SHAWN WESLEY	105 BEECHWOOD DRIVE - MECHANICSBURG PA 17055
49-	1	ABRAMS, CALVIN ROSS	BOX 974 - AMAGANSETT NY 11930
23-	1	ABRAMS, CALVIN ROSS	3012 CHERRY LANE - NORTHBROOK IL 60062
85-	1	ABREGO, JOHNNY RAY	563 WASATCH DRIVE - FREMONT CA 94536
42-	2	ABREU, JOSEPH LAWRENCE	26090 REGAL AVE - HAYWARD CA 94544
83-	1	ACKER, JAMES JUSTIN	BOX AA - FREER TX 78357
56-	1	ACKER, THOMAS JAMES	314 EVERS ST - WYCKOFF NJ 07481
63-	1	ACKLEY, FLORIAN FREDERICK 'FRITZ'	417 WEST 5TH ST - HAYWARD WI 54843
13-	1	ACOSTA, BALMADERO PEDRO 'CY'	D. NOVEMBER 17, 1963 MIAMI, FLA.
72-	1	ACOSTA, CECILIO 'CY'	AUG RAMIREZ 1420,COL GAB LEYVA-CULIACAN SINALOA MEX.
70-	1	ACOSTA, EDUARDO ELIXBET	22822 BOLTANA - MISSION VIEJO CA 92675
20-	1	ACOSTA, JOSE	OLD ADD: VUENA VISTA - MARIANAO CUBA
31-	1	ADAIR, JAMES AUBREY	D. DECEMBER 9, 1982 DALLAS, TEXAS
58-	1	ADAIR, KENNETH JERRY	D. MAY 31, 1987 TULSA, OKLA.
70-	2	ADAIR, MARION DANNE 'BILL'	1535 PINELLAS POINT S-ST PETERSBURG FL 33705
41-	1	ADAMS, ACE TOWNSEND	1005 SUMMETT DR-ALBANY GA 31705
46-	2	ADAMS, CHARLES DWIGHT 'RED'	1780 LAMBETH LANE - CONCORD CA 94518
14-	1	ADAMS, DANIEL LESLIE	D. OCTOBER 6, 1964 ST. LOUIS, MO.
22-	1	ADAMS, EARL JOHN 'SPARKY'	116 WASHINGTON ST - TREMONT PA 17981
39-	1	ADAMS, ELVIN CLARK 'BUSTER'	74390 ALLESANDRO #5 - PALM DESERT CA 92260
75-	1	ADAMS, GLENN CHARLES	RR 1 - SEDAN NM 88436
69-	1	ADAMS, HAROLD DOUGLAS 'DOUG'	1129 HARMONY CIR NE - JANESVILLE WI 53545
48-	1	ADAMS, HERBERT LOREN	903 SOUTH WILLISTON - WHEATON IL 60187
12-	1	ADAMS, JAMES IRVIN 'WILLIE'	D. JUNE 18, 1937 ALBANY, N.Y.
10-	2	ADAMS, JOHN BERTRAM	D. JUNE 24, 1940 LOS ANGELES, CALIF.
14-	2	ADAMS, KARL TUTWILER	D. SEPTEMBER 17, 1967 EVERETT, WASH.
47-	2	ADAMS, RICHARD LEROY	4650 DULIN ROAD #136 - FALLBROOK CA 92028
82-	1	ADAMS, RICKY LEE	10195 BOLTON - MONTCLAIR CA 91763
31-	2	ADAMS, ROBERT ANDREW	D. MARCH 6, 1970 JACKSONVILLE, FLA.
25-	1	ADAMS, ROBERT BURDETTE	357 WALTON ST - LEMOYNE PA 17043
46-	3	ADAMS, ROBERT HENRY	3828 PUEBLO WAY - SCOTTSDALE AZ 85251
77-	2	ADAMS, ROBERT MELVIN JR.	7653 DESOTO AVE - CANOGA PARK CA 91304
72-	2	ADAMS, ROBERT MICHAEL 'MIKE'	3828 PUEBLO WAY - SCOTTSDALE AZ 85251
23-	2	ADAMS, SPENCER DEWEY	D. NOVEMBER 25, 1970 FT. LAUDERDALE, FLA.
67-	1	ADAMSON, JOHN MICHAEL 'MIKE'	4408 SKY GLEN CT - MOORPARK CA 93021
50-	2	ADCOCK, JOSEPH WILBUR	BOX 385 - COUSHATTA LA 71019
50-	3	ADDIS, ROBERT GORDON	7466 HOLLYCROFT LN - MENTOR OH 44060
83-	2	ADDUCI, JAMES DAVID	10429 SOUTH LAMON - OAK LAWN IL 60453
39-	2	ADERHOLT, MORRIS WOODROW	D. MARCH 18, 1955 SARASOTA, FLA.
28-	1	ADKINS, GRADY EMMETT	D. MARCH 31, 1966 LITTLE ROCK, ARK.
42-	3	ADKINS, JOHN DEWEY	2627 WESTWOOD BLVD-LOS ANGELES CA 90064
42-	4	ADKINS, RICHARD EARL	D. SEPTEMBER 12, 1955 ELECTRA, TEX.
63-	2	ADLESH, DAVID GEORGE	9770 AVENIDA MONTEREY - CYPRESS CA 90630
87-	2	AFENIR, MICHAEL TROY	804 CHERRY COURT - SAN MARCOS CA 92069
62-	2	AGEE, TOMMIE LEE	POLICE DEPT.,94-41 43RD AVE - EAST ELMHURST NY 11369
54-	2	AGGANIS, HARRY	D. JUNE 27, 1955 CAMBRIDGE, MASS.
12-	2	AGLER, JOSEPH ABRAM	D. APRIL 26, 1971 MASSILLON, O.
13-	2	AGNEW, SAMUEL LESTER	D. JULY 19, 1951 SONOMA, CALIF.
81-	1	AGOSTO, JUAN R	VIA LETICIA 4LS8 - CAROLINA PR 00630
80-	1	AGUAYO, LUIS (MURIEL)	BOX 9036, SABANA BRANCH - VEGA BAJA PR 00764
85-	2	AGUILERA, RICHARD WARREN	%FRATTO,6506 HALM AVENUE - LOS ANGELES CA 90056
55-	2	AGUIRRE, HENRY JOHN	31101 SUNSET DR - FRANKLIN MI 48025
77-	3	AIKENS, WILLIE MAYS	P.O. BOX 1141 - SENECA SC 29678
79-	1	AINGE, DANIEL RAY	10 ORDWAY ROAD - WELLESLEY MA 02181
10-	3	AINSMITH, EDWARD WILBUR	D. SEPTEMBER 6, 1981 FORT LAUDERDALE, FLA.
11-	1	AITCHISON, RALEIGH LEONIDAS	D. SEPTEMBER 26, 1958 COLUMBUS, KAN.
12-	3	AITON, GEORGE WILSON 'BILL'	D. AUGUST 16, 1976 VAN NUYS, CALIF.
64-	1	AKER, JACK DELANE	11900 EDGEWATER DR #1009 - LAKEWOOD OH 44107
86-	1	AKERFELDS, DARREL WAYNE	7054 WEST ROXBURY PLACE - LITTLETON CO 80123
12-	4	AKERS, ALBERT EARL 'JERRY'	D. MAY 15, 1979 BAY PINES, FLA.
29-	1	AKERS, THOMAS ERNEST 'BILL'	D. APRIL 13, 1962 CHATTANOOGA, TENN.
58-	2	ALBANESE, JOSEPH PETER	54 LONGFELLOW DR - COLONIA NJ 07067
78-	1	ALBERTS, FRANCIS BURT 'BUTCH'	3063 AMBERLEA LN - BALDWINSVILLE NY 13027
10-	4	ALBERTS, FREDERICK JOSEPH 'CY'	D. AUGUST 27, 1917 FORT WAYNE, IND.

WILLIE MAYS AIKENS 18 OF

8" X 10" FULL—COLOR PHOTOGRAPHS

1 to 9 at $ 2.50 each plus postage & handling
10 to 24 at $ 2.00 each plus postage & handling
25 or more at $ 1.75 each plus postage & handling

RETIRED PLAYERS

Hank Aaron	Bobby Doerr (Sepia)
Dick Allen	Rocky Colavito
Walt Alston	Early Wynn
Luis Aparicio	Bill Mazerowski
Ernie Banks	Jim Bunning
Hank Bauer	Jim "Catfish" Hunter
Yogi Berra	Cookie Rojas
Lou Boudreau	Billy Williams
Lou Brock	Babe Ruth (Sepia)

Rod Carew
Orlando Cepeda
Roberto Clemente
Joe DiMaggio
Don Drysdale
Carl Erskine
Bob Feller
Whitey Ford
Bob Gibson
Elston Howard
Monte Irvin
Al Kaline
Harmon Killebrew
Ralph Kiner
Ted Kluzewski
Sandy Koufax
Bob Lemon
Al Lopez
Mickey Mantle
Juan Marichal
Roger Maris
Eddie Mathews
Willie Mays
Willie McCovey
Thurman Munson
Stan Musial
Jim Palmer
Gaylord Perry
Jim Perry
Boog Powell
Pee Wee Reese
Bobby Richardson
Phil Rizzuto
Robin Roberts
Brooks Robinson
Frank Robinson
Jackie Robinson
Red Schoendienst
Bobby Schantz
Enos Slaughter
Duke Snider
Warren Spahn
Willie Stargell
Bobby Thomson
Earl Weaver
Ted Williams
Carl Yastrzemski

TINTED PHOTOS

Ty Cobb
Bob Feller (Doug West Artwork)
Lou Gehrig

POSTAGE & HANDLING SCHEDULE
$ .01 to $ 20.00 add $ 2.00
$ 20.01 to $ 29.99 add $ 2.50
$ 30.00 to $ 49.99 add $ 3.00
$ 50.00 or more add $ 4.00

MARYLAND RESIDENTS ADD 5% SALES TAX
CANADIAN ORDERS – BOOKS ONLY
Canadian orders, orders outside the contiguous
United States, APO and FPO add 25% additional
U.S. FUNDS ONLY

MULTI—PLAYER PHOTOS

Mickey Mantle & Roger Maris
1951 Giants - Lockman, Westrum, Mays,
Irvin, Thomson, etc.
1960's Yankees Infield - Boyer, Kubek,
Richardson & Pepitone
1961 Yankee Sluggers - Maris, Berra, Mantle,
Howard, Skowron, Blanchard
1964 Cardinals Infield - Boyer, Groat,
Javier & White
1969 Mets Outfield - Agee, Jones, Swoboda

CURRENT PLAYERS

Tony Armas
Don Baylor
George Bell
Wade Boggs
George Brett
Jose Canseco
Steve Carlton
Gary Carter
Jack Clark
Will Clark
Roger Clemens
Eric Davis
Andre Dawson
Dwight Evans
Carlton Fisk
Steve Garvey
Kirk Gibson
Dwight Gooden
Ron Guidry
Tony Gwynn
Rickey Henderson
Keith Hernandez
Sam Horn
Kent Hrbek
Bo Jackson
Greg Jeffries
Wally Joyner
Ron Kittle
Dave Kingman
Fred Lynn
Bill Madlock
Don Mattingly
Willie McGee
Mark McGwire
Paul Molitor
Jack Morris
Dale Murphy
Eddie Murray
Mike Pagliarulo
Lance Parrish
Kirby Puckett
Tim Raines
Willie Randolph
Jim Rice
Dave Righetti
Cal Ripken, Jr.
Cal, Sr., Cal, Jr., Billy Ripken
Pete Rose
Nolan Ryan
Ryan Sandberg
Steve Sax
Mike Schmidt
Mike Scott
Tom Seaver
Larry Sheets
Ozzie Smith
Cory Snyder
Darryl Strawberry
Jim Traber
Alan Trammell
Fernando Valenzuela
Dave Winfield
Robin Yount

SEND
ONLY $ 1.00
for DEN'S
BIG CATALOGUE
CATALOGUE
sent FREE
with each ORDER

17

GENE ALLEY

41-	2	ALBOSTA, EDWARD JOHN	5360 FORT RD-SAGINAW MI 48601
49-	2	ALBRECHT, EDWARD ARTHUR	D. 1979 CENTERVILLE, ILL.
47-	3	ALBRIGHT, JOHN HAROLD	5433 HEWLETT DR - SAN DIEGO CA 92115
73-	2	ALBURY, VICTOR	6205 ALCOT CT - TAMPA FL 33624
76-	1	ALCALA, SANTO	RAMON MOTA #18 - SAN PEDRO DE MACORIS DOM. REP.
67-	2	ALCARAZ, ANGEL LUIS	1968 ADD: BOX 423 - HUMACAO PR 00661
14-	3	ALCOCK, JOHN FORBES 'SCOTTY'	D. JANUARY 30, 1973 WOOSTER, O.
43-	1	ALDERSON, DALE LEONARD	D. FEBRUARY 12, 1982 GARDEN GROVE, CALIF.
86-	2	ALDRETE, MICHAEL PETER	231 VIA DEL PINAR - MONTEREY CA 93940
87-	3	ALDRICH, JAY ROBERT	168 SALISBURY ROAD - WAYNE NJ 07470
17-	1	ALDRIDGE, VICTOR EDDINGTON	D. APRIL 17, 1973 TERRE HAUTE, IND.
41-	3	ALENO, CHARLES	601 MARION CT-DELAND FL 32720
29-	2	ALEXANDER, DAVID DALE	D. MARCH 2, 1979 GREENEVILLE, TENN.
71-	1	ALEXANDER, DOYLE LAFAYETTE	6412 SADDLE RIDGE ROAD - ARLINGTON TX 76016
75-	2	ALEXANDER, GARY WAYNE	5701 BOWCROFT ST - LOS ANGELES CA 90016
11-	2	ALEXANDER, GROVER CLEVELAND	D. NOVEMBER 4, 1950 ST. PAUL, NEB.
37-	1	ALEXANDER, HUGH	7211 ULMERTON RD #2159 - LARGO FL 33541
73-	3	ALEXANDER, MATTHEW	2419 STONEWALL - SHREVEPORT LA 71103
55-	3	ALEXANDER, ROBERT SOMERVILLE	350 54 EL CAMINO REAL - ENCINITAS CA 92024
12-	5	ALEXANDER, WALTER ERNEST	D. DECEMBER 29, 1978 FORT WORTH, TEXAS
86-	3	ALLANSON, ANDREW NEAL	1701 EAST 12TH STREET - CLEVELAND OH 44114
79-	2	ALLARD, BRIAN MARSHALL	110 RICHARD ST - HENRY IL 61537
14-	4	ALLEN, ARTEMUS WARD 'NICK'	D. OCTOBER 16, 1939 HINES, ILL.
62-	3	ALLEN, BERNARD KEITH	9120 MOHICAN TRAIL - NEGLEY OH 44441
26-	1	ALLEN, ETHAN NATHAN	STRATFORD HILL APTS #40C-CHAPEL HIL NC 27514
10-	5	ALLEN, FLETCHER MANSON 'SLEP'	D. OCTOBER 16, 1959 LUBBOCK, TEX.
12-	6	ALLEN, FRANK LEON	D. JULY 30, 1933 GAINESVILLE, ALA.
66-	1	ALLEN, HAROLD ANDREW 'HANK'	15 STATON DR - UPPER MARLBORO MD 20870
19-	1	ALLEN, HORACE TANNER 'PUG'	D. JULY 5, 1981 CANTON, N. C.
83-	3	ALLEN, JAMES BRADLEY 'JAMIE'	1203 FOLSOM AVE - YAKIMA WA 98902
14-	5	ALLEN, JOHN MARSHALL	D. SEPTEMBER 24, 1967 HAGERSTOWN, MD.
32-	1	ALLEN, JOHN THOMAS	D. MARCH 29, 1959 ST. PETERSBURG, FLA.
80-	2	ALLEN, KIM BRYANT	1651 N. RIVERSIDE AVE #614 - RIALTO CA 92376
69-	2	ALLEN, LLOYD CECIL	OLD ADD: 1678 MARGUERITE AVE - CORONA DEL MAR CA 92625
79-	3	ALLEN, NEIL PATRICK	1402 ARMSTRONG - KANSAS CITY KS 66102
63-	3	ALLEN, RICHARD ANTHONY	P.O. BOX 204 - SELLERSVILLE PA 18960
19-	2	ALLEN, ROBERT	B. 1896
37-	2	ALLEN, ROBERT EARL	1888 WEST AMES CIR-CHESAPEAKE VA 23321
61-	1	ALLEN, ROBERT GRAY	515 WOODLAWN - HENDERSON TX 75652
83-	4	ALLEN, RODERICK BERNET	1959 CLOVERFIELD BL #103-SANTA MONICA CA90405
72-	3	ALLEN, RONALD FREDRICK	917 WINONA DR - YOUNGSTOWN OH 44511
79-	4	ALLENSON, GARY MARTIN	95 RIVER STREET - ONEONTA NY 13820
63-	4	ALLEY, LEONARD EUGENE 'GENE'	10236 STEUBEN DRIVE - GLEN ALLEN VA 23060
54-	3	ALLIE, GAIR ROOSEVELT	1802 TOWN OAK DRIVE - SAN ANTONIO TX 78232
75-	3	ALLIETTA, ROBERT GEORGE	25 ROBINSON RD - FALMOUTH MA 02540
11-	3	ALLISON, MACK PENDLETON	D. MARCH 13, 1964 ST. JOSEPH, MO.
13-	3	ALLISON, MILO HENRY	D. JUNE 18, 1957 KENOSHA, WIS.
58-	3	ALLISON, WILLIAM ROBERT 'BOB'	2750 EAGANDALE BLVD - ST. PAUL MN 55121
33-	1	ALMADA, BALDOMERO MELO	OLD ADD: DICKENS 76, 201-POLANCO 5 MEXICO DF
11-	4	ALMEIDA, RAFAEL D.	D. MARCH, 1968 HAVANA, CUBA
74-	1	ALMON, WILLIAM FRANCIS	88 CLAFLIN COURT - WARWICK RI 02886
50-	4	ALOMA, LUIS BARBA	8414 NORTH MARMORA - MORTON GROVE IL 60053
64-	2	ALOMAR, SANTOS CONDES 'SANDY'	P.O. BOX 367 - SALINAS PR 00751
58-	4	ALOU, FELIPE ROJAS	BOX 1287 - SANTO DOMINGO DOMINICAN REP.
63-	5	ALOU, JESUS MARIA	APARTADO POSTAL 539/2 LAFARIA - SANTO DOMINGO DOM REP.
60-	1	ALOU, MATEO ROJAS	APARTADO POSTAL 30063 - SANTO DOMINGO DOMINICAN REP.
54-	4	ALSTON, THOMAS EDISON	616 ELLWOOD DR - HIGH POINT NC 27260
36-	1	ALSTON, WALTER EMMONS 'SMOKEY'	D. OCTOBER 1, 1984 OXFORD, O.
77-	4	ALSTON, WENDELL 'DEL'	17 LAMBERT RD - WHITE PLAINS NY 10605
82-	2	ALTAMARINO, PORFIRIO	B. MAY 17, 1952 ESTELI, NICARAGUA
20-	2	ALTEN, ERNEST MATTHIAS	D. SEPTEMBER 9, 1981 NAPA, CALIF.
16-	1	ALTENBURG, JESSE HOWARD	D. MARCH 12, 1973 LANSING, MICH.
59-	1	ALTMAN, GEORGE LEE	3601 BRIAR LANE - HAZEL CREST IL 60429
55-	4	ALTOBELLI, JOSEPH	17 ADEANE DR WEST - ROCHESTER NY 14624
58-	5	ALUSIK, GEORGE JOSEPH	581 GARDEN AVE - WOODRIDGE NJ 07095
68-	1	ALVARADO, LUIS CESAR	BOX 853 - LAJAS PR 00667
73-	4	ALVAREZ, JESUS ORLANDO	CUMMUNIDAD DOLORES 37 - RIO GRANDE PR 00745
81-	2	ALVAREZ, JOSE LINO	1105 ANDORA - CORAL GABLES FL 33146
58-	6	ALVAREZ, OSWALDO GONZALES 'OSSIE'	SANTUARIO 3137,COL. CHAPALITA-GUADALAJARA JALISCO MEX.
60-	2	ALVAREZ, ROGELIO	5010 NW 183RD ST - CAROL CITY FL 33055
62-	4	ALVIS, ROY MAXWELL 'MAX'	806 HUNTERWOOD DR - JASPER TX 75951
65-	1	ALYEA, BRANT RYERSON	P.O. BOX 25 - COLUMBUS NC 28722
54-	5	AMALFITANO, JOHN JOSEPH 'JOE'	3432 PECK AVE #202 - SAN PEDRO CA 90731
58-	7	AMARO, RUBEN	2333 BRICKELL AVE #616 - MIAMI FL 33129

37-	3	AMBLER, WAYNE HARPER	305 TOURNAMENT RD - PONTE VEDRA BEACH FL 32082
84-	1	AMELUNG, EDWARD ALLEN	17045 ROYAL VIEW DR - HACIENDA HEIGHTS CA 91745
55-	5	AMOR, VINCENTE ALVAREZ	3905 WEST 8TH COURT - HIALEAH FL 33012
52-	2	AMOROS, EDMUNDO ISASI 'SANDY'	1730 WINDSOR WAY - TAMPA FL 33619
15-	1	ANCKER, WALTER	D. FEBRUARY 13, 1954 ENGLEWOOD, N.J.
75-	4	ANDERSEN, LARRY EUGENE	17016 NE 2ND PL - BELLEVUE WA 98004
41-	4	ANDERSON, ALFRED WALTON	D. JUNE 23, 1985 ALBANY, GA.
86-	4	ANDERSON, ALLAN LEE	265 WHITTIER DRIVE WEST - LANCASTER OH 43130
48-	2	ANDERSON, ANDY HOLM	D. JULY 18, 1982 SEATTLE, WASH.
37-	4	ANDERSON, ARNOLD REVOLA 'RED'	D. AUGUST 7, 1972 SIOUX CITY, IA.
83-	5	ANDERSON, DAVID CARTER	5044 VIA DONALDO - YORBA LINDA CA 92686
71-	2	ANDERSON, DWAIN CLEAVEN	4996 LLANO DR - WOODLAND HILLS CA 91343
46-	4	ANDERSON, FERRELL JACK 'ANDY'	D. MARCH 12, 1978 JOPLIN, MO.
14-	6	ANDERSON, GEORGE ANDREW JENDRUS	D. MAY 28, 1962 CLEVELAND, O.
59-	2	ANDERSON, GEORGE LEE 'SPARKY'	4077 NORTH VERDE VISTA DR-THOUSAND OAKS CA 91360
32-	2	ANDERSON, HAROLD	D. MAY 1, 1974 ST. LOUIS, MO.
57-	1	ANDERSON, HARRY WALTER	4823 KENNETT PIKE - GREENVILLE DE 19807
78-	2	ANDERSON, JAMES LEA	3931 CALLE VALLE VISTA-NEWBURY PARK CA 91320
58-	8	ANDERSON, JOHN CHARLES	OLD ADD: BOX 49 - BROWNING MT 59417
82-	3	ANDERSON, KARL ADAM 'BUD'	196 WEST CYPRUS LANE - WESTBURY NY 11590

74-	2	ANDERSON, LAWRENCE DENNIS	8037 WORTHY DR - WESTMINSTER CA 92683
71-	3	ANDERSON, MICHAEL ALLEN	RR ONE - TIMMONSVILLE SC 29161
61-	2	ANDERSON, NORMAN CRAIG	RR 7, 6 WILLOWBROOK DR EAST - BETHLEHEM PA 18015
86-	5	ANDERSON, RICHARD ARLEN	3818 100TH STREET SE - EVERETT WA 98204
79-	5	ANDERSON, RICHARD LEE	3915 WEST 105TH ST - INGLEWOOD CA 90303
57-	2	ANDERSON, ROBERT CARL	4209 EAST 104TH - TULSA OK 74137
87-	4	ANDERSON, SCOTT RICHARD	5635 116TH AVENUE SOUTHEAST - BELLEVUE WA 98006
17-	2	ANDERSON, WALTER CARL	1811 MORNINGSIDE DR SE - GRAND RAPIDS MI 49506
25-	2	ANDERSON, WILLIAM EDWARD	D. MARCH 13, 1983 MEDFORD, MASS.
10-	6	ANDERSON, WINGO CHARLIE	D. DECEMBER 19, 1950 FORT WORTH, TEX.
55-	6	ANDRE, JOHN EDWARD	D. NOVEMBER 25, 1976 CENTERVILLE, MASS.
46-	5	ANDRES, ERNEST HENRY	5714 GARDEN LAKES DRIVE - BRADENTON FL 34203
75-	5	ANDREW, KIM DARRELL	10052 DENSMORE AVE - SEPULVEDA CA 91343
25-	3	ANDREWS, ELBERT DEVORE	D. NOVEMBER 25, 1979 GREENWOOD, S. C.
76-	2	ANDREWS, FRED	8239 SOUTH KINGSTON - CHICAGO IL 60617
47-	4	ANDREWS, HERBERT CARL 'HUB'	2305 2ND ST - DODGE CITY KS 67801
31-	1	ANDREWS, IVY PAUL	D. NOVEMBER 23, 1970 DORA, ALA.
73-	5	ANDREWS, JOHN RICHARD	9292 GORDON AVE - LAHABRA CA 90631
66-	2	ANDREWS, MICHAEL JAY	29 PAUL AVE - PEABODY MA 01960
37-	5	ANDREWS, NATHAN HARDY	RR 3 BOX 271 - KING NC 27021
75-	6	ANDREWS, ROBERT PATRICK	1280 MOUNTBATTEN CT - CONCORD CA 94518
39-	3	ANDREWS, STANLEY JOSEPH	3840 IRONWOOD LN #403 - BRADENTON FL 33505
31-	4	ANDRUS, WILLIAM MORGAN	D. MARCH 12, 1982 WASHINGTON, D. C.
76-	3	ANDUJAR, JOAQUIN	400 RANDAL WAY #106 - SPRING TX 77388
72-	4	ANGELINI, NORMAN STANLEY	16196 EAST BAILS PL - AURORA CO 80012
29-	3	ANGLEY, THOMAS SAMUEL	D. OCTOBER 26, 1952 WICHITA, KAN.
36-	2	ANKENMAN, FRED NORMAN 'PAT'	4014 UNDERWOOD - HOUSTON TX 77025
44-	1	ANTOLICK, JOSEPH	723 2ND ST - CATASAUQUA PA 18032
48-	3	ANTONELLI, JOHN AUGUST	12 WOODBURY PLACE - ROCHESTER NY 14618
44-	2	ANTONELLI, JOHN LAWRENCE	5539 BARFIELD RD - MEMPHIS TN 38117

53-	1	ANTONELLO, WILLIAM JAMES
56-	2	APARICIO, LUIS ERNEST
73-	6	APODACA, ROBERT JOHN
80-	3	APONTE, LUIS EDUARDO
15-	2	APPLETON, EDWARD SAMUEL
27-	1	APPLETON, PETER WILLIAM
30-	1	APPLING, LUCIUS BENJAMIN 'LUKE'
86-	6	AQUINO, LUIS ANTONIO
41-	5	ARAGON, ANGEL VALDES 'JACK'
14-	7	ARAGON, ANGEL VALDES SR. 'JACK'
23-	3	ARCHDEACON, MAURICE BRUCE
36-	3	ARCHER, FREDERICK MARVIN
61-	3	ARCHER, JAMES WILLIAM
38-	1	ARCHIE, GEORGE ALBERT
68-	2	ARCIA, JOSE RAIMUNDO
61-	4	ARDELL, DANIEL MIERS
47-	5	ARDIZOIA, RINALDO JOSEPH 'RUGGER'
48-	4	ARFT, HENRY IRVIN
59-	3	ARIAS, RODOLFO MARTINEZ 'RUDY'
31-	5	ARLETT, RUSSELL LORIS 'BUZZ'
65-	2	ARLICH, DONALD LOUIS
69-	3	ARLIN, STEPHEN RALPH
76-	4	ARMAS, ANTONIO RAFAEL
73-	7	ARMBRISTER, EDISON ROSANDER
34-	1	ARMBRUST, ORVILLE MARTIN
46-	6	ARMSTRONG, GEORGE NOBLE
11-	5	ARMSTRONG, HOWARD ELMER
80-	4	ARMSTRONG, MICHAEL DENNIS
71-	4	ARNOLD, CHRISTOPHER PAUL
86-	7	ARNOLD, TONY DALE
36-	4	ARNOVICH, MORRIS
86-	8	ARNSBERG, BRADLEY JEFF
43-	2	ARNTZEN, ORIE EDGAR
61-	5	ARRIGO, GERALD WILLIAM
75-	7	ARROYO, FERNANDO
55-	7	ARROYO, LUIS ENRIQUE
71-	5	ARROYO, RUDOLPH
86-	9	ASADOOR, RANDALL CARL
38-	2	ASBELL, JAMES MARION
28-	2	ASBJORNSON, ROBERT ANTHONY
25-	4	ASH, KENNETH LOWTHER
48-	5	ASHBURN, DON RICHARD 'RICHIE'
73-	8	ASHBY, ALAN DEAN
76-	5	ASHFORD, THOMAS STEVEN 'TUCKER'
57-	3	ASPROMONTE, KENNETH JOSEPH
56-	3	ASPROMONTE, ROBERT THOMAS
76-	6	ASSELSTINE, BRIAN HANLY
86-	10	ASSENMACHER, PAUL ANDRE
45-	1	ASTROTH, JOSEPH HENRY
83-	6	ATHERTON, KEITH ROWE
50-	5	ATKINS, JAMES CURTIS
27-	2	ATKINSON, HUBERT BURLEY 'LEFTY'
76-	7	ATKINSON, WILLIAM CECIL GLENN
26-	2	ATTREAU, RICHARD GILBERT
52-	3	ATWELL, MAURICE DAILEY 'TOBY'
36-	5	ATWOOD, WILLIAM FRANKLIN
71-	6	AUERBACH, FREDERICK STEVEN 'RICK'
73-	9	AUGUSTINE, DAVID RALPH
75-	8	AUGUSTINE, GERALD LEE
33-	2	AUKER, ELDEN LEROY
47-	6	AULDS, LEYCESTER DOYLE
76-	8	AULT, DOUGLAS REAGAN
65-	3	AUST, DENNIS KAY
70-	3	AUSTIN, RICK GERALD
76-	9	AUTRY, ALBERT

4054 VALENTINE CT - ST PAUL MN 55112
CALLE 67 #26-82 - MARACAIBO VENEZUELA S.A.
BOX 7845 - COLUMBIA SC 29202
CALLE BELLA VISTA 48-LA SABANITA,BOLIVAR VENEZUELA S.A.
D. JANUARY 27, 1932 ARLINGTON, TEX.
D. JANUARY 18, 1974 TRENTON, N.J.
RR 7, BRAGG RD - CUMMINGS GA 30130
30 S.O. 1506 CAPARRA TERRACE - RIO PIEDRAS PR 00921
P.O. BOX 596 - CLEARWATER FL 33515
D. JANUARY 24, 1952 NEW YORK, N.Y.
D. SEPTEMBER 5, 1954 ST. LOUIS, MO.
D. OCTOBER 31, 1981 CHARLOTTE, N. C.
1414 OLEANDER DR - TARPON SPRINGS FL 33589
820 MARQUETTE DRIVE - NASHVILLE TN 37205
7325 NW 3RD ST - MIAMI FL 33125
4966 PORT CLARIDGE - NEWPORT BEACH CA 92660
130 SANTA ROSA AVE - SAN FRANCISCO CA 94112
109 SUNNYSIDE LANE - BALLWIN MO 63021
3911 NW 11TH ST - MIAMI FL 33126
D. MAY 16, 1964 MINNEAPOLIS, MINN.
7877 SOUTH 73RD ST - COTTAGE GROVE MN 55016
6338 CAMINO CORTO - SAN DIEGO CA 92120
LOS MERCEDES #37,P.PIRITU EDO. - ANZOATEQUI VENEZ
MCQUAY ST, BOX 2003 - NASSAU BAHAMAS W.I.
D. OCTOBER 2, 1967 MOBILE, ALA.
16 FRANKLIN ST - EAST ORANGE NJ 07017
D. MARCH 8, 1926 CANISTEO, N.Y.
BOX 846 - HALIFAX VA 24558
2219 EL CAPITAN - ARCADIA CA 91006
1224 ELBY - IRVING TX 75061
D. JULY 20, 1959 SUPERIOR, WIS.
2450 HILLCREST ROAD - MEDFORD OR 97504
D. JANUARY 28, 1970 CEDAR RAPIDS, IA.
3740 REDTHORNE DR - AMELIA OH 45102
4917 FIRST PARKWAY - SACRAMENTO CA 95823
BOX 354 - PENUELAS PR 00724
828 SIERRA VISTA - MOUNTAIN VIEW CA 94040
1459 WEST MESA - FRESNO CA 93711
D. JULY 6, 1967 SAN MATEO, CAL.
D. JANUARY 21, 1970 WILLIAMSPORT, PA.
D. NOVEMBER 15, 1979 CLARKSBURG, W. VA.
PHILLIES ANNOUNCER - ARDMORE PA 19003
3151 COUNTRY CLUB BLVD - SUGARLAND TX 77478
502 MAPLE ST - COVINGTON TN 38019
% COORS, 10400 HARWIN - HOUSTON TX 77036
251 SUGARBERRY CIR - HOUSTON TX 77024
1488 COUNTRY CT - SANTA YNEZ CA 93460
6404 BALFOUR - ALLEN PARK MI 48101
151 SOUTH MOYER RD - CHALFONT PA 18914
ROUTE 198 BLAKES - MATHEWS VA 23020
RR 14 BOX 3635 - CULLMAN AL 35055
D. FEBRUARY 12, 1961 CHICAGO, ILL.
RR 2 - CHATHAM ONT. N7M 5S2 CAN.
D. JULY 5, 1964 CHICAGO, ILL.
BOX 686 - PURCELLVILLE VA 22132
3100 EL PASO-SNYDER TX 79549
4724 ABARGO ST - WOODLAND HILLS CA 91364
OLD ADD: 14850 SW 280TH ST #25-HOMESTEAD FL
569 WEST 13442 HALES PK CT-HALES CORNER WI 53130
15 SAILFISH RD - VERO BEACH FL 32960
YANCEY STAR RT BOX 16 - HONDO TX 78861
2990 BONAVENTURE CIRCLE - PALM HARBOR FL 33563
6917 SENOJ STREET - TAMPA FL 33610
BOX 347 - BROOKFIELD MO 64628
1119 PRINCETON - MODESTO CA 95350

24-	1	AUTRY, MARTIN GORDON
56-	4	AVERILL, EARL DOUGLAS
29-	4	AVERILL, HOWARD EARL
49-	3	AVILA, ROBERTO FRANCISCO GONZALEZ
77-	5	AVILES, RAMON ANTONIO
50-	6	AVREA, JAMES EPHERIUM
74-	3	AYALA, BENIGNO 'BENNIE'
47-	7	AYERS, WILLIAM OSCAR
13-	4	AYERS, YANCEY WYATT 'DOC'

D. JANUARY 26, 1950 SAVANNAH, GA.
1806 19TH DR NE - AUBURN WA 98002
D. AUGUST 16, 1983 EVERETT, WASH.
NAVEGANTES FR-19 REFORMA - VERACRUZ VERACRUZ MEX.
26 PADIAL ST - MANATI PR 00701
927 GLENSTONE - DALLAS TX 75232
BOX 814 - BAYAMON PR 00619
D. SEPTEMBER 24, 1980 NEWNAN, GA.
D. MAY 26, 1968 PULASKI, VA.

20

53-	2	AYLWARD, RICHARD JOHN	D. JUNE 11, 1983 SPRING VALLEY, CALIF.
60-	3	AZCUE, JOSE JOAQUIN	7609 WEST 115TH ST - OVERLAND PARK KS 66210
79-	6	BABCOCK, ROBERT ERNEST	4652 OLD PITTSBURGH RD - NEW CASTLE PA 16101
52-	4	BABE, LOREN ROLLAND	D. FEBRUARY 14, 1984 OMAHA, NEB.
34-	2	BABICH, JOHN CHARLES	6111 ROSALIND AV - RICHMOND CA 94803
15-	3	BABINGTON, CHARLES PERCY	D. MARCH 22, 1957 PROVIDENCE, R.I.
81-	3	BABITT, MACK NEAL 'SHOOTY'	2530 MATHEWS ST - BERKELEY CA 94702
80-	5	BACKMAN, WALTER WAYNE	160 SE 39TH - HILLSBORO OR 97123
17-	3	BACON, EDGAR SUTER	D. OCTOBER 2, 1963 FRANKFORT, KY.
75-	9	BACSIK, MICHAEL JAMES	935 GREEN RIDGE DR - DUNCANVILLE TX 75137
53-	3	BACZEWSKI, FREDERICK JOHN	D. NOVEMBER 14, 1976 CULVER CITY, CALIF.
12-	7	BADER, LORE VERNE 'KING'	D. JUNE 2, 1973 LEROY, KAN.
29-	5	BADGRO, MORRIS HIRAM 'RED'	1010 EAST TEMPERANCE ST - KENT WA 98031
26-	3	BAECHT, EDWARD JOSEPH	D. AUGUST 15, 1957 QUARRY TWP., ILL.
77-	6	BAEZ, JOSE ANTONIO	27 DEFEBRERO #15 - SAN CRISTOBAL DOMINICAN REP.
12-	8	BAGBY, JAMES CHARLES JACOB SR.	D. JULY 28, 1954 MARIETTA, GA.
38-	3	BAGBY, JAMES CHARLES JACOB JR.	1910 SOUTH COBB DR #4B - MARIETTA GA 30060
23-	4	BAGWELL, WILLIAM MALLORY	D. OCTOBER 5, 1976 CHOUDRANT, LA.
66-	3	BAHNSEN, STANLEY RAYMOND	780 NE 76TH ST - BOCA RATON FL 33431
46-	7	BAHR, EDSON GARFIELD	OLD ADD: STAR RT 1 BOX 51 - ONALASKA WA
14-	8	BAICHLEY, GROVER CLEVELAND	D. JUNE 30, 1956 SAN JOSE, CALIF.
86-	11	BAILES, SCOTT ALAN	4724 SOUTH STEWARTA - SPRINGFIELD MO 65807
19-	3	BAILEY, ABRAHAM LINCOLN	D. SEPTEMBER 27, 1939 JOLIET, ILL.
17-	4	BAILEY, ARTHUR EUGENE	D. NOVEMBER 14, 1973 HOUSTON, TEX.
16-	2	BAILEY, FRED MIDDLETON	D. AUGUST 16, 1972 HUNTINGTON, W. VA.
11-	6	BAILEY, HARRY LEWIS	D. OCTOBER 27, 1967 SEATTLE, WASH.
81-	4	BAILEY, HOWARD L.	12596 LAKE SHORE DRIVE - GRAND HAVEN MI 49417
59-	4	BAILEY, JAMES HOPKINS	4375 STONEWALL TELL RD - COLLEGE PARK GA 30349
84-	2	BAILEY, JOHN MARK	OLD ADD: 829 SOUTH LINK - SPRINGFIELD MO 65804
53-	4	BAILEY, LONAS EDGAR 'ED'	642 BROOME RD - KNOXVILLE TN 37919
62-	5	BAILEY, ROBERT SHERWOOD	7065 SEAWIND DR - LONG BEACH CA 90803
67-	3	BAILEY, STEVEN JOHN	1005 EUCLID AVE - LORAIN OH 44052
75-	10	BAILOR, ROBERT MICHAEL	P.O. BOX 1154 - PARK CITY UT 84060
45-	2	BAIN, HERBERT LOREN	OLD ADD: 1926 ARTHUR ST NE - MINNEAPOLIS MN
80-	6	BAINES, HAROLD DOUGLAS	107 TRUSTY ST - SAINT MICHAELS MD 21663
76-	10	BAIR, CHARLES DOUGLAS 'DOUG'	6401 PHEASANT RD - LOVELAND OH 45140
17-	5	BAIRD, ALBERT WELLS	D. NOVEMBER 27, 1976 SHREVEPORT, LA.
15-	4	BAIRD, HOWARD DOUGLASS	D. JUNE 13, 1967 THOMASVILLE, GA.
62-	6	BAIRD, ROBERT ALLEN	D. APRIL 11, 1974 CHATTANOOGA, TENN.
64-	3	BAKENHASTER, DAVID LEE	3237 MCKINLEY - COLUMBUS OH 43204
38-	4	BAKER, ALBERT JONES	D. NOVEMBER 6, 1982 KENEDY, TEXAS
78-	3	BAKER, CHARLES JOSEPH	1521 CHALGROVE DR - CORONA CA 91720
82-	4	BAKER, DAVID GLENN	RR TWO - LACONA IA 50139
14-	9	BAKER, DELMAR DAVID	D. SEPTEMBER 11, 1973 SAN ANTONIO, TEX.
84-	3	BAKER, DOUGLAS LEE	19377 WINGED FOOT CIRCLE - NORTHRIDGE CA 91326
53-	5	BAKER, EUGENE WALTER	2202 E. 48TH ST - DAVENPORT IA 52807
43-	5	BAKER, FLOYD WILSON	3033 IDLEWOOD AVE-YOUNGSTOWN OH 44511
69-	4	BAKER, FRANK	383 GIRARD AVE - SOMERSET NJ 08873
70-	4	BAKER, FRANK WATTS	BOX 3066 - MERIDIAN MS 39301
12-	9	BAKER, HOWARD FRANCIS	D. JANUARY 16, 1964 BRIDGEPORT, CONN.
76-	11	BAKER, JACK EDWARD	4536 SWALLOW PL - BIRMINGHAM AL 35213
19-	4	BAKER, JESSE EUGENE	D. JULY 25, 1960 POMONA, CALIF.
11-	7	BAKER, JESSE ORMAND	D. SEPTEMBER 26, 1972 TACOMA, WASH.
68-	3	BAKER, JOHNNIE B. "DUSTY"	24525 PALERMO DR - CALABASAS CA 91302
27-	3	BAKER, NEAL VERNON	D. JANUARY 5, 1982 HOUSTON, TEX.
78-	4	BAKER, STEVEN BYRNE	27527 EASY ACRES DRIVE - EUGENE OR 97405
35-	1	BAKER, THOMAS CALVIN	2002 GOULD ST-FORT WORTH TX 76106
63-	6	BAKER, THOMAS HENRY	D. MARCH 9, 1980 PORT TOWNSEND, WASH.

MIKE BACSIK

Ed Bailey—Cincinnati Redlegs

11-	8	BAKER, TRACY LEE	D. MARCH 14, 1975 PLACERVILLE, CAL.
40-	1	BAKER, WILLIAM PRESLEY	412 MELROSE ST SW - LENOIR NC 28645
38-	5	BALAS, MITCHELL FRANCIS	CHAMBERLAIN ROAD - WESTFORD MA 01886
74-	4	BALAZ, JOHN LARRY	2819 WORDEN ST - SAN DIEGO CA 92110
81-	5	BALBONI, STEPHEN CHARLES	126 WOOD GLEN LANE - LEES SUMMIT MO 64063
56-	5	BALCENA, ROBERT RUDOLPH	2602 CALIFORNIA AVE SW #1 - SEATTLE WA 98116
61-	6	BALDSCHUN, JACK EDWARD	492 BADER ST - GREEN BAY WI 54302
66-	4	BALDWIN, DAVID GEORGE	4025 PULITZER PLACE #308 - SAN DIEGO CA 92122
53-	6	BALDWIN, FRANK DEWITT	7298 ELKWOOD PL - WESTCHESTER OH 45069
27-	4	BALDWIN, HENRY CLAY	D. FEBRUARY 24, 1964 PHILADELPHIA, PA.
24-	2	BALDWIN, HOWARD EDWARD 'HARRY'	D. JANUARY 23, 1958 BALTIMORE, MD.
78-	5	BALDWIN, REGINALD CONRAD	763 LIEBOLD - DETROIT MI 48217
75-	11	BALDWIN, RICK ALAN	3713 WINDWOOD PLACE - MODESTO CA 95355
75-	12	BALDWIN, ROBERT HARVEY 'BILLY'	878 PACKARD DR - AKRON OH 44320
11-	9	BALENTI, MICHAEL RICHARD	D. AUGUST 4, 1955 ALTUS, OKLA.

GEORGE BAMBERGER

66-	5	BALES, WESLEY OWEN 'LEE'	7223 AUGUSTINE - HOUSTON TX 77036
87-	5	BALLARD, JEFFREY SCOTT	4828 RIMROCK ROAD - BILLINGS MT 59102
28-	3	BALLENGER, PELHAM ASHBY	D. DECEMBER 8, 1948 WEST GANTT TWP., S. C.
82-	5	BALLER, JAY SCOT	816 NORTH FIFTH STREET - READING PA 19601
71-	7	BALLINGER, MARK ALAN	%D.BALLINGER,176 DALE - NEWBURY PARK CA 91320
25-	5	BALLOU, NOBLE WINFIELD 'WIN'	D. JANUARY 30, 1963 SAN FRANCISCO, CAL.
62-	7	BALSAMO, ANTHONY FRED	160-15 86TH ST - HOWARD BEACH NY 11414
51-	1	BAMBERGER, GEORGE IRVIN	455 N. BATH CLUB BLVD - NORTH REDINGTON BEACH FL 33708
48-	6	BAMBERGER, HAROLD EARL	RR 1 BOX 317 - BIRDSBORO PA 19508
15-	5	BANCROFT, DAVID JAMES	D. OCTOBER 9, 1972 SUPERIOR, WIS.
81-	6	BANDO, CHRISTOPHER MICHAEL	35640 BRUSHWOOD DR - SOLON OH 44139
66-	6	BANDO, SALVATORE LEONARD	104 WEST JUNIPER LN - MEQUON WI 53092
73-	10	BANE, EDWARD NORMAN	3129 EAST TARO LANE - PHOENIX AZ 85024
69-	5	BANEY, RICHARD LEE	1412 DAMON AVE - ANAHEIM CA 92802
47-	8	BANKHEAD, DANIEL ROBERT	D. MAY 2, 1976 HOUSTON, TEX.
86-	12	BANKHEAD, MICHAEL SCOTT	2020 GUM TREE ROAD - ASHEBORO NC 27203
53-	7	BANKS, ERNEST	P.O. BOX 24302 - LOS ANGELES CA 90024
62-	8	BANKS, GEORGE EDWARD	D. MARCH 1, 1985 SPARTANBURG, S. C.
15-	6	BANKSTON, WILBORN EVERETT 'BILL'	D. FEBRUARY 26, 1970 GRIFFIN, GA.
74-	5	BANNISTER, ALAN	405 48TH ST NW - BRADENTON FL 33529
77-	7	BANNISTER, FLOYD FRANKLIN	6701 EAST CABALLO DRIVE - PARADISE VALLEY AZ 85253
47-	9	BANTA, JOHN KAY	3215 EAST 30TH AVE - HUTCHINSON KS 67502
14-	10	BARBARE, WALTER LAWRENCE	D. OCTOBER 28, 1965 GREENVILLE, S.C.
43-	4	BARBARY, DONALD ODELL 'RED'	402 WEST CURTIS - SIMPSONVILLE SC 29681
26-	4	BARBEE, DAVID MONROE	D. JULY 1, 1968 ALBEMARLE, N. C.
60-	4	BARBER, STEPHEN DAVID	3084 E. VAN BUSKIRK CIR - LAS VEGAS NV 89121
70-	5	BARBER, STEVEN LEE	1517 CUSHMAN DR - SIERRA VISTA AZ 85635
15-	7	BARBER, TYRUS TURNER	D. OCTOBER 20, 1968 MILAN, TENN.
66-	7	BARBIERI, JAMES PATRICK	13619 EAST 5TH AVE - SPOKANE WA 99216
57-	4	BARCLAY, CURTIS CORDELL	D. MARCH 27, 1985 MISSOULA, MONT.
72-	5	BARE, RAYMOND DOUGLAS	911 NORTH IVY ST - JENKS OK 74037
81-	7	BARFIELD, JESSE LEE	4208 CANTERWOOD DRIVE - HOUSTON TX 77068
22-	2	BARFOOT, CLYDE RAYMOND	D. MARCH 11, 1971 HIGHLAND PARK, CAL.
83-	7	BARGAR, GREG ROBERT	23005 KATHRYN AVENUE - TORRANCE CA 90505
76-	12	BARKER, LEONARD HAROLD	1339 BEECHWOOD HILLS CT NW - ATLANTA GA 30327
60-	5	BARKER, RAYMOND HAROLD	% GENERAL MOTORS - MARTINSBURG WV 25401
84-	4	BARKLEY, JEFFREY CARVER	264 THIRD AVE NE - HICKORY NC 28601
37-	6	BARKLEY, JOHN DUNCAN 'RED'	1200 LAWRENCE DR - WACO TX 76710
75-	13	BARLOW, MICHAEL ROSWELL	%SHEFTIC,4524 FRANCIS RD - CAZENOVIA NY 13035
53-	8	BARMES, BRUCE RAYMOND	509 MCDONALD AVE - CHARLOTTE NC 28203
37-	7	BARNA, HERBERT PAUL 'BABE'	D. MAY 18, 1972 CHARLESTON, W. VA.
27-	5	BARNABE, CHARLES EDWARD	D. AUGUST 16, 1977 WACO, TEX.
27-	6	BARNES, EMILE DEERING 'RED'	D. JULY 3, 1959 MOBILE, ALA.
23-	5	BARNES, EVERETT DUANE 'EPPIE'	D. NOVEMBER 17, 1980 MINEOLA, N. Y.
57-	5	BARNES, FRANK	1508 BRAZIL - GREENVILLE MS 38701
29-	6	BARNES, FRANK SAMUEL 'LEFTY'	D. SEPTEMBER 27, 1967 HOUSTON, TEX.
15-	8	BARNES, JESSE LAWRENCE	D. SEPTEMBER 9, 1961 SANTA ROSA, N.MEX.
26-	5	BARNES, JOHN FRANCIS 'HONEY'	D. JUNE 18, 1981 LOCKPORT, N. Y.
34-	3	BARNES, JUNIE SHOAF	D. DECEMBER 31, 1963 JACKSONVILLE, N. C.
72-	6	BARNES, LUTHER OWEN	6190 CULVER DRIVE SE - SALEM OR 97301
82-	6	BARNES, RICHARD MONROE	4357 DAVIS ROAD - LAKE WORTH FL 33461
24-	3	BARNES, ROBERT AVERY	BOX 68 - LACON IL 61540
21-	1	BARNES, SAMUEL THOMAS	D. FEBRUARY 19, 1981 MONTGOMERY, ALA.
19-	5	BARNES, VIRGIL JENNINGS	D. JULY 24, 1958 WICHITA, KAN.
83-	8	BARNES, WILLIAM HENRY 'SKEETER'	6626 RAVENAL CT - CINCINNATI OH 45213
15-	9	BARNEY, EDMUND J.	D. OCTOBER 4, 1967 RICE LAKE, WIS.
43-	5	BARNEY, REX EDWARD	MEMORIAL STADIUM - BALTIMORE MD 21218
20-	3	BARNHART, CLYDE LEE	D. JANUARY 21, 1980 HAGERSTOWN, MD.
24-	4	BARNHART, EDGAR VERNON	D. SEPTEMBER 14, 1984 COLUMBIA, MO.
28-	4	BARNHART, LESLIE EARL	D. OCTOBER 7, 1971 SCOTTSDALE, ARIZ.
44-	3	BARNHART, VICTOR DEE	RR 5 - HAGERSTOWN MD 21741
39-	4	BARNICLE, GEORGE BERNARD	9981 88TH ST NORTH - SEMINOLE FL 33543
65-	4	BARNOWSKI, EDWARD ANTHONY	311 RED OAK DRIVE - WILLIAMSVILLE NY 14221
82-	7	BAROJAS, SALOME ROMERO	B. JUNE 16, 1957 COROVA, VERACRUZ, MEXICO
60-	6	BARONE, RICHARD ANTHONY	403 GLENFORD PARK CT - SAN JOSE CA 95136
71-	8	BARR, JAMES LELAND	6335 OAK HILL DRIVE - ROSEVILLE CA 95661
35-	2	BARR, ROBERT ALEXANDER	BARRINGTON MOBILE HOMES-BARRINGTON NH 03825
74-	6	BARR, STEVEN CHARLES	OLD ADD: 550 AVENUE NORTH SE - WINTER HAVEN FL 33880
61-	7	BARRAGAN, FACUNDO ANTHONY 'CUNO'	1824 ST. ANN COURT - CARMICHAEL CA 95608
79-	7	BARRANCA, GERMAN MICHAEL	CALLE PINO SUAREZ #1642 - VERACRUZ VERACRUZ MEX.
37-	8	BARRETT, CHARLES HENRY 'RED'	410 MONTICELLO DR - WILSON NC 27893
39-	5	BARRETT, FRANCIS JOSEPH	434 NORTH 3RD ST-LEESBURG FL 32748
42-	5	BARRETT, JOHN JOSEPH	D. AUGUST 17, 1974 SEABROOK BEACH, N. H.
82-	8	BARRETT, MARTIN GLENN	3140 CLAMDIGGER - LAS VEGAS NV 89117

23- 6 BARRETT, ROBERT SCHLEY
33- 3 BARRETT, TRACEY SOUTER 'DICK'
21- 2 BARRETT, WILLIAM JOSEPH
74- 7 BARRIOS, FRANCISCO XAVIER
82- 9 BARRIOS, JOSE MANUEL
29- 7 BARRON, DAVID IRENUS 'RED'
14- 11 BARRON, FRANK JOHN
12- 10 BARRY, HARDIN
69- 6 BARRY, RICHARD DONOVAN
27- 7 BARTELL, RICHARD WILLIAM
44- 4 BARTHELSON, ROBERT EDWARD
28- 5 BARTHOLOMEW, LESTER JUSTIN
52- 5 BARTIROME, ANTHONY JOSEPH
43- 6 BARTLEY, BOYD OWEN
38- 6 BARTLING, IRVING HENRY
65- 5 BARTON, ROBERT WILBUR
31- 6 BARTON, VINCENT DAVID
45- 3 BARTOSCH, DAVID ROBERT
48- 7 BASGALL, ROMANUS 'MONTY'
12- 11 BASHANG, ALBERT C.
36- 6 BASHORE, WALTER FRANKLIN
44- 5 BASINSKI, EDWIN FRANK

D. JANUARY 18, 1982 ATLANTA, GA.
D. NOVEMBER 7, 1966 SEATTLE, WASH.
D. JANUARY 26, 1951 CAMBRIDGE, MASS.
D. APRIL 9, 1982 HERMOSILLO SONORA MEXICO
6484 SW 25TH ST - MIAMI FL 33155
D. OCTOBER 4, 1982 ATLANTA, GA.
D. SEPTEMBER 18, 1964 PLEASANTS CO., W. VA.
D. NOVEMBER 5, 1969 CARSON CITY, NEV.
47275 MIO MIO LOOP - KANEOHE HI 96744
1118 ISLAND DR - ALAMEDA CA 94501
40 MEADOWLARK LN - NORTHFORD CT 06472
D. SEPTEMBER 19, 1972 MADISON, WIS.
1104 PALMA SOLA BLVD - BRADENTON FL 34209
7500 NOREAST DR - FORT WORTH TX 76118
D. JUNE 12, 1973 WESTLAND, MICH.
777 DOROTHEA AVE - SAN MARCOS CA 92069
D. SEPTEMBER 13, 1973 TORONTO, ONT.
25212 AVENIDA DORENA - NEWHALL CA 91321
1965 LAUREL LN - SIERRA VISTA AZ 85635
D. JUNE 23, 1967 CINCINNATI, O.
D. SEPTEMBER 26, 1984 SEBRING, FLA.
6585 SW 67TH ST - PORTLAND OR 97223

11- 10 BASKETTE, JAMES BLAINE
82- 10 BASS, KEVIN CHARLES
61- 8 BASS, NORMAN DELANEY
77- 8 BASS, RANDY WILLIAM
39- 6 BASS, RICHARD WILLIAM
18- 1 BASS, WILLIAM CAPERS 'DOC'
13- 5 BASSLER, JOHN LANDIS
23- 7 BATCHELDER, JOSEPH EDMUND
63- 7 BATEMAN, JOHN ALVIN
69- 7 BATES, CHARLES RICHARD 'DICK'
27- 8 BATES, CHARLES WILLIAM
70- 6 BATES, DELBERT OAKLEY
39- 7 BATES, HUBERT EDGAR
13- 6 BATES, RAYMOND
86- 13 BATHE, WILLIAM DAVID
73- 11 BATISTA, RAFAEL
16- 3 BATSCH, WILLIAM MCKINLEY
12- 12 BATTEN, GEORGE BERNARD
55- 8 BATTEY, EARL JESSE
27- 9 BATTLE, JAMES MILTON
76- 13 BATTON, CHRISTOPHER SEAN
47- 10 BATTS, MATTHEW DANIEL
48- 8 BAUER, HENRY ALBERT
18- 2 BAUER, LOUIS WALTER
36- 7 BAUERS, RUSSELL LEE
11- 11 BAUMANN, CHARLES JOHN 'PADDY'
55- 9 BAUMANN, FRANK MATTHEW
49- 4 BAUMER, JAMES SLOAN
12- 13 BAUMGARDNER, GEORGE WASHINGTON
78- 6 BAUMGARTEN, ROSS
20- 4 BAUMGARTNER, HARRY E.
53- 9 BAUMGARTNER, JOHN EDWARD
14- 13 BAUMGARTNER, STANWOOD FULTON
47- 11 BAUMHOLTZ, FRANK CONRAD
60- 7 BAUTA, EDUARDO
59- 5 BAXES, DIMITRIOS SPEROS 'JIM'
56- 6 BAXES, MICHAEL
70- 7 BAYLOR, DON EDWARD
19- 6 BAYNE, WILLIAM LEAR
13- 7 BEALL, JOHN WOOLF
75- 14 BEALL, ROBERT BROOKS
24- 5 BEALL, WALTER ESAU
56- 7 BEAMON, CHARLES ALONZO SR.
78- 7 BEAMON, CHARLES ALONZO JR.
30- 2 BEAN, BELVEDERE BENTON
87- 6 BEAN, WILLIAM DARO
84- 5 BEANE, WILLIAM LAMAR
80- 7 BEARD, CHARLES DAVID 'DAVE'
48- 9 BEARD, CRAMER THEODORE 'TED'
74- 8 BEARD, MICHAEL RICHARD

D. JULY 30, 1942 ATHENS, TENN.
1971 BYERS DR - MENLO PARK CA 94025
8814 THIRD AVE - INGLEWOOD CA 90305
RR 3 BOX 23C - LAWTON OK 73501
P.O. BOX 291 - GREENWOOD FL 32443
D. JANUARY 12, 1970 MACON, GA.
D. JUNE 29, 1979 SANTA MONICA, CALIF.
%JOSLIN,222 CABOT ST - BEVERLY MA 01915
903 N. GARFIELD - SAND SPRING OK 74063
8601 EAST BONNIE ROSE AVE - SCOTTSDALE AZ 85253
D. JANUARY 29, 1980 TOPEKA, KANS.
8336 133RD NE - REDMOND WA 98052
D. APRIL 29, 1987 LONG BEACH, CALIF.
D. AUGUST 15, 1970 TUCSON, ARIZ.
11027 KENTUCKY AVENUE - WHITTIER CA 90603
BOX 211 - SAN PEDRO DE MACORIS DOMINICAN REP.
D. DECEMBER 31, 1963 CANTON, O.
D. AUGUST 4, 1972 NEW PORT RICHEY, FLA.
2501 SW 3RD STREET - OCALA FL 32674
D. SEPTEMBER 30, 1965 CHICO, CAL.
6109 WEST 77TH ST - LOS ANGELES CA 90045
838 NORTH ALLYSON - BATON ROUGE LA 70815
12705 WEST 108TH ST - OVERLAND PARK KS 66210
D. FEBRUARY 4, 1979 POMONA, N. J.
1924 GARDNER RD-WESTCHESTER IL 60156
D. NOVEMBER 20, 1969 INDIANAPOLIS, IND.
7712 SUNRAY LN - ST LOUIS MO 63123
303 PAOLI WOODS - PAOLI PA 19301
D. DECEMBER 13, 1970 BARBOURSVILLE, W. VA.
1020 BLUFF RD - GLENCOE IL 60022
D. DECEMBER 3, 1930 AUGUSTA, GA.
237 KENT LANE - BIRMINGHAM AL 35209
D. OCTOBER 4, 1955 PHILADELPHIA, PA.
4327 JENNINGS RD - CLEVELAND OH 44109
1087 E. JERSEY ST - ELIZABETH NJ 07201
6211 HUNTLEY AVE - GARDEN GROVE CA 92645
303 WICKMAN DR - MILL VALLEY CA 94941
5 FIELDSTONE LN - SOUTH NATICK MA 01760
D. MAY 27, 1981 ST. LOUIS, MO.
D. JUNE 13, 1926 BELTSVILLE, MD.
513 BIRCHWOOD RD - HILLSBORO OR 97123
D. JANUARY 28, 1959 SUITLAND, MD.
1717 WOODLAND AVE #3 - EAST PALO ALTO CA 94303
421 OAKLAND AVE #6 - OAKLAND CA 94611
901 WEST WRIGHT - COMANCHE TX 76442
1102 EAST JOANA - SANTA ANA CA 92701
1720 KNOLL FIELD WAY - ENCINITAS CA 92024
3703 MADRID CIR - NORCROSS GA 30092
10517 STELOR CT - INDIANAPOLIS IN 46256
5901 JFK BLVD #1603 - NORTH LITTLE ROCK AR 72116

```
54-  6 BEARD, RALPH WILLIAM              1367 BERKSHIRE DR - WEST PALM BEACH FL 33406
47- 12 BEARDEN, HENRY EUGENE 'GENE'      BOX 176 - HELENA AR 72342
76- 14 BEARE, GARY RAY                   2752 ELYSSEE ST - SAN DIEGO CA 92123
63-  8 BEARNARTH, LAWRENCE DONALD        85-18 143RD LN - SEMINOLE FL 33542
77-  9 BEASLEY, LEWIS PAIGE   TEX'       RR 1 BOX 65 - BOWLING GREEN VA 22427
78-  8 BEATTIE, JAMES LOUIS              9610 SE 34TH ST - MERCER ISLAND WA 98040
14- 14 BEATTY, DESMOND A                 D. OCTOBER 6, 1969 NORWAY, ME.
63-  9 BEAUCHAMP, JAMES EDWARD           BOX 1790 - PHENIX CITY AL 36867
41-  6 BEAZLEY, JOHN ANDREW              23 LYMINGTON COURT - BRENTWOOD TN 37027
26-  6 BECK, CLYDE EUGENE                BOX 147 - RANDSBURG CA 93554
14- 15 BECK, GEORGE F.                   1915 ADD: 22ND AVE- MOLINE ILL
65-  6 BECK, RICHARD HENRY               2151 HOXIE - RICHLAND WA 99352
24-  6 BECK, WALTER WILLIAM 'BOOM BOOM'  D. MAY 7, 1987 CHAMPAIGN, ILL.
13-  8 BECK, ZINN BERTRAM                D. MARCH 19, 1981 WEST PALM BEACH, FLA.
11- 12 BECKER, CHARLES S.                D. JULY 30, 1928 WASHINGTON, D.C.
43-  7 BECKER, HEINZ REINHARD            302 CLARENDON DR-DALLAS TX 75208
36-  8 BECKER, JOSEPH EDWARD             2800 21ST PLACE - VERO BEACH FL 32960
```

```
15- 10 BECKER, MARTIN HENRY              D. SEPTEMBER 25, 1957 CINCINNATI, O.
65-  7 BECKERT, GLENN ALFRED             870 VIRGINA LAKE CT - PALATINE IL 60067
27- 10 BECKMAN, JAMES JOSEPH             6989 BENNETT ROAD - CINCINNATI OH 45230
39-  8 BECKMANN, WILLIAM ALOYSIUS        111 FIESTA CIR-CREVE COEUR MO 63141
79-  8 BECKWITH, THOMAS JOSEPH 'JOE'     2057 COUNTRY SQUIRE RD - AUBURN AL 36830
55- 10 BECQUER, JULIO VELLEGAS           829 VINCENT AVE - MINNEAPOLIS MN 55411
62-  9 BEDELL, HOWARD WILLIAM            1187 CRESTWOOD DR - POTTSTOWN PA 19464
25-  6 BEDFORD, WILLIAM EUGENE           D. OCTOBER 6, 1977 SAN ANTONIO, TEXAS
22-  3 BEDGOOD, PHILIP BURLETTE          D. NOVEMBER 8, 1927 FORT PIERCE, FLA.
12- 14 BEDIENT, HUGH CARPENTER           D. JULY 21, 1965 JAMESTOWN, N.Y.
30-  3 BEDNAR, ANDREW JACKSON            D. NOVEMBER 26, 1937 GRAHAM, TEX.
81-  8 BEDROSIAN, STEPHEN WAYNE          5490 CHEISENWOOD DRIVE - DULUTH GA 30136
44-  6 BEELER, JOSEPH SAM 'JODIE'        3709 NABHOLTZ - MESQUITE TX 75150
68-  4 BEENE, FREDERICK RAY              BOX 143 - OAKHURST TX 77359
83-  9 BEENE, RAMON ANDREW 'ANDY'        5702 SECOND STREET - LUBBOCK TX 79416
48- 10 BEERS, CLARENCE SCOTT             4701 ANDERSON RD #30 - HOUSTON TX 77045
38-  7 BEGGS, JOSEPH STANLEY             D. JULY 19, 1983 INDIANAPOLIS, IND.
24-  7 BEGLEY, JAMES LAWRENCE            D. FEBRUARY 22, 1957 SAN FRANCISCO, CAL.
21-  3 BEHAN, CHARLES FREDERICK 'PETIE'  D. JANUARY 21, 1957 BRADFORD, PA.
83- 10 BEHENNA, RICHARD KIPP             9451 TONI DRIVE - CUTLER RIDGE FL 33157
70-  8 BEHNEY, MELVIN BRIAN              241 GROVE AVE - VERONA NJ 07042
46-  8 BEHRMAN, HENRY BERNARD            D. JANUARY 20, 1987 NEW YORK, N. Y.
34-  4 BEJMA, ALOYSIUS FRANK 'OLLIE'     4510 WEST WASHINGTON #107 - SOUTH BEND IN 46619
65-  8 BELANGER, MARK HENRY              2028 POT SPRING RD - TIMONIUM MD 21093
50-  7 BELARDI, CARROLL WAYNE            1467 PHANTOM AVE - SAN JOSE CA 95125
87-  7 BELCHER, TIMOTHY WAYNE            SPRING STREET - SPARTA OH 43350
62- 10 BELINSKY, ROBERT 'BO'            P.O. BOX 671 - WAIALUA HI 96791
72-  7 BELL, DAVID GUS 'BUDDY'          6485 HUNTERS TRAIL - CINCINNATI OH 45243
50-  8 BELL, DAVID RUSSELL 'GUS'        MINUTEMAN, 1010 RACE ST - CINCINNATI OH 45202
85-  3 BELL, ERIC ALVIN                  1601 COUCHMAN LANE - MODESTO CA 95355
39-  9 BELL, FERN LEE                    1975 ADD: 122 WEST 59TH PL - LOS ANGELES CA
58-  9 BELL, GARY                        AMERICAN SPTS,617 N. ST.MARYS - SAN ANTONIO TX 78205
24-  8 BELL, HERMAN S. 'HI'              D. JUNE 7, 1949 GLENDALE, CAL.
86- 14 BELL, JAY STUART                  9752 QUAIL HOLLOW COURT - PENSACOLA FL 32514
71-  9 BELL, JERRY HOUSTON               RR 3 BOX 609 - MOUNT JULIET TN 37122
81-  9 BELL, JORGE ANTONIO               BARIO REST. CLE T #179-SAN PEDRO DE MACORIS DOM. REP.
76- 15 BELL, KEVIN ROBERT                OLD ADD: ALGONQUIN - ROLLING MEADOWS IL
23-  8 BELL, LESTER ROWLAND              D. NOVEMBER 26, 1985 HARRISBURG, PA.
12- 15 BELL, RALPH A.                    D. OCTOBER 18, 1959 BURLINGTON, IA.
35-  3 BELL, ROY CHESTER 'BEAU'          D. SEPTEMBER 14, 1977 COLLEGE STATION, TEXAS
86- 15 BELL, TERENCE WILLIAM             4317 FERNMONT STREET - KETTERING OH 45440
52-  6 BELL, WILLIAM SAMUEL              D. OCTOBER 11, 1962 DURHAM, N. C.
57-  6 BELLA, JOHN 'ZEKE'                24 TAYLOR DR - COS COB CT 06807
82- 11 BELLIARD, RAFAEL LEONIDAS         DOMINGO CASTELLANO 17,GURABITO-SANTIAGO DOMINICAN REP.
75- 15 BELLOIR, ROBERT EDWARD            3246 WEST MANOR LN SW - ATLANTA GA 30311
67-  4 BENCH, JOHN LEE                   %TAFT HAMILTON,617 TAFT ST #1307 - CINCINNATI OH 45202
78-  9 BENEDICT, BRUCE EDWIN             335 QUIET WATER LANE - DUNWOODY GA 30338
31-  7 BENES, JOSEPH ANTHONY             D. MARCH 7, 1975 ELMHURST N. Y.
25-  7 BENGE, RAYMOND ADELPHIA           RR1 BOX 134A - JEWETT TX 75846
23-  9 BENGOUGH, BERNARD OLIVER          D. DECEMBER 22, 1968 PHILADELPHIA, PA.
71- 10 BENIQUEZ, JUAN JOSE               CALLE 99A BLK.87 #12 - CAROLINA PR 00630
39- 10 BENJAMIN, ALFRED STANLEY 'STAN'   46 ALLEN ST - GREENFIELD MA 01301
14- 16 BENN, HOMER OMER                  D. JUNE 4, 1967 MENDOTA, WIS.
64-  4 BENNETT, DAVID ,HANS              408 FAIRCHILD ST - YREKA CA 96097
62- 11 BENNETT, DENNIS JOHN              630 NORTH 5TH - KLAMATH FALLS OR 97601
```

Johnny Bund

27- 11	BENNETT, FRANCIS ALLEN	D. MARCH 18, 1966 WILMINGTON, DEL.
23- 10	BENNETT, HERSCHELL EMMETT	D. SEPTEMBER 9, 1964 SPRINGFIELD, MO.
28- 6	BENNETT, JAMES FRED	D. MAY 12, 1957 ATKINS, ARK.
18- 3	BENNETT, JOSEPH HARLEY	D. NOVEMBER 21, 1957 JOEL, MO.
23- 11	BENNETT, JOSEPH ROSENBLUM	D. JULY 11, 1987 MORRO BAY, CALIF.
34- 5	BENSON, ALLEN WILBERT	HURLEY SD 57036
43- 8	BENSON, VERNON ADAIR	BOX 127-GRANITE QUARRY NC 28072
13- 9	BENTLEY, JOHN NEEDLES	D. OCTOBER 24, 1969 OLNEY, MD.
78- 10	BENTON, ALFRED LEE 'BUTCH'	OLD ADD: 895 VIL LAKES#102 - ST PETERSBURG FL
34- 6	BENTON, JOHN ALTON 'AL'	D. APRIL 14, 1968 I'NWOOD, CAL.
10- 7	BENTON, JOHN CLEBON 'RUBE'	D. DECEMBER 12, 1937 DOTHAN, ALA.
23- 12	BENTON, LAWRENCE JAMES	D. APRIL 3, 1953 CINCINNATI, O.
22- 4	BENTON, SIDNEY WRIGHT	D. MARCH 8, 1977 FAYETTEVILLE, ARK.
22- 5	BENTON, STANLEY 'RABBIT'	D. JUNE 7, 1984 DALLAS, TEXAS
11- 13	BENZ, JOSEPH LOUIS	D. APRIL 23, 1957 CHICAGO, ILL.
87- 8	BENZINGER, TODD ERIC	3502 BEHMER ROAD - CINCINNATI OH 45245
12- 16	BERAN, DENNIS MARTIN	D. APRIL 28, 1943 BOSTON, MASS.
39- 11	BERARDINO, JOHN	1719 AMBASSADOR AVE - BEVERLY HILLS CA 90210
54- 7	BERBERET, LOUIS JOSEPH	4025 MARDON AVE - LAS VEGAS NV 89118
78- 11	BERENGUER, JUAN BAUTISTA	18241 GLENWOOD - LATHRUP VILLAGE MI 48076
80- 8	BERENYI, BRUCE MICHAEL	BOX 133 - SHERWOOD OH 43556
23- 13	BERG, MORRIS 'MOE'	D. MAY 29, 1972 BELLEVILLE, N. J.
44- 7	BERGAMO, AUGUST SAMUEL	D. AUGUST 19, 1974 GROSSE POINTE CITY, MICH.
14- 17	BERGER, CLARENCE EDWARD	D. JUNE 30, 1959 WASHINGTON, D. C.
22- 6	BERGER, JOHN HENNE	D. MAY 7, 1979 LAKE CHARLES, LA.
13- 10	BERGER, JOSEPH AUGUST	D. MARCH 5, 1956 ROCK ISLAND, ILL.
32- 3	BERGER, LOUIS WILLIAM 'BOZE'	11914 RENWOOD LN - ROCKVILLE MD 20852
30- 4	BERGER, WALTER ANTONE	124 21ST ST - MANHATTAN BCH CA 90266
11- 14	BERGHAMMER, MARTIN ANDREW	D. DECEMBER 21, 1957 PITTSBURGH, PA.
16- 4	BERGMAN, ALFRED HENRY	D. JUNE 21, 1961 FORT WAYNE, IND.
75- 16	BERGMAN, DAVID BRUCE	728 CANTERBURY COURT - GROSSE POINTE WOODS MI 48236
24- 9	BERLY, JOHN CHAMBERS	D. JUNE 26, 1977 HOUSTON, TEX.
18- 4	BERMAN, ROBERT LEON	24 CENTERVIEW DR - HUNTINGTON CT 06484
77- 10	BERNAL, VICTOR HUGO	4632 ABNER ST - LOS ANGELES CA 90032
78- 12	BERNARD, DWIGHT VERN	RURAL ROUTE 1 - BELLE RIVE IL 62810
79- 9	BERNAZARD, ANTONIO (GARCIA)	SANTA AV D-25,URB SANTA ELVIRA-CAGUAS PR00625
76- 16	BERNHARDT, JUAN RAMON	PROL. SERGIO A. BERA #13-SAN PEDRO DE MACORIS DOM REP.
18- 5	BERNHARDT, WALTER JACOB	D. JULY 26, 1958 WATERTOWN, N. Y.
53- 10	BERNIER, CARLOS RODRIGUEZ	3D5 JARDINER SANTO DOMINGO - JUANA DIAZ PR 00665
48- 11	BERO, JOHN GEORGE	D. MAY 11, 1985 GARDENA, CALIF.
77- 11	BERRA, DALE ANTHONY	517 RIDGEWOOD AVENUE - GLEN RIDGE NJ 07028
46- 9	BERRA, LAWRENCE PETER 'YOGI'	19 HIGHLAND AVE - MONTCLAIR NJ 07042
34- 7	BERRES, RAYMOND	111 HAWTHORNE RD - TWIN LAKES WI 53181
62- 12	BERRY, ALLEN KENNETH 'KEN'	3421 BRIARWOOD LN - TOPEKA KS 66611
25- 8	BERRY, CHARLES FRANCIS	D. SEPTEMBER 6, 1972 EVANSTON, ILL.
48- 12	BERRY, CORNELIUS JOHN 'CONNIE'	407 INKSTER AVE - KALAMAZOO MI 49001
42- 6	BERRY, JONAS ARTHUR	D. SEPTEMBER 27, 1958 ANAHEIM, CAL.
21- 4	BERRY, JOSEPH HOWARD JR	D. APRIL 29, 1976 PHILADELPHIA, PA.
87- 9	BERRYHILL, DAMON SCOTT	61 SOUTH LASENDA - SOUTH LAGUNA CA 92677
64- 5	BERTAINA, FRANK LOUIS	2340 HILLTOP COURT - SANTA ROSA CA 95405
60- 8	BERTELL, RICHARD GEORGE	25332 REMESA DR - MISSION VIEJO CA 92675
53- 11	BERTOIA, RENO PETER	3400 ERSKINE ST #906 - WINDSOR ONTARIO CAN.
36- 9	BERTRAND, ROMAN MATHIAS	1909 MOUNT HOOD - THE DALLES OR 97058
56- 8	BESANA, FREDERICK CYRIL	222 DIAMOND OAKS DR - ROSEVILLE CA 95678

40- 2 BESSE, HERMAN   D. AUGUST 13, 1972 LOS ANGELES, CAL.
55- 11 BESSENT, FRED DONALD 'DON'   5139 110TH STREET - JACKSONVILLE FL 32244
83- 11 BEST, KARL JOHN   11132 SE 129TH - KIRKLAND WA 98034
78- 13 BESWICK, JAMES WILLIAM   12519 DOMINGO RD NE - ALBUQUERQUE NM 87123
10- 8 BETCHER, FRANKLIN LYLE   D. NOVEMBER 27, 1981 WYNNEWOOD, PA.
64- 6 BETHEA, WILLIAM LAMAR   4001 WYLDWOOD - AUSTIN TX 78739
65- 9 BETHKE, JAMES CHARLES   419 NORTH OAKLEY ST - KANSAS CITY MO 64123
28- 7 BETTENCOURT, LAWRENCE JOSEPH   D. SEPTEMBER 15, 1978 NEW ORLEANS, LA.
84- 6 BETTENDORF, JEFFREY ALLEN   916 WEST LIME - LOMPOC CA 93436
20- 5 BETTS, WALTER MARTIN 'HUCK'   D. JUNE 13, 1987 MILLSBORO, DEL.

14- 18 BETZEL, CHRISTIAN FREDERICK ALBERT   D. FEBRUARY 7, 1965 WEST HOLLYWOOD,FLA
71- 11 BEVACQUA, KURT ANTHONY   6618 GRULLA ST - CARLSBAD CA 92008
52- 7 BEVAN, HAROLD JOSEPH   D. OCTOBER 5, 1968 NEW ORLEANS, LA.
44- 8 BEVENS, FLOYD CLIFFORD 'BILL'   5067 8TH NE - SALEM OR 97303
42- 7 BEVIL, LOUIS EUGENE   D. FEBRUARY 1, 1973 DIXON, ILL.
17- 6 BEZDEK, HUGH FRANCIS   D. SEPTEMBER 19, 1952 ATLANTIC CITY, N.J.
82- 12 BIANCALANA, ROLAND AMERICO 'BUDDY'   4120 SAN SAVERA DR NORTH - JACKSONVILLE FL 32217
75- 17 BIANCO, THOMAS ANTHONY   OLD ADD: 4 CURVEWOOD RD - PORT WASHINGTON NY 11050
49- 5 BIASATTI, HENRY ARCADO   9024 ALLEN RD - ALLEN PARK MI 48101
72- 8 BIBBY, JAMES BLAIR   RR 6 BOX 402 - MADISON HEIGHTS VA 24572
48- 13 BICKFORD, VERNON EDGELL   D. MAY 8, 1960 RICHMOND, VA.
48- 14 BICKNELL, CHARLES STEPHEN   6981 FORDS STATION RD - GERMANTOWN TN 38138
84- 7 BIELECKI, MICHAEL JOSEPH   1932 EASTFIELD RD - BALTIMORE MD 21222
20- 6 BIEMILLER, HARRY LEE   D. MAY 25, 1965 ORLANDO, FLA.
16- 5 BIGBEE, CARSON LEE   D. OCTOBER 17, 1964 PORTLAND, ORE.
20- 7 BIGBEE, LYLE RANDOLPH   D. AUGUST 5, 1942 PORTLAND, ORE.
29- 8 BIGELOW, ELLIOT ALLARDICE   D. AUGUST 10, 1933 TAMPA, FLA.
32- 4 BIGGS, CHARLES ORVAL   D. MAY 24, 1954 FRENCH LICK, IND.
70- 9 BIITTNER, LARRY DAVID   169 CRESTVIEW CT - BARRINGTON IL 60010
49- 6 BILBREY, JAMES MELVIN   D. DECEMBER 26, 1985 TOLEDO, O.
37- 9 BILDILLI, EMIL   D. SEPTEMBER 16, 1946 HARTFORD CITY, IND.
49- 7 BILKO, STEPHEN THOMAS   D. MARCH 7, 1978 WILKES-BARRE, PA.
83- 12 BILLARDELLO, DANN JAMES   836 BLUEBERRY DRIVE - WEST PALM BEACH FL 33414
68- 5 BILLINGHAM, JOHN EUGENE   8945 LAKE IRMA POINTE - ORLANDO FL 32817
27- 12 BILLINGS, HASKELL CLARK   D. DECEMBER 26, 1983 GREENBRAE, CALIF.
13- 11 BILLINGS, JOHN AUGUSTUS 'JOSH'   D. DECEMBER 30, 1981 SANTA MONICA, CALIF.
68- 6 BILLINGS, RICHARD ARLIN   1917 CREEKWOOD DR - ARLINGTON TX 76010
44- 9 BINKS, GEORGE EUGENE   4803 BELMONT RD - DOWNERS GROVE IL 60515
44- 10 BIRAS, STEPHEN ALEXANDER   D. APRIL 21, 1965 ST. LOUIS, MO.
73- 12 BIRD, JAMES DOUGLAS 'DOUG'   OLD ADD: 5542-3 MALT DR - FORT MYERS FL
21- 5 BIRD, JAMES EDWARD 'RED'   D. MARCH 23, 1972 MURFREESBORO, ARK.
86- 16 BIRKBECK, MICHAEL LAURENCE   1705 WEST HILL DRIVE - ORRVILLE OH 44667
33- 4 BIRKOFER, RALPH JOSEPH   D. MARCH 16, 1971 CINCINNATI, O.
55- 12 BIRRER, WERNER JOSEPH 'BABE'   115 RANCH TRAIL WEST - WILLIAMSVILLE NY 14221
85- 4 BIRTSAS, TIMOTHY DEAN   43 ROBERTSON COURT - CLARKSTON MI 48016
42- 8 BISCAN, FRANK STEPHEN   D. MAY 22, 1959 ST. LOUIS, MO.
25- 9 BISCHOFF, JOHN GEORGE   D. DECEMBER 28, 1981 GRANITE CITY, ILL.
52- 8 BISHOP, CHARLES TULLER   2705 ADDISON DR - DORAVILLE GA 30040

23- 14	BISHOP, JAMES MORTON	D. SEPTEMBER 20, 1973 MEXICO, MO.
14- 19	BISHOP, LLOYD CLIFTON	D. JUNE 17, 1968 WICHITA, KAN.
24- 10	BISHOP, MAX FREDERICK	D. FEBRUARY 4, 1962 WAYNESBORO, PA.
83- 13	BISHOP, MICHAEL DAVID	497 EAST NEWLOVE #D - SANTA MARIA CA 93454
21- 6	BISHOP, WILLIAM HENRY	D. FEBRUARY 14, 1956 ST. JOSEPH, MO.
12- 17	BISLAND, RIVINGTON MARTIN	D. JANUARY 11, 1973 SALZBURG, AUSTRIA
28- 8	BISSONETTE, DELPHIA LOUIS	D. JUNE 9, 1972 AUGUSTA, ME.
42- 9	BITHORN, HIRAM GABRIEL	D. JANUARY 1, 1952 EL MANTE, MEX.
86- 17	BITTIGER, JEFFREY SCOTT	821 HUDSON AVENUE - SECAUCUS NJ 07094
35- 4	BIVIN, JAMES NATHANIEL	D. NOVEMBER 7, 1982 PUEBLO, COLO.
83- 14	BJORKMAN, GEORGE ANTON	749 E. HARVARD - ONTARIO CA 91764
14- 20	BLACK, DAVID	D. OCTOBER 27, 1936 PITTSBURGH, PA.
43- 9	BLACK, DONALD PAUL	D. APRIL 21, 1959 CUYAHOGA FALLS, O.
81- 10	BLACK, HARRY RALSTON 'BUD'	75-707 HWY 111 #C-6 - PALM DESERT CA 92260
11- 15	BLACK, JOHN FALCNOR	D. MARCH 19, 1962 RUTHERFORD, N. J.
24- 11	BLACK, JOHN WILLIAM 'BILL'	D. JANUARY 14, 1968 PHILADELPHIA, PA.
52- 9	BLACK, JOSEPH	1904 GREYHOUND TOWERS - PHOENIX AZ 85077
52- 10	BLACK, WILLIAM CARROLL	1233 MT OLIVE AVE - UNIVERSITY CITY MO 63130
62- 13	BLACKABY, ETHAN ALLEN	2308 EAST ORANGEWOOD - PHOENIX AZ 85020
12- 18	BLACKBURN, EARL STUART	D. AUGUST 4, 1966 MANSFIELD, O.
15- 11	BLACKBURN, FOSTER EDWIN 'BABE'	D. MARCH 9, 1984 NEWPORT RICHEY, FLA.
48- 15	BLACKBURN, JAMES RAY	D. OCTOBER 26, 1969 CINCINNATI, O.
58- 10	BLACKBURN, RONALD HAMILTON	RR 10 BOX 67 - MORGANTON NC 28655
10- 9	BLACKBURNE, RUSSELL AUBREY 'LENA'	D. FEBRUARY 29, 1968 RIVERSIDE, N. J.
28- 9	BLACKERBY, GEORGE FRANKLIN	2527 FAIN - WICHITA FALLS TX 76308
42- 10	BLACKWELL, EWELL	84 ULOQUE CT - BREVARD NC 28712
17- 8	BLACKWELL, FREDRICK WILLIAM	D. DECEMBER 8, 1975 MORGANTOWN, KY.
74- 9	BLACKWELL, TIMOTHY P	1933 MAPLEBROOK - EL CAJON CA 92021
22- 7	BLADES, FRANCIS RAYMOND	D. MAY 18, 1979 LINCOLN, ILL.
69- 8	BLADT, RICHARD ALAN	620 SOUTH WATER ST - SILVERTON OR 97381
25- 10	BLAEHOLDER, GEORGE FRANKLIN	D. DECEMBER 29, 1947 GARDEN GROVE, CALIF.
41- 7	BLAEMIRE, RAE BERTRUM	D. DECEMBER 23, 1975 CHAMPAIGN, ILL.
29- 9	BLAIR, CLARENCE VICK	D. JULY 1, 1982 TEXARKANA, TEX.
74- 10	BLAIR, DENNIS HERMAN	612 FAIRWAY - REDLANDS CA 92373
42- 11	BLAIR, LOUIS NATHAN 'BUDDY'	700 FILHOIL - MONROE LA 71203
64- 7	BLAIR, PAUL L. D.	OLD ADD: DAMCO, 307 5TH AVE,6TH FLR.-NEW YORK NY 10016
51- 2	BLAKE, EDWARD JAMES	208 WILLOW CREEK COURT - BELLEVILLE IL 62223
20- 8	BLAKE, JOHN FREDERICK 'SHERIFF'	D. OCTOBER 31, 1982 BECKLEY, W. VA.
34- 8	BLAKELY, LINCOLN HOWARD	D. SEPTEMBER 28, 1976 OAKLAND, CALIF.
55- 13	BLANCHARD, JOHN EDWIN	15541 LARKIN DR - MINNETONKA MN 55343
35- 5	BLANCHE, PROSPER ALBERT 'AL'	81 EVERETT ST - ARLINGTON MA 02174
72- 9	BLANCO, DAMASO	OLD ADD: 659 CATAMARAN ST #2 - FOSTER CITY CA
65- 10	BLANCO, GILBERT HENRY	360 EAST MONTE VISTA RD - PHOENIX AZ 85004
70- 10	BLANCO, OSVALDO CARLOS	OLD ADD: DE LOZADA B1 E16,SAN JOSE DE AVILAVZ
10- 10	BLANDING, FRED JAMES	D. JULY 16, 1950 SALEM, VA.
22- 8	BLANKENSHIP, HOMER	D. JUNE 22, 1974 LONGVIEW, TEX.
22- 9	BLANKENSHIP, THEODORE	D. JANUARY 14, 1945 ATOKA, OKLA.
72- 10	BLANKS, LARVELL	408 WATERS AVE - DEL RIO TX 78840

34- 9	BLANTON, DARRELL ELIJAH 'CY'	D. SEPTEMBER 13, 1945 NORMAN, OKLA.
55- 14	BLASINGAME, DONALD LEE	9795 EAST MISSION LN - SCOTTSDALE AZ 85258
63- 10	BLASINGAME, WADE ALLEN	5207 RIVERHILL RD NE - MARIETTA GA 30067
64- 8	BLASS, STEPHEN ROBERT	1756 QUIGG DR - PITTSBURGH PA 15241
71- 12	BLATERIC, STEPHEN LAWRENCE	1662 SOUTH UTICA - DENVER CO 80219
48- 16	BLATNIK, JOHN LOUIS	CHERMONT RD, BOX 427 - LANSING OH 43934
42- 12	BLATTNER, ROBERT GARNETT	RR 73 BOX 205 - LAKE OZARK MO 65049
87- 10	BLAUSER, JEFFREY MICHAEL	12525 KILLARNEY WAY - AUBURN CA 95603
59- 6	BLAYLOCK, GARY NELSON	BOX 241 - MALDEN MO 63863
50- 9	BLAYLOCK, MARVIN EDWARD	2200 ANDOVER CT #602 - LITTLE ROCK AR 72207
56- 9	BLAYLOCK, ROBERT EDWARD	RR 2 BOX 460 - MULDROW OK 74948
65- 11	BLEFARY, CURTIS LEROY	1808 SW 4TH COURT - FORT LAUDERDALE FL 33312
60- 9	BLEMKER, RAYMOND 'BUDDY'	2363 DUNDEE DR - HENDERSON KY 42420
72- 11	BLESSITT, ISAIAH 'IKE'	19712 ANGLIN - DETROIT MI 48234
23- 15	BLETHEN, CLARENCE WALDO	D. APRIL 11, 1973 FREDERICK, MD.
42- 13	BLOCK, SEYMOUR 'CY'	4 OLDFIELD LN - LAKE SUCCESS NY 11020
85- 5	BLOCKER, TERRY FENNELL	823 PINEY WOODS ROAD - COLUMBIA SC 29210
69- 9	BLOMBERG, RONALD MARK	11660 MOUNTAIN LAUREL DR - ROSWELL GA 30075
37- 10	BLOODWORTH, JAMES HENRY	BOX 232-APALACHICOLA FL 32320
63- 11	BLOOMFIELD, CLYDE STALCUP 'BUD'	RR 8 BOX 592 - ROGERS AR 72756
24- 12	BLOTT, JACK LEONARD	D. JUNE 11, 1964 ANN ARBOR, MICH.
21- 7	BLUE, LUZERNE ATWELL	D. JULY 28, 1958 ALEXANDRIA, VA.
69- 10	BLUE, VIDA ROCHELLE	P.O. BOX 14438 - OAKLAND CA 94614
22- 10	BLUEGE, OSWALD LOUIS	D. OCTOBER 15, 1985 EDINA, MINN.
32- 5	BLUEGE, OTTO ADAM	D. JUNE 28, 1977 CHICAGO, ILL.
14- 21	BLUEJACKET, JAMES	D. MARCH 26, 1947 PEKIN, ILL.

```
18-  6 BLUHM, HARVEY FRED 'RED'          D. MAY 7, 1952 FLINT, MICH.
22- 11 BLUME, CLINTON WILLIS            D. JUNE 12, 1973 ISLIP, N. Y.
70- 11 BLYLEVEN, RIKALBERT BERT         18992 CANYON DR - VILLA PARK CA 92667
53- 12 BLYZKA, MICHAEL JOHN             1615 EAST 13TH ST #1 - CHEYENNE WY 82001
60- 10 BOAK, CHESTER ROBERT "CHET"      D. NOVEMBER 28, 1983 EMPORIUM, PA.
13- 12 BOARDMAN, CHARLES LOUIS          D. AUGUST 10, 1968 SACRAMENTO, CALIF.
68-  7 BOBB, MARK RANDALL 'RANDY'       D. JUNE 13, 1982 CARNELIAN BAY, CALIF.
63- 12 BOCCABELLA, JOHN DOMINIC         1035 LEA DR - SAN RAFAEL CA 94903
33-  5 BOCEK, MILTON FRANK              2342 SOUTH 61ST CT - CICERO IL 60650
74- 11 BOCHTE, BRUCE ANTON              6475 SOUTH MAXWELTON RD - CLINTON WA 98236
78- 14 BOCHY, BRUCE DOUGLAS             115 EAST AVENUE B - MELBOURNE FL 32901
46- 10 BOCKMAN, JOSEPH EDWARD 'EDDIE'   1400 MILBRAE AVE #2 - MILLBRAE CA 94030
86- 18 BOCKUS, RANDY WALTER             9313 CHESTNUT STREET - EAST SPARTA OH 44626
80-  9 BODDICKER, MICHAEL JAMES         BOX 21 - NORWAY IA 52318
11- 16 BODIE, FRANK STEPHAN 'PING'      D. DECEMBER 12, 1961 SAN FRANCISCO, CALIF.
17-  9 BOECKEL, NORMAN DOXIE            D. FEBRUARY 16, 1924 TORREY PINES, CALIF.
12- 19 BOEHLER, GEORGE HENRY            D. JUNE 23, 1958 LAWRENCEBURG, IND.
12- 20 BOEHLING, JOHN JOSEPH            D. SEPTEMBER 8, 1941 RICHMOND, VA.
67-  5 BOEHMER, LEONARD JOSEPH          3570 HIGHWAY P - WENTZVILLE MO 63385
32-  6 BOERNER, LAWRENCE HYER           D. OCTOBER 16, 1969 STAUNTON, VA.
85-  6 BOEVER, JOSEPH MARTIN            5141 TOWNE SOUTH ROAD - ST.LOUIS MO 63128
20-  9 BOGART, JOHN RENZIE              D. DECEMBER 7, 1986 CLARENCE, N. Y.
82- 13 BOGENER, TERRY WAYNE             411 MCCABE - PALMYRAMO 63461
28- 10 BOGGS, RAYMOND JOSEPH            1135 HILL AVE - GRAND JUNCTION CO 81501
76- 17 BOGGS, THOMAS WINSTON            8805 POINT WEST - AUSTIN TX 78759
82- 14 BOGGS, WADE ANTHONY              14615 VILLAGE GLEN CIRCLE - TAMPA FL 33606
68-  8 BOGLE, WARREN FREDERICK          11605 SW 103RD AVE - MIAMI FL 33156
13- 13 BOHEN, LEO IGNATIUS 'PAT'        D. APRIL 8, 1942 NAPA, CALIF.
16-  6 BOHNE, SAMUEL ARTHUR             D. MAY 23, 1977 PALO ALTO, CALIF.
82- 15 BOHNET, JOHN KELLY               224 PANORAMA DR - BENICIA CA 94510
74- 12 BOISCLAIR, BRUCE ARMAND          29064 W. SADDLE BROOK - AGOURA CA 91301
78- 15 BOITANO, DANNY JON               15400 WINCHESTER BLVD #43-LOS GATOS CA 95030
51-  3 BOKELMANN, RICHARD WERNER        629 NORTH BELMONT AV - ARLINGTON HEIGHTS IL 60004
33-  6 BOKEN, ROBERT ANTHONY            4011 TACOMA - LAS VEGAS NV 89121
36- 10 BOKINA, JOSEPH                   1901 EAST 25TH ST-CHATTANOOGA TN 37404
15- 12 BOLAND, BERNARD ANTHONY          D. SEPTEMBER 12, 1973 DETROIT, MICH.
34- 10 BOLAND, EDWARD JOHN              1655 S. HIGHLAND AVE #J196 - CLEARWATER FL 33516
14- 22 BOLD, CHARLES DICKENS            D. JULY 29, 1978 CHELSEA, MASS.
19-  7 BOLDEN, WILLIAM HORACE           D. DECEMBER 8, 1966 JEFFERSON CITY, TENN.
26-  7 BOLEN, STEWART O'NEAL            D. AUGUST 30, 1969 JACKSON, ALA.
62- 14 BOLES, CARL THEODORE             18020 CASTLEWOOD CT - HAYWARD CA 94541
27- 13 BOLEY, JOHN PETER 'JOE'          D. DECEMBER 30, 1962 MAHANOY CITY, PA.
50- 10 BOLGER, JAMES CYRIL              5524 SIDNEY RD - CINCINNATI OH 45238
61-  9 BOLIN, BOBBY DONALD              BOX EAST - SIX MILE SC 29682
54-  8 BOLLING, FRANK ELMORE            171 FENWICK RD - MOBILE AL 36608
39- 12 BOLLING, JOHN EDWARD             BOX 9266 - PANAMA CITY BEACH FL 32407
52- 11 BOLLING, MILTON JOSEPH           2752 FONTAINEBLEAU DR SOUTH - MOBILE AL 36606
65- 12 BOLLO, GREGORY GENE              15207 REGINA ST - ALLEN PARK MI 48101
50- 11 BOLLWEG, DONALD RAYMOND          513 TIMBER RIDGE DR #206 - CAROL STREAM IL 60188
28- 11 BOLTON, CECIL GLENFORD           419 SOUTH MAIN ST - GREENVILLE MS 38701
87- 11 BOLTON, THOMAS EDWARD            RURAL ROUTE 1, NOLENSVILLE ROAD - BRENTWOOD TN 37027
31-  8 BOLTON, WILLIAM CLIFTON          D. APRIL 21, 1979 LEXINGTON, N. C.
78- 16 BOMBACK, MARK VINCENT            %H.BOMBACK, 87 SMITH ST - FALL RIVER MA 02721
60- 11 BOND, WALTER FRANKLIN            D. SEPTEMBER 14, 1967 HOUSTON, TEX.
86- 19 BONDS, BARRY LAMAR               175 LYNDHURST AVENUE - SAN CARLOS CA 94070
68-  9 BONDS, BOBBY LEE                 175 LYNDHURST - SAN CARLOS CA 94076
37- 11 BONETTI, JULIO G                 D. JUNE 17, 1952 BELMONT, CAL.
27- 14 BONEY, HENRY TATE                BOX 906 - LAKE WORTH FL 33460
38-  8 BONGIOVANNI, ANTHONY THOMAS 'NINO' 416 ROSEWOOD AVE - SAN JOSE CA 95117
```

```
40-  3 BONHAM, ERNEST EDWARD 'TINY'     D. SEPTEMBER 15, 1949 PITTSBURGH, PA.
71- 13 BONHAM, WILLIAM GORDON           1605 SYCAMORE WAY - SOLVANG CA 93463
62- 15 BONIKOWSKI, JOSEPH PETER         6701 OLD REID RD - CHARLOTTE NC 28210
81- 11 BONILLA, JUAN GUILLERMO          RR 3 BOX 262 - QUINCY FL 32351
86- 20 BONILLA, ROBERTO MARTIN ANTONIO  2648 BAINBRIDGE AVENUE - BRONX NY 10458
13- 14 BONIN, ERNEST LUTHER             D. JANUARY 3, 1965 SYCAMORE, O.
77- 12 BONNELL, ROBERT BARRY            2102 179TH COURT NE - REDMOND WA 98052
80- 10 BONNER, ROBERT AVERILL           39 CEDAR TERRACE - HILTON NY 14468
44- 11 BONNESS, WILLIAM JOHN            D. DECEMBER 3, 1977 CLEVELAND, O.
20- 10 BONO, ADLAI WENDELL 'GUS'        D. DECEMBER 3, 1948 DEARBORN, MICH.
34- 11 BONURA, HENRY JOHN 'ZEKE'        D. MARCH 9, 1987 NEW ORLEANS, LA.
13- 15 BOOE, EVERETT LITTLE             D. MAY 21, 1969 KENNEDY, TEX.
83- 15 BOOKER, GREGORY SCOTT            14261 DALHOUSIE RD - SAN DIEGO CA 92129
```

66- 8	BOOKER, RICHARD LEE	BOX 59 - BROOKNEAL VA 24528
87- 12	BOOKER, RODERICK STEWART	526 WEST ALTADENA DRIVE - ALTADENA CA 91001
28- 12	BOOL, ALBERT	D. SEPTEMBER 27, 1981 LINCOLN, NEB.
81- 12	BOONE, DANIEL HUGH	RR 2 BOX 111A - ATOKA OK 74525
22- 12	BOONE, ISAAC MORGAN 'IKE'	D. AUGUST 1, 1958 NORTHPORT, ALA.
19- 8	BOONE, JAMES ALBERT 'DANNY'	D. MAY 11, 1968 TUSCALOOSA, ALA.
13- 16	BOONE, LUTE JOSEPH	D. JULY 29, 1982 PITTSBURGH, PA.
48- 17	BOONE, RAYMOND OTIS	15420 OLDE HWY 80 #137 - EL CAJON CA 92021
72- 12	BOONE, ROBERT RAYMOND	18571 VILLA DR - VILLA PARK CA 92667
62- 16	BOOZER, JOHN MORGAN	D. JANUARY 24, '986 LEXINGTON, S. C.
69- 11	BORBON, PEDRO RODRIGUEZ	LAS PALMAS,CORRAZOND DEJESUS #2-SANTO DOMINGO DOM. REP.
34- 12	BORDAGARAY, STANLEY GEORGE 'FRENCHY'	395 CRESTWOOD AV - VENTURA CA 93003
80- 11	BORDI, RICHARD ALBERT 'RICH'	206 ARROYO DR - SOUTH SAN FRANCISCO CA 94080
80- 12	BORDLEY, WILLIAM CLARKE	5314 PASEO DE PABLO - TORRANCE CA 90505
72- 13	BORGMANN, GLENN DENNIS	16 LUNDY TER - BUTLER NJ 07405
82- 16	BORIS, PAUL STANLEY	12 WOODLAND DR - COLINIA NJ 07067
64- 9	BORK, FRANK BERNARD	5754 STRATHMORE LANE - DUBLIN OH 43017
50- 12	BORKOWSKI, ROBERT VILARIAN	1031 GERHARD ST - DAYTON OH 45404
60- 12	BORLAND, THOMAS BRUCE	624 CHEROKEE DR - STILLWATER OK 74074
44- 12	BOROM, EDWARD JONES 'RED'	827 HIGHLAND OAKS - DALLAS TX 75232
57- 7	BOROS, STEPHEN	13121 DECANT - POWAY CA 92064
42- 14	BOROWY, HENRY LUDWIG	210 WEST PASSAIC AVENUE - BLOOMFIELD NJ 07003
12- 21	BORTON, WILLIAM BAKER 'BABE'	D. JULY 29, 1954 BERKELEY, CALIF.
66- 9	BOSCH, DONALD JOHN	1600 MCKINLEY RD - NAPA CA 94558
76- 18	BOSETTI, RICHARD ALAN 'RICK'	1233 HILL ST - ANDERSON CA 96007
86- 21	BOSIO, CHRISTOPHER LOUIS	10425 AMBASSADOR DRIVE - RANCHO CORDOVA CA 95670
77- 13	BOSLEY, THADDIS	1965 VALLEY RD - OCEANSIDE CA 92054
66- 10	BOSMAN, RICHARD ALLEN	12997 ORLEANS ST - WOODBRIDGE VA 22192
28- 13	BOSS, ELMER HARLEY	D. MAY 15, 1964 NASHVILLE, TENN.
45- 4	BOSSER, MELVIN EDWARD	RR 14 BOX 291 - CROSSVILLE TN 38555
15- 13	BOSTICK, HENRY LANDERS	D. SEPTEMBER 16, 1968 DENVER, COLO.
75- 18	BOSTOCK, LYMAN WESLEY	D. SEPTEMBER 24, 1978 GARY, IND.
84- 8	BOSTON, DARYL LAMONT	1016 VALLEY LANE - CINCINNATI OH 45229
64- 10	BOSWELL, DAVID WILSON	309 ROXBURY CT - JOPPA MD 21085
67- 6	BOSWELL, KENNETH GEORGE	2301 MATTERHORN LN - AUSTIN TX 78704
82- 17	BOTELHO, DEREK WAYNE	OLD ADD: 4900 NW 5TH AVE - BOCA RATON FL 33432
37- 12	BOTTARINI, JOHN CHARLES	D. OCTOBER 8, 1976 SPRING, N. MEX.
79- 10	BOTTING, RALPH WAYNE	1154 THOMPSON AVE - GLENDALE CA 91201
22- 13	BOTTOMLEY, JAMES LEROY	D. DECEMBER 11, 1959 SAINT LOUIS, MO.
62- 17	BOTZ, ROBERT ALLEN	4592 MONCHES RD - COLGATE WI 53017
56- 10	BOUCHEE, EDWARD FRANCIS	2036 SPRUCE AVE - DES PLAINES IL 60018
14- 23	BOUCHER, ALEXANDER FRANCIS	D. JUNE 23, 1974 TORRANCE, CALIF.
14- 24	BOUCHER, MEDRIC CHARLES FRANCIS	D. MARCH 12, 1974 MARTINEZ, CALIF.
38- 9	BOUDREAU, LOUIS	15600 ELLIS AVENUE - DOLTON IL 60419
61- 10	BOULDIN, CARL EDWARD	37 AUDUBON - FORT THOMAS KY 41075
80- 13	BOURJOS, CHRISTOPHER	3451 NORTH NEWCASTLE - CHICAGO IL 60634
71- 14	BOURQUE, PATRICK DANIEL	2013 EAST HARVARD DR - TEMPE AZ 85283
62- 18	BOUTON, JAMES ALAN	6 MYRON CT - TEANECK NJ 07666

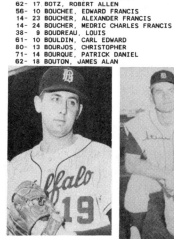

70-	12	BOWA, LAWRENCE ROBERT	1029 MORRIS AVENUE - BRYN MAWR PA 19010
14-	25	BOWDEN, DAVID TIMON	D. OCTOBER 25, 1949 EMORY, GA.
19-	9	BOWEN, EMMONS JOSEPH 'CHICK'	D. AUGUST 9, 1948 NEW HAVEN, CONN.
77-	14	BOWEN, SAMUEL THOMAS	8 HIGH HILL DR - BRUNSWICK GA 31520
63-	13	BOWENS, SAMUEL EDWARD	RR 4 BOX 27 NATIONAL AVE - LELAND NC 28451
49-	8	BOWERS, GROVER BILL	P. O. BOX 401 - WYNNE AR 72396
35-	6	BOWERS, STEWART COLE	1620 RIDGWAY RD - HAVERTOWN PA 19083
31-	9	BOWLER, GRANT TIERNEY	D. JUNE 25, 1968 DENVER, COLO.
43-	10	BOWLES, CHARLES JAMES	3004 NORTH CENTER ST-HICKORY NC 28601
22-	14	BOWLES, EMMETT JEROME	D. SEPTEMBER 3, 1959 FLAGSTAFF, ARIZ.
67-	7	BOWLIN, LOIS WELDON 'HOSS'	BOX 1026 - LIVINGSTON AL 35470
76-	19	BOWLING, STEPHEN SHADDON	1784 WEST 63RD - TULSA OK 74132
14-	26	BOWMAN, ALVAH EDSON	D. OCTOBER 11, 1979 LONGVIEW, TEXAS
20-	11	BOWMAN, ELMER WILHELM	17870 HOLIDAY DR,%BACE BOWMAN - MORGAN HILL CA 95037
61-	11	BOWMAN, ERNEST FERRELL 'BUDDY'	ROUTE 17, EAST SHORE APT #8 - JOHNSON CITY TN 37601
32-	7	BOWMAN, JOSEPH EMIL	2001 WEST 83RD ST - LEAWOOD KS 66206
39-	13	BOWMAN, ROBERT JAMES	D. SEPTEMBER 4, 1972 BLUEFIELD, W. VA.
55-	15	BOWMAN, ROBERT LEROY	2911 VIA CARMEN - SAN JOSE CA 95124
49-	9	BOWMAN, ROGER CLINTON	2210 SOUTH SEPULVEDA BLVD - LOS ANGELES CA 90064
10-	11	BOWSER, JAMES H. 'RED'	B. 1886 GREENSBURG, PA.
58-	11	BOWSFIELD, EDWARD OLIVER 'TED'	900 FAIRVIEW ROAD - PENTICTON BRITISH COL. CAN.
82-	18	BOYD, DENNIS RAY 'OIL CAN'	1611 20TH ST - MERIDIAN MS 39301
69-	12	BOYD, GARY LEE	15227 CHANERA AVE - GARDENA CA 90249
10-	12	BOYD, RAYMOND C.	D. FEBRUARY 11, 1920 HOUTONVILLE, ILL.
51-	4	BOYD, ROBERT RICHARD	2811 NORTH VASSAR AVE - WICHITA KS 67220
55-	16	BOYER, CLETIS LEROY	695 CLEARWATER HARBOR DR - LARGO FL 33540
49-	10	BOYER, CLOYD VICTOR	RR ONE BOX 231-A - WEBB CITY MO 64870
55-	17	BOYER, KENTON LLOYD	D. SEPTEMBER 7, 1982 ST. LOUIS, MO.
78-	17	BOYLAND, DORIAN SCOTT 'DOE'	OLD ADD: 1205 SW 18TH - PORTLAND OR 97205
26-	8	BOYLE, JAMES JOHN	D. DECEMBER 24, 1958 CINCINNATI, O.
12-	22	BOYLE, JOHN BELLEW	D. APRIL 3, 1971 FORT LAUDERDALE, FLA.
29-	10	BOYLE, RALPH FRANCIS 'BUZZ'	D. NOVEMBER 12, 1978 CINCINNATI, O.
38-	10	BOYLES, HARRY	101 SIOUX RD #473 - PHARR TX 78577
66-	11	BRABENDER, EUGENE MATHEW	10969 AMENDA ROAD - MAZOMANIA WI 53560
37-	13	BRACK, GILBERT HERMAN 'GIB'	D. JANUARY 20, 1960 GREENVILLE, TEX.
64-	11	BRADEY, DONALD EUGENE	3686 OAKLEAF ROAD - WEST BLOOMFIELD MI 48033
66-	12	BRADFORD, CHARLES WILLIAM 'BUDDY'	6440 SPRING PARK AVE - LADERA HEIGHTS CA90056
43-	11	BRADFORD, HENRY VICTOR 'VIC'	259 STONEY POINT RD - PARIS KY 40361
77-	15	BRADFORD, LARRY	4998 GREENTREE TRAIL - COLLEGE PARK GA 30349
56-	11	BRADFORD, WILLIAM D	BOX 3043 - FAIRFIELD BAY AR 72153
48-	18	BRADLEY, FREDERICK LANGDON	4540 SOUTH LAYMAN AVE - PICO RIVERA CA 90660
46-	11	BRADLEY, GEORGE WASHINGTON	D. OCTOBER 19, 1982 LAWRENCEBURG, TENN.
27-	15	BRADLEY, HERBERT THEODORE	D. OCTOBER 16, 1959 CLAY CENTER, KAN.
10-	13	BRADLEY, HUGH FREDERICK	D. JANUARY 26, 1949 WORCESTER, MASS.
16-	7	BRADLEY, JOHN THOMAS	D. MARCH 18, 1969 TULSA, OKLA.
81-	13	BRADLEY, MARK ALLEN	413 PIERCE ST - ELIZABETHTOWN KY 42701
83-	16	BRADLEY, PHILIP POOLE	207 MEADOW DRIVE - MACOMB IL 61455
84-	9	BRADLEY, SCOTT WILLIAM	30 ESSEX ROAD - ESSEX FALLS NJ 07021
83-	17	BRADLEY, STEVEN BERT	RURAL ROUTE 1 - TOLEDO IL 62468
69-	13	BRADLEY, THOMAS WILLIAM	6306 WHISPERING OAKS DR - JACKSONVILLE FL 32211
17-	10	BRADSHAW, DALLAS CARL	D. DECEMBER 11, 1939 HERRIN, ILL.
52-	12	BRADSHAW, GEORGE THOMAS	258 BRUNSWICK AVENUE WEST - HOLDEN BEACH NC 28462
29-	11	BRADSHAW, JOE SIAH	D. JANUARY 30, 1985 TAVARES, FLA.
20-	12	BRADY, CLIFFORD FRANCIS	D. SEPTEMBER 25, 1974 BELLEVILLE, ILL.
15-	14	BRADY, CORNELIUS JOSEPH 'NEAL'	D. JUNE 19, 1947 FORT MITCHELL, KY.
56-	12	BRADY, JAMES JOSEPH	6418 WHISPERING OAKS DR - JACKSONVILLE FL 32211
46-	12	BRADY, ROBERT JAY	42 OVERLAND ST - MANCHESTER CT 06040
12-	23	BRADY, WILLIAM A.	
40-	4	DRAGAN, ROBERT RANDALL	1901 INDIAN CREEK DR - FORT WORTH TX 76107
86-	22	BRAGGS, GLENN ERICK	2876 STATE STREET - SAN BERNARDINO CA 92405
14-	27	BRAINARD, FREDERICK	D. APRIL 17, 1959 GALVESTON, TEX.
15-	15	BRAITHWOOD, ALFRED	D. NOVEMBER 24, 1960 ROWLESBURG, W. VA.
28-	14	BRAME, ERVIN BECKHAM	D. NOVEMBER 22, 1949 HOPKINSVILLE, KY.
35-	7	BRAMHALL, ARTHUR WASHINGTON	D. SEPTEMBER 4, 1985 MADISON, WIS.
44-	13	BRANCA, RALPH THEODORE JOSEPH	WESTCHESTER COUNTRY CLUB - RYE NY 10580
39-	14	BRANCATO, ALBERT	108 GREEN VALLEY RD-UPPER DARBY PA 19082

62- 19 BRANCH, HARVEY ALFRED	4995 JOLLY DR - MEMPHIS TN 38101
41- 8 BRANCH, NORMAN DOWNS	D. NOVEMBER 21, 1971 NAVASOTA, TEX.
79- 11 BRANCH, ROY	5322 TERRY AVE - SAINT LOUIS MO 63120
63- 14 BRAND, RONALD GEORGE	1500 PINE VALLEY CIR - ROSEVILLE CA 95678
66- 13 BRANDON, DARRELL G	196 OLD FARM RD - HANOVER MA 02339
28- 15 BRANDT, EDWARD ARTHUR	D. NOVEMBER 1, 1944 SPOKANE, WASH.
56- 13 BRANDT, JOHN GEORGE 'JACKIE'	611 OSAGE DR - PAPILLION NE 68046
41- 9 BRANDT, WILLIAM GEORGE	D. MAY 16, 1968 FORT WAYNE, IND.
28- 16 BRANNAN, OTIS OWEN	D. JUNE 6, 1967 LITTLE ROCK, ARK.
27- 16 BRANOM, EDGAR DUDLEY 'DUD'	D. FEBRUARY 4, 1980 SUN CITY, ARIZ.
80- 14 BRANT, MARSHALL LEE	301 OAK ST - PENNGROVE CA 94951
86- 23 BRANTLEY, MICHAEL CHARLES 'MICKEY'	102 SUMMIT - CATSKILL NY 12414
21- 8 BRATCHE, FREDERICK OSCAR	D. JANUARY 7, 1962 MASSILLON, O.
24- 13 BRATCHER, JOSEPH WARLICK	D. OCTOBER 13, 1977 FORT WORTH, TEX.
64- 12 BRAUN, JOHN PAUL	1014 AMSTERDAM AVE - MADISON WI 53716
71- 15 BRAUN, STEPHEN RUSSELL	OLD ADD: 3108 167TH AVE NE - BELLEVUE WA 98008
69- 14 BRAVO, ANGEL ALFONSO	OLD ADD: CALLE CAMINO NUEVO #208-MARACAIBO VZ
21- 9 BRAXTON, EDGAR GARLAND	D. FEBRUARY 25, 1966 NORFLOK, VA.
41- 10 BRAY, CLARENCE WILBUR 'BUSTER'	D. SEPTEMBER 4, 1982 EVANSVILLE, IND.
21- 10 BRAZILL, FRANK LEO	D. NOVEMBER 3, 1976 OAKLAND, CALIF.
43- 12 BRAZLE, ALPHA EUGENE	D. OCTOBER 24, 1973 GRAND JUNCTION , COL.
83- 18 BREAM, SIDNEY EUGENE	2516 ELKRIDGE DRIVE - WEXFORD PA 15090
69- 15 BREAZEALE, JAMES LEO	717 BOLLING LANE - HOUSTON TX 77076
40- 5 BRECHEEN, HARRY DAVID	1134 SOUTH HIGHSCHOOL - ADA OK 74820
29- 12 BRECKINRIDGE, WILLIAM ROBERTSON	D. AUGUST 23, 1958 TULSA, OKLA.
69- 16 BREEDEN, DANNY RICHARD	111 "B" AVENUE - LOXLEY AL 36551
71- 16 BREEDEN, HAROLD NOEL	RR1 BOX 311 - LEESBURG GA 31763
60- 13 BREEDING, MARVIN EUGENE	BOX 1061 - DECATUR AL 35601
80- 15 BREINING, FRED LAWRENCE	1218 33RD AVE - SAN FRANCISCO CA 94122
37- 14 BREMER, HERBERT FREDERICK	D. NOVEMBER 28, 1979 COLUMBUS, GA.
14- 28 BRENEGAN, OLAF SELMAR	D. APRIL 20, 1956 GALESVILLE, WIS.
81- 14 BRENLY, ROBERT EARL	936 ORANGE ST - COSHOCTON OH 43812
10- 14 BRENNAN, ADDISON FOSTER	D. JANUARY 7, 1962 KANSAS CITY, MO.
33- 7 BRENNAN, JAMES DONALD 'DON'	D. APRIL 2L, 1953 BOSTON, MASS.
81- 15 BRENNAN, THOMAS MARTIN	5500 OAK CENTER DR - OAK LAWN IL 60453
65- 13 BRENNEMAN, JAMES LEROY	OLD ADD: 1855 EAST ROSE #12A - ORANGE CA 92667
12- 24 BRENNER, DELBERT HENRY	D. APRIL 11, 1971 ST. LOUIS PARK, MINN.
13- 17 BRENTON, LYNN DAVIS	D. OCTOBER 14, 1968 LOS ANGELES, CALIF.
32- 8 BRENZEL, WILLIAM RICHARD	D. JUNE 12, 1979 OAKLAND, CALIF.
14- 29 BRESSLER, RAYMOND BLOOM 'RUBE'	D. NOVEMBER 7, 1966 MT. WASHINGTON, O.
56- 14 BRESSOUD, EDWARD FRANCIS	10455 CRESTON DR - LOS ALTOS CA 94022
13- 18 BRETON, JOHN FREDERICK 'JIM'	D. MAY 30, 1973 BELOIT, WIS.
73- 13 BRETT, GEORGE HOWARD	3201 WEST 98TH - LEAWOOD KS 66206
24- 14 BRETT, HERBERT JAMES	D. NOVEMBER 25, 1974 ST PETERSBURG, FLA.
67- 8 BRETT, KENNETH ALVEN	1504 STRAND - HERMOSA BEACH CA 90254
39- 15 BREUER, MARVIN HOWARD	1106 JOYCE AVE-ROLLA MO 65401
84- 10 BREWER, ANTHONY BRUCE	659 WILDWOOD LANE - PALO ALTO CA 94303
60- 14 BREWER, JAMES THOMAS	D. NOVEMBER 16, 1987 TYLER, TEXAS
44- 14 BREWER, JOHN HERNDON	28271 WORCESTER - SUN CITY CA 92381
86- 24 BREWER, MICHAEL QUINN	2260 BRENTWOOD COURT - EAST PALO ALTO CA 94303
54- 9 BREWER, THOMAS AUSTIN	409 STATE RD - CHERAW SC 29520
43- 13 BREWSTER, CHARLES LAWRENCE	RR 2 BOX 165A - BLACKSHEAR GA 31516
61- 12 BRICE, ALAN HEALEY	7807 16TH AVE NW - BRADENTON FL 33505
58- 12 BRICKELL, FRITZ DARRELL	D. OCTOBER 15, 1965 WICHITA, KAN.
26- 9 BRICKELL, GEORGE FREDERICK 'FRED'	D. APRIL 8, 1961 WICHITA, KAN.
13- 19 BRICKLEY, GEORGE VINCENT	D. FEBRUARY 23, 1947 EVERETT, MASS.
52- 13 BRICKNER, RALPH HAROLD	3967 ROBINHILL DR - CINCINNATI OH 45211
51- 5 BRIDEWESER, JAMES EHRENFELD	24326 PARK PLACE DR - LAGUNA NIGUEL CA 92677
51- 6 BRIDGES, EVERETT LAMAR 'ROCKY'	2445 E. GATEWAY RD - COUER D'ALENE ID 83814
59- 7 BRIDGES, MARSHALL	1195 RATROND RO #10H - JACKSON MS 39521
30- 5 BRIDGES, THOMAS JEFFERSON DAVIS	D. APRIL 19, 1968 NASHVILLE, TENN.
12- 25 BRIEF, ANTHONY VINCENT 'BUNNY'	D. FEBRUARY 10, 1963 MILWAUKEE, WIS.
75- 19 BRIGGS, DANIEL LEE	231 FRANCE ST - SONOMA CA 95476
64- 13 BRIGGS, JOHN EDWARD	432 E. 27TH - PATERSON NJ 07514
56- 15 BRIGGS, JOHN TIFT	8724 SHERRY DR - ORANGEVALE CA 95662
58- 13 BRIGHT, HARRY JAMES	2048 50TH AVE - SACRAMENTO CA 95827
65- 14 BRILES, NELSON KELLEY	1324 CLEARVIEW DR - GREENSBURG PA 15501
22- 15 BRILLHEART, JAMES BENSON	D. SEPTEMBER 2, 1972 RADFORD, VA.
12- 26 BRINKER, WILLIAM HUTCHINSON	D. FEBRUARY 5, 1965 ARCADIA, CAL.

RALPH BRANCA

JACK BRANDT

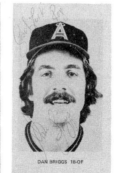

DAN BRIGGS 1B-OF

69- 17 BRINKMAN, CHARLES ERNEST	332 INGALLS ST - CINCINNATI OH 45204
61- 13 BRINKMAN, EDWIN ALBERT	7106 WYANDOTTE DR - CINCINNATI OH 45238
52- 14 BRINKOPF, LEON CLARENCE	915 SOUTH MINNESOTA - CAPE GIRARDEAU MO 63701
47- 13 BRISSIE, LELAND VICTOR 'LOU'	1908 WHITEPINE DR - NORTH AUGUSTA SC 29841
66- 14 BRISTOL, JAMES DAVID 'DAVE'	RR1 - ANDREWS NC 28901

```
37- 15 BRITTAIN, AUGUST SCHUSTER          D. FEBRUARY 16, 1974 WILMINGTON, N. C.
50- 13 BRITTIN, JOHN ALBERT               1036 FRANCELLA CT - SPRINGFIELD IL 62702
67-  9 BRITTON, JAMES ALAN               10455 SW 112TH ST - MIAMI FL 33176
13- 20 BRITTON, STEPHEN GILBERT           D. JUNE 20, 1983 PARSONS, KAN.
79- 12 BRIZZOLARA, ANTHONY JOHN           1638 PRINCESS CIR NE - ATLANTA GA 30345
34- 13 BROACA, JOHN JOSEPH                D. MAY 16, 1985 LAWRENCE, MASS.
71- 17 BROBERG, PETER SVEN                220 MONTEREY RD - PALM BEACH FL 33480
82- 19 BROCK, GREGORY ALLEN              700 HOLLY HOCK LANE - PLACENTIA CA 92670
17- 11 BROCK, JOHN RAY                    D. OCTOBER 27, 1951 CLAYTON, MO.
61- 14 BROCK, LOUIS CLARK                12595 DURBIN DR - ST LOUIS MO 63141
52- 15 BRODOWSKI, RICHARD STANLEY         90 FORD ST - LYNN MA 01904
59-  8 BROGLIO, ERNEST GILBERT           2838 VIA CARMEN - SAN JOSE CA 95124
72- 14 BROHAMER, JOHN ANTHONY            1236 LEXINGTON DR - VISTA CA 92083
44- 15 BRONDELL, KENNETH LEROY           7029 DECELIS PL - VAN NUYS CA 91401
10- 15 BRONKIE, HERMAN CHARLES            D. MAY 27, 1968 SOMERS, CONN.
59-  9 BRONSTAD, JAMES WARREN            693 QUAIL RIDGE ROAD - ALEDO TX 76008
75- 20 BROOKENS, EDWARD DWAIN             RR 1 - FAYETTEVILLE PA 17222
79- 13 BROOKENS, THOMAS DALE             120 HILLSIDE DR - FAYETTEVILLE PA 17222
80- 16 BROOKS, HUBERT                    1502 SPRING AVE - COMPTON CA 90221
25- 11 BROOKS, JONATHAN JOSEPH 'MANDY'    D. JUNE 17, 1962 KIRKWOOD, MO.
69- 18 BROOKS, ROBERT                    1130 WEST 252ND ST - HARBOR CITY CA 90710
40-  6 BROSKIE, SIGMUND THEODORE          D. MAY 17, 1975 CANTON, O.
54- 10 BROSNAN, JAMES PATRICK            7742 WEST CHURCHILL ST - MORTON GROVE IL 60053
69- 19 BROSSEAU, FRANKLIN LEE            41 ISLAND RD - SAINT PAUL MN 55110
16-  8 BROTTEM, ANTON CHRISTIAN 'TONY'    D. AUGUST 5, 1929 CHICAGO, ILL.
80- 17 BROUHARD, MARK STEVEN             6289 JACKIE AVE - WOODLAND HILLS CA 91367
55- 18 BROVIA, JOSEPH JOHN               142 ACADIA ST - SANTA CRUZ CA 95060
20- 13 BROWER, FRANK WILLARD              D. NOVEMBER 20, 1960 BALTIMORE, MD.
31- 10 BROWER, LOUIS LESTER              308 SUNRISE RD - ROSWELL NM 88201
86- 25 BROWER, ROBERT RICHARD            2110 GUNNELL FARMS DRIVE - VIENNA VA 22180
51-  7 BROWN, ALTON LEO                  253 CONSUL AVE - VIRGINIA BEACH VA 23462
11- 17 BROWN, CARROLL WILLIAM 'BOARDWALK' D. FEBRUARY 8, 1977 BURLINGTON, N. J.
11- 18 BROWN, CHARLES ROY 'CURLY'         D. JUNE 10, 1968 SPRING HILL, KAN.
28- 17 BROWN, CLINTON HAROLD              D. DECEMBER 31, 1955 ROCKY RIVER,O.
73- 14 BROWN, CURTIS                     3745 HAYWOOD ST - SACRAMENTO CA 95838
83- 19 BROWN, CURTIS STEVEN              104 EAST HEMINGWAY CIRCLE - COCONUT CREEK FL 33063
81- 16 BROWN, DARRELL WAYNE              5843 FIFTH AVE - LOS ANGELES CA 90043
14- 30 BROWN, DELOS HIGHT                 D. DECEMBER 21, 1964 CARBONDALE, ILL.
15- 16 BROWN, DONALD G                   1917 ADD: 712 ELLAS ST - BEATRICE NE
13- 21 BROWN, DRUMMOND NICOL              D. JANUARY 27, 1927 PLATTE CO., MO.
20- 14 BROWN, EDWARD WILLIAM              D. SEPTEMBER 10, 1956 VALLEJO, CAL.
69- 20 BROWN, EDWIN RANDOLPH 'RANDY'     2039 LAKE ALDEN DRIVE - APOPKA FL 32703
11- 19 BROWN, ELMER YOUNG                 D. JANUARY 23, 1955 INDIANAPOLIS, IND.
51-  8 BROWN, HECTOR HAROLD 'HAL'        BOX 1626 - GREENSBORO NC 27402
69- 21 BROWN, ISAAC 'IKE'                LINCOLN CT #A-4 - LAKELAND FL 33805
70- 13 BROWN, JACKIE GENE                RR 3 BOX 50B - HOLDENVILLE OK 74848
37- 16 BROWN, JAMES ROBERSON             D. DECEMBER 29, 1977 BATH, N. C.
75- 21 BROWN, JERALD RAY 'JAKE'           D. DECEMBER 18, 1981 HOUSTON, TEXAS
84- 11 BROWN, JOHN CHRISTOPHER           5015 BRIGHTON AVE - LOS ANGELES CA 90062
86- 26 BROWN, JOHN KEVIN                 MCINTYRE GA 31054
37- 17 BROWN, JOHN LINDSAY                D. JANUARY 1, 1967 SAN ANTONIO, TEX.
68- 10 BROWN, JOPHERY CLIFFORD           3008 WEST 81ST ST - INGLEWOOD CA 90305
27- 17 BROWN, JOSEPH HENRY                D. MARCH 7, 1950 LOS ANGELES, CALIF.
63- 15 BROWN, LARRY LESLEY              13158 LAMIRADA CIRCLE - WEST PALM BEACH FL 33414
76- 20 BROWN, LEON                       7537 SOUTH LAROSA - TEMPE AZ 85283
25- 12 BROWN, LLOYD ANDREW                D. JANUARY 14, 1974 OPALOCKA, FLA
35-  8 BROWN, MACE STANLEY               305 NORTH HOLDEN RUAD-GREENSBORO NC 27410
84- 12 BROWN, MARK ANTHONY               59 CHURCH ST - NORTH WALPOLE NH 03608
83- 20 BROWN, MICHAEL CHARLES            312 COPCO LANE - SAN JOSE CA 95123
82- 20 BROWN, MICHAEL GARY               8712 PINE NEEDLES CT - VIENNA VA 22180
22- 16 BROWN, MYRL LINCOLN                D. FEBRUARY 23, 1981 HARRISBURG, PA.
43- 14 BROWN, NORMAN                     106 EAST MAIN ST-BENNETTSVILLE SC 29512
65- 15 BROWN, OLLIE LEE                  8462 COUNTRY CLUB DR - BUENA PARK CA 90621
69- 22 BROWN, OSCAR LEE                 19113 GUNLOCK AVE - CARSON CA 90746
61- 15 BROWN, PAUL DWAYNE                RR 4 - HOLDENVILLE OK 74848
57-  8 BROWN, RICHARD ERNEST             D. APRIL 12, 1970 BALTIMORE, MD.
14- 31 BROWN, ROBERT M.                  B. 1891
```

TOM BROOKENS

```
30-  6 BROWN, ROBERT MURRAY              %M.REMONDINI,123 RICHARD DRIVE - HANOVER MA 02339
46- 13 BROWN, ROBERT WILLIAM             1324 THOMAS PL - FORT WORTH TX 76107
79- 14 BROWN, ROGERS LEE 'BOBBY'         OLD ADD: BOX 874 - EASTVILLE VA 23307
81- 17 BROWN, SCOTT EDWARD               BOX 608 - DEQUINCY LA 70633
83- 21 BROWN, STEPHEN ELBERT            1203 WEST 8TH STREET - DAVIS CA 95616
78- 18 BROWN, THOMAS DALE                248 GLORIA DR - BATON ROUGE LA 70815
44- 16 BROWN, THOMAS MICHAEL             315 SHADY PL - BRENTWOOD TN 37027
```

63- 16 BROWN, THOMAS WILLIAM	9104 WOODLAND DR - SILVER SPRING MD 20910
25- 13 BROWN, WALTER GEORGE 'JUMBO'	D. OCTOBER 2, 1966 FREEPORT, N. Y.
47- 14 BROWN, WALTER IRVING	RR ORIENTAL PARK - BEMUS POINT NY 14712
47- 15 BROWN, WILLARD JESSE	2217 BRECKENRIDGE - HOUSTON TX 77026
63- 17 BROWN, WILLIAM JAMES 'GATES'	17206 SANTA BARBARA - DETROIT MI 48221
12- 27 BROWN, WILLIAM VERNA	D. MAY 15, 1965 LUBBOCK, TEX.
65- 16 BROWNE, BYRON ELLIS	OLD ADD: 1015 NORTH 31ST ST - BATON ROUGE LA 7080
35- 9 BROWNE, EARL JAMES	1405 FAIR PARK BLVD - LITTLE ROCK AR 72204
86- 27 BROWNE, JEROME AUSTIN	2A PRINCE STREET - CHRISTIANSTED VI 00820
62- 20 BROWNE, PRENTICE ALMONT 'PIDGE'	187-23 CASPER DR - SPRING TX 77373
60- 15 BROWNING, CALVIN DUANE	1000 CAMELOT - CLINTON OK 73601
10- 16 BROWNING, FRANK	D. MAY 19, 1948 SAN ANTONIO, TEX.
84- 13 BROWNING, THOMAS LEO	4135 MURPHY - BILLINGS MT 59101
67- 10 BRUBAKER, BRUCE ELLSWORTH	2026 BAHAMA ROAD - LEXINGTON KY 40509
32- 9 BRUBAKER, WILBUR LEE 'BILL'	D. APRIL 2, 1978 LAGUNA HILLS, CALIF.
59- 10 BRUCE, ROBERT JAMES	RR 4 BOX 363X - CANYON LAKE TX 78130
61- 16 BRUCKBOWER, FREDERICK JOHN	404 MCHUGH - HOLMES WI 54636
48- 19 BRUCKER, EARLE FRANCIS JR.	629 MUNDY TERRACE - EL CAJON CA 92020
37- 18 BRUCKER, EARLE FRANCIS SR	D. MAY 8, 1981 SAN DIEGO, CALIF.
21- 11 BRUGGY, FRANK LEO	D. APRIL 5, 1959 ELIZABETH, N. J.
78- 19 BRUHERT, MICHAEL EDWIN	143-35 95TH AVE - JAMAICA NY 11435
87- 13 BRUMLEY, ANTHONY MICHAEL 'MIKE'	2618 WEST QUINCY CIRCLE - BROKEN ARROW OK 74012
64- 14 BRUMLEY, TONY MIKE	5415 FOURTH AVE DR NW - BRADENTON FL 33529
81- 18 BRUMMER, GLENN EDWARD	RR 2 BOX 175 - MOUNTAIN GROVE MO 65711
81- 19 BRUNANSKY, THOMAS ANDREW	1319 SOUTH HILLWARD AVE - WEST COVINA CA 91791
49- 11 BRUNER, JACK RAYMOND	1641 NORTH 76TH - LINCOLN NE 68505
39- 16 BRUNER, WALTER ROY	305 SOUTH LYNDON LN-LOUISVILLE KY 40222
56- 16 BRUNET, GEORGE STUART	1511 EAST DIANA AVENUE - ANAHEIM CA 92805
76- 21 BRUNO, THOMAS MICHAEL	OLD ADD: 4609 LINSCOTT - DOWNERS GROVE IL
66- 15 BRUNSBERG, ARLO ADOLPH	1164 128TH AVE NORTH - BLAINE MN 55434
77- 16 BRUSSTAR, WARREN SCOTT	3320 REDWOOD RD - NAPA CA 94558
53- 13 BRUTON, WILLIAM HARON	6122 WEST OUTER DR - DETROIT MI 48235
61- 17 BRYAN, WILLIAM RONALD	3313 GRACE DR - OPELIKA AL 36801
35- 10 BRYANT, CLAIBORNE HENRY	1380 NW 43RD TER #102-FORT LAUDERDALE FL33313
79- 15 BRYANT, DEREK ROSZELL	OLD ADD: C-12 COOPERSTOWN - LEXINGTON KY
66- 16 BRYANT, DONALD RAY	OLD ADD: 4023 SW 328TH - FEDERAL WAY WA 98003
85- 7 BRYANT, RALPH WENDELL	RR 4 BOX 374 - LEESBURG GA 31763
67- 11 BRYANT, RONALD RAYMOND	2318 SHIRE LN - DAVIS CA 95616
86- 28 BRYDEN, THOMAS RAY	2205 SUMNER POINT DRIVE - SUMNER WA 98390
70- 14 BRYE, STEPHEN ROBERT	200 STANTONVILLE RD - OAKLAND CA 94619
22- 17 BUBSER, HAROLD FRED	D. JUNE 22, 1959 MELROSE PARK, ILL.
48- 20 BUCHA, JOHN GEORGE	1215 NORTH MINK RD - DANIELSVILLE PA 18038
85- 8 BUCHANAN, ROBERT GORDON	4704 HIGHWAY 30 - ELY IA 52227
61- 18 BUCHEK, GERALD PETER	3950A WILMINGTON AVE - ST. LOUIS MO 63116
34- 14 BUCHER, JAMES QUINTER	RR 1 BOX 599 - PALMYRA PA 17078
18- 7 BUCKEYE, GARLAND MAIERS	D. NOVEMBER 14, 1975 STONE LAKE, WIS.
16- 9 BUCKLES, JESS ROBERT	D. AUGUST 2, 1975 WESTMINSTER, CAL.
84- 14 BUCKLEY, KEVIN JOHN	34 CALVIN ST - BRAINTREE MA 02184
69- 23 BUCKNER, WILLIAM JOSEPH	3 MCDONALD CIR - ANDOVER MA 01810
78- 20 BUDASKA, MARK DAVID	702 WASHINGTON STREET #43 - MARINA DEL REY CA 90292
56- 17 BUDDIN, DONALD THOMAS	BOX 186 - FOUNTAIN INN SC 29644
46- 14 BUDNICK, MICHAEL JOE	307 WEST BLAINE - SEATTLE WA 98119
85- 9 BUECHELE, STEVEN BERNARD	1730 MIRAMAR - FULLERTON CA 92631
13- 22 BUES, ARTHUR FREDERICK	D. NOVEMBER 7, 1954 WHITEFISH BAY, WIS.
63- 18 BUFORD, DONALD ALVIN	15412 VALLEY VISTA BLVD-SHERMAN OAKS CA 91403
53- 14 BUHL, ROBERT RAY	8644 SW 63RD COURT - OCALA FL 32676
87- 14 BUHNER, JAY CAMPBELL	1511 DAVON LANE - HOUSTON TX 77058
87- 15 BUICE, DEWAYNE ALLISON	422F SOUTH CHATHAM CIRCLE - ANAHEIM CA 92806
45- 5 BUKER, CYRIL OWEN	108 CENTRAL AVE - GREENWOOD WI 54437
54- 11 BULLARD, GEORGE DONALD	7 DYER COURT - DANVERS MA 01923
77- 17 BULLING, TERRY CHARLES 'BUD'	OLD ADD: 15591 ASTER ST - WESTMINSTER CA
85- 10 BULLOCK, ERIC JERALD	17503 HARWICK COURT - CARSON CA 90746
36- 11 BULLOCK, MALTON JOSEPH 'RED'	BOX 727 - MOSS POINT MS 39563
72- 15 BUMBRY, ALONZO BENJAMIN	28 TREMBLANT CT - LUTHERVILLE MD 21093

TOM BRUNO

63- 19 BUNKER, WALLACE EDWARD	502 FIRST ST - LANGLEY WA 98260
55- 19 BUNNING, JAMES PAUL DAVID	30 WINSTON HILL RD - FORT THOMAS KY 41075
69- 24 BURBACH, WILLIAM DAVID	BOX 3 - DICKEYVILLE WI 53808
55- 20 BURBRINK, NELSON EDWARD	9895 88TH WAY NORTH - SEMINOLE FL 33543
69- 25 BURCHART, LARRY WAYNE	6305 SOUTH 114 EAST AVE - TULSA OK 74133
62- 21 BURDA, EDWARD ROBERT 'BOB'	8737 EAST KEIM DR - SCOTTSDALE AZ 85253
62- 22 BURDETTE, FREDDIE THOMASON	1200 HIGGINS CT #Q5 - ALBANY GA 31707
50- 14 BURDETTE, SELVA LEWIS 'LOU'	2837 GULF OF MEXICO DR - LONGBOAT KEY FL33548
10- 17 BURG, JOSEPH PETER	D. APRIL 28, 1969 JOLIET, ILL.
49- 12 BURGESS, FORREST HARRILL 'SMOKEY'	717 CAROLEEN RD - FOREST CITY NC 28043

54- 12	BURGESS, THOMAS ROLAND	3201 WALNUT ST NE - ST PETERSBURG FL 33704
68- 11	BURGMEIER, THOMAS HENRY	12104 WEST 100TH ST - LENEXA KS 66214
43- 15	BURGO, WILLIAM ROSS	231 GLENWOOD ST - MORGAN LA 70380
42- 15	BURICH, WILLIAM MAX	1175 LAMOREE RD #62 - SAN MARCOS CA 92069
10- 18	BURK, CHARLES SANFORD	D. OCTOBER 11, 1934 BROOKLYN, N.Y.
56- 18	BURK, MACK EDWIN	4310 BRAZIL CIR - PASADENA TX 77502
15- 17	BURKAM, CHAUNCEY DEPEW	D. MAY 9, 1964 KALAMAZOO, MICH.
36- 12	BURKART, ELMER ROBERT	139 OTHORIDGE - LUTHERVILLE MD 21093
76- 22	BURKE, GLENN LAWRENCE	279 COLLINGWOOD - SAN FRANCISCO CA 94114
58- 14	BURKE, LEO PATRICK	1729 WOODBURN DRIVE - HAGERSTOWN MD 21740
23- 16	BURKE, LESLIE KINGSTON	D. MAY 6, 1975 DANVERS, MASS.
24- 15	BURKE, PATRICK EDWARD	D. JULY 7, 1965 ST. LOUIS, MO.
27- 18	BURKE, ROBERT JAMES	D. FEBRUARY 8, 1971 JOLIET, ILL.
77- 18	BURKE, STEVEN MICHAEL	4656 HIBISCUS RD - STOCKTON CA 95205
85- 11	BURKE, TIMOTHY PHILIP	53244 SOUTH 155TH STREET - OMAHA NE 68137
10- 19	BURKE, WILLIAM IGNATIUS	D. FEBRUARY 9, 1967 WORCESTER, MASS.
87- 16	BURKETT, JOHN DAVID	104 CRANDON CIRCLE - BEAVER PA 15010
45- 6	BURKHART, WILLIAM KENNETH 'KEN'	3708 SPLENDOR DRIVE, RR 7 - KNOXVILLE TN 37918
87- 17	BURKS, ELLIS RENA	2709 GALEMEADOW DRIVE - FORT WORTH TX 76123
74- 13	BURLESON, RICHARD PAUL 'RICK'	270 EAST MIRA VERDE DR - LAHABRA HEIGHTS CA 90631
27- 19	BURNETT, JOHN HENDERSON	D. AUGUST 12, 1959 TAMPA, FLA.
56- 19	BURNETTE, WALLACE HARPER	RR 1 BOX 168 - BLAIRS VA 24527
23- 17	BURNS, DENNIS	D. MAY 21, 1969 TULSA, OKLA.
12- 28	BURNS, EDWARD JAMES	D. JUNE 1, 1942 MONTEREY, CALIF.
14- 32	BURNS, GEORGE HENRY	D. JANUARY 7, 1978 KIRKLAND, WASH.
11- 20	BURNS, GEORGE JOSEPH	D. AUGUST 15, 1966 GLOVERSVILLE, N.Y.
30- 7	BURNS, JOHN IRVING	D. APRIL 18, 1975 BOSTON, MASS.
24- 16	BURNS, JOSEPH FRANCIS	D. JANUARY 7, 1986 TRENTON, N. J.
10- 20	BURNS, JOSEPH FRANCIS	D. JULY 12, 1987 BEVERLY, MASS.
43- 16	BURNS, JOSEPH JAMES	D. JUNE 24, 1974 BRYN MAWR, PA.
78- 21	BURNS, ROBERT BRITT	913 CORLEY DRIVE - HUNTSVILLE AL 35802
55- 21	BURNSIDE, PETER WILLITS	1945 CHESTNUT - WILMETTE IL 60091
78- 22	BURNSIDE, SHELDON JOHN	4351 BLOOR ST #34 - ETOBICKE ONT. M9C 2A4 CAN.
46- 15	BURPO, GEORGE HARVIE	8981 EAST PALMS DR - TUCSON AZ 85715
14- 33	BURR, ALEXANDER THOMSON	D. NOVEMBER 1, 1918 FRANCE
62- 23	BURRIGHT, LARRY ALLEN	1239 EAST PALM DR - GLENDORA CA 91740
73- 15	BURRIS, BERTRAM RAY	4214 TICINO VALLEY DR - ARLINGTON TX 76016
48- 21	BURRIS, PAUL ROBERT	RR 2 BOX 348 - HUNTERSVILLE NC 28078
70- 15	BURROUGHS, JEFFREY ALAN	6155 LAGUNA CT - LONG BEACH CA 90803
43- 17	BURROWS, JOHN	D. APRIL 27, 1987 COAL RUN, O.
19- 10	BURRUS, MAURICE LENNON 'DICK'	D. DECEMBER 2, 1972 ELIZABETH CITY, N. C.
58- 15	BURTON, ELLIS NARRINGTON	BERTH 202 EAST BASIN - WILMINGTON CA 90744
75- 22	BURTON, JAMES SCOTT	700 PEACH TREE LN - ROCHESTER MI 48063
50- 15	BURTSCHY, EDWARD FRANK 'MOE'	620 PEDRETTE APT A-6 - CINCINNATI OH 45238
85- 12	BURTT, DENNIS ALLEN	1079 NORTH MALLARD STREET - ORANGE CA 92667
60- 16	BURWELL, RICHARD MATTHEW	P. O. BOX 1825 - TWIN FALLS ID 83301
20- 15	BURWELL, WILLIAM EDWIN	D. JUNE 11, 1973 ORMOND BEACH, FLA.
50- 16	BUSBY, JAMES FRANKLIN	BOX 97 - YALAHA FL 32797
41- 11	BUSBY, PAUL MILLER	2011 35TH AVE-MERIDIAN MS 39301
72- 16	BUSBY, STEVEN LEE	OLD ADD: BOX 783 - BLUE SPRINGS MO
43- 18	BUSCH, EDGAR JOHN	D. JANUARY 17, 1987 SHILOH VALLEY TWP,ST. CLAIR CO,ILL.
65- 17	BUSCHHORN, DONALD LEE	17804 EAST 26TH ST - INDEPENDENCE MO 64057
23- 18	BUSH, GUY TERRELL	D. JULY 2, 1985 SHANNON, MISS.
12- 29	BUSH, LESLIE AMBROSE 'JOE'	D. NOVEMBER 1, 1974 FORT LAUDERDALE, FLA.
82- 21	BUSH, ROBERT RANDALL 'RANDY'	OLD ADD: 38 OLYMPIC COURT - NEW ORLEANS LA 70114
27- 20	BUSHEY, FRANCIS CLYDE	D. MARCH 18, 1972 TOPEKA, KAN.
26- 10	BUSKEY, JOSEPH HENRY	D. APRIL 11, 1949 CUMBERLAND, MD.
77 19	BUSKEY, MICHAEL THOMAS	315 OXFORD ST - SAN FRANCISCO CA 94134
73- 16	BUSKEY, THOMAS WILLIAM	476 ALLEGHENY DR - HARRISBURG PA 17111
71- 18	BUSSE, RAYMOND EDWARD	OLD ADD: 501 MYRTLE LN SOUTH - DAYTONA BEACH FL
36- 13	BUTCHER, ALBERT MAXWELL 'MAX'	D. SEPTEMBER 15, 1957 LOGAN, W. VA.
11- 21	BUTCHER, HENRY JOSDPH	D. DECEMBER 28, 1979 HAZEL CREST, ILL.
80- 18	BUTCHER, JOHN DANIEL	302 WINCHESTER COURT - LAKE BLUFF IL 60044
80- 19	BUTERA, SALVATORE PHILIP	38 HILL DR- BOHEMIA NY 11716
43- 19	BUTKA, EDWARD LUKE	131 WEST COLLEGE ST-CANONSBURG PA 15317
40- 7	BUTLAND, WILBURN RUE 'BILL'	2735 CRUFT-TERRE HAUTE IN 47803
11- 22	BUTLER, ARTHUR EDWARD	D. OCTOBER 7, 1984 FALL RIVER, MASS.
81- 20	BUTLER, BRETT MORGAN	215 FRASHER WAY - DULUTH GA 30136
62- 24	BUTLER, CECIL DEAN	RR4 - DALLAS GA 30132
33- 8	BUTLER, CHARLES THOMAS	D. MAY 10, 1964 BRUNSWICK, GA.
26- 11	BUTLER, JOHN STEPHEN	D. APRIL 29, 1967 LONG BEACH, CAL.
69- 26	BUTLER, WILLIAM FRANKLIN	HC 3 BOX 122 - CROSS JUNCTION VA 22625
62- 25	BUTTERS, THOMAS ARDEN	46 APPLETON PL - DURHAM NC 27705
38- 11	BUXTON, RALPH STANLEY	348 BOWLING GREEN-SAN LEANDRO CA 94577
45- 7	BUZAS, JOSEPH JOHN	BOX 5010 - READING PA 19612
58- 16	BUZHARDT, JOHN WILLIAM	RR 2 BOX 1684 - PROSPERITY SC 29127
43- 20	BYERLY, ELDRED WILLIAM 'BUD'	8611 SAPPINGTON RD-ST LOUIS MO 63126
87- 18	BYERS, RANDELL PARKER	31 WALDEN DRIVE(P.O. BOX 304) - BRIDGETON NJ 08302

ENOS CABELL

50- 17 BYRD, HARRY GLADWIN	D. MAY 14, 1985 DARLINGTON, S. C.
77- 20 BYRD, JEFFREY ALAN	11085 MORNING DOVE RD - LAKESIDE CA 92040
29- 13 BYRD, SAMUEL DEWEY	D. MAY 11, 1981 MESA, ARIZ.
29- 14 BYRNE, GERALD WILFORD	D. AUGUST 11, 1955 LANSING, MICH.
43- 21 BYRNE, THOMAS JOSEPH	442 PINEVIEW AVE-WAKE FOREST NC 27587
43- 22 BYRNES, MILTON JOHN	D. FEBRUARY 1, 1979 ST. LOUIS, MO.
80- 20 BYSTROM, MARTIN EUGENE	P.O. BOX 26 - GEIGERTOWN PA 19523
44- 17 CABALLERO, RALPH JOSEPH 'PUTSY'	6773 MILNE ST - NEW ORLEANS LA 70119
72- 17 CABELL, ENOS MILTON	7011 COUNTRY CLUB LN - ANAHEIM CA 92807
13- 23 CABRERA, ALFREDO A	D. HAVANA, CUBA
77- 21 CACEK, CRAIG THOMAS	8916 GLORIA AVE - SEPULVEDA CA 91343
87- 19 CADARET, GREGORY JAMES	5665 CAROLINE DRIVE - LAKEVIEW MI 48850
15- 18 CADORE, LEON JOSEPH	D. MARCH 16, 1958 SPOKANE, WASH.
12- 30 CADY, FORREST LEROY 'HICK'	D. MARCH 3, 1946 CEDAR RAPIDS, IA.
37- 19 CAFEGO, THOMAS	D. OCTOBER 29, 1961 DETROIT, MICH.
56- 20 CAFFIE, JOSEPH CLIFFORD	P.O. BOX 1932 - WARREN OH 44482
78- 23 CAGE, WAYNE LEVELL	RR 1 BOX 62 - CHOUDRANT LA 71227
68- 12 CAIN, LESLIE	4516 CYPRESS AVE - RICHMOND CA 91804
32- 10 CAIN, MERRITT PATRICK 'SUGAR'	D. APRIL 3, 1975 ATLANTA, GA.
49- 13 CAIN, ROBERT MAX	161 EAST 226TH ST - EUCLID ON 44123
34- 15 CAITHAMER, GEORGE THEODORE	D. JUNE 1, 1954 CHICAGO, ILL.
84- 15 CALDERON, IVAN	OLD ADD: 334 EST. 34 BUZON - LOIZA PR 00672
50- 18 CALDERONE, SAMUEL FRANCIS	1000 SOUTH COOPER ST - BEVERLY NJ 08010
28- 18 CALDWELL, BRUCE	D. FEBRUARY 15, 1959 WEST HAVEN, CONN.
25- 14 CALDWELL, CHARLES WILLIAM	D. NOVEMBER 1, 1957 PRINCETON, N. J.
28- 19 CALDWELL, EARL WELTON	D. SEPTEMBER 15, 1981 MISSION, TEXAS
71- 19 CALDWELL, RALPH MICHAEL 'MIKE'	1645 BROOK RUN DR - RALEIGH NC 27614
10- 21 CALDWELL, RAYMOND BENJAMIN	D. AUGUST 17, 1967 SALAMANCA, N. Y.
84- 16 CALHOUN, JEFFREY WILTON	1212 PARK ST - MCCOMB MS 39648
13- 24 CALHOUN, WILLIAM DAVITTE	D. FEBRUARY 11, 1955 SANDERSVILLE, GA.
41- 12 CALIGIURI, FREDERICK JOHN	BOX 429 - RIMERSBURG PA 16248
22- 18 CALLAGHAN, MARTIN FRANCIS	D. JUNE 24, 1975 NORWOOD, MASS.
83- 22 CALLAHAN, BENJAMIN FRANKLIN	BOX 676 - DOBSON NC 27017
10- 22 CALLAHAN, DAVID JOSEPH	D. OCTOBER 28, 1969 OTTAWA, ILL.
39- 17 CALLAHAN, JOSEPH THOMAS	D. MAY 24, 1949 SOUTH BOSTON, MASS.
13- 25 CALLAHAN, LEO DAVID	D. MAY 2, 1982 ERIE, PA.
15- 19 CALLAHAN, RAYMOND JAMES	D. JANUARY 23, 1973 OLYMPIA, WASH.
13- 26 CALLAHAN, WESLEY LEROY	D. SEPTEMBER 13, 1953 DAYTON,O.
21- 12 CALLAWAY, FRANK BURNETT	D. AUGUST 21, 1987 KNOXVILLE, TENN.
58- 17 CALLISON, JOHN WESLEY	2316 OAKDALE ST - GLENSIDE PA 19038
63- 20 CALMUS, RICHARD LEE	3823 SOUTH 28TH WEST AVE - TULSA OK 74107
83- 23 CALVERT, MARK	RR 4 BOX 314J - BROKEN ARROW OK 74012
42- 16 CALVERT, PAUL LEO EMILE	364 CHATELAINE ST #7 - SHERBROOKE QUE J1G 1Z6 CAN.
13- 27 CALVO, JACINTO 'JACK'	D. JUNE 15, 1965 MIAMI, FLA.
80- 21 CAMACHO, ERNEST CARLOS	OLD ADD: 746 ST REGIS - AVON LAKE OH 44012
70- 16 CAMBRIA, FREDERICK DENNIS	12 IRIS CT - NORTHPORT NY 11768
43- 23 CAMELLI, HENRY RICHARD	6 LARCH RD-WELLESLEY MA 02181
33- 9 CAMILLI, ADOLF LOUIS	2831 HACIENDA ST - SAN MATEO CA 94403
60- 17 CAMILLI, DOUGLAS JOSEPH	872 ORIOLE DRIVE SE - WINTER HAVEN FL 33880
69- 27 CAMILLI, LOUIS STEVEN	4700 OAHU DR NE - ALBUQUERQUE NM 87111
87- 20 CAMINITI, KENNETH GENE	5129 CORDOY LANE - SAN JOSE CA 95124
17- 12 CAMP, HOWARD LEE	D. MAY 8, 1950 EASTABOGA, ALA.
76- 23 CAMP, RICK LAMAR	6 CANTEY PLACE NW - ATLANTA GA 30327
48- 22 CAMPANELLA, ROY	6213 CAPISTRANO - WOODLAND HILLS CA 91367
64- 15 CAMPANERIS, DAGOBERTO 'BERT'	P.O. BOX 8232 - SCOTTSDALE AZ 85252
43- 24 CAMPANIS, ALEXANDER SEBASTIAN	3113 CORONADO DR - FULLERTON CA 92632
66- 17 CAMPANIS, JAMES ALEXANDER	17082 CASCADES AVE - YORBA LINDA CA 92686
28- 20 CAMPBELL, ARCHIBALD STEWART	630 MARGRAVE DRIVE - RENO NV 89502
30- 8 CAMPBELL, BRUCE DOUGLAS	4011 BAYSIDE RD - FORT MYERS BEACH FL 33931
40- 8 CAMPBELL, CLARENCE 'SOUP'	SPARTA VA 22552
77- 22 CAMPBELL, DAVID ALLEN	OLD ADD: RR 10 LYNN TER #2 - JOHNSON CITY TN 37601
67- 12 CAMPBELL, DAVID WILSON	9978 WALDGROVE PLACE - SAN DIEGO CA 92131
62- 26 CAMPBELL, JAMES ROBERT	1924 KNOLLWOOD LN - LOS ALTOS CA 94022
70- 17 CAMPBELL, JAMES ROBERT	RR 1 BOX 194 - LAMAR SC 29069
33- 10 CAMPBELL, JOHN MILLARD 'WHITEY'	100 SILVER BEACH #4 - DAYTONA BEACH FL 32081
67- 13 CAMPBELL, JOSEPH EARL	2151 SMALLHOUSE RD - BOWLING GREEN KY 42101
87- 21 CAMPBELL, MICHAEL THOMAS	6412 SOUTHWEST HINDS - SEATTLE WA 98116
41- 13 CAMPBELL, PAUL MCLAUGHLIN	BOX 1724 - FAIRFIELD GLADE TN 38555
64- 16 CAMPBELL, RONALD THOMAS	2254 LAUREL HILLS DRIVE NW - CLEVELAND TN 37311
33- 11 CAMPBELL, WILLIAM GILTHORPE 'GILLY'	D. FEBRUARY 21, 1973 LOS ANGELES, CAL.
73- 17 CAMPBELL, WILLIAM RICHARD	217 BEAUMONT LN - BARRINGTON IL 60010
77- 23 CAMPER, CARDELL	175 EAST EASTON #33 - RIALTO CA 92376
69- 28 CAMPISI, SALVATORE JOHN	3303 LAKEWOOD DR - HOLIDAY FL 33590
51- 9 CAMPOS, FRANCISCO JOSE LOPEZ	2840 NW 4TH ST - MIAMI FL 33125
18- 8 CANAVAN, HUGH EDWARD	D. SEPTEMBER 4, 1967 BOSTON, MASS.

86- 29	CANDAELE, CASEY TODD	1001 EAST MAPLE - LOMPOC CA 93436
75- 23	CANDELARIA, JOHN ROBERT	25732 BUCKLESTONE COURT - LAGUNA HILLS CA 92633
43- 25	CANDINI, MILO CAIN	641 MANOR - MANTECA CA 95336
83- 24	CANDIOTTI, THOMAS CAESER	1700 FOUNTAIN SPRINGS CIRCLE - DANVILLE CA 94526
77- 24	CANEIRA, JOHN CASCAES	18 SPRUCE ST - NAUGATUCK CT 06770
85- 13	CANGELOSI, JOHN ANTHONY	183 SE 4TH AVENUE - HIALEAH FL 33010
60- 18	CANNIZZARO, CHRISTOPHER JOHN	576 DOLORES - SAN LEANDRO CA 94577
77- 25	CANNON, JOSEPH JEROME	6426 WAGNER RD - PENSACOLA FL 32505
85- 14	CANSECO, JOSE	2530 SW 102ND AVE - MIAMI FL 33165
25- 15	CANTRELL, DEWEY GUY	D. JANUARY 31, 1961 MCALESTER, OKLA.
27- 21	CANTWELL, BENJAMIN CALDWELL	D. DECEMBER 4, 1962 SALEM, MO.
16- 10	CANTWELL, MICHAEL JOSEPH	D. JANUARY 9, 1953 OTEEN, N.C.
76- 24	CAPILLA, DOUGLAS EDMOND	3178 MANDA DR - SAN JOSE CA 95124
81- 21	CAPPUZZELLO, GEORGE ANGELO	1625 DOWN LAKE DRIVE - WINDERMERE FL 32786
71- 20	CAPRA, LEE WILLIAM 'BUZZ'	7112 RIVERSIDE DR - BERWYN IL 60402
82- 22	CAPRA, NICK LEE	3201 SOUTH UTICA - DENVER CO 80236
44- 18	CAPRI, PATRICK NICHOLAS	935 41ST ST - BROOKLYN NY 11219
12- 31	CAPRON, RALPH EARL	D. SEPTEMBER 19, 1980 LOS ANGELES, CALIF.
30- 9	CARAWAY, CECIL BRADFORD PATRICK 'PAT'	D. JUNE 9, 1974 EL PASO, TEX.
69- 29	CARBO, BERNARDO	1637 FORT STREET - WYANDOTTE MI 48192
46- 16	CARDEN, JOHN BRUTON	D. FEBRUARY 8, 1949 MEXIA, TEX.
63- 21	CARDENAL, JOSE DOMEC	5701 NORTH SHERIDAN - CHICAGO IL 60660
60- 19	CARDENAS, LEONARDO LAZARO 'CHICO'	OLD ADD: 11696 HINKLEY DR - FOREST PARK OH 45240
63- 22	CARDINAL, CONRAD SETH 'RANDY'	3810 VERDE WAY - NORTH LAS VEGAS NV 89030
43- 26	CARDONI, ARMAND JOSEPH 'BEN'	D. APRIL 2, 1969 JESSUP, PA.
57- 9	CARDWELL, DONALD EUGENE	BOX 474 - CLEMMONS NC 27012
67- 14	CAREW, RODNEY CLINE	5144 EAST CRESCENT DR - ANAHEIM CA 92807
52- 16	CAREY, ANDREW ARTHUR	1601 DOVE STREET #220 - NEWPORT BEACH CA 92660
10- 23	CAREY, MAX GEORGE	D. MAY 30, 1976 MIAMI, FLA.
35- 11	CAREY, THOMAS FRANCIS ALOYSIUS	D. FEBRUARY 21, 1970 ROCHESTER, N. Y.
32- 11	CARLETON, JAMES OTTO 'TEX'	D. JANUARY 11, 1977 FORT WORTH, TEX.
41- 14	CARLIN, JAMES ARTHUR	1215 33RD ST-BIRMINGHAM AL 35218
67- 15	CARLOS, FRANCISCO MANUEL 'CISCO'	OLD ADD: 1229 SESMAS ST - DUARTE CA 91010
48- 23	CARLSEN, DONALD HERBERT	3600 EAST EASTER AVE - LITTLETON CO 80122
17- 13	CARLSON, HAROLD GUST	D. MAY 28, 1930 CHICAGO, ILL.
20- 16	CARLSON, LEON ALTON	D. SEPTEMBER 15, 1961 JAMESTOWN, N. Y.
11- 23	CARLSTROM, ALBIN OSCAR 'SWEDE'	D. APRIL 23, 1935 ELIZABETH, N.J.
65- 18	CARLTON, STEVEN NORMAN	16240 HOLTS LAKE DR - CHESTERFIELD MO 63017
27- 22	CARLYLE, HIRAM CLEO	D. NOVEMBER 12, 1967 LOS ANGELES, CAL.
25- 16	CARLYLE, ROY EDWARD	D. NOVEMBER 22, 1956 NORCROSS, GA.
83- 25	CARMAN, DONALD WAYNE	6 COOPER RUN DRIVE - CHERRY HILL NJ 08003
59- 11	CARMEL, LEON JAMES 'DUKE'	10 PHEASANT VALLEY DR - CORAM NY 11727
41- 15	CARNETT, EDWIN ELLIOTT	1010 INDIAN CREEK DR - LEBANON MO 65536
43- 27	CARPENTER, LEWIS EMMETT	D. APRIL 25, 1979 MARIETTA, GA.
16- 11	CARPENTER, PAUL CALVIN	D. MARCH 14, 1968 NEWARK, O.
40- 9	CARPENTER, ROBERT LOUIS	9321 SOUTH SACRAMENTO AVE - EVERGREEN PARK IL 60642
65- 19	CARPIN, FRANK DOMINIC	5202 RIVERSIDE DR - RICHMOND VA 23225
39- 18	CARRASQUEL, ALEJANDRO ALEXANDER	D. AUGUST 19, 1969 CARACAS, VENEZUELA
50- 19	CARRASQUEL, ALFONSO COLON 'CHICO'	1432 NORTH LAWNDALE AVE - CHICAGO IL 60657
59- 12	CARREON, CAMILO GARCIA	D. SEPTEMBER 2, 1987 TUCSON, ARIZ.
87- 22	CARREON, MARK STEVEN	4450 EAST COOPER STREET - TUCSON AZ 85711
70- 18	CARRITHERS, DONALD GEORGE	1851 HARRIS AVE - SAN JOSE CA 95124
64- 17	CARROLL, CLAY PALMER	RR 6 BOX 784 - CLANTON AL 35045
19- 11	CARROLL, DORSEY LEE 'DIXIE'	D. OCTOBER 13, 1984 JACKSONVILLE, FLA.
29- 15	CARROLL, EDGAR FLEISCHER	D. OCTOBER 13, 1984 ROSSVILLE, MD.
25- 17	CARROLL, OWEN THOMAS	D. JUNE 8, 1975 ORANGE, N. J.
16- 12	CARROLL, RALPH ARTHUR 'DOC'	D. JUNE 27, 1983 WORCESTER, MASS.
55- 22	CARROLL, THOMAS EDWARD	607 BAYSIDE - ROCKAWAY POINT NY 11697
74- 14	CARROLL, THOMAS MICHAEL	RR 1 BOX 857 - WATERFORD VA 22190
10- 24	CARSON, ALBERT JAMES	D. NOVEMBER 26, 1962 SAN DIEGO, CALIF.
34- 16	CARSON, WALTER LLOYD 'KIT'	D. JUNE 21, 1983 LONG BEACH, CALIF.
53- 15	CARSWELL, FRANK WILLIS	3517 STANFORD - HOUSTON TX 77006
44- 19	CARTER, ARNOLD LEE	8102 PEBBLE BROOK LN - LOUISVILLE KY 40219
74- 15	CARTER, GARY EDMUND	15 HUNTLY DRIVE - PALM BEACH GARDENS FL 33418
26- 12	CARTER, JOHN HOWARD 'HOWIE'	430 EAST 86TH ST - NEW YORK NY 10028
83- 26	CARTER, JOSEPH CHRIS	1800 NE 51ST - OKLAHOMA CITY OK 73111
25- 18	CARTER, OTIS LEONARD 'BLACKIE'	D. SEPTEMBER 10, 1978 GREENVILLE, S. C.
14- 34	CARTER, PAUL WARREN 'NICK'	D. SEPTEMBER 11, 1984 LAKE PARK, GA.
31- 11	CARTER, SOLOMON MOBLEY	2402 GALE PL - EL DORADO AR 71730
63- 23	CARTY, RICARDO ADOLFO JACABO 'RICO'	5 ENS ENRIQUILLO-SAN PEDRO DE MACORIS DOM. REP.
85- 15	CARY, CHARLES DOUGLAS	3323 CASA GRANDE DRIVE - SAN RAMON CA 94583
47- 16	CARY, SCOTT RUSSELL	RR 4 - BRONSON MI 49028
58- 18	CASALE, JERRY JOSEPH	145 DURANT AVE - STATEN ISLAND NY 10306
65- 20	CASANOVA, ORTIZ PAULINO 'PAUL'	OLD ADD: 413 CHERRY - SYRACUSE NY 13210
34- 17	CASCARELLA, JOSEPH THOMAS	7111 PARK HEIGHTS AVE - BALTIMORE MD 21215

JOSE CARDENAL

Greetings from
GARY CARTER

```
37- 20 CASE, GEORGE WASHINGTON            1108 EVERGREEN RD - MORRISVILLE PA 19067
35- 12 CASEY, HUGH THOMAS                 D. JULY 3, 1951 ATLANTA, GA.
69- 30 CASH, DAVID                        1165 MCKINNEY LN #1405 - GREENTREE PA 15220
58- 19 CASH, NORMAN DALTON                D. OCTOBER 12, 1986 BEAVER ISLAND, MICH.
73- 18 CASH, RONALD FOREST                277 EARLY PARKWAY SE - SMYRNA GA 30080
11- 24 CASHION, JAY CARL                  D. NOVEMBER 17, 1935 LAKE MILLICENT, WIS.
73- 19 CASKEY, CRAIG DOUGLAS              836 YVONNE PL - ANAHEIM CA 92801
49- 14 CASSINI, JACK DEMPSEY              1500 ROAD 1 #42 - DUNEDIN FL 33528
34- 18 CASTER, GEORGE JASPER              D. DECEMBER 18, 1955 LAKEWOOD, CAL.
42- 17 CASTIGLIA, JAMES VINCENT           5301 WESTBARD CIR #313 - WASHINGTON DC 20016
47- 17 CASTIGLIONE, PETER PAUL            1320 NE 26TH TERRACE - POMPANO BEACH FL 33062
78- 24 CASTILLO, ANTHONY BELTRAN          10300 JOYCE CT - SAN JOSE CA 95127
80- 22 CASTILLO, ESTEBAN MANUEL 'MANNY'   COSTA RICA 112,ENS. OZAMA - SANTO DOMINGO DOM. REP.
86- 30 CASTILLO, JUAN                     CALLE ELIA CAMARENA 100-SAN PEDRO DE MACORIS DOM. REP.
81- 22 CASTILLO, MARTIN HORACE            2669 BAYLOR ST - ANAHEIM CA 92801
82- 23 CASTILLO, MONTE CARMELO            189 AUDUBON AVENUE #3N - NEW YORK NY 10032
77- 26 CASTILLO, ROBERT ERNIE             2837 SIERRA ST - LOS ANGELES CA 90031
79- 16 CASTINO, JOHN ANTHONY              6624 GLEASON RD - EDINA MN 55435
43- 28 CASTINO, VINCENT CHARLES           D. MARCH 6, 1967 SACRAMENTO, CAL.
73- 20 CASTLE, DONALD HARDY               RR 2 BOX 34AA - COLDWATER MS 38618
10- 25 CASTLE, JOHN FRANCIS               D. APRIL 13, 1929 PHILADELPHIA, PA.
34- 19 CASTLEMAN, CLYDELL                 BOX 140601 - DONELSON TN 37214
54- 13 CASTLEMAN, FOSTER EPHRAIM          8250 GRAVES ROAD - CINCINNATI OH 45243
23- 19 CASTNER, PAUL HENRY                D. MARCH 3, 1986 ST. PAUL, MINN.
74- 16 CASTRO, WILLIAMS RADHAMES          5231 RAVEN DR - GREENDALE WI 53129
64- 18 CATER, DANNY ANDERSON              1016 CAMINO LA COSTA #2606 - AUSTIN TX 78752
12- 33 CATHER, THEODORE P.                D. APRIL 9, 1945 ELKTON, MD.
42- 18 CATHEY, HARDIN                     561 ELAINE DR - NASHVILLE TN 37211
83- 27 CATO, JOHN KEEFE                   98 MARYTON ROAD - WHITE PLAINS NY 10603
17- 14 CATON, JAMES HOWARD 'BUSTER'       D. JANUARY 8, 1948 ZANESVILLE, O.
79- 17 CAUDILL, WILLIAM HOLLAND           1200 MANHATTAN BEACH BLVD - MANHATTAN BEACH CA 90266
46- 17 CAULFIELD, JOHN JOSEPH             D. DECEMBER 16, 1986 SAN FRANCISCO, CALIF.
18-  9 CAUSEY, CECIL ALGERNON 'RED'       D. NOVEMBER 11, 1960 TAMPA, FLA.
55- 23 CAUSEY, JAMES WAYNE                2905 PAYNTER DR - RUSTON LA 71270
19- 12 CAVANAUGH, JOHN J.                 D. JANUARY 14, 1961 NEW BRUNSWICK, N. J.
34- 20 CAVARRETTA, PHILIP JOSEPH          2206 PORTSIDE PASSAGE - PALM HARBOR FL 33563
22- 19 CAVENEY, JAMES CHRISTOPHER 'IKE'   D. JULY 6, 1949 SAN FRANCISCO, CAL.
11- 25 CAVET, TILLER 'PUG'                D. AUGUST 4, 1966 SAN LUIS OBISPO, CALIF.
55- 24 CECCARELLI, ARTHUR EDWARD          63 HALL DR - ORANGE CT 06477
44- 20 CECIL, REX HOLSTON                 D. OCTOBER 30, 1966 LONG BEACH, CAL.
70- 19 CEDENO, CESAR EUGENITO             9919 SAGE DOWNE - HOUSTON TX 77034
42- 19 CENTER, MARVIN EARL 'PETE'         BOX 64 - CAMPTON KY 41301
```

```
58- 20 CEPEDA, ORLANDO MANUEL                   3 SOMMER RIDGE DRIVE #156 - ROSEVILLE CA 95678
75- 25 CERONE, RICHARD 'RICK'                   63 EISENHOWER - CRESSKILL NJ 07626
85- 16 CERUTTI, JOHN JOSEPH                     43 SOUTH MAIN AVENUE - ALBANY NY 12208
51- 10 CERV, ROBERT HENRY                       2601 WINCHESTER S. - LINCOLN NE 68512
71- 21 CEY, RONALD CHARLES                      22714 CREOLE RD - WOODLAND HILLS CA 91364
60- 20 CHACON, ELIO RODRIGUEZ                   OLD ADD: AVE ANDALUCIA,ED. MARICAY-CARACAS VZ
86- 31 CHADWICK, RAY CHARLES                    607 GADDIS STREET - DURHAM NC 27702
29- 16 CHAGNON, LEON WILBUR                     D. JULY 30, 1953 AMESBURY, MASS.
51- 11 CHAKALES, ROBERT EDWARD                  206 MORELAND DR - RICHMOND VA 23229
73- 21 CHALK, DAVID LEE                         6126 SUMMER CREEK CIR - DALLAS TX 75231
10- 26 CHALMERS, GEORGE W.                      D. AUGUST 5, 1960 BRONX, N. Y.
79- 18 CHAMBERLAIN, CRAIG PHILIP                10408 SANTA CLARA STREET - CYPRESS CA 90630
32- 12 CHAMBERLAIN, WILLIAM VINCENT             404 SPADARO DR - VENICE FL 33595
34- 21 CHAMBERLIN, JOSEPH JEREMIAH              D. JANUARY 28, 1983 SAN FRANCISCO, CALIF.
83- 28 CHAMBERS, ALBERT EUGENE                  1303 NORTH 14TH ST - HARRISBURG PA 17103
48- 24 CHAMBERS, CLIFFORD DAY                   10237 PRAIRIE RD - BOISE ID 83702
37- 21 CHAMBERS, JOHNNIE MONROE                 D. MAY 11, 1977 PALATKA, FLA.
10- 27 CHAMBERS, WILLIAM CHRISTOPHER            D. MARCH 27, 1962 FORT WAYNE, IND.
71- 22 CHAMBLISS, CARROLL CHRISTOPHER 'CHRIS'   19 ORATAM ROAD - UPPER SADDLE RIVER NJ 07458
69- 31 CHAMPION, BUFORD BILLY                    304 NE LOWER CREEK DR - LENOIR NC 28645
76- 25 CHAMPION, ROBERT MICHAEL 'MIKE'          17965 FIESTA WAY - TUSTIN CA 92680
63- 24 CHANCE, ROBERT                           2258 OAK RIDGE DR - CHARLESTON WV 25311
61- 19 CHANCE, WILMER DEAN                      9505 W. SMITHVILLE WESTERN - WOOSTER OH 44691
47- 18 CHANDLER, EDWARD OLIVER                  5811 SOUTH HALM AVENUE - LOS ANGELES CA 90056
37- 22 CHANDLER, SPURGEON FERDINAND 'SPUD'      1591 77TH ST NORTH - ST PETERSBURG FL 33710
69- 32 CHANEY, DARREL LEE                       5196 CLEARWATER DR - STONE MOUNTAIN GA 30087
13- 28 CHANEY, ESTEY CLEON                      D. FEBRUARY 5, 1952 CLEVELAND, O.
10- 28 CHANNELL, LESTER CLARK                   D. MAY 7, 1954 DENVER, COLO.
75- 24 CHANT, CHARLES JOSEPH                    13426 SUNFLOWER CT - SUNNYMEAD CA 92388
20- 17 CHAPLIN, BERT EDGAR                      D. AUGUST 15, 1978 SANFORD, FLA.
28- 21 CHAPLIN, JAMES BAILEY 'TINY'             D. MARCH 25, 1939 NATIONAL CITY, CAL.
35- 13 CHAPMAN, CALVIN LOUIS                    D. APRIL 1, 1983 BATESVILLE, MISS.
33- 12 CHAPMAN, EDWIN VOLNEY                    RURAL ROUTE 2 - LAMBERT MS 38643
```

39- 19 CHAPMAN, FREDERICK WILLIAM   112 NORTH RIDGE AVE - KANNAPOLIS NC 28081
34- 22 CHAPMAN, GLENN JUSTICE   2 FAIROAK DRIVE - RICHMOND IN 47374
12- 34 CHAPMAN, HARRY E.   D. OCTOBER 21, 1918 NEVADA, MO.
24- 17 CHAPMAN, JOHN JOSEPH   D. NOVEMBER 3, 1953 PHILADELPHIA, PA.
79- 19 CHAPMAN, KELVIN KEITH   300 ROAD NORTH - REDWOOD VALLEY CA 94570
12- 35 CHAPMAN, RAYMOND JOHNSON   D. AUGUST 17, 1920 NEW YORK, N.Y.
38- 12 CHAPMAN, SAMUEL BLAKE   11 ANDREW DR #39 - TIBURON CA 94920
30- 10 CHAPMAN, WILLIAM BENJAMIN 'BEN'   401 SHADESWOOD CIR - BIRMINGHAM AL 35226
78- 25 CHAPPAS, HARRY PERRY   1440 NW 52ND AVE - LAUDERHILL FL 33313
13- 29 CHAPPELL, LAVERNE ASHFORD 'LARRY'   D. NOVEMBER 8, 1918 SAN FRANCISCO, CALIF.
80- 23 CHARBONEAU, JOSEPH   OLD ADD: 450 HARVARD AVE #412 - SANTA CLARA CA 95051
62- 27 CHARLES, EDWIN DOUGLAS   57 PARK TERRACE EAST #B58 - NEW YORK NY 10034
40- 10 CHARTAK, MICHAEL GEORGE   D. JULY 25, 1967 OAKDALE, IA.
64- 19 CHARTON, FRANK LANE "PETE"   27 VINCINDA LN - HARRIMAN TN 37748
36- 14 CHASE, KENDALL FAY   D. JANUARY 16, 1985 ONEONTA, N. Y.
30- 11 CHATHAM, CHARLES L. 'BUSTER'   D. DECEMBER 15, 1975 WACO, TEXAS
66- 18 CHAVARRIA, OSWALDO QUIJANO   5771 WINCH STREET - NORTH BARNEBY B.C. CAN.
67- 16 CHAVEZ, NESTOR ISAIAS SILVA   D. MARCH 16, 1969 MARACAIBO, VENEZ.
73- 22 CHEADLE, DAVID BAIRD   4236 BATTERY RD - VIRGINIA BEACH VA 23455
10- 29 CHEEK, HARRY G.   D. JUNE 25, 1956 PARAMUS, N. J.
20- 18 CHEEVES, VIRGIL EARL 'CHIEF'   D. MAY 5, 1979 DALLAS, TEXAS
35- 14 CHELINI, ITALO VINCENT   D. AUGUST 25, 1972 SAN FRANCISCO, CAL.
11- 26 CHENEY, LAURANCE RUSSELL   D. JANUARY 6, 1969 DAYTONA BEACH, FLA.
57- 10 CHENEY, THOMAS EDGAR   607 EUGEMAR - ALBANY GA 31707
37- 23 CHERVINKO, PAUL   D. JUNE 3, 1976 DANVILLE, ILL.
48- 25 CHESNES, ROBERT VINCENT   D. MAY 23, 1979 EVERETT, WASH.
45- 8 CHETKOVICH, MITCHELL   D. AUGUST 24, 1971 GRASS VALLEY, CAL.
77- 27 CHEVEZ, ANTONIO SILVIO   TELIA D PTO. - LEON NICARAGUA C.A.
82- 24 CHIFFER, FLOYD JOHN   4325 LEVELSIDE AVE - LAKESIDE CA 90712
30- 12 CHILD, HARRY PATRICK   D. NOVEMBER 8, 1972 ALEXANDRIA, VA.
85- 17 CHILDRESS, RODNEY OSBORNE 'ROCKY'   5 MEADOWGLEN COURT - SANTA ROSA CA 95404
71- 23 CHILES, RICHARD FRANCIS   4501 SAN RAMON DR - DAVIS CA 95616
35- 15 CHIOZZA, DINO JOSEPH   D. APRIL 23, 1972 MEMPHIS, TENN.
34- 23 CHIOZZA, LOUIS PEO   D. FEBRUARY 28, 1971 MEMPHIS, TENN.
41- 16 CHIPMAN, ROBERT HOWARD   D. NOVEMBER 8, 1973 HUNTINGTON, N.Y.
45- 9 CHIPPLE, WALTER JOHN   D. JUNE 8, 1988 TONAWANDA, N. Y.
79- 20 CHISM, THOMAS RAYMOND   1311 ELSON ROAD - CHESTER PA 19013
50- 20 CHITI, HARRY   5968 AUSTIN COVE - MEMPHIS TN 38134
58- 21 CHITTUM, NELSON BOYD   616 BONITA PARKWAY - HENDERSONVILLE TN 37075
70- 20 CHLUPSA, ROBERT JOSEPH   RR1 - SOUND BEACH NY 11789
60- 21 CHOATE, DONALD LEON   7105 STATE STREET REAR - EAST SAINT LOUIS IL 62203
10- 30 CHOUINARD, FELIX GEORGE   D. APRIL 28, 1955 HINES, ILL.
10- 31 CHOUNEAU, WILLIAM 'CHIEF'   D. SEPTEMBER 17, 1948 CLOQUET, MINN.
37- 24 CHOZEN, HARRY KENNETH   2208 20TH ST - LAKE CHARLES LA 70601
79- 21 CHRIS, MICHAEL   12437 WOODGREEN ST - LOS ANGELES CA 90066
57- 11 CHRISLEY, BARBRA O'NEIL 'NEIL'   104 WOODLAND WAY - GREENWOOD SC 29646
19- 13 CHRISTENBURY, LLOYD REID   D. DECEMBER 13, 1944 BIRMINGHAM, ALA.
71- 24 CHRISTENSEN, BRUCE RAY   BOX 178 - MORONI UT 84646
84- 17 CHRISTENSEN, JOHN LAWRENCE   2223 E. COMMONWEALTH AVE - FULLERTON CA 92631
26- 13 CHRISTENSEN, WALTER NIELS   D. DECEMBER 20, 1984 MENLO PARK, CALIF.
79- 22 CHRISTENSON, GARY RICHARD   1610 WASHINGTON AVE - NEW HYDE PARK NY 11040
73- 23 CHRISTENSON, LARRY RICHARD   250 SOUTH 17TH #601 - PHILADELPHIA PA 19103
68- 13 CHRISTIAN, ROBERT CHARLES   D. FEBRUARY 20, 1974 SAN DIEGO, CAL.

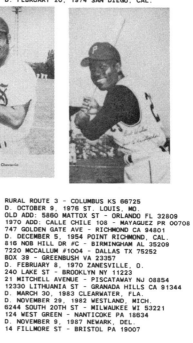

Ozzie Chavarria

84- 18 CHRISTIANSEN, CLAY C.   RURAL ROUTE 3 - COLUMBUS KS 66725
38- 13 CHRISTMAN, MARQUETTE JOSEPH   D. OCTOBER 9, 1976 ST. LOUIS, MO.
83- 29 CHRISTMAS, STEPHEN RANDALL   OLD ADD: 5860 MATTOX ST - ORLANDO FL 32809
59- 13 CHRISTOPHER, JOSEPH O'NEAL   1970 ADD: CALLE CHILE 108 - MAYAGUEZ PR 00708
45- 10 CHRISTOPHER, LOYD EUGENE   747 GOLDEN GATE AVE - RICHMOND CA 94801
42- 20 CHRISTOPHER, RUSSELL ORMAND   D. DECEMBER 5, 1954 POINT RICHMOND, CAL.
50- 21 CHURCH, EMORY NICHOLAS 'BUBBA'   816 NOB HILL DR #C - BIRMINGHAM AL 35209
66- 19 CHURCH, LEONARD   7220 MCCALLUM #1004 - DALLAS TX 75252
57- 12 CHURN, CLARENCE NOTTINGHAM 'CHUCK'   BOX 39 - GREENBUSH VA 23357
24- 18 CHURRY, JOHN   D. FEBRUARY 8, 1970 ZANESVILLE, O.
51- 12 CIAFFONE, LAWRENCE THOMAS   240 LAKE ST - BROOKLYN NY 11223
87- 23 CIARDI, MARK THOMAS   21 MITCHELL AVENUE - PISCATAWAY NJ 08854
83- 30 CIAS, DARRYL RICHARD   12330 LITHUANIA ST - GRANADA HILLS CA 91344
29- 17 CICERO, JOSEPH FRANCIS   D. MARCH 30, 1983 CLEARWATER, FLA.
57- 13 CICOTTE, ALVA WARREN   D. NOVEMBER 29, 1982 WESTLAND, MICH.
44- 21 CIESLAK, THADDEUS WALTER 'TED'   6244 SOUTH 20TH ST - MILWAUKEE WI 53221
45- 11 CIHOCKI, ALBERT JOSEPH   124 WEST GREEN - NANTICOKE PA 18634
32- 13 CIHOCKI, EDWARD JOSEPH   D. NOVEMBER 9, 1987 NEWARK, DEL.
65- 21 CIMINO, PETER WILLIAM   14 FILLMORE ST - BRISTOL PA 19007

56- 21 CIMOLI, GINO NICHOLAS	30 LINDA VISTA - TIBURON CA 94920
43- 29 CIOLA, LOUIS ALEXANDER	2105 8TH AVE NW-AUSTIN MN 55912
61- 20 CIPRIANI, FRANK DOMINICK	62 BARLOW - LACKAWANNA NY 14218
37- 25 CISAR, GEORGE JOSEPH	2520 SOUTH 56TH COURT-CICERO IL 60650
61- 21 CISCO, GALEN BERNARD	RR 1 BOX 150 - SAINT MARYS OH 45885
28- 22 CISSELL, CHALMER WILLIAM 'BILL'	D. MARCH 15, 1949 CHICAGO, ILL.
83- 31 CITARELLA, RALPH ALEXANDER	29 EAST SHERMAN AVE - COLONIA NJ 07067
26- 14 CLABAUGH, JOHN WILLIAM 'MOOSE'	D. JULY 11, 1984 TUCSON, ARIZ.
20- 19 CLAIRE, DAVID MATTHEW	D. JANUARY 7, 1956 LAS VEGAS, NEV.
11- 27 CLANCY, ALBERT HARRISON	D. OCTOBER 17, 1951 LAS CRUCES, N. MEX.
77- 28 CLANCY, JAMES	6147 ROBROY ST - OAK FOREST IL 60452
24- 19 CLANCY, JOHN WILLIAM 'BUD'	D. SEPTEMBER 26, 1968 OTTUMWA, IA.
22- 20 CLANTON, UCAL CURT	D. FEBRUARY 24, 1960 ANTLERS, OKLA.
76- 26 CLAREY, DOUGLAS WILLIAM	506 NORTH ARDEN BLVD - LOS ANGELES CA 90040
47- 19 CLARK, ALFRED ALOYSIUS 'ALLIE'	250 NORTH STEVENS AVE - SOUTH AMBOY NJ 08879
27- 23 CLARK, BAILEY EARL	D. JANUARY 16, 1938 WASHINGTON, D. C.
81- 23 CLARK, BRYAN DONALD	700 STARKEY ROAD #511 - LARGO FL 33541
22- 21 CLARK, DANIEL CURRAN	D. MAY 23, 1937 MERIDIAN, MISS.
86- 32 CLARK, DAVID EARL	RURAL ROUTE 3 BOX 248 - TUPELO MS 38801
13- 30 CLARK, GEORGE MYRON	D. NOVEMBER 14, 1940 SIOUX CITY, IA.
67- 17 CLARK, GLEN ESTER	3110 EAST 14TH - AUSTIN TX 78702
75- 26 CLARK, JACK ANTHONY	1048 WINDJAMMER CIRCLE - FOSTER CITY CA 94404
48- 26 CLARK, JAMES	1040 MACARTHUR BLVD #116 - SANTA ANA CA 92707
71- 25 CLARK, JAMES EDWARD	1322 WEST ECKERMAN - WEST COVINA CA 91790
11- 28 CLARK, JAMES FRANCIS	D. MARCH 20, 1969 BEAUMONT, TEX.
38- 14 CLARK, JOHN CARROLL 'CAP'	D. FEBRUARY 16, 1957 FAYETTEVILLE, N. C.
51- 13 CLARK, MELVIN EARL	BOX 97 - WEST COLUMBIA WV 25287
52- 17 CLARK, MICHAEL JOHN	3 ASPEN AVE - BELLMAWR NJ 08030
58- 22 CLARK, PHILIP JAMES	1103 6TH ST - ALBANY GA 31701
67- 18 CLARK, RICKEY CHARLES	16132 MEADOWBROOK - DETROIT MI 48240
79- 23 CLARK, ROBERT CALE	1030 PERVISITO ST - PERRIS CA 92370
20- 20 CLARK, ROBERT WILLIAM	D. MAY 18, 1944 CARLSBAD, N. M.
66- 20 CLARK, RONALD BRUCE	700 STARKEY RD #511 - LARGO FL 33541
86- 33 CLARK, WILLIAM NUSCHLER	6526 VIRGILIAN STREET - NEW ORLEANS LA 70126
45- 12 CLARK, WILLIAM OTIS 'OTEY'	2735 EAST BASS LAKE RD - GRAND RAPIDS MN 55744
24- 20 CLARK, WILLIAM WATSON 'WATTY'	D. MARCH 4, 1972 CLEARWATER, FLA.
21- 13 CLARKE, ALAN THOMAS	D. MARCH 11, 1975 CHEVERLY, MD.
65- 22 CLARKE, HORACE MEREDITH	BOX 891 - FREDERIKSTED VI 00840
44- 22 CLARKE, RICHARD GREY	2122 GLENWOOD ST - KANNAPOLIS NC 28081
23- 20 CLARKE, RUFUS RIVERS	D. FEBRUARY 8, 1983 COLUMBIA, S. C.
83- 32 CLARKE, STANLEY MARTEN	37 EAST LAKE STREET - TOLEDO OH 43608
20- 21 CLARKE, SUMPTER MILLS	D. MARCH 16, 1962 KNOXVILLE, TENN.
55- 25 CLARKE, VIBERT ERNESTO 'WEBBO'	D. JUNE 14, 1970 CRISTOBAL, CANAL ZONE
29- 18 CLARKE, WILLIAM STUART 'STU'	D. AUGUST 26, 1985 HAYWARD, CALIF.
52- 18 CLARKSON, JAMES BUSTER 'BUZZ'	639 SIXTH ST - JEANETTE PA 15644
27- 24 CLARKSON, WILLIAM HENRY	D. AUGUST 27, 1971 RALEIGH, N. C.
42- 21 CLARY, ELLIS	206 WEST ALDEN ST-VALDOSTA GA 31603
87- 24 CLARY, MARTIN KEITH	254 PARE - CLAWSON MI 48017
33- 13 CLASET, GOWELL SYLVESTER	D. MARCH 8, 1981 ST. PETERSBURG, FLA.
13- 31 CLAUSS, ALBERT STANLEY	D. SEPTEMBER 13, 1952 NEW HAVEN, CONN.
43- 30 CLAY, DAIN ELMER	462 PARKWAY - CHULA VISTA CA 92010
77- 29 CLAY, KENNETH EARL	1665 GOLDENTREE PLACE - CHARLOTTESVILLE VA 22901

MARK CLEAR   RHP

79- 24 CLEAR, MARK ALAN	4005 E. ROLLING GREEN LN - ORANGE CA 92667
45- 13 CLEARY, JOSEPH CHRISTOPHER	135 WEST 225 STREET - NEW YORK NY 10463
39- 20 CLEMENS, CHESTER SPURGEON	423 CRESPI - SAN CLEMENTE CA 92672
14- 35 CLEMENS, CLEMENT LAMBERT	D. NOVEMBER 18, 1967 ST PETERSBURG, FLA.
60- 22 CLEMENS, DOUGLAS HORACE	RR 2 BOX 174 - NEW HOPE PA 18938
84- 19 CLEMENS, WILLIAM ROGER	1818 BROOKCHESTER - KATY TX 77450
39- 21 CLEMENSEN, WILLIAM MELVILLE	7555 MYRTLE VISTA AVE - SACRAMENTO CA 95831
55- 26 CLEMENTE, ROBERTO WALKER	D. DECEMBER 31,1972 SAN JUAN, P. R.
85- 18 CLEMENTS, PATRICK BRIAN	125 PARMAC ROAD #5 - CHICO CA 95926
71- 26 CLEMONS, LANCE LEVIS	1346 LODGE CIR - SPRING HILL FL 33512
14- 36 CLEMONS, ROBERT BAXTER	D. APRIL 5, 1964 LOS ANGELES, CALIF.
16- 13 CLEMONS, VERNE JAMES	D. MAY 5, 1959 BAY PINES, FLA.
61- 22 CLENDENON, DONN ALVIN	765 CEDARWOOD DR - PITTSBURGH PA 15235
69- 33 CLEVELAND, REGINALD LESLIE	OLD ADD: 1 EDGEWOOD DR NW - CALGARY ALBERTA T3A 2T3
54- 19 CLEVENGER, TRUMAN EUGENE 'TEX'	74 NORTH CARMELITA - PORTERVILLE CA 93257
80- 24 CLIBURN, STANLEY GENE	727 NIMITZ DR - JACKSON MS 39209
84- 20 CLIBURN, STEWART WALKER	5720 MEDALLION DR - JACKSON MS 39211
34- 24 CLIFT, HARLOND BENTON	915 NORTH 15TH AVE #5 - YAKIMA WA 98902
34- 25 CLIFTON, HERMAN EARL 'FLEA'	4077 RACE RD - CINCINNATI OH 45211
60- 23 CLINE, TYRONE ALEXANDER	676 AYERS - CHARLESTON SC 29412
70- 21 CLINES, EUGENE ANTHONY	245 DARLENE ST - YORK PA 17402
60- 24 CLINTON, LUCIEAN LOUIS	330 N. ARMOUR - WICHITA KS 67206
61- 23 CLONINGER, TONY LEE	RR 2 BOX 381-A - IRON STATION NC 28080

66- 21 CLOSTER, ALAN EDWARD
24- 21 CLOUGH, EDGAR GEORGE
26- 15 CLOWERS, WILLIAM PERRY
86- 34 CLUTTERBUCK, BRYAN RICHARD
73- 24 CLYDE, DAVID EUGENE
43- 31 CLYDE, THOMAS KNOX
46- 18 COAN, GILBERT FITZGERALD
56- 22 COATES, JAMES ALTON
29- 19 COBB, HERBERT EDWARD
18- 10 COBB, JOSEPH STANLEY
39- 22 COBLE, DAVID LAMAR
83- 33 COCANOWER, JAMES STANLEY 'JAIME'
15- 20 COCHRAN, ALVAH JACKSON
18- 11 COCHRAN, GEORGE LESLIE
86- 35 COCHRANE, DAVID CARTER
25- 19 COCHRANE, GORDON STANLEY 'MICKEY'
13- 32 COCREHAM, EUGENE
82- 25 CODIROLI, CHRISTOPHER ALLEN
12- 36 COFFEY (JOHN JOSEPH SMITH) 'JACK'
37- 26 COFFMAN, GEORGE DAVID
87- 25 COFFMAN, KEVIN REESE
27- 25 COFFMAN, SAMUEL RICHARD 'DICK'
67- 19 COGGINS, FRANKLIN
72- 18 COGGINS, RICHARD ALLEN
31- 12 COHEN, ALTA ALBERT
26- 16 COHEN, ANDREW HOWARD
55- 27 COHEN, HYMAN
34- 26 COHEN, SYDNEY HARRY
58- 23 COKER, JIMMIE GOODWIN
55- 28 COLAVITO, ROCCO DOMENICO
78- 26 COLBERN, MICHAEL MALLOY
66- 22 COLBERT, NATHAN
70- 22 COLBERT, VINCENT NORMAN
69- 34 COLBORN, JAMES WILLIAM
21- 14 COLE, ALBERT GEORGE
50- 22 COLE, DAVID BRUCE
38- 15 COLE, EDWARD WILLIAM
51- 14 COLE, RICHARD ROY
61- 24 COLEMAN, CLARENCE 'CHOO CHOO'

6518 JESSUP ROAD - RICHMOND VA 23234
D. JANUARY 30, 1944 HARRISBURG, PA.
D. JANUARY 13, 1978 SWEENY, TEX.
OLD ADD: 2360 OLTESVIG LANE - HIGHLAND MI 48031
402 HICKORY POST - HOUSTON TX 77024
3612 GARDEN BROOK DR - DALLAS TX 75234
P.O. BOX 668 - BREVARD NC 28712
BOX 57 - LANCASTER VA 22503
D. JANUARY 8, 1980 TARBORO, N. C.
D. DECEMBER 24, 1947 ALLENTOWN, PA.
D. OCTOBER 15, 1971 ORLANDO, FLA.
1609 STONEHENGE - LITTLE ROCK AR 72212
D. MAY 23, 1947 ATLANTA, GA.
D. MAY 21, 1960 HARBOR CITY, CALIF.
5362 EUCALYPTUS HILL ROAD - YORBA LINDA CA 92686
D. JUNE 2, 1962 LAKE FOREST, ILL.
D. DECEMBER 27, 1945 LULING, TEX.
43650 EXCELSO PLACE - FREMONT CA 94539
D. DECEMBER 4, 1962 NEW YORK, N. Y.
1120 BEACON PKWY EAST #202 - BIRMINGHAM AL 35209
203 EDINBURGH - VICTORIA TX 77904
D. MARCH 24, 1972 ATHENS, ALA.
106 ARMSTEDD CIR - GRIFFIN GA 30223
OLD ADD: 3801 PARKVIEW - IRVINE CA 92713
1 CLARIDGE DR - VERONA NJ 07044
4341 NORTH STANTON - EL PASO TX 79902
22610 FLAMINGO ST - WOODLAND HILLS CA 91364
D. APRIL 9, 1988 EL PASO, TEXAS
BOX TWO - THROCKMORTON TX 76083
OLD ADD: TEMPLE PA 19560
1059 EAST FAIRMONT - TEMPE AZ 85282
OLD ADD: 17369 RUETTE ABETO - SAN DIEGO CA 92128
1417 'E' STREET SE - WASHINGTON DC 20003
2932 SOLIMAR BEACH DR - VENTURA CA 93001
D. MAY 30, 1975 SAN MATEO, CAL.
30 SOUTH CONOCOCHEAGUE ST - WILLIAMSPORT MD 21795
OLD ADD: 6853 LARMANDA - DALLAS TX 75231
3149 MADEIRA - COSTA MESA CA 92626
4038 SUN VALLEY CRESENT - CHESAPEAKE VA 23321

12- 37 COLEMAN, CURTIS HANCOCK
77- 30 COLEMAN, DAVID LEE
49- 15 COLEMAN, GERALD FRANCIS
59- 14 COLEMAN, GORDON CALVIN
65- 23 COLEMAN, JOSEPH HOWARD
42- 22 COLEMAN, JOSEPH PATRICK
32- 14 COLEMAN, PARKE EDWARD 'ED'
47- 20 COLEMAN, RAYMOND LEROY
13- 33 COLEMAN, ROBERT HUNTER
85- 19 COLEMAN, VINCENT MAURICE
55- 29 COLEMAN, WALTER GARY
14- 37 COLES, CADWALLADER R.
58- 24 COLES, CHARLES EDWARD
83- 34 COLES, DARNELL
72- 19 COLETTA, CHRISTOPHER MICHAEL
11- 29 COLLAMORE, ALLAN EDWARD
27- 26 COLLARD, EARL CLINTON 'HAP'
31- 13 COLLIER, ORLIN EDWARD
13- 34 COLLINS, CYRIL WILSON
75- 27 COLLINS, DAVID SCOTT
77- 31 COLLINS, DONALD EDWARD
39- 23 COLLINS, EDWARD TROWBRIDGE JR.
20- 22 COLLINS, HARRY WARREN 'RIP'
31- 14 COLLINS, JAMES ANTHONY 'RIP'
14- 38 COLLINS, JOHN EDGAR "ZIP"
10- 32 COLLINS, JOHN FRANCIS 'SHANO'
48- 27 COLLINS, JOSEPH EDWARD
65- 24 COLLINS, KEVIN MICHAEL
23- 21 COLLINS, PHILIP EUGENE
40- 11 COLLINS, ROBERT JOSEPH
19- 14 COLLINS, THARON LESLIE 'PAT'
10- 33 COLLINS, WILLIAM SHIRLEY
51- 15 COLLUM, JACK DEAN
42- 23 COLMAN, FRANK LOYD
70- 23 COLPAERT, RICHARD CHARLES

D. JULY 1, 1980 NEWPORT, ORE.
4303 DELHI DR - DAYTON OH 45432
1004 HAVENHURST DR - LAJOLLA CA 92037
8698 ZENITH CT - CINCINNATI OH 45231
2372 CHANDLER AVE - FORT MYERS FL 33907
1751 CORAL WAY - NORTH FORT MYERS FL 33917
D. AUGUST 5, 1964 OREGON CITY, ORE.
BOX 8 - HORNBROOK CA 96044
D. JULY 16, 1959 BOSTON, MASS.
11510 SAVO VIEW DRIVE - ST.LOUIS MO 63146
207 PAWLING AVE - TROY NY 12180
D. JUNE 30, 1942 MIAMI, FLA.
BOX 32 - JEFFERSON PA 15344
4282 WEST GAIL DR - CHANDLER AZ 85226
136 SW 38TH TER - CAPE CORAL 33914
D. AUGUST 8, 1980 BATTLE CREEK, MI.
D. JULY 14, 1968 JAMESTOWN, N. Y.
D. SEPTEMBER 9, 1944 MEMPHIS, TENN.
D. FEBRUARY 28, 1941 KNOXVILLE, TENN.
95 SPRINGWOOD DRIVE - SPRINGBORO OH 45066
BOX 208 - LYONS GA 30436
BOX 206 - KENNETT SQUARE PA 19348
D. MAY 27, 1968 BRYAN, TEX.
D. APRIL 16, 1970 NEW HAVEN, N. Y.
D. DECEMBER 19, 1983 MANASSAS, VA.
D. SEPTEMBER 10, 1955 NEWTON, MASS.
731 SUBURBAN RD - UNION NJ 07083
97 W. ELMWOOD ST - CLAWSON MI 48017
D. AUGUST 14, 1948 CHICAGO, ILL.
D. APRIL 19, 1969 PITTSBURGH, PA.
D. MAY 19, 1960 KANSAS CITY, KAN.
D. JUNE 26, 1961 SAN BERNARDINO, CALIF.
523 11TH AVE - GRINNELL IA 50112
D. FEBRUARY 19, 1983, LONDON, ONT.
47412 ELDON - UTICA MI 48087

70- 24	COLSON, LOYD ALBERT	RR ONE - GOULD OK 73544
68- 14	COLTON, LAWRENCE ROBERT	4015 SW 52ND AVE - PORTLAND OR 97221
73- 25	COLUCCIO, ROBERT PASQUALI	1333 PARADISE CT SE - OLYMPIA WA 98503
80- 25	COMBE, GEOFFREY WADE	2384 E. AVENIDA OTONO - THOUSAND OAKS CA 91362
24- 22	COMBS, EARLE BRYAN	D. JULY 21, 1976 RICHMOND, KY.
47- 21	COMBS, MERRILL RUSSELL	D. JULY 8, 1981 RIVERSIDE, CALIF.
45- 14	COMELLAS, JORGE	13015 SW 50TH ST - MIAMI FL 33165
67- 20	COMER, HARRY WAYNE	RR 1 BOX 4F - SHENANDOAH VA 22849
78- 27	COMER, STEVEN MICHAEL	20500 SUMMERVILLE RD - EXCELSIOR MN 55331
54- 15	COMMAND, JAMES DALTON	1743 MATILDA ST NE - GRAND RAPIDS MI 49503
26- 17	COMORSKY, ADAM ANTHONY	D. MARCH 2, 1951 SWOYERSVILLE, PA.
11- 30	COMPTON, ANNA SEBASTIAN 'PETE'	D. FEBRUARY 3, 1978 KANSAS CITY, MO.
11- 31	COMPTON, HARRY LEROY 'JACK'	D. JULY 4, 1974 LANCASTER, O.
70- 25	COMPTON, MICHAEL LYNN	8624 LEIGHTON DR - TAMPA FL 33614
72- 20	COMPTON, ROBERT CLINTON	OLD ADD: 45 KENT ST - MONTGOMERY AL
84- 21	COMSTOCK, KEITH MARTIN	968 TAMARACK - SAN CARLOS CA 94070
13- 35	COMSTOCK, RALPH REMICK	D. SEPTEMBER 13, 1966 TOLEDO, O.
48- 28	CONATSOR, CLINTON ASTOR	26701 QUAIL CREEK #191 - LAGUNA HILLS CA 92653
70- 26	CONCEPCION, DAVID ISMAEL	URB. LOS CAOBOS BOTALON 5D, 5 PISO-MARACAY VENEZ
80- 26	CONCEPCION, ONIX (CARDONA)	PARCELA 61AA-BO.HIGUILLAR - DORADO PR 00646
62- 28	CONDE, RAMON LUIS	BOX 57 - JUANA DIAZ PR 00665
86- 36	CONE, DAVID BRIAN	3612 BIRCHWOOD DRIVE - KANSAS CITY MO 64137
15- 21	CONE, ROBERT EARL	D. MAY 24, 1955 GALVESTON, TEX.
40- 12	CONGER, RICHARD	D. FEBRUARY 16, 1970 LOS ANGELES, CAL.
64- 20	CONIGLIARO, ANTHONY RICHARD	25 KNOLL WAY - SAN RAFAEL CA 94903
69- 35	CONIGLIARO, WILLIAM MICHAEL	ROSEMARY RD - NAHANT MA 01908
20- 23	CONKWRIGHT, ALLEN HOWARD	7835 COWLES MT CT #B-2 - SAN DIEGO CA 92119
34- 27	CONLAN, JOHN BERTRAND 'JOCKO'	7810 E. MARIPOSA DR - SCOTTSDALE AZ 85251
52- 19	CONLEY, DONALD EUGENE 'GENE'	4 BIRCHTREE RD - FOXBORO MA 02035
14- 39	CONLEY, JAMES PATRICK 'SNIPE'	D. JANUARY 7, 1978 DESOTO, TEX.
58- 25	CONLEY, ROBERT BURNS	OLD ADD: 75 TOWNE SQUARE DR - NEWPORT NEWS VA 23607
23- 22	CONLON, ARTHUR JOSEPH	P.O. BOX 141 - POCASSET MA 02559
83- 35	CONNALLY, FRITZIE LEE	714 CARDINAL CIRCLE - PASADENA TX 77502
21- 15	CONNALLY, GEORGE WALTER 'SARGE'	D. JANUARY 27, 1978 TEMPLE, TEXAS
25- 20	CONNALLY, MERVIN THOMAS	D. JUNE 12, 1964 BERKELEY, CAL.
31- 15	CONNATSER, BROADUS MILBURN 'BRUCE'	D. JANUARY 27, 1971 TERRE HAUTE, IND.
31- 16	CONNELL, EUGENE JOSEPH	D. AUGUST 31, 1937 WAVERLY, N. Y.
26- 18	CONNELL, JOSEPH BERNARD	D. SEPTEMBER 21, 1977 TREXLERTOWN, PA.
20- 24	CONNELLY, THOMAS MARTIN	D. FEBRUARY 18, 1941 HINES, ILL.
45- 15	CONNELLY, WILLIAM WIRT	D. NOVEMBER 27, 1980 RICHMOND, VA.
29- 20	CONNOLLY, EDWARD JOSEPH	D. NOVEMBER 14, 1963 PITTSFIELD, MASS.
64- 21	CONNOLLY, EDWARD JOSEPH JR.	14 HIGHRIDGE ROAD - WILBRAHAM MA 01095
13- 36	CONNOLLY, JOSEPH ALOYSIUS	D. SEPTEMBER 1, 1943 SPRINGFIELD, R.I.
21- 16	CONNOLLY, JOSEPH GEORGE	D. MARCH 30, 1960 SAN FRANCISCO, CALIF.
15- 22	CONNOLLY, THOMAS FRANCIS	D. MAY 14, 1966 BOSTON, MASS.
49- 16	CONNORS, KEVIN WILLIAM 'CHUCK'	STAR ROUTE 3-4400 BOX 73 - TEHACHAPI CA 93561
37- 27	CONNORS, MERVYN JAMES	1131 ADDISON ST-BERKELEY CA 94702
66- 23	CONNORS, WILLIAM JOSEPH	895 N. VILLAGE DR #101 - ST. PETERSBURG FL 33702
78- 26	CONROY, TIMOTHY JAMES	416 LUZERNE DR - MONROEVILLE PA 15146
23- 23	CONROY, WILLIAM FREDERICK 'PEP'	D. JANUARY 23, 1970 CHICAGO, ILL.
35- 16	CONROY, WILLIAM GORDON	7194 CRAIL CT - CITRUS HEIGHTS CA 95610
53- 16	CONROY, WILLIAM ANGELO	1266 WILLSBROOK CT - WESTLAKE VILLAGE CA91360
56- 23	CONSTABLE, JAMES LEE	RR 14 - BOX 540 - JONESBORO TN 37659
50- 23	CONSUEGRA, SANDALIO SIMEON	3255 FLAGLER STREET #14 - MIAMI FL 33125
80- 27	CONTRERAS, ARNALDO JUAN 'NARDIE'	1540 RIVER LN - TAMPA FL 33603
11- 32	CONWAY, CHARLES CONNELL	D. SEPTEMBER 12, 1968 YOUNGSTOWN, O.
41- 17	CONWAY, JACK CLEMENTS	3545 PINE - WACO TX 76708
20- 25	CONWAY, JEROME PATRICK	D. APRIL 16, 1980 HOLYOKE, MASS.
15- 23	CONWAY, OWEN SYLVESTER	D. MARCH 12, 1942 PHILADELPHIA, PA.
18- 12	CONWAY, RICHARD DANIEL 'RIP'	D. DECEMBER 3, 1971 ST PAUL, MINN.
11- 33	CONWELL, EDWARD JAMES	D. MAY 1, 1926 NORWOOD PARK, ILL.
50- 24	CONYERS, HERBERT LEROY	D. SEPTEMBER 16, 1964 CLEVELAND, O.
13- 37	CONZELMAN, JOSEPH HARRISON	D. APRIL 17, 1979 MOUNTAIN BROOK, ALA.
50- 25	COOGAN, DALE ROGER	16940 'B' STREET - HUNTINGTON BEACH CA 92647
41- 18	COOK, EARL DAVIS	RR 4 - STOUFFVILLE ONTARIO CAN.
85- 20	COOK, GLEN PATRICK	34 JOHNSON ST - TONAWQANDA NY 14150
13- 38	COOK, LUTHER ALMUS 'DOC'	D. JUNE 30, 1973 LAWRENCEBURG, TENN.
86- 37	COOK, MICHAEL HORACE	518 SARAH STREET - CHARLESTON SC 29407
59- 15	COOK, RAYMOND CLIFFORD 'CLIFF'	605 WILLIAMSBURG MANOR - ARLINGTON TX 76014
15- 24	COOK, ROLLIN EDWARD	D. AUGUST 11, 1975 TOLEDO, O.
70- 27	COOK, RONALD WAYNE	913 FLANAGAN - LONGVIEW TX 75602
30- 13	COOKE, ALLEN LINDSEY 'DUSTY'	D. NOVEMBER 21, 1987 RALEIGH, N. C.
14- 40	COOMBS, CECIL LYSANDER	D. NOVEMBER 25, 1975 FORT WORTH, TEX.
63- 25	COOMBS, DANIEL BERNARD	14130 CLEOBROOK - HOUSTON TX 77070

33- 14 COOMBS, RAYMOND FRANKLIN 'BOBBY'	BOX 782 - OGUNQUIT ME 03907
17- 15 COONEY, JAMES EDWARD	34 WOODSIA RD - SAUNDERSTOWN RI 02874
21- 17 COONEY, JOHN WALTER	D. JULY 8, 1986 SARASOTA, FLA.
31- 17 COONEY, ROBERT DANIEL	D. MAY 4, 1976 GLEN FALLS, N. Y.
12- 38 COOPER, ARLEY WILBUR	D. AUGUST 7, 1973 ENCINO, CALIF.
48- 29 COOPER, CALVIN ASA	330 POPLAR ST - CLINTON SC 29325
71- 27 COOPER, CECIL CELESTER	1431 MISTY BEND - KATY TX 77450
13- 39 COOPER, CLAUDE WILLIAM	D. JANUARY 21, 1974 PLAINVIEW, TEX.
81- 24 COOPER, DONALD JAMES	66-10 52ND AVE - MASPETH NY 11378
80- 28 COOPER, GARY NATHANIEL	127 OGLESBY AVE - GARDEN CITY GA 31408
14- 41 COOPER, GUY EVANS	D. AUGUST 2, 1951 SANTA MONICA, CALIF.
38- 16 COOPER, MORTON CECIL	D. NOVEMBER 17, 1958 LITTLE ROCK, ARK.
46- 19 COOPER, ORGE PATTERSON 'PAT'	4424 HOBBS HILL DR - CHARLOTTE NC 28212
40- 13 COOPER, WILLIAM WALKER	12514 BONANZA DRIVE - SUN CITY WEST AZ 85375
35- 17 COPELAND, MAYS	D. NOVEMBER 29, 1982 INDIO, CALIF.
35- 18 COPPOLA, HENRY PETER	42 PLEASANT STREET-MILFORD MA 01757
87- 26 CORA, JOSE MANUEL	CALLE 17, F12 VILLA NUEVA - CAGUAS PR 00625
80- 29 CORBETT, DOUGLAS MITCHELL	108 STONEBROOK CT - LONGWOOD FL 32779
36- 15 CORBETT, EUGENE LOUIS	BOX 904 - SALISBURY MD 21801
71- 28 CORBIN, ALTON RAY	922 LIBERTY ST - LIVE OAK FL 32060
45- 16 CORBITT, CLAUDE ELLIOTT	D. MAY 1, 1978 CINCINNATI, O.
15- 25 CORCORAN, ARTHUR ANDREW	D. JULY 27, 1958 CHELSEA, MASS.
10- 34 CORCORAN, MICHAEL JOSEPH 'MICKEY'	D. DECEMBER 9, 1950 BUFFALO, N.Y.
77- 32 CORCORAN, TIMOTHY MICHAEL	4349 FRIAR CIRCLE - LAVERNE CA 91750
18- 13 COREY, EDWARD NORMAN	D. SEPTEMBER 17, 1970 KENOSHA, WIS.
79- 25 COREY, MARK MUNDELL	BOX 161 - EVERGREEN CO 80439
25- 21 CORGAN, CHARLES HOWARD	D. JUNE 13, 1928 WAGONER, OKLA.
11- 34 CORHAN, ROY GEORGE	D. NOVEMBER 24, 1958 SAN FRANCISCO, CALIF.
69- 36 CORKINS, MICHAEL PATRICK	6354 DUCHESS DR - RIVERSIDE CA 92509
78- 29 CORNEJO, NEIVES MARDIE	1510 EAST FORTUNA - WICHITA KS 67216
84- 22 CORNELL, JEFFERY RAY	5207 MCCOY - KANSAS CITY MO 64133
77- 33 CORNUTT, TERRY STANTON	179 WEST HAZEL - ROSEBURG OR 97470
64- 22 CORRALES, PATRICK	2499 PEACHTREE ROAD NE - ATLANTA GA 30305
85- 21 CORREA, EDWIN JOSUE	BUZON 749 RUTA 649 - CAROLINA PR 00630

JIM COX

72- 21 CORRELL, VICTOR CROSBY	9 EAST MOORE ST - STATESBORO GA 30458
10- 35 CORRIDEN, JOHN MICHAEL SR. 'RED'	D. SEPTEMBER 28, 1959 INDIANAPOLIS, IND.
46- 20 CORRIDEN, JOHN MICHAEL JR	5441 EAST 17TH ST - INDIANAPOLIS IN 46218
77- 34 CORT, BARRY LEE	OLD ADD: 8707 SEAHAWK LN - TAMPA FL
23- 24 CORTAZZO, JOHN FRANK 'SHINE'	D. MARCH 4, 1963 PITTSBURGH, PA.
51- 16 CORWIN, ELMER NATHAN 'AL'	1412 SHERWOOD - GENEVA IL 60134
35- 19 COSCARART, JOSEPH MARVIN	127A SPATH RD - SEQUIM WA 98382
38- 17 COSCARART, PETER JOSEPH	2808 JULINDA WAY - ESCONDIDO CA 92025
80- 30 COSEY, DONALD RAY	139 BYXBEE ST - SAN FRANCISCO CA 94132
72- 22 COSGROVE, MICHAEL JOHN	2226 WEST PALO VERDE DR - PHOENIX AZ 85015
66- 24 COSMAN, JAMES HARRY	6520 ROBBINS RIDGE LN - MEMPHIS TN 38119
13- 40 COSTELLO, DANIEL FRANCIS	D. MARCH 26, 1936 PITTSBURGH, PA.
26- 19 COTE, WARREN PETER 'PETE'	D. OCTOBER 17, 1987 MIDDLETON, MASS.
26- 20 COTTER, EDWARD CHRISTOPHER	D. JUNE 14, 1959 HARTFORD, CONN.
22- 22 COTTER, HARVEY LOUIS	D. AUGUST 6, 1955 LOS ANGELES, CAL.
11- 35 COTTER, RICHARD RAPHAEL	D. APRIL 4, 1945 BROOKLYN, N. Y.
59- 16 COTTIER, CHARLES KEITH	7129 LAKE BALLINGER WAY - EDMONDS WA 98020
84- 23 COTTO, HENRY	JUAN J. GARCIA ED. 21 #201 - CAGUAS PR 00625
11- 36 COTTRELL, ENSIGN STOVER	D. FEBRUARY 27, 1947 SYRACUSE, N.Y.
17- 16 COUCH, JOHN DANIEL	D. DECEMBER 8, 1975 PALO ALTO, CALIF.
83- 36 COUCHEE, MICHAEL EUGENE	16900 CYPRESS WAY - LOS GATOS CA 95030
60- 25 COUGHTRY, JAMES MARLAN	4232 SAN VICENTE - CHINO CA 91709
69- 37 COULTER, THOMAS LEE 'SKIP'	809 TRENTON ST - TORONTO OH 43964
14- 42 COUMBE, FREDERICK NICHOLAS 'FRITZ'	D. MARCH 21, 1978 PARADISE, CALIF.
51- 17 COURTNEY, CLINTON DAWSON	D. JUNE 16, 1975 ROCHESTER, N. Y.
19- 15 COURTNEY, HENRY SEYMOUR	D. DECEMBER 11, 1954 LYME, CT.
23- 25 COUSINEAU, ED 'D'	D. JULY 14, 1951 WATERTOWN, MASS.
12- 39 COVELESKI, STANLEY ANTHONY	D. MARCH 20, 1984 SOUTH BEND, IND.
44- 23 COVINGTON, CHESTER ROGERS	D. JUNE 11, 1976 PEMBROKE PARK, FLA.
13- 41 COVINGTON, CLARENCE CALVERT 'TEX'	D. JANUARY 4, 1963 DENISON, TEX.
56- 24 COVINGTON, JOHN WESLEY 'WES'	905 10145 119TH STREET - EDMONTON ALBERTA T5K 1Z2 CAN.
11- 37 COVINGTON, WILLIAM WILKES	D. DECEMBER 10, 1931 DENISON, TEX.
63- 26 COWAN, BILLY ROLAND	1539 VIA CORONEL-PALOS VERDES ESTATES CA90274
74- 17 COWENS, ALFRED EDWARD	5723 KENISTON AVE - LOS ANGELES CA 90043
82- 26 COWLEY, JOSEPH ALAN	146 RUGBY RD - LEXINGTON KY 40504
83- 37 COX, DANNY BRADFORD	306 FEAGIN MILL RD - WARNER ROBINS GA 31093
25- 22 COX, ELMER JOSEPH 'DICK'	D. JUNE 1, 1966 MORRO BAY, CALIF.
22- 23 COX, ERNEST THOMPSON	D. APRIL 29, 1974 BIRMINGHAM, ALA.
28- 23 COX, GEORGE MELVIN	1525 NORTH WHARTON - SHERMAN TX 75090
55- 30 COX, GLENN MELVIN	BOX 487 - LOS MOLINOS CA 96055
73- 26 COX, JAMES CHARLES	916 SOUTH VALE - BLOOMINGTON IL 61701

80- 31 COX, JEFFREY LINDON	2727 VANDERHOOF DR - WEST COVINA CA 91791
66- 25 COX, JOSEPH CASEY	630 GRAND AVE - LONG BEACH CA 90814
73- 27 COX, LARRY EUGENE	246 VALLEY WAY - LIMA OH 45804
26- 21 COX, LESLIE WARREN	D. OCTOBER 14, 1934 SAN ANGELO, TEX.
20- 26 COX, PLATEAU REX	D. OCTOBER 15, 1984 ROANOKE, VA.
68- 15 COX, ROBERT JOE	4030 RIVER RIDGE CHASE - MARIETTA GA 30067
70- 28 COX, TERRY LEE	216 HOLLAND - CARLSBAD NM 88220
36- 16 COX, WILLIAM DONALD	45 CIRCLE DR-CHARLESTON IL 61920
41- 19 COX, WILLIAM RICHARD	D. MARCH 30, 1978 HARRISBURG, PA.
77- 35 COX, WILLIAM TED	113 WEST PRATT DR - MIDWEST CITY OK 73110
14- 43 COYNE, "TOOTS"	
45- 17 COZART, CHARLES RHUBIN	RR 2 BOX 212-A - HUDSON NC 28638
12- 40 CRABB, JAMES ROY	D. MARCH 30, 1940 LEWISTON, MONT.
10- 36 CRABLE, GEORGE E	B. 1886 BROOKLYN, N.Y.
29- 21 CRABTREE, ESTEL CRAYTON	D. JANUARY 4, 1967 LOGAN, O.
55- 31 CRADDOCK, WALTER ANDERSON	D. JULY 6, 1980 PARMA HEIGHTS OHIO
37- 28 CRAFT, HARRY FRANCIS	716 GLEN HAVEN DR - CONROE TX 77301
16- 14 CRAFT, MAURICE MONTAGUE 'MOLLY'	D. OCTOBER 25, 1978 LOS ANGELES, CALIF.
31- 18 CRAGHEAD, HOWARD OLIVER	D. JULY 15, 1962 SAN ZIELOE, CAL.
64- 23 CRAIG, PETER JOEL	801 SILVERLEAF PL - RALEIGH NC 27609
79- 26 CRAIG, RODNEY PAUL 'ROCKY'	OLD ADD: 23230 SESAME ST - TORRANCE CA
55- 32 CRAIG, ROGER LEE	26658 SAN FELIPE RD - WARNER SPRING CA 92086
69- 38 CRAM, GERALD ALLEN	2748 NORTH 121ST AVE - OMAHA NE 68164
29- 22 CRAMER, ROGER MAXWELL 'DOC'	5 HILLIARD DR - MANAHAWKIN NJ 08050
12- 41 CRAMER, WILLIAM WENDELL	D. SEPTEMBER 11, 1966 FORT WAYNE, IND.
49- 17 CRANDALL, DELMAR WESLEY	623 ROSARITA DR - FULLERTON CA 92635
14- 44 CRANE, SAMUEL BYREN	D. NOVEMBER 12, 1955 PHILADELPHIA, PA.
37- 29 CRAWFORD, CHARLES LOWRIE 'LARRY'	B. APRIL 27, 1914 SWISSVALE, PA.
29- 23 CRAWFORD, CLIFFORD RANKIN 'PAT'	900 ACADEMY HEIGHTS #3 - KINSTON NC 28501
45- 18 CRAWFORD, GLENN MARTIN	D. JANUARY 2, 1972 SAGINAW, MICH.
73- 28 CRAWFORD, JAMES FREDERICK	OLD ADD: 48621 I-94 S'CE DR DR-BELLKEVILLE MI
15- 26 CRAWFORD, KENNETH DANIEL	D. NOVEMBER 11, 1976 PITTSBURGH, PA.
52- 20 CRAWFORD, RUFUS 'JAKE'	2928 WESTBROOK - FORT WORTH TX 76111
80- 32 CRAWFORD, STEVE RAY	RR 2 BOX 7-8 - SALINA OK 74365
64- 24 CRAWFORD, WILLIE MURPHY	P.O. BOX 491054 - LOS ANGELES CA 90049
43- 32 CREEDEN, CORNELIUS STEPHEN	D. NOVEMBER 30, 1969 SANTA ANA, CAL.
31- 19 CREEDON, PATRICK FRANCIS	622 NORTH MAIN ST - BROCKTON MA 02401
45- 19 CREEL, JACK DALTON	7119 OAK ARBOR - HOUSTON TX 77088
82- 27 CREEL, STEVEN KEITH	527 TRAIL RIDGE DR - DUNCANVILLE TX 75116
47- 22 CREGER, BERNARD ODELL	15 GREENWELL CT - LYNCHBURG VA 24502
27- 27 CREMINS, ROBERT ANTHONY	415 MANOR RIDGE RD - PELHAM NY 10803
38- 18 CRESPI, FRANK ANGELO JOSEPH	1710 FERNBROOK - FLORISSANT MO 63031
48- 30 CRESS, WALKER JAMES	14177 WINTERSET - GREENWELL SPRINGS LA 70739
87- 27 CREWS, STANLEY TIMOTHY 'TIM'	8103 19TH AVENUE - TAMPA FL 33619
69- 39 CRIDER, JERRY STEPHEN	821 KENSINGTON DR - ORLANDO FL 32808
87- 28 CRIM, CHARLES ROBERT	25800 SAND CYN - CANYON COUNTRY CA 91350
51- 18 CRIMIAN, JOHN MELVIN	3012 GREEN ST - CLAYMONT DE 19703
78- 30 CRIPE, DAVID GORDON	40657 OAKLAND AVE - HEMET CA 92343
77- 36 CRISCIONE, DAVID GERALD	87 HAMLET ST - FREDONIA NY 14063
42- 24 CRISCOLA, ANTHONY PAUL	4025 BAYARD-SAN DIEGO CA 92109
10- 37 CRISP, JOSEPH SHELBY	D. FEBRUARY 5, 1939 KANSAS CITY, MO.
51- 19 CRISTANTE, LEO DANTE	D. AUGUST 24, 1977 DEARBORN, MICH.
24- 23 CRITZ, HUGH MELVILLE	D. JANUARY 10, 1980 GREENWOOD, MISS.
44- 24 CROCKER, CLAUDE ARTHUR	MERRIE OAKS - CLINTON SC 29325
74- 18 CROMARTIE, WARREN LIVINGSTON	%BOOTH,1751 NW 36TH ST - MIAMI FL 33142
37- 30 CROMPTON, HERBERT BRYAN	D. AUGUST 5, 1963 MOLINE, ILL.
54- 16 CRONE, RAYMOND HAYES	916 NW PANORAMA LOOP - WAXAHACHIE TX 75165
29- 24 CRONIN, JAMES JOHN	D. JUNE 10, 1983 RICHMOND, CALIF.
26- 22 CRONIN, JOSEPH EDWARD	D. SEPTEMBER 7, 1984 OSTERVILLE, MASS.
28- 24 CRONIN, WILLIAM PATRICK	D. OCTOBER 26, 1966 NEWTON, MASS.
70- 29 CROSBY, EDWARD CARLTON	11463 ANTICOST WAY - CYPRESS CA 90630
75- 28 CROSBY, KENNETH STEWART	BOX 680306 - PARK CITY UT 84068
32- 15 CROSETTI, FRANK PETER JOSEPH	65 WEST MONTEREY AV - STOCKTON CA 95204
42- 25 CROSS, JOFFRE JAMES 'JEFF'	6154 LONGMONT-HOUSTON TX 77027
12- 42 CROSSIN, FRANK PATRICK	D. DECEMBER 6, 1965 KINGSPORT, PA.
30- 14 CROUCH, JACK ALBERT	D. AUGUST 25, 1972 LEESBURG, FLA.
39- 24 CROUCH, WILLIAM ELMER	D. DECEMBER 26, 1980 HOWELL, MICH.
10- 38 CROUCH, WILLIAM HENRY	D. DECEMBER 22, 1945 HIGHLAND PARK, MICH.
39- 25 CROUCHER, FRANK DONALD	D. MAY 21, 1980 HOUSTON, TEXAS
23- 26 CROUSE, CLYDE ELLSWORTH 'BUCK'	D. OCTOBER 23, 1983 MUNCIE, IND.
82- 28 CROW, DONALD LEROY	7605 WESTBROOK AVE - YAKIMA WA 98908
26- 23 CROWDER, ALVIN FLOYD 'GEN'	D. APRIL 3, 1972 WINSTON-SALEM, N. C.
52- 21 CROWE, GEORGE DANIEL	3820 SE 73RD ST - OCALA FL 32671
15- 27 CROWELL, MINOT JOY 'CAP'	D. SEPTEMBER 30, 1962 CENTRAL FALLS, R.I.
28- 25 CROWLEY, EDGAR JEWEL	D. APRIL 14, 1970 BIRMINGHAM, ALA.
69- 40 CROWLEY, TERRENCE MICHAEL	10626 ANGLOHILL RD - COCKEYSVILLE MD 21030
45- 20 CROWSON, THOMAS WOODROW WILSON 'WOODY'	D. AUGUST 14, 1947 MAYODAN, N. C.
14- 45 CRUISE, WALTON EDWIN	D. JANUARY 9, 1975 SYLACAUGA ALA.
17- 17 CRUM, CALVIN CARL	D. DECEMBER 7, 1945 TULSA, OKLA.
45- 21 CRUMLING, EUGENE LEON	RR 24 BOX 809 - YORK PA 17406
24- 24 CRUMP, ARTHUR ELLIOTT	D. SEPTEMBER 7, 1976 RALEIGH, N. C.
20- 27 CRUMPLER, RAY MAXTON	D. OCTOBER 6, 1969 FAYETTEVILLE, N. C.
14- 46 CRUTCHER, RICHARD LOUIS	D. JUNE 19, 1952 FRANKFORT, KY.
13- 42 CRUTHERS, CHARLES PRESTON 'PRESS'	D. DECEMBER 27, 1976 KENOSHA, WISC.
73- 29 CRUZ, CIRILO 'TOMMY'	CALLE H-E-8 - ARROYO PR 00615
73- 30 CRUZ, HECTOR LUIS	CALLE H-E-8 - ARROYO PR 00615
75- 29 CRUZ, HENRY ACOSTA	OLD ADD: MONTRE BRISAS CALLE T-O-6 - FAJARDO PR 00648
70- 30 CRUZ, JOSE DELAN	B-15 JARDINES LAFAYETTE - ARROYO PR 00615
77- 37 CRUZ, JULIO LOUIS	40 ORCAS KEY - BELLEVUE WA 98006
78- 31 CRUZ, TODD RUBEN	868 WEST OLIVE STREET - COLTON CA 92324
78- 32 CRUZ, VICTOR MANUEL	ALEXANDER FLEMING NO. 67 - SANTO DOMINGO DOMINICAN REP.
74- 19 CUBBAGE, MICHAEL LEE	BOX 126 - RUCKERSVILLE VA 22968
35- 20 CUCCINELLO, ALFRED EDWARD	106 LWGION PLACE - MALVERNE NY 11565
30- 15 CUCCINELLO, ANTHONY FRANCIS	3610 BEACH DR - TAMPA FL 33629
43- 33 CUCCURULLO, ARTHUR JOSEPH 'COOKIE'	D. JANUARY 23, 1983 WEST ORANGE, N. J.
77- 38 CUELLAR, BOBBY	705 EAST SIXTH STREET - ALICE TX 78332
50- 26 CUELLAR, CHARLES JESUS PATRICK	3209 GRACE ST - TAMPA FL 33607
59- 17 CUELLAR, MIGUEL 'MIKE'	BOX 50016 - LEVITTOWN PR 00950
61- 25 CUETO, DAGOBERTO CONCEPCION	EL COROJO - SAN LUIS PINAR DEL RIO CUBA

14- 47 CUETO, MANUEL MELO — D. JUNE 29, 1942 REGLA, HAVANA CUBA
43- 34 CULBERSON, DELBERT LEON 'LEE' — 34 GLENRISE TER - ROME GA 30161
62- 29 CULLEN, JOHN PATRICK — 164 ALEXANDER AVE - NUTLEY NJ 07110
66- 26 CULLEN, TIMOTHY LEO — 789 SOLANA DR - LAFAYETTE CA 94549
38- 19 CULLENBINE, ROY JOSEPH — 24638 MEADOW LN - MOUNT CLEMENS MI 48043
36- 17 CULLER, RICHARD BROADUS — D. JUNE 16, 1964 CHAPEL HILL, N. C.
26- 24 CULLOP, HENRY 'NICK' — D. DECEMBER 8, 1978 WESTERVILLE, O.
13- 43 CULLOP, NORMAN ANDREW 'NICK' — D. APRIL 15, 1961 TAZEWELL, VA.
25- 23 CULLOTON, BERNARD ALOYSIUS 'BUD' — D. NOVEMBER 9, 1976 KINGSTON, N. Y.
83- 38 CULMER, WILFRED HILLARD — BOX N9762 - NASSAU BAHAMAS W.I.
42- 26 CULP, BENJAMIN BALDY — 3827 KAREN ST-PHILADELPHIA PA 19114
63- 27 CULP, RAY LEONARD — 7400 WATERLINE - AUSTIN TX 78731
10- 39 CULP, WILLIAM EDWARD — D. SEPTEMBER 3, 1969 ARNOLD, PA.
66- 27 CULVER, GEORGE RICHARD — 4800 TREANNA AVENUE #2A - BAKERSFIELD CA 93301
68- 16 CUMBERLAND, JOHN SHELDON — 3250 MCMULLEN BOOTH ROAD - CLEARWATER FL 33519
26- 25 CUMMINGS, JOHN WILLIAM — D. OCTOBER 5, 1962 WEST MIFFLIN, PA.
29- 25 CUNNINGHAM, BRUCE LEE — D. MARCH 8, 1984 HAYWARD, CALIF.
16- 15 CUNNINGHAM, GEORGE HAROLD — D. MARCH 10, 1972 CHATTANOOGA, TENN.
54- 17 CUNNINGHAM, JOSEPH ROBERT — BOX 8787 - ST.LOUIS MO 63102
31- 20 CUNNINGHAM, RAYMOND LEE — 1007 CHRISTINE - HOUSTON TX 77017
21- 18 CUNNINGHAM, WILLIAM ALOYSIUS — D. SEPTEMBER 26, 1953 COLUSA, CAL.
10- 40 CUNNINGHAM, WILLIAM JAMES — D. FEBRUARY 21, 1946 SCHENECTADY, N. Y.
75- 30 CURRENCE, DELANCY LAFAYETTE — 1238 STANLEY DR - ROCK HILL SC 29730
16- 16 CURRIE, MURPHY ARCHIBALD — D. JUNE 22, 1939 ASHEBORO, N.C.
55- 33 CURRIE, WILLIAM CLEVELAND — ARLINGTON GA 31713
47- 23 CURRIN, PERRY GILMORE — 1967 ADD: 1615 SIGMON NW - ROANOKE VA 24017
60- 26 CURRY, GEORGE ANTHONY 'TONY' — BOX 7054 - NASSAU BAHAMAS W.I.
11- 38 CURRY, GEORGE JAMES — D. OCTOBER 5, 1963 STRATFORD, CONN.
61- 26 CURTIS, JACK PATRICK — RR 3 BOX 458 - GRANITE FALLS NC 28630
70- 31 CURTIS, JOHN DUFFIELD — 858 ANDROMEDA LN - FOSTER CITY CA 94404
43- 35 CURTIS, VERNON EUGENE — 724 21ST ST - CAIRO IL 62914
43- 36 CURTRIGHT, GUY PAXTON — 1620 BENTWOOD DR - SUN CITY CENTER FL 33570
51- 20 CUSICK, JOHN PETER — 46 NORTHWOOD AVE - DEMAREST NJ 07627
12- 43 CUTSHAW, GEORGE WILLIAM — D. AUGUST 22, 1973 SAN DIEGO, CALIF.
21- 19 CUYLER, HAZEN SHIRLEY 'KIKI' — D. FEBRUARY 11, 1950 ANN ARBOR, MICH.
22- 24 CVENGROS, MICHAEL JOHN — D. AUGUST 2, 1970 HOT SPRINGS, ARK.
14- 48 CYPERT, ALFRED BOYD — D. JANUARY 9, 1973 WASHINGTON, D.C.
73- 31 DACQUISTO, JOHN FRANCIS — 3440 FIR ST - SAN DIEGO CA 92104
75- 31 DADE, LONNIE PAUL — OLD ADD: 15829 SE 171ST PL - RENTON WA 98055
43- 37 DAGENHARD, JOHN DOUGLAS — 10511 HALBRENT AVE - MISSION HILLS CA 91345
32- 16 DAGLIA, PETER GEORGE — D. MARCH 11, 1952 WILLITS, CAL.
55- 34 DAGRES, ANGELO GEORGE — GREENTREE LN RFD - ROWLEY MA 01969
63- 28 DAHL, JAY STEVEN — D. JUNE 20, 1965 SALISBURY, N. C.
35- 21 DAHLGREN, ELLSWORTH TENNEY 'BABE' — 17 WOODLYN LN - BRADBURY CA 91010
56- 25 DAHLKE, JEROME ALEXANDER 'JOE' — 3643 HALLBROOK ST - MEMPHIS TN 38127
29- 26 DAILEY, SAMUEL LAURENCE — D. DECEMBER 2, 1979 COLUMBIA, MO.
61- 27 DAILEY, WILLIAM GARLAND — RR 1 BOX M8 - DUBLIN VA 24084
67- 21 DAL CANTON, JOHN BRUCE — 624 RAY DR - CARNEGIE PA 15106
11- 39 DALE, EMMETT EUGENE 'GENE' — D. MARCH 20, 1958 ST. LOUIS, MO.
55- 35 DALEY, BUDDY LEO — RR 62-C BOX 205 - LANDER WY 82520
12- 44 DALEY, JOHN FRANCIS — %K.METZ, 104 MASSA AVENUE - MANSFIELD OH 44907
11- 40 DALEY, JUD LAWRENCE — D. JANUARY 26, 1967 GADSDEN, ALA.
55- 36 DALEY, PETER HARVEY — 4019 CALLE MIRA MONTE - NEWBURY PARK CA 91320
37- 31 DALLESSANDRO, NICHOLAS DOMINIC 'DOM' — D. APRIL 29, 1988 INDIANAPOLIS, IND.
60- 27 DALRYMPLE, CLAYTON ERROL — 710 BRUCE LANE - CHICO CA 95928
15- 28 DALRYMPLE, WILLIAM DUNN — D. JULY 14, 1967 SAN DIEGO, CALIF.
10- 41 DALTON, TALBOT PERCY 'JACK' — OLD ADD: 2 PROSPECT AVE - CATONSVILLE MD
13- 44 DALY, THOMAS DANIEL — D. NOVEMBER 7, 1946 MEDFORD, MASS.
63- 29 DAMASKA, JACK LLOYD — 252 BLACKHAWK RD - BEAVER FALLS PA 15010
15- 29 DAMRAU, HARRY ROBERT — D. AUGUST 21, 1957 STATEN ISLAND, N. Y.

JOHN D'ACQUISTO

28- 26 DANEY, ARTHUR LEE — D. MARCH 11, 1988 SCOTTSDALE, ARIZ.
11- 41 DANFORTH, DAVID CHARLES — D. SEPTEMBER 19, 1970 BALTIMORE, MD.
57- 14 DANIEL, CHARLES EDWARD — 1640 BABS RD - MEMPHIS TN 38116
37- 32 DANIEL, HANDLEY JACOB 'JAKE' — 990 NEW HUTCHINSON MILL RD - LAGRANGE GA 30240
57- 15 DANIELS, BENNIE — P.O. BOX 4444 - COMPTON CA 90221
10- 42 DANIELS, BERNARD ELMER 'BERT' — D. JUNE 6, 1958 CEDAR GROVE, N.J.
45- 22 DANIELS, FREDERICK CLINTON — 522 SALISBURY RD - STATESVILLE NC 28677
52- 22 DANIELS, HAROLD JACK — 3715 ELMRIDGE DR - EVANSVILLE IN 47711
86- 38 DANIELS, KALVOSKI — 151 IGNICI DRIVE #2L - WARNER ROBINS GA 31093
15- 30 DANNER, HENRY FREDERICK 'BUCK' — D. SEPTEMBER 21, 1949 BOSTON, MASS.
33- 15 DANNING, HARRY — 212 FOX CHAPEL COURT - VALPARAISO IN 46383
28- 27 DANNING, IKE — D. MARCH 28, 1983 SANTA MONICA, CALIF.
44- 25 DANTONIO, JOHN JAMES 'FATS' — 430 SOUTH CLARK ST - NEW ORLEANS LA 70119
42- 27 DAPPER, CLIFFORD ROLAND — 733 BURMA RD-FALLBROOK CA 92028

74- 20 DARCY, PATRICK LEONARD
14- 49 DARINGER, CLIFFORD CLARENCE
14- 50 DARINGER, ROLLA HARRISON
46- 21 DARK, ALVIN RALPH
83- 39 DARLING, RONALD MAURICE
54- 18 DARNELL, ROBERT JACK
77- 39 DARR, MICHAEL EDWARD
34- 28 DARROW, GEORGE OLIVER
62- 30 DARWIN, ARTHUR BOBBY LEE
78- 33 DARWIN, DANNY WAYNE
24- 25 DASHIELL, JOHN WALLACE 'WALLY'
13- 45 DASHNER, LEE CLAIRE
45- 23 DASSO, FRANCIS JOSEPH NICHOLAS
15- 31 DAUBERT, HARRY J.
10- 43 DAUBERT, JACOB ELSWORTH
76- 27 DAUER, RICHARD FREMONT
51- 21 DAUGHERTY, HAROLD RAY
87- 29 DAUGHERTY, JOHN MICHAEL
37- 33 DAUGHTERS, ROBERT FRANCIS
83- 40 DAULTON, DARREN ARTHUR
12- 45 DAUSS, GEORGE AUGUST 'HOOKS'
53- 17 DAVALILLO, POMPEYO ANTONIO 'YO-YO'
63- 30 DAVALILLO, VICTOR JOSE
69- 41 DAVANON, FRANK GERALD
20- 28 DAVENPORT, CLAUDE EDWIN
14- 51 DAVENPORT, DAVID W.
58- 26 DAVENPORT, JAMES HOUSTON
21- 20 DAVENPORT, JOUBERT LUM
77- 40 DAVEY, MICHAEL GERARD
62- 31 DAVIAULT, RAYMOND JOSEPH ROBERT
84- 24 DAVID, ANDRE ANTER
18- 14 DAVIDSON, CLAUDE BOUCHER
86- 39 DAVIDSON, JOHN MARK
65- 25 DAVIDSON, THOMAS EUGENE 'TED'
59- 18 DAVIE, GERALD LEE
14- 52 DAVIES, LLOYD GARRISON 'CHICK'
84- 25 DAVIS, ALVIN GLENN
65- 26 DAVIS, ARTHUR WILLARD 'BILL'
63- 31 DAVIS, BRYSHEAR BARNETT 'BROCK'
81- 25 DAVIS, CHARLES THEODORE 'CHILI'
34- 29 DAVIS, CURTIS BENTON
84- 26 DAVIS, ERIC KEITH
12- 46 DAVIS, FRANK TALMADGE 'DIXIE'
12- 47 DAVIS, GEORGE ALLEN
82- 29 DAVIS, GEORGE EARL 'STORM'

515 SOUTH COLUMBUS BLVD - TUCSON AZ 85711
D. DECEMBER 12, 1971 SACRAMENTO, CALIF.
D. MAY 23, 1974 SEYMOUR, IND.
103 CRAMBERRY WAY - EASLEY SC 29640
19 WOODLAND STREET - MILLBURY MA 01527
509 MAPLE DR - SPRINGDALE AR 72764
OLD ADD: 5862 "B" FULLERTON AVE - BUENA PARK CA 90621
D. MARCH 24, 1983 SUN CITY, ARIZ.
17509 ALORA STREET - CERRITOS CA 90701
2218 FALL RIVER DRIVE - ARLINGTON TX 76006
D. MAY 20, 1972 PENSACOLA, FLA.
D. DECEMBER 16, 1960 EL DORADO, KAN.
1413 MADISON - WENATCHEE WA 98801
D. JANUARY 8, 1944 DETROIT, MICH.
D. OCTOBER 9, 1924 CINCINNATI, O.
6880 GALA - HIGHLAND CA 92346
OLD ADD: 66 ELDRED AVENUE - BEDFORD OH 44014
8633 SOMERSET AVE - SAN DIEGO CA 92123
1003B HERITAGE VILLAGE - SOUTHBURY CT 06488
RURAL ROUTE 3 BOX 21 - ARKANSAS CITY KS 67005
D. JULY 27, 1963 ST. LOUIS, MO.
CENTRO COMMERCIAL #8 - MAIQUETIA VENEZUELA S.A.
CLE TRUJILLO 7,MARIPEREZ,Q.V.-CARACAS VENEZ
5751 CHEENA - HOUSTON TX 77096
D. JUNE 13, 1976 CORPUS CHRISTI, TEX.
D. OCTOBER 16, 1954 EL DORADO, ARK.
1016 HEWITT DR - SAN CARLOS CA 94070
D. APRIL 21, 1961 DALLAS, TEX.
SOUTH 5118 MADELIA - SPOKANE WA 99203
12116 ONTARIO E. - POINTES AUX TREMBLES QUE CAN.
1428 CALLE LINDA - SAN DIMAS CA 91773
D. APRIL 18, 1956 WEYMOUTH, MASS.
P.O. BOX 1001 - MOORESVILLE NC 28115
515 DE ARMOND PLACE - SANTA MARIA CA 93454
19380 SAVAGE ROAD - BELLEVILLE MI 48111
D. SEPTEMBER 5, 1973 MIDDLETOWN, CONN.
14945 SE 60TH STREET - BELLEVUE WA 98006
6638 KNOX AVE SOUTH - MINNEAPOLIS MN 55423
2080 WEST ONTARIO AVE - CORONA CA 91720
4227 DON ORTEGA PLACE - LOS ANGELES CA 90008
D. OCTOBER 12, 1965 COVINA, CAL.
6606 DENVER AVE #1 - LOS ANGELES CA 90044
D. FEBRUARY 4, 1944 RALEIGH, N.C.
D. JUNE 4, 1961 BUFFALO, N.Y.
P.O. BOX 14025 - SAVANNAH GA 31416

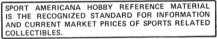

SPORT AMERICANA HOBBY REFERENCE MATERIAL IS THE RECOGNIZED STANDARD FOR INFORMATION AND CURRENT MARKET PRICES OF SPORTS RELATED COLLECTIBLES.

Pat Darcy
Cincinnati Reds

26- 26 DAVIS, GEORGE WILLIS 'KIDDO'
83- 41 DAVIS, GERALD EDWARD
84- 27 DAVIS, GLENN EARL
32- 17 DAVIS, HARRY ALBERT
59- 19 DAVIS, HERMAN THOMAS 'TOMMY'
19- 16 DAVIS, ISAAC MARION
62- 32 DAVIS, JACKE SYLVESTA
54- 19 DAVIS, JAMES BENNETT
81- 26 DAVIS, JODY PACKARD
85- 22 DAVIS, JOEL CLARK
41- 20 DAVIS, JOHN HUMPHREY 'RED'
87- 30 DAVIS, JOHN KIRK
15- 32 DAVIS, JOHN WILBUR 'BUD'
40- 14 DAVIS, LAWRENCE COLUMBUS 'CRASH'
80- 33 DAVIS, MARK WILLIAM
80- 34 DAVIS, MICHAEL DWAYNE
80- 35 DAVIS, ODIE ERNEST
46- 22 DAVIS, OTIS ALLEN
36- 18 DAVIS, RAY THOMAS 'PEACHES'
77- 41 DAVIS, RICHARD EARL
52- 23 DAVIS, ROBERT BRANDON 'BRANDY'
58- 27 DAVIS, ROBERT EDWARD
73- 32 DAVIS, ROBERT JOHN EUGENE
62- 33 DAVIS, RONALD EVERETTE
78- 34 DAVIS, RONALD GENE
85- 23 DAVIS, STEVEN KENNON
79- 27 DAVIS, STEVEN MICHAEL
49- 18 DAVIS, THOMAS OSCAR 'TOD'
85- 24 DAVIS, TRENCH NEAL

D. MARCH 4, 1983 BRIDGEPORT, CONN.
72 THERESA STREET - TRENTON NJ 08618
2241 14TH STREET - COLUMBUS GA 31906
2002 LINE STREET - SHREVEPORT LA 71104
9767 WHIRLAWAY - ALTA LOMA CA 91701
D. APRIL 2, 1984 TUCSON, ARIZ.
1131 LYNNWOOD DR - CARTHAGE TX 75633
3327 COUNTRYSIDE DR - SAN MATEO CA 94403
RR 1 BEN HILL DR - OAKWOOD GA 30566
4117 PACKARD DRIVE - JACKSONVILLE FL 32216
P.O. BOX 2742 - LAUREL MS 39440
9840 AURA - NORTHRIDGE CA 91324
D. MAY 26, 1967 LIGHTFOOT, VA.
4767 CHAMPION CT - GREENSBORO NC 27410
1620 READING BLVD - WYOMISSING PA 19610
7312 CANTON DRIVE - LEMON GROVE CA 92045
1014 MONTANA ST - SAN ANTONIO TX 78203
3078 EASTLAND BLVD #202A - CLEARWATER FL 33519
1802 BEECH ST-DUNCAN OK 73533
2415 WEST ALONDRA - COMPTON CA 90220
222 CHELTENHAM RD - NEWARK DE 19712
37 WEST 12TH ST - NEW YORK NY 10003
BOX 132 - LOCUST GROVE OK 74352
10811 SHAWNBROOK - HOUSTON TX 77071
8103 COYTON - HOUSTON TX 77061
802 SERENADE DRIVE - SAN ANTONIO TX 78216
1377 ANTONIO LANE - SAN JOSE CA 95117
D. DECEMBER 31, 1978 WEST COVINA, CALIF.
OLD ADD: 916 SEAGULL AVE - BALTIMORE MD 21225

ANDRE DAWSON
Voltigeur/Outfielder

28- 28	DAVIS, VIRGIL LAWRENCE 'SPUD'	D. AUGUST 14, 1984 BIRMINGHAM, ALA.
83- 42	DAVIS, WALLACE MCARTHUR 'BUTCH'	112 PRICE STREET - WILLIAMSTON NC 27892
60- 28	DAVIS, WILLIAM HENRY	4419 BUENA VISTA #203 - DALLAS TX 75202
38- 20	DAVIS, WOODROW WILSON	BOX 87-ODUM GA 31555
69- 42	DAVISON, MICHAEL LYNN	578 PROSPECT - HUTCHINSON MN 55350 .
83- 43	DAWLEY, WILLIAM CHESTER	RR 2, KENDALL ROAD EXT - LISBON CT 06417
76- 28	DAWSON, ANDRE NOLAN	10301 SW 144TH STREET - MIAMI FL 33176
24- 26	DAWSON, RALPH FENTON 'JOE'	D. JANUARY 4, 1978 LONGVIEW, TEX.
13- 46	DAWSON, REXFORD PAUL	D. OCTOBER 20, 1958 INDIANAPOLIS, IND.
69- 43	DAY, CHARLES FREDERICK 'BOOTS'	11972 CHARTER OAK PKWY - ST. LOUIS MO 63146
24- 27	DAY, CLYDE HENRY 'PEA RIDGE'	D. MARCH 21, 1934 KANSAS CITY, MO.
83- 44	DAYETT, BRIAN KELLY	45 VILLAGE ST - DEEP RIVER CT 06417
82- 30	DAYLEY, KENNETH GRANT	1601 MOUNT HOOD ST - THE DALLES OR 97058
12- 48	DEAL, CHARLES ALBERT	D. SEPTEMBER 16, 1979 COVINA, CALIF.
47- 24	DEAL, ELLIS FERGUSON 'COT'	4710 HEMLOCK CIRCLE - OKLAHOMA CITY OK 73162
39- 26	DEAL, LINDSAY FRED	D. APRIL 18, 1979 LITTLE ROCK, ARK.
36- 19	DEAN, ALFRED LOVILL 'CHUBBY'	D. DECEMBER 21, 1970 RIVERSIDE, N. J.
41- 21	DEAN, JAMES HARRY	D. JUNE 1, 1960 ROCKMART, GA.
30- 16	DEAN, JAY HANNA 'DIZZY'	D. JULY 17, 1974 RENO, NEV.
34- 30	DEAN, PAUL DEE	D. MARCH 17, 1981 SPRINGDALE, ARK.
67- 22	DEAN, TOMMY DOUGLAS	RR2 - IUKA MS 38852
24- 28	DEAN, WAYLAND OGDEN	D. APRIL 10, 1930 HUNTINGTON, W. VA.
27- 28	DEAR, PAUL STANFORD 'BUDDY'	BOX 2475 - CHRISTIANSBURG VA 24073
77- 42	DEBARR, DENNIS LEE	6292 MOCK ORANGE CT - NEWARK CA 94560
16- 17	DEBERRY, JOHN HERMAN 'HANK'	D. SEPTEMBER 10, 1951 SAVANNAH, TENN.
20- 29	DEBERRY, JOSEPH GADDY	D. OCTOBER 9, 1944 SOUTHERN PINES, N. C.
17- 18	DEBUS, ADAM JOSEPH	D. MAY 13, 1977 CHICAGO, ILL.
62- 34	DEBUSSCHERE, DAVID ALBERT	90 3RD ST - GARDEN CITY NY 11530
22- 25	DECATUR, ARTHUR RUE	D. APRIL 25, 1966 TALLADEGA, ALA.
73- 33	DECINCES, DOUGLAS VERNON	9411 HAZEL CIR - VILLA PARK CA 92667
83- 45	DECKER, DEE MARTIN 'MARTY'	920 GATE LANE - PILOT HILL CA 95664
69- 44	DECKER, GEORGE HENRY 'JOE'	4507 SOUTH 12TH STREET - TACOMA WA 98405
16- 18	DEDE, ARTHUR RICHARD	D. SEPTEMBER 6, 1971 KEENE, N.H.
35- 22	DEDEAUX, RAOUL MARTIAL 'ROD'	1430 SOUTH EASTMAN AVE - LOS ANGELES CA 90023
83- 46	DEDMON, JEFFREY LINDEN	21102 SOUTH BROADWELL - TORRANCE CA 90502
15- 33	DEE, MAURICE LEO 'SHORTY'	D. AUGUST 12, 1971 JAMAICA PLAINS, MASS.
84- 28	DEER, ROBERT GEORGE	2028 MARSH ROAD - SANTA ROSA CA 95405
63- 32	DEES, CHARLES HENRY	23412 DORSET PL - HARBOR CITY CA 90710
17- 19	DEFATE, CLYDE HERBERT 'TONY'	D. SEPTEMBER 3, 1963 NEW ORLEANS, LA.
78- 35	DEFREITES, ARTURO SIMON	HERMONOS MIRABEL #21 - SAN PEDRO DE MACORIS DOM. REP.
61- 28	DEGERICK, MICHAEL ARTHUR	353 RIDGEDALE AVE - EAST HANOVER NJ 07936
74- 21	DEIDEL, JAMES LAWRENCE	OLD ADD: 2545 SOUTH PATTON CT - DENVER CO
40- 15	DEJAN, MIKE DAN	D. FEBRUARY 2, 1953 WEST LOS ANGELES, CALIF.
74- 22	DEJESUS, IVAN	GAUTHIER #1753,SANTIAGO IGLESAIS - RIO PIEDRAS PR 00921
82- 31	DEJOHN, MARK STEPHEN	966 WORTHINGTON RIDGE - BERLIN CT 06037
45- 24	DEKONING, WILLIAM CALLAHAN	D. JULY 26, 1979 PALM HARBOR, FLA.
44- 26	DELACRUZ, TOMAS	D. SEPTEMBER 6, 1958 HAVANA, CUBA
60- 29	DELAHOZ, MIGUEL ANGEL	1367 SW 14TH STREET - MIAMI FL 33145
32- 18	DELANCEY, WILLIAM PINKNEY	D. NOVEMBER 28, 1946 PHOENIX, ARIZ.
24- 29	DELANEY, ARTHUR DEWEY	D. MAY 2, 1970 HAYWARD, CALIF.
75- 32	DELAROSA, JESUS	20 #28 LOS MINOS - SANTO DOMINGO DOMINICAN REP.
83- 47	DELEON, JOSE	216 BRIGHTON AVENUE - PERTH AMBOY NJ 08861
81- 27	DELEON, LUIS ANTONIO	SAN ANTON 120,CLE E.CABRERRA - PONCE PR 00731
77- 43	DELGADO, LUIS FELIPE	VILLA DEL CARMEN, BOX 879 - AY HATILLO PR 00659
52- 24	DELGRECO, ROBERT GEORGE	625 SOUTHVIEW DR - PITTSBURGH PA 15226
12- 49	DELHI, LEE WILLIAM 'FLAME'	D. MAY 9, 1966 GREENBRAE, CALIF.
55- 37	DELIS, JUAN FRANCISCO	1963 ADD:3A #24508, REPARTO DOLORES - HAVANA
29- 27	DELKER, EDWARD ALBERTS	1 SOUTH FRONT ST - ST CLAIR PA 17970
12- 50	DELL, WILLIAM GEORGE 'WHEEZER'	D. AUGUST 24, 1966 INDEPENDENCE, CALIF.
33- 16	DELMAS, ALBERT CHARLES	D. DECEMBER 4, 1979 HUNTINGTON BEACH, CALIF.
52- 25	DELOCK, IVAN MARTIN 'IKE'	147 PARKER RD - NEEDHAM MA 02194
74- 23	DELOS SANTOS, RAMON GENERO	OZAMA ESTE #13 - SANTO DOMINGO DOMINICAN REP.
43- 38	DELSAVIO, GARTON ORVILLE	48 ROOSEVELT DR-BLAUVELT NY 10913
48- 31	DELSING, JAMES HENRY	1569 WALPOLE DR - CHESTERFIELD MO 63017
51- 22	DEMAESTRI, JOSEPH PAUL	50 FAIRWAY - NOVATO CA 94947

12- 51 DEMAREE, ALBERT WENTWORTH D. MAY 2, 1962 LONG BEACH, CALIF.
32- 19 DEMAREE, JOSEPH FRANKLIN D. AUGUST 30, 1958 LOS ANGELES, CAL.
48- 32 DEMARS, WILLIAM LESTER 661 POINSETTIA #207 - CLEARWATER FL 33515
57- 16 DEMERIT, JOHN STEPHEN 550 WEST WALTERS ST - PORT WASHINGTON WI 53074
74- 24 DEMERY, LAWRENCE CALVIN 3745 O FAIRBURN RD SW - ATLANTA GA 30331
56- 26 DEMETER, DONALD LEE 1521 SW 56TH ST - OKLAHOMA CITY OK 73119
59- 20 DEMETER, STEVEN 2805 MARIONCLIFF DR - PARMA OH 44134
74- 25 DEMOLA, DONALD JOHN 500-184A PECONIC - LAKE RONKONKOMA NY 11779
10- 44 DEMOTT, BENYEW HARRISON D. JULY 5, 1963 SOMERVILLE, N.J.
51- 23 DEMPSEY, CORNELIUS FRANCIS 'CON' 1530 CORDILLERAS RD - REDWOOD CITY CA 94062
69- 45 DEMPSEY, JOHN RIKARD "RICK" 5641 MASON AVE - WOODLAND HILLS CA 91364
82- 32 DEMPSEY, MARK STEVEN OLD ADD: 30 E. LANE AVE - DAYTON OH 45406
67- 23 DENEHY, WILLIAM FRANCIS 1520 SAYBROOK RD - MIDDLETOWN CT 06457
82- 33 DENMAN, BRIAN JOHN 654 PARKHURST BLVD - BUFFALO NY 14223
23- 27 DENNEHEY, THOMAS FRANCIS 'TOD' D. AUGUST 8, 1977 PHILADELPHIA, PA.
42- 28 DENNING, OTTO GEORGE 3434 WEST MELROSE-CHICAGO IL 60618
65- 27 DENNIS, DONALD RAY RR2 - UNIONTOWN KS 66779
74- 26 DENNY, JOHN ALLEN OLD ADD: 14551 BURNLEA ST - CHESTERFIELD MO 63017
73- 34 DENT, RUSSELL EARL 'BUCKY' 5540 EAST COACH HOUSE CIRCLE - BOCA RATON FL 33432
47- 25 DENTE, SAMUEL JOSEPH 19 REDMAN TER - WEST CALDWELL NJ 07006
43- 39 DEPHILLIPS, ANTHONY ANDREW 26 TIMBERLINE CIRCLE - PORT JEFFERSON NY 11777
80- 36 DERNIER, ROBERT EUGENE 9509 EAST 77TH ST - RAYTOWN MO 64138
10- 45 DERRICK, CLAUD LESTER D. JULY 15, 1974 CLAYTON, GA.
70- 32 DERRICK, JAMES MICHAEL 1117 ONTARIO AVE - WEST COLUMBIA SC 29169
31- 21 DERRINGER, PAUL D. NOVEMBER 17, 1987 SARASOTA, FLA.
56- 27 DERRINGTON, CHARLES JAMES 'JIM' 10509 BRYSON AVE - SOUTH GATE CA 90281

Greetings from
DON DeMOLA

BUCKY DENT

44- 27 DERRY, ALVA RUSSELL 'RUSS' PRINCETON MO 64673
80- 37 DESA, JOSEPH D. DECEMBER 20, 1986 SAN JUAN, P. R.
30- 17 DESAUTELS, EUGENE ABRAHAM 2802 MANSFIELD AV - FLINT MI 48503
84- 29 DESHAIES, JAMES JOSEPH 24 CHASE ST - MASSENA NY 13662
32- 20 DESHONG, JAMES BROOKLYN 99 SOUTH 31ST ST - HARRISBURG PA 17109
16- 19 DESJARDIEN, PAUL RAYMOND 'SHORTY' D. MARCH 7, 1956 MONROVIA, CALIF.
87- 31 DESTRADE, ORESTES 3015 SOUTHWEST 92ND PLACE - MIAMI FL 33165
80- 38 DETHERAGE, ROBERT WAYNE OLD ADD: 2325 NORTH BENTON - SPRINGFIELD MO 65803
30- 18 DETORE, GEORGE FRANCIS RR 1 - NEW HARTFORD NY 13413
73- 35 DETTORE, THOMAS ANTHONY 1120 MCEWEN AVE - CANONSBURG PA 15317
42- 29 DETWEILER, ROBERT STERLING 'DUCKY' 312 HOLT ST-FEDERALSBURG MD 21632
46- 23 DEUTSCH, MELVIN ELLIOTT RR 2 BOX 373A - CALDWELL TX 77836
32- 21 DEVENS, CHARLES 1 POST OFFICE SQUARE #900 - BOSTON MA 02110
87- 32 DEVEREAUX, MICHAEL OLD ADD: P.O. BOX 7789 - TUCSON AZ 85725
73- 36 DEVINE, PAUL ADRIAN 271 TIMBER LAUREL LANE - LAWRENCEVILLE GA 30245
18- 15 DEVINE, WILLIAM PATRICK 'MICKEY' D. OCTOBER 1, 1957 ALBANY, N. Y.
20- 30 DEVINEY, JOHN HAROLD 'HAL' D. JANUARY 4, 1933 WESTWOOD, MASS.
24- 30 DEVIVEIROS, BERNARD JOHN 3520 REDDING ST - OAKLAND CA 94619
44- 28 DEVLIN, JAMES RAYMOND 130 WORMAN ST, ESPY - BLOOMSBURG PA 17815
13- 47 DEVOGT, REX EUGENE D. NOVEMBER 9, 1935 ALMA, MICH.
18- 16 DEVORMER, ALBERT E. D. AUGUST 29, 1966 GRAND RAPIDS, MICH.
87- 33 DEWILLIS, JEFFREY ALLEN 3105 YOST ROAD - PEARLAND TX 77581
77- 44 DIAZ, BAUDILIO JOSE 'BO' LA VEGA #40 - CUA., ESTADO MIRANDA VENEZUELA S.A.
82- 34 DIAZ, CARLOS ANTHONY 1204 NORTH C STREET - LOMPOC CA 93436
86- 40 DIAZ, EDGAR SERRANO CALLE DIAMANTE #32 VILLA BLANCA - CAGUAS PR 00625
87- 34 DIAZ, MARIO RAFAEL URB. JAIME C. RODRIGUEZ STR 2 - YABUCOA PR 00767
83- 48 DIAZ, MICHAEL ANTHONY 1032 BANYAN WAY - PACIFICA CA 94044
24- 31 DIBUT, PEDRO D. DECEMBER 4, 1979 HIALEAH, FLA.
64- 25 DICKEN, PAUL FRANKLIN 7253 ST ANDREWS RD - LAKE WORTH FL 33460
23- 28 DICKERMAN, LEO LOUIS D. APRIL 30, 1982 ATKINS, ARK.
17- 20 DICKERSON, GEORGE CLARK D. JULY 9, 1938 LOS ANGELES, CALIF.
35- 23 DICKEY, GEORGE WILLARD 'SKEETS' D. JUNE 16, 1976 DEWITT, ARK.
28- 29 DICKEY, WILLIAM MALCOLM 7611 CHOCTAW ROAD - LITTLE ROCK AR 72205
36- 20 DICKMAN, GEORGE EMERSON D. APRIL 27, 1981 NEW YORK, N. Y.
36- 21 DICKSHOT, JOHN OSCAR 1530 JENKINSON CT - WAUKEGAN IL 60085
63- 33 DICKSON, JAMES EDWARD 685 FRANKLIN - ASTORIA OR 97103
39- 27 DICKSON, MURRY MONROE 721 OLIVE - LEAVENWORTH KS 66048
10- 46 DICKSON, WALTER R. D. DECEMBER 9, 1918 ARDMORE, OKLA.
69- 46 DIDIER, ROBERT DANIEL 153 OAK PARK DR - ALAMEDA CA 94501
42- 30 DIEHL, GEORGE KRAUSE D. AUGUST 24, 1986 KINGSPORT, TENN.
47- 26 DIERING, CHARLES EDWARD ALLEN 1 NOB HILL DR - ST LOUIS MO 63138
64- 26 DIERKER, LAWRENCE EDWARDS 9019 COLLEEN - HOUSTON TX 77035
33- 17 DIETRICH, WILLIAM JOHN D. JUNE 20, 1978 PHILADELPHIA, PA.
27- 29 DIETRICK, WILLIAM ALEXANDER D. MAY 6, 1946 BETHESDA, MD.
40- 16 DIETZ, LLOYD ARTHUR 'DUTCH' D. OCTOBER 29, 1972 BEAUMONT, TEX.
66- 28 DIETZ, RICHARD ALLEN %J.HENRYS,1475 TERRILL MILL SE - MARIETTA GA 30349
54- 20 DIETZEL, LEROY LOUIS 2331 CARTWRIGHT PL - CHARLOTTE NC 28208
48- 33 DIFANI, CLARENCE JOSEPH 'JAY' 808 NORTH MILL - FESTUS MO 63028

```
34- 31 DIGGS, REESE WILSON                        D. OCTOBER 30, 1978 BALTIMORE, MD.
69- 47 DILAURO, JACK EDWARD                        168 EAST MOHAWK - MALVERN OH 44644
59- 21 DILLARD, DAVID DONALD 'DON'                 RR1 - WATERLOO SC 29384
75- 33 DILLARD, STEPHEN BRADLEY                     6217 48TH DR EAST - BRADENTON FL 33508
17- 21 DILLHOEFER, WILLIAM MARTIN 'PICKLES'        D. FEBRUARY 22, 1922 ST. LOUIS, MO.
14- 54 DILLINGER, HARLEY HUGH                       D. JANUARY 8, 1959 CLEVELAND, O.
46- 24 DILLINGER, ROBERT BERNARD                   15380 RHODODENDRON DR-CANYON COUNTY CA 91351
67- 24 DILLMAN, WILLIAM HOWARD                      44 HOLLY HILL RD - RICHBORO PA 18954
63- 34 DILLON, STEPHEN EDWARD                       130 WEST 228TH ST - BRONX NY 10463
74- 27 DILONE, MIGUEL ANGEL                         CALLE EL SOL #190 - SANTIAGO DOMINICAN REP.
40- 17 DIMAGGIO, DOMINIC PAUL                       162 POINT RD - MARION MA 02738
36- 22 DIMAGGIO, JOSEPH PAUL                        2150 BEACH ST - SAN FRANCISCO CA 94123
37- 34 DIMAGGIO, VINCENT PAUL                       D. OCTOBER 3, 1986 NORTH HOLLYWOOD, CALIF.
77- 45 DIMMEL, MICHAEL WAYNE                        1705 BIG CANYON TRAIL - CARROLLTON TX 75007
75- 34 DINEEN, KERRY MICHAEL                        702 ELDER AVE - CHULA VISTA CA 92010
45- 25 DINGES, VANCE GEORGE                         274 SOUTH HIGH ST - HARRISONBURG VA 22801
73- 37 DIORIO, RONALD MICHAEL                       2 WHITE OAK LN - WATERBURY CT 06705
51- 24 DIPIETRO, ROBERT LOUIS PAUL                  909 CARRIAGE HILL DR - YAKIMA WA 98902
81- 28 DIPINO, FRANK MICHAEL                        141 NORTHWOOD WAY - CAMILLUS NY 13031
69- 48 DISTASO, ALEC JOHN                           25156 AVENIDA RONDEL - VALENCIA CA 91355
84- 30 DISTEFANO, BENITO JAMES                      16 LOCUST DR - THIELLS NY 10984
18- 17 DISTEL, GEORGE ADAM 'DUTCH'                  D. FEBRUARY 12, 1967 MADISON, IND.
54- 21 DITMAR, ARTHUR JOHN                          14 CINNAMON FERN LANE - MYRTLE BEACH SC 29577
52- 26 DITTMER, JOHN DOUGLAS                        200 NORTH MAIN ST - ELKADER IA 52043
53- 18 DIXON, JOHN CRAIG 'SONNY'                    7920 STEELE CREEK - CHARLOTTE NC 28210
84- 31 DIXON, KENNETH JOHN                          40 CLINTON HILL COURT - BALTIMORE MD 21228
25- 24 DIXON, LEO MOSES                             D. APRIL 11, 1984 CHICAGO, ILL.
77- 46 DIXON, THOMAS EARL                           2945 SOUTH DELANEY ST - ORLANDO FL 32806
12- 52 DOAK, WILLIAM LEOPOLD                        D. NOVEMBER 26, 1954 BRADENTON, FLA.
24- 32 DOBB, JOHN KENNETH                           973 HAMPDEN RD - MUSKEGON MI 49441
59- 22 DOBBEK, DANIEL JOHN                          4042 SE YAMHILL - PORTLAND OR 97214
29- 28 DOBENS, RAYMOND JOSEPH                       D. APRIL 21, 1980 STUART, FLA.
39- 28 DOBERNIC, ANDREW JOSEPH 'JESS'              2906 MISSOURI - SAINT LOUIS MO 63118
66- 29 DOBSON, CHARLES THOMAS                       2604 LACLEDE STATION RD - MAPLEWOOD MO 63143
39- 29 DOBSON, JOSEPH EDWARD                        7605 LOWRY STREET - JACKSONVILLE FL 32256
67- 25 DOBSON, PATRICK EDWARD                       2123 SE 13TH TERRACE - CAPE CORAL FL 33904
47- 27 DOBY, LAWRENCE EUGENE                        NISHUANE RD 45 - MONTCLAIR NJ 07042
45- 26 DOCKINS, GEORGE WOODROW                      BOX 3 - CLYDE KS 66938
12- 53 DODD, ORAN A. 'ONA'                          D. MARCH 31, 1929 NEWPORT, ARK.
86- 41 DODD, THOMAS MARION                          3735 NORTHEAST SHAVER - PORTLAND OR 97212
12- 54 DODGE, JOHN LEWIS                            D. JUNE 19, 1916 MOBILE, ALA.
21- 21 DODGE, SAMUEL EDWARD                         OLD ADD: WYALUSING, PA.
86- 42 DODSON, PATRICK NEAL                         844 GLENWAY DRIVE - INGLEWOOD CA 90302
37- 35 DOERR, ROBERT PERSHING                       33705 ILLAMO-AGNESS RD - AGNESS OR 97406
74- 28 DOHERTY, JOHN MICHAEL                        109 WAKEFIELD ST - READING MA 01867
14- 55 DOLAN, E. L. 'BIDDY'
30- 19 DOLJACK, FRANK JOSEPH                        D. JANUARY 23, 1948 CLEVELAND, O.
35- 24 DOLL, ARTHUR JAMES                           D. APRIL 28, 1978 CALUMET CITY, ILL.
23- 29 DONAHUE, JOHN FREDERICK                      D. OCTOBER 3, 1949 BOSTON, MASS.
43- 40 DONAHUE, JOHN STEPHEN MICHAEL                415 N. BELMONT AVE - ARLINGTON HGTS IL 60004
38- 21 DONALD, RICHARD ATLEY                        RR 2 BOX 132-CHOUDRANT LA 71227
12- 55 DONALDS, EDWARD ALEXANDER                    D. JULY 3, 1950 COLUMBUS, O.
66- 30 DONALDSON, JOHN DAVID                        3331 BENARD AVE - CHARLOTTE NC 28206
29- 29 DONDERO, LEONARD PETER                       BOX 2224 - FREMONT CA 94536
11- 42 DONNELLY, EDWARD                             D. NOVEMBER 28, 1957 RUTLAND, VT.
59- 23 DONNELLY, EDWARD VINCENT                     823 ROPER - HOUSTON TX 77034
44- 29 DONNELLY, SYLVESTER URBAN 'BLIX'            D. JUNE 20, 1976 OLIVIA, MINN.
61- 29 DONOHUE, JAMES THOMAS                        16 HUNTLEIGH DOWNS - ST LOUIS MO 63131
```

```
21- 22 DONOHUE, PETER JOSEPH                        D. FEBRUARY 23, 1988 FORT WORTH, TEXAS
79- 28 DONOHUE, THOMAS JAMES                        29 RUGBY RD - WESTBURY NY 11590
55- 38 DONOSO, LINO GALATA                          1971 ADD: CALLE SANTA MARIA - HAVANA CUBA
50- 27 DONOVAN, RICHARD EDWARD                      61 DEEP RUN RD - COHASSET MA 02025
42- 31 DONOVAN, WILLARD EARL                        1611 SOUTH 10TH AVE-MAYWOOD IL 60153
85- 25 DOPSON, JOHN ROBERT                          3337 OLD GAMBER ROAD - FINKSBURG MD 21048
82- 35 DORAN, WILLIAM DONALD                        1402 PLANTATION DRIVE - RICHMOND TX 77469
22- 26 DORAN, WILLIAM JAMES                         D. MARCH 9, 1978 SANTA MONICA, CALIF.
47- 28 DORISH, HARRY                                68 ELEY ST - KINGSTON PA 18704
23- 30 DORMAN, CHARLES WILLIAM                      D. NOVEMBER 15, 1928 SAN FRANCISCO, CAL.
28- 30 DORMAN, DWIGHT DEXTER                        D. DECEMBER 7, 1974 ANAHEIM, CAL.
87- 35 DORSETT, BRIAN RICHARD                       3123 EMERALD ROAD - TERRE HAUTE IN 47805
40- 18 DORSETT, CALVIN LEAVELLE                     D. OCTOBER 22, 1970 ELK CITY, OKLA.
80- 39 DORSEY, JAMES EDWARD                         335 ELM STREET - SEEKONK MA 02771
11- 43 DORSEY, JEREMIAH                             B. 1885 OAKLAND, CALIF.
79- 29 DOTSON, RICHARD ELLIOTT                      4240 PALOMINO CIR %HICKS - RENO NV 89509
61- 30 DOTTER, GARY RICHARD                         1639 HURSCH - WICHITA FALLS TX 76302
```

57- 17 DOTTERER, HENRY JOHN 'DUTCH'	10592 DAVITT AVE - GARDEN GROVE CA 92643
21- 23 DOUGLAS, ASTYANAX SAUNDERS	D. JANUARY 26, 1975 EL PASO, TEXAS
57- 18 DOUGLAS, CHARLES WILLIAM 'WHAMMY'	135 ASH ST - HUBERT NC 28539
45- 27 DOUGLAS, JOHN FRANKLIN	D. FEBRUARY 11, 1984 MIAMI, FLA.
12- 56 DOUGLAS, PHILIPS BROOKS	D. AUGUST 1, 1952 SEQUATCHIE VALLEY, TENN.
15- 34 DOUGLASS, HOWARD LAWRENCE 'LARRY'	D. NOVEMBER 4, 1949 JELLICO, TENN.
23- 31 DOUTHIT, TAYLOR LEE	D. MAY 28, 1986 FREMONT, CALIF.
10- 47 DOWD, JAMES JOSEPH 'SKIP'	D. DECEMBER 20, 1960 HOLYOKE, MASS.
19- 17 DOWD, RAYMOND BERNARD	D. APRIL 4, 1962 NORTHAMPTON, MASS.
87- 36 DOWELL, KENNETH ALLEN	2720 CASTRO WAY - SACRAMENTO CA 95818
64- 27 DOWLING, DAVID BARCLAY	1802 24TH - LONGVIEW WA 98632
61- 31 DOWNING, ALPHONSO ERWIN	2800 NEILSON WAY #412 - SANTA MONICA CA 90405
73- 38 DOWNING, BRIAN JAY	4861 SILVER SPURS - YORBA LINDA CA 92686
72- 23 DOWNS, DAVID RALPH	925 EAST 1050 NORTH - BOUNTIFUL UT 84010
86- 43 DOWNS, KELLY ROBERT	925 EAST 1050 NORTH - BOUNTIFUL UT 84010
78- 36 DOYLE, BRIAN REED	1310 MEADOW CIR NE - WINTER HAVEN FL 33880
43- 41 DOYLE, HOWARD JAMES 'DANNY'	322 SOUTH PAYNE - STILLWATER OK 74074
10- 48 DOYLE, JAMES FRANCIS	D. FEBRUARY 1, 1912 SYRACUSE, N. Y.
83- 49 DOYLE, JEFFREY DONALD	28851 LINGO LANE - JUNCTION CITY OR 97448
25- 25 DOYLE, JESSE HERBERT	D. APRIL 15, 1961 BELLEVILLE, ILL.
69- 49 DOYLE, PAUL SINNOTT	5832 WOODBORO DR - HUNTINGTON BEACH CA 92649
70- 33 DOYLE, ROBERT DENNIS 'DENNY'	6756 WINTERSET GARDENS-WINTER HAVEN FL 33880
35- 30 DOYLE, WILLIAM CARL	D. SEPTEMBER 4, 1951 KNOXVILLE, TENN.
86- 44 DOZIER, THOMAS DEAN	3804 DON WAY - RICHMOND CA 94806
47- 29 DOZIER, WILLIAM JOSEPH 'BUZZ'	2609 BRAEMER - WACO TX 76710
86- 45 DRABEK, DOUGLAS DEAN	1803 TRAVIS - VICTORIA TX 77901
56- 28 DRABOWSKY, MYRON WALTER 'MOE'	530 AUDUBON PLACE - HIGHLAND PARK IL 60035
69- 50 DRAGO, RICHARD ANTHONY	%CASA YBEL,P.O. BOX 353 - SANIBEL ISLAND FL 33957
11- 44 DRAKE, DELOS DANIEL	D. OCTOBER 3, 1965 FINDLAY, O.
45- 28 DRAKE, LARRY FRANCIS	D. JULY 14, 1985 HOUSTON, TEXAS
22- 27 DRAKE, LOGAN GAFFNEY	D. JUNE 1, 1940
60- 30 DRAKE, SAMUEL HARRISON	4415 SPRINGDALE DR - LOS ANGELES CA 90043
56- 29 DRAKE, SOLOMON LOUIS	1732 CORNING ST - LOS ANGELES CA 90035
39- 30 DRAKE, THOMAS KENDALL	4121 50TH AVE N-BIRMINGHAM AL 35217
82- 36 DRAVECKY, DAVID FRANCIS	11474 CAMINITO MAGNIFICA - SAN DIEGO CA 92131
31- 22 DREESEN, WILLIAM RICHARD	D. NOVEMBER 9, 1971 MOUNT VERNON, N. Y.
44- 30 DREISEWERD, CLEMENT JOHN	45 SNIPE ST - NEW ORLEANS LA 70124
44- 31 DRESCHER, WILLIAM CLAYTON	D. MAY 15, 1968 CONGERS, N. Y.
25- 26 DRESSEN, CHARLES WALTER	D. AUGUST 10, 1966 DETROIT, MICH.
14- 56 DRESSEN, LEO AUGUST	D. JUNE 30, 1931 DILLER, NEB.
75- 35 DRESSLER, ROBERT ALAN	OLD ADD: 3002 N. 46TH ST - PHOENIX AZ 85018
44- 32 DREWS, FRANK JOHN	D. APRIL 22, 1972 BUFFALO, N. Y.
46- 25 DREWS, KARL AUGUST	D. AUGUST 15, 1963 DANIA, FLA.
73- 39 DRIESSEN, DANIEL	BOX 1001 - HILTON HEAD ISLAND SC 29928
70- 34 DRISCOLL, JAMES BERNARD	55 FARRELL STREET #21 - NEWTONVILLE MA 02160
17- 22 DRISCOLL, JOHN LEO 'PADDY'	D. JUNE 28, 1968 CHICAGO, ILL.
16- 20 DRISCOLL, MICHAEL COLUMBUS	D. MARCH 22, 1953 FOXBORO, MASS.
13- 48 DROHAN, THOMAS F.	D. SEPTEMBER 17, 1926 KEWANEE, ILL.
49- 19 DROPO, WALTER	65 EAST INDIA ROW #31C - BOSTON MA 02109
57- 19 DROTT, RICHARD FRED	D. AUGUST 16, 1985 GLENDALE HEIGHTS, ILL.
87- 37 DRUMMOND, TIMOTHY DARNELL	HIGHWAY 925S BOX 335E - WALDORF MD 20601
78- 37 DRUMRIGHT, KEITH ALAN	422 EAST DOWNING - SPRINGFIELD MO 65807
56- 30 DRYSDALE, DONALD SCOTT	2 LACERRA CIR - RANCHO MIRAGE CA 92270
44- 33 DUBIEL, WALTER JOHN 'MONK'	D. OCTOBER 25, 1969 HARTFORD, CONN.
87- 38 DUCEY, ROBERT THOMAS	47 ELGIN STREET NORTH - CAMBRIDGE ONT. N1R 5H1 CAN.
63- 35 DUCKWORTH, JAMES RAYMOND	2929 GRINNELL DR - DAVIS CA 95616
29- 30 DUDLEY, ELISE CLISE	P.O. BOX 4859 - PINOPOLIS SC 29469
41- 22 DUDRA, JOHN JOSEPH	D. OCTOBER 24, 1965 PANA, ILL.
77- 47 DUES, HAL JOSEPH	DRAWER R - DICKINSON TX 77539
22- 28 DUFF, CECIL ELBA 'LARRY'	D. NOVEMBER 10, 1969 BEND, ORE.
61- 32 DUFFALO, JAMES FRANCIS	4109 CHILDRESS #101 - MESQUITE TX 75150
67- 26 DUFFIE, JOHN BROWN	3453 GLEN RD - DECATUR GA 30032
13- 49 DUFFY, BERNARD ALLEN	D. FEBRUARY 9, 1962 ABILENE, TEX.
70- 35 DUFFY, FRANK THOMAS	1740 EAST SILVER STREET - TUCSON AZ 85719
28- 31 DUGAN, DANIEL PHILLIP	D. JUNE 25, 1968 GREEN BROOK, N. J.
17- 23 DUGAN, JOSEPH ANTHONY	D. JULY 7, 1982 NORWOOD, MASS.
30- 20 DUGAS, AUGUSTIN JOSEPH	46 SOUTH "A" ST - TAFTVILLE CT 06380
13- 50 DUGEY, OSCAR JOSEPH	D. JANUARY 1, 1966 DALLAS, TEX.
11- 45 DUGGAN, JAMES ELMER	D. DECEMBER 5, 1951 INDIANAPOLIS, IND.
69- 51 DUKES, JAN NOBLE	1242 MILLBRAE AVENUE - MILLBRAE CA 94030
67- 27 DUKES, THOMAS EARL	325 MONTE VISTA RD - ARCADIA CA 91007
59- 24 DULIBA, ROBERT JOHN	610 SPRUCE STREET - WEST PITTSTON PA 18643
15- 35 DUMONT, GEORGE HENRY	D. OCTOBER 13, 1956 MINNEAPOLOS, MINN.
77- 48 DUMOULIN, DANIEL LYNN	304 IVY DR - KOKOMO IN 46902
23- 32 DUMOVICH, NICHOLAS	D. DECEMBER 12, 1979 LAGUNA HILLS, CALIF.
83- 50 DUNBAR, THOMAS JEROME	558 SOUTH PALM DRIVE - AIKEN SC 29801

HAL DUES
Lanceur/Pitcher

TOMMY DUNBAR
TEXAS Rangers

49

64- 28 DUNCAN, DAVID EDWIN	455 WEST RAPA - TUCSON AZ 85704
15- 36 DUNCAN, LOUIS BAIRD 'PAT'	D. JULY 17, 1960 COLUMBUS, O.
85- 26 DUNCAN, MARIANO	INGENIO ANGELINA #137 - SAN PEDRO DE MACORIS DOM REP.
77- 49 DUNCAN, TAYLOR MCDOWELL	176 SHILOH RD - ASHEVILLE NC 28803
13- 51 DUNCAN, VERNON VAN DYKE	D. JUNE 1, 1954 DAYTONA BEACH, FLA.
70- 36 DUNEGAN, JAMES WILLIAM	1405 SOUTH 12TH ST - BURLINGTON IA 52601
26- 27 DUNHAM, LELAND HUFFIELD	D. MAY 11, 1961 ATLANTA, ILL.
53- 19 DUNLAP, GRANT LESTER	6401 EL PATO COURT - CARLSBAD CA 92007
29- 31 DUNLAP, WILLIAM JAMES	D. NOVEMBER 29, 1980 READING, PA.
13- 52 DUNLOP, GEORGE HENRY	D. DECEMBER 12, 1972 MERIDEN, CONN.
52- 27 DUNN, JAMES WILLIAM	1656 SUMMIT DR - GADSDEN AL 35901
74- 29 DUNN, RONALD RAY	OLD ADD: 236 E. CALIMYRNA ST - FRESNO CA 93726
87- 39 DUNNE, MICHAEL DENNIS	4807 WANDA - BARTONVILLE IL 61607
70- 37 DUNNING, STEVEN JOHN	23 PLYMOUTH - IRVINE CA 92714
85- 27 DUNSTON, SHAWON DONNELL	6145 NORTH SHERIDAN #157 - CHICAGO IL 60660
76- 29 DUPREE, MICHAEL DENNIS	5164 E. ASHLAN #129 - FRESNO CA 93727
81- 29 DURAN, DANIEL JAMES	201 DEL NORTE - SUNNYVALE CA 94086
54- 22 DUREN, RINOLD GEORGE	7606 WEST HAMPSTEAD DRIVE - MIDDLETON WI 53562
72- 24 DURHAM, DONALD GARY	2627 PENNINGTON BEND RD - NASHVILLE TN 37214
29- 32 DURHAM, EDWARD FANT	D. APRIL 27, 1976 CHESTER, S. C.
54- 23 DURHAM, JOSEPH VANN	9715 MENDOZA RD - RANDALLSTOWN MD 21133
80- 40 DURHAM, LEON	3932 DICKSON AVE - CINCINNATI OH 45229
57- 20 DURNBAUGH, ROBERT EUGENE	1638 NORTH CENTRAL DR - DAYTON OH 45432
25- 27 DURNING, GEORGE DEWEY	D. APRIL 18, 1986 TAMPA, FLA.
17- 24 DURNING, RICHARD KNOTT	D. SEPTEMBER 23, 1948 CASTLE POINT, N. Y.
25- 28 DUROCHER, LEO ERNEST	1400 EAST PALM CANYON #210-PALM SPRINGS CA 92262
44- 34 DURRETT, ELMER CHARLES 'RED'	RR 3 BOX 93 - WAXAHACHIE TX 75165
22- 29 DURST, CEDRIC MONTGOMERY	D. FEBRUARY 16, 1971 SAN DIEGO, CAL.
41- 23 DUSAK, ERVIN FRANK	241 EAST PRAIRIE AVE - LOMBARD IL 60148
56- 31 DUSER, CARL ROBERT	3021 CORMWALL RD - BETHLEHEM PA 18017
63- 36 DUSTAL, ROBERT ANDREW	4919 CACHET BLVD - LAKELAND FL 33806
73- 40 DWYER, JAMES EDWARD	7607 WEST 159TH PL - TINLEY PARK IL 60477
37- 36 DWYER, JOSEPH MICHAEL	56 HIGH ST - WEST ORANGE NJ 07052
80- 41 DYBZINSKI, JEROME MATTHEW	OLD ADD: 89 245 DERBY - NAPERVILLE IL 60540
51- 25 DYCK, JAMES ROBERT	1704 SECOND STREET - CHENEY WA 99004
14- 57 DYER, BENJAMIN FRANKLIN	D. AUGUST 7, 1959 KENOSHA, WIS.
68- 17 DYER, DONALD ROBERT 'DUFFY'	742 WEST LAS PALMARITAS - PHOENIX AZ 85021
22- 30 DYER, EDWIN HAWLEY	D. APRIL 20, 1964 HOUSTON, TEX.
18- 18 DYKES, JAMES JOSEPH	D. JUNE 15, 1976 PHILADELPHIA, PA.
85- 28 DYKSTRA, LENNY KYLE	908 RASHFORD DRIVE - PLACENTIA CA 92670
59- 25 EADDY, DONALD JOHNSON	%J.EADDY,3440 POINSETTIA-GRAND RAPIDS MI49508
15- 37 EAKLE, CHARLES EMORY	D. JUNE 15, 1959 BALTIMORE, MD.
84- 32 EARL, WILLIAM SCOTT	BOX 63 - NORTH VERNON IN 47265
60- 31 EARLEY, ARNOLD CARL	4341 CAPTAINS LN - FLINT MI 48507
38- 22 EARLEY, THOMAS FRANCIS ALOYSIUS	D. APRIL 5, 1988 NANTUCKET ISLAND, MASS.
86- 46 EARLEY, WILLIAM ALBERT	3120 ROOSEVELT AVE - CINCINNATI OH 45211
39- 31 EARLY, JACOB WILLARD	D. MAY 31, 1985 MELBOURNE, FLA.
28- 32 EARNSHAW, GEORGE LIVINGSTON	D. DECEMBER 1, 1976 LITTLE ROCK, ARK.
73- 41 EASLER, MICHAEL ANTHONY	14901 MILVERTON - CLEVELAND OH 44120
87- 40 EASLEY, KENNETH LOGAN	RURAL ROUTE 1 BOX 35 - KIMBERLY ID 83341
15- 38 EAST, CARLTON WILLIAM	D. JANUARY 15, 1953 WHITESBURG, GA.
41- 24 EAST, GORDON HUGH	D. NOVEMBER 2, 1981 CHARLESTON, S. C.
49- 20 EASTER, LUSCIOUS LUKE	D. MARCH 29, 1979 EUCLID, O.
28- 33 EASTERLING, PAUL	% TATTNALL, BOX 860 - REIDSVILLE GA 30453
74- 30 EASTERLY, JAMES MORRIS 'JAMIE'	1306 PLANTATION - CROCKETT TX 75835
44- 35 EASTERWOOD, ROY CHARLES	D. AUGUST 24, 1984 GRAHAM, TEXAS
55- 39 EASTON, JOHN DAVID	SCOTCH RD BOX 418 RR1 - PENNINGTON NJ 08534
74- 31 EASTWICK, RAWLINS JACKSON	224 CHESTNUT STREET - HADDONFIELD NJ 08033
79- 30 EATON, CRAIG	3307 BALTUSROL LN - LAKE WORTH FL 33467
44- 36 EATON, ZEBULON VANCE	146 LINCOLN BOULEVARD - KENMORE NY 14217
35- 26 EAVES, VALLIE ENNIS	D. APRIL 19, 1960 NORMAN, OKLA.
13- 53 EAYRS, EDWIN	D. NOVEMBER 30, 1969 WARWICK, R.I.
15- 39 ECCLES, HARRY JOSIAH	D. JUNE 28, 1955 JAMESTOWN, N.Y.
39- 32 ECHOLS, JOHN GRESHAM	D. NOVEMBER 13, 1972 ATLANTA, GA.
75- 36 ECKERSLEY, DENNIS LEE	263 MORSE RD - SUDBURY MA 01776
30- 21 ECKERT, ALBERT GEORGE	D. APRIL 20, 1974 MILWAUKEE, WIS.

19- 18 ECKERT, CHARLES WILLIAM	D. AUGUST 22, 1986 TREVOSE, PA.
32- 22 ECKHARDT, OSCAR GEORGE 'OX'	D. APRIL 22, 1651 YORKTOWN, TEX.
70- 38 EDDY, DONALD EUGENE	BOX 537 - ROCKWELL IA 50469
79- 31 EDDY, STEVEN ALLEN	OLD ADD: 2332 14TH AVE - MOLINE IL 61265
81- 30 EDELEN, BENNY JOE	BOX 13 - GRACEMONT OK 73042
32- 23 EDELEN, EDWARD JOSEPH	D. FEBRUARY 1, 1982 LAPLATA, MD.
55- 40 EDELMAN, JOHN ROGERS	922 MONTE VISTON DR - WEST CHESTER PA 19380

76- 30	EDEN, EDWARD MICHAEL 'MIKE'	OLD ADD: 6705 NORTH HINES AVE - TAMPA FL 33614
87- 41	EDENS, THOMAS PATRICK	RURAL ROUTE 2 BOX ?424 - FRUITLAND ID 83619
79- 32	EDGE, CLAUDE LEE 'BUTCH'	3728 MARCONI AVENUE - SACRAMENTO CA 95821
66- 31	EDGERTON, WILLIAM ALBERT	2838 FIR LANE - SOUTH BEND IN 46615
12- 57	EDINGTON, JACOB FRANK 'STUMP'	D. NOVEMBER 29, 1969 BASTROP,LA.
80- 42	EDLER, DAVID DELMAR	1504 SOUTH 34TH AVE - YAKIMA WA 98902
13- 54	EDMONDSON, EDWARD EARL	D. MAY 10, 1971 LEESBURG, FLA.
22- 31	EDMONDSON, GEORGE HENDERSON	D. JULY 11, 1973 WACO, TEX.
69- 52	EDMONDSON, PAUL MICHAEL	D. FEBRUARY 13, 1970 SANTA BARBARA, CALIF.
15- 40	EDWARDS, ALBERT	B. 1896 FREEPORT, N.Y.
46- 26	EDWARDS, CHARLES BRUCE	D. APRIL 25, 1975 SACRAMENTO, CALIF.
78- 38	EDWARDS. DAVID LEONARD	16061 GAMBLE AVENUE - RIVERSIDE CA 92504
25- 29	EDWARDS, FOSTER HAMILTON	D. JANUARY 4, 1980 ORLEANS, MASS.
41- 25	EDWARDS, HENRY ALBERT	360 BEDFORD ROAD - ORANGE CA 92668
62- 35	EDWARDS, HOWARD RODNEY 'DOC'	4717 HUMPHREY ROAD - GREAT VALLEY NY 14741
22- 32	EDWARDS, JAMES CORBETTE 'JIM JOE'	D. JANUARY 19, 1965 CALHOUN COUNTY, MISS.
61- 33	EDWARDS, JOHN ALBAN	10118 SPRINGWOOD FOREST DR - HOUSTON TX 77055
81- 31	EDWARDS, MARSHALL LYNN	16061 GAMBLE AVE #O - RIVERSIDE CA 92504
77- 50	EDWARDS, MICHAEL LEWIS	3216 WADSWORTH AVE - LOS ANGELES CA 90011
34- 32	EDWARDS, SHERMAN STANLEY	1223 WEST FIRST - ELDORADO AR 71730
63- 37	EGAN, RICHARD WALLIS	3508 CHEROKEE DRIVE - CARSON CITY NV 89701
65- 28	EGAN, THOMAS PATRICK	16318 EAST HALBURTON RD-HACIENDA HEIGHTS CA91745
27- 30	EGGERT, ELMER ALBERT	D. APRIL 9, 1971 ROCHESTER, N. Y.
15- 41	EHMKE, HOWARD JONATHAN	D. MARCH 17, 1959 PHILADELPHIA, PA.
24- 33	EHRHARDT, WELTON CLAUDE 'RUBE'	D. APRIL 27, 1980 CHICAGO HEIGHTS, ILL.
12- 58	EIBEL, HENRY HACK	D. OCTOBER 16, 1945 MACON, GA.
78- 39	EICHELBERGER, JUAN TYRONE	14674 SILVERSET ST - POWAY CA 92064
82- 37	EICHHORN, MARK ANTHONY	132 WINGFOOT COURT - APTOS CA 95003
25- 30	EICHRODT, FREDERICK GEORGE	D. JULY 14, 1965 INDIANAPOLIS, IND.
64- 29	EILERS, DAVID LOUIS	1500 LEE - BRENHAM TX 77833
44- 37	EISENHART, JACOB HENRY 'HANK'	HCR-61 BOX 354 - MILL CREEK PA 17060
82- 37	EISENREICH, JAMES DONALD	2006 11TH AVENUE SOUTH - ST. CLOUD MN 56301
35- 27	EISENSTAT, HARRY	3333 WARRENSVILLE CTR #214 - SHAKER HEIGHTS OH 44122
49- 21	ELDER, GEORGE REZIN	40200 BROOKSIDE AVE - CHERRY VALLEY CA 92223
13- 55	ELDER, HENRY KNOX 'HEINIE'	D. NOVEMBER 13, 1958 LONG BEACH, CALIF.
66- 32	ELIA, LEE CONSTANTINE	1201 NORWOOD AVE - CLEARWATER FL 33516
43- 42	ELKO, PETER	133 MADISON ST -WILKES BARRE PA 18702
17- 25	ELLER, HORACE OWEN 'HOD'	D. JULY 18, 1961 INDIANAPOLIS, IND.
19- 19	ELLERBE, FRANCIS ROGERS	LATTA SC 29565
74- 32	ELLINGSEN, HAROLD BRUCE	5873 DANELAND - LAKEWOOD CA 90713
62- 36	ELLIOT, LAWRENCE LEE	13278 STONE CANYON RD #B - POWAY CA 92064
23- 33	ELLIOTT, ALLEN CLIFFORD	D. MAY 6, 1979 ST. LOUIS, MO.
21- 24	ELLIOTT, CARTER WARD	D. MAY 21, 1959 PALM SPRINGS, CAL.
11- 46	ELLIOTT, EUGENE BIRMINGHOUSE	D. JANUARY 5, 1976 HUNTINGDON, PA.
10- 49	ELLIOTT, HAROLD B. 'ROWDY'	D. FEBRUARY 12, 1934 SAN FRANCISCO, CALIF.
29- 33	ELLIOTT, HAROLD WILLIAM	D. APRIL 25, 1963 HONOLULU, HAW.
53- 20	ELLIOTT, HARRY LEWIS	1154 RANDOM - EL CAJON CA 92020
47- 30	ELLIOTT, HERBERT GLENN	D. JULY 27, 1969 PORTLAND, ORE.
23- 34	ELLIOTT, JAMES THOMPSON	D. JANUARY 7, 1970 TERRE HAUTE, IND.
72- 25	ELLIOTT, RANDY LEE	P.O. BOX 834 - SOMIS CA 93066
39- 33	ELLIOTT, ROBERT IRVING	D. MAY 4, 1966 SAN DIEGO, CAL.
68- 18	ELLIS, DOCK PHILIP	121 E. 139TH ST - LOS ANGELES CA 90061
67- 28	ELLIS, JAMES RUSSELL	13608 AVE 224 - TULARE CA 93274
69- 53	ELLIS, JOHN CHARLES	15 WHITNEY LN - EAST LYME CT 06333
71- 29	ELLIS, ROBERT WALTER	OLD ADD: 13210 LAKEWOOD DR NE - AURORA OR 97002
62- 37	ELLIS, SAMUEL JOSEPH	6111 WHITEWAY - TEMPLE TERRACE FL 33617
20- 31	ELLISON, GEORGE RUSSELL	D. JANUARY 20, 1978 SAN FRANCISCO, CALIF.
16- 21	ELLISON, HERBERT SPENCER 'BABE'	D. AUGUST 11, 1955 SAN FRANCISCO, CALIF.
58- 28	ELLSWORTH, RICHARD CLARK	1099 WEST MORRIS - FRESNO CA 93705
24- 34	ELMORE, VERDO WILSON	D. AUGUST 5, 1969 BIRMINGHAM, ALA.
23- 35	ELSH, EUGENE ROY	D. NOVEMBER 12, 1978 PHILADELPHIA, PA.
86- 47	ELSTER, KEVIN DANIEL	5801 MARSHALL DRIVE - HUNTINGTON BEACH CA 92649
53- 21	ELSTON, DONALD RAY	2436 MAPLE ST - NORTHBROOK IL 60062
41- 26	EMBREE, CHARLES WILLIAM 'RED'	5500 N. BANK RD - CRESCENT CITY CA 95531
23- 36	EMBRY, CHARLES AKIN 'SLIM'	D. OCTOBER 10, 1947 NASHVILLE, TENN.
11- 47	EMERSON, CHESTER ARTHUR	D. JULY 2, 1971 AUGUSTA, ME.
63- 38	EMERY, CALVIN WAYNE	RR 1 BOX 24 - CENTRE HALL PA 16828
24- 35	EMERY, HERRICK SMITH 'SPOKE'	D. JUNE 2, 1975 CAPE CANAVERAL, FLA.
16- 22	EMMER, FRANK WILLIAM	D. OCTOBER 18, 1963 HOMESTEAD, FLA.
23- 37	EMMERICH, ROBERT G.	D. NOVEMBER 22, 1948 BRIDGEPORT, CONN.
45- 29	EMMERICH, WILLIAM PETER 'SLIM'	257 EAST FAIRVIEW ST - ALLENTOWN PA 18103
46- 27	ENDICOTT, WILLIAM FRANKLIN	BOX 48, 5 MILE LANDING - TOPOCK AZ 86436
12- 59	ENGEL, JOSEPH WILLIAM	D. JUNE 12, 1969 CHATTANOOGA, TENN.
85- 29	ENGEL, STEVEN MICHAEL	1657 TRILLIUM COURT - READING OH 45215

Pete Elko

25- 31	ENGLE, CHARLES AUGUST	D. OCTOBER 12, 1983 SAN ANTONIO, TEX.
81- 32	ENGLE, RALPH DAVID 'DAVE'	5343 CASTLE HILLS DRIVE - SAN DIEGO CA 92109
81- 33	ENGLE, RICHARD DOUGLAS	2634 JACKSON PIKE - BATAVIA OH 45103
32- 24	ENGLISH, CHARLES DEWIE	1600 S. BALDWIN AVE #32 - ARCADIA CA 91006
27- 31	ENGLISH, ELWOOD GEORGE	14 NORTH ELEVENTH ST - NEWARK OH 43055
31- 23	ENGLISH, GILBERT RAYMOND	RR 2 BOX 356 - TRINITY NC 27370
46- 28	ENNIS, DELMAR	712 WOODSIDE RD - JENKINTOWN PA 19046
26- 28	ENNIS, RUSSELL ELWOOD	D. JANUARY 29, 1949 SUPERIOR, WIS.
76- 31	ENRIGHT, GEORGE ALBERT	6046 LAKE WORTH RD #969-LAKE WORTH FL 33463
17- 26	ENRIGHT, JOHN PERCY	D. AUGUST 18, 1975 POMPANO BEACH, FLA.
12- 60	ENS, ANTON 'MUTZ'	D. JUNE 28, 1950 ST. LOUIS, MO.
22- 33	ENS, JEWEL WINKLEMEYER	D. JANUARY 17, 1950 SYRACUSE, N. Y.
74- 33	ENYART, TERRY GENE	520 SEAL AVE - PIKETON OH 45661
14- 58	ENZENROTH, CLARENCE HERMAN 'JACK'	D. FEBRUARY 21, 1944
14- 59	ENZMANN, JOHN	D. MARCH 14, 1984 RIVERHEAD, N. Y.
87- 42	EPPARD, JAMES GERHARD	332 ASHBY STREET - AZUSA CA 91702
38- 23	EPPERLY, ALBERT PAUL	2621 IOWA ST - DAVENPORT IA 52803
35- 28	EPPS, AUBREY LEE	D. NOVEMBER 13, 1984 ACKERMAN, MISS.
38- 24	EPPS, HAROLD FRANKLIN	4500 CYPRESSWOOD #406 - SPRING TX 77379
66- 33	EPSTEIN, MICHAEL PETER	7775 SOUTH BISCAY ST - AURORA CO 80016
77- 51	ERARDI, JOSEPH GREGORY	204 HANOVER AVE - LIVERPOOL NY 13088
47- 31	ERAUTT, EDWARD LORENZ	7252 WAITE DR - LAMESA CA 92041
50- 28	ERAUTT, JOSEPH MICHAEL	D. OCTOBER 6, 1976 PORTLAND, ORE.
58- 29	ERICKSON, DON LEE	2717 INTERLACHEN - SPRINGFIELD IL 62704
14- 60	ERICKSON, ERIC GEORGE ADOLPH	D. MAY 19, 1965 JAMESTOWN, N. Y.
53- 22	ERICKSON, HAROLD JAMES	333 BAYSHORE DR - OSPREY FL 33559
35- 29	ERICKSON, HENRY NELS	D. DECEMBER 13, 1964 LOUISVILLE, KY.
41- 27	ERICKSON, PAUL WALFORD	363 BOYD ST - FOND DU LAC WI 54935
29- 34	ERICKSON, RALPH LIEF	3307 QUAIL MEADOWS DRIVE - SANTA MARIA CA 93455
78- 40	ERICKSON, ROGER FARRELL	2506 ARROWHEAD DRIVE - SPRINGFIELD IL 62702
47- 32	ERMER, CALVIN COOLIDGE	1009 PANORAMA DR - CHATTANOOGA TN 37421
57- 21	ERNAGA, FRANK JOHN	50 NORTH ROOP ST - SUSANVILLE CA 96130
38- 25	ERRICKSON, RICHARD MERRIWELL	2976 DOUGLAS LANE - VINELAND NJ 08360
48- 34	ERSKINE, CARL DANIEL	6214 SOUTH MADISON AVE - ANDERSON IN 46013
83- 51	ESASKY, NICHOLAS ANDREW	1048 JUMPERS RIDGE - MARIETTA GA 30064
54- 24	ESCALERA, SATURNINO CUADRADO 'NINO'	P.O. BOX 30168 - RIO PIEDRAS PR 00928
82- 39	ESCARREGA, ERNESTO	APARTADO POSTAL 48G - LOS MOCHIS SINOLOA MEX.
15- 42	ESCHEN, JAMES GODRICH	D. SEPTEMBER 27, 1960 SLOATSBURG, N.Y.
42- 32	ESCHEN, LAWRENCE EDWARD	346 36TH AVE NE - ST. PETERSBURG FL 33704
11- 48	ESMOND, JAMES J.	D. JUNE 26, 1948 TROY, N.Y.
82- 40	ESPINO, JUAN	EUGENIO M. DE CESTOS #50 - BONAO DOMINICAN REP.
74- 34	ESPINOSA, ARNULFO ACEVEDO 'NINO'	27 DE BEBRERO #9 - VILLA ALTAGRACIA DOMINICAN REP.
84- 33	ESPINOZA, ALVARO ALBERTO	URB. MICHELENA C/93 #86-74 - VALENCIA VENEZUELA S.A.
52- 28	ESPOSITO, SAMUEL	ATH DEPT N. C. ST U - RALEIGH NC 27607
83- 52	ESPY, CECIL EDWARD	2401 WILLOW GLEN DRIVE - EL CAJON CA 92020
58- 30	ESSEGIAN, CHARLES ABRAHAM	144 NORTH HOBART BLVD - LOS ANGELES CA 90004
79- 33	ESSER, MARK GERALD	4 JACKSON DR - POUGHKEEPSIE NY 12603
73- 42	ESSIAN, JAMES SARKIS	22959 GAUKLER - ST CLAIR SHORES MI 48080
35- 30	ESTALELLA, ROBERTO MENDEZ	3297 WEST 14TH LN - HIALEAH FL 33012
64- 30	ESTELLE, RICHARD HARRY	2221 TAYLOR AVE - POINT PLEASANT NJ 08742
51- 26	ESTOCK, GEORGE JOHN	595 RAY STREET - SEBASTIAN FL 32958
60- 32	ESTRADA, CHARLES LEONARD	459 NORTH TASSAJARA - SAN LUIS OBISPO CA 93401
71- 30	ESTRADA, FRANCISCO (SOTO)	MANUEL DOBLADO PTE 605-A - NAVAJOA SONORA MEX.
29- 35	ESTRADA, OSCAR	D. JANUARY 2, 1978 HAVANA, CUBA
62- 38	ETCHEBARREN, ANDREW AUGUSTE	915 PROMONTORY DRIVE - NEWPORT BEACH CA 92660
43- 43	ETCHISON, CLARENCE HAMPTON 'BUCK'	D. JANUARY 24, 1980 EAST NEW MARKET, MD.
67- 29	ETHERIDGE, BOBBY LAMAR	2633 WILLOW DRIVE - GREENVILLE MS 38701
38- 26	ETTEN, NICHOLAS RAYMOND TOM	21 SPINNING WHEEL RD - HINSDALE IL 60521
22- 34	EUBANKS, UEL MELVIN	D. NOVEMBER 21, 1954 DALLAS, TEX.
85- 30	EUFEMIA, FRANK ANTHONY	71 DELFORD AVENUE - BERGENFIELD NJ 07621
17- 27	EUNICK, FERNANDES BOWEN	D. DECEMBER 9, 1959 BALTIMORE, MD.
39- 34	EVANS, ALFRED HUBERT	D. APRIL 6, 1979 WILSON, N. C.
78- 41	EVANS, BARRY STEVEN	8060 WOODS LANE - JONESBORO GA 30236
69- 54	EVANS, DARRELL WAYNE	354 PROVENCAL - DETROIT MI 48231
72- 26	EVANS, DWIGHT MICHAEL	3 JORDAN RD - LYNNFIELD MA 01940
15- 43	EVANS, JOSEPH PATTON	D. AUGUST 9, 1953 GULFPORT, MISS.
36- 23	EVANS, RUSSELL EDISON 'RED'	D. JUNE 14, 1982 LAKEVIEW, ARK.
32- 25	EVANS, WILLIAM ARTHUR	D. JANUARY 8, 1952 WICHITA, KANS.
16- 23	EVANS, WILLIAM JAMES	D. DECEMBER 21, 1946 BURLINGTON, N. C.
49- 22	EVANS, WILLIAM LAWRENCE	D. NOVEMBER 30, 1983 GRAND JUNCTION, COLO.
69- 55	EVERITT, EDWARD LEON	RR 1 BOX 417 - MARSHALL TX 75670
13- 56	EVERS, JOSEPH FRANCIS	D. JANUARY 4, 1949 ALBANY, N.Y.
41- 28	EVERS, WALTER ARTHUR 'HOOT'	637 SOUTH RIPPLE CREEK - HOUSTON TX 77057
21- 25	EWING, REUBEN	D. OCTOBER 5, 1970 WEST HARTFORD, CONN.

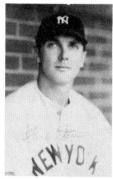

```
73- 43  EWING, SAMUEL JAMES                        RR 4, POWELL RD - LEWISBURG TN 37091
19- 20  EWOLDT, ARTHUR LEE                         D. DECEMBER 8, 1977 DES MOINES, IA.
43- 44  EYRICH, GEORGE LINCOLN                     565 SOUTH 15TH ST-READING PA 19602
23- 38  EZZELL, HOMER ESTELL                       D. AUGUST 3, 1976 SAN ANTONIO, TEX.
14- 61  FABER, URBAN CHARLES 'RED'                 D. SEPTEMBER 25, 1976 CHICAGO, ILL.
16- 24  FABRIQUE, ALBERT LAVERNE 'BUNNY'           D. JANUARY 10, 1960 ANN ARBOR, MICH.
53- 23  FACE, ELROY LEON                           608 DELLA DR #5F - NORTH VERSAILLES PA 15137
80- 43  FAEDO, LEONARDO LAGO 'LENNY'               2920 COLLINS ST - TAMPA FL 33607
19- 21  FAETH, ANTHONY JOSEPH                      D. DECEMBER 22, 1982 ST. PAUL, MINN.
43- 45  FAGAN, EVERETT JOSEPH                      D. FEBRUARY 16, 1983 MORRISTOWN, N.J.
18- 19  FAHEY, FRANCIS RAYMOND                     D. MARCH 19, 1954 BOSTON, MASS.
12- 61  FAHEY, HOWARD SIMPSON                      D. OCTOBER 24, 1971 CLEARWATER, FLA.
71- 31  FAHEY, WILLIAM ROGER                       5740 MONA LN - DALLAS TX 75236
51- 27  FAHR, GERALD WARREN 'RED'                  816 WEST PARK ST - PARAGOULD AR 72450
14- 62  FAHRER, CLARENCE WILLIE 'PETE'             D. JUNE 10, 1967 FREMONT, MICH.
47- 33  FAIN, FERRIS ROY                           BOX 1357 - GEORGETOWN CA 95634
19- 22  FAIRCLOTH, JAMES LAMAR 'RAGS'              D. OCTOBER 5, 1953 TUCSON, ARIZ.
68- 19  FAIREY, JAMES BURKE                        218 STRAWBERRY ST - CLEMSON SC 29361
58- 31  FAIRLY, RONALD RAY                         23140 PARK SORRENTO - CALABASAS CA 91302
75- 37  FALCONE, PETER FRANK                       3179 BOLERO DR - ATLANTA GA 30341
20- 32  FALK, BIBB AUGUST                          4213 AVE 'D ' - AUSTIN TX 78751
25- 32  FALK, CHESTER EMANUEL 'CHET'               D. JANUARY 7, 1982 AUSTIN, TEXAS
31- 24  FALLENSTIN, EDWARD JOSEPH                  D. NOVEMBER 24, 1971 ORANGE, N.J.
37- 37  FALLON, GEORGE DECATUR                     71 PLAINVIEW DR - STRATFORD CT 06497
84- 34  FALLON, ROBERT JOSEPH                      2114 NORTH 44TH AVE - HOLLYWOOD FL 33021
14- 63  FALSEY, PETER JAMES                        D. MAY 23, 1976 LOS ANGELES, CALIF.
45- 30  FANNIN, CLIFFORD BRYSON                    D. DECEMBER 11, 1966 SANDUSKY, O.
54- 25  FANNING, WILLIAM JAMES 'JIM'               BOX 500 STATION M - MONTREAL QUEBEC H1V 3P2 CAN.
63- 39  FANOK, HARRY MICHAEL                       16 FANOK RD - WHIPPANY NJ 07981
49- 23  FANOVICH, FRANK JOSEPH                     3 FAIRGREEN AVENUE - NEW SMYRNA BEACH FL 32069
86- 48  FANSLER, STANLEY ROBERT                    RURAL ROUTE 2 BOX 550-1 - ELKINS WV 26241
10- 50  FANWELL, HARRY CLAYTON                     D. JULY 15, 1965 BALTIMORE, MD.
70- 39  FANZONE, CARMEN                            5114 RANCHITO AVE - SHERMAN OAKS CA 91423
61- 34  FARLEY, ROBERT JACOB                       RR 3 BOX 190 - MONTOURSVILLE PA 17754
71- 32  FARMER, EDWARD JOSEPH                      1825 IDAHO AVENUE - SANTA MONICA 90403
16- 25  FARMER, FLOYD HASKELL 'JACK'               D. MAY 21, 1970 COLUMBIA, LA.
82- 41  FARR, JAMES ALFRED                         RR 1 BOX 98 - ATHENS PA 18810
84- 35  FARR, STEVEN MICHAEL                       RR 2 BOX 2365CC - LAPLATA MD 20646
25- 33  FARRELL, EDWARD STEPHEN 'DOC'              D. DECEMBER 20, 1966 LIVINGSTON, N. J.
87- 43  FARRELL, JOHN EDWARD                       12 HIGHLAND AVENUE - MONMOUTH BEACH NJ 07750
14- 64  FARRELL, JOHN J.                           D. MARCH 24, 1918 CHICAGO, ILL.
43- 46  FARRELL, MAJOR KERBY                       D. DECEMBER 17, 1975 NASHVILLE, TENN.
56- 32  FARRELL, RICHARD JOSEPH                    D. JUNE 11, 1977 GREAT YARMOUTH, ENGLAND
68- 20  FAST, DARCY RAE                            7241 RIDGEMONT DRIVE SE - LACEY WA 98503
53- 24  FASZHOLZ, JOHN EDWARD                      7108 GENEVA - AUSTIN TX 78723
62- 39  FAUL, WILLIAM ALVAN                        RR1 BOX 7 - PLEASANT PLAIN OH 45162
27- 32  FAULKNER, JAMES LEROY                      D. JUNE 2, 1962 WEST PALM BEACH, FLA.
44- 38  FAUSETT, ROBERT SHAW                       503 SOUTHWEST PARKWAY #711 - COLLEGE STATION TX 77840
11- 49  FAUST, CHARLES VICTOR                      D. JUNE 18, 1915 FORT STEILACOOM, WASH.
16- 26  FAUTSCH, JOSEPH ROAMON                     D. MARCH 16, 1971 NEW HOPE, MINN.
62- 40  FAZIO, ERNEST JOSEPH                       2626 NICHOLSON ST - SAN LEANDRO CA 94577
52- 29  FEAR, LUVERN CARL                          D. SEPTEMBER 6, 1976 SPENCER, IA.
51- 28  FEDEROFF, ALFRED                           10150 MORTONVIEW - TAYLOR MI 48080
34- 33  FEHRING, WILLIAM PAUL 'DUTCH'              1735 POPPY AVE - MENLO PARK CA 94023
38- 27  FEINBERG, EDWARD                           D. APRIL 20, 1986 HOLLYWOOD, FLA.
85- 31  FELDER, MICHAEL OTIS                       322 SOUTH 17TH STREET - RICHMOND CA 94804
42- 33  FELDERMAN, MARVIN WILFRED                  4342 WEST 177TH ST-TORRANCE CA 90504
41- 29  FELDMAN, HARRY                             D. MARCH 16, 1962 FORT SMITH, ARK.
23- 39  FELIX, AUGUST GUENTHER                     D. MAY 12, 1960 MONTGOMERY, ALA.
58- 32  FELLER, JACK LELAND                        LUKES POINT DRIVE - QUINCY MI 49082
36- 24  FELLER, ROBERT WILLIAM ANDREW              BOX 157 - GATES MILLS OH 44040
15- 44  FELSCH, OSCAR EMIL 'HAPPY'                 D. AUGUST 17, 1964 MILWAUKEE, WIS.
68- 21  FELSKE, JOHN FREDRICK                      600 LIVINGSTON - MCHENRY IL 60050
79- 34  FELTON, TERRY LANE                         BOX 533 - BAKER LA 70714
21- 26  FENNER, HORACE ALFRED 'HOD'                D. NOVEMBER 20, 1954 DETROIT, MICH.
72- 27  FENWICK, ROBERT RICHARD                    1223 FIFTH AVE SOUTH - ANOKA MN 55303
42- 34  FERENS, STANLEY                            BOX 261-YUKON PA 15698
18- 20  FERGUSON, JAMES ALEXANDER                  D. APRIL 28, 1976 SEPULEVEDA, CALIF.
70- 40  FERGUSON, JOSEPH VANCE                     6036 STONEYBROOK DRIVE - FORT WORTH TX 76112
44- 39  FERGUSON, ROBERT LESTER                    2332 EAST THIRD - MONTGOMERY AL 36106
87- 44  FERMIN, FELIX JOSE                         CALLE CAPOTILLO #24 - MAO, VALVERDE, DOMINICAN REP.
40- 19  FERNANDES, EDWARD PAUL                     D. NOVEMBER 27, 1968 HAYWARD, CAL.
83- 53  FERNANDEZ, CHARLES SIDNEY 'SID'            992C AWAAWAANOA PLACE - HONOLULU HI 96825
```

67- 30 FERNANDEZ, FRANK	37 COUGHLAN AVE - STATEN ISLAND NY 10310
42- 35 FERNANDEZ, FROILAN 'NANNY'	26229 MONTE VISTA-LOMITA CA 90717
56- 33 FERNANDEZ, HUMBERTO PEREZ 'CHICO'	3322 24TH ST - DETROIT MI 48208
68- 22 FERNANDEZ, LORENZO MARTO	1310 SW 97TH AVE - MIAMI FL 33175
83- 54 FERNANDEZ, OCTAVIO ANTONIO 'TONY'	CALLE N#3,B.RESTAURACION-SAN PEDRO DE MACORIS DOM. REP.
63- 40 FERRARA, ALFRED JOHN	BOX 69263 - LOS ANGELES CA 90069
55- 41 FERRARESE, DONALD HUGH	14140 GAYHEAD RD - APPLE VALLEY CA 92307
66- 34 FERRARO, MICHAEL DENNIS	6195-B LAUREL LANE - TAMARAC FL 33319
35- 31 FERRAZZI, WILLIAM JOSEPH	13 ARI WOODS - KEYSTONE HEIGHTS FL 32656
85- 32 FERREIRA, ANTHONY ROSS	3756 LOFTON PLACE - RIVERSIDE CA 92501
29- 36 FERRELL, RICHARD BENJAMIN 'RICK'	2199 GOLFVIEW #203 - TROY MI 48084
27- 33 FERRELL, WESLEY CHEEK	D. DECEMBER 9, 1976 SARASOTA, FLA.
74- 35 FERRER, SERGIO	P.AREILAGE NX-8,LEVITTOWN LAKES - TOA BAJA PR 00632
41- 30 FERRICK, THOMAS JEROME	517 HARRINGTON RD-HAVERTOWN PA 19083
79- 35 FERRIS, ROBERT EUGENE	9718 IRONMASTER DR - BURKE VA 22015
45- 31 FERRISS, DAVID MEADOW 'BOO'	510 ROBINSON DR - CLEVELAND MS 38732
10- 51 FERRY, JOHN FRANCIS	D. AUGUST 29, 1954 PITTSFIELD, MASS.
37- 38 FETTE, LOUIS HENRY WILLIAM	D. JANUARY 3, 1981 WARRENSBURG, MO.
17- 28 FEWSTER, WILSON LLOYD 'CHICK'	D. APRIL 16, 1945 BALTIMORE, MD.
81- 34 FIALA, NEIL STEPHEN	3715 ANDORA - ST.LOUIS MO 63125
44- 40 FICK, JOHN RALPH	D. JUNE 9, 1958 SOMERS POINT, N. J.
76- 32 FIDRYCH, MARK STEVEN	171 CRESCENT ST #B - SHREWSBURY MA 01545
32- 26 FIEBER, CLARENCE THOMAS 'LEFTY'	D. AUGUST 20, 1985 REDWOOD CITY, CALIF.
85- 33 FIELDER, CECIL GRANT	426 REDCOAT LANE - ARLINGTON TX 76018
86- 49 FIELDS, BRUCE ALAN	1003 GORDON AVENUE - LANSING MI 48910
73- 44 FIFE, DANNY WAYNE	5037 TIMBER RIDGE - CLARKSTON MI 48016
74- 36 FIGUEROA, EDUARDO	CALLE 41 A-N15 - SANTA JUANITA PR 00619
80- 44 FIGUEROA, JESUS MARIA	SANTA CRUZ VILLA MELLA KM 8 - SANTO DOMINGO DOM. REP.
40- 20 FILE, LAWRENCE SAMUEL	550 OCEAN PINES - BERLIN MD 21811
82- 42 FILER, THOMAS CARSON	9748 SUSAN RD - PHILADELPHIA PA 19115
44- 41 FILIPOWICZ, STEPHEN CHARLES	D. FEBRUARY 21, 1975 WILKES-BARRE, PA.
34- 34 FILLEY, MARCUS LUCIUS	1011 HOOSICK ROAD - ¡ROY NY 12180
15- 45 FILLINGIM, DANA	D. FEBRUARY 3, 1961 TUSKEGEE, ALA.
82- 43 FILSON, WILLIAM PETER 'PETE'	1034 10TH AVE - FOLSOM PA 19033
83- 55 FIMPLE, JOHN JOSEPH	930 8TH ST - EUREKA CA 95501
79- 36 FINCH, JOEL D	68571 OAK SPRING RD - EDWARDSBURG MI 49112
16- 27 FINCHER, WILLIAM ALLEN	D. MAY 7, 1946 SHREVEPORT, LA.
47- 34 FINE, THOMAS MORGAN	13130 BLANCO RD #1001 - SAN ANTONIO TX 78216
68- 23 FINGERS, ROLAND GLEN	11582 AVENIDA SIRVITA - SAN DIEGO CA 92128

54- 26 FINIGAN, JAMES LEROY	D. MAY 16, 1981 QUINCY, ILL.
35- 32 FINK, HERMAN ADAM	D. AUGUST 24, 1980 SALISBURY, N. C.
86- 50 FINLEY, CHARLES EDWARD	RURAL ROUTE 1 BOX 165 - WEST MONROE LA 71291
43- 47 FINLEY, ROBERT EDWARD	D. JANUARY 2, 1986 WEST COVINA, CALIF.
30- 22 FINN, CORNELIUS FRANCIS 'MICKEY'	D. JULY 7, 1933 ALTOONA, PA.
12- 62 FINNERAN, JOSEPH IGNATIUS 'HAPPY'	D. FEBRUARY 3, 1942 ORANGE, N.J.
31- 25 FINNEY, HAROLD WILSON	RR 2 BOX 195 - LAFAYETTE AL 36862
31- 26 FINNEY, LOUIS KLOPSCHE	D. APRIL 22, 1966 LAFAYETTE, ALA.
68- 24 FIORE, MICHAEL GARY JOSEPH	17 SILVER ST - MALVERNE NY 11565
81- 35 FIREOVID, STEPHEN JOHN	RR 5 - BRYAN OH 43506
81- 36 FIROVA, DANIEL MICHAEL	202 ST JOHN - REFUGIO TX 78377
19- 23 FISBURN, SAMUEL	D. APRIL 11, 1965 BETHLEHEM, PA.
30- 23 FISCHER, CHARLES WILLIAM 'CARL'	D. DECEMBER 10, 1963 MEDINA, N. Y.
62- 41 FISCHER, HENRY WILLIAM	2304 PEBBLE BEACH DR - LAKE WORTH FL 33467
87- 45 FISCHER, JEFFREY THOMAS	124 GREGORY PLACE - WEST PALM BEACH FL 33405
41- 31 FISCHER, REUBEN WALTER	RR 1 BOX 1517 - HUDSON WI 54016
86- 51 FISCHER, TODD RICHARD	1520 FOUNTAIN AVENUE - FORT MYERS FL 33907
56- 34 FISCHER, WILLIAM CHARLES	139 UPLAND DRIVE - COUNCIL BLUFFS IA 51501
13- 57 FISCHER, WILLIAM CHARLES	D. SEPTEMBER 4, 1945 RICHMOND, VA.
77- 52 FISCHLIN, MICHAEL THOMAS	4410 CIRCULO DE LAS CHACRAS - TUCSON AZ 85718
11- 50 FISHER, AUGUSTUS HARRIS	D. APRIL 8, 1972 PORTLAND, ORE.
85- 34 FISHER, BRIAN KEVIN	629 JASPER ST - AURORA CO 80011
19- 24 FISHER, CLARENCE HENRY	D. NOVEMBER 2, 1965 POINT PLEASANT, W. VA.
45- 32 FISHER, DONALD RAYMOND	D. JULY 29, 1973 MAYFIELD HEIGHTS, O.
59- 26 FISHER, EDDIE GENE	408 CARDINAL CIRCLE SOUTH - ALTUS OK 73521
64- 31 FISHER, FREDERICK BROWN 'FRITZ'	3703 BARCELONA DRIVE - TOLEDO OH 43615
23- 40 FISHER, GEORGE ALOYS 'SHOWBOAT'	BARACUDA AVE S. (BOX 203) - AVON MN 56310
51- 29 FISHER, HARRY DEVEREAUX	D. SEPTEMBER 20, 1981 WATERLOO, ONT.
10- 52 FISHER, JOHN GUS 'RED'	D. JANUARY 1, 1940 LOUISVILLE, KY.
59- 27 FISHER, JOHN HOWARD	611 HAMILTON ST - EASTON PA 18042
55- 42 FISHER, MAURICE WAYNE	15920 LUCERNE RD - FREDERICKTOWN OH 43019
10- 53 FISHER, RAYMOND LYLE	D. NOVEMBER 3, 1982 ANN ARBOR, MICH.
12- 63 FISHER, ROBERT TAYLOR	D. AUGUST 4, 1963 JACKSONVILLE, FLA.
67- 31 FISHER, THOMAS GENE	8233 HUMMINGBIRD COURT - INDIANAPOLIS IN 46256

16- 28 FISHER, WILBUR MCCULLOUGH   D. OCTOBER 24, 1960 WELCH, W. VA.
69- 56 FISK, CARLTON ERNEST   16612 CATAWBA RD - LOCKPORT IL 60441
14- 65 FISKE, MAXIMILIAN PATRICK   D. MAY 15, 1928 CHICAGO, ILL.
14- 66 FITTERY, PAUL CLARENCE   D. JANUARY 28, 1974 CARTERSVILLE, GA.
28- 34 FITZBERGER, CHARLES CASPAR   D. JANUARY 25, 1965 BALTIMORE, MD.
48- 35 FITZGERALD, EDWARD RAYMOND   431 CHRISTOPHER ST - FOLSOM CA 95630
22- 35 FITZGERALD, HOWARD CHUMNEY   D. FEBRUARY 26, 1959 EAGLE FALLS, TEX.
58- 33 FITZGERALD, JOHN FRANCIS   RR 1 BOX 351 - WESTTOWN NY 10998
11- 51 FITZGERALD, JUSTIN HOWARD 'MIKE' D. JANUARY 17, 1945 SAN MATEO, CALIF.
83- 56 FITZGERALD, MICHAEL ROY   3641 MANOR DR - LAKEWOOD CA 90712
31- 27 FITZGERALD, RAYMOND FRANCIS   D. SEPTEMBER 6, 1977 WESTFIELD, MASS.
24- 36 FITZKE, PAUL FREDERICK HERMAN   D. JUNE 30, 1950 SACRAMENTO, CAL.
66- 35 FITZMAURICE, SHAUN EARLE   12107 MOUNTAIN LAUREL DRIVE - RICHMOND VA 23236
69- 57 FITZMORRIS, ALAN JAMES   3545 MOUNT EVEREST AVE - SAN DIEGO CA 92111
15- 46 FITZPATRICK, EDWARD HENRY   D. OCTOBER 23, 1965 BETHLEHEM, PA.
25- 33 FITZSIMMONS, FREDERICK LANDIS   D. NOVEMBER 18, 1979 YUCCA VALLEY, CALIF.
19- 25 FITZSIMMONS, THOMAS WILLIAM   D. DECEMBER 20, 1971 OAKLAND, CALIF.
14- 67 FLACK, MAX JOHN   D. JULY 31, 1975 BELLEVILLE, ILL.
45- 33 FLAGER, WALTER LEONARD   3087 PORTLAND RD NE #1 - SALEM OR 97303
17- 29 FLAGSTEAD, IRA JAMES   D. MARCH 13, 1940 OLYMPIA, WASH.
41- 32 FLAIR, ALBERT DELL   2538 CALHOUN ST-NEW ORLEANS LA 70118
75- 38 FLANAGAN, MICHAEL KENDALL   6 WYNDHAM COURT - TIMONIUM MD 21093
13- 58 FLANIGAN, CHARLES JAMES   D. JANUARY 8, 1930 SAN FRANCISCO, CALIF.
46- 29 FLANIGAN, RAYMOND ARTHUR   1416 GLENDALE RD - BALTIMORE MD 21239
54- 27 FLANIGAN, THOMAS ANTHONY   114 EAST 40TH - COVINGTON KY 41015

DEE FONDY
Cincinnati Redlegs

BARRY FOOTE

77- 53 FLANNERY, JOHN MICHEAL   6222 GREEN MEADOW ROAD - LAKEWOOD CA 90713
79- 37 FLANNERY, TIMOTHY EARL   1835 BEL AIR TER - ENCINITAS CA 92024
27- 34 FLASKAMPER, RAYMOND HAROLD   D. FEBRUARY 3, 1978 SAN ANTONIO, TEX.
64- 32 FLAVIN, JOHN THOMAS   2027 CALIMYRNA AVE #101 - FRESNO CA 93711
48- 36 FLEITAS, ANGEL FELIX HUSTA   689 EBONY STREET - MELBOURNE FL 32935
40- 21 FLEMING, LESLIE FLETCHERD 'BILL' 2750 WEST HOLCOMB LN - RENO NV 89511
39- 35 FLEMING, LESLIE HARVEY 'BILL' D. MARCH 5, 1980 CLEVELAND, TEXAS
34- 35 FLETCHER, ELBURT PRESTON   131 OTIS AVE - MILTON MA 02186
14- 68 FLETCHER, OLIVER FRANK   D. OCTOBER 7, 1974 ST. PETERSBURG, FLA.
81- 37 FLETCHER, SCOTT BRIAN   2063 PANOLA RD,%O.BELLAMY - ELLENWOOD GA 30049
62- 42 FLETCHER, THOMAS WAYNE   RR 1 BOX 408 - OAKWOOD IL 61858
55- 43 FLETCHER, VANOIDE   P.O. BOX 368 - YADKINVILLE NC 27055
43- 48 FLICK, LEWIS MILLER   1712 ECHO DR - KINGSPORT TN 37665
17- 30 FLINN, DON RAPHIEL   D. MARCH 9, 1959 WACO, TEX.
78- 42 FLINN, JOHN RICHARD   173 RIVO ALTO CANAL - LONG BEACH CA 90803
42- 36 FLITCRAFT, HILDRETH MILTON 'HILLY' 50 EAST AVENUE(BOX 260) - WOODSTOWN NJ 08098
34- 36 FLOHR, MORITZ HERMAN 'MORT'   5522 ORDWAY LANE - CANISTEO NY 14823
56- 35 FLOOD, CURTIS CHARLES   4139 CLOVERDALE AVE - LOS ANGELES CA 90008
26- 29 FLORENCE, PAUL ROBERT   D. MAY 28, 1986 GAINESVILLE, FLA.
77- 54 FLORES, GILBERTO   BDA SALAZAR 1 #38 - PONCE PR 00731
42- 37 FLORES, JESSE SANDOVAL   1930 EL PORTAL DR - LAHABRA CA 90632
51- 30 FLOWERS, BENNETT   901 TREMONT RD - WILSON NC 27895
40- 22 FLOWERS, CHARLES WESLEY   1622 DODD DR - WYNNE AR 72396
23- 41 FLOWERS, D'ARCY RAYMOND 'JAKE' D. DECEMBER 27, 1962 CLEARWATER, FLA.
44- 42 FLOYD, LESLIE ROE 'BUBBA'   BELVEDERE STONEY BROOK #B4 - HOT SPRINGS AR 71901
68- 25 FLOYD, ROBERT NATHAN   1319 HALIFAX - MESA AZ 85203
15- 47 FLUHRER, JOHN L.   D. JULY 17, 1946 COLUMBUS, O.
10- 54 FLYNN, JOHN ANTHONY   D. MARCH 23, 1935 PROVIDENCE, R.I.
75- 39 FLYNN, ROBERT DOUGLAS   428 MCKENNA CT - LEXINGTON KY 40505
36- 25 FLYTHE, STUART MCGUIRE   D. OCTOBER 18, 1963 DURHAM, N. C.
58- 34 FODGE, EUGENE ARLEN   1505 NORTH CHICAGO ST - SOUTH BEND IN 46628
53- 25 FOILES, HENRY LEE   BOX 1021 - VIRGINIA BEACH VA 23451
78- 43 FOLEY, MARVIS EDWIN   4058 LANCASTER DRIVE - SARASOTA FL 34241
28- 35 FOLEY, RAYMOND KIRWIN   D. MARCH 22, 1980 VERO BEACH, FLA.
83- 57 FOLEY, THOMAS MICHAEL   11723 SW 95TH TERRACE - MIAMI FL 33186
70- 41 FOLI, TIMOTHY JOHN   105 WILLOW BEND LANE - ORMOND BEACH FL 32074
70- 42 FOLKERS, RICHARD NEVIN   7100 3RD AVENUE NORTH - ST. PETERSBURG FL 33710
51- 31 FONDY, DEE VIRGIL   1422 BELLA VISTA CIR - REDLANDS CA 92373
21- 22 FONSECA, LEWIS ALBERT   7504 NORTH AJO ROAD - SCOTTSDALE AZ 85258
83- 58 FONTENOT, SILTON RAY   904 LAKE RIDGE LN - LAKE CHARLES LA 70605
71- 33 FOOR, JAMES EMERSON   42 SOUTH SCHLUETER - ST LOUIS MO 63135
73- 45 FOOTE, BARRY CLIFTON   5300 CASTLEBROOK DR - RALEIGH NC 27604
85- 35 FORD, CURTIS GLENN   11890 BRAMPTON HUNT ROAD - FLORISSANT MO 63033
75- 40 FORD, DARNELL GLENN 'DANNY'   1250 72ND AVE NE #206 - FRIDLEY MN 55432
78- 44 FORD, DAVID ALAN   OLD ADD: 3585 WEST 49TH ST - CLEVELAND OH 44102
50- 29 FORD, EDWARD CHARLES 'WHITEY' 38 SCHOOLHOUSE LANE - LAKE SUCCESS NY 11020
36- 26 FORD, EUGENE MATTHEW   D. SEPTEMBER 7, 1970 EMMETSBURG, IA.
19- 26 FORD, HORACE HILLS 'HOD'   D. JANUARY 29, 1977 WINCHESTER, MASS.
73- 46 FORD, PERCIVAL EDMUND WENTWORTH D. JULY 8, 1980 NASSAU BAHAMAS

70- 43 FORD, THEODORE HENRY — 430 NORTH 4TH STREET - VINELAND NJ 08360
24- 37 FOREMAN, AUGUST — D. FEBRUARY 13, 1953 NEW YORK, N. Y.
52- 30 FORNIELES, JOSE MIGUEL 'MIKE' — 29 OAK SQUARE AVE - BRIGHTON MA 02135
70- 44 FORSCH, KENNETH ROTH — 7445 STONE CREEK LN - ANAHEIM CA 92807
74- 37 FORSCH, ROBERT HERBERT — 428 HICKORY GLEN LN - ST LOUIS MO 63141
71- 34 FORSTER, TERRY JAY — 3504 MOUNT LAURENCE - SAN DIEGO CA 92117
15- 48 FORSYTHE, CLARENCE D — B. ST. LOUIS, MO.
16- 29 FORTUNE, GARRETT REESE — D. SEPTEMBER 23, 1955 WASHINGTON, D. C.
64- 33 FOSNOW, GERALD EUGENE 'JERRY' — 253 WHOOPING LOOP - ALTAMONTE SPRINGS FL 32701
21- 28 FOSS, GEORGE DUEWARD — D. NOVEMBER 10, 1969 MIAMI, FLA.
61- 35 FOSS, LAWRENCE CURTIS — P.O. BOX 775027 - STEAMBOAT SPRINGS CO 80477
67- 32 FOSSE, RAYMOND EARL — 7950 WEST BATES RD - TRACY CA 95376
67- 33 FOSTER, ALAN BENTON — 1515 STALKER CT - EL CAJON CA 92020
10- 55 FOSTER, EDWARD CUNNINGHAM — D. JANUARY 15, 1937 WASHINGTON, D.C.
13- 59 FOSTER, GEORGE 'RUBE' — D. MARCH 1, 1976 BOKOSHE, OKLA.
69- 58 FOSTER, GEORGE ARTHUR — BOX 11098 - GREENWICH CT 06830
63- 41 FOSTER, LARRY LYNN — BOX 97 - WHITEHALL MI 49461
71- 35 FOSTER, LEONARD NORRIS — 36 JACOB PRICE APTS - COVINGTON KY 41012
70- 45 FOSTER, ROY — OLD ADD: 1321 E. 276TH STREET - EUCLID OH 44132
22- 36 FOTHERGILL, ROBERT ROY 'FATTY' — D. MARCH 20, 1938 DETROIT, MICH.
73- 47 FOUCAULT, STEVEN RAYMOND — 1525 SW 87TH AVENUE - MIAMI FL 33174
12- 64 FOURNIER, JOHN FRANK — D. SEPTEMBER 5, 1973 TACOMA, WASH.
24- 38 FOWLER, JESSE — D. SEPTEMBER 23, 1973 COLUMBIA, S. C.
54- 28 FOWLER, JOHN ARTHUR 'ART' — 3046 EAST MAIN EXTENSION - SPARTANBURG SC 29301
23- 42 FOWLER, JOSEPH CHESTER 'CHET' — 5550 HARVEST HILL #W264 - DALLAS TX 75230
41- 33 FOWLER, RICHARD JOHN — D. MAY 22, 1972 ONEONTA, N. Y.
82- 44 FOWLKES, ALAN KIM — OLD ADD: 1333 N. 68TH ST #224 - SCOTTSDALE AZ 85257
42- 38 FOX, CHARLES FRANCIS — 50 MOUNDS ROAD - SAN MATEO CA 94402
33- 18 FOX, ERVIN 'PETE' — D. JULY 5, 1966 DETROIT, MICH.

44- 43 FOX, HOWARD FRANCIS — D. OCTOBER 9, 1955 SAN ANTONIO, TEX.
47- 35 FOX, JACOB NELSON 'NELLIE' — D. DECEMBER 1, 1975 BALTIMORE, MD.
60- 33 FOX, TERRENCE EDWARD — STAR ROUTE A BOX 196-D - NEW IBERIA LA 70560
25- 35 FOXX, JAMES EMORY — D. JULY 21, 1967 MIAMI, FLA.
68- 36 FOY, JOSEPH ANTHONY — 1655 UNDERCLIFF DR - BRONX NY 10453
53- 26 FOYTACK, PAUL EUGENE — 5590 HICKORY PL - WEST BLOOMFIELD MI 48033
72- 28 FRAILING, KENNETH DOUGLAS — 4137 PRESCOTT - SARASOTA FL 33582
60- 34 FRANCIS, EARL COLEMAN — 28 QUAIL HILL RD - PITTSBURGH PA 15214
22- 37 FRANCIS, RAY JAMES — D. JULY 14, 1932 ATLANTA, GA.
84- 36 FRANCO, JOHN ANTHONY — 54 BAY 46TH ST - BROOKLYN NY 11214
82- 45 FRANCO, JULIO CESAR — CF 16 B.LIBRE ING CONS-SAN PEDRO DE MACORIS DOM. REP.
56- 36 FRANCONA, JOHN PATSY 'TITO' — 2206 MERCER RD - NEW BRIGHTON PA 15066
81- 38 FRANCONA, TERRY JON — 2206 MERCER RD - NEW BRIGHTON PA 15066
27- 35 FRANKHOUSE, FREDRICK MELOY — BOX 297 - PORT ROYAL PA 17082
44- 44 FRANKLIN, JAMES WILFORD 'JACK' — 105 WATER OAK COURT - PANAMA CITY BEACH FL 32407
71- 36 FRANKLIN, JOHN WILLIAM 'JAY' — OLD ADD: 2305 STRYKER AVE - VIENNA VA
41- 34 FRANKLIN, MURRAY ASHER — D. MARCH 16, 1978 HARBOR CITY, CALIF.
39- 36 FRANKS, HERMAN LOUIS — 2745 COMANCHE DR-SALT LAKE CITY UT 84108
86- 52 FRASER, WILLIAM PATRICK 'WILLIE' — 855 SEAGULL LANE #A301 - NEWPORT BEACH CA 92663
31- 28 FRASIER, VICTOR PATRICK — D. JANUARY 10, 1977 JACKSONVILLE, TEX.
78- 45 FRAZIER, GEORGE ALLEN — 13802 EAST 29TH PLACE - TULSA OK 74134
47- 36 FRAZIER, JOSEPH FILMORE — 519 FAIRWAY DR - BROKEN ARROW OK 74012
29- 37 FREDERICK, JOHN HENRY — D. JUNE 18, 1977 TIGARD, ORE.
42- 39 FREED, EDWIN CHARLES — 840 MCDOW DR-ROCK HILL SC 29730
70- 46 FREED, ROGER VERNON — 1329 SOUTH WILLOW AVE - WEST COVINA CA 91790
61- 36 FREEHAN, WILLIAM ASHLEY — 4248 SUNNINGDALE - BLOOMFIELD HILLS MI 48013
21- 29 FREEMAN, ALEXANDER VERNON 'BUCK' — D. FEBRUARY 21, 1953 FORT SAM HOUSTON, TEXAS
21- 30 FREEMAN, HARVEY BAYARD — D. JANUARY 10, 1970 KALAMAZOO, MICH.
52- 31 FREEMAN, HERSHELL BASKIN — 5437 SAN MARINO PL - ORLANDO FL 32807
72- 29 FREEMAN, JIMMY LEE — 2144 SOUTH FULTON PL - TULSA OK 74114
27- 36 FREEMAN, JOHN EDWARD — D. APRIL 14, 1958 WASHINGTON, D. C.
59- 28 FREEMAN, MARK PRICE — 6 BROOKSIDE DR - LITTLETON CO 80120
86- 53 FREEMAN, MARVIN — 7314 SOUTH LOWE STREET - CHICAGO IL 60621
55- 44 FREESE, EUGENE LEWIS — 6504 GLENDALE - METAIRIE LA 70003
53- 27 FREESE, GEORGE WALTER — 3341 SW MARIGOLD ST - PORTLAND OR 97219
25- 36 FREEZE, CARL ALEXANDER 'JAKE' — D. APRIL 9, 1983 SAN ANGELO, TEX.
61- 37 FREGOSI, JAMES LOUIS — 5730 MIDNIGHT PASS RD #408B - SARASOTA FL 34242
41- 35 FREIBURGER, VERNON DONALD — 15490 DEVONSHIRE CIR - WESTMINSTER CA 92683
22- 38 FREIGAU, HOWARD EARL — D. JULY 18, 1932 CHATTANOOGA, TENN.
74- 38 FREISLEBEN, DAVID JAMES — 2119 PEACH LN - PASADENA TX 77502
32- 27 FREITAS, ANTONIO — 5648 GREENACRES WAY - ORANGEVALE CA 95662
17- 31 FRENCH, FRANK ALEXANDER 'PAT' — D. JULY 13, 1969 BATH, ME.
29- 38 FRENCH, LAWRENCE ROBERT — D. FEBRUARY 9, 1987 SAN DIEGO, CALIF.
20- 33 FRENCH, RAYMOND EDWARD — D. APRIL 3, 1978 ALAMEDA, CALIF.
65- 29 FRENCH, RICHARD JAMES 'JIM' — 6960 GLORIA DR - PENNGROVE CA 94951

```
23- 43 FRENCH, WALTER EDWARD                      D. MAY 13, 1984 MOUNTAIN HOME, ARK.
29- 39 FREY, BENJAMIN RUDOLPH                      D. NOVEMBER 1, 1937 JACKSON, MICH.
80- 45 FREY, JAMES GOTTFRIED                       1805 REUTER RD - TIMONIUM MD 21093
33- 19 FREY, LINUS REINHARD 'LONNY'                14424 127TH AVE SE - SNOHOMISH WA 98290
73- 48 FRIAS, JESUS MARIA 'PEPE'                   CALLE 4 #9 - SAN PEDRO DE MACORIS DOM. REP.
19- 27 FRIBERG, GUSTAF BERNHARD                    D. DECEMBER 8, 1958 LYNN, MASS.
52- 32 FRICANO, MARION JOHN                        D. MAY 18, 1976 TIJUANA, MEX.
23- 44 FRIDAY, GRIER WILLIAM 'SKIPPER'             D. AUGUST 25, 1962 GASTONIA, N. C.
52- 33 FRIDLEY, JAMES RILEY                        540 JOSMINE NW AVE - PORT CHARLOTTE FL 33952
20- 34 FRIED, ARTHUR EDWIN 'CY'                    D. OCTOBER 10, 1970 SAN ANTONIO, TEX.
32- 28 FRIEDRICHS, ROBERT GEORGE                   NORRIS ROAD - SUGAR GROVE IL 60554
49- 24 FRIEND, OWEN LACEY                          2917 HALSTED - WICHITA KS 67204
51- 32 FRIEND, ROBERT BARTMESS                     4 SALEM CIR - FOX CHAPEL PA 15238
41- 36 FRIERSON, ROBERT LAWRENCE 'BUCK'            RR 1 BOX 257 - ARTHUR CITY TX 75411
10- 56 FRILL, JOHN EDMUND                          D. SEPTEMBER 28, 1918 WESTERLY, R. I.
34- 37 FRINK, FREDERICK FERDINAND                  2830 JEFFERSON STREET - COCONUT GROVE FL 33133
19- 28 FRISCH, FRANK FRANCIS                       D. MARCH 12, 1973 WILMINGTON, DEL.
67- 34 FRISELLA, DANIEL VINCENT                    D. JANUARY 1, 1977 PHOENIX, ARIZ.
13- 60 FRITZ, HARRY KOCH                           D. NOVEMBER 4, 1974 COLUMBUS, O.
75- 41 FRITZ, LAURENCE JOSEPH                      2632 SCHRAGE AVE - WHITING IN 46394
55- 45 FROATS, WILLIAM JOHN                        OLD ADD: 16 ASHTON RD - YONKERS NY 10705
82- 46 FROBEL, DOUGLAS STEPHEN                     63 GLENRIDGE RD - OTTAWA ONT. K2G 2Z8 CAN.
87- 46 FROHWIRTH, TODD GERARD                      6608 WEST CHAMBERS STREET - MILWAUKEE WI 53210
77- 55 FROST, CARL DAVID 'DAVE'                    2206 OCANA DR - LONG BEACH CA 90815
78- 46 FRY, JERRY RAY                              405 EAST MULBERRY #12 - CHATHAM IL 62629
23- 45 FRY, JOHNSON                                D. APRIL 7, 1959 CARMI, ILL.
40- 23 FRYE, CHARLES ANDREW                        D. MAY 25, 1945 HICKORY, N. C.
66- 37 FRYMAN, WOODROW THOMPSON                    RR 1 BOX 21 - EWING KY 41039
42- 40 FUCHS, CHARLES RUDOLPH                      D. JUNE 10, 1969 WEEHAWKEN, N. J.
```

LINUS FREY

```
29- 40 FUCHS, EMIL EDWIN                           D. DECEMBER 5, 1961 BOSTON, MASS.
83- 59 FUENTES, MICHAEL JAY                        6001 CELLINI STREET - CORAL GABLES FL 33146
69- 59 FUENTES, MIGUEL                             D. JANUARY 29, 1970 LOIZA ALDEA, P. R.
65- 30 FUENTES, RIGOBERTO PEAT 'TITO'              1080 HATTERAS - FOSTER CITY CA 94404
21- 31 FUHR, OSCAR LAWRENCE                        D. MARCH 27, 1975 DALLAS, TEX.
22- 39 FUHRMAN, ALFRED GEORGE 'OLLIE'              D. JANUARY 11, 1969 PEORIA, ILL.
21- 32 FULGHUM, JAMES LAVOISIER 'DOT'              D. NOVEMBER 11, 1947 MIAMI, FLA.
79- 38 FULGHUM, JOHN THOMAS                        301 S. BRYANT AVE #C200 - EDMOND OK 73034
15- 49 FULLER, FRANK EDWARD                        D. OCTOBER 29, 1965 WARREN, MICH.
73- 49 FULLER, JAMES H                             2844 POINSETTIA DR - SAN DIEGO CA 92106
74- 39 FULLER, JOHN EDWARD                         33022 CHRISTINA - DANA POINT CA 92629
64- 34 FULLER, VERN GORDON                         %REGISTRY,7901 24TH AVE SOUTH - MINNEAPOLIS MN 55420
21- 33 FULLERTON, CURTIS HOOPER                    D. JANUARY 2, 1975 WINTHROP, MASS.
28- 36 FULLIS, CHARLES PHILIP 'CHICK'              D. MARCH 28, 1946 ASHLAND, PA.
87- 47 FULTON, WILLIAM DAVID                       217 DOROTHY DRIVE - PITTSBURGH PA 15235
81- 39 FUNDERBURK, MARK CLIFFORD                   6924 OLD PROVIDENCE RD - CHARLOTTE NC 28226
29- 41 FUNK, ELIAS CALVIN 'LIZ'                    D. JANUARY 17, 1968 OKLAHOMA CITY, OKLA.
60- 35 FUNK, FRANKLIN RAY                          4452 EAST BELLVIEW ST - PHOENIX AZ 85008
86- 54 FUNK, THOMAS JAMES                          2905 NE 56TH TERRACE - KANSAS CITY MO 64119
46- 30 FURILLO, CARL ANTHONY                       1415 CARSONIA AVE - STONY CREEK MILLS PA19606
22- 40 FUSSELL, FREDERICK MORRIS                   D. OCTOBER 23, 1966 SYRACUSE, N. Y.
52- 34 FUSSELMAN, LESTER LEROY                     D. MAY 21, 1970 CLEVELAND, O.
35- 33 GABLER, FRANK HAROLD                        D. NOVEMBER 1, 1967 LONG BEACH, CAL.
59- 29 GABLER, JOHN RICHARD                        8606 WEST 81ST ST - OVERLAND PARK KS 66204
58- 35 GABLER, WILLIAM LOUIS                       729 POPE - ST. LOUIS MO 63147
45- 34 GABLES, KENNETH HARLIN                      D. JANUARY 2, 1960 WALNUT GROVE, MO.
39- 37 GABRIELSON, LEONARD HILBOURNE               1387 GLEN DR - SAN LEANDRO CA 94577
60- 36 GABRIELSON, LEONARD GARY                    24230 HILLVIEW DR - LOS ALTOS HILLS CA 94022
38- 28 GADDY, JOHN WILSON                          D. MAY 3, 1966 ALBEMARLE, N. C.
51- 33 GAEDEL, EDWARD CARL                         D. JUNE 19, 1961 CHICAGO, ILL.
81- 40 GAETTI, GARY JOSEPH                         OLD ADD: 1420 JONQUIL STREET - CENTRALIA IL 62801
82- 47 GAFF, BRENT ALLEN                           RR 2 BOX 122A - ALBION IN 46701
36- 27 GAFFKE, FABIAN SEBASTIAN                    4305 SOUTH PENNSYLVANIA AVE-MILWAUKEE WI 53207
63- 42 GAGLIANO, PHILIP JOSEPH                     730 OAKHILL LANE - MANCHESTER MO 63021
65- 31 GAGLIANO, RALPH MICHAEL                     845 DICKINSON ST - MEMPHIS TN 38107
83- 60 GAGNE, GREGORY CARPENTER                    8318 17TH AVE SOUTH - BLOOMINGTON MN 55420
14- 69 GAGNIER, EDWARD J.                          D. SEPTEMBER 13, 1946 DETROIT, MICH.
22- 41 GAGNON, HAROLD DENNIS 'CHICK'               D. APRIL 30, 1970 WILMINGTON, DEL.
60- 37 GAINES, ARNESTA JOE                         4759 MELDON AVE - OAKLAND CA 94619
21- 34 GAINES, WILLARD ROLAND 'NEMO'               D. JANUARY 26, 1979 WARRENTON, VA.
85- 36 GAINEY, TELMANCH 'TY'                       131 JERICHO ST - CHERAW SC 29520
34- 38 GALAN, AUGUST JOHN                          1345 NOB HILL - PINOLE CA 94564
85- 37 GALARRAGA, ANDRES JOSE PADOVANI             BARRIO NUEVO CHAPELLIN CLEJON SOLEDAD #5-CARACAS VENEZ
77- 56 GALASSO, ROBERT JOSE                        915 REED ROAD NE - SMYRNA GA 30080
33- 20 GALATZER, MILTON                            D. JANUARY 29, 1976 SAN FRANCISCO, CALIF.
```

78- 47	GALE, RICHARD BLACKWELL	FOX RIDGE RD - LITTLETON NH 03561
34- 39	GALEHOUSE, DENNIS WARD	121 HUFFMAN AVE - DOYLESTOWN OH 44230
70- 47	GALLAGHER, ALAN MITCHELL	1852 BEVERLY AVE - CLOVIS CA 93612
87- 48	GALLAGHER, DAVID THOMAS	OLD ADD: 444 EAST FRANKLIN STREET - TRENTON NJ 08610
62- 43	GALLAGHER, DOUGLAS EUGENE	1690 MAPLE LN - FREMONT OH 43420
32- 29	GALLAGHER, EDWARD MICHAEL	D. DECEMBER 22, 1981 HYANNIS PORT, MASS.
15- 50	GALLAGHER, JOHN CARROLL	D. MARCH 30, 1952 NORFOLK, VA.
23- 46	GALLAGHER, JOHN LAURENCE	D. SEPTEMBER 10, 1984 GLADWYN, PA.
39- 38	GALLAGHER, JOSEPH EMMETT	2525 MCCUE #121 - HOUSTON TX 77056
22- 42	GALLAGHER, LAWRENCE KIRBY 'GIL'	D. JANUARY 6, 1957 WASHINGTON, D. C.
72- 30	GALLAGHER, ROBERT COLLINS	315 FAIR AVE - SANTA CRUZ CA 95060
42- 41	GALLE, STANLEY JOSEPH	7 NORTH REED AVE - MOBILE AL 36604
85- 38	GALLEGO, MICHAEL ANTHONY	3700 SOUTH PLAZA DRIVE #E102 - SANTA ANA CA 92704
12- 65	GALLIA, MELVIN ALLYS 'BERT'	D. MARCH 19, 1976 DEVINE, TEX.
31- 29	GALLIVAN, PHILIP JOSEPH	D. NOVEMBER 24, 1969 ST. PAUL, MINN.
19- 29	GALLOWAY, CLARENCE EDWARD 'CHICK'	D. NOVEMBER 7, 1969 CLINTON, S. C.
12- 66	GALLOWAY, JAMES CATO 'BAD NEWS'	D. MAY 3, 1950 FORT WORTH, TEX.
86- 55	GALVEZ, BALVINO	BATEY LABOMBA DIV PORV'IR-SAN PEDRO DE MACORIS DOM REP.
30- 24	GALVIN, JAMES JOSEPH	D. SEPTEMBER 30, 1969 MARIETTA, GA.
72- 31	GAMBLE, JOHN ROBERT	3740 AMADOR WAY - RENO NV 89502
35- 34	GAMBLE, LEE JESSE	237 JENKS AVE-PUNXATAWNEY PA 15767
69- 60	GAMBLE, OSCAR CHARLES	108 TENSAW RD - MONTGOMERY AL 36117
10- 57	GANDIL, CHARLES ARNOLD 'CHICK'	D. DECEMBER 12, 1970 CALISTOGA, CALIF.
16- 30	GANDY, ROBERT BRINKLEY	D. JUNE 19, 1945 JACKSONVILLE, FLA.
87- 49	GANT, RONALD EDWIN	512 MONTERREY - VICTORIA TX 77904
39- 39	GANTENBEIN, JOSEPH STEPHEN	535 ORANGE AVE - SOUTH SAN FRANCISCO CA 94080
76- 33	GANTNER, JAMES ELMER	BOX 156 - EDEN WI 53019
27- 37	GANZEL, FOSTER PIRIE 'BABE'	D. FEBRUARY 6, 1978 JACKSONVILLE FLA.
46- 31	GARAGIOLA, JOSEPH HENRY	6221 EAST HUNTRESS DR - PARADISE VALLEY AZ 85253
44- 45	GARBARK, NATHANIEL MICHAEL 'MIKE'	2015 QUEENS ROAD #1 - CHARLOTTE NC 28207
34- 40	GARBARK, ROBERT MICHAEL	267 JEFFERSON ST - MEADVILLE PA 16335
69- 61	GARBER, HENRY EUGENE 'GENE'	771 STONEMILL DRIVE - ELIZABETHTOWN PA 17022
56- 37	GARBER, ROBERT MITCHELL	101 ACACIA LN - REDWOOD CITY CA 94062
84- 37	GARBEY, BARBARO GARBEY	OLD ADD: 181-10 NW 56TH ST - MIAMI FL 33178
52- 35	GARBOWSKI, ALEXANDER	110 ELLIOTT ST - YONKERS NY 10705
76- 34	GARCIA, ALFONSO RAFAEL	526A NORTH CIVIC DR - WALNUT CREEK CA 94596
78- 48	GARCIA, DAMASO DOMINGO	SANCHEZ NO. 104 - MOCA DOMINICAN REP.
81- 41	GARCIA, DANIEL RAPHAEL	72 MEADE AVENUE - BETHPAGE NY 11714
77- 57	GARCIA, DAVID	15420 OLDE HWY 80 #129 - EL CAJON CA 92021
48- 37	GARCIA, EDWARD MIGUEL 'MIKE'	D. JANUARY 13, 1986 FAIRVIEW PARK, O.
87- 50	GARCIA, LEONARDO ANTONIO	JUAN SALTITOPA #28 E.BOLIVAL-SANTIAGO DOMINICAN REP.
87- 51	GARCIA, MIGUEL ANGEL	CARLOS DELGADO CHALBAUD BLQ6 LETRA C #6-CARACAS VENEZ
73- 50	GARCIA, PEDRO MODESTO	OLD ADD: BARRIOS PUENTO DE JOBOS-GUAYAMA PR
72- 32	GARCIA, RALPH	725 EL CENTAURO DR - EL PASO TX 79922
48- 38	GARCIA, RAMON GARCIA	FALGUERAS 256 - HAVANA CUBA
54- 29	GARCIA, VINICIO UZCANGA	R. CAMPOAMOR 805,COL ANAHUAC-MONTEREY NUEVO LEON MEX.
45- 35	GARDELLA, ALFRED STEVE	3761 NW 35TH STREET - COCONUT CREEK FL 33066
44- 46	GARDELLA, DANIEL LEWIS	16 MORSEMERE PL - YONKERS NY 10701
81- 42	GARDENHIRE, RONALD CLYDE	7701 QUAIL - WICHITA KS 67212
23- 47	GARDINER, ARTHUR CECIL	D. OCTOBER 21, 1954 COPIAGUE, N. Y.
75- 42	GARDNER, ARTHUR JUNIOR	RR 2 BOX 41 - WALNUT GROVE MS 39189
45- 36	GARDNER, GLENN MILESO	D. JULY 7, 1964 ROCHESTER, N. Y.
11- 52	GARDNER, HARRY RAY	D. AUGUST 2, 1961 CANBY, ORE.
29- 42	GARDNER, RAYMOND VINCENT	D. MAY 3, 1968 FREDERICK, MD.
65- 32	GARDNER, RICHARD FRANK 'ROB'	OLD ADD: 129 CHAPIN ST - BINGHAMTON NY 13905
84- 38	GARDNER, WESLEY BRIAN	305 RUTH STREET - BENTON AR 72015
54- 30	GARDNER, WILLIAM FREDERICK	35 DAYTON RD - WATERFORD CT 06385
36- 28	GARIBALDI, ARTHUR EDWARD	D. OCTOBER 20, 1967 SACRAMENTO, CAL.
62- 44	GARIBALDI, BOB ROY	2143 OREGON AVENUE - STOCKTON CA 95204
31- 30	GARLAND, LOUIS LYMAN	BOX 492 - IDAHO FALLS ID 83401
73- 51	GARLAND, MARCUS WAYNE	8529 NEWSON STATION ROAD - NASHVILLE TN 37221
69- 62	GARMAN, MICHAEL DOUGLAS	3806 AIRPORT AVE - CALDWELL ID 83605
32- 30	GARMS, DEBS C.	D. DECEMBER 16, 1984 GLEN ROSE, TEXAS
73- 52	GARNER, PHILIP MASON	BOX 288 - HOUSTON TX 77001
68- 26	GARR, RALPH ALLAN	7819 CHASEWAY DR - MISSOURI CITY TX 77459
82- 48	GARRELTS, SCOTT WILLIAM	206 EAST ELM - BUCKLEY IL 60918
15- 51	GARRETT, CLARENCE RAYMOND	D. FEBRUARY 11, 1977 MOUNDSVILLE, W. VA.
70- 48	GARRETT, GREGORY	14963 SANDRA - SAN FERNANDO CA 91340
66- 38	GARRETT, HENRY ADRIAN 'ADE'	BOX 201 - MANCHACA TX 78652
69- 63	GARRETT, RONALD WAYNE	716 DEAN AVE - SARASOTA FL 33577
64- 35	GARRIDO, GIL GONZALO	SHERIFF DEPT. ,556 N. MCDONOUGH - DECATUR GA 30030
46- 32	GARRIOTT, CECIL VIRGIL	31750 MACHADO #71 - LAKE ELSINORE CA 92330
28- 37	GARRISON, CLIFFORD WILLIAM	815 CAPAY ST - ESPARTO CA 95627
43- 49	GARRISON, ROBERT FORD	5075 65TH AVENUE NORTH - PINELLAS PARK FL 34665
31- 31	GARRITY, FRANCIS JOSEPH 'HANK'	D. SEPTEMBER 3, 1962 BOSTON, MASS.
48- 39	GARVER, NED FRANKLIN	BOX 114 - NEY OH 43549

WAYNE GARLAND

69- 64 GARVEY, STEVEN PATRICK	4320 LAJOLLA VILLAGE DR - SAN DIEGO CA 92122
77- 58 GARVIN, THEODORE JARED 'JERRY'	167 SANDPIPER LANE - MORRO BAY CA 93442
69- 65 GASPAR, RODNEY EARL	28771 PEACH BLOSSOM - MISSION VIEJO CA 92692
44- 47 GASSAWAY, CHARLES CASON	10925 WESTWOOD LAKE DR - MIAMI FL 33165
55- 46 GASTALL, THOMAS EVERETT	D. SEPTEMBER 20, 1956 CHESAPEAKE BAY, MD.
20- 35 GASTON, ALEXANDER NATHANIEL	D. FEBRUARY 8, 1979 SANTA MONICA, CALIF.
67- 35 GASTON, CLARENCE EDWIN 'CITO'	65 HILTON AVE - TORONTO ONTARIO M5R 3E5 CAN.
24- 39 GASTON, NATHANIEL MILTON 'MILT'	5064 WHITE OAK CT - BRADENTON FL 33507
78- 49 GATES, JOSEPH DANIEL	1517 EAST NINETEENTH AVE - GARY IN 46407
81- 43 GATES, MICHAEL GRANT	8149 GARDEN GROVE - RESEDA CA 91335
63- 43 GATEWOOD, AUBREY LEE	5 PINE TREE LOOP - NORTH LITTLE ROCK AR 72116
78- 50 GAUDET, JAMES JENNINGS	969 UNDERWOOD DRIVE - MACON GA 31210
25- 37 GAUTREAU, WALTER PAUL 'DOC'	D. AUGUST 23, 1970 SALT LAKE CITY, UTAH
36- 29 GAUTREAUX, SIDNEY ALLEN	D. APRIL 19, 1980 MORGAN CITY, LA.
20- 36 GAW, GEORGE JOSEPH 'CHIPPY'	D. MAY 26, 1968 BOSTON, MASS.
23- 48 GAZELLA, MICHAEL	D. SEPTEMBER 11, 1978 ODESSA, TEX.
47- 37 GEARHART, LLOYD WILLIAM	206 HOME AVE - XENIA OH 45385
23- 49 GEARIN, DENNIS JOHN 'DINTY'	D. MARCH 11, 1959 PROVIDENCE, R. I.
42- 42 GEARY, EUGENE FRANCIS JOSEPH 'HUCK'	D. JANUARY 27, 1981 CUBA, N. Y.
18- 21 GEARY, ROBERT NORTON	D. JANUARY 31, 1980 CINCINNATI, O.
71- 37 GEBHARD, ROBERT HENRY	117 MARQUETTE AVE -NORTH MANKATO MN 56001
47- 38 GEBRIAN, PETER	103 RIVER RD #E-4 - NUTLEY NJ 07110
72- 33 GEDDES, JAMES LEE	4129 ZUBER RD - ORIENT OH 43146
39- 40 GEDEON, ELMER JOHN	D. APRIL 15, 1944 FRANCE
13- 61 GEDEON, ELMER JOSEPH	D. MAY 19, 1941 SAN FRANCISCO, CALIF.
80- 46 GEDMAN, RICHARD LEO	32 LAFAYETTE - WORCESTER MA 01608
39- 41 GEE, JOHN ALEXANDER	D. JANUARY 23, 1988 CORTLAND, N. Y.
23- 50 GEHRIG, HENRY LOUIS 'LOU'	D. JUNE 2, 1941 RIVERDALE, N. Y.
24- 40 GEHRINGER, CHARLES LEONARD	32301 LAHSER RD - BIRMINGHAM MI 48010
37- 39 GEHRMAN, PAUL ARTHUR	D. OCTOBER 23, 1986 BEND, ORE.
58- 36 GEIGER, GARY MERLE	7327 SOUTH 69TH EAST CT - TULSA OK 74133
78- 51 GEISEL, JOHN DAVID 'DAVE'	59 COSHWAY PLACE - TONAWANDA NY 14150
69- 66 GEISHERT, VERNON WILLIAM	RR 4 - RICHLAND CENTER WI 53581
29- 43 GELBERT, CHARLES MAGNUS	D. JANUARY 13, 1967 EASTON, PA.
64- 36 GELNAR, JOHN RICHARD	312 SOUTH ROBINSON - MANGUM OK 73554
22- 43 GENEWICH, JOSEPH EDWARD	D. DECEMBER 21, 1985 LOCKPORT, N. Y.
50- 30 GENOVESE, GEORGE MICHAEL	11474 ERWIN ST - HOLLYWOOD CA 91606
57- 22 GENTILE, JAMES EDWARD	1016 NEPTUNE - EDMOND OK 73034
43- 50 GENTILE, SAMUEL CHRISTOPHER	123 CENTRAL AVE-EVERETT MA 02149
69- 67 GENTRY, GARY EDWARD	205 STAR ROUTE TWO - CAVE CREEK AZ 85331
54- 31 GENTRY, HARVEY WILLIAM	109 EATON LN - BRISTOL TN 37620
43- 51 GENTRY, JAMES RUFFUS	4929 FULP ST - WINSTON SALEM NC 27105
55- 47 GEORGE, ALEX THOMAS	1001 ROMANY ROAD - KANSAS CITY MO 64113
35- 35 GEORGE, CHARLES PETER 'GREEK'	RR 2 BOX 39E - BRUNSWICK GA 31520
11- 53 GEORGE, THOMAS EDWARD 'LEFTY'	D. MAY 13, 1955 YORK, PA.
38- 29 GEORGY, OSCAR JOHN	302 BAYLOR PLACE - KENNER LA 70062
36- 30 GERAGHTY, BENJAMIN RAYMOND	D. JUNE 18, 1963 JACKSONVILLE, FLA.
62- 45 GERARD, DAVID FREDERICK	318 DOONE PL - FAIRLESS HILLS PA 19030
85- 39 GERBER, CRAIG STUART	4297 PERSHING AVENUE - SAN BERNARDINO CA 92407
14- 70 GERBER, WALTER	D. JUNE 19, 1951 COLUMBUS, O.
62- 46 GERBERMAN, GEORGE ALOIS	1501 MICHAEL - EL CAMPO TX 77437
74- 40 GERHARDT, ALLEN RUSSELL 'RUSTY'	2003 HEATHERWAY - ARLINGTON TX 76012
86- 56 GERHART, HAROLD KENNETH 'KEN'	707 ELLIOT STREET - MURFREESBORO TN 37130
43- 52 GERHEAUSER, ALBERT	D. MAY 28, 1972 SPRINGFIELD, MO.
27- 38 GERKEN, GEORGE HERBERT	D. OCTOBER 23, 1977 ARCAIDA, CALIF.
45- 37 GERKIN, STEPHEN PAUL	D. NOVEMBER 8, 1978 BAY PINES, FLA.
38- 30 GERLACH, JOHN GLENN	5721 DOGWOOD PL - MADISON WI 53705
19- 30 GERNER, EDWIN FREDERICK	D. MAY 15, 1970 PHILADELPHIA, PA.
52- 36 GERNERT, RICHARD EDWARD	1420 ROSE VIRGINIA RD - READING PA 19615
69- 68 GERONIMO, CESAR FRANCISCO	TEFADA FLO. #56 - SANTO DOMINGO DOMINICAN REP.
13- 62 GERVAIS, LUCIEAN EDWARD 'LEFTY'	D. OCTOBER 19, 1950 LOS ANGELES, CALIF.
45- 38 GETTEL, ALLEN JONES	5620 PARLIAMENT DR - VIRGINIA BEACH VA 23452
10- 58 GEYER, JACOB BOWMAN 'RUBE'	D. OCTOBER 12, 1962 WAHKON, MINN.
24- 41 GEYGAN, JAMES EDWARD 'CHAPPIE'	D. MARCH 16, 1966 COLUMBUS, O.
16- 31 GHARRITY, EDWARD PATRICK 'PATSY'	D. OCTOBER 10, 1966 BELOIT, WIS.
83- 61 GHELFI, ANTHONY PAUL	3414 GENEVA LANE - LACROSSE WI 54601
58- 37 GIALLOMBARDO, ROBERT PAUL	60 BAY 41ST STREET - BROOKLYN NY 11214
11- 54 GIANNINI, JOSEPH FRANCIS	D. SEPTEMBER 26, 1942 SAN FRANCISCO, CALIF.
25- 38 GIARD, JOSEPH OSCAR	D. JULY 10, 1956 WORCESTER, MASS.
60- 38 GIBSON, JOSEPH CHARLES	RR 2 - NEWTON MS 39345
84- 39 GIBBONS, JOHN MICHAEL	95 DUNCAN ST #A - BOLLING AIR FORCE BASE DC 20366
62- 47 GIBBS, JERRY DEAN 'JAKE'	219 ST. ANDREWS CIR - OXFORD MS 38655
24- 42 GIBSON, CHARLES GRIFFIN	713 RIDGECREST RD - LAGRANGE GA 30241
13- 63 GIBSON, FRANK GILBERT	D. APRIL 27, 1961 AUSTIN, TEX.

Lou Gehrig

George Gerken

67- 36 GIBSON, JOHN RUSSELL 'RUSS'   495 GARDNERS NOOK RD - SWANSEA MA 02777
79- 39 GIBSON, KIRK HAROLD   1082 OAK POINTE DR - PONTIAC MI 48054
59- 30 GIBSON, ROBERT   215 BELLEVIEW BLVD SOUTH - BELLEVIEW NE 68005
83- 62 GIBSON, ROBERT LOUIS   261 POWELL ROAD - SPRINGFIELD PA 19064
26- 30 GIBSON, SAMUEL BRAXTON   D. JANUARY 31, 1983 HIGH POINT, N. C.
37- 40 GICK, GEORGE EDWARD   3 BRADY CT - LAFAYETTE IN 47905
87- 52 GIDEON, BYRON BRETT   P.O. BOX 822 - GEORGETOWN TX 78627
75- 43 GIDEON, JAMES LESLIE   5623 BRAESVALLEY - HOUSTON TX 77035
13- 64 GIEBEL, JOSEPH HENRY   D. MARCH 17, 1981 SILVER SPRING, MD.
39- 42 GIEBELL, FLOYD GEORGE   RR 1 BOX 111, LAURELWOOD DR - WILKESBORO NC 28697
54- 32 GIEL, PAUL ROBERT   13400 MCGINTZ RD - MINNEAPOLIS MN 55343
59- 31 GIGGIE, ROBERT THOMAS   89 MCANDREW RD - BRAINTREE MA 02184
67- 37 GIGON, NORMAN PHILLIP   205 PAXINOSA RD EAST - EASTON PA 18042
67- 38 GIL, TOMAS GUSTAVO 'GUS'   URB. URDAVETA, VEREDA 15#1 - CARACAS VENEZUELA S.A.
42- 43 GILBERT, ANDREW   803 WALNUT DR-LATROBE PA 15650
40- 24 GILBERT, CHARLES MADER   D. AUGUST 13, 1983 NEW ORLEANS, LA.
59- 32 GILBERT, DREW EDWARD 'BUDDY'   1913 BELCARO DR - KNOXVILLE TN 37918
50- 31 GILBERT, HAROLD JOSEPH 'TOOKIE'   D. JUNE 23, 1967 NEW ORLEANS, LA.
72- 34 GILBERT, JOE DENNIS   1952 NORTH BOWIE ST - JASPER TX 75951
14- 71 GILBERT, LAWRENCE WILLIAM   D. FEBRUARY 17, 1965 NEW ORLEANS, LA.
85- 40 GILBERT, MARK DAVID   OLD ADD: 3151 N. COURSE LN #201 - POMPANO BEACH FL 3306
28- 38 GILBERT, WALTER JOHN   D. SEPTEMBER 8, 1959 DULUTH, MINN.
72- 35 GILBREATH, RODNEY JOE   1438 RIDGELAND WAY - LILBURN GA 30247
71- 38 GILBRETH, WILLIAM FREEMAN   690 EAST NORTH 16TH ST - ABILENE TX 79601
59- 33 GILE, DONALD LOREN   3145 PORTER DR - PALO ALTO CA 94304
81- 44 GILES, BRIAN JEFFREY   8607 GLEN HAVEN ST - SAN DIEGO CA 92125
20- 37 GILHAM, GEORGE LEWIS   D. APRIL 25, 1937 LANSDOWNE, PA.
11- 55 GILHOOLEY, FRANK PATRICK   D. JULY 11, 1959 TOLEDO, O.
19- 31 GILL, EDWARD JAMES   27 FEDERICO CIR - STOUGHTON MA 02072
37- 41 GILL, GEORGE LLOYD   RAYMOND MS 39154
23- 51 GILL, HAROLD EDWARD   D. AUGUST 1, 1932 BROCKTON, MASS.
27- 39 GILL, JOHN WESLEY   D. DECEMBER 26, 1984 NASHVILLE, TENN.
40- 25 GILLENWATER, CARDEN EDISON   49 COUNTRY CLUB DR - LARGO FL 33543
23- 52 GILLENWATER, CLARAL LEWIS   D. FEBRUARY 26, 1978 PENSACOLA, FLA.
22- 44 GILLESPIE, JOHN PATRICK   D. FEBRUARY 15, 1954 VALLEJO, CAL.
42- 44 GILLESPIE, PAUL ALLEN   D. AUGUST 11, 1970 ANNISTON, ALA.
44- 48 GILLESPIE, ROBERT WILLIAM   123 CAROL RD - WINSTON SALEM NC 27106
53- 28 GILLIAM, JAMES WILLIAM 'JUNIOR'   D. OCTOBER 8, 1978 INGLEWOOD, CALIF.
67- 39 GILLIFORD, PAUL GANT   7 WOODLAND DR - MALVERN PA 19355
27- 40 GILLIS, GRANT   D. FEBRUARY 4, 1981 THOMASVILLE, ALA.
14- 72 GILMORE, ERNEST GROVER   D. NOVEMBER 25, 1919 SIOUX CITY, IA.
44- 49 GILMORE, LEONARD PRESTON   RR 2 BOX 213C - JONES OK 73049
68- 27 GILSON, HAROLD   OLD ADD: 1509 JULIE ST #B - BERKELEY CA 94703
15- 52 GINGRAS, JOSEPH ELZEAD JOHN   D. SEPTEMBER 6, 1947 JERSEY CITY, N.J.
14- 73 GINN, TINSLEY RUCKER   D. AUGUST 30, 1931 ATLANTA, GA.
48- 40 GINSBERG, MYRON NATHAN 'JOE'   243 COLDWAY DRIVE #B9 - PUNTA GORDA FL 33950
44- 50 GIONFRIDDO, ALBERT FRANCIS   64 BRISTOL PLACE - GOLETA CA 93117
53- 29 GIORDANO, THOMAS ARTHUR   1026 CARLL DR - BAYSHORE NY 11706
10- 59 GIRARD, CHARLES AUGUST   D. AUGUST 6, 1936 BROOKLYN, N. Y.
36- 31 GIULIANI, ANGELO JOHN   1985 NORFOLK AVE - ST PAUL MN 55116
62- 48 GIUSTI, DAVID JOHN   524 CLAIR DR - PITTSBURGH PA 15241
46- 33 GLADD, JAMES WALTER   D. NOVEMBER 8, 1977 LONG BEACH, CALIF.
83- 63 GLADDEN, CLIFTON DANIEL 'DAN'   888 BROOK GROVE LN - CUPERTINO CA 95014
61- 38 GLADDING, FRED EARL   4721 MACMONT CIR - POWELL TN 37819
44- 51 GLADU, ROLAND EDWIN   OLD ADD: 4368 BERRIE - MONTREAL QUEBEC

20- 38 GLAISER, JOHN BURKE   D. MARCH 7, 1959 HOUSTON, TEX.
25- 39 GLASS, THOMAS JOSEPH   D. DECEMBER 5, 1981 GREENSBORO, N. C.
13- 65 GLAVENICH, LUKE FRANK   D. MAY 22, 1935 STOCKTON, CALIF.
49- 25 GLAVIANO, THOMAS GIATANO   23905 HITCHING POST RD - SONORA CA 95370
87- 53 GLAVINE, THOMAS MICHAEL   89 TREBLE COVE ROAD - BILLERICA MA 01862
20- 39 GLAZNER, CHARLES FRANKLIN   850 MAURY RD BOX 4 - ORLANDO FL 32804
20- 40 GLEASON, JOSEPH PAUL   18 EXCHANGE - PHELPS NY 14532
63- 44 GLEASON, ROY WILLIAM   1115 WILCOX AVE - MONTEREY PARK CA 91754
16- 32 GLEASON, WILLIAM PATRICK   D. JANUARY 9, 1957 HOLYOKE, MASS.
79- 40 GLEATON, JERRY DON   121 GARMAN DR - EARLY TX 76801
36- 32 GLEESON, JAMES JOSEPH   545 EAST 129TH TER - KANSAS CITY MO 64145
19- 32 GLEICH, FRANK ELMER   D. MARCH 27, 1949 COLUMBUS, O.
20- 41 GLENN, BURDETTE 'BOB'   D. JUNE 3, 1977 RICHMOND, CALIF.
15- 53 GLENN, HARRY MELVILLE   D. OCTOBER 12, 1918 ST. PAUL, MINN.
60- 39 GLENN, JOHN   32 EDGEWATER BEACH APTS - BEVERLY NJ 08010
32- 31 GLENN, JOSEPH CHARLES   D. MAY 6, 1985 TUNKHANNOCK, PA.
30- 25 GLIATTO, SALVADOR MICHAEL   6031D ARBOLEDA WAY - DALLAS TX 75248
14- 74 GLOCKSON, NORMAN STANLEY   D. AUGUST 5, 1955 MAYWOOD, ILL.
39- 43 GLOSSOP, ALBAN   120 SOUTH RUBY LANE - FAIRVIEW HEIGHTS IL 62208

```
75- 44  GLYNN, EDWARD PAUL                        157 SAN CARLOS STREET - TOMS RIVER NJ 08757
49- 26  GLYNN, WILLIAM VINCENT                    6916 51ST - SAN DIEGO CA 92120
74- 41  GODBY, DANNY RAY                          RR 2 BOX 28A - CHAPMANVILLE WV 25508
72- 36  GODDARD, JOSEPH HAROLD                    302 RIDGE PARK DR - BECKLEY WV 25801
22- 45  GOEBEL, EDWIN                             D. AUGUST 12, 1959 BROOKLYN, N. Y.
60- 40  GOETZ, JOHN HARDY                         3253 MYDDLETON - TROY MI 48084
72- 37  GOGGIN, CHARLES FRANCIS                   6008 ROBERT E. LEE DR - NASHVILLE TN 37215
70- 49  GOGOLEWSKI, WILLIAM JOSEPH                1522 GRAHAM AVE - OSHKOSH WI 54901
60- 41  GOLDEN, JAMES EDWARD                      8630 SW 10TH - TOPEKA KS 66606
10- 60  GOLDEN, ROY KRAMER                        D. OCTOBER 4, 1961 NORWOOD, O.
28- 39  GOLDMAN, JONAH JOHN                       D. AUGUST 17, 1980 PALM BEACH, FLA.
49- 27  GOLDSBERRY, GORDON FREDERICK              22772 BAY FRONT LN - LAKE FOREST CA 92630
26- 31  GOLDSMITH, HAROLD EUGENE                  %GENE GOLDSMITH,8 GRANDVIEW TER - ESSEX CT 06426
32- 32  GOLDSTEIN, ISADORE                        944 FLANDERS T - DELRAY BEACH FL 33446
43- 53  GOLDSTEIN, LESLIE ELMER 'LONNIE'          6516 SABROSA CT WEST - FORT WORTH TX 76133
62- 49  GOLDY, PURNAL WILLIAM                     1318 CHERRYVILLE RD - LITTLETON CO 80120
41- 37  GOLETZ, STANLEY                           14513 SOUTH ROBINSON - OKLAHOMA CITY OK 73170
49- 28  GOLIAT, MIKE MITCHEL                      2650 GREEN LAWN DR - SEVEN HILLS OH 44131
72- 38  GOLTZ, DAVID ALLAN                        RR 6 BOX 230 - FERGUS FALLS MN 56537
22- 46  GOLVIN, WALTER GEORGE                     D. JUNE 11, 1973 GARDENA, CALIF.
35- 36  GOMEZ, JOSE LUIS RODRIGUEZ 'CHILE'        GONZALEZ DE COSIO 359-3 - MEXICO CITY D.F. MEX.
74- 42  GOMEZ, LUIS JOSE                          676 CHESTERFIELD DRIVE - LAWRENCEVILLE GA 30245
44- 52  GOMEZ, PRESTON MARTINEZ                   23 BELCOURT DRIVE SOUTH - NEWPORT BEACH CA 92660
84- 40  GOMEZ, RANDALL SCOTT 'ROCKY'              801 BARNESON AVE - SAN MATEO CA 94402
53- 30  GOMEZ, RUBEN                              T2-8 IQUAZA PARK GARDENS-RIO PIEDRAS PR 00928
30- 26  GOMEZ, VERNON LOUIS 'LEFTY'               26 SAN BENITO WAY - NOVATO CA 94947
60- 42  GONDER, JESSE LEMAR                       5937 WHITNEY ST - OAKLAND CA 94609
79- 41  GONZALES, DANIEL DAVID                    OLD ADD: 12319 CULLMAN AVE-WHITTIER CA 90604
18- 22  GONZALES, EUSEBIO MIGUEL                  D. FEBRUARY 14, 1976 HAVANA, CUBA
37- 42  GONZALES, JOE MADRID                      30715 COCOS PALM AVE - HOMELAND CA 92348
77- 59  GONZALES, JULIO CESAR                     BO. RIO CANAS, BOX 86 - CAGUAS PR 00625
49- 29  GONZALES, JULIO ENRIQUE                   OLD ADD: CALIXTO GARCIA 37 - ORIENTE CUBA
84- 41  GONZALES, RENE ADRIAN                     755 ORANGEWOOD - COVINA CA 91723
55- 48  GONZALES, WENCESLAO O'REILLY 'VINCE'      D. MARCH 11, 1981 CIUDAD DEL CARMEN,CAMP.MEX
60- 43  GONZALEZ, ANDRES ANTONIO 'TONY'           8011 SW 196TH TER - MIAMI FL 33189
84- 42  GONZALEZ, DENIO MARIANO                   CALLE SAN LUIS #131, GUALEY - SANTO DOMINGO DOM. REP.
72- 39  GONZALEZ, JOSE FERNANDO                   URB VISTA ANGEL CALLE 4-A-48-ARECIBO PR 00612
85- 41  GONZALEZ, JOSE RAFAEL                     CALLE ANTERA MOTA #35 - PUERTO PLATA DOMINICAN REP.
12- 67  GONZALEZ, MIGUEL ANGEL CORDERO 'MIKE'     D. FEBRUARY 19, 1977 HAVANA, CUBA
76- 35  GONZALEZ, ORLANDO EUGENE                  OLD ADD: 2352 SW 26TH LN - MIAMI FL
63- 45  GONZALEZ, PEDRO                           104 GEN CABRAL - SAN PEDRO DE MACORIS DOM. REP.
29- 44  GOOCH, CHARLES FURMAN                     D. MAY 30, 1982 LANHAM, MD.
21- 35  GOOCH, JOHN BEVERLEY                      D. MAY 15, 1975 NASHVILLE, TENN.
15- 54  GOOCH, LEE CURRIN                         D. MAY 18, 1966 RALEIGH, N.C.
10- 61  GOOD, RALPH NELSON                        D. NOVEMBER 24, 1965 WATERVILLE, ME.
28- 40  GOODELL, JOHN HENRY WILLIAM 'BILL'        10 LITTLE DRIVE, BELLA VISTA - BENTONVILLE AR 72714
84- 43  GOODEN, DWIGHT EUGENE                     3101 EAST ELM ST - TAMPA FL 33610
35- 37  GOODMAN, IVAL RICHARD                     D. NOVEMBER 25, 1984 CINCINNATI, O.
47- 39  GOODMAN, WILLIAM DALE                     D. OCTOBER 1, 1984 SARASOTA, FLA.
70- 50  GOODSON, JAMES EDWARD 'ED'                RR 2 BOX 12-0 - INDEPENDENCE VA 24348
14- 75  GOODWIN, CLAIRE VERNON 'PEP'              D. FEBRUARY 15, 1972 OAKLAND, CALIF.
75- 45  GOODWIN, DANNY KAY                        2001 NORTH BOURLAND - PEORIA IL 61601
48- 41  GOODWIN, JAMES PATRICK                    11533 FRANCETTA LN - ST. LOUIS MO 63138
16- 33  GOODWIN, MARVIN MARDO                     D. OCTOBER 21, 1925 HOUSTON, TES.
46- 34  GOOLSBY, RAYMOND DANIEL                   OLD ADD: 1101 LEE RD #3 - WINTER PARK FL
65- 33  GOOSSEN, GREGORY BRYANT                   12321 BLIX ST - NORTH HOLLYWOOD CA 91607
55- 49  GORBOUS, GLEN EDWARD                      1511 CAYUGA DRIVE NW - CALGARY ALBERTA T2L ON1 CAN.
86- 57  GORDON, DONALD THOMAS                     87-13 95TH STREET - WOODHAVEN NY 11421
38- 31  GORDON, JOSEPH LOWELL                     D. APRIL 14, 1978 SACRAMENTO, CALIF.
77- 60  GORDON, MICHAEL WILLIAM                   161 BISHOP ST - BROCKTON MA 02401
41- 38  GORDON, SIDNEY                            D. JUNE 17, 1975 NEW YORK, N.Y.
21- 36  GORDONIER, RAYMOND CHARLES                D. NOVEMBER 15, 1960 ROCHESTER, N. Y.
54- 33  GORIN, CHARLES PERRY                      2617 FISET DR - AUSTIN TX 78731
77- 61  GORINSKI, ROBERT JOHN                     BOX 133 - CALUMET PA 15621
52- 37  GORMAN, HERBERT ALLEN                     D. APRIL 5, 1953 SAN DIEGO, CAL.
37- 43  GORMAN, HOWARD PAUL                       D. APRIL 29, 1984 HARRISBURG, PA.
52- 38  GORMAN, THOMAS ALOYSIUS                   474 WEST VLY STRM BLVD - VALLEY STREAM NY 11581
39- 44  GORMAN, THOMAS DAVID                      D. AUGUST 11, 1986 CLOSTER, N. J.
81- 45  GORMAN, THOMAS PATRICK                    2523 NORTH BOONES FERRY RD - WOODBURN OR 97071
41- 39  GORNICKI, HENRY FRANK                     5510 TAMBERLANE DRIVE - PALM BEACH GARDENS FL 33418
40- 26  GORSICA, JOHN JOSEPH PERRY                BOX 1518 - BECKLEY WV 25801
57- 23  GORYL, JOHN ALBERT                        3282 YOTHERS RD - APOPKA FL 32703
63- 46  GOSGER, JAMES CHARLES                     1527 LYONS STREET - PORT HURON MI 48060
21- 37  GOSLIN, LEON ALLEN 'GOOSE'                D. MAY 15, 1971 BRIDGETON, N. J.
```

```
62- 50  GOSS, HOWARD WAYNE                         11511 SANTA GERTRUDES #20 - WHITTIER CA 90604
72- 40  GOSSAGE, RICHARD MICHAEL 'GOOSE'           10565 VIACHA WAY - SAN DIEGO CA 92124
13- 66  GOSSETT, JOHN STAR 'DICK'                  D. OCTOBER 6, 1962 MASSILLON, O.
60- 44  GOTAY, JULIO ENRIQUE                       JUAN JOSE CARTAGENA ST #L34 - PONCE PR 00731
82- 49  GOTT, JAMES WILLIAM                        1840 LOS ROBLES AVE - SAN MARINO CA 91108
12- 68  GOULAIT, THEODORE LEE                      D. JULY 15, 1936 ST. CLAIR, MICH.
16- 34  GOULD, ALBERT FRANK                        D. AUGUST 8, 1982 SAN JOSE, CALIF.
44- 53  GOULISH, NICHOLAS EDWARD                   D. MAY 15, 1984 YOUNGSTOWN, O.
10- 62  GOWDY, HARRY 'HANK'                        D. AUGUST 1, 1966 COLUMBUS, O.
72- 41  GOWELL, LAWRENCE CLYDE                     45 SEVENTH ST - AUBURN ME 04210
69- 69  GRABARKEWITZ, BILLY CORDELL                P.O. BOX 670685 - DALLAS TX 75367
58- 38  GRABER, RODNEY BLAINE                      4674 MOUNT ARMET DR - SAN DIEGO CA 92117
29- 45  GRABOWSKI, ALFONS FRANCIS                  D. OCTOBER 29, 1966 MEMPHIS, N. Y.
24- 43  GRABOWSKI, JOHN PATRICK                    D. MAY 23, 1946 ALBANY, N. Y.
32- 33  GRABOWSKI, REGINALD JOHN                   D. APRIL 2, 1955 SYRACUSE, N. Y.
38- 32  GRACE, JOSEPH LAVERNE                      D. SEPTEMBER 18, 1969 MURPHYSBORO, ILL.
78- 52  GRACE, MICHAEL LEE                         3514 SHELBY - PONTIAC MI 48054
29- 46  GRACE, ROBERT EARL                         D. DECEMBER 22, 1980 PHOENIX, ARIZ.
13- 67  GRAF, FREDERICK GOTTLIEB                   D. OCTOBER 4, 1979 CHATTANOOGA, TENN.
57- 24  GRAFF, MILTON EDWARD                       3602 TANGLEWOOD DRIVE - BRYAN TX 77802
34- 41  GRAHAM, ARTHUR WILLIAM 'SKINNY'            D. JULY 10, 1967 ARLINGTON, MASS.
10- 63  GRAHAM, BERT                               D. JUNE 17, 1971 COTTONWOOD, ARIZ.
79- 42  GRAHAM, DANIEL JAY                         BOX 728 - WINKELMAN AZ 85298
14- 76  GRAHAM, DAWSON FRANK 'TINY'                D. DECEMBER 29, 1962 NASHVILLE, TENN.
46- 35  GRAHAM, JOHN BERNARD                       1521 INTERLACHEN #258K - SEAL BEACH CA 90740
24- 44  GRAHAM, KYLE                               D. DECEMBER 1, 1973 OAK GROVE, ALA.
83- 64  GRAHAM, LEE WILLIAM                        OLD ADD: BOX 1012 - BELLEVIEW FL 32620
22- 47  GRAHAM, ROY VINCENT                        D. APRIL 26, 1933 MANILLA, PHILLIPINES
63- 47  GRAHAM, WAYNE LEON                         13218 SOUTH THORNTREE - HOUSTON TX 77015
66- 39  GRAHAM, WILLIAM ALBERT                     RR 2 BOX 275 - FLEMINGSBURG KY 41041
68- 28  GRAMLY, BERT THOMAS 'TOM'                  16485 REDWOOD CIR, RR 1 - MCKINNEY TX 75069
54- 34  GRAMMAS, ALEXANDER PETER                   3432 OAKDALE DR - BIRMINGHAM AL 35223
27- 41  GRAMPP, HENRY ERCHARDT                     D. MARCH 24, 1986 NEW YORK, N. Y.
68- 29  GRANGER, WAYNE ALLEN                       BOX 134, ALDRICH AVE - HUNTINGTON MA 01050
23- 53  GRANT, GEORGE ADDISON                      D. MARCH 25, 1986 MONTGOMERY, ALA.
42- 45  GRANT, JAMES CHARLES                       D. JULY 8, 1970 ROCHESTER, MINN.
23- 54  GRANT, JAMES RONALD                        D. NOVEMBER 30, 1985 DES MOINES, IOWA
58- 39  GRANT, JAMES TIMOTHY 'MUDCAT'              1020 SOUTH DUNSMUIR - LOS ANGELES CA 90019
84- 44  GRANT, MARK ANDREW                         123 FAIRLANE DR - JOLIET IL 60435
83- 65  GRANT, THOMAS RAYMOND                      BOX 113 - MENDON MA 01756
22- 48  GRANTHAM, GEORGE FARLEY                    D. MARCH 16, 1954 KINGMAN, ARIZ.
83- 66  GRAPENTHIN, RICHARD RAY                    RURAL ROUTE 1 - LINN GROVE IA 51033
```

```
48- 42  GRASMICK, LOUIS JUNIOR                     6715 QUAD AVE - BALTIMORE MD 21237
46- 36  GRASSO, NEWTON MICHAEL 'MICKEY'            D. OCTOBER 15, 1975 MIAMI FLA.
45- 39  GRATE, DONALD                              1245 NW 203RD ST - MIAMI FL 33169
26- 32  GRAVES, JOSEPH EBENEZER                    D. DECEMBER 22, 1980 SALEM, MASS.
27- 42  GRAVES, SAMUEL SIDNEY 'SID'                D. DECEMBER 26, 1983 BIDDEFORD, ME.
64- 37  GRAY, DAVID ALEXANDER                      539 BRINKER AVE - OGDEN UT 84404
77- 62  GRAY, GARY GEORGE                          BOX 98 - LAPLACE LA 70068
54- 35  GRAY, JOHN LEONARD                         6320 SW 138TH COURT #206 - MIAMI FL 33183
82- 50  GRAY, LORENZO                              3263 PALM AVE #A - LYNWOOD CA 90262
37- 44  GRAY, MILTON MARSHALL                      D. JUNE 30, 1969 QUINCY, FLA.
45- 40  GRAY, PETER                                203 PHILLIPS ST - NANTICOKE PA 18634
58- 40  GRAY, RICHARD BENJAMIN                     503 SOUTH HAMPTON - ANAHEIM CA 92804
24- 45  GRAY, SAMUEL DAVID                         D. APRIL 16, 1953 MCKINNEY, TEX.
12- 69  GRAY, STANLEY OSCAR                        D. OCTOBER 11, 1964 SNYDER, TEX.
46- 37  GRAY, THEODORE GLENN                       21 EAST WASHINGTON - CLARKSTON MI 48016
59- 34  GRBA, ELI                                  332 E. 17TH - VANCOUVER BC V7L 2V9 CAN.
54- 36  GREASON, WILLIAM HENRY                     4536 HILLMAN DR SW - BIRMINGHAM AL 35221
84- 45  GREEN, CHRISTOPHER DEWAYNE                 3740 59TH AVE WEST - BRADENTON FL 33507
81- 46  GREEN, DAVID ALEJANDRO                     COLINIA MANAGUA GRUPO H#47 - MANAGUA NICARAGUA C.A.
59- 35  GREEN, ELIJAH JERRY 'PUMPSIE'              BERKELEY H.S. 2246 MILVA-BERKELEY CA 94704
59- 36  GREEN, FRED ALLAN                          BOX 161 - TITUSVILE NJ 08560
86- 58  GREEN, GARY ALLEN                          562 SOUTH TRENTON AVENUE - PITTSBURGH PA 15221
57- 25  GREEN, GENE LEROY                          D. MAY 23, 1981 ST. LOUIS, MO.
60- 45  GREEN, GEORGE DALLAS                       1060 W. ADDISON ST - CHICAGO IL 60613
35- 38  GREEN, HARVEY GEORGE                       D. JULY 24, 1970 FRANKLIN, LA.
24- 46  GREEN, JOSEPH HENRY                        D. FEBRUARY 4, 1972 BRYN MAWR, PA.
28- 41  GREEN, JULIUS FOUST 'JUNE'                 D. MARCH 19, 1974 GLENDORA, CALIF.
57- 26  GREEN, LEONARD CHARLES                     18693 SUNSET ST - DETROIT MI 48234
63- 48  GREEN, RICHARD LARRY                       525 38TH - RAPID CITY SD 57701
30- 27  GREENBERG, HENRY BENJAMIN                  D. SEPTEMBER 4, 1986 BEVERLY HILLS, CALIF.
79- 43  GREENE, ALTAR ALPHONSE                     18294 MARLOWE - DETROIT MI 48235
24- 47  GREENE, NELSON GEORGE                      D. APRIL 6, 1983 LEBANON, PA.
```

24- 48	GREENFIELD, KENT	D. MARCH 14, 1978 GUTHRIE, KY.
52- 39	GREENGRASS, JAMES RAYMOND	2930 OCTAVIA CIR - MARIETTA GA 30062
85- 42	GREENWELL, MICHAEL LEWIS	954 EAST HYACINTH ST - NORTH FORT MYERS FL 33903
54- 37	GREENWOOD, ROBERT CHANDLER	35800 MOLINA CT - FREMONT CA 94536
77- 63	GREER, BRIAN KEITH	914 CARLSON DR - BREA CA 92621
13- 68	GREGG, DAVID CHARLES	D. NOVEMBER 12, 1965 CLARKSTON, WASH.
43- 54	GREGG, HAROLD DANA	KEOUGHS RR 1 #1 - BISHOP CA 93514
11- 56	GREGG, SYLVEANUS AUGUSTUS 'VEAN'	D. JULY 29, 1964 ABERDEEN, WASH.
87- 54	GREGG, WILLIAM THOMAS	3924 OLD VINEYARD ROAD #35 - WINSTON SALEM NC 27104
12- 70	GREGORY, FRANK ERNST	D. NOVEMBER 5, 1955 BELOIT, WIS.
64- 38	GREGORY, GROVER LEROY 'LEE'	6456 NORTH TEILMAN - FRESNO CA 93705
11- 57	GREGORY, HOWARD WATTERSON	D. MAY 30, 1970 TULSA, OKLA.
32- 34	GREGORY, PAUL EDWIN	P.O. BOX 921 - STARKVILLE MS 39759
71- 39	GREIF, WILLIAM BRILEY	807 EAST 31ST - AUSTIN TX 78705
40- 27	GREMP, LOUIS EDWARD 'BUDDY'	205 FLOYD AVENUE #2 - MODESTO CA 95350
19- 33	GREVELL, WILLIAM	D. JUNE 21, 1923 SPRINGFIELD TWP., PA.
70- 51	GRICH, ROBERT ANTHONY	206 PROSPECT AVE - LONG BEACH CA 90803
20- 42	GRIESENBECK, CARLOS PHILIPPE TIMOTHY	D. MARCH 25, 1953 SAN ANTONIO, TEX.
70- 52	GRIEVE, THOMAS ALAN	3206 HERITAGE CT - ARLINGTON TX 76016
46- 38	GRIFFETH, LEON CLIFFORD	BOX 335 - PATTERSON NY 12563
73- 53	GRIFFEY, GEORGE KENNETH 'KEN'	5385 CROSS BRIDGE DR - WESTCHESTER OH 45069
76- 36	GRIFFIN, ALFREDO CLAUDINO	B#3 B HATOMAYOR ING CONS-SAN PEDRO DE MACORIS DOM. REP.
70- 53	GRIFFIN, DOUGLAS LEE	6005 GREENLEAF CIRCLE - WINTER HAVEN FL 33880
17- 32	GRIFFIN, FRANCIS ARTHUR 'PUG'	D. OCTOBER 12, 1951 COLORADO SPRINGS COLO.
19- 34	GRIFFIN, IVY MOORE	D. AUGUST 25, 1957 GAINESVILLE, FLA.
11- 58	GRIFFIN, JAMES LINTON 'HANK'	D. FEBRUARY 11, 1950 TERRELL, TEX.
28- 42	GRIFFIN, MARTIN JOHN	D. NOVEMBER 19, 1951 LOS ANGELES, CAL.
79- 44	GRIFFIN, MICHAEL LEROY	1620 GROVE AVE - WOODLAND CA 95695
14- 77	GRIFFIN, PATRICK RICHARD	D. JUNE 7, 1927 YOINGSTOWN, O.
69- 70	GRIFFIN, THOMAS JAMES	13147 AVENIDA LAVELENCIA - POWAY CA 92064
22- 49	GRIFFITH, BARTHOLOMEW JOSEPH	D. MAY 5, 1973 BISHOP, CALIF.
63- 49	GRIFFITH, ROBERT DERRELL	515 1/2 WEST TEXAS - ANADARKO OK 73005
13- 69	GRIFFITH, THOMAS HERMAN	D. APRIL 13, 1967 CINCINNATI, O.
56- 38	GRIGGS, HAROLD LLOYD	2781 NE SECOND AVENUE - POMPANO BEACH FL 33064
23- 55	GRIGSBY, DENVER CLARENCE	D. NOVEMBER 10, 1973 SAPULPA, OKLA.

66- 40	GRILLI, GUIDO JOHN	4636 LORECE - MEMPHIS TN 38117
75- 46	GRILLI, STEPHEN JOSEPH	3040 WALPOLE LN - BALDWINSVILLE NY 13027
54- 38	GRIM, ROBERT ANTON	7118 CODY STREET - SHAWNEE MISSION KS 66214
16- 35	GRIMES, BURLEIGH ARLAND	D. DECEMBER 6, 1985 CLEAR LAKE, WIS.
31- 32	GRIMES, EDWARD ADELBERT	D. OCTOBER 4, 1974 CHICAGO, ILL.
38- 33	GRIMES, OSCAR RAY JR.	25151 BROOKPARD RD #203 - NORTH OLMSTED OH 44070
20- 43	GRIMES, OSCAR RAY SR.	D. MAY 25, 1953 MINERVA, O.
20- 44	GRIMES, ROY AUSTIN	D. SEPTEMBER 13, 1954 HANOVERTON, O.
16- 36	GRIMM, CHARLES JOHN	D. NOVEMBER 15, 1983 SCOTTSDALE, ARIZ.
51- 34	GRIMSLEY, ROSS ALBERT	1538 FRAYSER BLVD - MEMPHIS TN 38127
71- 40	GRIMSLEY, ROSS ALBERT II	39 JUDGES LN - TOWSON MD 21204
12- 71	GRINER, DONALD DEXTER 'DAN'	D. JUNE 3, 1950 BISHOPVILLE, S.C.
34- 42	GRISSOM, LEE THEO	BOX 875 - CORNING CA 96021
46- 39	GRISSOM, MARVIN EDWARD	13975 NOBLE WAY - RED BLUFF CA 96080
52- 40	GROAT, RICHARD MORROW	320 BEACH ST - PITTSBURGH PA 15218
56- 39	GROB, CONRAD GEORGE	5047 ENCHANTED VALLEY RD - CROSS PLAINS WI 53528
41- 40	GRODZICKI, JOHN	5927 RIVERSIDE DRIVE - DAYTONA BEACH FL 32019
12- 72	GROH, HENRY KNIGHT 'HEINIE'	D. AUGUST 22, 1968 CINCINNATI,O.
19- 35	GROH, LEWIS CARL	D. OCTOBER 20, 1960 ROCHESTER, N. Y.
41- 41	GROMEK, STEPHEN JOSEPH	21455 CORSAUT - BIRMINGHAM MI 48010
55- 50	GROSS, DONALD JOHN	9859 BIRDIE DRIVE - STANWOOD MI 49346
25- 40	GROSS, EWELL 'TURKEY'	D. JANUARY 22, 1936 DALLAS, TEX.
73- 54	GROSS, GREGORY EUGENE	16 RABBIT RUN ROAD - MALVERN PA 19355
83- 67	GROSS, KEVIN FRANK	402 FOURTH ST - FILLMORE CA 93015
76- 37	GROSS, WAYNE DALE	45 LEONARD COURT - DANVILLE CA 94526
30- 28	GROSSKLOS, HOWARD HOFFMAN 'HOWDIE'	310 LLWYD'S LANE - VERO BEACH FL 32960
52- 41	GROSSMAN, HARLEY JOSEPH	1032 OAKWOOD LN - EVANSVILLE IN 47710
63- 50	GROTE, GERALD WAYNE	148-26 WILLOW BEND - SAN ANTONIO TX 78232
47- 40	GROTH, ERNEST WILLIAM	BLACKHAWK-NEGLY RD - BEAVER FALLS PA 15010
46- 40	GROTH, JOHN THOMAS	177 QUEENS LN - PALM BEACH FL 33480
40- 28	GROVE, ORVAL LEROY	2743 POPE AVE - SACRAMENTO CA 95821
25- 41	GROVE, ROBERT MOSES 'LEFTY'	D. MAY 22, 1975 NORWALK, O.
13- 70	GROVER, CHARLES BERT	D. MAY 24, 1971 EMMETT TWP., CALHOUN CO.,MICH
16- 37	GROVER, ROY ARTHUR	D. FEBRUARY 7, 1978 MILWAUKIE, ORE.
12- 73	GRUBB, HARVEY HARRISON	D. JANUARY 25, 1970 CORPUS CHRISTI, TEX.
72- 42	GRUBB, JOHN MAYWOOD	3920 COGBILL RD - RICHMOND VA 23234
20- 45	GRUBBS, THOMAS DILLARD	D. JANUARY 28, 1986 MOUNT STERLING, KY.
31- 33	GRUBE, FRANKLIN THOMAS	D. JULY 2, 1945 NEW YORK, N. Y.
84- 46	GRUBER, KELLY WAYNE	1205 FALCON LEDGE - AUSTIN TX 78746

55- 51 GRUNWALD, ALFRED HENRY	7120 BOTHWELL RD - RESEDA CA 91335
38- 34 GRYSKA, SIGMUND STANLEY	4527 SOUTH DRAKE-CHICAGO IL 60632
61- 39 GRZENDA, JOSEPH CHARLES	GOULDSBORO PA 18424
82- 51 GUANTE, CECILIO (MAGALLANE)	JALISCO 67 SIMON BOLIVAR-SANTO DOMINGO DOMINICAN REP.
84- 47 GUBICZA, MARK STEVEN	593 MONASTERY AVE - PHILADELPHIA PA 19128
29- 47 GUDAT, MARVIN JOHN	D. MARCH 2, 1954 LOS ANGELES, CAL.
37- 45 GUERRA, FERMIN ROMERO 'MIKE'	4025 NW 3RD ST - MIAMI FL 33126
73- 55 GUERRERO, MARIO MIGUEL	CALLE DUARTE #450 - SANTO DOMINGO DOMINICAN REP.
78- 53 GUERRERO, PEDRO	535 S. PLYMOUTH BLVD - LOS ANGELES CA 90020
84- 48 GUETTERMAN, ARTHUR LEE	P.O. BOX 1594 - KENT WA 98032
75- 47 GUIDRY, RONALD AMES	109 CONWAY - LAFAYETTE LA 70507
85- 43 GUILLEN, OSWALDO JOSE	CLE SAN JOSE #52,EL RODEO DEL TUY-MIRANDO VENEZ
64- 39 GUINDON, ROBERT JOSEPH	THORNHILL INN - JACKSON NH 03846
68- 30 GUINN, DRANNON EUGENE 'SKIP'	6060 MONTEVERDE DRIVE - SAN JOSE CA 95120
46- 41 GUINTINI, BENJAMIN JOHN	OLD ADD: 735 SHADOW RIDGE #4 - ROSEVILLE CA 95678
40- 29 GUISE, WITT ORISON	D. AUGUST 13, 1968 NORTH LITTLE ROCK, ARK.
16- 38 GUISTO, LOUIS JOSEPH	2037 WAVERLY - NAPA CA 94558
78- 54 GULDEN, BRADLEY LEE	BOX 254 (LIME STREET) - CARVER MN 55315
70- 54 GULLETT, DONALD EDWARD	RURAL ROUTE 2 - MALONETON KY 41158
23- 56 GULLEY, THOMAS JEFFERSON	D. NOVEMBER 24, 1966 ST. CHARLES, ARK.
30- 29 GULLIC, TEDD JOSEPH	BOX 703 - WEST PLAINS MO 65775
79- 45 GULLICKSON, WILLIAM LEE	OLD ADD: BOX 6263 - CHAMPAIGN IL 61820
82- 52 GULLIVER, GLENN JAMES	8123 CORTLAND - ALLEN PARK MI 48101
35- 39 GUMBERT, HARRY EDWARD	BOX 377 - WIMBERLEY TX 78676
82- 53 GUMPERT, DAVID LAWRENCE	921 CHAMBERS ST - SOUTH HAVEN MI 49090
36- 33 GUMPERT, RANDALL PENNINGTON	MONOCACY STATION PA 19542
16- 39 GUNKEL, WOODROW WILLIAM 'RED'	D. APRIL 19, 1954 NORTH CHICAGO, ILL.
11- 59 GUNNING, HYLAND	D. MARCH 28, 1975 TOGUS, ME.
70- 55 GURA, LARRY CYRIL	9 NW CIRCLE DR - JOLIET IL 60432
11- 60 GUST, ERNEST HERMAN FRANK	D. OCTOBER 26, 1945 MAUPIN, ORE.
39- 45 GUSTINE, FRANK WILLIAM	1130 GREENTREE RD - PITTSBURGH PA 15220
72- 43 GUTH, CHARLES HENRY 'BUCKY'	202 MORRIS DR - SALISBURY MD 21801
67- 40 GUTIERREZ, CESAR DARIO	PINTO A MISERIA #100 - CARACAS VENEZUELA S.A.
83- 68 GUTIERREZ, JOAQUIN FERNANDO	AMBERES 3ER CALLEJON # 29-35-CARTAGENA COLOMBIA S.A.
36- 34 GUTTERIDGE, DONALD JOSEPH	804 LAKEVIEW DR - PITTSBURG KS 66762
85- 44 GUZMAN, JOSE ALBERTO	BO. PLAYA #28 - SANTA ISABEL PR 00757
69- 71 GUZMAN, SANTIAGO DONOVAN	ENS RESTAUROSIN M4TA#12-SAN PEDRO DE MACORIS DOM. REP.
81- 47 GWOSDZ, DOUGLAS WAYNE	14503 ROYAL HILL DR - HOUSTON TX 77083
82- 54 GWYNN, ANTHONY KEITH	3524 DELTA - LONG BEACH CA 90810
87- 55 GWYNN, CHRISTOPHER KARLTON	3524 DELTA AVENUE - LONG BEACH CA 90810
33- 21 GYSELMAN, RICHARD RENALD	5212 54TH AV SOUTH - SEATTLE WA 98118
37- 46 HAAS, BERTHOLD JOHN	4604 KENSINGTON AVE - TAMPA FL 33629
15- 55 HAAS, BRUNO PHILIP	D. JUNE 5, 1952 SARASOTA, FLA.
76- 38 HAAS, BRYAN EDMUND 'MOOSE'	9961 EAST DOUBLETREE RANCH RD - SCOTTSDALE AZ 85258
57- 27 HAAS, GEORGE EDWIN 'EDDIE'	100 HILLMONT DR, RR 10 - PADUCAH KY 42001
25- 42 HAAS, GEORGE WILLIAM 'MULE'	D. JUNE 30, 1974 NEW ORLEANS, LA.
51- 35 HABENICHT, ROBERT JULIUS	D. DECEMBER 24, 1980 RICHMOND, VA.
85- 45 HABYAN, JOHN GABRIEL	122 PLUNKETT ST - BRENTWOOD NY 11717
32- 35 HACK, STANLEY CAMFIELD	D. DECEMBER 15, 1979 DIXON, ILL.
71- 41 HACKER, RICHARD WARREN	930 EAST MAIN - BELLEVILLE IL 62220
48- 43 HACKER, WARREN LOUIS	BOX 41 - LENZBURG IL 62255
52- 42 HADDIX, HARVEY	4001 VERNON ASHBURY RD-SOUTH VIENNA OH 45369
26- 33 HADLEY, IRVING DARIUS 'BUMP'	D. FEBRUARY 15,1963 LYNN, MASS.
58- 41 HADLEY, KENT WILLIAM	549 HYDE - POCATELLO ID 83201
15- 56 HAEFFNER, WILLIAM BERNHARD	D. JANUARY 27, 1982 DELAWARE CO., PA.
43- 55 HAEFNER, MILTON ARNOLD 'MICKEY'	504 JACKSON-NEW ATHENS IL 62264
24- 49 HAFEY, CHARLES JAMES 'CHICK'	D. JULY 2, 1973 CALISTOGA, CAL.
35- 40 HAFEY, DANIEL ALBERT 'BUD'	D. JULY 27, 1986 SACRAMENTO, CALIF.
39- 46 HAFEY, THOMAS FRANCIS	7747 TERRACE DR - EL CERRITO CA 94532
11- 61 HAGEMAN, KURT MORITZ 'CASEY'	D. APRIL 1, 1964 NEW BEDFORD, PA.
83- 69 HAGEN, KEVIN EUGENE	OLD ADD: 15232 SE 272ND #15 - KENT WA 98031
68- 31 HAGUE, JOE CLARENCE	14027 FAIRWAY OAKS - SAN ANTONIO TX 78217
69- 72 HAHN, DONALD ANTONE	1046 BOISE DR - CAMPBELL CA 95008
52- 43 HAHN, FREDERICK ALOYS	D. AUGUST 16, 1984 VALHALLA, N.Y.
40- 30 HAHN, RICHARD FREDERICK	1616 ORIOLE AVE - ORLANDO FL 32803
19- 36 HAID, HAROLD AUGUSTINE	D. AUGUST 13, 1952 LOS ANGELES, CAL.
23- 57 HAINES, HENRY LUTHER 'HINKEY'	D. JANUARY 9, 1979 SHARON HILL, PA.
18- 23 HAINES, JESSE JOSEPH 'POP'	D. AUGUST 5, 1978 DAYTON, O.
73- 56 HAIRSTON, JERRY WAYNE	900 CARLSON COURT - NAPERVILLE IL 60540
69- 73 HAIRSTON, JOHN LOUIS	3612 4TH ST WEST - BIRMINGHAM AL 35207
51- 36 HAIRSTON, SAMUEL	3800 CENTERPLACE WEST - BIRMINGHAM AL 35207
13- 71 HAISLIP, JAMES CLIFTON	D. JANUARY 22, 1970 DALLAS, TEX.
41- 42 HAJDUK, CHESTER	6838 CONCORD LN-NILES IL 60648
19- 37 HALAS, GEORGE STANLEY	D. OCTOBER 31, 1983 CHICAGO, ILL.
31- 34 HALE, ARVEL ODELL	D. JUNE 9, 1980 EL DORADO, ARK.
14- 78 HALE, GEORGE WAGNER	D. NOVEMBER 1, 1945 WICHITA, KAN.
74- 43 HALE, JOHN STEVEN	2715 CLEMSON COURT - BAKERSFIELD CA 93306
55- 52 HALE, ROBERT HOUSTON	2919 W. SIBLEY - PARK RIDGE IL 60068
20- 46 HALE, SAMUEL DOUGLAS	D. SEPTEMBER 6, 1974 WHEELER, TEX.
15- 57 HALEY, RAYMOND TIMOTHY	D. OCTOBER 8, 1973 BRADENTON, FLA.
74- 44 HALICKI, EDWARD LOUIS	273 HICKORY ST - KEARNEY NJ 07032
81- 48 HALL, ALBERT	1628 SPAULDING RD - BIRMINGHAM AL 35211
86- 59 HALL, ANDREW CLARK 'DREW'	RR 1 BOX 195 - RUSH KY 41168
11- 62 HALL, HERBERT ERNEST	D. JULY 18, 1948 SEATTLE, WASH.
18- 24 HALL, HERBERT SILAS	D. JULY 1, 1970 FRESNO, CAL.
43- 56 HALL, IRVIN GLADSTONE	1153 DEANWOOD RD - BALTIMORE MD 21234
63- 51 HALL, JIMMIE RANDOLPH	4001 LADY MARIAN DRIVE - WILSON NC 27893
48- 44 HALL, JOHN SYLVESTER	300 BELL DR - MIDWEST CITY OK 73110
10- 64 HALL, MARCUS	D. FEBRUARY 24, 1915 JOPLIN, MO.
81- 49 HALL, MELVIN	RR 1 ROUTE 90 - CAYAGA NY 13034
52- 44 HALL, RICHARD WALLACE	2131 FOLKSTONE RD - TIMONIUM MD 21093
49- 30 HALL, ROBERT LEWIS	D. MARCH 12, 1983 ST. PETERSBURG, FLA.
68- 32 HALL, THOMAS EDWARD	3592 LILLIAN AVENUE - RIVERSIDE CA 92504
13- 72 HALL, WILLIAM BERNARD	D. AUGUST 15, 1947 NEWPORT, KY.
54- 39 HALL, WILLIAM LEE	D. JANUARY 1, 1986 MOULTRIE, GA.
25- 43 HALLAHAN, WILLIAM ANTHONY	D. JULY 8, 1981 BINGHAMTON, N.Y.
61- 40 HALLER, THOMAS FRANK	745 COLUMBIA DR - SAN MATEO CA 94402
40- 31 HALLETT, JACK PRICE	D. JUNE 11, 1982 TOLEDO, O.
16- 40 HALLIDAY, NEWTON REESE	D. APRIL 6, 1918 GREAT LAKES, ILL.

```
11- 63 HALLINAN, EDWARD S              D. AUGUST 24, 1940 SAN FRANCISCO, CALIF.
14- 79 HALT, ALVA WILLIAM             D. JANUARY 22, 1973 SANDUSKY, O.
22- 50 HAMANN, ELMER JOSEPH 'DOC'     D. JANUARY 11, 1973 MILWAUKEE, WIS.
71- 42 HAMBRIGHT, ROGER DEE           OLD ADD: 523 NORTH 39 TH ST - SPRINGFIELD OR
26- 34 HAMBY, JAMES SANFORD           1117 SOUTH 11TH ST - SPRINGFIELD IL 62703
72- 44 HAMILTON, DAVID EDWARD         9464 CHERRY HILLS LN - SAN RAMON CA 94583
11- 64 HAMILTON, EARL ANDREW          D. NOVEMBER 17, 1968 ANAHEIM, CALIF.
62- 51 HAMILTON, JACK EDWIN           HCR 2 BOX 1035 - HOLLISTER MO 65672
86- 60 HAMILTON, JEFFREY ROBERT       6216 KNOLLWOOD #172 - FLINT MI 48507
61- 41 HAMILTON, STEVE ABSHER         RR 5 - MOREHEAD KY 40351
52- 45 HAMILTON, THOMAS BALL          D. NOVEMBER 29, 1973 TYLER, TEX.
57- 28 HAMLIN, KENNETH LEE            TALL TIMBERS - CLIMAX MI 49034
33- 22 HAMLIN, LUKE DANIEL            D. FEBRUARY 18,1978 CLARE, MICH.
70- 56 HAMM, PETER WHITFIELD          525 LOCKHART BULCH RD - SANTA CRUZ CA 95060
81- 50 HAMMAKER, CHARLTON ATLEE       2739 STUBB BLUFF RD - KNOXVILLE TN 37932
82- 55 HAMMOND, STEVEN BEN            OLD ADD: 2555 FOX HALL LN - COLLEGE PARK GA 30349
15- 58 HAMMOND, WALTER CHARLES 'JACK' D. MARCH 4, 1942 KENOSHA, WIS.
44- 54 HAMNER, GRANVILLE WILBUR       401 EAST SHORE DRIVE - CLEARWATER FL 33515
46- 42 HAMNER, RALPH CONANT           BOX 236 - BRADLEY AR 71826
45- 41 HAMNER, WESLEY GARVIN 'GAR'    RR 2 BOX 91 - MECHANICSVILLE VA 23111
74- 45 HAMPTON, ISAAC BERNARD 'IKE'   1604 LEE ST - CAMDEN SC 29020
55- 53 HAMRIC, ODBERT HERMAN 'BERT'   D. AUGUST 8, 1984 SPRINGBORO, O.
43- 57 HAMRICK, RAYMOND BERNARD       3125 SHANE DRIVE - RICHMOND CA 94806
40- 32 HANCKEN, MORRIS MEDLOCK 'BUDDY' BOX 288 - HOUSTON TX 77001
49- 31 HANCOCK, FRED JAMES            D. MARCH 12, 1986 CLEARWATER, FLA.
78- 55 HANCOCK, RONALD GARRY          2217 GREEN HILLS DR - VALRICO FL 33594
70- 57 HAND, RICHARD ALLEN            2103 OAKWOOD LN - ARLINGTON TX 76012
11- 65 HANDIBOE, ALOYSIUS JAMES 'MIKE' D. JANUARY 31, 1953 SAVANNAH, GA.
46- 43 HANDLEY, EUGENE LOUIS          8656 FRESNO DR #506A - HUNTINGTON BEACH CA 92646
36- 35 HANDLEY, LEE ELMER             D. APRIL 8, 1970 PITTSBURGH, PA.
64- 40 HANDRAHAN, JAMES VERNON 'VERN' 36 NEWLAND CRESCENT - CHARLOTTETOWN PEI C1A 4H5 CAN.
65- 34 HANDS, WILLIAM ALFRED          WILLOW TERRACE - ORIENT NY 11957
53- 31 HANEBRINK, HARRY ALOYSIUS      10400 RENFREW DR - ST LOUIS MO 63137
22- 51 HANEY, FRED GIRARD             D. NOVEMBER 9, 1977 BEVERLY HILLS, CALIF.
66- 41 HANEY, WALLACE LARRY           BOX 97 - BARBOURSVILLE VA 22923
14- 80 HANFORD, CHARLES JOSEPH        D. JULY 19, 1963 TRENTON, N.J.
27- 43 HANKINS, DONALD WAYNE          D. MAY 16, 1963 WINSTON-SALEM, N. C.
61- 42 HANKINS, JAY NELSON            9309 EAST 84TH TER - RAYTOWN MO 64138
13- 73 HANLEY, JOSEPH PATRICK         D. MAY 1, 1961 ELMHURST, N. Y.
75- 48 HANNA, PRESTON LEE             5555 MAYFAIR DR - PENSACOLA FL 32506
18- 25 HANNAH, JAMES HARRISON 'TRUCK' D. APRIL 27, 1982 FOUNTAIN VALLEY, CALIF.
76- 39 HANNAHS, GERALD ELLIS          26 LORNA DR - LITTLE ROCK AR 72205
62- 52 HANNAN, JAMES JOHN             3907 CHERRY HILL WAY - ANNANDALE VA 22003
39- 47 HANNING, LOY VERNON            D. JULY 8, 1986 ANACONDA, MO.
44- 55 HANSEN, ANDREW VIGGO           362 YORKTOWN CIR - ATLANTIS FL 33462
51- 37 HANSEN, DOUGLAS WILLIAM        16706 EAST ROCKY KNOLL RD - HACIENDA HEIGHTS CA 91745
74- 46 HANSEN, ROBERT JOSEPH          19 NORTH KELSEY AVE - EVANSVILLE IN 47711
```

GERALD HANNAHS
Lanceur/Pitcher

LARRY HARLOW

```
58- 42 HANSEN, RONALD LAVERN          13602 ALLISTON DR - BALDWIN MD 21013
30- 30 HANSEN, ROY EMIL FREDERICK 'SNIPE' D. SEPTEMBER 11, 1978 CHICAGO, ILL.
18- 26 HANSEN, ROY INGLOF             D. FEBRUARY 9, 1977 BELOIT, WIS.
43- 58 HANSKI, DONALD THOMAS          D. SEPTEMBER 2, 1957 WORTH, ILL.
21- 38 HANSON, EARL SYLVESTER 'OLLIE' D. AUGUST 19, 1951 CLIFTON, N.J.
13- 74 HANSON, HARRY                  B. ST. LOUIS, MO.
42- 46 HANYZEWSKI, EDWARD MICHAEL     RR 1 BOX 120 - VERGAS MN 56587
23- 58 HAPPENNY, JOHN CLIFFORD        208 EVERNIA ST - WEST PALM BEACH FL 33401
28- 43 HARDER, MELVIN LEROY           130 CENTER ST #6A - CHARDON OH 44024
18- 27 HARDGROVE, WILLIAM HENRY 'PAT' D. JANUARY 26, 1973 JACKSON, MISS.
67- 41 HARDIN, JAMES WARREN           3000 NORTH OCEAN DRIVE - RIVIERA BEACH FL 33404
52- 46 HARDIN, WILLIAM EDGAR          29500 HEATHERCLIFF ROAD #271 - MALIBU CA 90265
13- 75 HARDING, CHARLES HAROLD        D. OCTOBER 30, 1971 BOLD SPRINGS, TENN.
58- 43 HARDY, CARROLL WILLIAM         213 VAQUERO DR - BOULDER CO 80302
51- 38 HARDY, FRANCIS JOSEPH 'RED'    5620 NORTH 12TH ST - PHOENIX AZ 85014
74- 47 HARDY, HOWARD LAWRENCE 'LARRY' 2402 DRAWBRIDGE RD - ARLINGTON TX 76012
65- 35 HARGAN, STEVEN LOWELL          2502 MORANGO TRAIL - PALM SPRINGS CA 92262
80- 47 HARGESHEIMER, ALAN ROBERT      7400 WEST MYRTLE - CHICAGO IL 60631
79- 46 HARGIS, GARY LYNN              157 GEMINI AVE - LOMPOC CA 93436
13- 76 HARGRAVE, EUGENE FRANKLIN 'BUBBLES' D. FEBRUARY 23, 1969 CINCINNATI, O.
23- 59 HARGRAVE, WILLIAM MCKINLEY 'PINKY' D. OCTOBER 3, 1942 FT. WAYNE, IND.
23- 60 HARGREAVES, CHARLES RUSSELL    D. MAY 9, 1979 NEPTUNE, N. J.
74- 48 HARGROVE, DUDLEY MICHAEL 'MIKE' RR 3 BOX 94C - PERRYTON TX 79070
10- 65 HARKNESS, FREDERICK HARVEY 'SPECS' D. MAY 18, 1952 COMPTON, CALIF.
61- 43 HARKNESS, THOMAS WILLIAM 'TIM' 2725 LOUIS PERE - LACHINE QUEBEC CAN.
75- 49 HARLOW, LARRY DUANE            OLD ADD: 1002 TOWNSEND AVE - AZTEC NM
41- 43 HARMAN, WILLIAM BELL           9 GUYENNE RD - WILMINGTON DE 19807
```

```
54- 40 HARMON, CHARLES BYRON                          6035A RIDGEACRE DR - CINCINNATI OH 45237
67- 42 HARMON, TERRY WALTER                           OAKWOOD DR - MEDFORD NJ 08055
79- 47 HARPER, BRIAN DAVID                            6 SILVERLEAF DR - ROLLING HILLS CA 90274
16- 41 HARPER, GEORGE WASHINGTON                      D. AUGUST 18, 1978 MAGNOLIA, ARK.
13- 77 HARPER, HARRY CLAYTON                          D. APRIL 23, 1963 LAYTON, N.J.
15- 59 HARPER, JOHN WESLEY                            D. JUNE 18, 1927 HALSTEAD, KAN.
80- 48 HARPER, TERRY JOE                              1685 DORRIS RD - DOUGLAS GA 30134
62- 53 HARPER, THOMAS                                 3 CHRISTOPHER DR - STOUGHTON MA 02072
11- 66 HARPER, WILLIAM HOMER                          D. JUNE 17, 1951 SOMERVILLE, TENN.
69- 74 HARRAH, COLBERT DALE 'TOBY'                    6120 TEN MILE BRIDGE ROAD - FORT WORTH TX 76115
69- 75 HARRELL, JOHN ROBERT                           756 ERIE CIR - MILPITAS CA 95035
12- 74 HARRELL, OSCAR MARTIN 'SLIM'                   D. APRIL 30, 1971 HILLSBORO, TEX.
35- 41 HARRELL, RAYMOND JAMES                         D. JANUARY 28, 1984 ALEXANDRIAS, LA.
55- 54 HARRELL, WILLIAM                               253 MOUNT HOPE DRIVE - ALBANY NY 12202
65- 36 HARRELSON, DERRELL MCKINLEY 'BUD'              25 FALCON DR - HAUPPAUGE NY 11787
63- 52 HARRELSON, KENNETH SMITH 'HAWK'                150 CROSSWAYS PARK WEST - WOODBURY NY 11797
68- 33 HARRELSON, WILLIAM CHARLES                     5804 FAIR OAKS DRIVE - BAKERSFIELD CA 93306
13- 78 HARRINGTON, ANDREW FRANCIS                     D. NOVEMBER 12, 1938 MALDEN, MASS.
25- 44 HARRINGTON, ANDREW MATTHEW                     D. JANUARY 26, 1979 BOISE, IDAHO
63- 53 HARRINGTON, CHARLES MICHAEL 'MIKE'             RR 7 BOX 626 - HATTIESBURG MS 39401
53- 32 HARRINGTON, WILLIAM WOMBLE                     17 CLEVELAND SCHOOL RD - GARNER NC 27529
67- 43 HARRIS, ALONZO                                 7753 S. HOOPER - LOS ANGELES CA 90001
25- 46 HARRIS, ANTHONY SPENCER                        D. JULY 3, 1982 MINNEAPOLIS, MINN.
14- 81 HARRIS, BENJAMIN FRANKLIN                      D. APRIL 29, 1927 ST. LOUIS, MO.
55- 55 HARRIS, BOYD GAIL                              7625 JORDON HOLLOW COURT - MANASSAS VA 22110
41- 44 HARRIS, CHALMER LUMAN 'LUM'                    RR 1 BOX 280 - VINCENT AL 35178
48- 45 HARRIS, CHARLES 'BUBBA'                        P. O. BOX 159 - NOBLETON FL 34263
25- 45 HARRIS, DAVID STANLEY                          D. SEPTEMBER 18, 1973 ATLANTA, GA.
81- 51 HARRIS, GREG ALLEN                             11248 BARBI LANE - LOS ALAMITOS CA 90720
36- 36 HARRIS, HERBERT BENJAMIN                       545 WOODMAR TERRACE - CRYSTAL LAKE IL 60014
68- 34 HARRIS, JAMES WILLIAM                          114 WEST BRANDYWINE CIRCLE - WILMINGTON NC 28403
79- 48 HARRIS, JOHN THOMAS                            3609 LINKWOOD - CLOVIS NM 88101
14- 82 HARRIS, JOSEPH                                 D. DECEMBER 10, 1959 RENTON, PA.
40- 33 HARRIS, MAURICE CHARLES 'MICKEY'               D. APRIL 15, 1971 FARMINGTON, MICH.
38- 35 HARRIS, ROBERT ARTHUR                          BOX 492 - NORTH PLATTE NE 69101
41- 45 HARRIS, ROBERT NED                             D. DECEMBER 18, 1976 WEST PALM BEACH, FLA.
19- 38 HARRIS, STANLEY RAYMOND 'BUCKY'                D. NOVEMBER 8, 1977 BETHESDA, MD.
72- 45 HARRIS, VICTOR LANIER                          6329 GREEN VALLEY CIR - CULVER CITY CA 90230
70- 58 HARRIS, WALTER FRANCIS 'BUDDY'                 2305 CAROL LN - NORRISTOWN PA 19403
23- 61 HARRIS, WILLIAM MILTON                         D. AUGUST 21, 1965 INDIAN TRAIL, N. C.
57- 29 HARRIS, WILLIAM THOMAS                         322 SOUTH REED - KENNEWICK WA 99336
65- 37 HARRISON, CHARLES WILLIAM                      3201 SOUTH 23RD ST #112 - ABILENE TX 79605
55- 56 HARRISON, ROBERT LEE                           253 BRIERLEY WAY - INDIANAPOLIS IN 46032
72- 46 HARRISON, RORIC EDWARD                         1103 CONCORDA DRIVE - TEMPE AZ 85281
65- 38 HARRISON, THOMAS JAMES                         6822 SHERMAN WAY - BELL CA 90203
20- 47 HARRISS, WILLIAM JENNINGS BRYAN 'SLIM          D. SEPTEMBER 19, 1963 TEMPLE, TEXAS
45- 42 HARRIST, EARL                                  BOX 238 - SIMSBORO LA 71275
37- 47 HARSHANEY, SAMUEL                              419 THELMA DR-SAN ANTONIO TX 78212
48- 46 HARSHMAN, JOHN ELVIN                           2227 COMMONWEALTH - SAN DIEGO CA 92104
15- 60 HARSTAD, OSCAR THEANDER                        D. NOVEMBER 14, 1985 CORVALLIS, ORE.
80- 49 HART, JAMES MICHAEL 'MIKE'                     409 LARKSPUR - PORTAGE MI 49081
63- 54 HART, JAMES RAY                                6769 CEDAR BOULEVARD - NEWARK CA 94560
84- 49 HART, MICHAEL LAWRENCE                         16552 WEST CRESCENT DR - NEW BERLIN WI 53151
43- 59 HART, WILLIAM WOODROW                          D. JULY 29, 1968 LYKINS,PA.
65- 39 HARTENSTEIN, CHARLES OSCAR                     6815 DEPAUL COVE - AUSTIN TX 78723
12- 75 HARTER, FRANKLIN PIERCE                        D. APRIL 14, 1959 BREESE, ILL.
14- 83 HARTFORD, BRUCE DANIEL                         D. MAY 25, 1975 LOS ANGELES, CAL.
39- 48 HARTJE, CHRISTIAN HENRY                        D. JUNE 26, 1946 SEATTLE, WASH.
11- 67 HARTLEY, GROVER ALLEN                          D. OCTOBER 19, 1964 DAYTONA BEACH, FLA.
62- 54 HARTMAN, J. C.                                 3425 ROSEDALE ST - HOUSTON TX 77004
59- 37 HARTMAN, ROBERT LOUIS                          2732 LINCOLN RD - KENOSHA WI 53140
22- 52 HARTNETT, CHARLES LEO 'GABBY'                  D. DECEMBER 20, 1972 PARK RIDGE, ILL.
13- 79 HARTRANFT, RAYMOND CHARLES                     D. FEBRUARY 10, 1955 CHESTER CO., PA.
73- 57 HARTS, GREGORY RUDOLPH                         OLD ADD: 160 WOODARD AVE SE - ATLANTA GA
50- 32 HARTSFIELD, ROY THOMAS                         150 HUNTERS COVE - ROSWELL GA 30076
47- 41 HARTUNG, CLINTON 'HONDO'                       1018 EAST FULTON - SINTON TX 78387
76- 40 HARTZELL, PAUL FRANKLIN                        610 NEWPORT CENTER RD #1290 - NEWPORT BEACH CA 92660
28- 44 HARVEL, LUTHER RAYMOND                         D. APRIL 10, 1986 KANSAS CITY, MO.
87- 56 HARVEY, BRYAN STANLEY                          RURAL ROUTE 1 BOX 144K - CATAWBA NC 28609
16- 42 HASBROOK, ROBERT LYNDON 'ZIGGY'                D. FEBRUARY 9, 1976 GARLAND, TEX.
45- 43 HASENMAYER, DONALD IRVIN                       721 GOLF DRIVE - WARRINGTON PA 18976
40- 34 HASH, HERBERT HOWARD                           RR ONE BOX 3 - BOSTON VA 22713
33- 23 HASLIN, MICHAEL JOSEPH 'MICKEY'                171 GEORGE AV - PLAINS PA 18705
36- 37 HASSETT, JOHN ALOYSIUS 'BUDDY'                 114 STONY RIDGE DR-HILLSDALE NJ 07642
```

```
78- 56 HASSEY, RONALD WILLIAM              5935 EAST PLACITA ESQUINA - TUCSON AZ 85718
71- 43 HASSLER, ANDREW EARL               OLD ADD: BOX 17101 - TUCSON AZ
28- 45 HASSLER, JOSEPH FREDERICK          D. SEPTEMBER 4, 1971 DUNCAN, OKLA.
37- 48 HASSON, CHARLES EUGENE 'GENE'      5205 SAN BERARDINO RD #513 - MONTCLAIR CA 91763
19- 39 HASTY, ROBERT KELLER               D. MAY 28, 1972 DALLAS, GA.
79- 49 HATCHER, MICHAEL VAUGHN 'MICKEY'   720 SOUTH DOBSON #59 - MESA AZ 85202
84- 50 HATCHER, WILLIAM AUGUSTUS          P.O. BOX 207 - WILLIAMS AZ 86046
50- 33 HATFIELD, FRED JAMES               STAR ROUTE 1 BOX 3025 - TALLAHASSEE FL 32304
45- 44 HATHAWAY, RAY WILSON               25 LEISURE MOUNT RD - ASHEVILLE NC 28804
46- 44 HATTEN, JOSEPH HILARIAN            RR 2 BOX 678 - SHINGLETOWN CA 96088
35- 42 HATTER, CLYDE MELNO                D. OCTOBER 16, 1937 YOSEMITE, KY.
46- 45 HATTON, GRADY EDGEBERT             BOX 97 - WARREN TX 77664
12- 76 HAUGER, JOHN ARTHUR                D. AUGUST 2, 1944 REDWOOD CITY, CALIF.
43- 60 HAUGHEY, CHRISTOPHER FRANCIS       46728 CRAWFORD ST #25 - FREMONT CA 94539
47- 42 HAUGSTAD, PHILIP DONALD            RR 4 BOX 180 - BLACK RIVER FALLS WI 54615
10- 66 HAUSER, ARNOLD GEORGE              D. MAY 22, 1956 AURORA, ILL.
22- 53 HAUSER, JOSEPH JOHN                919 NORTH 15TH STREET #14 - SHEBOYGAN WI 53081
75- 50 HAUSMAN, THOMAS MATTHEW            3165 WESTFIELD CIR - LAS VEGAS NV 89121
44- 56 HAUSMANN, CLEMENS RAYMOND          D. AUGUST 29, 1972 BAYTOWN, TEX.
44- 57 HAUSMANN, GEORGE JOHN              218 FAWN VALLEY - BOERNE TX 78006
81- 52 HAVENS, BRADLEY DAVID              1304 MONTROSE AVENUE - ROYAL OAK MI 48073
51- 39 HAWES, ROY LEE                     BOX 912 - RINGGOLD GA 30736
11- 68 HAWK, EDWARD                       D. MARCH 26, 1936 NEOSHO, MO.
82- 56 HAWKINS, MELTON ANDREW 'ANDY'      P.O. BOX 8812 - WACO TX 76714
60- 46 HAWKINS, WYNN FIRTH                5326 COTTAGE LN - CORTLAND OH 44410
21- 39 HAWKS, NELSON LOUIS 'CHICK'        D. MAY 26, 1973 SAN RAFAEL, CAL.
15- 61 HAWORTH, HOMER HOWARD              D. JANUARY 28, 1953 TROUTDALE, ORE.
70- 59 HAYDEL, JOHN HAROLD 'HAL'          304 LYNWOOD DR - HOUMA LA 70360
58- 44 HAYDEN, EUGENE FRANKLIN            1597 ALAMO DR #188 - VACAVILLE CA 95688
82- 57 HAYES, BEN JOSEPH                  3501 10TH ST NE - ST PETERSBURG FL 33704
33- 24 HAYES, FRANKLIN WITMAN             D. JUNE 22, 1955 POINT PLEASANT, N. J.
35- 43 HAYES, JAMES MILLARD              6180 ROCKLAND RD - LITHONIA GA 30058
27- 44 HAYES, MINTER CARNEY 'JACKIE'      D. FEBRUARY 9, 1983 BIRMINGHAM, ALA.
81- 53 HAYES, VON FRANK                   OLD ADD: 312 N. GULF BLVD #C-TADIAN ROCK BEACH FL 34635
80- 50 HAYES, WILLIAM ERNEST              8 SOUTH ASH ST - NORTH PLATTE NE 69101
39- 49 HAYNES, JOSEPH WALTER              D. JANUARY 6, 1967 HOPKINS, MINN.
86- 61 HAYWARD, RAYMOND ALTON             7417 NORTHWEST 121ST - OKLAHOMA CITY OK 73132
68- 35 HAYWOOD, WILLIAM KIERNAN           18113 194TH AVE NE - WOODINVILLE WA 98072
44- 58 HAYWORTH, MYRON CLAUDE 'RED'       507 OAK VIEW RD - HIGH POINT NC 27260
26- 35 HAYWORTH, RAYMOND HALL             1408 CARDIFF LANE - HIGH POINT NC 27260
80- 51 HAZEWOOD, DRUNGO LARUE             5130 DEL NORTE BLVD - SACRAMENTO CA 95820
55- 57 HAZLE, ROBERT SIDNEY               164 DORSET DR - COLUMBIA SC 29210
40- 35 HEAD, EDWARD MARVIN                D. JANUARY 31, 1980 BASTROP, LA.
23- 62 HEAD, RALPH                        D. OCTOBER 8, 1962 MUSCADINE, ALA.
30- 31 HEALEY, FRANCIS JEREMIAH           71 PENACOOK STREET - SPRINGFIELD MA 01104
69- 76 HEALY, FRANCIS XAVIER              1 PRIMROSE LN - HOLYOKE MA 01040
15- 62 HEALY, THOMAS FITZGERALD           D. JANUARY 15, 1974 CLEVELAND, O.
54- 41 HEARD, JEHOSIE                     6465 3RD AVE SOUTH - BIRMINGHAM AL 35212
10- 67 HEARN, BUNN 'BUNNY'                D. OCTOBER 11, 1959 WILSON, N.C.
10- 68 HEARN, EDMUND                      D. SEPTEMBER 8, 1952 SAWTELLE, CALIF.
86- 62 HEARN, EDWARD JOHN                 P.O. BOX 3201 - FORT PIERCE FL 34948
26- 36 HEARN, ELMER LAFAYETTE 'BUNNY'     D. MARCH 31, 1974 VENICE, FLA.
47- 43 HEARN, JAMES TOLBERT               1678 BEVERLY WOOD CT - CHAMBLEE GA 30341
85- 46 HEARRON, JEFFREY VERNON            13176 EAST HEDDA DR - CERRITOS CA 90701
36- 38 HEATH, JOHN GEOFFREY 'JEFF'        D. DECEMBER 9, 1975 SEATTLE, WASH.
82- 58 HEATH, KELLY MARK                  202 WOODSTOCK DR - GREENVILLE NC 27834
78- 57 HEATH, MICHAEL THOMAS              12137 FRUITWOOD DRIVE - RIVERVIEW FL 33569
31- 36 HEATH, MINOR WILSON 'MICKEY'       D. JULY 30, 1986 DALLAS, TEXAS
20- 48 HEATH, SPENCER PAUL                D. JANUARY 25, 1930 CHICAGO, ILL.
35- 44 HEATH, THOMAS GEORGE               D. FEBRUARY 26, 1967 LOS GATOS, CAL.
65- 40 HEATH, WILLIAM CHRIS               2111 PLANTATION DR - RICHMOND TX 77469
83- 70 HEATHCOCK, RONALD JEFFREY 'JEFF'   12861 ASPENWOOD LN - GARDEN GROVE CA 92640
18- 28 HEATHCOTE, CLIFTON EARL            D. JANUARY 19, 1939 YORK, PA.
82- 59 HEATON, NEAL                       611 BLUE POINT DR - HOLTSVILLE NY 11742
75- 51 HEAVERLO, DAVID WALLACE            3720 WEST LAKESHORE DR - MOSES LAKE WA 98837
31- 36 HEBERT, WALLACE ANDREW             3408 WESTWOOD RD - WEST LAKE LA 70665
68- 36 HEBNER, RICHARD JOSEPH             510 NATHAN ST - NORWOOD MA 02062
12- 77 HECHINGER, MICHAEL VINCENT         D. AUGUST 13, 1967 CHICAGO, ILL.
13- 80 HEDGEPETH, HARRY MALCOLM           D. JULY 30, 1966 RICHMOND, VA.
65- 41 HEDLUND, MICHAEL DAVID             2412 KLINGER RD - ARLINGTON TX 76016
79- 50 HEEP, DANIEL WILLIAM               327 TEAKWOOD LN - SAN ANTONIO TX 78216
34- 43 HEFFNER, DONALD HENRY              816 SOUTHVIEW ROAD #C - ARCADIA CA 91006
63- 55 HEFFNER, ROBERT FREDERICK          910 NORTH TWELFTH - ALLENTOWN PA 18102
45- 45 HEFLIN, RANDOLPH RUTHERFORD        115 23RD STREET NW #25 - HICKORY NC 28601
41- 46 HEGAN, JAMES EDWARD                D. JUNE 17, 1984 SWAMPSCOTT, MASS.
64- 41 HEGAN, JAMES MICHAEL 'MIKE'        9648 OLD BARN RD - MEQUON WI 53092
```

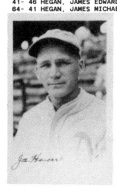

85- 47	HEGMAN, ROBERT HILMER	RURAL ROUTE 5 - SAINT CLOUD MN 56301
18- 29	HEHL, HERMAN JACOB 'JAKE'	D. JULY 4, 1961 BROOKLYN, N. Y.
69- 77	HEIDEMANN, JACK SEALE	925 WEST SYCAMORE - CHANDLER AZ 85224
14- 84	HEILMANN, HARRY EDWIN	D. JULY 9, 1951 SOUTHFIELD, MICH.
42- 47	HEIM, VAL RAYMOND	1050 LOUDON - SUPERIOR NE 68978
20- 49	HEIMACH, FRED AMOS	D. JUNE 1, 1973 FORT MYERS, FLA.
83- 71	HEIMUELLER, GORMAN JOHN	8134 CALABAR AVE - PLAYA DEL REY CA 90291
21- 40	HEINE, WILLIAM HENRY 'BUD'	D. SEPTEMBER 2, 1976 FORT LAUDERDALE, FLA.
37- 49	HEINTZELMAN, KENNETH ALPHONSE	406 S. CHURCH - SAINT PETERS MO 63376
73- 58	HEINTZELMAN, THOMAS KENNETH	406 SOUTH CHURCH - ST PETERS MO 63376
34- 44	HEISE, CLARENCE EDWARD 'LEFTY'	5 WEST NIGHTINGALE STREET - APOPKA FL 32712
57- 30	HEISE, JAMES EDWARD	4021 HARGILL DR - ORLANDO FL 32806
67- 44	HEISE, ROBERT LOWELL	832 EIGHTH AVENUE S - ST. PETERSBURG FL 33701
61- 44	HEISER, LEROY BARTON	1038 GROVE HILL RD - BALTIMORE MD 21227
60- 47	HEIST, ALFRED MICHAEL	P.O. BOX 70 - COOKSON OK 74427
18- 30	HEITMANN, HENRY ANTON	D. DECEMBER 15, 1958 BROOKLYN, N. Y.
56- 40	HELD, MELVIN NICHOLAS	BOX 204 - EDON OH 43518
54- 42	HELD, WOODSON GEORGE	BIG DIAMOND RANCH - DUBOIS WY 82513
38- 36	HELF, HENRY HARTZ	D. OCTOBER 27, 1984 AUSTIN, TEXAS
15- 63	HELFRICH, EMORY WILBUR 'TY'	D. MARCH 18, 1955 PLEASANTVILLE, N.J.
64- 42	HELMS, TOMMY VANN	5427 BLUE SKY DR - CINCINNATI OH 45247
43- 61	HELTZEL, WILLIAM WADE 'HEINIE'	RR 2-YORK PA 17403
61- 45	HEMAN, RUSSELL FREDRICK	1410 NORTH MARLES DR - SANTA ANA CA 92706
14- 85	HEMINGWAY, EDSON MARSHALL	D. JULY 5, 1969 EAST GRAND RAPIDS, MICH
28- 46	HEMSLEY, RALSTON BURDETT 'ROLLIE'	D. JULY 31, 1972 WASHINGTON, D. C.
49- 32	HEMUS, SOLOMON JOSEPH 'SOLLY'	6565 WEST LOOP SOUTH #555 - BELLAIRE TX 77401
30- 32	HENDERSON WILLIAM MAXWELL	D. OCTOBER 6, 1966 PENSACOLA, FLA.
21- 41	HENDERSON, BERNARD	D. JUNE 4, 1966 LINDEN, TEXAS
81- 54	HENDERSON, DAVID LEE	BOX 21 - SOUTH DOD PALOS CA 93665
14- 86	HENDERSON, EDWARD J.	D. JANUARY 15, 1964 NEW YORK, N. Y.
74- 49	HENDERSON, JOSEPH LEE	OLD ADD: 125 INQUERO LN #38 - EL PASO TX
65- 42	HENDERSON, KENNETH JOSEPH	947 WILLOWLEAF DR #1305 - SAN JOSE CA 95128
79- 51	HENDERSON, RICKEY HENLEY	10561 ENGLEWOOD DR - OAKLAND CA 94621
77- 64	HENDERSON, STEPHEN CURTIS	5003 BEEKMAN COURT - TAMPA FL 33624
61- 46	HENDLEY, CHARLES ROBERT 'BOB'	645 WIMBISH - MACON GA 31204
71- 44	HENDRICK, GEORGE ANDREW	20893 STARSHINE ROAD - WALNUT CA 91789
23- 63	HENDRICK, HARVEY LEE	D. OCTOBER 29, 1941 COVINGTON, TENN.
10- 69	HENDRICKS, EDWARD	D. NOVEMBER 28, 1930 JACKSON, MICH.
68- 37	HENDRICKS, ELROD JEROME	3709 BROWNBROOK COURT - RANDALLSTOWN MD 21133
45- 46	HENDRICKSON, DONALD WILLIAMSON	D. JANUARY 19, 1977 NORFOLK, VA.
11- 69	HENDRIX, CLAUDE RAYMOND	D. MARCH 22, 1944 ALLENTOWN, PA.
11- 70	HENDRYX, TIMOTHY GREEN	D. AUGUST 14, 1957 CORPUS CHRISTI, TEX.
86- 63	HENGEL, DAVID LEE	1501 QUINTANA WAY - FREMONT CA 94538
19- 40	HENION, LAFAYETTE MARION	D. JULY 22, 1955 SAN LUIS OBISPO, CALIF.
82- 60	HENKE, THOMAS ANTHONY	RR SIX - JEFFERSON CITY MO 65101
54- 43	HENLEY, GAIL CURTICE	10150 DAINES DR - TEMPLE CITY CA 91780
21- 42	HENLINE, WALTER JOHN 'BUTCH'	D. OCTOBER 9, 1957 SARASOTA, FLA.
87- 57	HENNEMAN, MICHAEL ALAN	1515 WESTVALE DRIVE - FESTUS MO 63028
37- 50	HENNESSEY, GEORGE	D. JANUARY 15, 1988 PRINCETON, N. J.
13- 81	HENNESSY, LESTER BAKER	D. NOVEMBER 20, 1976 NEW YORK, N. Y.
69- 78	HENNIGAN, PHILLIP WINSTON	P.O. BOX 1212 - CENTER TX 75935
14- 87	HENNING, ERNEST HERMAN 'PETE'	D. NOVEMBER 9, 1939 DYER, IND.
73- 59	HENNINGER, RICHARD LEE	RR 1 BOX 271 - HASTINGS NE 68901
24- 50	HENRICH, FRANK WILDE 'FRITZ'	D. MAY 1, 1959 PHILADELPHIA, PA.
57- 31	HENRICH, ROBERT EDWARD	1531 VIA LOS COYOTES - LAHABRA CA 90631
37- 51	HENRICH, THOMAS DAVID	1347 ALBINO TRAIL - DEWEY AZ 86327
11- 71	HENRIKSEN, OLAF	D. OCTOBER 17, 1962 NORWOOD, MASS.
84- 51	HENRY, DWAYNE ALLEN	502 HAMPSTEAD ROAD - MIDDLETOWN DE 19709
44- 59	HENRY, EARL CLIFFORD	BOX 43 - WHITE COTTAGE OH 43791
21- 43	HENRY, FRANK JOHN 'DUTCH'	D. AUGUST 23, 1968 EAST CLEVELAND, O.
22- 54	HENRY, FREDERICK MARSHALL 'SNAKE'	BOX 333 - WENDELL NC 27591
36- 39	HENRY, JAMES FRANCIS	D. AUGUST 15, 1976 MEMPHIS, TENN.
10- 70	HENRY, JOHN PARK	D. NOVEMBER 24, 1941 FORT HUACHUCA, ARIZ.
61- 47	HENRY, RONALD BAXTER	878 SOUTH DEXTER #508 - DENVER CO 80222
66- 42	HENRY, WILLIAM FRANCIS	190 BOULEVARD - KENILWORTH NJ 07033

52- 47	HENRY, WILLIAM RODMAN	302 CHRISTINE - HOUSTON TX 77017
33- 25	HENSHAW, ROY KNIKELBINE	4221 GARDEN AVE - WESTERN SPRINGS IL 60558
35- 45	HENSIEK, PHILIP FRANK	D. FEBRUARY 21, 1972 ST. LOUIS, MO.
86- 64	HENSLEY, CHARLES FLOYD	P.O. BOX 439 - TULARE CA 93277
66- 43	HEPLER, WILLIAM LEWIS	10271 BLOSSOM LAKE DR - SEMINOLE FL 33542
63- 56	HERBEL, RONALD SAMUEL	105 CHINOOK LANE #F - STEILACOOM WA 98388
13- 82	HERBERT, ERNIE ALBERT	D. JANUARY 13, 1968 DALLAS, TEX.
15- 64	HERBERT, FREDERICK	D. MAY 29, 1963 TICE, FLA.
50- 34	HERBERT, RAYMOND ERNEST	32629 FIVE MILE RD - LIVONIA MI 48150

87- 58 HEREDIA, UBALDO JOSE	CLE ESPIRITO SANTO ISLA MARG.-NUEVA ESPARTA VENEZ
26- 37 HERMAN, FLOYD CAVES 'BABE'	D. NOVEMBER 27, 1987 GLENDALE, CALIF.
31- 37 HERMAN, WILLIAM JENNINGS BRYAN	3111 GARDEN EAST #33-PALM BEACH GARDENS FL 33410
23- 64 HERMANN, ALBERT BARTEL	D. AUGUST 20, 1980 LEWES, DEL.
43- 62 HERMANSKI, EUGENE VICTOR	100 HALLOCK AVE.FOX HALL #14 - MIDDLESEX NJ 08846
67- 45 HERMOSO, ANGEL REMIGIO	CALLE BOUKTON #7 - CARABOBO VENEZ
74- 50 HERNAIZ, JESUS RAFAEL	24 ST BLOCK 76 #47 VILLA - CAROLINA PR 00630
71- 45 HERNANDEZ, ENZO OCTAVIO	VEREDA NORTH 5E-4,GUANTRA-PUERTA LACRUZ ANZ, VENEZ
56- 41 HERNANDEZ, GREGORIO EVELIO	3004 SW 113TH AVE - MIAMI FL 33165
77- 65 HERNANDEZ, GUILLERMO 'WILLIE'	BO ESPINA CALLE C BOX 125 - AGUADA PR 00602
65- 43 HERNANDEZ, JACINTO 'JACKIE'	850 NW FOURTH AVENUE - MIAMI FL 33136
74- 51 HERNANDEZ, KEITH	255 EAST 49TH #28D - NEW YORK NY 10017
82- 61 HERNANDEZ, LEONARDO JESUS	URB. EL MILAGRO,CALLE SUCRE 38 - EDO MIRANDA VENEZ
86- 65 HERNANDEZ, MANUEL ANTONIO	EUGENIO A. ALFIONADA #35 - LAROMANA DOMINICAN REP.
79- 52 HERNANDEZ, PEDRO JULIO	JULIO A. GARCIA #43 - LA ROMANA DOMINICAN REP.
67- 46 HERNANDEZ, RAMON GONZALEZ	REPARTO, ROSAMARIA CLE 5F-19-CAROLINA PRO0630
72- 47 HERNANDEZ, RODOLFO 'RUDY'	CARVAJAL #1802 NORTE - MAZATLAN SINOLOA MEX.
60- 48 HERNANDEZ, RUDOLPH ALBERT	8 CALLE RODRIGUEZ SERRA - CONDADO PR 00907
42- 48 HERNANDEZ, SALVADOR JOSE RAMOS	D. JANUARY 3, 1986 HAVANA, CUBA
84- 52 HERNANDEZ, TOBIAS RAFAEL	IRA CALLE GUAMACHITO #47-49 - CALABOZO, GUARICO VENEZ
74- 52 HERNDON, LARRY DARNELL	6915 SKYLINE BLVD - HILLSBOROUGH CA 94010
79- 53 HERR, THOMAS MITCHELL	1077 OLDE FORGE CROSSING - LANCASTER PA 17601
11- 72 HERRELL, WALTER WILLIAM	D. JANUARY 23, 1949 FRONT ROYAL, VA.
67- 47 HERRERA, JOSE CONCEPCION	MARAVEN ADRI 12,CEN.COM. LAGUNILLAS - E. ZULIA VENEZ
58- 45 HERRERA, JUAN FRANCISCO 'PANCHO'	2930 NW 21ST AVE - MIAMI FL 33142
51- 40 HERRERA, PROCOPIO RODRIGUEZ 'TITO'	APDO POSTAL 257-CIUDAD SATELITE, EDO MEX.
25- 47 HERRERA, RAMON 'MIKE'	D. FEBRUARY 3, 1978 HAVANA, CUBA
56- 42 HERRIAGE, WILLIAM TROY	3204 TAMWORTH COURT - MODESTO CA 95350
54- 44 HERRIN, THOMAS EDWARD	BOX 550 - SAN JOSE CA 95125
29- 48 HERRING, ARTHUR L.	296 HIGHWAY DR - MARION IN 46952
12- 78 HERRING, HERBERT LEE	D. APRIL 22, 1964 TUCSON, ARIZ.
15- 65 HERRING, WILLIAM FRANCIS	D. SEPTEMBER 10, 1962 HONESDALE, PA.
67- 48 HERRMANN, EDWARD MARTIN	16935 ALONDRA DR - SAN DIEGO CA 92128
32- 36 HERRMANN, LEROY GEORGE	D. JULY 3, 1972 LIVERMORE, CAL.
18- 31 HERRMANN, MARTIN JOHN	D. SEPTEMBER 11, 1956 CINCINNATI, O.
62- 55 HERRNSTEIN, JOHN ELLETT	603 SEMINOLE RD - CHILLICOTHE OH 45602
62- 56 HERRSCHER, RICHARD FRANKLIN 'RICK'	4024 DRUID - DALLAS TX 75205
56- 43 HERSH, EARL WALTER	3201 MURKLE RD - WESTMINSTER MD 21157
61- 48 HERSHBERGER, NORMAN MICHAEL 'MIKE'	4130 MEADOWVIEW DR - CANTON OH 44709
38- 37 HERSHBERGER, WILLARD MCKEE	D. AUGUST 3, 1940 BOSTON, MASS.
83- 72 HERSHISER, OREL LEONARD QUINTON	549 LYONS WAY - PLACENTIA CA 92670
52- 48 HERTWECK, NEAL CHARLES	3030 ST CLAIRE RD - WINSTON SALEM NC 27106
64- 43 HERTZ, STEVE ALLAN	10211 SW 96TH TER - MIAMI FL 33156
56- 44 HERZOG, DORREL HORMAN ELVERT 'WHITEY'	3613 SOUTH FOREST - INDEPENDENCE MO 64052
84- 53 HESKETH, JOSEPH THOMAS	3690 SALISBURY AVE - BLASDELL NY 14219
16- 43 HESSELBACHER, GEORGE EDWARD	D. FEBRUARY 18, 1980 RYDAL, PA.
45- 47 HETKI, JOHN EDWARD	4004 STARY DR - PARMA OH 44134
35- 46 HEUSSER, EDWARD BURLETON	D. MARCH 1, 1956 AURORA, COLO.
20- 50 HEVING, JOHN ALOYSIUS	D. DECEMBER 24, 1968 SALISBURY, N. C.
30- 33 HEVING, JOSEPH WILLIAM	D. APRIL 11, 1970 COVINGTON, KY.
73- 60 HEYDEMAN, GREGORY GEORGE	61 VIA PARAISO - MONTEREY CA 93940
64- 44 HIATT, JACK E	STAR ROUTE BOX 341 - PINE AZ 85544
67- 49 HIBBS, JAMES KERR	2821 SOUTH MAIN ST - VENTURA CA 93003

WILLIE HERNANDEZ

42- 49 HICKEY, JAMES ROBERT	163 CHESTER ST - EAST HARTFORD CT 06108
81- 55 HICKEY, KEVIN JOHN	5715 SOUTH MASON - CHICAGO IL 60638
15- 66 HICKMAN, DAVID JAMES	D. DECEMBER 30, 1958 BROOKLYN, N. Y.
62- 57 HICKMAN, JAMES LUCIUS	BOX 355 - HENNING TN 38041
65- 44 HICKMAN, JESSE OWENS	1801 JEWEL STREET - PINEVILLE LA 71360
56- 45 HICKS, CLARENCE WALTER 'BUDDY'	7600 COOLGROVE DR - DOWNEY CA 90240
64- 45 HICKS, JAMES EDWARD	3717 EUCLID AVE - EAST CHICAGO IN 46312
59- 38 HICKS, WILLIAM JOSEPH 'JOE'	2707 BROOKMERE RD - CHARLOTTESVILLE VA 22901
37- 52 HIGBE, WALTER KIRBY	D. MAY 6, 1985 COLUMBIA, S. C.
22- 55 HIGBEE, MAHLON JESSE	D. APRIL 7, 1968 DEPAUW, IND.
49- 33 HIGDON, WILLIAM TRAVIS	D. AUGUST 30, 1986 PASCAGOULA, MISS.
66- 44 HIGGINS, DENNIS DEAN	2204 ANDERSON DR - JEFFERSON CITY MO 65101
30- 34 HIGGINS, MICHAEL FRANKLIN 'PINKY'	D. MARCH 21, 1969 DALLAS, TEX.
22- 56 HIGH, ANDREW AIRD	D. FEBRUARY 22, 1981 TOLEDO, O.
19- 41 HIGH, CHARLES EDWIN	D. SEPTEMBER 11, 1960 PORTLAND, ORE.
13- 83 HIGH, HUGH JENKEN	D. NOVEMBER 16, 1962 ST. LOUIS CO., MO.
85- 48 HIGUERA, TEODORO VALENZUELA	OLD ADD: CIUDAD DE JUAREZ CHIHUAHUA MEX.
31- 38 HILCHER, WALTER FRANK	D. NOVEMBER 21, 1962 MINNEAPOLIS, MINN.
31- 39 HILDEBRAND, ORAL CLYDE	D. SEPTEMBER 8, 1977 SOUTHPORT, IND.
13- 84 HILDEBRAND, PALMER MARION	D. JANUARY 25, 1960 NORTH CANTON, O.
69- 79 HILGENDORF, THOMAS EUGENE	BOX 1131 - COTTAGE GROVE OR 97424

15- 67	HILL, CARMEN PROCTOR 'BUNKER'	2913 BROADWAY - INDIANAPOLIS IN 46205
17- 33	HILL, CLIFFORD JOSEPH 'RED'	D. AUGUST 11, 1938 EL PASO, TEX.
57- 32	HILL, DAVID BURNHAM	827 WEST WOODCHASE DRIVE - KNOXVILLE TN 37922
83- 73	HILL, DONALD EARL	5607 E. NAPLES CANAL ST - LONG BEACH CA 90803
69- 80	HILL, GARRY ALTON	3538 BACK CREEK CHURCH RD - CHARLOTTE NC 28213
15- 68	HILL, HERBERT LEE	D. SEPTEMBER 2, 1970 FARMERS BRANCH, TEX.
69- 81	HILL, HERMAN ALEXANDER	D. DECEMBER 14, 1970 MAGALLANES, VEN.
35- 41	HILL, JESSE TERRILL	245 SOUTH EL MOLINO #208 - PASADENA CA 91101
39- 50	HILL, JOHN CLINTON	D. SEPTEMBER 20, 1970 DECATUR, GA.
73- 61	HILL, MARC KEVIN	804 LINCOLN - ELSBERRY MO 63343
87- 59	HILLEGAS, SHAWN PATRICK	RURAL ROUTE 1 BOX 39A - SOUTH FORK PA 15956
61- 49	HILLER, CHARLES JOSEPH	6830 BURNING TREE DR - SEMINOLE FL 33543
46- 46	HILLER, FRANK WALTER	D. JANUARY 8, 1987 WEST CHESTER, PA.
20- 51	HILLER, HARVEY MAX 'HOB'	D. DECEMBER 27, 1956 LEHIGHTON, PA.
65- 45	HILLER, JOHN FREDERICK	P.O. BOX 1013 - IRON MOUNTAIN MI 49801
24- 51	HILLIS, MALCOLM DAVID 'MACK'	D. JUNE 16, 1961 CAMBRIDGE, MASS.
55- 58	HILLMAN, DARIUS DUTTON 'DAVE'	849 MIMOSA DR - KINGSPORT TN 37660
14- 88	HILLY, WILLIAM EDWARD	D. JULY 25, 1953 EUREKA, MO.
72- 48	HILTON, JOHN DAVID 'DAVE'	10508 WEST CORTEZ CIRCLE #13 - FRANKLIN WI 53132
61- 50	HIMSL, AVITUS BERNARD 'VEDIE'	5127 WEST HUTCHINSON - CHICAGO IL 60641
77- 66	HINDS, SAMUEL RUSSELL	2165 SAN JOSE - CLOVIS CA 93612
34- 45	HINKLE, DANIEL GORDON 'GORDIE'	D. MARCH 19, 1972 HOUSTON, TEX.
51- 41	HINRICHS, PAUL EDWIN	824 NORTH MONROE - LITCHFIELD IL 62056
10- 71	HINRICHS, WILLIAM LOUIS	D. AUGUST 18, 1972 SELMA, CALIF.
82- 62	HINSHAW, GEORGE ADDISON	1927 NORTH SLATER AVE - COMPTON CA 90220
64- 46	HINSLEY, JERRY DEAN	3115 EL CAMINO REAL #31 - LAS CRUCES NM 88001
28- 47	HINSON, JAMES PAUL	D. SEPTEMBER 23, 1960 MUSKOGEE, OKLA.
61- 51	HINTON, CHARLES EDWARD	6330 16TH ST NW - WASHINGTON DC 20011
71- 46	HINTON, RICHARD MICHAEL	OLD ADD: 730 AGAVE PLACE - TUCSON AZ 85718
87- 60	HINZO, THOMAS LEE	82 MILLAN COURT - CHULA VISTA CA 92010
66- 45	HIPPAUF, HERBERT AUGUST	1781 KIMBERLY DR - SUNNYVALE CA 94087
47- 47	HISER, GENE TAYLOR	1450 CALDWELL LANE - HOFFMAN ESTATES IL 60194
68- 38	HISLE, LARRY EUGENE	P.O. BOX 84 %FERGUSON - PORTSMOUTH OH 45662
51- 42	HISNER, HARLEY PARNELL	RR 2 BOX 253A - MONROEVILLE IN 46773
38- 38	HITCHCOCK, JAMES FRANKLIN	D. JUNE 23, 1959 MONTGOMERY, ALA.
42- 50	HITCHCOCK, WILLIAM CLYDE	1117 WEST COLLINWOOD CIR-OPELIKA AL 36801
17- 34	HITT, BRUCE SMITH	D. NOVEMBER 10, 1973 PORTLAND, ORE.
49- 34	HITTLE, LLOYD ELDON	2031 WEST ELM STREET - LODI CA 95242
31- 40	HOAG, MYRIL OLIVER	D. JULY 28, 1971 HIGH SPRINGS, FLA.
54- 45	HOAK, DONALD ALBERT	D. OCTOBER 9, 1969 PITTSBURGH, PA.
61- 52	HOBAUGH, EDWARD RUSSELL	527 5TH AVE - FORD CITY PA 16226
57- 33	HOBBIE, GLEN FREDERICK	RR 2, NORTHWOOD HEIGHTS - HILLSBORO IL 62049
81- 56	HOBBS, JOHN DOUGLAS	3 WADE DR - CHERRY HILL NJ 08034
13- 85	HOBBS, WILLIAM LEE	D. JANUARY 5, 1945 HAMILTON, O.
75- 52	HOBSON, CLELL LAVERN 'BUTCH'	1422 CLARENDON AVENUE - BESSEMER AL 35020
20- 52	HOCK, EDWARD FRANCIS	D. NOVEMBER 21, 1963 PORTSMOUTH, O.
75- 53	HOCKENBERY, CHARLES MARION	1112 PIERCE ST - ONALASKA WI 54650
38- 39	HOCKETT, ORIS LEON	D. MARCH 23, 1969 HAWTHORNE, CAL.
34- 46	HOCKETTE, GEORGE EDWARD	D. JANUARY 20, 1974 PLANTATION, FLA.
25- 48	HODAPP, URBAN JOHN	D. JUNE 14, 1980 CINCINNATI, O.
51- 43	HODERLEIN, MELVIN ANTHONY	535 CINTI BATAVIA PIKE - CINCINNATI OH 45244
20- 53	HODGE, CLARENCE CLEMET 'SHOVEL'	D. DECEMBER 31, 1967 FORT WALTON BEACH, FLA.
84- 54	HODGE, ED OLIVER	12043 LEMMING ST - LAKEWOOD CA 90715
42- 51	HODGE, EDWARD BURTON 'BERT'	RR 19-KNOXVILLE TN 37920
71- 48	HODGE, HAROLD MORRIS 'GOMER'	501 WISCONSIN STREET - SPINDALE NC 28160
43- 63	HODGES, GILBERT RAYMOND	D. APRIL 2, 1972 WEST PALM BEACH, FLA.
73- 62	HODGES, RONALD WRAY	LAKE VIEW DR - ROCKY MOUNT VA 24157
39- 51	HODGIN, ELMER RALPH	3203 FARMINGTON DR-GREENSBORO NC 27407

CHUCK HOCKENBERY P

80- 52	HODGSON, PAUL JOSEPH DENIS	110 CHANDLER DRIVE - FREDERICTON NEW BRUN. E3B 5S7 CAN.
46- 47	HODKEY, ALOYSIUS JOSEPH 'ELI'	5163 BROADWAY - LORAIN OH 44052
52- 49	HOEFT, WILLIAM FREDERICK	36427 SHERWOOD - LIVONIA MI 48154
63- 57	HOERNER, JOSEPH WALTER	6344 TIDEWATER DR - FLORISSANT MO 63033
40- 36	HOERST, FRANK JOSEPH	31 VILLAGE LANE - MOUNT LAUREL NJ 08054
11- 73	HOFF, CHESTER CORNELIUS	1825 S. RIDGEWOOD AVE #206 - ORMOND BEACH FL 32074
44- 60	HOFFERTH, STEWART EDWARD	BOX 283 - KOUTS IN 46347
29- 49	HOFFMAN, CLARENCE CASPER 'DUTCH'	D. DECEMBER 6, 1962 BELLEVILLE, ILL.
15- 69	HOFFMAN, EDWARD ADOLPH 'TEX'	D. MAY 19, 1947 NEW ORLEANS, LA.
80- 53	HOFFMAN, GLENN EDWARD	217 NORTH DALE ST - ANAHEIM CA 92801
79- 54	HOFFMAN, GUY ALAN	1111 WALNUT STREET - OTTAWA IL 61350
64- 47	HOFFMAN, JOHN EDWARD	2315 NW 85TH - SEATTLE WA 98117
42- 52	HOFFMAN, RAYMOND LAMONT	3509 SILVER LACE LANE #53 - BOYNTON BEACH FL 33436
39- 52	HOFFMAN, WILLIAM JOSEPH	3234 NORTH 25TH ST-PHILADELPHIA PA 19129
49- 35	HOFMAN, ROBERT GEORGE	14 BROOK HOLLOW - OAKLAND NJ 07436

19- 42 HOFMANN, FRED	D. NOVEMBER 19, 1964 ST. HELENA, CAL.
14- 89 HOGAN, GEORGE A.	D. FEBRUARY 28, 1922 BARTLESVILLE, OKLA.
25- 49 HOGAN, JAMES FRANCIS 'SHANTY'	D. APRIL 7, 1967 BOSTON, MASS.
21- 44 HOGAN, KENNETH SYLVESTER	D. JANUARY 2, 1980 CLEVELAND, O.
11- 74 HOGAN, WILLIAM HENRY 'HAPPY'	D. SEPTEMBER 28, 1974 SAN JOSE, CALIF.
11- 75 HOGG, CARTER BRADLEY	D. APRIL 2, 1935 BUENA VISTA, GA.
34- 47 HOGG, WILBERT GEORGE 'BERT'	D. NOVEMBER 5, 1973 DETROIT, MICH.
29- 50 HOGSETT, ELON CHESTER 'CHIEF'	115 WEST 16TH ST - HAYS KS 67601
52- 50 HOGUE, CALVIN GREY	1050 BERKSHIRE RD - DAYTON OH 45419
48- 47 HOGUE, ROBERT CLINTON	D. DECEMBER 22, 1987 MIAMI, FLA.
27- 45 HOHMAN, WILLIAM HENRY	D. OCTOBER 29, 1968 BALTIMORE, MD.
10- 72 HOHNHURST, EDWARD HENRY	D. MARCH 26, 1916 COVINGTON, KY.
44- 61 HOLBOROW, WALTER ALBERT	D. JULY 14, 1986 FORT LAUDERDALE, FLA.
35- 48 HOLBROOK, JAMES MARBURY 'SAMMY'	1215 21ST AVE - MERIDIAN MS 39301
45- 48 HOLCOMBE, KENNETH EDWARD	32 BOTANY DR - ASHEVILLE NC 28805
34- 48 HOLDEN, JOSEPH FRANCIS	424 SOUTH 2ND ST - ST CLAIR PA 17970
13- 86 HOLDEN, WILLIAM PAUL	D. SEPTEMBER 14, 1971 PENSACOLA, FLA.
72- 49 HOLDSWORTH, FREDRICK WILLIAM	47300 WEST MAIN ST - NORTHVILLE MI 48167
14- 90 HOLKE, WALTER HENRY	D. OCTOBER 12, 1954 ST LOUIS, MO.
20- 54 HOLLAHAN, WILLIAM JAMES	D. NOVEMBER 27, 1965 NEW YORK, NEW YORK
77- 67 HOLLAND, ALFRED WILLIS	28 ACORN HILL DRIVE - VOORHEES NJ 08043
26- 38 HOLLAND, HOWARD ARTHUR 'MUL'	D. FEBRUARY 16, 1969 WESTCHESTER, VA.
32- 37 HOLLAND, ROBERT CLYDE 'DUTCH'	D. JUNE 16, 1967 LUMBERTON, N.C.
39- 53 HOLLAND, WILLIAM DAVID	504 CASHWELL PL - GOLDSBORO NC 27530
79- 55 HOLLE, GARY CHARLES	820 FIFTH AVE - WATERVLIET NY 12189
28- 48 HOLLEY, EDWARD EDGAR	D. OCTOBER 26, 1986 PADUCAH, KY.
21- 45 HOLLING, CARL	D. JULY 28, 1962 SONOMA, CAL.
35- 49 HOLLINGSWORTH, ALBERT WAYNE	728B YARSA BLVD - AUSTIN TX 78748
22- 57 HOLLINGSWORTH, JOHN BURNETT 'BONNIE'	801 VANOSDALE ROAD NW #203 - KNOXVILLE TN 37919
49- 36 HOLLMIG, STANLEY ERNEST	D. DECEMBER 4, 1981 SAN ANTONIO, TEXAS
18- 32 HOLLOCHER, CHARLES JACOB	D. AUGUST 14, 1940 STRATMAN, MO.
53- 33 HOLLOMAN, ALVA LEE 'BOBO'	D. MAY 1, 1987 ATHENS, GA.
29- 51 HOLLOWAY, JAMES MADISON	RR 1 BOX 3285 - MARINGOUIN LA 70757
22- 58 HOLLOWAY, KENNETH EUGENE	D. SEPTEMBER 25, 1968 THOMASVILLE, GA.
77- 68 HOLLY, JEFFREY OWEN	2601 ALVORD ST - REDONDO BEACH CA 90278
24- 52 HOLM, ROSCOE ALBERT 'WATTIE'	D. MAY 19, 1950 EVERLY, IA.
43- 64 HOLM, WILLIAM FRED	D. JULY 27, 1977 EAST CHICAGO, IND.
68- 39 HOLMAN, GARY RICHARD	24842 LAKEFIELD - EL TORO CA 93010
80- 54 HOLMAN, RANDY SCOTT	OLD ADD: 750 MOBILE AVE #48 - CAMARILLO CA 93010
18- 33 HOLMES, ELWOOD MARTER	D. APRIL 15, 1954 CAMDEN, N. J.
42- 53 HOLMES, THOMAS FRANCIS	1 PINE DR-WOODBURY NY 11797
30- 36 HOLSHAUSER, HERMAN ALEXANDER	90 WINECOFF AVE NE - CONCORD NC 28025
25- 50 HOLT, JAMES EMMETT MADISON 'RED'	D. FEBRUARY 2, 1961 BIRMINGHAM, ALA.
68- 40 HOLT, JAMES WILLIAM	RR 3 BOX 335 - GRAHAM NC 27253
80- 55 HOLT, ROGER BOYD	1615 SAILFISH AVE - FRUITLAND PARK FL 32731
65- 46 HOLTGRAVE, LAVERN GEORGE 'VERN'	389 NORTH 8TH ST - BREESE IL 62230
85- 49 HOLTON, BRIAN JOHN	829 MAURICE - ISHPEMING MI 49849
65- 47 HOLTZMANN, KENNETH DALE	933 PROVIDENCE - BUFFALO GROVE IL 60089
77- 69 HONEYCUTT, FREDERICK WAYNE 'RICK'	2237 VALLE DR - LAHABRA HEIGHTS CA 90631
25- 51 HOOD, AUBREY LARRISON 'ABE'	807 PEPPER MILL PLACE - VIRGINIA BEACH VA 23464
73- 63 HOOD, DONALD HARRIS	708 FIRESTONE DR - FLORENCE SC 29501
49- 37 HOOD, WALLACE JAMES JR.	966 EILINITA AVE - GLENDALE CA 91208
20- 55 HOOD, WALLACE JAMES SR.	D. MAY 2, 1965 HOLLYWOOD, CAL.
57- 34 HOOK, JAMES WESLEY 'JAY'	768 SUFFIELD - BIRMINGHAM MI 48000
35- 50 HOOKS, ALEXANDER MARCUS	BOX 123-EDGEWOOD TX 75117
50- 35 HOOPER, ROBERT NELSON	D. MARCH 17, 1980 NEW BRUNSWICK, N. J.
74- 53 HOOTEN, MICHAEL LEON	461 NORTH 11TH ST - COOS BAY OR 97420
71- 49 HOOTON, BURT CARLTON	3619 GRANBY COURT - SAN ANTONIO TX 78217
52- 51 HOOVER, RICHARD LLOYD	D. APRIL 12, 1981 LAKE PLACID, FLA.
43- 65 HOOVER, ROBERT JOE	D. SEPTEMBER 2, 1965 LOS ANGELES, CAL.
75- 54 HOPKINS, DONALD	5014 HAWAIIAN TRAIL - CINCINNATI OH 45223
68- 41 HOPKINS, GAIL EASON	131 SOUTH ROSE STREET - LODI CA 95240
34- 49 HOPKINS, MEREDITH HILLIARD 'MARTY'	D. NOVEMBER 20, 1963 DALLAS, TEX.
27- 46 HOPKINS, PAUL HENRY	131 MAIN ST - DEEP RIVER CT 06417
39- 54 HOPP, JOHN LEONARD	715 EAST 5TH ST-HASTINGS NE 68901
46- 48 HOPPER, JAMES MCDANIEL	D. JANUARY 23, 1982 CHARLOTTE, N. C.
13- 87 HOPPER, WILLIAM BOOTH	D. JANUARY 14, 1965 ALLEN PARK, MICH.
24- 53 HORAN, JOSEPH PATRICK 'SHAGS'	D. FEBRUARY 13, 1969 LOS ANGELES, CAL.
61- 53 HORLEN, JOEL EDWARD	3718 CHARTWELL DR - SAN ANTONIO TX 78230
87- 61 HORN, SAMUEL LEE	7463 BLACK OAK RD - SAN DIEGO CA 92114
29- 52 HORNE, BERLYN DALE 'TRADER'	D. FEBRUARY 3, 1983 FRANKLIN, O.
78- 58 HORNER, JAMES ROBERT 'BOB'	209 STEEPLECHASE DRIVE - IRVING TX 75062
15- 70 HORNSBY, ROGERS	D. JANUARY 5, 1963 CHICAGO, ILL.
12- 79 HORSEY, HANSON	D. DECEMBER 1, 1949 MILLINGTON, MD.
17- 35 HORSTMAN, OSCAR THEODORE	D. MAY 11, 1977 SALINA, KAN.
64- 48 HORTON, ANTHONY DARRIN	17001 LIVORNO DR - PACIFIC PALISADES CA 90272
84- 55 HORTON, RICKY NEAL	15703 LAMAR RIDGE ROAD - CHESTERFIELD MO 63017
63- 58 HORTON, WILLIAM WATTERSN	%REID,15124 WARWICK - DETROIT MI 48223
53- 34 HOSKINS, DAVID TAYLOR	D. APRIL 2, 1970 FLINT, MICH.
70- 60 HOSLEY, TIMOTHY KENNETH	401 WEST HENRY ST - SPARTANBURG SC 29301
56- 46 HOST, EUGENE EARL	1415 FULTON ST - NASHVILLE TN 37206
44- 62 HOSTETLER, CHARLES CLOYD	D. FEBRUARY 18, 1971 FORT COLLINS, COLO.
81- 57 HOSTETLER, DAVID ALAN	424 WEST NORMAN - ARCADIA CA 91006
71- 50 HOTTMAN, KENNETH ROGER	7960 BAR DU LN - SACRAMENTO CA 95828
12- 80 HOUCK, BYRON SIMON	D. JUNE 17, 1969 SANTA CRUZ, CALIF.
70- 61 HOUGH, CHARLES OLIVER	2266 SHADE TREE CIR - BREA CA 92621
47- 44 HOUK, RALPH GEORGE	1084 PELHAM COURT - WINTER HAVEN FL 33884
50- 36 HOUSE, HENRY FRANKLIN 'FRANK'	2564 DOLLY RIDGE RD - BIRMINGHAM AL 35243
67- 50 HOUSE, PATRICK LORY	4205 GREEN MEADOWS DR - MERIDIAN ID 83642
71- 51 HOUSE, THOMAS ROSS	12794 VIA FELINO - DEL MAR CA 92014
13- 88 HOUSE, WILLARD EDWIN	D. NOVEMBER 16, 1923 KANSAS CITY, MO.
80- 56 HOUSEHOLDER, PAUL WESLEY	BOX 236 - NORTH MONMOUTH ME 04265
10- 73 HOUSER, BENJAMIN FRANKLIN	D. JANUARY 15, 1952 AUGUSTA, ME.
14- 91 HOUSER, JOSEPH WILLIAM	D. JANUARY 3, 1953 ORLANDO, FLA.
45- 49 HOUTTEMAN, ARTHUR JOSEPH	1755 WEST BUELL RD - LAKE ORION MI 48035
69- 82 HOVLEY, STEPHEN EUGENE	1400 MCANDREW RD #11 - OJAI CA 93023
18- 34 HOVLIK, EDWARD C.	D. MARCH 20, 1955 PAINESVILLE, O.
63- 59 HOWARD, BRUCE ERNEST	3114 BOUGAINVILLEA - SARASOTA FL 33579
12- 81 HOWARD, DAVID AUSTIN	D. JANUARY 26, 1956 DALLAS, TEX.

72- 50	HOWARD, DOUGLAS LYNN	OLD ADD: 352 SOUTH 1200 EAST - SALT LAKE CITY
18- 35	HOWARD, EARL NYCUM	D. APRIL 4, 1937 EVERETT, PA.
55- 59	HOWARD, ELSTON GENE	D. DECEMBER 14, 1980 NEW YORK, N. Y.
58- 46	HOWARD, FRANK OLIVER	560 ST MARYS BLVD - GREEN BAY WI 54301
79- 56	HOWARD, FRED IRVING	88 SCAMMAN ST - SOUTH PORTLAND ME 04106
14- 92	HOWARD, IVAN CHESTER	D. MARCH 30, 1967 MEDFORD, ORE.
70- 62	HOWARD, LARRY RAYFORD	OLD ADD: 2201 BROOKHOLLOW - ABILENE TX 79605
46- 49	HOWARD, LEE VINCENT	1221 SONOMA DRIVE - ALTADENA CA 91001
81- 58	HOWARD, MICHAEL FREDRIC	OLD ADD: 4981 46TH ST - SACRAMENTO CA 95820
73- 64	HOWARD, WILBUR LEON	OLD ADD: 12500 DUNLAP #423 - HOUSTON TX 77031
71- 52	HOWARTH, JAMES EUGENE	606 SANTINI ST - BILOXI MS 39530
74- 54	HOWE, ARTHUR HENRY	711 KAHLDON COURT - HOUSTON TX 77079
52- 52	HOWE, CALVIN EARL	7325 HESSLER DRIVE NE - ROCKFORD MI 49341
23- 65	HOWE, LESTER CURTIS	D. JULY 16, 1976 WOODMERE, N. Y.
80- 57	HOWE, STEVEN ROY	318 WEST 6TH STREET - WHITEFISH MT 59937
47- 45	HOWELL, HOMER ELLIOTT 'DIXIE'	216 STONEHENGE DR - LOUISVILLE KY 40207
85- 50	HOWELL, JACK ROBERT	6401 EAST MALVERN - TUCSON AZ 85718
80- 58	HOWELL, JAY CANFIELD	2920 WASHINGTON ST - MIAMI FL 33133
84- 56	HOWELL, KENNETH	16845 PLAINVIEW - DETROIT MI 48219
40- 37	HOWELL, MILLARD FILLMORE 'DIXIE'	D. MARCH 18, 1960 HOLLYWOOD, FLA.
41- 47	HOWELL, MURRAY DONALD 'RED'	D. OCTOBER 1, 1950 GREENVILLE, S. C.
12- 82	HOWELL, ROLAND BOATNER	D. MARCH 31, 1973
74- 55	HOWELL, ROY LEE	1201 EAST CYPRESS - LOMPOC CA 93436
49- 38	HOWERTON, WILLIAM RAY	1430 BUCKINGHAM WAY - HAYWARD CA 94544
13- 89	HOWLEY, DANIEL PHILIP	D. MARCH 10, 1944 EAST WEYMOUTH, MASS.
61- 54	HOWSER, RICHARD DALTON	D. JUNE 17, 1987 KANSAS CITY, MO.
52- 53	HOYLE, ROLAND EDISON 'TEX'	695 CHURCH ST - CARBONDALE PA 18407
79- 57	HOYT, DEWEY LAMARR	329 PINECLIFF COURT - COLUMBIA SC 29209
18- 36	HOYT, WAITE CHARLES	D. AUGUST 25, 1984 CINCINNATI, O.
70- 63	HRABOSKY, ALAN THOMAS	8800 PLEASANT HILL RD - LITHONIA GA 30058
81- 59	HRBEK, KENT ALAN	OLD ADD: 9108 4TH AVENUE SOUTH - BLOOMINGTON MN 55420
68- 42	HRINIAK, WALTER JOHN	18 STACY DR NORTH - ANDOVER MA 01845
78- 59	HUBBARD, GLENN DEE	127 PEACHTREE APT,⅝CHURCH - ATLANTA GA 30303
28- 49	HUBBELL, CARL OWEN	SUNCREST APT #8,130 NORTH LESEUER #1 - MESA AZ 83205
19- 43	HUBBELL, WILBERT WILLIAM 'BILL'	D. AUGUST 3, 1980 LAKEWOOD, CO.
61- 55	HUBBS, KENNETH DOUGLASS	D. FEBRUARY 15, 1964 UTAH LAKE, UTAH
20- 56	HUBER, CLARENCE BILL	D. FEBRUARY 22, 1965 LAREDO, TEX.
39- 55	HUBER, OTTO	225 MIDLAND AVE - GARFIELD NJ 07026
35- 51	HUCKLEBERRY, EARL EUGENE	RR 2-MAUD OK 74854
83- 74	HUDGENS, DAVID MARK	6550 EAST OSBORN - SCOTTSDALE AZ 85032
23- 66	HUDGENS, JAMES PRICE	D. AUGUST 26, 1955 ST. LOUIS, MO.
84- 57	HUDLER, REX ALLEN	503 EAST MENLO - FRESNO CA 93710
26- 39	HUDLIN, GEORGE WILLIS	14 BETSEY LN - LITTLE ROCK AR 72205
72- 51	HUDSON, CHARLES	RR 5 BOX 50 - COALGATE OK 74538
83- 75	HUDSON, CHARLES LYNN	2124 HEATHER GLEN - DALLAS TX 75232
52- 54	HUDSON, HAL CAMPBELL	15 FARMER ST - NEWNAN GA 30263
69- 83	HUDSON, JESSIE JAMES	1101 ELOISE - MANSFIELD LA 71052
36- 40	HUDSON, JOHN WILSON	D. NOVEMBER 7, 1970 BRYAN, TEX.
74- 56	HUDSON, REX HAUGHTON	5100 NORTH AVENUE A #331 - MIDLAND TX 79705
40- 38	HUDSON, SIDNEY CHARLES	1309 WESTWOOD DR - WACO TX 76710
14- 93	HUENKE, ALBERT A.	D. SEPTEMBER 20, 1974 SAINT MARYS O.
37- 53	HUFFMAN, BENJAMIN FRANKLIN	2 CEDAR LN-LURAY VA 22835
79- 58	HUFFMAN, PHILLIP LEE	334 CALADIUM ST - LAKE JACKSON TX 77566
74- 57	HUGHES, JAMES MICHAEL	7526 EL MANOR AVE - LOS ANGELES CA 90045
52- 55	HUGHES, JAMES ROBERT	4521 WEST 83RD ST - CHICAGO IL 60652
87- 62	HUGHES, KEITH WILLS	309 FRIENDSHIP DRIVE - PAOLI PA 19301
66- 46	HUGHES, RICHARD HENRY	BOX 598 - STEPHENS AR 71764
35- 52	HUGHES, ROY JOHN	4730 BRANDT PIKE-DAYTON OH 45424
70- 64	HUGHES, TERRY WAYNE	432 PIERPONT AVE EXT - SPARTANBURG SC 29303
59- 39	HUGHES, THOMAS EDWARD	OLD ADD: 5921 SOUTHCREST ST - HOUSTON TX
30- 36	HUGHES, THOMAS FRANKLIN	790 19TH ST - BEAUMONT TX 77706
41- 48	HUGHES, THOMAS OWEN	RR 4-MOUNTAINTOP PA 18707
14- 94	HUGHES, VERNON ALEXANDER	D. SEPTEMBER 26, 1961 SEWICKLEY, PA.
21- 46	HUGHES, WILLIAM NESBERT	D. FEBRUARY 25, 1963 BIRMINGHAM, ALA.
41- 49	HUGHSON, CECIL CARLTON 'TEX'	135 WEST SIERRA LN - SAN MARCOS TX 78666
15- 71	HUHN, EMIL HUGO	D. SEPTEMBER 5, 1925 CAMDEN, S.C.
83- 76	HUISMAN, MARK LAWRENCE	1711 F STREET - SCHUYLER NE 68661
83- 77	HULETT, TIMOTHY CRAIG	RR 5 - SPRINGFIELD IL 62707
22- 59	HULIHAN, HARRY JOSEPH	D. SEPTEMBER 11, 1980 RUTLAND, VT.
23- 67	HULVEY, JAMES HENSEL 'HANK'	D. APRIL 9, 1982 MOUNT SIDNEY, VA.
77- 70	HUME, THOMAS HUBERT	1803 WEST 7TH ST - PALMETTO FL 33561
11- 76	HUMPHREY, ALBERT	D. MAY 13, 1961 ASHTABULA, O.
38- 40	HUMPHREY, BYRON WILLIAM 'BILL'	3248 SOUTH CLAY - SPRINGFIELD MO 65807

71- 53 HUMPHREY, TERRYAL GENE	21 ENSUENO WEST - IRVINE CA 92701
62- 58 HUMPHREYS, ROBERT WILLIAM	FARM DEPT., COUNTY STADIUM - MILWAUKEE WI 53246
10- 74 HUMPHRIES, ALBERT	D. SEPTEMBER 21, 1945 ORLANDO, FLA.
38- 41 HUMPHRIES, JOHN WILLIAM	D. JUNE 24, 1965 NEW ORLEANS, LA.
64- 49 HUNDLEY, CECIL RANDOLPH 'RANDY'	122 EAST FOREST LN - PALATINE IL 60067
22- 60 HUNGLING, BERNARD HERMAN	D. MARCH 30, 1968 DAYTON, O.
26- 40 HUNNEFIELD, WILLIAM FENTON	D. AUGUST 28, 1976 NANTUCKET, MASS.
10- 75 HUNT, BENJAMIN FRANKLIN	OLD ADD: 730 K ST - SACRAMENTO CA
85- 51 HUNT, JAMES RANDALL 'RANDY'	117 DESTIN ST - MONTGOMERY AL 36110
59- 40 HUNT, KENNETH LAWRENCE	1464 WEST 170TH ST - GARDENA CA 90247
61- 56 HUNT, KENNETH RAYMOND	268 EAST 300 NORTH - MORGAN UT 84050
31- 41 HUNT, OLIVER JOEL	D. JULY 24, 1978 TEAGUE, TEXAS
63- 60 HUNT, RONALD KENNETH	2806 JACKSON RD - WENTZVILLE MO 63385
33- 26 HUNTER, EDISON FRANKLIN	D. MARCH 14, 1967 COLERAIN TWP., O.
11- 77 HUNTER, FREDERICK CREIGHTON 'NEWT'	D. OCTOBER 26, 1963 COLUMBUS, O.
53- 35 HUNTER, GORDON WILLIAM 'BILLY'	104 EAST SEMINARY AVE - LUTHERVILLE MD 21093
71- 54 HUNTER, HAROLD JAMES 'BUDDY'	5407 SOUTH 15TH ST - OMAHA NE 68107
16- 44 HUNTER, HERBERT HARRISON	D. JULY 26, 1970 ORLANDO, FLA.
65- 48 HUNTER, JAMES AUGUSTUS 'CATFISH'	RR ONE BOX 895 - HERTFORD NC 27944
62- 59 HUNTER, WILLARD MITCHELL	2562 POPPLETON AVE - OMAHA NE 68105
12- 83 HUNTER, WILLIAM ELLSWORTH	D. APRIL 10, 1934 BUFFALO, N.Y.
67- 51 HUNTZ, STEPHEN MICHAEL	4425 FAIRVIEW PKWY - CLEVELAND OH 44126
23- 68 HUNTZINGER, WALTER HENRY	D. AUGUST 11, 1981 UPPER DARBY, PA.
83- 78 HUPPERT, DAVID BLAINE	OLD ADD: ZEPHYRHILLS FL 34283
54- 46 HURD, THOMAS CARR	D. SEPTEMBER 5, 1982 WATERLOO, IOWA
77- 71 HURDLE, CLINTON MERRICK	515 MARGARET ST - MERRITT ISLAND FL 32952
80- 59 HURST, BRUCE VEE	46 PLEASANT ST - WELLESLEY MA 02181
28- 50 HURST, FRANK O'DONNELL 'DON'	D. DECEMBER 6, 1952 LOS ANGELES, CAL.
25- 52 HUSTA, CARL LAWRENCE	D. NOVEMBER 6, 1951 KINGSTON, N. Y.
37- 54 HUSTON, WARREN LLEWELLYN	12 ROBINWOOD ROAD, RR 3 - BUZZARD BAY MA 02532
33- 27 HUTCHESON, JOSEPH JOHNSON	2400 BELL AVE - DENTON TX 76201
40- 39 HUTCHINGS, JOHN RICHARD JOSEPH	D. APRIL 27, 1963 INDIANAPOLIS, IND.
39- 56 HUTCHINSON, FREDERICK CHARLES	D. NOVEMBER 12, 1964 BRADENTON, FLA.
33- 28 HUTCHINSON, IRA KENDALL	D. AUGUST 21, 1973 CHICAGO, ILL.
74- 58 HUTSON, GEORGE HERBERT	7203 WEST SUGARTREE CT - SAVANNAH GA 31410

FRED HUTCHINSON
Cincinnati Reds

HERB HUTSON

25- 53 HUTSON, ROY LEE	D. MAY 20, 1957 LAMESA, CAL.
70- 65 HUTTO, JAMES NEAMON	P.O. BOX 86 - DAYTONA BEACH FL 32015
66- 47 HUTTON, THOMAS GEORGE	1713 LYNDON ST - SOUTH PASADENA CA 91030
55- 60 HYDE, RICHARD ELDE	1506 CAMBRIDGE - CHAMPAIGN IL 61820
73- 65 IGNASIAK, GARY RAYMOND	3084 ANGELUS DRIVE - PONTIAC MI 48055
13- 90 IMLAY, HARRY MILLER 'DOC'	D. OCTOBER 7, 1948 BORDENTOWN, N.J.
86- 66 INCAVIGLIA, PETER JOSEPH	P.O. BOX 526 - PEBBLE BEACH CA 93953
87- 63 INFANTE, FERMIN ALEXIS	EL HATILLO CALLE SVCR #33 - CARACAS VENEZUELA S.A.
14- 95 INGERSOLL, ROBERT RANDOLPH	D. JANUARY 13, 1927 MINNEAPOLIS, MINN.
11- 78 INGERTON, WILLIAM JOHN 'SCOTTY'	D. JUNE 15, 1956 CLEVELAND, O.
29- 53 INGRAM, MELVIN DAVID	D. OCTOBER 28, 1979 MEDFORD, ORE.
87- 64 INNIS, JEFFREY DAVID	3024 GREENLAKE DRIVE - DECATUR IL 62521
77- 72 IORG, DANE CHARLES	1330 NORTH 100 EAST - PLEASANT GROVE UT 84062
78- 60 IORG, GARTH RAY	BOX 1074 - BLUE LAKE CA 95525
41- 50 IOTT, CLARENCE EUGENE 'HOOKS'	D. AUGUST 17, 1980 ST. PETERSBURG, FLA.
14- 96 IRELAN, HAROLD '	D. JULY 16, 1944 CARMEL, IND.
81- 60 IRELAND, TIMOTHY NEAL	20932 TIMES AVE - HAYWARD CA 94541
49- 39 IRVIN, MONFORD MERRILL 'MONTE'	104 SYCAMORE CIR - HOMOSASSA FL 32646
12- 84 IRVIN, WILLIAM EDWARD	D. FEBRUARY 18, 1916 PHILADELPHIA, PA.
38- 42 IRWIN, THOMAS ANDREW	508 50TH ST-ALTOONA PA 16602
21- 47 IRWIN, WALTER KINGSLEY	D. AUGUST 18, 1976 SPRING LAKE, MICH.
80- 60 ISALES, ORLANDO	OLD ADD: 16 SE 1171 CABARRA TER - RIO PIEDRAS PR 00921
71- 55 IVIE, MICHAEL WILSON	534 MIDLAND PARK DR - STONE MOUNTAIN GA 30083
67- 52 IZQUIERDO, ENRIQUE ROBERTO 'HANK'	6011 SW 97TH AVE - MIAMI FL 33173
53- 36 JABLONSKI, RAYMOND LEO	D. NOVEMBER 25, 1985 CHICAGO, ILL.
59- 41 JACKSON, ALVIN NEIL	ONE SAINT MARKS PL - DIX HILLS NY 11746
15- 72 JACKSON, CHARLES HERBERT	D. MAY 27, 1968 RATFORD, VA.
87- 65 JACKSON, CHARLES LEO	5727 37TH AVENUE SOUTH - SEATTLE WA 98118
83- 79 JACKSON, DANNY LYNN	12784 EAST ASBURY CIRCLE #P203 - AURORA CO 80014
78- 61 JACKSON, DARRELL PRESTON	1310 JARVIS AVE - LOS ANGELES CA 90061
85- 52 JACKSON, DARRIN JAY	OLD ADD: 11238 HANNUM AVENUE - CULVER CITY CA 90230
11- 79 JACKSON, GEORGE CHRISTOPHER	D. NOVEMBER 25, 1972 CLEBURNE, TEX.
65- 49 JACKSON, GRANT DWIGHT	212 MESA CIRCLE - UPPER SAINT CLAIR PA 15241
33- 29 JACKSON, JOHN LEWIS	D. OCTOBER 24, 1956 SOMERS POINT, N. J.
87- 66 JACKSON, KENNETH BERNARD	P.O. BOX 613 - WASKOM TX 75692
55- 61 JACKSON, LAWRENCE CURTIS	1861 SHORELINE DR #110 - BOISE ID 83706
58- 47 JACKSON, LOUIS CLARENCE	D. MAY 27, 1969 TOKYO, JAPAN
86- 67 JACKSON, MICHAEL RAY	7234 WILEY STREET - HOUSTON TX 77016
70- 66 JACKSON, MICHAEL WARREN	626 N. 13TH ST - HUMBOLDT TN 38343

50- 37 JACKSON, RANSOM JOSEPH 'RANDY'   250 HUNNICUT DR - ATHENS GA 30601
67- 53 JACKSON, REGINALD MARTINEZ   2449 F. UNION BLVD #11A - ISLIP NY 11751
63- 61 JACKSON, ROLAND THOMAS 'SONNY'   3377 BOBOLINK DR - ATLANTA GA 30311
54- 47 JACKSON, RONALD ALLEN   2828 SPRINGBROOK DR - KALAMAZOO MI 49004
75- 55 JACKSON, RONNIE D   2944 PEMBROKE CT - FULLERTON CA 92631
77- 73 JACKSON, ROY LEE   711 DOGWOOD AVE - OPELIKA AL 36801
22- 61 JACKSON, TRAVIS CALVIN   D. JULY 27, 1987 WALDO, ARK.
86- 68 JACKSON, VINCENT EDWARD 'BO'   P.O. BOX 2517 - AUBURN AL 36831
14- 97 JACKSON, WILLIAM RILEY   D. SEPTEMBER 26, 1958 PEORIA, ILL.
48- 48 JACOBS, ANTHONY ROBERT   D. DECEMBER 21, 1980 NASHVILLE, TENN.
39- 57 JACOBS, ARTHUR EVAN   D. JUNE 8, 1967 INGLEWOOD, CAL.
54- 48 JACOBS, FORREST VANDERGRIFT 'SPOOK' BOX 66 - MILFORD DE 19963
60- 49 JACOBS, LAMAR GARY 'JAKE'   BOX 340 - CANFIELD OH 44406
37- 55 JACOBS, NEWTON SMITH 'BUCKY'   1437 GREYCOURT AVE-RICHMOND VA 23227
18- 37 JACOBS, OTTO ALBERT   D. NOVEMBER 19, 1955 CHICAGO, ILL.
28- 51 JACOBS, RAYMOND F.   D. APRIL 5, 1952 LOS ANGELES, CAL.
14- 98 JACOBS, WILLIAM ELMER   D. FEBRUARY 10, 1958 SALEM , MO.
15- 73 JACOBSON, MERWIN JOHN WILLIAM   D. JANUARY 13, 1978 BALTIMORE, MD.
15- 74 JACOBSON, WILLIAM CHESTER 'BABY DOLL' D. JANUARY 16, 1977 ORION, ILL.
18- 38 JACOBUS, STUART LOUIS 'LARRY'   D. AUGUST 19, 1965 NORTH COLLEGE HILL, OHIO
81- 61 JACOBY, BROOK WALLACE   1027 ROSEWOOD DR - OXNARD CA 93030
71- 56 JACQUEZ, PATRICK THOMAS   8351 COLONIAL - STOCKTON CA 95209
64- 50 JAECKEL, PAUL HENRY   250 SOUTH ROSE DR #141 - PLACENTIA CA 92690
20- 57 JAEGER, JOSEPH PETER   D. DECEMBER 13, 1963 HAMPTON, IA.
25- 54 JAHN, ARTHUR CHARLES   D. JANUARY 9, 1948 LITTLE ROCK, ARK.
36- 41 JAKUCKI, SIGMUND   D. MAY 28, 1979 GALVESTON, TEXAS
24- 54 JAMERSON, CHARLEY DEWEY   D. AUGUST 4, 1980 MOCKSVILLE, N. C.
75- 56 JAMES, ARTHUR   4531 GARLAND AVE - DETROIT MI 48214

JESSE JEFFERSON

60- 50 JAMES, CHARLES WESLEY   104 COLLIER ST - FULTON MO 65221
68- 43 JAMES, CLEO JOEL   6020 KITTYHAWK DR - RIVERSIDE CA 92504
83- 80 JAMES, DION   804 NINTH AVENUE - SACRAMENTO CA 95818
86- 69 JAMES, DONALD CHRISTOPHER 'CHRIS' RURAL ROUTE 2 BOX 231 - ALTO TX 75925
68- 44 JAMES, JEFFREY LYNN   25649 LAWRENCE ROAD - JUNCTION CITY OR 97448
58- 48 JAMES, JOHN PHILLIP   6037 EAST LARKSPUR - SCOTTSDALE AZ 85254
77- 74 JAMES, PHILIP ROBERT 'SKIP'   7716 W. 72ND TER - OVERLAND PARK KS 66204
67- 54 JAMES, RICHARD LEE   2358 FOXWORTH DR - PANAMA CITY FL 32405
29- 54 JAMES, ROBERT BYRNE 'BERNIE'   12222 BLANCO #1507 - SAN ANTONIO TX 78216
78- 62 JAMES, ROBERT HARVEY   7838 KYLE - SUNLAND CA 91040
12- 85 JAMES, WILLIAM A. 'LEFTY'   D. MAY 3, 1933 PORTSMOUTH, O.
11- 80 JAMES, WILLIAM HENRY   D. MAY 24, 1942 VENICE, CALIF.
13- 91 JAMES, WILLIAM LAWRENCE   D. MARCH 10, 1971 OROVILLE, CALOF.
15- 75 JAMIESON, CHARLES DEVINE   D. OCTOBER 27, 1969 PATERSON, N.J.
70- 67 JANESKI, GERALD JOSEPH   317 NORTH MISSION DR - SAN GABRIEL CA 91711
53- 37 JANOWICZ, VICTOR FELIX   1966 JERVIS RD - COLUMBUS OH 43221
47- 46 JANSEN, LAWRENCE JOSEPH   RR 2 BOX 413A - FOREST GROVE OR 97116
10- 76 JANSEN, RAYMOND WILLIAM   D. MARCH 19, 1934 ST. LOUIS, MO.
12- 86 JANTZEN, WALTER C. 'HEINIE'   D. APRIL 1, 1948 HINES, ILL.
11- 81 JANVRIN, HAROLD CHANDLER   D. MARCH 1, 1962 BOSTON, MASS.
44- 63 JARVIS, LEROY GILBERT   2605 NORTH HUDSON - OKLAHOMA CITY OK 73103
69- 84 JARVIS, RAYMOND ARNOLD   OLD ADD: 266 FRUITHILL AVE - NORTH PROVIDENCE RI 02911
66- 48 JARVIS, ROBERT PATRICK 'PAT'   4425 EAST KINGSPOINTS CIR - DUNWOOD GA 30338
14- 99 JASPER, HARRY W. 'HI'   D. MAY 22, 1937 ST. LOUIS, MO.
65- 50 JASTER, LARRY EDWARD   1105 MATTES DRIVE - MIDLAND MI 48640
72- 52 JATA, PAUL   1598 BIRARD STREET - WANTAGH NY 11793
40- 40 JAVERY, ALVA WILLIAM   D. SEPTEMBER 13, 1977 WOODSTOCK, CONN.
76- 41 JAVIER, IGNACIO ALFREDO   BARRIO LIBRE #96 ING CON-SAN PEDRO DE MACORIS DOM. REP.
60- 51 JAVIER, MANUEL JULIAN   B#12 URB. PINA - SAN FRANCISCO DE MACORIS DOM. REP.
84- 58 JAVIER, STANLEY JULIAN ANTONIO   B#12 URB. PINA-SAN FRANCISCO DE MACORIS DOMINICAN REP.
53- 38 JAY, JOSEPH RICHARD   3660 STATE ROAD 580 #80 - OLDSMAR FL 34677
21- 48 JEANES, ERNEST LEE 'TEX'   D. APRIL 5, 1973 LONGVIEW, TEX.
36- 42 JEFFCOAT, GEORGE EDWARD   D. OCTOBER 13, 1978 LEESVILLE, S. C.
48- 49 JEFFCOAT, HAROLD BENTLEY   4016 WISCONSIN AVE - TAMPA FL 33616
83- 81 JEFFCOAT, JAMES MICHAEL 'MIKE'   RURAL ROUTE 1 BOX 289 - PINE BLUFF AR 71603
87- 67 JEFFERIES, GREGORY SCOTT   70 DUMONT COURT - MILLBRAE CA 94030
73- 66 JEFFERSON, JESSE HARRISON   1421 RAILROAD AVE - MIDLOTHIAN VA 23113
86- 70 JEFFERSON, STANLEY   2420-3E HUNTER AVENUE - BRONX NY 10475
30- 37 JEFFRIES, IRVINE FRANKLIN   D. JUNE 8, 1982 LOUISVILLE, KY.
41- 51 JELINCICH, FRANK ANTHONY   LIBERTY TOWER 99, 890 MAIN ST - SANTA CLARA CA 95050
87- 68 JELKS, GREGORY DION   615 BAY SPRINGS ROAD - CENTRE AL 35960
83- 82 JELTZ, LARRY STEVEN 'STEVE'   615 WEST 28TH PLACE - LAWRENCE KS 66044
65- 51 JENKINS, FERGUSON ARTHUR   P.O. BOX 1937 - BLENHEIM ONTARIO NOP 1AO CAN.
22- 62 JENKINS, JOHN ROBERT   D. AUGUST 3, 1968 COLUMBIA, MO.
14-100 JENKINS, JOSEPH DANIEL   D. JUNE 21, 1974 FRESNO, CALIF.

25- 55	JENKINS, THOMAS GRIFFIN	D. MAY 3, 1979 WEYMOUTH, MASS.
62- 60	JENKINS, WARREN WASHINGTON 'JACK'	3810 OBISPO - TAMPA FL 33609
51- 44	JENNINGS, WILLIAM LEE	7065 FOXCROFORT DR - AFFTON MO 63123
31- 42	JENSEN, FORREST DUCENUS 'WOODY'	1311 NORTH PARKWOOD LANE - WICHITA KS 67208
50- 38	JENSEN, JACK EUGENE	D. JULY 14, 1982 CHARLOTTESVILLE, VA.
12- 87	JENSEN, WILLIAM CHRISTIAN	D. MARCH 27, 1917 PHILADELPHIA, PA.
29- 55	JESSEE, DANIEL EDWARD	D. APRIL 30, 1970 VENICE, FLA.
69- 85	JESTADT, GARRY ARTHUR	825 PARNELL PL - SUNNYVALE CA 94087
52- 56	JESTER, VIRGIL MILTON	8130 RALEIGH PL - WESTMINSTER CO 80030
69- 86	JETER, JOHN	1590 METRPOLIAN AVE #2F - BRONX NY 10462
50- 39	JETHROE, SAMUEL	340 EAST 14TH ST - ERIE PA 16503
83- 83	JIMENEZ, ALFONSO 'HOUSTON'	OLD ADD: NAVOJOA MEXICO
64- 51	JIMENEZ, FELIX ELVIO	SIMON BOLIVAR #24 - SAN PEDRO DE MACORIS DOM. REP.
62- 61	JIMENEZ, MANUEL EMILIO	24 SIMON BOLIVAR - SAN PEDRO DE MACORIS DOM. REP.
74- 59	JIMINEZ, JUAN ANTONIO	CALLE 9,CASA 1N EL ENSUENO - SANTIAGO DOMINICAN REP.
63- 62	JOHN, THOMAS EDWARD	3133 N. 16TH ST - TERRE HAUTE IN 47804
26- 41	JOHNS, AUGUSTUS FRANCIS	D. SEPTEMBER 12, 1975 SAN ANTONIO, TEX.
15- 76	JOHNS, WILLIAM R. 'PETE'	D. AUGUST 9, 1964 CLEVELAND, O.
14-101	JOHNSON, ADAM RANKIN SR	D. JULY 2, 1972 WILLIAMSPORT, PA.
41- 52	JOHNSON, ADAM RANKIN 'RANK' JR.	1308 1/2 WARREN AVENUE - WILLIAMSPORT PA 17701
64- 52	JOHNSON, ALEXANDER	7650 GRAND RIVER - DETROIT MI 48206
81- 62	JOHNSON, ANTHONY CLAIR	OLD ADD: 4446 JANSSEN DR - MEMPHIS TN 38128
27- 47	JOHNSON, ARTHUR GILBERT	D. JUNE 7, 1982 SARASOTA, FLA.
40- 41	JOHNSON, ARTHUR HENRY	23 HEMLOCK DR-HOLDEN MA 01520
59- 42	JOHNSON, BENJAMIN FRANKLIN	112 LOCKSLEY DR - GREENWOOD SC 29646
81- 63	JOHNSON, BOBBY EARL	OLD ADD: 3432 SOUTH LOOP 12 - DALLAS TX 75224
46- 50	JOHNSON, CHESTER LILLIS	D. APRIL 10, 1983 SEATTLE, WASH.
69- 87	JOHNSON, CLAIR BARTH 'BART'	904 INDIAN BOUNDARY DRIVE - WESTMONT IL 60559
72- 53	JOHNSON, CLIFFORD	318 GLEN OAK - SAN ANTONIO TX 78220
53- 39	JOHNSON, CLIFFORD 'CONNIE'	1900 EAST 54TH ST - KANSAS CITY MO 64130
52- 57	JOHNSON, DARRELL DEAN	3 BUSSELL PARK ROAD - ORD NE 68862
65- 52	JOHNSON, DAVID ALLEN	4245 BEAR GULLEY RD - WINTER PARK FL 32789
74- 60	JOHNSON, DAVID CHARLES	2402 MARCHALL ST - ABILENE TX 79605
87- 69	JOHNSON, DAVID WAYNE	9747 BIRD RIVER ROAD - MIDDLE RIVER MD 21220
60- 52	JOHNSON, DERON ROGER	13847 TWIN PEAKS RD - POWAY CA 92064
47- 47	JOHNSON, DONALD ROY	1925 NE 19TH AVENUE #5A - PORTLAND OR 97212
43- 66	JOHNSON, DONALD SPORE	580 BROOKS - LAGUNA BEACH CA 92651
40- 42	JOHNSON, EARL DOUGLAS	9541 25TH AVE NW-SEATTLE WA 98107
20- 58	JOHNSON, EDWIN CYRIL	D. JULY 3, 1975 MORGANFIELD, KY.
12- 88	JOHNSON, ELLIS WATT	D. JANUARY 14, 1965 MINNEAPOLIS, MINN.
14-102	JOHNSON, ELMER ELLSWORTH	D. OCTOBER 31, 1966 HOLLYWOOD, FLA.
12- 89	JOHNSON, ERNEST RUDOLPH	D. MAY 1, 1952 MONROVIA, CALIF.
50- 40	JOHNSON, ERNEST THORWALD	500 DORRIS RD - ALPHARETTA GA 30201
66- 49	JOHNSON, FRANK HERBERT	568 NORTH CENTER ST - MESA AZ 85201
22- 63	JOHNSON, FREDERICK EDWARD	D. JUNE 14, 1973 KERRVILLE, TEX.
13- 92	JOHNSON, GEORGE HOWARD 'CHIEF'	D. JUNE 12, 1922 DES MOINES, IA.
25- 56	JOHNSON, HENRY WARD	D. AUGUST 20, 1982 BRADENTON, FLA.
82- 63	JOHNSON, HOWARD MICHAEL	7 WAGAMAN DRIVE - WOODBURY NY 11797
70- 68	JOHNSON, JAMES BRIAN	1459 MADISON ST - MUSKEGON MI 49442
68- 45	JOHNSON, JERRY MICHAEL	4566 DEL MAR AVE - SAN DIEGO CA 92107
44- 64	JOHNSON, JOHN CLIFFORD	810 MINE STREET - NORWAY MI 49870
78- 63	JOHNSON, JOHN HENRY	7578 YOUNG CIR - RENO NV 89511
85- 53	JOHNSON, JOSEPH RICHARD	14 EVERGREEN RD - PLAINVILLE MA 02762
87- 70	JOHNSON, KENNETH LANCE	1109 VAN BUREN #D - LINCOLN HEIGHTS OH 45215
58- 49	JOHNSON, KENNETH TRAVIS	121 MYRTLEWOOD DR - PINEVILLE LA 71360
47- 48	JOHNSON, KENNETH WANDERSEE	326 BROOKFIELD - WICHITA KS 67206
74- 61	JOHNSON, LAMAR	5105 YUCCA COURT - ARLINGTON TX 76017
72- 54	JOHNSON, LARRY DOBY	3115 EAST 98TH ST - CLEVELAND OH 44104
34- 50	JOHNSON, LLOYD WILLIAM	D. OCTOBER 8, 1980 STOCKTON, CALIF.
60- 53	JOHNSON, LOUIS BROWN	5830 GREEN VALLEY CIR - CULVER CITY CA 90230
74- 62	JOHNSON, MICHAEL NORTON	OLD ADD: RR 1 - FARIBAULT MN 55021
11- 82	JOHNSON, OTIS L.	D. NOVEMBER 9, 1915 JOHNSON CITY, N. Y.
20-136	JOHNSON, PAUL OSCAR	D. FEBRUARY 14, 1973 MCALLEN, TEX.
82- 64	JOHNSON, RANDALL GLENN	852 WEST 11TH AVE - ESCONDIDO CA 92025
80- 61	JOHNSON, RANDALL STUART	40 WEST 64TH ST - HIALEAH FL 33012
58- 50	JOHNSON, RICHARD ALLAN	808-B NORTH BEELINE - PAYSON AZ 85541
69- 88	JOHNSON, ROBERT DALE	12862 MALENA DR - SANTA ANA CA 92705
33- 30	JOHNSON, ROBERT LEE	D. JULY 6, 1982 TACOMA, WASH.
60- 54	JOHNSON, ROBERT WALLACE	1474 BARCLAY ST - ST PAUL MN 55106
82- 65	JOHNSON, RONALD DAVID	11371 KATHY LN - GARDEN GROVE CA 92640
86- 71	JOHNSON, RONDIN ALLEN	3620 SOUTHWEST 102 ND - SEATTLE WA 98146
29- 56	JOHNSON, ROY CLEVELAND	D. SEPTEMBER 10, 1973 TACOMA, WASH.
82- 66	JOHNSON, ROY EDWARD	902 NORTH ST. LOUIS - CHICAGO IL 60651

18- 40 JOHNSON, ROY J. 'HARDROCK'	D. JANUARY 10, 1986 SCOTTSDALE, ARIZ.
16- 45 JOHNSON, RUSSELL CONWELL 'JING'	D. DECEMBER 6, 1950 POTTSTOWN, PA.
28- 52 JOHNSON, SILAS KENNETH	BOX 291 - SHERIDAN IL 60551
60- 55 JOHNSON, STANLEY LUCIUS	56 MORNINGSIDE DR - DALY CITY CA 94015
22- 64 JOHNSON, SYLVESTER	D. FEBRUARY 20, 1985 PORTLAND, ORE.
74- 63 JOHNSON, THOMAS RAYMOND	27415 SANTA FE STREET - HEMET CA 92343
73- 67 JOHNSON, TIMOTHY EWALD	7004 JENNER COURT - CITRUS HEIGHTS CA 95610
44- 65 JOHNSON, VICTOR OSCAR	1515 DRURY AVE - EAU CLAIRE WI 54701
81- 64 JOHNSON, WALLACE DARNELL	2512 ADAMS ST - GARY IN 46407
83- 84 JOHNSON, WILLIAM CHARLES	OLD ADD: 1701 N. LINCOLN ST - WILMINGTON DE 19806
16- 46 JOHNSON, WILLIAM LAWRENCE	D. NOVEMBER 5, 1950 LOS ANGELES, CALIF.
43- 67 JOHNSON, WILLIAM RUSSEL	2903 LAKE FOREST DR-AUGUSTA GA 30904
79- 59 JOHNSTON, GREGORY BERNARD	1406 PROSPECT DRIVE - POMONA CA 91766
11- 83 JOHNSTON, JAMES HARLE	D. FEBRUARY 14, 1967 CHATTANOOGA, TENN.
13- 93 JOHNSTON, JOHN THOMAS	15117 ILLINOIS ST - PARAMOUNT CA 90723
64- 53 JOHNSTON, REX DAVID	D. JULY 14, 1959 TYLER, TEX.
24- 55 JOHNSTON, WILFRED IVEY 'FRED'	1300 WENTWORTH AVE - PASADENA CA 91106
66- 50 JOHNSTONE, JOHN WILLIAM 'JAY'	BOX 153 - VINA CA 96092
34- 51 JOINER, ROY MERRILL	D. MARCH 6, 1972 BUFFALO, N. Y.
54- 49 JOK, STANLEY EDWARD	2020 SANTA CLARA AVE #402 - ALAMEDA CA 94501
30- 38 JOLLEY, SMEAD POWELL	D. MAY 27, 1963 DURHAM, N. C.
53- 40 JOLLY, DAVID	RURAL ROUTE 1 BOX 63 - CHARLESTON MS 38921
83- 85 JONES, ALFORNIA	D. NOVEMBER 25, 1980 COLUMBIA, S. C.
32- 38 JONES, ARTHUR LENOX	411 SOUTH MORTON AVENUE - CENTERVILLE IN 47330
86- 72 JONES, BARRY LOUIS	D. DECEMBER 28, 1952 PITTSBURG, KAN.
16- 47 JONES, CARROLL ELMER 'DEACON'	1821 WESTWARD HO CIR - EL CAJON CA 92021
85- 54 JONES, CHRISTOPHER DALE	P.O. BOX 4064 - ATLANTA GA 30302
67- 55 JONES, CLARENCE WOODROW	751 EDWARD ST - MOBILE AL 36610
63- 63 JONES, CLEON JOSEPH	D. JUNE 3, 1969 DENVER, COLO.
28- 53 JONES, COBURN DYAS	D. NOVEMBER 8, 1980 ORLANDO, FLA.
41- 53 JONES, DALE ELDON	BOX 175 - HARMONSBURG PA 16422
79- 60 JONES, DARRYL LEE	125 MCAULEY DR - VICKSBURG MS 39180
26- 42 JONES, DECATUR POINDEXTER 'DICK'	3107 FAITH - WEST COVINA CA 91792
82- 67 JONES, DOUGLAS REID	4054 MONTECITO AVE - FRESNO CA 93702
45- 50 JONES, EARL LESLIE	475 S. WESTRIDGE CIR - ANAHEIM HILLS CA 92807
70- 69 JONES, GARY HOWELL	53 MOONLIT CIR - SACRAMENTO CA 95831
54- 50 JONES, GORDON BASSETT	1015 GOLDFINCH - SUGARLAND TX 77478
62- 62 JONES, GROVER WILLIAM 'DEACON'	4125 PALMYRA RD - LOS ANGELES CA 90008
61- 57 JONES, HAROLD MARION	D. JULY 15, 1972 JEANNETTE, PA.
21- 49 JONES, HOWARD	3054 NEWCASTLE DRIVE - DALLAS TX 75220
86- 73 JONES, JAMES CONDIA	10155 MAMMOTH AVE - BATON ROUGE LA 70814
64- 54 JONES, JAMES DALTON	BOX 156-EPPS LA 71237
41- 54 JONES, JAMES MURRELL 'JAKE'	311 WHITE HORSE PL - HADDON HEIGHTS NJ 08035
83- 86 JONES, JEFFERY RAYMOND	15626 DRAKE - SOUTHGATE MI 48198
80- 62 JONES, JEFFREY ALLEN	D. SEPTEMBER 7, 1977 LEWES, DEL.
23- 69 JONES, JESSE F. 'BROADWAY'	D. MAY 13, 1961 ST. LOUIS, MO.
24- 56 JONES, JOHN JOSEPH 'BINKY'	D. JUNE 5, 1980 RUSTON, LA.
19- 44 JONES, JOHN PAUL	D. NOVEMBER 3, 1956 BALTIMORE, MD.
23- 70 JONES, JOHN WILLIAM	4 RIDGE ROAD - SIMSBURY CT 06070
24- 57 JONES, KENNETH FREDERICK	BOX 175 - HARMONSBURG PA 16422
79- 61 JONES, LYNN MORRIS	184 NATHAN RD - ATLANTA GA 30331
61- 58 JONES, MACK	OLD ADD: 6182 HILLVIEW COURT - JACKSONVILLE FL 32210
80- 63 JONES, MICHAEL CARL	D. JUNE 30, 1975 LINCOLN, CALIF.
40- 43 JONES, MORRIS E. 'RED'	17800 LYSANDER DR - CARSON CA 90746
75- 57 JONES, ODELL	D. MARCH 18, 1979 DALLAS, TEXAS
20- 59 JONES, PERCY LEE	15358 MIDLAND RD - POWAY CA 92064
73- 68 JONES, RANDALL LEO	4071 GREENSTONE COURT - DECATUR GA 30035
86- 74 JONES, RICKY MIRON	2107 ABEYTA CT - LOVELAND CO 80537
74- 64 JONES, ROBERT OLIVER	D. AUGUST 30, 1964 SAN DIEGO, CAL.
17- 36 JONES, ROBERT WALTER	5371 WEST 12TH AVE - HIALEAH FL 33012
84- 59 JONES, ROSS A.	P.O. BOX 1149 - POWAY CA 92064
76- 42 JONES, RUPPERT SANDERSON	D. NOVEMBER 5, 1971 MORGANTOWN, W. VA.
51- 45 JONES, SAMUEL	D. JULY 6, 1966 BARNESVILLE, O.
14-103 JONES, SAMUEL POND 'SAD SAM'	506 MATTOX DR #23 - GREENVILLE NC 27834
46- 51 JONES, SHELDON LESLIE 'AVAILABLE'	WYANDOTTE COUNTY POLICE DEPT. - KANSAS CITY KS 66101
60- 56 JONES, SHERMAN JARVIS 'ROADBLOCK'	8116 KINGSDALE DR - KNOXVILLE TN 37919
67- 56 JONES, STEVEN HOWELL	4835 MANVILLE CIRCLE - JACKSONVILLE FL 32210
76- 43 JONES, THOMAS FREDERICK ;RICK'	6204 GREENEYES WAY - ORANGEVALE CA 95662
77- 75 JONES, TIMOTHY BYRON	13727 JUDAH AVENUE - HAWTHORNE CA 90250
86- 75 JONES, TRACY DONALD	7322 ALCEDO CIR - SACRAMENTO CA 95823
46- 52 JONES, VERNAL LEROY 'NIPPY'	D. OCTOBER 10, 1946 BOSTON, MASS.
11- 84 JONES, WILLIAM DENNIS	D. FEBRUARY 26, 1938 WICHITA, KAN.
11- 85 JONES, WILLIAM RODERICK 'TEX'	D. OCTOBER 18, 1983 CINCINNATI, O.
47- 49 JONES, WILLIE EDWARD	D. AUGUST 23, 1977 NEW YORK, N. Y.
20- 60 JONNARD, CLARENCE JAMES 'BUBBER'	D. AUGUST 27, 1959 NASHVILLE, TENN.
21- 50 JONNARD, CLAUDE ALFRED	245 BELGREEN PLACE - SANTA ROSA CA 95405
36- 43 JOOST, EDWIN DAVID	2004-D LINCOLNTON RD - SALISBURY NC 28144
27- 48 JORDAN, BAXTER BYERLY 'BUCK'	D. DECEMBER 4, 1957 GASTONIA, N. C.
33- 31 JORDAN, JAMES WILLIAM	57 LAKESHORE RD - LANSING NY 14881
53- 41 JORDAN, MILTON MIGNOT	1114 METCALF - SEDRO WOOLLEY WA 98284
51- 46 JORDAN, NILES CHAPMAN	D. JUNE 5, 1960 MERIDEN, CONN.
12- 90 JORDAN, RAYMOND WILLIS 'RIP'	2909 SOUTH WYOMING - ROSWELL NM 88201
44- 66 JORDAN, THOMAS JEFFERSON	D. MARCH 1, 1980 WILMETTE, ILL.
29- 57 JORGENS, ARNDT LUDWIG 'ART'	129 SOUTH SPRUCE ST-WOOD DALE IL 60191
35- 53 JORGENS, ORVILLE EDWARD	8267 KIRKWOOD CT - CUCAMONGA CA 91730
47- 50 JORGENSEN, JOHN DONALD 'SPIDER'	1604 LILLIAN AVE - ARLINGTON TX 76013
68- 46 JORGENSEN, MICHAEL	119 MINNIE ST - SANTA CRUZ CA 95062
37- 56 JORGENSON, CARL 'PINKY'	D. SEPTEMBER 8, 1979 SANTIAGO DOM REP
64- 55 JOSEPH, RICARDO EMELINDO	511 NORTH WALNUT - NEW HAMPTON IA 50659
65- 53 JOSEPHSON, DUANE CHARLES	1896 REDDING AVE - UPLAND CA 91786
69- 89 JOSHUA, VON EVERETT	D. SEPTEMBER 23, 1961 NEW ORLEANS, LA.
16- 48 JOURDAN, THEODORE CHARLES	1609 WHITMAN LN - WHEATON IL 60187
62- 63 JOYCE, MICHAEL LEWIS	20 HILLSIDE AVENUE - UPPER SADDLE RIVER NJ 07458
65- 54 JOYCE, RICHARD EDWARD	D. DECEMBER 10, 1981 SAN FRANCISCO, CALIF.
39- 58 JOYCE, ROBERT EMMETT	2186 TUDOR CASTLE WAY - DECATUR GA 30035
86- 76 JOYNER, WALLACE KEITH	D. MAY 6, 1957 LAPEER, MICH.
27- 49 JUDD, RALPH WESLEY	CATERBURY ST 64 - INGERSOLL ONTARIO CAN.
41- 55 JUDD, THOMAS WILLIAM OSCAR	

Curt Kaufman

15- 77	JUDGE, JOSEPH IGNATIUS	D. MARCH 11, 1963 WASHINGTON, D.C.
40- 44	JUDNICH, WALTER FRANKLIN	D. JULY 12, 1971 GLENDALE, CAL..
48- 50	JUDSON, HOWARD KOLLS	239 FAIRWAY CIRCLE NE - WINTER HAVEN FL 33881
35- 54	JUDY, LYLE LEROY	410 FLAGLER BLVD - SAINT AUGUSTINE FL 32084
39- 59	JUELICH, JOHN WALTER	D. DECEMBER 25, 1970 ST. LOUIS, MO.
40- 45	JUMONVILLE, GEORGE BENEDICT	5507 WILLIAM & MARY - MOBILE AL 36608
37- 57	JUNGELS, KENNETH PETER	D. SEPTEMBER 9, 1975 WEST BEND, WIS.
82- 68	JURAK, EDWARD JAMES	3650 SOUTH WALKER AVE - SAN PEDRO CA 90731
65- 55	JUREWICZ, MICHAEL ALLEN	17826 IXONIA AVE WEST - LAKEVILLE MN 55044
31- 43	JURGES, WILLIAM FREDERICK	7001 142ND AVE #74 - LARGO FL 33541
44- 67	JURISICH, ALVIN JOSEPH	D. NOVEMBER 3, 1981 NEW ORLEANS, LA.
44- 68	JUST, JOSEPH ERWIN	7708 WEST KANGAROO LAKE-BAILEYS HARBOR WI 54202
72- 55	JUTZE, ALFRED HENRY 'SKIP'	3395 ZEPHYR CT - WHEAT RIDGE CO 80033
14-104	JUUL, EARL HERBERT	D. JANUARY 4, 1942 CHICAGO, ILL.
11- 86	JUUL, HERBERT VICTOR	D. NOVEMBER 14, 1928 CHICAGO, ILL.
59- 43	KAAT, JAMES LEE	1355 ERROL PKWY #140 - APOPKA FL 32712
10- 77	KADING, JOHN FREDERICK	D. JUNE 2, 1964 CHICAGO, ILL.
13- 94	KAFORA, FRANK JACOB 'JAKE'	D. MARCH 23, 1928 CHICAGO, ILL.
22- 65	KAHDOT, ISAAC LEONARD 'IKE'	2218 NW 42ND - OKLAHOMA CITY OK 73112
38- 43	KAHLE, ROBERT WAYNE	5311 GLASGOW CT-LOS ANGELES CA 90045
10- 78	KAHLER, GEORGE RANNELS	D. FEBRUARY 14, 1924 BATTLE CREEK, MICH.
30- 39	KAHN, OWEN EARLE 'JACK'	D. JANUARY 17, 1981 RICHMOND, VA.
80- 64	KAINER, DONALD WAYNE	10 DARNELL - CONROE TX 77301
11- 87	KAISER, ALFRED EDWARD	D. APRIL 11, 1969 CINCINNATI, O.
55- 62	KAISER, CLYDE DONALD 'DON'	2901 EAST 12TH - ADA OK 74820
85- 55	KAISER, JEFFREY PATRICK	15324 DUMAY - SOUTHGATE MI 48195
71- 57	KAISER, ROBERT THOMAS	30606 LAKE ROAD - BAY VILLAGE OH 44140
14-105	KAISERLING, GEORGE	D. MARCH 2, 1918 STEUBENVILLE, O.
37- 58	KALFASS, WILLIAM PHILIP	D. SEPTEMBER 8, 1968 BROOKLYN, N. Y.
40- 46	KALIN, FRANK BRUNO	D. JANUARY 12, 1975 WEIRTON, W. VA.
53- 42	KALINE, ALBERT WILLIAM	945 TIMBERLAKE DR - BLOOMFIELD HILLS MI 48013
18- 41	KALLIO, RUDOLPH	D. APRIL 6, 1979 NEWPORT, ORE.
23- 71	KAMM, WILLIAM EDWARD 'WILLIE'	22 BRIARWOOD WAY - BELMONT CA 94002
78- 64	KAMMEYER, ROBERT LYNN	4711 DEL RIO RD - SACRAMENTO CA 95822
24- 58	KAMP, ALPHONSE FRANCIS	D. FEBRUARY 25, 1955 BOSTON, MASS.
34- 52	KAMPOURIS, ALEX WILLIAM	2776 17TH ST - SACRAMENTO CA 95818
15- 78	KANE, FRANCIS THOMAS	D. DECEMBER 2, 1962 BROCKTON, MASS.
25- 57	KANE, JOHN FRANCIS	D. JULY 25, 1956 CHICAGO, ILL.
38- 44	KANE, THOMAS JOSEPH	D. NOVEMBER 26, 1973 CHICAGO, ILL.
62- 64	KANEHL, RODERICK EDWIN	2186 STARR ROAD - PALM SPRINGS CA 92262
14-106	KANTLEHNER, ERVINE LESLIE	66-2 BARRANCE AVE - SANTA BARBARA CA 93109
36- 44	KARDOW, PAUL OTTO	D. APRIL 27, 1968 SAN ANTONIO, TEXAS
86- 77	KARKOVICE, RONALD JOSEPH	4531 SHELDRAKE DRIVE - ORLANDO FL 32806
43- 68	KARL, ANTON ANDREW	8 CANDLEWOOD ROAD - NEW FAIRFIELD CT 06812
30- 40	KARLON, WILLIAM JOHN 'JACK'	D. DECEMBER 7, 1964 WARE, MASS.
27- 50	KAROW, MARTIN GREGORY	D. APRIL 27, 1986 BRYAN, TEXAS
46- 53	KARPEL, HERBERT	6922 BABCOCK AVE - NORTH HOLLYWOOD CA 91605
20- 61	KARR, BENJAMIN JOYCE	D. DECEMBER 8, 1968 MEMPHIS, TENN.
15- 79	KARST, JOHN GOTTLIEB	D. MAY 21, 1976 CAPE MAY COURT HOUSE, N. J.
57- 35	KASKO, EDWARD MICHAEL	317 BURNWICK RD - RICHMOND VA 23227
52- 58	KATT, RAYMOND FREDERICK	711 RUDELOFF RD - SEGUIN TX 78155
44- 69	KATZ, ROBERT CLYDE	D. DECEMBER 14, 1962 ST. JOSEPH, MICH.
12- 91	KAUFF, BENJAMIN MICHAEL	D. NOVEMBER 17, 1961 COLUMBUS,O.
14-107	KAUFFMAN, HOWARD RICHARD 'DICK'	D. APRIL 17, 1948 LEWISBURG, PA.
21- 51	KAUFMAN, ANTHONY CHARLES	D. JUNE 4, 1982 ELGIN, ILL.
82- 69	KAUFMAN, CURT GERRARD	RR 3 BOX 33 - HARLAN IA 51537
14-108	KAVANAGH, CHARLES HUGH	D. SEPTEMBER 6, 1973 REEDSBURG, WIS.
14-109	KAVANAGH, LEO DANIEL	D. AUGUST 10, 1950 CHICAGO, ILL.
14-110	KAVANAGH, MARTIN JOSEPH	D. JULY 28, 1960 TAYLOR, MICH.
48- 51	KAZAK, EDWARD TERRANCE	802 NEWMAN DR - AUSTIN TX 78703
53- 43	KAZANSKI, THEODORE STANLEY	40008 CROSSWIND - NOVI MI 48050
68- 47	KEALEY, STEVEN WILLIAM	RR 1 BOX 6 - HILLSBORO KS 67063
61- 59	KEANE, JOHN JOSEPH	D. JANUARY 6, 1967 HOUSTON, TEX.
79- 62	KEARNEY, ROBERT HENRY	11611 PICCADILLY CIRCLE - SAN ANTONIO TX 78251
24- 59	KEARNS, EDWARD PAUL 'TED'	D. DECEMBER 21, 1949 TRENTON, N. J.
42- 54	KEARSE, EDWARD PAUL	D. JULY 15, 1968 EUREKA, CALIF.
12- 92	KEATING, RAYMOND HERBERT	D. DECEMBER 28, 1963 SACRAMENTO, CALIF.
13- 95	KEATING, WALTER FRANCIS 'CHICK'	D. JULY 13, 1959 PHILADELPHIA, PA.
81- 65	KEATLEY, GREGORY STEVEN	120 LONGITUDE LN - LEXINGTON SC29072
22- 66	KECK, FRANK JOSEPH 'CACTUS'	D. FEBRUARY 6, 1981 ST. LOUIS, MO.
85- 56	KEEDY, CHARLES PATRICK 'PAT'	1958 BRACKETT LOOP - BIRMINGHAM AL 35214
17- 37	KEEFE, DAVID EDWIN	D. FEBRUARY 4, 1978 KANSAS CITY, MO.
59- 44	KEEGAN, EDWARD CHARLES	BOX 71-A, HARRISONVILLE RD - MULLICA HILL NJ 08067
53- 44	KEEGAN, ROBERT CHARLES	101 SANDSTONE DR - ROCHESTER NY 14616

44- 70 KEELY, ROBERT WILLIAM   313 BRYN MAWR ISLAND - BRADENTON FL 33507
18- 42 KEEN, HOWARD VICTOR   D. DECEMBER 10, 1976 SALISBURY, MD.
11- 88 KEEN, WILLIAM BROWN   D. JULY 16, 1947 SOUTH POINT, O.
20- 62 KEENAN, JAMES WILLIAM   D. JUNE 5, 1980 SEMINOLE, FLA.
82- 70 KEENER, JEFFREY BRUCE   31607 102ND AVE SE - AUBURN WA 98002
76- 44 KEENER, JOSEPH DONALD   STAR ROUTE 79 - ADELANTO CA 92301
25- 58 KEESEY, JAMES WARD   D. SEPTEMBER 5, 1951 BOISE, IDA.
80- 65 KEETON, RICKEY   3433 STATHEM AVE - CINCINNATI OH 45211
42- 55 KEHN, CHESTER LAURENCE   D. APRIL 5, 1984 SAN DIEGO, CALIF.
14-111 KEIFER, SHERMAN C. 'KATIE'   B. 1892
65- 56 KEKICH, MICHAEL DENNIS   OLD ADD: 408 MAPLE ST SE - ALBUQUERQUE NM 87106
11- 89 KELIHER, MAURICE MICHAEL   D. SEPTEMBER 7, 1930 WASHINGTON, D.C.
52- 59 KELL, EVERETT LEE 'SKEETER'   3101 OLIVE - PINE BLUFF AR 71603
43- 69 KELL, GEORGE CLYDE   BOX 158 - SWIFTON AR 72471
16- 49 KELLEHER, ALBERT ALOYSIUS 'DUKE'   D. SEPTEMBER 28, 1947 STATEN ISLAND, N. Y.
42- 56 KELLEHER, FRANCIS EUGENE   D. APRIL 13, 1979 STOCKTON, CALIF.
35- 55 KELLEHER, HAROLD JOSEPH   220 23RD ST - AVALON NJ 08202
12- 93 KELLEHER, JOHN PATRICK   D. AUGUST 21, 1960 BRIGHTON, MASS.
72- 56 KELLEHER, MICHAEL DENNIS   2429 ANACAPA ST - SANTA BARBARA CA 93105
39- 60 KELLER, CHARLES ERNEST   8238 YELLOW SPRING RD - FREDERICK MD 21701
49- 40 KELLER, HAROLD KEFAUVER   2018 245TH AVE SE - ISSAQUAH WA 98027
66- 51 KELLER, RONALD LEE   4280 ROLAND RD - INDIANAPOLIS IN 46208
53- 45 KELLERT, FRANK WILLIAM   D. NOVEMBER 19, 1976 OKLAHOMA CITY, OKLA.
23- 72 KELLETT, ALFRED HENRY   D. JULY 14, 1960 NEW YORK, N. Y.
34- 53 KELLETT, DONALD STAFFORD 'RED'   D. NOVEMBER 5, 1970 FT. LAUDERDALE, ALA.
25- 59 KELLEY, HARRY LEROY   D. MARCH 23, 1958 PARKIN, ARK.
64- 56 KELLEY, RICHARD ANTHONY   OLD ADD: 13630 ADDISON ST - SHERMAN OAKS CA 91423
64- 57 KELLEY, THOMAS HENRY   2933 FINCH DR - DANVILLE VA 24540
19- 45 KELLIHER, FRANCIS MORTIMER   D. MARCH 4, 1956 SOMERVILLE, MASS.
48- 52 KELLNER, ALEXANDER RAYMOND   3716 NORTH JACKSON AVE - TUCSON AZ 85719
52- 60 KELLNER, WALTER JOSEPH   3737 NORTH TUCSON BLVD - TUCSON AZ 85716
14-112 KELLOGG, WILLIAM DEARSTYNE   D. DECEMBER 12, 1971 BALTIMORE, MD.
10- 79 KELLY, ALBERT MICHAEL 'RED'   D. JANUARY 29, 1961 ZEPHYRHILLS, FLA.
86- 78 KELLY, BRYAN KEITH   8012 ROSE AVENUE - ORLANDO FL 32810
80- 66 KELLY, DALE PATRICK 'PAT'   5176 SAN SIMEON DR - SANTA BARBARA CA 93111
14-113 KELLY, EDWARD LEO   D. NOVEMBER 4, 1928 RED LODGE, MONT.
15- 80 KELLY, GEORGE LANGE   D. OCTOBER 13, 1984 BURLINGAME, CALIF.
67- 57 KELLY, HAROLD PATRICK 'PAT'   836 EAST HAINES ST - PHILADELPHIA PA 19138
14-114 KELLY, HERBERT BARRETT   D. MAY 18, 1973 TORRANCE, CALIF.
14-115 KELLY, JAMES ROBERT   D. APRIL 10, 1961 KINGSPORT, TENN.
75- 58 KELLY, JAY THOMAS 'TOM'   57 KIERST STREET - PARLIN NJ 08859
14-116 KELLY, JOSEPH HENRY   D. AUGUST 16, 1977 ST. JOSEPH, MO.
26- 43 KELLY, JOSEPH JAMES   D. NOVEMBER 24, 1967 LYNBROOK, N. Y.
26- 44 KELLY, MICHAEL J.   OLD ADD: 5853 VON VESSEN AVE - ST LOUIS MO
23- 73 KELLY, REYNOLDS JOSEPH 'REN'   D. AUGUST 24, 1963 MILLBRAE, CAL.
87- 71 KELLY, ROBERT CONRADO   4 CIUDAD RADIAL - JUANA DIAZ PANAMA C.A.
51- 47 KELLY, ROBERT EDWARD   9 MOHAWK DR - NIENTIC CT 06359
69- 90 KELLY, VAN HOWARD   11 BEAUREGARD DR - SPENCER NC 28159
20- 63 KELLY, WILLIAM HENRY   37 QUEENS WAY - CAMILLUS NY 13031
10- 80 KELLY, WILLIAM JOSEPH   D. JUNE 3, 1940 DETROIT, MICH.

Charlie Keller   NEW YO   [Cincinnati Reds]   Bob Kennedy

64- 58 KELSO, WILLIAM EUGENE   419 NW BRIARCLIFF ROAD - KANSAS CITY MO 64116
37- 59 KELTNER, KEN FREDERICK   3220 KING ARTHURS CT WEST - GREENFIELD WI 53221
54- 51 KEMMERER, RUSSELL PAUL   RR 4, HICKORY HILLS - NORTH VERNON IN 47265
29- 58 KEMNER, HERMAN JOHN 'DUTCH'   418 WASHINGTON - QUINCY IL 62301
77- 76 KEMP, STEVE F   12979 CLAYMONT COURT - SAN DIEGO CA 92130
69- 91 KENDALL, FRED LYNN   1219 HICKORY AVE - TORRANCE CA 90503
61- 60 KENDERS, ALBERT DANIEL GEORGE   8744 MATILIJA AVE - VAN NUYS CA 91402
28- 54 KENNA, EDWARD ALOYSIUS   D. AUGUST 21, 1972 SAN FRANCISCO, CALIF.
70- 70 KENNEDY, JAMES EARL   OLD ADD: 2573 NW NORTHRUP - PORTLAND OR 97210
62- 65 KENNEDY, JOHN EDWARD   2 RODNEY ROAD - WEST PEABODY MA 01960
57- 36 KENNEDY, JOHN IRVIN   %E.WHITE,4166 LOCKHART-JACKSONVILLE FL 32209
74- 65 KENNEDY, JUNIOR RAYMOND   OLD ADD: 25459 JUDITH CT - ARVIN CA 93203
34- 54 KENNEDY, LLOYD VERNON 'VERN'   RR 1 BOX 164 - MENDON MO 64660
46- 54 KENNEDY, MONTIA CALVIN   5735 BERRYWOOD - RICHMOND VA 23224
16- 50 KENNEDY, RAYMOND LINCOLN   D. JANUARY 18, 1969 CASSELBERRY, FLA.
39- 61 KENNEDY, ROBERT DANIEL   3708 EAST OMEGA CIR - MESA AZ 85205
78- 65 KENNEDY, TERRENCE EDWARD   P.O. BOX 220 - RIDERWOOD MD 21139
48- 53 KENNEDY, WILLIAM AULTON   D. APRIL 8, 1983 SEATTLE, WASH.
42- 57 KENNEDY, WILLIAM GORMAN   2500 N. VAN DORN ST #621 - ALEXANDRIA VA 22304
38- 45 KENNEY, ARTHUR JOSEPH   #3 TIMBER LANE - NORTH READING MA 01864
67- 58 KENNEY, GERALD T   1980 HARRISON - BELOIT WI 53511
12- 94 KENT, MAURICE ALLEN   D. APRIL 19, 1966 IOWA CITY, IA.
62- 66 KENWORTHY, RICHARD LEE   3745 TADE LN - INDIANAPOLIS IN 46234
12- 95 KENWORTHY, WILLIAM JENNINGS 'DUKE'   D. SEPTEMBER 21, 1950 EUREKA, CALIF.

68- 48 KEOUGH, JOSEPH WILLIAM   2958 LIBERTY DRIVE - PLEASANTON CA 94566
77- 77 KEOUGH, MATTHEW LON   6281 FRONT SOUTH RD - LIVERMORE CA 94550
56- 47 KEOUGH, RICHARD MARTIN 'MARTY' 2 TIVOLI - IRVINE CA 92720
84- 60 KEPSHIRE, KURT DAVID   27 OAKWOOD DRIVE - SEYMOUR CT 06483
85- 57 KERFELD, CHARLES PATRICK   1001 SONOMA ST - CARSON CITY NV 89701
50- 41 KERIAZAKOS, CONSTANTINE NICHOLAS 'GUS 238 CLAREMONT AVE - MONTCLAIR NJ 07042
39- 62 KERKSIECK, WAYMAN WILLIAM 'BILL' D. MARCH 11, 1970 LITTLE ROCK, ARK.
15- 81 KERLIN, ORIE MILTON   D. OCTOBER 29, 1974 SHREVEPORT, LA.
74- 66 KERN, JAMES LESTER   6009 AMBERWOOD CT - ARLINGTON TX 76016
62- 67 KERN, WILLIAM GEORGE   625 GREEN ST - ALLENTOWN PA 18102
65- 57 KERNEK, GEORGE BOYD   210 NORTH GULF - HOLDENVILLE OK 74848
20- 64 KERNS, DANIEL P.   B. PHILADELPHIA, PA.
45- 51 KERNS, RUSSELL ELDON   22000 LAWRENCE RD - FIDDLETOWN CA 95629
23- 74 KERR, JOHN FRANCIS   2812 EAST 220TH PL - LONG BEACH CA 90810
14-117 KERR, JOHN JONAS 'DOC'   D. JUNE 9, 1937 BALTIMORE, MD.
43- 70 KERR, JOHN JOSEPH 'BUDDY'   341 GROVE ST-ORADELL NJ 07649
25- 60 KERR, JOHN MELVILLE 'MEL'   D. AUGUST 9, 1980 VERO BEACH, FLA.
19- 46 KERR, RICHARD HENRY   D. MAY 4, 1963 HOUSTON, TEX.
76- 45 KERRIGAN, JOSEPH THOMAS   95 MONTEREY BLVD - SAN FRANCISCO CA 94131
64- 59 KESSINGER, DONALD EULON   1010 JUNE ROAD #201 - MEMPHIS TN 38119
68- 49 KESTER, RICHARD LEE   BOX 623 - GARDNERVILLE NV 89410
22- 67 KETCHUM, AUGUST FRANKLIN 'GUS' D. SEPTEMBER 10, 1980 OKLAHOMA CITY, OKLA.
12- 96 KETTER, PHILIP   B. HUTCHINSON, KAN.
14-118 KEUPPER, HENRY J.   D. AUGUST 14 1960 MARION, ILL.
84- 61 KEY, JAMES EDWARD   3301 AVERY AVE SW - HUNTSVILLE AL 35805
85- 58 KHALIFA, SAM   8825 EAST SECOND PLACE - TUCSON AZ 85710
25- 61 KIBBIE, HORACE KENT 'HOD'   D. OCTOBER 19, 1975 FORT WORTH, TEX.
12- 97 KIBBLE, JOHN WESTLY   D. DECEMBER 13, 1969 ROUNDUP, MONT.
20- 65 KIEFER, JOSEPH WILLIAM   D. JULY 5, 1975 UTICA, N. Y.
84- 62 KIEFER, STEVEN GEORGE   11822 OLD FASHION - GARDEN GROVE CA 92640
51- 48 KIELY, LEO PATRICK   D. JANUARY 18, 1984 GLEN RIDGE, N. J.
17- 38 KILDUFF, PETER JOHN   D. FEBRUARY 14, 1930 PITTSBURG, KAN.
87- 72 KILGUS, PAUL NELSON   2102 SMALLHOUSE ROAD - BOWLING GREEN KY 42101
14-119 KILHULLEN, JOSEPH ISADORE 'PAT' D. NOVEMBER 2, 1922 OAKLAND, CALIF.
69- 92 KILKENNY, MICHAEL DAVID   274 HOLLAND ST WEST - BRADFORD ONTARIO CAN.
54- 52 KILLEBREW, HARMON CLAYTON   BOX 626 - ONTARIO OR 97914
59- 45 KILLEEN, EVANS HENRY   123 MAIN ST - WESTHAMPTON NY 11978
11- 90 KILLILAY, JOHN WILLIAM   D. OCTOBER 21, 1968 TULSA, OKLA.
37- 60 KIMBALL, NEWELL W. 'NEWT'   1425 GRIFFITH AVE - LAS VEGAS NV 89104
36- 45 KIMBERLIN, HARRY LYDLE   1028 KINZER ST #201B - POPLAR BLUFF MO 63901
45- 52 KIMBLE, RICHARD LOUIS   3733 LARCHMONT PARKWAY - TOLEDO OH 43613
20- 66 KIME, HAROLD LEE   D. MAY 16, 1939 COLUMBUS, O.
76- 46 KIMM, BRUCE EDWARD   RR 1 BOX 13A - AMANA IA 52203
19- 47 KIMMICK, WALTER LYONS   RR 2 BOX 371 - BOSWELL PA 15531
29- 59 KIMSEY, CLYDE ELIAS 'CHAD'   D. DECEMBER 3, 1942 PRYOR, OKLA.
56- 48 KINDALL, GERALD DONALD   ATH DEPT, UNIV OF ARIZONA - TUCSON AZ 85721
46- 55 KINDER, ELLIS RAYMOND   D. OCTOBER 16, 1968 JACKSON, TENN.

46- 56 KINER, RALPH MCPHERRAN   17 LEGRANDE AVE #17 - GREENWICH CT 06830
54- 53 KING, CHARLES GILBERT 'CHICK'   RURAL ROUTE 1 BOX 68B - PARIS TN 38242
44- 71 KING, CLYDE EDWARD   103 STRATFORD RD - GOLDSBORO NC 27530
16- 52 KING, EDWARD LEE   D. SEPTEMBER 7, 1938 CHELSEA, MASS.
16- 51 KING, EDWARD LEE   D. SEPTEMBER 16, 1967 SHINNSTOWN, W. VA.
86- 79 KING, ERIC STEVEN   1063 STANFORD DRIVE - SIMI VALLEY CA 93065
67- 59 KING, HAROLD   1027 WEST SOUTH ST - ORLANDO FL 32805
55- 63 KING, JAMES HUBERT   RR 2 BOX 15 - ELKINS AR 72727
35- 56 KING, LYNN PAUL   D. MAY 11, 1972 ATLANTIC, IA.
54- 54 KING, NELSON JOSEPH   126 JAMES PL - PITTSBURGH PA 15228
32- 39 KINGDON, WESCOTT WILLIAM   D. APRIL 19, 1975 CAPISTRANO, CALIF.
86- 80 KINGERY, MICHAEL SCOTT   411 SOUTH THIRD - ATWATER MN 56209
79- 63 KINGMAN, BRIAN PAUL   11 TOKENEKE TRAIL - DARIEN CT 06820
71- 58 KINGMAN, DAVID ARTHUR   P.O. BOX 209 - GLENBROOK NV 89413
14-120 KINGMAN, HENRY LEES   D. DECEMBER 27, 1982 OAKLAND, CALIF.
78- 66 KINNEY, DENNIS PAUL   7440 CROESSCREEKS #3 - TEMPERANCE MI 48182
18- 43 KINNEY, WALTER WILLIAM   D. JULY 1, 1971 ESCONDIDO, CAL.
80- 67 KINNUNEN, MICHAEL JOHN   5818 MCKINLEY PL NORTH - SEATTLE WA 98103
19- 48 KINSELLA, ROBERT FRANCIS   D. DECEMBER 30, 1951 LOS ANGELES, CALIF.
34- 55 KINZY, HENRY HENSEL 'HARRY'   3721 ARROYO RD - FORT WORTH TX 76109
57- 37 KIPP, FRED LEO   6510 WEST 69TH ST - OVERLAND PARK KS 66204
85- 59 KIPPER, ROBERT WAYNE   2145 BILTER ROAD - AURORA IL 60505
53- 46 KIPPER, THORNTON JOHN   8780 EAST MCKELLOPS #340 - SCOTTSDALE AZ 85257
14-121 KIPPERT, EDWARD AUGUST   D. JUNE 3, 1980 DETROIT, MICH.
69- 93 KIRBY, CLAYTON LAWS   949 NORTH POTOMAC ST - ARLINGTON VA 22205
49- 41 KIRBY, JAMES HERSCHEL   729 DOVER RD - NASHVILLE TN 37211
12- 98 KIRBY, LARUE   D. JUNE 10, 1961 LANSING, MICH.

19- 49 KIRCHER, MICHAEL ANDREW D. JUNE 26, 1972 ROCHESTER, N. Y.
47- 51 KIRK, THOMAS DANIEL D. AUGUST 1, 1974 PHILADELPHIA, PA.
61- 61 KIRK, WILLIAM PARTHEMORE 365 FOLKSTONE WAY - YORK PA 17402
10- 81 KIRKE, JUDSON FABIAN 'JAY' D. AUGUST 31, 1968 NEW ORLEANS, LA.
58- 51 KIRKLAND, WILLIE CHARLES 17155 SANTA ROSA - DETROIT MI 48221
62- 68 KIRKPATRICK, EDGAR LEON 24791 VIA LARGA - LAGUNA NIGUEL CA 92677
12- 99 KIRKPATRICK, ENOS CLAIRE D. APRIL 14, 1964 PITTSBURGH, PA.
74- 67 KIRKWOOD, DONALD PAUL 455 WEST ELMWOOD - CLAWSON MI 48017
50- 42 KIRRENE, JOSEPH JOHN 2340 MARSHALL WAY - SACRAMENTO CA 95819
10- 82 KIRSCH, HARRY LOUIS D. DECEMBER 25, 1925 PITTSBURGH, PA.
45- 53 KISH, ERNEST ALEXANDER 6619 S.O.M. CENTER RD - SOLON OH 44139
71- 59 KISON, BRUCE EUGENE 1403 RIVERVIEW CIRCLE - BRADENTON FL 33529
54- 55 KITSOS, CHRISTOPHER ANESTOS 1219 ANCHOR DR - MOBILE AL 36609
82- 71 KITTLE, RONALD DALE 8080 E. 109TH - CROWN POINT IN 46307
34- 56 KLAERNER, HUGO EMIL D. JANUARY 3, 1982 FREDERICKSBURG, TEXAS
66- 52 KLAGES, FRED ANTHONY OLD ADD: 261 BERRY ST - BADEN PA 15005
64- 60 KLAUS, ROBERT FRANCIS 10661 GABACHO DR - SAN DIEGO CA 92124
52- 61 KLAUS, WILLIAM JOSEPH 1655 SOUTH DR - SARASOTA FL 33579
85- 60 KLAWITTER, THOMAS CARL 2506 KENWOOD - JANESVILLE WI 53545
25- 62 KLEE, OLLIE CHESTER D. FEBRUARY 9, 1977 TOLEDO, O.
28- 55 KLEIN, CHARLES HERBERT D. MARCH 28, 1958 INDIANAPOLIS, IND.
44- 72 KLEIN, HAROLD JOHN D. DECEMBER 10, 1957 ST. LOUIS, MO.
43- 71 KLEIN, LOUIS FRANK D. JUNE 20, 1976 METAIRIE, LA.
34- 57 KLEINHANS, THEODORE OTTO D. JULY 24, 1985 REDINGTON BEACH, FLA.
35- 57 KLEINKE, NORBERT GEORGE 'NUB' D. MARCH 16, 1950 MARIN, CAL.
11- 91 KLEPFER, EDWARD LLOYD D. AUGUST 9, 1950 TULSA, OKLA.
76- 47 KLEVEN, JAY ALLEN 118 VIA BOLSA - SAN LORENZO CA 94580
43- 72 KLIEMAN, EDWARD FREDERICK D. NOVEMBER 15, 1979 HOMOS ASSA, FLA.
58- 52 KLIMCHOCK, LOUIS STEPHEN 1913 EAST MYRNA LANE - TEMPE AZ 85284

69- 94 KLIMKOWSKI, RONALD BERNARDO 791 EDGEWOOD DR - WESTBURY NY 11590
55- 64 KLINE, JOHN ROBERT 'BOBBY' 5924 47TH AVE NORTH -ST PETERSBURG FL 33703
30- 41 KLINE, ROBERT GEORGE D. MARCH 16, 1987 WESTERVILLE, O.
52- 62 KLINE, RONALD LEE MAIN ST BOX 155 - CALLERY PA 16024
70- 71 KLINE, STEVEN JACK BOX 429 - CHELAN WA 98816
27- 51 KLINGER, JOSEPH JOHN D. JULY 31, 1960 LITTLE ROCK, ARK.
38- 46 KLINGER, ROBERT HAROLD D. AUGUST 19, 1977 VILLA RIDGE, MO.
87- 73 KLINK, JOSEPH CHARLES 2115 NORTH 35TH AVENUE - HOLLYWOOD FL 33021
50- 43 KLIPPSTEIN, JOHN CALVIN 1176 ABERDEEN RD - PALATINE IL 60067
44- 73 KLOPP, STANLEY HAROLD D. MARCH 11, 1980 ROBESONIA, PA.
31- 44 KLOZA, JOHN CLARENCE 'NAP' D. JUNE 11, 1962 MILWAUKEE, WIS.
21- 52 KLUGMANN, JOSIE D. JULY 18, 1951 MOBERLY, MO.
34- 58 KLUMPP, ELMER EDWARD N67 W27085 HWY 74 - SUSSEX WI 53089
47- 52 KLUSZEWSKI, THEODORE BERNARD D. MARCH 29, 1988 CINCINNATI, O.
76- 48 KLUTTS, GENE ELLIS "MICKEY" 20701 BECH BLVD #259-HUNTINGTON BCH CA 92648
42- 58 KLUTTZ, CLYDE FRANKLIN D. MAY 12, 1979 SALISBURY, N. C.
75- 59 KNAPP, ROBERT CHRISTIAN 'CHRIS' 1415 CASTLE CT - ST JOSEPH MI 49085
10- 83 KNAUPP, HENRY ANTONE 'COTTON' D. JULY 6, 1967 NEW ORLEANS, LA.
26- 45 KNEISCH, RUDOLPH FRANK D. APRIL 6, 1965 BALTIMORE, MD.
76- 49 KNEPPER, ROBERT WESLEY 2045 OAKHILL ROAD - ROSEBURG OR 97470
45- 54 KNERR, WALLACE LUTHER 'LOU' D. MARCH 23, 1980 LANCASTER, P A.
79- 64 KNICELY, ALAN LEE BOX 433 - DAYTON VA 22821
47- 53 KNICKERBOCKER, AUSTIN JAY P.O. BOX 236 - CLINTON CORNERS NY 12514
33- 32 KNICKERBOCKER, WILLIAM HART D. SEPTEMBER 8, 1963 SEBASTOPOL, CALIF.
74- 68 KNIGHT, CHARLES RAY 2308 TARA DRIVE - ALBANY NY 31707
22- 58 KNIGHT, ELMA RUSSELL 'JACK' D. JULY 30, 1976 SAN ANTONIO, TEX.
12-100 KNISELY, PETER C. D. JULY 1, 1948 BROWNSVILLE, PA.
20- 67 KNODE, KENNETH THOMSON 'MIKE' D. DECEMBER 20, 1980 SOUTH BEND, IND.
23- 75 KNODE, ROBERT TROXELL 'RAY' D. APRIL 13, 1982 BATTLE CREEK, MICH.
64- 61 KNOOP, ROBERT FRANK 3 RIDGEROCK - LAGUNA NIGUEL CA 92677
32- 40 KNOTHE, GEORGE BERTRAM D. JULY 3, 1981 DOVER, N. J.
32- 41 KNOTHE, WILFRED EDGAR 'FRITZ' D. MARCH 22, 1963 PASSAIC, N. J.
33- 33 KNOTT, JOHN HENRY D. OCTOBER 13, 1981 BROWNWOOD, TEXAS
65- 58 KNOWLES, DAROLD DUANE 5261 42ND ST - ST.PETERSBURG FL 33711
15- 82 KNOWLSON, THOMAS HERBERT D. APRIL 11, 1943 MIAMI SHORES, FLA.
20- 68 KNOWLTON, WILLIAM YOUNG D. FEBRUARY 25, 1944 PHILADELPHIA, PA.
24- 60 KNOX, CLIFFORD HIRAM 'BUD' D. SEPTEMBER 24, 1965 OSKALOOSA, IA.
72- 57 KNOX, JOHN CLINTON OLD ADD: 34 PELL MELL DRIVE - BETHEL CT 06801
85- 61 KNUDSON, MARK RICHARD 881 WEST 100TH AVE - NORTHGLENN CO 80221
53- 47 KOBACK, NICHOLAS NICHOLIA 52 STONEHEDGE DR - NEWINGTON CT 06111
73- 69 KOBEL, KEVIN RICHARD EDDY RD - COLDEN NY 14033
63- 64 KOCH, ALAN GOODMAN 1517 RIDGELAND RD EAST - MOBILE AL 36609
44- 74 KOCH, BARNETT D. JUNE 6, 1987 TACOMA, WASH.
12-101 KOCHER, BRADLEY WILSON D. JANUARY 13, 1965 WHITE HAVEN, PA.

46- 57	KOECHER, RICHARD FINLAY	2000 VALLEY FORGE CIR-KING OF PRUSSIA PA19406
70- 72	KOEGEL, PETER JOHN	OLD ADD: 1205 NORTH 48TH - PHOENIX AZ 85008
25- 63	KOEHLER, HORACE LEVERING 'POP'	D. DECEMBER 8, 1986 TACOMA, WASH.
32- 42	KOENECKE, LEONARD GEORGE	D. SEPTEMBER 17, 1935 TORONTO, ONT.
25- 64	KOENIG, MARK ANTHONY	RURAL ROUTE 3 #3654 - ORLAND CA 95963
19- 50	KOENIGSMARK, WILLIS THOMAS	D. JULY 1, 1972 WATERLOO, ILL.
10- 84	KOESTNER, ELMER JOSEPH	D. OCTOBER 27, 1959 FAIRBURY, ILL.
37- 61	KOHLMAN, JOSEPH JAMES	D. MARCH 16, 1974 PHILADELPHIA, PA.
48- 54	KOKOS, RICHARD JEROME	D. APRIL 9, 1986 CHICAGO, ILL.
60- 57	KOLB, GARY ALAN	164 CIRCLE DR - CROSS LANE WV 25356
40- 43	KOLLOWAY, DONALD MARTIN	2236 WEST 121ST STREET PL - BLUE ISLAND IL 60406
21- 53	KOLP, RAYMOND CARL	D. JULY 29, 1967 NEW ORLEANS, LA.
15- 83	KOLSETH, KARL DICKEY	D. MAY 3, 1956 CUMBERLAND, MD.
62- 69	KOLSTAD, HAROLD EVERETTE	15149 BEL ESCOU DR - SAN JOSE CA 95124
13- 96	KOMMERS, FRED RAYMOND	D. JUNE 14, 1943 CHICAGO, ILL.
83- 87	KOMMINSK, BRAD LYNN	2987 HANOVER DRIVE - LIMA OH 45805
73- 70	KONIECZNY, DOUGLAS	8341 RIVERLAND DRIVE #6 - STERLING HEIGHTS MI 48078
48- 55	KONIKOWSKI, ALEXANDER JAMES	81 BANK STREET - SEYMOUR CT 06483
42- 59	KONOPKA, BRUCE BRUNO	3212 SOUTH ADAMS - DENVER CO 80210
44- 75	KONSTANTY, CASIMIR JAMES 'JIM'	D. JUNE 11, 1976 ONEONTA, N. Y.
15- 84	KOOB, ERNEST GERALD	D. NOVEMBER 12, 1941 LEMAY, MO.
62- 70	KOONCE, CALVIN LEE	3646 GOLFVIEW DR - HOPE MILLS NC 28348
67- 60	KOOSMAN, JERRY MARTIN	RR 2 BOX 67E - CHASKA MN 55318
66- 53	KOPACZ, GEORGE FELIX	14150 SOMERSET COURT - ORLAND PARK IL 60462
21- 54	KOPF, WALTER HENRY	D. APRIL 30, 1979 CINCINNATI, O.
13- 97	KOPF, WILLIAM LORENZ 'LARRY'	D. OCTOBER 15, 1986 ANDERSON TWP., HAMILTON CO., OHIO
61- 62	KOPLITZ, HOWARD DEAN	623 BOYD ST - OSHKOSH WI 54901
15- 85	KOPP, MERLIN HENRY	D. MAY 7, 1960 SACRAMENTO, CALIF.
58- 53	KOPPE, JOSEPH	7887 BEATRICE ST - WESTLAND MI 48185
23- 76	KOPSHAW, GEORGE KARL	D. DECEMBER 26, 1934 LYNCHBURG, VA.
54- 56	KORCHECK, STEPHEN JOSEPH	8018 WILLOW AVE - SARASOTA FL 33580
15- 86	KORES, ARTHUR EMIL	D. MARCH 26, 1974 MILWAUKEE, WIS.
66- 54	KORINCE, GEORGE EUGENE	OLD ADD: 83 SHORELINE DR - ST. CATHERINES ONT. L2N 5N7
65- 59	KOSCO, ANDREW JOHN	9329 NEW SPRINGFIELD RD - POLAND OH 44514
52- 63	KOSHOREK, CLEMENT JOHN	3951 AMHERST - ROYAL OAK MI 48072
51- 49	KOSKI, WILLIAM JOHN	2656 EL GRECO DR - MODESTO CA 95351
41- 56	KOSLO, GEORGE BERNARD 'DAVE'	D. DECEMBER 1, 1975 MENASHA, WIS.
44- 76	KOSMAN, MICHAEL THOMAS	2110 S. 6TH - LAFAYETTE IN 47904
31- 45	KOSTER, FREDERICK CHARLES	D. APRIL 24, 1979 SAINT MATTHEWS, KY.
62- 71	KOSTRO, FRANK JERRY	36 STEELE ST #200- DENVER CO 80206
55- 65	KOUFAX, SANFORD 'SANDY'	1000 ELYSIAN PARK AVE - LOS ANGELES CA 90012
25- 65	KOUPAL, LOUIS LADDIE	D. DECEMBER 8, 1961 SAN GABRIEL, CAL.
32- 43	KOWALIK, FABIAN LORENZ	D..AUGUST 14, 1954 KARNES CITY, TEX.
38- 47	KOY, ERNEST ANYZ	BOX 476 1047 SOUTH OAK-BELLVILLE TX 77418
48- 56	KOZAR, ALBERT KENNETH	3004 VINCENT RD - WEST PALM BEACH FL 33405
39- 63	KRACHER, JOSEPH PETER	D. DECEMBER 25, 1981 SAN ANGELO, TEXAS
14-122	KRAFT, CLARENCE OTTO	D. MARCH 26, 1958 FORT WORTH, TEX.
37- 62	KRAKAUSKAS, JOSEPH VICTOR LAWRENCE	D. DECEMBER 8, 1960 HAMILTON, ONT.
59- 46	KRALICK, JOHN FRANCIS	BOX 3006 - SOLDOTNA AK 99669
53- 48	KRALY, STEVEN CHARLES	12 DAVIS AVENUE - JOHNSON CITY NY 13790
39- 64	KRAMER, JOHN HENRY	2126 PAULINE ST-NEW ORLEANS LA 70117
62- 72	KRANEPOOL, EDWARD EMIL	177 HIGH POND DRIVE - JERICHO NY 11753
11- 92	KRAPP, EUGENE H.	D. APRIL 13, 1923 DETROIT, MICH.
43- 73	KRAUS, JOHN WILLIAM 'TEX'	D. JANUARY 2, 1976 SAN ANTONIO, TEX.
31- 46	KRAUSSE, LEWIS BERNARD SR.	3680 EDGERTON CIR - SARASOTA FL 33581
61- 63	KRAUSSE, LOUIS BERNARD JR	RR 1 BOX 572C - HOLT MO 64048
75- 60	KRAVEC, KENNETH PETER	13599 MOHAWK TRAIL - MIDDLEBURG HGTS OH 44130
56- 49	KRAVITZ, DANIEL	RR1 - DUSHORE PA 18614
84- 63	KRAWCZYK, RAYMOND ALLEN	10032 RIDGLEY DR - GARDEN GROVE CA 92643
31- 47	KREEVICH, MICHAEL ANDREAS	RURAL ROUTE 2 BOX 220 - CECIL WI 54111
43- 74	KREITNER, ALBERT JOSEPH	313 CHURCH ST - NASHVILLE TN 37201
11- 93	KREITZ, RALPH WESLEY	D. JULY 20, 1941 PORTLAND, ORE.
24- 61	KREMER, REMY PETER 'RAY'	D. FEBRUARY 8, 1965 PINOLE, CAL.
73- 71	KREMMEL, JAMES LOUIS	EAST 12512 HOUK - SPOKANE WA 99216
79- 65	KRENCHICKI, WAYNE RICHARD	53 FARRELL AVE - TRENTON NJ 08618
47- 54	KRESS, CHARLES STEVEN	3102 DUNCAN - SAINT JOSEPH MO 64507
27- 52	KRESS, RALPH 'RED'	D. NOVEMBER 29, 1962 LOS ANGELES, CALIF.
46- 58	KRETLOW, LOUIS HENRY	3302 GOLDFINCH - ENID OK 73701
75- 61	KREUGER, RICHARD ALAN	1143 POWERS NW - GRAND RAPIDS MI 49504
62- 73	KREUTZER, FRANKLIN JAMES	21 SILVERWOOD CIR - ANNAPOLIS MD 21403
11- 94	KRICHELL, PAUL BERNARD	D. JUNE 4, 1957 NEW YORK, N.Y.
49- 42	KRIEGER, KURT FERDINAND	D. AUGUST 16, 1970 ST. LOUIS, MO.
37- 63	KRIST, HOWARD WILBUR	44 GROVE ST - DELAVAN NY 14042

Bill Virdon

```
78- 67  KROL, JOHN THOMAS                          3012 FLEET ST - WINSTON SALEM NC 27107
64- 62  KROLL, GARY MELVIN                         9038 EAST 40TH ST - TULSA OK 74145
35- 58  KRONER, JOHN HAROLD                        D. AUGUST 26, 1968 ST. LOUIS, MO.
60- 58  KRSNICH, MICHAEL                           1200 NW 43RD ST - POMPANO BEACH FL 33064
49- 43  KRSNICH, ROCCO PETER                       5701 WEST 92ND STREET - OVERLAND PARK KS 66207
13- 98  KRUEGER, ERNEST GEORGE                     D. APRIL 22, 1976 WAUKEGAN, ILL.
83- 88  KRUEGER, WILLIAM CULP                      1844 HARVEST RD - PLEASANTON CA 94566
65- 60  KRUG, EVERETT BEN 'CHRIS'                  401 ORANGEWOOD - ANAHEIM CA 92802
81- 66  KRUG, GARY EUGENE                          1327 BAYLOR DR - COLORADO SPRINGS CO 80909
12-102  KRUG, MARTIN JOHN                          D. JUNE 27, 1966 GLENDALE, CALIF.
86- 81  KRUK, JOHN MARTIN                          RURAL ROUTE 4 BOX 31 - KEYSER WV 26726
76- 50  KRUKOW, MICHAEL EDWARD                     416 ALABAMA STREET - SAN GABRIEL CA 91775
49- 44  KRYHOSKI, RICHARD DAVID                    18855 WARWICK RD - BIRMINGHAM MI 48009
57- 38  KUBEK, ANTHONY CHRISTOPHER                 3311 NORTH MCDONALD - APPLETON WI 54911
67- 61  KUBIAK, THEODORE ROGER                     15774 SUNSET DRIVE - POWAY CA 92064
61- 64  KUBISZYN, JACK JOSEPH                      2306 UNIVERSITY BLVD - TUSCALOOSA AL 35401
80- 68  KUBSKI, GILBERT THOMAS                     1565 SUNRISE CIR - CARLSBAD CA 92008
50- 44  KUCAB, JOHN ALBERT                         D. MAY 26, 1977 YOUNGSTOWN, O.
74- 69  KUCEK, JOHN ANDREW CHARLES                 1219 WARREN RD - NEWTON FALLS OH 44444
55- 66  KUCKS, JOHN CHARLES                        15 OAKLAND ST - HILLSDALE NJ 07642
49- 45  KUCZEK, STANISLAW LEO 'STEVE'              769 SACANDAGA RD - SCOTIA NY 12302
43- 75  KUCZYNSKI, BERNARD CARL                    1725 NORTH DOUGLAS DRIVE - ALLENTOWN PA 18103
76- 51  KUEHL, KARL OTTO                           8218 VIA DE LA ESCUELA - SCOTTSDALE AZ 85258
52- 64  KUENN, HARVEY EDWARD                       D. FEBRUARY 28, 1988 PEORIA, ARIZ.
77- 78  KUHAULUA, FRED MAHELE                      89-203 NALAKAHIKI PL - NANAKULI HI 96792
30- 42  KUHEL, JOSEPH ANTHONY                      D. FEBRUARY 26, 1984 KANSAS CITY, KAN.
24- 62  KUHN, BERNARD DANIEL 'BUB'                 D. NOVEMBER 20, 1956 LANSING, MICH.
55- 67  KUHN, KENNETH HAROLD                       69 SKYLINE TERRACE - MILL VALLEY CA 94941
12-103  KUHN, WALTER CHARLES                       D. JUNE 14, 1935 FRESNO, CALIF.
74- 70  KUIPER, DUANE EUGENE                       % SBROCCO,36931 EAGLE RD - WILLOUGHBY HILLS OH 44094
55- 68  KUME, JOHN MIKE                            RR2 WOODARD RD - ANDOVER OH 44003
84- 64  KUNKEL, JEFFREY WILLIAM                    1 NAUTILUS DR - LEONARDO NJ 07737
61- 65  KUNKEL, WILLIAM GUSTAVE JAMES              D. MAY 4, 1985 RED BANK, N. J.
79- 66  KUNTZ, RUSSELL JAY 'RUSTY'                 1666 CRESTVIEW CIR - SAN LUIS OBISPO CA 93401
23- 77  KUNZ, EARL DEWEY                           D. APRIL 14, 1963 SACRAMENTO, CAL.
75- 62  KUROSAKI, RYAN YOSHITOMO                   1324 HIGH VIEW PL - HONOLULU HI 96816
41- 57  KUROWSKI, GEORGE JOHN 'WHITEY'             310 SPRINGSIDE DR-SHILLINGTON PA 19607
68- 50  KURTZ, HAROLD JAMES                        BELLE POINT - QUEENSTOWN MD 21658
41- 58  KUSH, EMIL BENEDICT                        D. NOVEMBER 26, 1969 RIVER GROVE, ILL.
73- 72  KUSICK, CRAIG ROBERT                       306 HIGHWAY 70 EAST - ST. GERMAIN WI 54558
70- 73  KUSNYER, ARTHUR WILLIAM                    4316 MEADOWLAND CIR - SARASOTA FL 33583
86- 82  KUTCHER, RANDY SCOTT                       37618 DALZELL - PALMDALE CA 93550
11- 95  KUTINA, JOSEPH PETER                       D. APRIL 13, 1945 CHICAGO, ILL.
59- 47  KUTYNA, MARION JOHN 'MARTY'                2711 EAST CAMBRIA ST - PHILADELPHIA PA 19134
46- 59  KUZAVA, ROBERT LEROY                       1118 VINEWOOD AVE - WYANDOTTE MI 48192
42- 60  KVASNAK, ALEXANDER                         3265 HEMPSTEAD AVE-ARCADIA CA 91006
12-104  KYLE, ANDREW EWING                         D. SEPTEMBER 6, 1971 TORONTO, ONT.
37- 64  LAABS, CHESTER PETER                       D. JANUARY 26, 1983 WARREN, MICH.
50- 45  LABINE, CLEMENT WALTER                     BOX 643 - WOONSOCKET RI 02895
69- 95  LABOY, JOSE ALBERTO 'COCO'                 19TH ST. B20 #24 SABANA GDNS - CAROLINA PR 00630
77- 79  LACEY, ROBERT JOSEPH                       2525 EAST FOUNTAIN - MESA AZ 85201
69- 96  LACHEMANN, MARCEL ERNEST                   1449 BOOKMAN AVE - WALNUT CA 91789
65- 61  LACHEMANN, RENE GEORGE                     2736 WEST PLATA AVE - MESA AZ 85202
83- 89  LACHOWICZ, ALLEN ROBERT                    310 ROOSEVELT AVE - MCKEES ROCK PA 15136
14-128  LACLAIRE, GEORGE LEWIS                     D. OCTOBER 10, 1918 FARNHAM, QUE.
72- 58  LACOCK, RALPH PIERRE 'PETE'                9725 RIGGS - OVERLAND PARK KS 66212
75- 63  LACORTE, FRANK JOSEPH                      1667 EL DORADO DR - GILROY CA 95020
78- 68  LACOSS, MICHAEL JAMES                      4110 LAVIDA - VISALIA CA 93277
72- 59  LACY, LEONDAUS 'LEE'                       4450 PARK ALISAL - CALABASAS CA 91302
26- 46  LACY, OSCEOLA GUY                          D. NOVEMBER 19, 1953 CLEVELAND, TENN.
79- 67  LADD, PETER LINWOOD                        5665 GROVE TER - GREENDALE WI 53129
46- 60  LADE, DOYLE MARION                         445 NORTH 12TH ST - GENEVA NE 68361
47- 55  LAFATA, JOSEPH JOSEPH                      29321 BRITTANY CT WEST - ROSEVILLE MI 48066
45- 55  LAFOREST, BYRON JOSEPH 'TY'                D. MAY 5, 1947 ARLINGTON, MASS.
82- 72  LAFRANCOIS, ROGER VICTOR                   28 ASPINOOK ST - JEWETT CITY CT 06351
82- 73  LAGA, MICHAEL RUSSELL                      27 CENTER ST - RAMSEY NJ 07446
34- 59  LAGGER, EDWIN JOSEPH                       D. NOVEMBER 18, 1981 JOLIET, ILL.
70- 74  LAGROW, LERRIN HARRIS                      12271 EAST TURQUOISE - SCOTTSDALE AZ 85259
68- 51  LAHOUD, JOSEPH MICHAEL                     HUT HILL ROAD, BOX 165 - BRIDGEWATER CT 06752
82- 74  LAHTI, JEFFREY ALLEN                       OLD ADD: 90 SW SIXTH AVE - ONTARIO OR 97914
46- 61  LAJESKIE, RICHARD EDWARD                   D. AUGUST 15, 1976 RAMSEY, N. J.
39- 65  LAKE, EDWARD ERVING                        1840 NELSON ST - SAN LEANDRO CA 94579
83- 90  LAKE, STEVEN MICHAEL                       16445 NORTH 63RD DRIVE - GLENDALE AZ 85306
42- 61  LAKEMAN, ALBERT WESLEY                     D. MAY 25, 1976 SPARTANBURG, S.C
```

```
62- 74 LAMABE, JOHN ALEXANDER              16224 ANTIETAM AVE - BATON ROUGE LA 70816
43- 76 LAMACCHIA, ALFRED ANTHONY           13515 VISTA BONITA - SAN ANTONIO TX 78216
40- 48 LAMANNA, FRANK                      D. SEPTEMBER 1, 1980 SYRACUSE, N. Y.
41- 59 LAMANNO, RAYMOND SIMON              827 POLK ST-ALBANY CA 94706
35- 59 LAMANSKE, FRANK JAMES               D. AUGUST 4, 1971 OLNEY,ILL.
17- 39 LAMAR, WILLIAM HARMONG              D. MAY 24, 1970 ROCKPORT, MASS.
37- 65 LAMASTER, WAYNE LEE                 2525 EAST ELM ST NEW-ALBANY IN 47150
70- 75 LAMB, JOHN ANDREW                   SHARON VALLEY RD - SHARON CT 06069
20- 69 LAMB, LAYMAN RAYMOND                D. OCTOBER 5, 1955 FAYETTEVILLE, ARK.
69- 97 LAMB, RAYMOND RICHARD               1741 TUSTIN AVE #17C - COSTA MESA CA 92627
46- 62 LAMBERT, CLAYTON PATRICK            D. APRIL 3, 1981 OGDEN, UTAH
41- 60 LAMBERT, EUGENE MARION              268 MONTELO-MEMPHIS TN 38117
16- 53 LAMBETH, OTIS SAMUEL                D. JUNE 5, 1976 MORAN, KAN.
12-105 LAMLINE, FREDERICK ARTHUR           D. SEPTEMBER 20, 1970 PORT HURON, MICH.
70- 76 LAMONT, GENE WILLIAM                4110 TONGA - SARASOTA FL 33583
20- 70 LAMOTTE, ROBERT EUGENE              D. NOVEMBER 2, 1970 CHATHAM, GA.
77- 80 LAMP, DENNIS PATRICK                12100 MONTECITO RD #161-LOS ALAMITOS CA 90720
69- 98 LAMPARD, CHRISTOPHER KEITH          842 NE 74TH AVE - PORTLAND OR 97213
35- 60 LANAHAN, RICHARD ANTHONY            D. MARCH 12, 1975 ROCHESTER, MINN.
87- 74 LANCASTER, LESTER WAYNE             105 EAST 8TH STREET - IRVING TX 75060
77- 81 LANCE, GARY DEAN                    1802 OMEGA DR - COLUMBIA SC 29206
82- 75 LANCELOTTI, RICHARD ANTHONY 'RICK'  5 CIRCLE LN - CHERRY HILL NJ 08003
29- 60 LAND, WILLIAM GILBERT 'DOC'         D. APRIL 14, 1986 LIVINGSTON, ALA.
52- 65 LANDENBERGER, KENNETH HENRY         D. JULY 28, 1960 CLEVELAND, O.
77- 82 LANDESTOY, RAFAEL SIVIALDO CAMILO   KM 8 1/2 CARRET SANCHEZ,CLE#1 - SANTO DOMINGO DOM REP.
57- 39 LANDIS, JAMES HENRY                 2439 STONEHOUSE CT - NAPA CA 94558
63- 65 LANDIS, WILLIAM HENRY               525 SYCAMORE - HANFORD CA 93230
77- 83 LANDREAUX, KENNETH FRED             1840 S. MARENGO #56 - ALHAMBRA CA 91803
76- 52 LANDRETH, LARRY ROBERT              5 BURRITT ST - STRATFORD ONT. N5A 4W6 CAN.
50- 46 LANDRITH, HOBERT NEAL               4335 QUEENS WAY - BLOOMFIELD HILLS MI 48013
57- 40 LANDRUM, DONALD LEROY               19 BARRIE COURT - PITTSBURG CA 94565
38- 48 LANDRUM, JESSE GLENN                D. JUNE 27, 1983 BEAUMONT, TEX.
50- 47 LANDRUM, JOSEPH BUTLER              RR 5 BOX 339 - COLUMBIA SC 29203
80- 69 LANDRUM, TERRY LEE 'TITO'           1121 KENTUCKY SE - ALBUQUERQUE NM 87108
86- 83 LANDRUM, THOMAS WILLIAM 'BILL'      RURAL ROUTE 5 BOX 339 - COLUMBIA SC 29203
24- 63 LANE, JAMES HUNTER                  5720 HERALD SQUARE - MEMPHIS TN 38119
53- 49 LANE, JERALD HAL                    7306 ELAINE DR - CHATTANOOGA TN 37421
71- 60 LANE, MARVIN                        17191 ARDMORE - DETROIT MI 48235
49- 46 LANE, RICHARD HARRISON              26609 ACADEMY DR-PALOS VERDES PENIN CA 90274
41- 61 LANFRANCONI, WALTER OSWALD          D. AUGUST 18, 1986 BARRE, VT.
38- 49 LANG, DONALD CHARLES                5700 KIRKSIDE DR #F - BAKERSFIELD CA 93309
30- 43 LANG, MARTIN JOHN                   D. JANUARY 13, 1968 LAKEWOOD, COLO.
75- 64 LANG, ROBERT DAVID                  985 HOMER AVE - PITTSBURGH PA 15237
14-123 LANGE, ERWIN HENRY                  D. APRIL 24, 1971 MAYWOOD, ILL.
10- 85 LANGE, FRANK HERMAN                 D. DECEMBER 26, 1945 MADISON, WIS.
72- 60 LANGE, RICHARD OTTO                 3387 BROOKS RD, RR 2 - FREELAND MI 48623
26- 47 LANGFORD, ELTON L. 'SAM'            1012 ITASCA STREET - PLAINVIEW TX 79072
76- 50 LANGFORD, JAMES RICK                1119 59TH ST NW - BRADENTON FL 33505
84- 65 LANGSTON, MARK EDWARD               2935 MARIETTA DR - SANTA CLARA CA 95051
64- 63 LANIER, HAROLD CLIFTON              2207 GREENS COURT - RICHMOND TX 77469
38- 50 LANIER, HUBERT MAX                  RR 1 BOX 487 - DUNNELLON FL 32630
71- 61 LANIER, LORENZO                     2928 WOODHILL AVE - CLEVELAND OH 44104
36- 46 LANNING, JOHN YOUNG                 28 DEANWOOD CIR - ASHEVILLE NC 28803
16- 54 LANNING, LESTER ALFRED              D. JUNE 13, 1962 BRISTOL, CONN.
38- 51 LANNING, THOMAS NEWTON              D. NOVEMBER 4, 1967 MARIETTA, GA.
78- 69 LANSFORD, CARNEY RAY                821 REDWOOD DR - DANVILLE CA 94526
82- 76 LANSFORD, JOSEPH DALE 'JODY'        RR TWO - EUFAULA OK 74432
22- 69 LANSING, EUGENE HEWETT              D. JANUARY 18, 1945 RENSSELAER, N. Y.
51- 50 LAPALME, PAUL EDMORE                167 SMITH ST - LEOMINSTER MA 01453
22- 70 LAPAN, PETER NELSON                 D. JANUARY 5, 1953 NORWALK, CAL.
42- 62 LAPIHUSKA, ANDREW                   900 MULBERRY STREET-MILLVILLE NJ 08332
80- 70 LAPOINT, DAVID JEFFREY              21 WINDYHILL RD - GLENS FALLS NY 12801
47- 56 LAPOINTE, RALPH JOHN                D. SEPTEMBER 13, 1967 BURLINGTON, VT.
58- 54 LARKER, NORMAN HOWARD               4701 VILLAGE RD - LONG BEACH CA 90808
86- 84 LARKIN, BARRY LOUIS                 6818 ELWYNNE DRIVE - CINCINNATI OH 45236
87- 75 LARKIN, EUGENE THOMAS               916 BELLMORE ROAD - NORTH BELLMORE NY 11710
83- 91 LARKIN, PATRICK CLIBURN             1101 GREENFIELD AVENUE - ARCADIA CA 91006
34- 60 LARKIN, STEPHEN PATRICK             D. MAY 2, 1969 NORRISTOWN, PA.
18- 44 LARMORE, ROBERT MCCAHAN             D. JANUARY 15, 1964 ST. LOUIS, MO.
70- 77 LAROCHE, DAVID EUGENE               RR 5 BOX 61 - FORT SCOTT KS 66701
78- 70 LAROSE, HENRY JOHN                  99 ROLAND - CUMBERLAND RI 02864
68- 52 LAROSE, VICTOR RAYMOND              2908 EAST SYLVIA ST - PHOENIX AZ 85028
14-124 LAROSS, HARRY RAYMOND               D. MARCH 22, 1954 HINES, ILL.
53- 50 LARSEN, DON JAMES                   17090 COPPER HILL DR - MORGAN HILL CA 95037
36- 47 LARSEN, ERLING ADELI                2020 S. COLUMBUS BLVD #306 - TUCSON AZ 85711
```

CHIP LANG

76- 54 LARSON, DANIEL JAMES	1616 MONTEREY AVE - HERMOSA BEACH CA 90254
63- 66 LARUSSA, ANTHONY	338 GOLDEN MEADOW PLACE - DANVILLE CA 94526
54- 57 LARY, ALFRED ALLEN	RR 8 BOX 139 - NORTHPORT AL 35476
54- 58 LARY, FRANK STRONG	RR 8 BOX 142 - NORTHPORT AL 35476
29- 61 LARY, LYNFORD HOBART	D. JANUARY 9, 1973 DOWNEY, CAL.
63- 67 LASHER, FREDERICK WALTER	HIGHWAY EAST - MERRILLAN WI 54754
82- 77 LASKEY, WILLIAM ALAN	311 EAST WEBER ST - TOLEDO OH 43608
24- 64 LASLEY, WILLARD ALMOND	2565 DEXTER AVE NORTH #201 - SEATTLE WA 98109
54- 59 LASORDA, THOMAS CHARLES	1473 WEST MAXZIM - FULLERTON CA 92633
57- 41 LASSETTER, DONALD O'NEAL	406 GORDY ST - PERRY GA 31069
85- 62 LATHAM, WILLIAM CAROL	1312 BAROSWOOD TER - BIRMINGHAM AL 35235
10- 86 LATHERS, CHARLES TEN EYCK 'CHICK'	D. JULY 26, 1971 PETOSKEY, MICH.
13- 99 LATHROP, WILLIAM GEORGE	D. NOVEMBER 20, 1958 JANESVILLE, WIS.
57- 42 LATMAN, ARNOLD BARRY	13700 TAHITI WAY #340 - MARINA DEL REY CA 90291
56- 50 LAU, CHARLES RICHARD	D. MARCH 18, 1984 KEY COLONY BEACH, FLA.
81- 67 LAUDNER, TIMOTHY JON	6505 VALLEY VIEW ROAD - CORCORAN MN 55340
67- 62 LAUZERIQUE, GEORGE	601 OLEASTER AVE - WEST PALM BEACH FL 33414
34- 61 LAVAGETTO, HARRY ARTHUR 'COOKIE'	46 TARA RD - ORINDA CA 94563
84- 66 LAVALLIERE, MICHAEL EUGENE	12 SCOTT AVE - HOCKSETT NH 03106
13-100 LAVAN, JOHN LEONARD 'DOC'	D. MAY 29, 1952 DETROIT, MICH.
74- 71 LAVELLE, GARY ROBERT	1100 WORTHINGTON CIRCLE - VIRGINIA BEACH VA 23464
12-106 LAVENDER, JAMES SANFORD	D. JANUARY 12, 1960 CARTERSVILLE, GA.
14-125 LAVIGNE, ARTHUR DAVID	D. JULY 18, 1950 WORCESTER, MASS.
69- 99 LAW, RONALD DAVID	OLD ADD: 9000 YUCCA WAY - THORNTON CO
78- 71 LAW, RUDY KARL	10712 FELTON ST - INGLEWOOD CA 90304
80- 71 LAW, VANCE AARON	1748 NORTH COBBLESTONE DRIVE - PROVO UT 84604
50- 48 LAW, VERNON SANDERS	3885 NORTH LITTLE ROCK DR - PROVO UT 84601
48- 63 LAWING, GARLAND FREDERICK	5710 ORR RD #20 - CHARLOTTE NC 28213
82- 78 LAWLESS, THOMAS JAMES	1736 WEST 25TH ST - ERIE PA 16502
54- 60 LAWRENCE, BROOKS ULYSSES	716 NORTHLAND ROAD #E - CINCINNATI OH 45240
63- 68 LAWRENCE, JAMES ROSS	BOX 851 - CALEDONIA ONTARIO NOA 1AO CAN.
24- 65 LAWRENCE, ROBERT ANDREW	D. NOVEMBER 6, 1983 JAMAICA, N. Y.
32- 44 LAWRENCE, WILLIAM HENRY	135 GRAND ST - REDWOOD CITY CA 94062
16- 55 LAWRY, OTIS CARROLL	D. OCTOBER 23, 1965 CHINA, ME.
30- 44 LAWSON, ALFRED VOYLE 'ROXIE'	D. APRIL 9, 1977 STOCKPORT, IA.
72- 61 LAWSON, STEVEN GEORGE	3013 LIVE OAK CT - DANVILLE CA 94526
70- 78 LAXTON, WILLIAM HARRY	261 MANSION AVE - AUDUBON NJ 08106
15- 87 LAYDEN, EUGENE FRANCIS	D. DECEMBER 12, 1984 PITTSBURGH, PA.
48- 57 LAYDEN, PETER JOHN	D. JULY 18, 1982 EDNA, TEXAS
27- 53 LAYNE, HERMAN	D. AUGUST 27, 1973 GALLIPOLIS, O.
41- 62 LAYNE, IVORIA HILLIS 'HILLY'	4623 DORISA AVE-CHATTANOOGA TN 37411
48- 58 LAYTON, LESTER LEE	8780 EAST MCKELLIPS RD #27 - SCOTTSDALE AZ 85257
68- 53 LAZAR, JOHN DAN	8444 OAKWOOD AVE - MUNSTER IN 46321
43- 77 LAZOR, JOHN PAUL	8054 S. 116TH ST - SEATTLE WA 98178
84- 67 LAZORKO, JACK THOMAS	742 FIFTH AVE - RIVER EDGE NJ 07661
26- 48 LAZZERI, ANTHONY MICHAEL	D. AUGUST 6, 1946 SAN FRANCISCO, CAL.
80- 72 LEA, CHARLES WILLIAM	4237 FAIRMONT AVE - MEMPHIS TN 38108
23- 78 LEACH, FREDERICK M	D. DECEMBER 10, 1981 HAGERMAN, ID.
81- 68 LEACH, RICHARD MAX 'RICK'	4033 WEST COURT - FLINT MI 48504
81- 69 LEACH, TERRY HESTER	603 HOWELL AVE - SELMA AL 36701
80- 73 LEAL, LUIS ENRIQUE	CALLE 28 #30-60 - BARQUISMETO,EDO. LARA VENEZ
14-126 LEAR, CHARLES BERNARD 'KING'	D. OCTOBER 31, 1976 GREENCASTLE, PA.
15- 88 LEAR, FREDERICK FRANCIS	D. OCTOBER 13, 1955 EAST ORANGE, N.J.
17- 40 LEARD, WILLIAM WALLACE	D. JANUARY 15, 1970 SAN FRANCISCO, CAL.
14-127 LEARY, JOHN LOUIS	D. AUGUST 18, 1961 WALTHAM, MASS.
81- 70 LEARY, TIMOTHY JAMES	201 OCEAN AVE #1801B - SANTA MONICA CA 90402
20- 71 LEATHERS, HAROLD LANGFORD	D. APRIL 12, 1977 MODESTO, CALIF.
19- 51 LEBOURVEAU, DEWITT WILEY 'BEVO'	D. DECEMBER 19, 1947 NEVADA CITY, CAL.
15- 89 LEDBETTER, RALPH OVERTON 'RAZOR'	D. FEBRUARY 1, 1969 WEST PALM BEACH, FLA.
19- 52 LEE, CLIFFORD WALKER	D. AUGUST 25, 1980 DENVER, COLO.
57- 43 LEE, DONALD EDWARD	9101 PALM TREE DR - TUCSON AZ 85710
20- 72 LEE, ERNEST DUDLEY 'DUD'	D. JANUARY 7, 1971 DENVER, COLO.
30- 45 LEE, HAROLD BURNHAM	4118 RIVER RD - MOSS POINT MS 39563
69-100 LEE, LERON	2-2-33 HYAKUNINCHO SHIN JUKO-KU - TOKYO 160 JAPAN
85- 62 LEE, MANUEL LEE	3RA #86 VILLA MAGDALENA - SAN PEDRO DE MACORIS DOM REP.
78- 72 LEE, MARK LINDEN	RT VIGO BOX 89 -TULIA TX 79088
60- 59 LEE, MICHAEL RANDALL	2511 BUENA FLORES - FALLBROOK CA 92028
64- 64 LEE, ROBERT DEAN	P.O. BOX 0346 - TEHACHAPI CA 93461
45- 56 LEE, ROY EDWIN	D. NOVEMBER 11, 1985 ST. LOUIS, MO.
33- 34 LEE, THORNTON STARR	9054 CALLE NORLO EAST - TUCSON AZ 85710
34- 47 LEE, WILLIAM CRUTCHER	D. JUNE 15, 1977 PLAQUEMINE, LA.
69-101 LEE, WILLIAM FRANCIS	306 PINETREE CIR - BEACONSFIELD QUEBEC H9W 5E1 CAN.
15- 90 LEE, WILLIAM JOSEPH	D. JANUARY 6, 1984 WEST HAZELTON, PA.
59- 48 LEEK, EUGENE HAROLD	3327 BANCROFT ST - SAN DIEGO CA 92104
84- 68 LEEPER, DAVID DALE	1922 FERN - ORANGE CA 92667
21- 55 LEES, GEORGE EDWARD	D. JANUARY 2, 1980 MECHANICSBURG, PA.
65- 62 LEFEBVRE, JAMES KENNETH	9120 NORTH 106TH PLACE - SCOTTSDALE AZ 85258
80- 74 LEFEBVRE, JOSEPH HENRY	19 RIVER RD - PENACOOK NH 03301
38- 52 LEFEBVRE, WILFRID HENRY 'BILL'	7200 ULMERTON RD #1379 - LARGO FL 33541
20- 73 LEFEVRE, ALFREDO MODESTO	D. JANUARY 21, 1982 GLEN COVE, N. Y.
83- 92 LEFFERTS, CRAIG LINDSAY	1035 INSPIRATION LANE - ESCONDIDO CA 92025
24- 66 LEFLER, WADE HAMPTON	D. MARCH 6, 1981 HICKORY, N. C.
74- 72 LEFLORE, RONALD	5126 IROQUOIS - DETROIT MI 48213
29- 62 LEGETT, LOUIS ALFRED 'DOC'	D. MARCH 6, 1988 NEW ORLEANS, LA.
86- 85 LEGG, GREGORY LYNN	411 SOUTH UPAS - ESCONDIDO CA 92025
32- 45 LEHENY, REGIS FRANCIS	D. NOVEMBER 2, 1976 PITTSBURGH, PA.
61- 66 LEHEW, JAMES ANTHONY	398 ARMSTRONG LN - BALTIMORE MD 21221
52- 66 LEHMAN, KENNETH KARL	447 COIN LAKE RD -SEDRO WOOLLEY WA 98284
46- 64 LEHNER, PAUL EUGENE	D. DECEMBER 27, 1967 BIRMINGHAM, ALA.
11- 96 LEHR, CLARENCE EMANUEL	D. JANUARY 31, 1948 DETROIT, MICH.
26- 49 LEHR, NORMAN CARL MICHAEL	D. JULY 17, 1968 CONESUS LAKE, N. Y.
33- 35 LEIBER, HENRY EDWARD	RR 2 BOX 811 - TUCSON AZ 85749
13-101 LEIBOLD, HARRY LORAN 'NEMO'	D. FEBRUARY 4, 1977 DETROIT, MICH.
79- 68 LEIBRANDT, CHARLES LOUIS	1424 OVERLOOK DR - GOLF IL 60029
21- 56 LEIFER, ELMER EDWIN	D. SEPTEMBER 26, 1948 EVERETT, WASH.
12-107 LEINHAUSER, WILLIAM CHARLES	D. APRIL 14, 1978 ELKINS PARK, PA.
39- 66 LEIP, EDGAR ELLSWORTH	D. NOVEMBER 24, 1983 ZEPHYRHILLS, FLA.
84- 69 LEIPER, DAVID PAUL	1421 HURON TRAIL - PLANO TX 75075
87- 76 LEISTER, JOHN WILLIAM	2901 DELMAR - GREAT FALLS MT 59404

87- 77	LEITER, ALOIS TERRY	37 BROWN AVENUE - PINE BEACH NJ 08741
54- 61	LEJA, FRANK JOHN	118 WILSON RD - NAHANT MA 01908
11- 97	LEJEUNE, SHELDON ALDENBERT 'LARRY'	D. APRIL 21, 1952 CHATTANOOGA, TENN.
65- 63	LEJOHN, DONALD EVERETT	154 EDWARDS ST - BROWNSVILLE PA 15417
73- 73	LEMANCZYK, DAVID LAWRENCE	24 LEHIGH CT - ROCKVILLE CENTRE NY 11570
62- 75	LEMASTER, DENVER CLAYTON	4424 RIVERCLIFF DR - LILBURN GA 30247
75- 65	LEMASTER, JOHNNIE LEE	372 4TH ST - PAINTSVILLE KY 41240
61- 67	LEMAY, RICHARD PAUL	4821 SOUTH FLORENCE AVE - TULSA OK 74105
50- 49	LEMBO, STEPHEN NEAL	133-22 124TH ST - SOUTH OZONE PARK NY 11420
75- 66	LEMON, CHESTER EARL 'CHET'	4124 LAKE RIDGE LN - BLOOMFIELD HILLS MI 48013
50- 50	LEMON, JAMES ROBERT	95 FAIRWAY LAKES - MYRTLE BEACH SC 29577
41- 63	LEMON, ROBERT GRANVILLE	1141 CLAIBORNE DR-LONG BEACH CA 90807
69-102	LEMONDS, DAVID LEE	207 JACKSON DR - CHARLOTTE NC 28213
76- 55	LEMONGELLO, MARK	OLD ADD: 251 ATLANTIC ST #30A - KEYPORT NJ 07735
50- 51	LENHARDT, DONALD EUGENE	13317 WOODLAKE VILLAGE CT - ST LOUIS MO 63141
28- 56	LENNON, EDWARD FRANCIS	D. SEPTEMBER 13, 1947 PHILADELPHIA, PA.
54- 62	LENNON, ROBERT ALBERT	8 DUDLEY LANE - DIX HILLS NY 11746
78- 73	LENTINE, JAMES MATTHEW	1901 EAST LAHABRA BLVD - LAHABRA CA 90631
68- 54	LEON, EDUARDO ANTONIO	5616 N. CALLE DE LA REINA - TUCSON AZ 85718
45- 57	LEON, ISIDORO JUAN	CALLE O NO. 260, APT 5 - VADARO HAVANA CUBA
73- 74	LEON, MAXIMINO (MEDINA)	DOMICILIO CONOCIDO - VILLA ACULA VERACRUZ MEX.
74- 73	LEONARD, DENNIS PATRICK	4102 EVERGREEN LN - BLUE SPRINGS MO 64015
11- 98	LEONARD, ELMER ELLSWORTH 'TINY'	D. MAY 27, 1981 NAPA, CALIF.
33- 36	LEONARD, EMIL JOHN "DUTCH"	D. APRIL 17, 1983 SPRINGFIELD, ILL.
13-102	LEONARD, HUBERT BENJAMIN 'DUTCH'	D. JULY 11, 1952 FRESNO, CALIF.
77- 84	LEONARD, JEFFREY N	1626 NORTH FELTON ST - PHILADELPHIA PA 19151
14-129	LEONARD, JOSEPH HOWARD	D. MAY 1, 1920 WASHINGTON, D.C.
67- 63	LEONHARD, DAVID PAUL	87 CORNING ST - BEVERLY MA 01915
28- 57	LEOPOLD, RUDOLPH MATAS	D. SEPTEMBER 3, 1965 BATON ROUGE, LA.
41- 64	LEOVICH, JOHN JOSEPH	3531 NORTH REEF DR - LINCOLN CITY OR 97367
52- 67	LEPCIO, THADDEUS STANLEY 'TED'	263 GREENLODGE ST - DEDHAM MA 02026
55- 69	LEPPERT, DON EUGENE	5130 DURANT - MEMPHIS TN 38116
61- 68	LEPPERT, DONALD GEORGE	ROAD #1 BOX AA-7 - NINEVAH IN 46164
75- 67	LERCH, RANDY LOUIS	P.O. BOX 23 - KELSEY CA 95643
10- 87	LERCHEN, BERTRAM ROE	D. JANUARY 7, 1962 DETROIT, MICH.
52- 68	LERCHEN, GEORGE EDWARD	354 EAST ROSE - GARDEN CITY MI 48135
28- 58	LERIAN, WALTER IRVIN	D. OCTOBER 22, 1929 BALTIMORE, MD.
69-103	LERSCH, BARRY LEE	OLD ADD: 1617 1/2 PALMER ST - PUEBLO CO 81004
72- 62	LESHNOCK, DONALD LEE	464 LORA AVE - YOUNGSTOWN OH 44504
82- 79	LESLEY, BRADLEY JAY	BOX 1012 - TURLOCK CA 95381
17- 41	LESLIE, ROY REID	D. APRIL 9, 1972 SHERMAN, TEX.
29- 63	LESLIE, SAMUEL ANDREW	D. JANUARY 21, 1979 PASCAGOULA, MISS.
39- 67	LETCHAS, CHARLIE	1121 HIGHLAND ST - THOMASVILLE GA 31792
47- 57	LEVAN, JESSE ROY	255 LINCOLN RD - READING PA 19606
13-103	LEVERENZ, WALTER FRED	D. MARCH 19, 1973 ATASCADERO, CALIF.
22- 71	LEVERETT, GORHAM VANCE 'DIXIE'	D. FEBRUARY 20, 1957 BEAVERTON, ORE.
20- 74	LEVERETTE, HORACE WILBUR 'HOD'	D. APRIL 10, 1958 ST. PETERSBURG, FLA.
30- 46	LEVEY, JAMES JULIUS	D. MARCH 14, 1970 DALLAS, TEX.
23- 79	LEVSEN, EMIL HENRY 'DUTCH'	D. MARCH 12, 1972 MINNEAPOLIS, MINN.
40- 49	LEVY, EDWARD CLARENCE	BOX 1188 - LAGRANGE GA 30241
75- 68	LEWALLYN, DENNIS DALE	2900 BRECKENRIDGE DR - PENSACOLA FL 32506
51- 51	LEWANDOWSKI, DANIEL WILLIAM	370 MOUNT ALBION ROAD - HAMILTON ONTARIO L8K 5T2 CAN.
67- 64	LEWIS, ALLAN SYDNEY	PUERTO ARMUELLAS - CHIRIQUI GRANDE PANAMA C.A.
10- 88	LEWIS, GEORGE EDWARD 'DUFFY'	D. JUNE 17, 1979 SALEM, N. H.
79- 69	LEWIS, JAMES MARTIN	OLD ADD: 16049 NE 8TH AVE - NORTH MIAMI BEACH FL 33162
11- 99	LEWIS, JOHN DAVID	D. FEBRUARY 25, 1956 STEUBENVILLE, O.
35- 61	LEWIS, JOHN KELLY 'BUDDY'	BOX 788-GASTONIA NC 28052
64- 65	LEWIS, JOHNNY JOE	822 CARR #F - ST. LOUIS 63101
24- 67	LEWIS, WILLIAM BURTON	D. MARCH 24, 1950 TONAWANDA, N. Y.
33- 37	LEWIS, WILLIAM HENRY 'BUDDY'	D. OCTOBER 24, 1977 MEMPHIS, TENN.

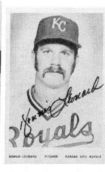

MARK LEMONGELLO

DENNIS LEONARD   PITCHER   KANSAS CITY ROYALS

71- 62	LEY, TERRENCE RICHARD	2914 NE 66TH - PORTLAND OR 97213
88- 86	LEYLAND, JAMES RICHARD	THORNBERRY, 708 WINDVUE DRIVE - PITTSBURGH PA 15205
80- 75	LEZCANO, CARLOS MANUEL	5240 SW 3RD ST - FORT LAUDERDALE FL 33317
74- 74	LEZCANO, SIXTO JOAQUIN	OLD ADD: 437 SOUTH HAWLEY RD #69-MILWAUKEE WI
45- 58	LIBKE, ALBERT WALTER	1117 SOUTH APPELAND DR - WENATCHEE WA 98801
69-104	LIBRAN, FRANCISCO	CALLE DR ESCADE #202 - MAYAGUEZ PR 00708
81- 71	LICKERT, JOHN WILBUR	922 WILHELM ST - PITTSBURGH PA 15220
53- 51	LIDDLE, DONALD EUGENE	1022 NORTH CHERRY ST - MOUNT CARMEL IL 62863
35- 62	LIEBER, CHARLES EDWIN 'DUTCH'	D. DECEMBER 31, 1961 LOS ANGELES, CAL.
30- 47	LIEBHARDT, GLENN IGNATIUS	2460 TANTELON PL - WINSTON SALEM NC 27107
10- 89	LIESE, FREDERICK RICHARD	D. JUNE 30, 1967 LOS ANGELES, CALIF.
36- 48	LILLARD, ROBERT EUGENE 'GENE'	5676 ENCINA RD - GOLETA CA 93117
39- 68	LILLARD, WILLIAM BEVERLY	340 OLD MILL ROAD #47 - SANTA BARBARA CA 93110
58- 55	LILLIS, ROBERT PERRY	P.O. BOX 111206 - CARROLLTON TX 75011

51- 52	LIMMER, LOUIS	100-11 DEBS PL - BRONX NY 10475
81- 72	LINARES, RUFINO DELACRUZ	QUIS QUEYA,LA LOMA 14 #23-SAN PEDRO DE MACORIS DOM REP.
27- 54	LIND, HENRY CARL	D. AUGUST 2, 1946 NEW YORK, N. Y.
74- 75	LIND, JACKSON HUGH	718 N. LINDEN CIR - MESA AZ 85203
87- 78	LIND, JOSE	VILLA CAITO #18 - DORADO PR 00646
60- 60	LINDBECK, EMERIT DESMOND	347 EAST GARFIELD ST - KEWANNEE IL 61443
65- 64	LINDBLAD, PAUL AARON	6512 SHOREWOOD DRIVE - ARLINGTON TX 76016
47- 58	LINDE, LYMAN GILBERT	607 WEST BURNETT ST - BEAVER DAM WI 53916
41- 65	LINDELL, JOHN HARLAN	D. AUGUST 27, 1985 NEWPORT BEACH, CALIF.
86- 87	LINDEMAN, JAMES WILLIAM	2278 SCOTT STREET - DES PLAINES IL 60018
50- 52	LINDEN, WALTER CHARLES	4432 HARVEY AVE - WESTERN SPRINGS IL 60558
43- 78	LINDQUIST, CARL EMIL	RR 1 BOX 185A - EMPORIUM PA 15834
11-100	LINDSAY, WILLIAM GIBBONS	D. JULY 14, 1963 GREENSBORO, N.C.
22- 72	LINDSEY, JAMES KENDRICK	D. OCTOBER 25, 1963 JACKSON, LA.
87- 79	LINDSEY, WILLIAM DONALD	9335 SOUTH HAMPTON PLACE - BOCA RATON FL 33434
16- 56	LINDSTROM, AXEL OLAF	D. JUNE 25, 1940 ASHEVILLE, N. C.
58- 56	LINDSTROM, CHARLES WILLIAM	220 PARK PLACE - LINCOLN IL 62656
24- 68	LINDSTROM, FRED CHARLES	D. OCTOBER 4, 1981 CHICAGO, ILL.
66- 55	LINES, RICHARD GEORGE	OLD ADD: 4220 N. FEDERAL HWY - FORT LAUDERDALE FL 33306
52- 69	LINHART, CARL JAMES	2647 DELMAR AVE - GRANITE CITY IL 62040
10- 90	LINK, FREDERICK THEODORE	D. MAY 22, 1939 HOUSTON, TEXAS
33- 38	LINKE, EDWARD KARL	D. JUNE 21, 1988 CHICAGO, ILL.
54- 63	LINT, ROYCE JAMES	6814 SE JACK RD - MILWAUKIE OR 97222
29- 64	LINTON, CLAUD CLARENCE 'BOB'	D. APRIL 3, 1980 DESTIN, FLA.
73- 75	LINTZ, LARRY	71 LACONIA CT - SAN JOSE CA 95139
62- 76	LINZ, PHILIP FRANCIS	1189 FIRST AVE - NEW YORK NY 10021
63- 69	LINZY, FRANK ALFRED	RR 2 BOX 395 - COWETA OK 74429
56- 51	LIPIETRI, MICHAEL ANGELO	150 YOAKUM AVE - FARMINGDALE NY 11735
42- 63	LIPON, JOHN JOSEPH	13315 ALCHESTER - HOUSTON TX 77079
37- 66	LIPSCOMB, GERARD 'NIG'	D. FEBRUARY 27, 1978 HUNTERSVILLE, N. C.
63- 70	LIPSKI, ROBERT PETER	1 SNOOK ST - SCRANTON PA 18505
87- 80	LIRIANO, NELSON ARTURO	MARTIRES 19 DE NOV.#7,ENS LUPERON-PUERTO PLATA DOM REP.
70- 79	LIS, JOSEPH ANTHONY	107 KIMBERLY RD - SOMERVILLE NJ 08876
27- 55	LISENBEE, HORACE MILTON 'HOD'	D. NOVEMBER 14, 1987 CLARKSVILLE, TENN.
81- 73	LISI, RICCARDO- PATRICK EMILIO	OLD ADD: 32 RIVERVIEW W. APTS#2-PITTSFIELD MA
29- 65	LISKA, ADOLPH JAMES	3831 NE WASCO - PORTLAND OR 97232
73- 76	LITTELL, MARK ALAN	BOX 35 - DEFIANCE MO 63341
80- 76	LITTLE, DONALD JEFFREY 'JEFF'	OLD ADD: 5550 C. R. 44 - WOODVILLE OH 43469
82- 80	LITTLE, RICHARD BRYAN	OLD ADD: 1003 MAGNOLIA - HEARNE TX 77859
12-108	LITTLE, WILLIAM ARTHUR 'JACK'	D. JULY 27, 1961 DALLAS, TEX.
80- 77	LITTLEFIELD, JOHN ANDREW	1214 N. ALAMEDA ST - AZUSA CA 91702
50- 53	LITTLEFIELD, RICHARD BERNARD	14838 KENTFIELD - DETROIT MI 48223
27- 56	LITTLEJOHN, CHARLES CARLISLE	D. OCTOBER 27, 1977 KANSAS CITY, MO.
78- 74	LITTLEJOHN, DENNIS GERALD	OLD ADD: 2244 WEST FREMONT DR - TEMPE AZ
81- 74	LITTLETON, LARRY MARVIN	2318 ARMAND RD NE - ATLANTA GA 30324
52- 70	LITTRELL, JACK NAPIER	7510 FLOYDSBURG RD - CRESTWOOD KY 40014
40- 50	LITWHILER, DANIEL WEBSTER	3810 PLAYER DRIVE - NEWPORT RICHEY FL 33553
47- 59	LIVELY, EVERETT ADRIAN 'BUD'	8605 ESSLINGER CT - HUNTSVILLE AL 35802
11-101	LIVELY, HENRY EVERETT 'JACK'	D. DECEMBER 5, 1967 ARAB, ALA.
39- 69	LIVENGOOD, WESLEY AMOS	2220 ELGIN RD - WINSTON SALEM NC 27103
38- 53	LIVINGSTON, THOMPSON ORVILLE 'MICKEY'	D. APRIL 3, 1983 HOUSTON, TEXAS
68- 55	LLENAS, WINSTON ENRIQUILLO	APARTADO #92 - SANTIAGO DOMINICAN REP.
22- 73	LLEWELLYN, CLEMENT MANLEY	D. NOVEMBER 27, 1969 CHARLOTTE, N. C.
12-109	LOAN, WILLIAM JOSEPH 'MIKE'	D. NOVEMBER 12, 1969 SPRINGFIELD, PA.
39- 70	LOANE, ROBERT KENNETH	BOX 246 - COOL CA 95614
14-130	LOBERT, FRANK JOHN	D. MAY 29, 1932 PITTSBURGH, PA.
62- 77	LOCK, DONALD WILSON	1330 NORTH WALNUT - KINGMAN KS 67068
55- 70	LOCKE, CHARLES EDWARD	805 OAKWOOD - POPLAR BLUFF MO 63901
59- 49	LOCKE, LAWRENCE DONALD 'BOBBY'	RR 1 BOX 400 - DUNBAR PA 15431
64- 66	LOCKE, RONALD THOMAS	P.O. BOX 229 - KENYON RI 02836
65- 65	LOCKER, ROBERT AWTRY	735 SILVERCREST CT - LAFAYETTE CA 94549
73- 77	LOCKLEAR, GENE	RR1 BOX 213 - PEMBROKE NC 28382
55- 71	LOCKLIN, STUART CARLTON	1823 SOUTH BOUTEN - APPLETON WI 54911
45- 59	LOCKMAN, CARROLL WALTER 'WHITEY'	8234 NORTH 75TH ST - SCOTTSDALE AZ 85253
65- 66	LOCKWOOD, CLAUDE EDWARD 'SKIP'	131 BUCKSKIN DR - WESTON MA 02193
38- 54	LODIGIANI, DARIO ANTHONY	745 LATHROP ST - NAPA CA 94558
28- 59	LOEPP, GEORGE HERBERT	D. SEPTEMBER 4, 1967 LOS ANGELES, CAL.
50- 54	LOES, WILLIAM 'BILLY'	33-08 84TH ST - JACKSON HEIGHTS NY 11372
26- 50	LOFTUS, FRANCIS PATRICK	D. OCTOBER 27, 1980 BELCHERTOWN, MASS.
24- 69	LOFTUS, RICHARD JOSEPH	D. JANUARY 21, 1972 CONCORD, MASS.
51- 53	LOGAN, JOHN	6115 WEST CLEVELAND AVE - MILWAUKEE WI 53219
35- 63	LOGAN, ROBERT DEAN 'LEFTY'	D. MAY 20, 1978 INDIANAPOLIS, IND.
14-131	LOHR, HOWARD SYLVESTER	D. JUNE 9, 1977 PHILADELPHIA, PA.
47- 60	LOHRKE, JACK WAYNE 'LUCKY'	2817 LUCENA DR - SAN JOSE CA 95132

34- 63	LOHRMAN, WILLIAM LEROY	250 ROUTE 208 - NEW PALTZ NY 12561
78- 75	LOIS, ALBERTO	INGENIO CONSUELO CALLE 5-SAN PEDRO DE MACORIS DOM. REP.
63- 71	LOLICH, MICHAEL STEPHEN 'MICKEY'	6252 ROBINHILL - WASHINGTON MI 48094
71- 63	LOLICH, RONALD JOHN	OLD ADD: 2436 N. SAVIER - PORTLAND OR 97210
46- 65	LOLLAR, JOHN SHERMAN 'SHERM'	D. SEPTEMBER 24, 1977 SPRINGFIELD, MO.
80- 78	LOLLAR, WILLIAM TIMOTHY 'TIM'	316 NORTH JEFFERSON - FARMINGTON MO 63640
84- 70	LOMAN, DOUGLAS EDWARD	25 LINCOLN STREET - BAKERSFIELD CA 93305
31- 48	LOMBARDI, ERNEST NATALI	D. SEPTEMBER 26, 1977 SANTA CRUZ, CALIF.
86- 88	LOMBARDI, PHILIP ARDEN	12444 CAROL PLACE - GRANADA HILLS CA 91344
45- 60	LOMBARDI, VICTOR ALVIN	5164 EAST ASHLAN #103 - FRESNO CA 93727
48- 59	LOMBARDO, LOUIS	1551 FIRST STREET S. #701 - JACKSONVILLE BEACH FL 32250
85- 64	LOMBARDOZZI, STEPHEN PAUL	2 HAND HEWN WAY - MANLIUS NY 13104
65- 67	LONBORG, JAMES REYNOLD	498 FIRST PARISH RD - SCITUATE MA 02066
11-102	LONERGAN, WALTER E.	D. JANUARY 23, 1958 LEXINGTON, MASS.
22- 74	LONG, JAMES ALBERT	D. SEPTEMBER 14, 1970 FORT DODGE, IA.
63- 72	LONG, JEOFFREY KEITH	11 FLOWER CT - LAKESIDE PARK KY 41017
11-103	LONG, LESTER 'LEP'	D. OCTOBER 21, 1958 BIRMINGHAM, ALA.
51- 54	LONG, RICHARD DALE	41 FIELDSTONE DRIVE - GANSEVOORT NY 12831
81- 75	LONG, ROBERT EARL	250 GLADIOLIS (BOX 951) - ANNA MARIA FL 33501
11-104	LONG, THOMAS AUGUSTUS	D. JUNE 15, 1972 MOBILE, ALA.
24- 70	LONG, THOMAS FRANCIS	D. SEPTEMBER 16, 1973 LOUISVILLE, KY.
85- 65	LONG, WILLIAM DOUGLAS	794 HIGHLAND AVENUE WEST - BUFFALO NY 14223
56- 52	LONNETT, JOSEPH PAUL	126 DUNCAN CIR - BEAVER PA 15009
68- 56	LOOK, BRUCE MICHAEL	1792 HAMILTON ROAD - OKEMOS MI 48864
61- 69	LOOK, DEAN ZACHARY	2103 BUTTERNUT - OKEMOS MI 48864
44- 77	LOPAT, EDMUND WALTER	99 OAK TRAIL RD - HILLSDALE NJ 07642
48- 60	LOPATA, STANLEY EDWARD	LEISURE WORLD MANOR #2239 - MESA AZ 85206
45- 61	LOPATKA, ARTHUR JOSEPH	7310 NORTH HARLEM - CHICAGO IL 60648
72- 63	LOPES, DAVID EARL 'DAVEY'	16984 AVE DE SANTA YNEZ-PACIFIC PALISADES CA 90272
28- 60	LOPEZ, ALFONSO RAMON	3601 BEACH DR - TAMPA FL 33609
65- 68	LOPEZ, ARTURO	57 WALNUT ST - OAKLAND NJ 07436
74- 76	LOPEZ, AURELIO RIOS	5 PONIENTE #8 - TEXAMACHALCO PUEBLA MEX.
76- 56	LOPEZ, CARLOS ANTONIO	MEXICI #33A, POINTE - MAZATLAN SINALOA MEX.
55- 72	LOPEZ, HECTOR HEADLEY	666 JANOS LN - WEST HEMPSTEAD NY 11552
66- 56	LOPEZ, JOSE RAMON	D. SEPTEMBER 4, 1982 MIAMI, FLA.
63- 73	LOPEZ, MARCELINO PONS	841 NW LITTLE RIVER DR - MIAMI FL 33150
23- 80	LORD, WILLIAM CARLTON 'CARL'	D. AUGUST 15, 1947 CHESTER, PA.
13-104	LORENZEN, ADOLPH ANDREAS 'LEFTY'	D. MARCH 5, 1963 DAVENPORT, IA.
16- 57	LOTZ, JOSEPH PETER	D. JANUARY 1, 1971 HAYWARD, CAL.
80- 79	LOUCKS, SCOTT GREGORY	1801 VIOLA DR - SIERRA VISTA AZ 85635
10- 91	LOUDELL, ARTHUR	D. FEBRUARY 19, 1961 KANSAS CITY, MO.
67- 65	LOUGHLIN, LAWRENCE JOHN	410 SOUTH 57TH - TACOMA WA 98408
64- 67	LOUN, DONALD NELSON	9095 WEXFORD DR - VIENNA VA 22180
13-105	LOVE, EDWARD HAUGHTON 'SLIM'	D. NOVEMBER 30, 1942 MEMPHIS, TENN.
22- 75	LOVELACE, THOMAS RIVERS	D. JULY 12, 1979 DALLAS, TEX.
55- 73	LOVENGUTH, LYNN RICHARD	13565 SW HART RD - BEAVERTON OR 97005
33- 39	LOVETT, MERRITT MARWOOD	1047 NORTH HARLEM AVE #1NA - OAK PARK IL 60302
80- 80	LOVIGLIO, JOHN PAUL 'JAY'	96 COUNTRY VILLAGE LN - EAST ISLIP NY 11730
72- 64	LOVITTO, JOSEPH	3803 SHADY CREEK NORTH - ARLINGTON TX 76013
63- 74	LOVRICH, PETER	19626 BEECHNUT DR - MOKENA IL 60448
15- 91	LOW, FLETCHER	D. JUNE 6, 1973 HANOVER, N.H.
11-105	LOWDERMILK, LOUIS BAILEY	D. DECEMBER 27, 1975 CENTRALIA, ILL.
20- 75	LOWE, GEORGE WESLEY	D. SEPTEMBER 2, 1981 SOMERS POINT, N. J.
70- 80	LOWENSTEIN, JOHN LEE	1208 STARKY - AUGUSTA KS 67010
51- 55	LOWN, OMAR JOSEPH 'TURK'	1106 VAN BUREN - PUEBLO CO 81004
42- 64	LOWREY, HARRY LEE 'PEANUTS'	D. JULY 2, 1986 INGLEWOOD, CALIF.
84- 71	LOWRY, DWIGHT	RR 2 BOX 225 - PEMBROKE NC 28372
42- 65	LOWRY, SAMUEL JOSEPH	263A HERMITAGE STREET - PHILADELPHIA PA 19127
86- 89	LOYND, MICHAEL WALLACE	19 RANDALL DRIVE - SHORT HILLS NJ 07078
84- 72	LOZADO, WILLIAM 'WILLIE'	551 EUCLID AVE - BROOKLYN NY 11208
81- 76	LUBRATICH, STEVEN GEORGE	910 CASTLE - SAN LEANDRO CA 94578
36- 49	LUBY, HUGH MAX	D. MAY 4, 1986 EUGENE, ORE.
38- 55	LUCADELLO, JOHN	103 OAKWOOD DR-SAN ANTONIO TX 78228
23- 81	LUCAS, CHARLES FREDERICK 'RED'	D. JULY 9, 1986 NASHVILLE, TENN.
35- 64	LUCAS, FREDERICK WARRINGTON	D. MARCH 11, 1987 CAMBRIDGE, MD.
80- 81	LUCAS, GARY PAUL	3356 AVENIDA SIERRA - ESCONDIDO CA 92025
31- 49	LUCAS, JOHN CHARLES	D. OCTOBER 31, 1970 MARYVILLE, ILL.
29- 66	LUCAS, RAY WESLEY	D. OCTOBER 9, 1969 HARRISON, MICH.
70- 81	LUCCHESI, FRANK JOSEPH	3027 GLASGOW DR - ARLINGTON TX 76013
23- 82	LUCE, FRANK EDWARD	D. FEBRUARY 3, 1942 MILWAUKEE, WIS.
20- 76	LUCEY, JOSEPH EARL	D. JULY 30, 1980 HOLYOKE, MASS.
43- 79	LUCIER, LOUIS JOSEPH	579 HIGHLAND ST - NORTHBRIDGE MA 01534
24- 71	LUDOLPH, WILLIAM FRANCIS	D. APRIL 8, 1952 OAKLAND, CAL.
25- 66	LUEBBE, ROY JOHN	D. AUGUST 21, 1985 PAPILLION, NEB.

JOE LONNETT

CARLOS LOPEZ

71- 64 LUEBBER, STEPHEN LEE	3302 MOOREHEAD DR - JOPLIN MO 64804
62- 78 LUEBKE, RICHARD RAYMOND	D. DECEMBER 4, 1974 SAN DIEGO, CALIF.
85- 66 LUGO, URBANO RAFAEL	ROOEVELT RES. TIUNA ENT BPH 44 ROSALES - CARACAS VENEZ
13-106 LUHRSEN, WILLIAM FERDINAND	D. AUGUST 15, 1973 NORTH LITTLE ROCK, ARK.
41- 66 LUKON, EDWARD PAUL	RR 3, CHERRY VALLEY RD - BURGETTSTOWN PA15021
67- 66 LUM, MICHAEL KEN-WAI	3476 COCHISE DR NW - ATLANTA GA 30339
57- 44 LUMENTI, RAPHAEL ANTHONY 'RALPH'	P.O. BOX 137 - WORCESTER MA 01519
56- 53 LUMPE, JERRY DEAN	732 PEARSON DRIVE - SPRINGFIELD MO 65804
54- 64 LUNA, GUILLERMO ROMERO "MEMO"	CARDENAS 50 OTE. - LOS MOCHIS SINOLOA MEX.
45- 62 LUND, DONALD ANDREW	1000 SOUTH STATE ST - ANN ARBOR MI 48109
67- 67 LUND, GORDON T	1717 ROBBIE LN - MOUNT PROSPECT IL 60056
24- 72 LUNDGREN, EBIN DELMAR 'DEL'	D. OCTOBER 19, 1984 LINDSBORG, KAN.
73- 78 LUNDSTEDT, THOMAS ROBERT	8645 HUNTERS WAY - ST. PAUL MN 55124
19- 53 LUNTE, HARRY AUGUST	D. JULY 27, 1965 ST. LOUIS, MO.
40- 51 LUPIEN, ULYSSES JOHN 'TONY'	BOX 351 - NORWICH VT 05055
61- 70 LUPLOW, ALVIN DAVID	2450 STARLITE DR - SAGINAW MI 48603
14-132 LUQUE, ADOLFO	D. JULY 3, 1957 HAVANA, CUBA
87- 81 LUSADER, SCOTT EDWARD	759 CAROLINE AVENUE - WEST PALM BEACH FL 33406
10- 92 LUSH, ERNEST BENJAMIN	D. FEBRUARY 26, 1937 DETROIT, MICH.
56- 54 LUTTRELL, LYLE KENNETH	D. JULY 11, 1984 CHATTANOOGA, TENN.
22- 76 LUTZ, LOUIS WILLIAM	D. FEBRUARY 22, 1984 CINCINNATI, O.
51- 56 LUTZ, ROLLIN JOSEPH 'JOE'	1411 QUAIL DR - SARASoTA FL 33581
23- 83 LUTZKE, WALTER JOHN 'RUBE'	D. MARCH 6, 1938 MILWAUKEE, WIS.
70- 82 LUZINSKI, GREGORY MICHAEL	320 JACKSON RD - MEDFORD NJ 08055
67- 68 LYLE, ALBERT WALTER 'SPARKY'	17 SIGNAL HILL DR - VOORHEES NJ 08043
25- 67 LYLE, JAMES CHARLES	D. OCTOBER 10, 1977 WILLIAMSPORT, PA.
20- 77 LYNCH, ADRIAN RYAN	D. MARCH 16, 1934 DAVENPORT, IA.
80- 82 LYNCH, EDWARD FRANCIS	5940 SW 120TH ST - MIAMI FL 33156
54- 65 LYNCH, GERALD THOMAS	120 DAVIS MILL COURT - LAWRENCEVILLE GA 30245
48- 61 LYNCH, MATT DANNY 'DUMMY'	D. JUNE 30, 1978 PLANO, TEXAS
22- 77 LYNCH, WALTER EDWARD	D. DECEMBER 21, 1976 DAYTONA BEACH, CALIF.
16- 58 LYNN, BYRD	D. FEBRUARY 5, 1940 NAPA, CAL.
74- 77 LYNN, FREDRIC MICHAEL	801 INVERNESS DRIVE - RANCHO MIRAGE CA 92270
39- 71 LYNN, JAPHET MONROE 'RED'	D. OCTOBER 27, 1977 BELLVILLE, TEX.
37- 67 LYNN, JEROME EDWARD	D. SEPTEMBER 25, 1972 SCRANTON, PA.
44- 78 LYON, RUSSELL MAYO	BOX 366 - CALHOUN FALLS SC 29629
44- 79 LYONS, ALBERT HAROLD	D. DECEMBER 20, 1965 INGLEWOOD, CAL.
86- 90 LYONS, BARRY STEPHEN	644 HOPKINS BOULEVARD - BILOXI MS 39530
47- 61 LYONS, EDWARD HOYT	1466 EBERT ST - WINSTON SALEM NC 27103
20- 78 LYONS, GEORGE TONY	D. AUGUST 12, 1981 NEVADA, MO.
41- 67 LYONS, HERSCHEL E	7900 DUNBARTON AVE-LOS ANGELES CA 90045
85- 67 LYONS, STEPHEN JOHN	OLD ADD: 8475 SW PARKVIEW LOOP - BEAVERTON OR 97005
29- 67 LYONS, TERENCE HILBERT	D. SEPTEMBER 9, 1959 DAYTON, O.
23- 84 LYONS, THEODORE AMAR	D. JULY 25, 1986 SULPHUR, LA.
83- 93 LYONS, WILLIAMS ALLEN	2621 GRANDVIEW AVENUE - ALTON IL 62002
80- 83 LYSANDER, RICHARD EUGENE	225 FLORENCE ST #1 - SUNNYVALE CA 94086
69-105 LYTTLE, JAMES LAWRENCE	751 CAMINO LAKE CIR - BOCA RATON FL 33432
55- 74 MAAS, DUANE FREDRICK 'DUKE'	D. DECEMBER 7, 1976 MOUNT CLEMENS, MICH.
58- 57 MABE, ROBERT LEE	90 BISHOP AVE - DANVILLE VA 24541
76- 57 MACCORMACK, FRANK LOUIS	2 SCHMIDT PL - SECAUCUS NJ 07094
28- 61 MACDONALD, HARVEY FORSYTH	D. OCTOBER 4, 1965 MANOA, PA.
50- 55 MACDONALD, WILLIAM PAUL	RR 1 BOX 13 - BELLEVUE ID 83313
87- 82 MACFARLANE, MICHAEL ANDREW	7421 WOODSIDE AVENUE - STOCKTON CA 95207
26- 51 MACFAYDEN, DANIEL KNOWLES	D. AUGUST 26, 1972 BRUNSWICK, ME.
74- 78 MACHA, KENNETH EDWARD	P.O. BOX 381 - EXPORT PA 15632
79- 70 MACHA, MICHAEL WILLIAM	117 PERTH - VICTORIA TX 77901
71- 65 MACHEMEHL, CHARLES WALTER	RR 5 BOX 234 - BRENHAM TX 77833
78- 76 MACHEMER, DAVID RITCHIE	1359 ST. JOSEPH CIR - ST. JOSEPH MI 49085
10- 93 MACK, EARLE THADDEUS	D. FEBRUARY 4, 1967 UPPER DARBY, PA.
22- 78 MACK, FRANK GEORGE	D. JULY 2, 1971 CLEARWATER, FLA.
45- 63 MACK, JOSEPH JOHN	OLD ADD: 2038 MULBERRY LN - ARLINGTON HEIGHTS IL 60004
38- 56 MACK, RAYMOND JAMES	D. MAY 7, 1969 BUCYRUS, O.
87- 83 MACK, SHANE LEE	13708 FELSON STREET - CERITOS CA 90701
85- 68 MACK, TONY LYNN	OLD ADD: 3304 MONTE VESTA #E32 - LEXINGTON KY 40502
73- 79 MACKANIN, PETER	2905 HOLLYBROOK DRIVE - WEST COVINA 91791
55- 75 MACKENZIE, ERIC HUGH	1224 EMILY ST - MOORETOWN ONTARIO CAN.
61- 71 MACKENZIE, HENRY GORDON 'GORDY'	RURAL ROUTE 1 BOX 1383 - FRUITLAND PARK FL 32731
60- 61 MACKENZIE, KENNETH PURVIS	232 YORK ST - NEW HAVEN CT 06520
41- 68 MACKIEWICZ, FELIX THADDEUS	33 NANTUCKET LN-OLIVETTE MO 63132
53- 52 MACKINSON, JOHN JOSEPH	17934 HATTON ST - RESEDA CA 91335
79- 71 MACKO, STEVEN JOSEPH	D. NOVEMBER 15, 1981 ARLINGTON, TEX.
62- 79 MACLEOD, WILLIAM DANIEL	136 BASS AVENUE - GLOUCESTER MA 01930
38- 57 MACON, MAX CULLEN	D. JANUARY 20, 1989 CHARLOTTE, N. C.
22- 79 MACPHEE, WALTER SCOTT 'WADDY'	825 WEST CENTER ST #16B - JUPITER FL 33458
44- 80 MACPHERSON, HARRY WILLIAM	971 BAY VISTA BLVD - ENGLEWOOD FL 33533
80- 84 MACWHORTER, KEITH	86B VILLAGE GREEN NORTH - EAST PROVIDENCE RI 02915
16- 59 MADDEN, EUGENE	D. APRIL 6, 1949 UTICA, N. Y.
14-133 MADDEN, FRANCIS A.	D. APRIL 30, 1952 PITTSBURGH, PA.
12-110 MADDEN, LEONARD JOSEPH	D. SEPTEMBER 9, 1949 TOLEDO, O.
83- 94 MADDEN, MICHAEL ANTHONY	4733 FRANKFORT WAY - DENVER CO 80239
87- 84 MADDEN, MORRIS DEWAYNE	105 JENNINGS - LAURENS SC 29360
46- 66 MADDERN, CLARENCE JAMES	D. AUGUST 9, 1986 TUCSON, ARIZ.
70- 83 MADDOX, ELLIOTT	109 HILTON AVE - VAUXHALL NJ 07088
72- 65 MADDOX, GARRY LEE	OLD ADD: 26 BRIARWOOD - BERLIN NJ 08091
78- 77 MADDOX, JERRY GLENN	5539 BAYWOOD - RIVERSIDE CA 92504
86- 91 MADDUX, GREGORY ALAN	4241 RAWHIDE - LAS VEGAS NV 89120
86- 92 MADDUX, MICHAEL AUSLEY	4241 RAWHIDE - LAS VEGAS NV 89120
85- 69 MADISON, CHARLES SCOTT 'SCOTTIE'	STAR ROUTE BOX 1605 - LILLIAN AL 36549
50- 56 MADISON, DAVID PLEDGER	D. DECEMBER 9, 1985 MACON, MISS.
32- 46 MADJESKI, EDWARD WILLIAM	%MONTGOMERY,9915 KNOLLWOOD DR - CINCINNATI OH 45242
73- 80 MADLOCK, BILL	453 EAST DECATUR ST - DECATUR IL 62521
87- 85 MADRID, ALEXANDER	1626 WEST FIFTH STREET - MESA AZ 85201
47- 62 MADRID, SALVADOR	D. FEBRUARY 24, 1977 FORT WAYNE, IND.
60- 62 MAESTRI, HECTOR ANIBAL	581 SW 89TH COURT - MIAMI FL 33174
86- 93 MAGADAN, DAVID JOSEPH	4505 NORTH A STREET - TAMPA FL 33609
11-106 MAGEE, LEO CHRISTOPHER	D. MARCH 14, 1966 COLUMBUS, O.
38- 58 MAGGERT, HARL WARREN	D. JULY 10, 1986 CITRUS HEIGHTS, CALIF.
45- 64 MAGLIE, SALVATORE ANTHONY	77 MORNINGSIDE DR - GRAND ISLAND NY 14072
11-107 MAGNER, EDMUND BURKE 'STUBBY'	D. SEPTEMBER 9, 1956 CHILLICOTHE, O.

70- 84 MAGNUSON, JAMES ROBERT   OLD ADD: 1014 EAST WALNUT - GREEN BAY WI 54301
87- 86 MAGRANE, JOSEPH DAVID   RR 5 BOX 544B - MOREHEAD KY 40351
66- 57 MAGRINI, PETER ALEXANDER   2402 RANCHO CABEZA DR - SANTA ROSA CA 95404
22- 80 MAGUIRE, FRED EDWARD   D. NOVEMBER 3, 1961 BOSTON, MASS.
50- 57 MAGUIRE, JACK   BOX 13947 - GAINESVILLE FL 32604
21- 57 MAHADY, JAMES BERNARD   D. AUGUST 9, 1936 CORTLAND, N. Y.
60- 63 MAHAFFEY, ARTHUR   3545 RHOADS AVE - NEWTOWN SQUARE PA 19073
26- 52 MAHAFFEY, LEE ROY   D. JULY 23, 1969 ANDERSON, S. C.
40- 52 MAHAN, ARTHUR LEO   1002 KENWYN ST-PHILADELPHIA PA 19124
12-111 MAHARG, WILLIAM JOSEPH   D. NOVEMBER 20, 1953 PHILADELPHIA, PA.
78- 78 MAHLBERG, GREGORY JOHN   5100 N. PLACITA DEL LAZO - TUCSON AZ 85715
77- 85 MAHLER, MICHAEL JAMES 'MICKEY'   6908 COUNTRY WOOD CIR #F - MIDVALE UT 84047
79- 72 MAHLER, RICHARD KEITH 'RICK'   7911 QUIRT DR - SAN ANTONIO TX 78227
30- 48 MAHON, ALFRED GWINN   D. DECEMBER 26, 1977 NEW HAVEN, CONN.
10- 94 MAHONEY, CHRISTOPHER JOHN   D. JULY 15, 1954 VISALIA, CALIF.
11-108 MAHONEY, DANIEL JOSEPH   D. SEPTEMBER 28, 1960 UTICA, N.Y.
59- 50 MAHONEY, JAMES THOMAS   150 SYCAMORE TER - GLEN ROCK NJ 07452
51- 51 MAHONEY, ROBERT PAUL   6901 LYNN - LINCOLN NE 68505
45- 65 MAIER, ROBERT PHILIP   334 DUNELLEN AVE - DUNELLAN NJ 08812
36- 50 MAILHO, EMIL PIERRE   566 SCOTT ST - FREMONT CA 94538
15- 92 MAILS, JOHN WALTER 'DUSTER'   D. JULY 5, 1974 SAN FRANCISCO, CALIF.
48- 62 MAIN, FORREST HARRY 'WOODY'   563 CAMINO DE TEODORO - WALNUT CA 91789
14-134 MAIN, MILES GRANT 'ALEX'   D. DECEMBER 29, 1965 ROYAL OAK, MICH.
43- 80 MAINS, JAMES ROYAL   D. MARCH 17, 1969 BRIDGTON, ME.
15-105 MAISEL, CHARLES LOUIS   D. AUGUST 25, 1953 BALTIMORE, MD.
13-107 MAISEL, FREDERICK CHARLES 'FRITZ'   D. APRIL 22, 1967 BALTIMORE, MD.
13-108 MAISEL, GEORGE JOHN   D. NOVEMBER 20, 1968 BALTIMORE, MD.
39- 72 MAJESKI, HENRY   12 ROOSEVELT ST - STATEN ISLAND NY 10304
37- 68 MAKOSKY, FRANK   D. JANUARY 10, 1987 STROUDSBURG, PA.
75- 69 MAKOWSKI, THOMAS ANTHONY   195 ROESCH AVE - BUFFALO NY 14201
33- 40 MALAY, JOSEPH CHARLES   233 SUCCESS PARK - BRIDGEPORT CT 06610
81- 77 MALDONADO, CANDIDO   HCO2 BOX 16800 - ARECIBO PR 00612
81- 78 MALER, JAMES MICHAEL   OLD ADD: 14408 SW 143RD CT - MIAMI FL 33186
37- 69 MALINOSKY, ANTHONY JOSEPH   5540 WEST FIFTH ST #60 - OXNARD CA 93030
34- 64 MALIS, CYRUS SOL   D. JANUARY 12, 1971 NORTH HOLLYWOOD, FLA.
57- 45 MALKMUS, ROBERT EDWARD   400 WALLINGFORD TER - UNION NJ 07083
59- 51 MALLETT, GERALD GORDON   7610 FOREST PARK DR - BEAUMONT TX 77707
50- 58 MALLETTE, MALCOLM FRANCIS   2419 SILVER FOX LN - RESTON VA 22091
87- 87 MALLICOAT, ROBBIN DALE   2820 SOUTHEAST BRODIAEA COURT - HILLSBORO OR 97123
31- 50 MALLON, LESLIE CLYDE   702 CIMMARON TRAIL - GRANBURY TX 76048
21- 58 MALLONEE, HOWARD BENNETT 'BEN'   D. FEBRUARY 19, 1978 BALTIMORE, MD.
25- 68 MALLONEE, JULIUS NORRIS   D. DECEMBER 26, 1934 CHARLOTTE, N. C.
40- 53 MALLORY, JAMES BAUGH   1905 FOREST HILLS DR - GREENVILLE NC 27834
77- 86 MALLORY, SHELDON   17604 S. OAKWOOD - HAZELCREST IL 60429
10- 95 MALLOY, ARCHIBALD ALEXANDER   D. MARCH 1, 1961 FERRIS, TEX.
43- 81 MALLOY, ROBERT PAUL   3850 KIRKUP AVE-CINCINNATI OH 45213
87- 88 MALLOY, ROBERT WILLIAM   OLD ADD: DALLAS TX
55- 76 MALMBERG, HARRY WILLIAM   D. OCTOBER 29, 1976 SAN FRANCISCO, CALIF.
49- 47 MALONE, EDWARD RUSSELL   224 AVENIDA MAJORCA #A - LAGUNA HILLS CA 92653
15- 93 MALONE, LEWIS ALOYSIUS   D. FEBRUARY 17, 1972 BROOKLYN, N.Y.

PEPE MANGUAL

28- 62 MALONE, PERCE LEIGH 'PAT'   D. MAY 13, 1943 ALTOONA, PA.
60- 64 MALONEY, JAMES WILLIAM   2217 WEST KEATS - FRESNO CA 93705
12-112 MALONEY, PATRICK WILLIAM   D. JUNE 27, 1979 PAWTUCKET, R. I.
13-109 MALOY, PAUL AUGUSTUS   D. MARCH 18, 1976 SANDUSKY, O.
43- 82 MALTZBERGER, GORDON RALPH   D. DECEMBER 11, 1974 RIALTO, CALIF.
55- 77 MALZONE, FRANK JAMES   16 ALETHA RD - NEEDHAM MA 02192
13-110 MAMAUX, ALBERT LEON   D. JANUARY 2, 1963 SANTA MONICA, .CALIF.
28- 63 MANCUSO, AUGUST RODNEY 'GUS'   D. OCTOBER 26, 1984 HOUSTON, TEXAS
44- 81 MANCUSO, FRANK OCTAVIUS   5126 CRIPPLE CREEK - HOUSTON TX 77017
14-135 MANDA, CARL ALAN   D. MARCH 9, 1983 ARTESIA, N. MEX.
41- 69 MANDERS, HAROLD CARL   BOX 149 - DALLAS CENTER IA 50063
52- 71 MANGAN, JAMES DANIEL   6878 TRINIDAD - SAN JOSE CA 95120
69-106 MANGUAL, ANGEL LUIS   LAS DELICIAS R10,ROD.DEL VALLE-PONCE PR 00731
72- 66 MANGUAL, JOSE MANUEL 'PEPE'   CALLE 41,AC19 LOS CAOBOS - PONCE PR 00731
24- 73 MANGUM, LEON ALLEN   D. JULY 9, 1974 LIMA, O.
12-113 MANGUS, GEORGE GRAHAM   D. AUGUST 10, 1933 RUTLAND, MASS.
20- 79 MANION, CLYDE JENNINGS   D. SEPTEMBER 4, 1967 DETROIT, MICH.
76- 58 MANKOWSKI, PHILIP ANTHONY   204 ROSEWOOD TER - CHEEKTOWAGA NY 14225
44- 82 MANN, BEN GARTH   RR 1 BOX 14 - ITALY TX 76651
28- 64 MANN, JOHN LEO   D. MARCH 31, 1977 TERRE HAUTE, IND.
13-111 MANN, LESLIE   D. JANUARY 14, 1962 PASADENA, CALIF.
14-136 MANNING, ERNEST DEVON   D. APRIL 28, 1973 PENSACOLA, FLA.
62- 80 MANNING, JAMES BENJAMIN   4341 SW 2ND CT - PLANTATION FL 33317
75- 70 MANNING, RICHARD EUGENE 'RICK'   150 MILES RD - CHAGRIN FALLS OH 44022

40- 54	MANNO, DONALD	1338 ELLIOTT ST-WILLIAMSPORT PA 17701
81- 79	MANRIQUE, FRED ELOI	CARRERA 6 #21 SANTE FE - CIUDAD BOLIVAR VENEZ
56- 55	MANTILLA, FELIX	6973 NORTH TACOMA ST - MILWAUKEE WI 53224
51- 58	MANTLE, MICKEY CHARLES	5730 WATSON CIR - DALLAS TX 75225
69-107	MANUEL, CHARLES FUQUA	4930 BOWER RD SW - ROANOKE VA 24018
75- 71	MANUEL, JERRY	9524 BEDINGTON WAY - SACRAMENTO CA 95827
23- 85	MANUSH, HENRY EMMETT 'HEINIE'	D. MAY 12, 1971 SARASOTA, FLA.
50- 59	MANVILLE, RICHARD WESLEY	479 MONTGOMERY RD - ALTAMONTE SPRINGS FL 32714
87- 89	MANWARING, KIRT DEAN	502 JOHN STREET - HORSEHEADS NY 14845
19- 54	MAPEL, ROLLA MAMILTON	D. APRIL 6, 1966 SAN DIEGO, CAL.
48- 63	MAPES, CLIFFORD FRANKLIN	BOX 872 - PRYOR OK 74362
32- 47	MAPLE, HOWARD ALBERT	D. NOVEMBER 9, 1970 PORTLAND, ORE.
60- 65	MARANDA, GEORGES HENRI	13 THIBEAULT #1 - LEVIS QUEBEC G6V 2J6 CAN.
12-114	MARANVILLE, WALTER JAMES VINCENT	D. JANUARY 5, 1954 NEW YORK, N.Y.
23- 86	MARBERRY, FREDRICK 'FIRPO'	D. JUNE 30, 1976 MEXIA, TEX.
13-112	MARBET, WALTER WILLIAM	D. SEPTEMBER 24, 1956 HOHENWALD, TENN.
40- 55	MARCHILDON, PHILIP JOSEPH	3 COURTWRIGHT ROAD - ETOBICOKE ONTARIO M9C 4B3 CAN.
33- 41	MARCUM, JOHN ALFRED	D. SEPTEMBER 10, 1984 LOUISVILLE, KY.
65- 69	MARENTETTE, LEO JOHN	4000 SYLVANIA #66 - TOLEDO OH 43623
56- 56	MARGONERI, JOSEPH EMANUEL	RR 1 BOX 177 - WEST NEWTON PA 15089
60- 66	MARICHAL, JUAN ANTONIO	3178 NW 19TH STREET - MIAMI FL 33125
14-137	MARION, DONALD G. 'DAN'	D. JANUARY 18, 1933 MILWAUKEE, WIS.
35- 65	MARION, JOHN WYETH 'RED'	D. MARCH 13, 1975 SAN JOSE, CALIF.
40- 56	MARION, MARTIN WHITEFORD 'SLATS'	8 FORCEE LANE - ST.LOUIS MO 63124
57- 46	MARIS, ROGER EUGENE	D. DECEMBER 14, 1985 HOUSTON, TEX.
51- 59	MARKELL, HARRY DUQUESNE 'DUKE'	D. JUNE 14, 1984 FORT LAUDERDALE, FLA.
50- 60	MARKLAND, CLENETH EUGENE 'GENE'	613 EAST OLEANDER CIR - SEBASTIAN FL 32958
15- 94	MARKLE, CLIFFORD MONROE	D. MAY 24, 1974 TEMPLE CITY, CALIF.
51- 60	MARLOWE, RICHARD BURTON	D. DECEMBER 30, 1968 TOLEDO, O.
40- 57	MARNIE, HARRY SYLVESTER 'HAL'	2715 SOUTH SMETLEY-PHILADELPHIA PA 19145
53- 53	MAROLEWSKI, FRED DANIEL	298 BENSLEY - CALUMET CITY IL 60409
69-108	MARONE, LOUIS STEPHEN	663 TYRONE ST - EL CAJON CA 92020
31- 51	MARQUARDT, ALBERT LUDWIG 'OLLIE'	D. FEBRUARY 7, 1968 PORT CLINTON, O.
72- 67	MARQUEZ, GONZALO	D. DECEMBER 20, 1984 VALENCIA, VENEZUELA
51- 61	MARQUEZ, LUIS ANGEL	D. MARCH 1, 1988 AGUADILLA, P. R.
25- 69	MARQUIS, JAMES MILBURN	BOX F - WEST POINT CA 95255
53- 54	MARQUIS, ROBERT RUDOLPH	2075 LONGFELLOW DR - BEAUMONT TX 77706
55- 78	MARQUIS, ROGER J	5 LINDBERGH AVE - HOLYOKE MA 01040
50- 61	MARRERO, CONRADO EUGENIO RAMOS	205 AVONTAMIENTO #1 - CERRO HAVANA CUBA
17- 42	MARRIOTT, WILLIAM EARL	D. AUGUST 11, 1969 BERKELEY, CALIF.
32- 48	MARROW, CHARLES KENNON 'BUCK'	D. NOVEMBER 21, 1982 NEWPORT NEWS, VA.
11-109	MARSANS, ARMANDO	D. SEPTEMBER 3, 1960 HAVANA, CUBA
49- 48	MARSH, FRED FRANCIS	RR4 - CORRY PA 16407
41- 70	MARSHALL, CHARLES ANDREW	1 RADCLIFF CT-WILMINGTON DE 19804
46- 67	MARSHALL, CLARENCE WESTLY	27642-I SUSAN BETH WAY - SAUGUS CA 91350
67- 69	MARSHALL, DAVID LEWIS	4433 CHARLEMAGNE - LONG BEACH CA 90808
29- 68	MARSHALL, EDWARD HARBERT 'DOC'	1840 FAIRWAY CIR CR - SAN MARCOS CA 92069
58- 58	MARSHALL, JIM RUFE	5761 N. CASA BLANCA - SCOTTSDALE AZ 85253
73- 81	MARSHALL, KEITH ALAN	RR 2, 334F BECKWITH ROAD - PINE CITY NY 14871
81- 80	MARSHALL, MICHAEL ALLEN	4641 FULTON AVE #105 - SHERMAN OAKS CA 92423
67- 70	MARSHALL, MICHAEL GRANT	ATH DEPT,HENDERSON STATE COL - ARKADELPHIA AR 71923
42- 66	MARSHALL, MILO MAX	4794 BOLIVAR CT - SALEM OR 97301
12-115	MARSHALL, ROY DEVERNE 'RUBE'	D. JUNE 11, 1980 DOVER, O.
42- 67	MARSHALL, WILLARD WARREN	204 MAIN ST-FORT LEE NJ 07024
31- 52	MARSHALL, WILLIAM HENRY	D. MAY 5, 1977 SACRAMENTO, CALIF.
50- 62	MARTIN, ALFRED MANUEL 'BILLY'	P.O. BOX 2889 - DANVILLE CA 94526
53- 55	MARTIN, BARNEY ROBERT	1617 TALL PINES CIR - COLUMBIA SC 29205
44- 83	MARTIN, BORIS MICHAEL 'BABE'	323 FAWN MEADOWS - BALLWIN MO 63011
79- 73	MARTIN, DONALD RENIE	504 FAIRVIEW AVE - DOVER DE 19901
17- 43	MARTIN, ELWOOD GOOD 'SPEED'	D. JUNE 14, 1983 LEMON GROVE, CALIF.
46- 68	MARTIN, FRED TURNER	D. JUNE 11, 1979 CHICAGO, ILL.
37- 70	MARTIN, HERSHEL RAY	D. NOVEMBER 17, 1980 CUBA, MO.
74- 79	MARTIN, JERRY LINDSEY	918 SOUTH BONHAM RD - COLUMBIA SC 29205
12-116	MARTIN, JOHN CHRISTOPHER	D. JULY 4, 1980 BRONX, N. Y.
28- 65	MARTIN, JOHN LEONARD ROOS. 'PEPPER'	D. MARCH 5, 1965 MCALESTER, OKLA.
80- 85	MARTIN, JOHN ROBERT	P.O. BOX 7281 - PORT SAINT LUCIE FL 34985
59- 52	MARTIN, JOSEPH CLIFTON 'J. C.'	%MARTIN LAUNDRY,2222 W. BELMONT - CHICAGO IL 60618
86- 94	MARTIN, JOSEPH MICHAEL 'MIKE'	21100 NE SANDY BLVD #62 - TROUTDALE OR 97060

49- 49	MARTIN, MORRIS WEBSTER	244 POTTERY RD - WASHINGTON MO 63090
19- 55	MARTIN, PATRICK FRANCIS	D. FEBRUARY 4, 1949 BROOKLYN, N. Y.
55- 79	MARTIN, PAUL CHARLES 'JAKE'	1529 33RD STREET - SAN DIEGO CA 92102
43- 83	MARTIN, RAYMOND JOSEPH	107 PELLANA RD-NORWOOD MA 02062
36- 51	MARTIN, STUART MCGUIRE	BOX 184 - SEVERN NC 27877
68- 57	MARTIN, THOMAS EUGENE 'GENE'	110 STANLEY DR - LEESBURG GA 31763

14-138 MARTIN, WILLIAM GLOYD   D. SEPTEMBER 15, 1949 WASHINGTON, D.C.
36- 52 MARTIN, WILLIAM JOSEPH 'JOE'   D. SEPTEMBER 28, 1960 BUFFALO, N. Y.
24- 74 MARTINA, JOSEPH JOHN   D. MARCH 22, 1962 NEW ORLEANS, LA.
80- 86 MARTINEZ, ALFREDO   2346 THOMAS - LOS ANGELES CA 90031
83- 95 MARTINEZ, CARMELO (SALGADO)   BUZON 1297 - DORADO PR 00646
86- 95 MARTINEZ, DAVID   360 TULIP TRAIL - CASSELBERRY FL 32707
87- 90 MARTINEZ, EDGAR   BO. MAGUAYO BUZON 1295RR - DORADO PR 00646
74- 80 MARTINEZ, FELIX ANTHONY 'TIPPY'   1524 DELLSWAY RD - TOWSON MD 21204
63- 75 MARTINEZ, GABRIEL ANTONIO 'TONY'   OLD ADD: 4599 NW 9TH ST - MIAMI FL 33126
69-109 MARTINEZ, JOHN ALBERT 'BUCK'   6213 VISTA AVE - SACRAMENTO CA 95824
69-110 MARTINEZ, JOSE AZCUIZ   11813 EAST 59TH TER CIR - KANSAS CITY MO 64133
76- 59 MARTINEZ, JOSE DENNIS 'DENNY'   3 BROOK FARM COURT - COCKEYSVILLE MD 21030
62- 82 MARTINEZ, ORLANDO OLIVO 'MARTY'   748 NORTH 23RD WEST AVE - TULSA OK 74127
62- 81 MARTINEZ, RODOLFO HECTOR   OLD ADD: MARIANAO - HAVANA CUBA
50- 63 MARTINEZ, ROGELIO ULLOA   9118 5TH AVE - BROOKLYN NY 11209
77- 87 MARTINEZ, SILVIO RAMON   OLD ADD: CARLOS DE LORA 25 - SANTIAGO DOMINICAN REP.
70- 85 MARTINEZ, TEODORE NOEL   CALLE ABREU 150 - SANTO DOMINGO DOMINICAN REP.
35- 66 MARTINI, GUIDO JOE 'WEDO'   D. OCTOBER 28, 1970
37- 71 MARTY, JOSEPH ANTON   D. OCTOBER 4, 1984 SACRAMENTO, CALIF.
57- 47 MARTYN, ROBERT GORDON   3365 SW 123RD - BEAVERTON OR 97005
75- 72 MARTZ, GARY ARTHUR   E 8003 EUCLID - SPOKANE WA 99212
80- 87 MARTZ, RANDY CARL   ATH. DEPT. MACMURRAY COLLEGE - JACKSONVILLE IL 62650
87- 91 MARZANO, JOHN ROBERT   1224 SOUTH 11TH STREET - PHILADELPHIA PA 19147
69-111 MASHORE, CLYDE WAYNE   14680 MARSH CREEK RD - CLAYTON CA 94517
39- 73 MASI, PHILIP SAMUEL   1 NORTH MAIN STREET - MOUNT PROSPECT IL 60056
66- 58 MASON, DONALD STETSON   8 FAWN ROAD - SOUTH YARMOUTH MA 02664
58- 59 MASON, HENRY   1136 SOUTH LINCOLN - MARSHALL MO 65340
71- 66 MASON, JAMES PERCY   RR 1 BOX 308 - THEODORE AL 36582
82- 81 MASON, MICHAEL PAUL   5955 STONEYBROOK DR - MINNETONKA MN 55343
84- 73 MASON, ROGER LEROY   5955 STONEYBROOK DR - MINNETONKA MN 55343
57- 48 MASSA, GORDON RICHARD   5905 KIMBERLY AVE - CINCINNATI OH 45213
18- 45 MASSEY, ROY HARDEE   D. JUNE 23, 1954 ATLANTA, GA.
17- 44 MASSEY, WILLIAM HERBERT 'MIKE'   D. OCTOBER 17, 1971 SHREVEPORT, LA.
31- 53 MASTERS, WALTER THOMAS   151 METCALFE ST #404 - OTTAWA ONTARIO K2P 1N8 CAN.
40- 58 MASTERSON, PAUL NICKALIS   3003 WEST 53RD ST-CHICAGO IL 60632
39- 74 MASTERSON, WALTER EDWARD   4515 CARTERET DR - NEW BERN NC 28560
84- 74 MATA, VICTOR JOSE   AVE DE LOS MARTIRES 131 - SANTO DOMINGO DOMINICAN REP.
52- 72 MATARAZZO, LEONARD   2715 CARLISLE ST - NEW CASTLE PA 16105
67- 71 MATCHICK, JOHN THOMAS 'TOM'   5523 BENTWOOD DRIVE - TOLEDO OH 43615
12-117 MATHES, JOSEPH JOHN   D. DECEMBER 21, 1978 ST. LOUIS, MO.
52- 73 MATHEWS, EDWIN LEE   13744 RECUERDO DR - DEL MAR CA 92014
86- 96 MATHEWS, GREGORY INMAN   5682 TAHOE CIRCLE - BUENA PARK CA 90621
60- 67 MATHEWS, NELSON ELMER   211 CRESTVIEW - COLUMBIA IL 62236
60- 68 MATHIAS, CARL LYNWOOD   RR 2 - OLEY PA 19567
85- 70 MATHIS, RONALD VANCE   OLD ADD: 10326 BON OAK DR - ST. LOUIS MO 63136
70- 86 MATIAS, JOHN ROY   98-1616 HOOLAUAE ST - AIEA HI 96701
71- 67 MATLACK, JONATHAN TRUMPBOUR   8100 SHELTON DR - FORT WORTH TX 76112
14-139 MATTESON, HENRY EDSON   D. AUGUST 31, 1943 BROCTON, N.Y.
72- 68 MATTHEWS, GARY NATHANIEL   13215 MERCER ST - PACOIMA CA 91331
22- 81 MATTHEWS, JOHN JOSEPH   D. FEBRUARY 8, 1968 HAGERSTOWN, MD.
23- 87 MATTHEWS, WID CURRY   D. OCTOBER 5, 1965 HOLLYWOOD, CAL.
43- 84 MATTHEWSON, DALE WESLEY   D. FEBRUARY 20, 1984 BLAIRSVILLE, GA.
38- 59 MATTICK, ROBERT JAMES   1721 159TH PLACE NE - BELLEVUE WA 98008
12-118 MATTICK, WALTER JOSEPH   D. NOVEMBER 5, 1968 LOS ALTOS, CALIF.
82- 82 MATTINGLY, DONALD ARTHUR   RR 5 BOX 74 - EVANSVILLE IN 47711
31- 54 MATTINGLY, LAURENCE EARL   4007 BEDFORD PLACE - SUITLAND MD 20746
14-140 MATTIS, RALPH L.   D. SEPTEMBER 13, 1960 WILLIAMSPORT, PA.
29- 69 MATTOX, CLOY MITCHELL   D. AUGUST 3, 1985 DANVILLE, VA.
22- 82 MATTOX, JAMES POWELL   D. OCTOBER 12, 1973 MYRTLE BEACH, S. C.
79- 74 MATULA, RICHARD CARLTON   1817 CHAPEL HEIGHTS DR - WHARTON TX 77488
81- 81 MATUSZEK, LEONARD JAMES   1875 BARCELONA DR - DUNEDIN FL 33528
34- 65 MATUZAK, HARRY GEORGE   D. NOVEMBER 26, 1978 HOPE, ALA.
44- 84 MAUCH, EUGENE WILLIAM   46 LA RONDA DR - RANCHO MIRAGE CA 92270
34- 66 MAULDIN, MARSHALL REESE 'MARK'   6545 HANEN ST - UNION CITY GA 30291
24- 75 MAUN, ERNEST GERALD   D. JANUARY 1, 1987 CORPUS CHRISTI, TEXAS
45- 66 MAUNEY, RICHARD   D. FEBRUARY 6, 1970 ALBEMARLE, N. C.
58- 60 MAURIELLO, RALPH   23644 DEL CER CIR - CANOGA PARK CA 91304
48- 64 MAURO, CARMEN LOUIS   536 STANFORD DR - SAN LUIS OBISPO CA 93401
49- 50 MAVIS, ROBERT HENRY   300 MARKWOOD DR - LITTLE ROCK AR 72205
69-112 MAXIE, LARRY HANS   296 VERDUSO WAY - UPLAND CA 91786
62- 83 MAXVILL, CHARLES DALLAN 'DAL'   6745 RYAN CREST RD - FLORISSANT MO 63031

50- 64 MAXWELL, CHARLES RICHARD   RR2 MAPLE LAKE - PAW PAW MI 49079
68- 58 MAY, CARLOS   5533 HILL AND DALE DR - CINCINNATI OH 45213
67- 72 MAY, DAVID LAFRANCE   915 GRAY ST - NEW CASTLE DE 19720
17- 45 MAY, FRANK SPRUIELL 'JAKIE'   D. JUNE 3, 1970 WENDELL, N. C.
64- 68 MAY, JERRY LEE   RR 2 BOX 318 - BRIDGEWATER VA 22812
65- 70 MAY, LEE ANDREW   5533 HILL & DALE DR - CINCINNATI OH 45213
39- 75 MAY, MERRILL GLEND 'PINKY'   5503 DASHING CREEK ST - SAN ANTONIO TX 78247
70- 87 MAY, MILTON SCOTT   6504 RIVERVIEW BLVD NW - BRADENTON FL 34209
65- 71 MAY, RUDOLPH   P.O. BOX 1290 - NORTH FORK CA 93643
24- 76 MAY, WILLIAM HERBERT 'BUCKSHOT'   D. MARCH 15, 1984 BAKERSFIELD, CALIF.
68- 59 MAYBERRY, JOHN CLAIBORN   11115 WEST 121ST TERRACE - OVERLAND PARK KS 66213
59- 53 MAYE, ARTHUR LEE   OLD ADD: 867 E. 52ND ST - LOS ANGELES CA 90011
57- 49 MAYER, EDWIN DAVID   440 OAKDALE AVE - CORTE MADERA CA 94925
12-119 MAYER, ERSKINE JOHN   D. MARCH 10, 1957 LOS ANGELES, CALIF.
15- 95 MAYER, SAMUEL FRANKEL   D. JULY 1, 1962 ATLANTA, GA.
11-110 MAYER, WALTER A.   D. NOVEMBER 18, 1951 MINNEAPOLIS, MINN.
11-111 MAYES, ADAIR BUSHYHEAD 'PADDY'   D. MAY 28, 1962 FAYETTEVILLE, ARK.
40- 59 MAYNARD, JAMES WALTER   D. SEPTEMBER 7, 1977 DURHAM, N. C.
22- 83 MAYNARD, LEROY EVANS 'CHICK'   D. JANUARY 31, 1957 BANGOR, ME.
36- 53 MAYO, EDWARD JOSEPH   825 OCEAN PINES - BERLIN MD 21811
48- 65 MAYO, JOHN LEWIS 'JACKIE'   719 MAPLERIDGE DR - YOUNGSTOWN OH 44512
15- 96 MAYS, CARL WILLIAM   D. APRIL 4, 1971 EL CAJON, CALIF.

THE SPORT AMERICANA FOOTBALL, HOCKEY, BAS-
KETBALL & BOXING CARD PRICE IS THE AUTHORI-
TATIVE SOURCE FOR INFORMATION AND CURRENT
PRICES FOR CARDS OF THESE SPORTS.

51- 62 MAYS, WILLIE HOWARD   51 MT VERNON LN - ATHERTON CA 94025
56- 57 MAZEROSKI, WILLIAM STANLEY   RR6 BOX 130 - GREENSBURG PA 15601
35- 67 MAZZERA, MELVIN LEONARD   6 WEST DUNMAR LN - STOCKTON CA 95207
76- 60 MAZZILLI, LEE LOUIS   12 CARPENTERS DRK RD - GREENWICH CT 06830
11-112 MCADAMS, GEORGE D. 'JACK'   D. MAY 21, 1937 SAN FRANCISCO, CALIF.
30- 49 MCAFEE, WILLIAM FORT   D. JULY 8, 1958 CULPEPPER, VA.
13-113 MCALLESTER, WILLIAM LUSK   D. MARCH 3, 1970 CHATTANOOGA, TENN.
71- 68 MCANALLY, ERNEST LEE   RR 4 BOX 61-A - MOUNT PLEASANT TX 75455
58- 61 MCANANY, JAMES   11066 RHODA WAY - CULVER CITY CA 90230
68- 60 MCANDREW, JAMES CLEMENT   5749 NORTH STETSON CT - PARKER CO 80134
14-141 MCARTHUR, OLAND ALEXANDER 'DIXIE' D. MAY 31, 1986 COLUMBUS, MISS.
14-142 MCAULEY, JAMES EARL 'IKE'   D. APRIL 6, 1928 DES MOINES, IA.
60- 69 MCAULIFFE, RICHARD JOHN   BOX 211 - WEST SIMSBURY CT 06092
14-143 MCAVOY, GEORGE H   OLD ADD: ARDMORE OK 73401
13-114 MCAVOY, JAMES EUGENE 'WICKEY'   D. JULY 5, 1973 ROCHESTER, N. Y.
59- 54 MCAVOY, THOMAS JOHN   CLINTON COURT - STILLWATER NY 12118
61- 72 MCBEAN, ALVIN O'NEAL   BOX 4475 - ST THOMAS VI 00801
26- 53 MCBEE, PRYOR EDWARD   D. APRIL 19, 1963 ROSEVILLE, CALIF.
73- 82 MCBRIDE, ARNOLD RAY "BAKE"   5210 NORTH HWY 67 - FLORISSANT MO 63033
59- 55 MCBRIDE, KENNETH FAYE   2138 DAVENPORT AVE - CLEVELAND OH 44114
43- 85 MCBRIDE, THOMAS RAYMOND   3219 CAROL ANN - WICHITA FALLS TX 76309
64- 69 MCCABE, JOE ROBERT   1001 CRESCENT DR - GREENCASTLE IN 46135
46- 69 MCCABE, RALPH HERBERT   D. MAY 4, 1974 WINDSOR, ONT.
18- 46 MCCABE, RICHARD JAMES   D. APRIL 11, 1950 BUFFALO, N. Y.
15- 97 MCCABE, TIMOTHY   D. APRIL 12, 1977 IRONTON, MO.
18- 47 MCCABE, WILLIAM FRANCIS   D. SEPTEMBER 2, 1969 CHICAGO, ILL.
46- 70 MCCAHAN, WILLIAM GLENN   D. JULY 3, 1986 FORT WORTH, TEXAS
62- 84 MCCALL, BRIAN ALLEN   105 UNION ST - ALEXANDRIA VA 22314
48- 66 MCCALL, JOHN WILLIAM   2959 PALMER DR - SIERRA VISTA AZ 85635
77- 88 MCCALL, LARRY STEPHEN   RR 5 BOX 354 - CANDLER NC 28715
48- 67 MCCALL, ROBERT LEONARD 'DUTCH'   2600 ASHLEY #A107-NORTH LITTLE ROCK AR 72114
27- 57 MCCALLISTER, JOHN   D. OCTOBER 18, 1946 COLUMBUS, O.
14-144 MCCANDLESS, SCOTT COOK 'JOHN'   D. AUGUST 17, 1861 PITTSBURGH, PA.
20- 80 MCCANN, ROBERT EMMETT   D. APRIL 15, 1937 PHILADELPHIA, PA.
59- 56 MCCARDELL, ROGER MORTON   16 WEST MAIN ST - RISING SUN MD 21911
23- 88 MCCARREN, WILLIAM JOSEPH   D. SEPTEMBER 11, 1983 DENVER, COLO.
10- 96 MCCARTHY, ALEXANDER GEORGE   D. MARCH 12, 1978 SALISBURY, MD.
48- 68 MCCARTHY, JEROME FRANCIS   D. OCTOBER 3, 1965 OCEANSIDE, N. Y.
34- 67 MCCARTHY, JOHN JOSEPH   D. SEPTEMBER 13, 1973 MUNDELEIN, ILL.
26- 54 MCCARTHY, JOSEPH VINCENT   D. JANUARY 13, 1978 BUFFALO,N. Y.
85- 71 MCCARTHY, THOMAS MICHAEL   5 CAROLYN DR, RR 8 - PLYMOUTH MA 02360
13-115 MCCARTY, GEORGE LEWIS   D. JUNE 9, 1930 READING, PA.
59- 57 MCCARVER, JAMES TIMOTHY 'TIM'   1518 YOUNGFORD RD - GLADWYNNE PA 19035
85- 72 MCCASKILL, KIRK EDWARD   15226 N. 51ST ST - SCOTTSDALE AZ 85254
77- 89 MCCATTY, STEVEN EARL   3595 CROOKS ROAD - TROY MI 48084
61- 73 MCCLAIN, JOE FRED   RR 8 BOX 109 - JOHNSON CITY TN 37601
31- 55 MCCLANAHAN, PETE   BOX 157 - MONT BELVIOU TX 77580
19- 56 MCCLELLAN, HERVEY MCDOWELL   D. NOVEMBER 6, 1925 CYNTHIANA, KY.
87- 92 MCCLENDON, LLOYD GLENN   2975 EAGLE WAY - BOULDER CO 80303
13-116 MCCLESKEY, JEFFERSON LAMAR   D. MAY 11, 1971 AMERICUS, GA.
36- 54 MCCLOSKEY, JAMES ELLWOOD   D. AUGUST 18, 1971 JERSEY CITY, N. J.

DEN'S
COLLECTORS DEN

PLASTIC CARD PROTECTING PAGES
LARGEST SELECTION IN THE HOBBY

TRY **DEN'S**

FINEST QUALITY PLASTIC SHEETS

Featuring:

NON—MIGRATING PLASTIC IN ALL SHEETS
PLASTIC THAT DOES NOT STICK TOGETHER
STIFFNESS TO RESIST CARD CURLING
INTELLIGENT DESIGN
RESISTANCE TO CRACKING
FULL COVERAGE OF CARDS, PHOTOS, ENVELOPES

NO MIX & MATCH

STYLE	POCKETS CAPACITY	RECOMMENDED FOR	PRICE EACH (DOES NOT INCLUDE P & H)			
			1 24	25 99	100 299	300 600
9	9/18	TOPPS (1957—PRESENT), FLEER, DONRUSS, TCMA, KELLOGG, POST CEREAL, LEAF (1960), RECENT NON-SPORTS CARDS, ALL STANDARD 2½" X 3½" CARDS	.25	.23	.21	.19
8	8/16	TOPPS (1952—1956), BOWMAN (1953—55)	.25	.23	.21	.19
12	12/24	BOWMAN (1948—50), TOPPS (1951 RED AND BLUE), RECENT TOPPS AND FLEER STICKERS	.25	.23	.21	.19
1	1/2	PHOTOGRAPHS (8X10)	25	.23	.21	.19
2	2/4	PHOTOGRAPHS (5x7), TOPPS SUPERSTAR PHOTOS	25	.23	.21	19
4	4/8	POSTCARDS, TOPPS SUPER (1964,70,71), EXHIBITS, DONRUSS (ACTION ALL STARS), PEREZ STEELE HOF	.25	.23	.21	.19
18	18/36	T CARDS, TOPPS COINS, BAZOOKA (1963—67 INDIVIDUAL CARDS)	.35	.35	.30	.27
9G	9/18	GOUDEY, DIAMOND STARS, LEAF (1948)	.35	.35	30	27
9PB	9/18	PLAY BALL, BOWMAN (1951—52), DOUBLE PLAY, TOPPS MINIS, ALL GUM, INC. SPORT AND NON—SPORT	.35	.35	30	27
1C	1/2	TURKEY REDS (T3), PEPSI (1977), PRESS GUIDES, MOST WRAPPERS SPORT AND NON—SPORT	.35	35	.30	27
3	3/6	HOSTESS PANELS, HIRES, ZELLERS PANELS	30	25	25	20
6V	6/12	TOPPS (DOUBLE HEADERS, GREATEST MOMENTS, 1951 TEAM, CONNIE MACK, CURRENT STARS, 1965 FOOT-BALL AND HOCKEY, BUCKS, 1969—70 BASKETBALL), DADS HOCKEY, DOUBLE FOLDERS, TRIPLE FOLDERS	.35	35	.30	.27
6D	6/12	RED MAN (WITH OR WITHOUT TABS), DISC, KAHN'S (1955—67)	.35	35	30	27
1Y	1/1	YEARBOOKS, PROGRAMS, MAGAZINES, HOBBYPAPERS TABLOIDS POCKET SIZE 9"X12"	35	.35	30	.27
1S	1/2	SMALL PROGRAMS, MAGAZINE PAGES AND PHOTOS, CRACKER JACK SHEETS, POCKET SIZE 8½" X 11"	.30	.30	25	20
10	10/10	MATCHBOOK COVERS, POCKET SIZE 1 3/4" X 4 3/4"	.35	.35	30	.27
3E	3/3	FIRST DAY COVERS, BASEBALL COMMEMORATIVE ENVELOPES, STANDARD SIZED ENVELOPES	.35	.35	.30	.27
3L	3/6	SQUIRT, PEPSI (1963), FLEER (STAMPS IN STRIPS), TOPPS (1964 AND 1969 STAMPS IN STRIPS),	.35	.35	.30	.27
6P	6/12	POLICE OR SAFETY CARDS (ALL SPORTS)	.25	.23	.21	.19

POSTAGE & HANDLING SCHEDULE
$ .01 to $ 20.00 add $ 2.00
$ 20.01 to $ 29.99 add $ 2.50
$ 30.00 to $ 49.99 add $ 3.00
$ 50.00 or more add $ 4.00

MARYLAND RESIDENTS ADD 5% TAX
CANADIAN ORDERS — BOOKS ONLY
CANADIAN BOOK ORDERS ADD 25% postage
Orders outside contiguous U.S.A. add 25% more
U.S. FUNDS ONLY

MAKE CHECK OR MONEY ORDER PAYABLE TO:

DEN'S COLLECTORS DEN
Dept. BAL
P.O. BOX 606, LAUREL, MD 20707

DON'T SETTLE FOR LESS THAN THE BEST. BE SURE THAT THE
STYLES 9,8,4,12,1 & 2 HAVE DEN'S COLLECTORS DEN EMBOSSED
ON THE BORDER OF THE SHEET.

MasterCard VISA

10- 97	MCCLURE, LAWRENCE LEDWITH	D. AUGUST 31, 1948 HUNTINGTON, W. VA.
75- 73	MCCLURE, ROBERT CRAIG	3419 STACEY COURT - MOUNTAIN VIEW CA 94040
15- 98	MCCLUSKEY, HARRY ROBERT	D. JUNE 7, 1962 TOLEDO, O.
33- 42	MCCOLL, ALEXANDER BOYD	1203 SHERMAN ST - GENEVA OH 44041
14-145	MCCONNAUGHEY, RALPH J.	D. JUNE 4, 1966 DETROIT, MICH.
15- 99	MCCONNELL, SAMUEL FAULKNER	D. JUNE 27, 1981 PHOENIXVILLE, PA.
64- 70	MCCOOL, WILLIAM JOHN	863 FERNSHIRE DR - CENTERVILLE OH 45459
80- 88	MCCORMACK, DONALD ROSS	RR 2 BOX 93 - OMAK WA 98841
34- 68	MCCORMICK, FRANK ANDREW	D. NOVEMBER 21, 1982 MANHASSET, N. Y.
56- 58	MCCORMICK, MICHAEL FRANCIS	410 LINCOLN CENTRE - FOSTER CITY CA 94404
40- 60	MCCORMICK, MYRON WINTHROP 'MIKE'	D. APRIL 14, 1976 LOS ANGELES, CALIF.
39- 76	MCCOSKY, WILLIAM BARNEY	33 PINE ARBOR LN #102 - VERO BEACH FL 32962
59- 58	MCCOVEY, WILLIE LEE	P.O. BOX 620342 - WOODSIDE CA 94062
38- 60	MCCOY, BENJAMIN JENISON	3932 EAST OMAHA DR SW-GRANDVILLE MI 49418
39- 77	MCCRABB, LESTER WILLIAM	412 SOUTH CHURCH ST - QUARRYVILLE PA 17566
63- 76	MCCRAW, TOMMY LEE	2225 CLYDE #1 - LOS ANGELES CA 90016
25- 70	MCCREA, FRANCIS WILLIAM	D. FEBRUARY 25, 1981 DOVER, N. J.
14-146	MCCREERY, ESLEY PORTERFIELD	D. OCTOBER 19, 1960 SACRAMENTO, CALIF.
22- 84	MCCUE, FRANK ALOYSIUS	D. JULY 5, 1953 EVERGREEN PARK, ILL.
85- 73	MCCULLERS, LANCE GRAYE	17606 WILLOW CREEK - LUTZ FL 33549
40- 61	MCCULLOUGH, CLYDE EDWARD	D. SEPTEMBER 18, 1982 SAN FRANCISCO, CALIF.
29- 70	MCCULLOUGH, PAUL WILLARD	D. NOVEMBER 7, 1970 NEWCASTLE, PA.
42- 68	MCCULLOUGH, PHILIP LAMAR	25 EXETER RD-AVONDALE ESTATES GA 30002
22- 85	MCCURDY, HARRY HENRY	D. JULY 21, 1972 HOUSTON, TEX.
55- 80	MCDANIEL, LYNDALL DALE	5024 SOUTH OSAGE - KANSAS CITY MO 64133
57- 50	MCDANIEL, MAX VON	33202 ROLLING WOOD - PINEHURST TX 77361
12-120	MCDERMOTT, FRANK A. 'RED'	D. SEPTEMBER 11, 1964 PHILADELPHIA, PA.
48- 69	MCDERMOTT, MAURICE JOSEPH 'MICKEY'	4950 BRILL - PHOENIX AZ 85008
72- 69	MCDERMOTT, TERRENCE MICHAEL	407 NORTH VILLAGE AVE - ROCKVILLE CENTRE NY 11552
57- 51	MCDEVITT, DANIEL EUGENE	2991 SALEM RD SE - CONYERS GA 30207
12-121	MCDONALD, CHARLES E. 'TEX'	D. MARCH 31, 1943 HOUSTON, TEX.
69-113	MCDONALD, DAVID BRUCE	32 NE 22ND AVE #204 - POMPANO BEACH FL 33062
11-113	MCDONALD, EDWARD C.	D. MARCH 11, 1946 ALBANY, N.Y.
31- 56	MCDONALD, HENRY MONROE	D. OCTOBER 17, 1982 HEMET, CALIF.
50- 65	MCDONALD, JIMMIE LEROY	3767 STIRRUP DRIVE - KINGMAN AZ 86401
10- 98	MCDONALD, MALCOLM JOSEPH	D. MAY 30, 1963 BAYTOWN, TEXAS
43- 86	MCDONNELL, JAMES WILLIAM	OLD ADD: 14238 SEYMOUR - DETROIT MI 48205
51- 63	MCDOUGALD, GILBERT JAMES	10 WARREN AVE - SPRING LAKE NJ 07762
87- 93	MCDOWELL, JACK BURNS	5443 VANNOORD AVENUE - VAN NUYS CA 91401
85- 74	MCDOWELL, ODDIBE	5240 SW 18TH ST - HOLLYWOOD FL 33023
85- 75	MCDOWELL, ROGER ALAN	5973 OAKMOST PLACE - STUART FL 34997
61- 74	MCDOWELL, SAMUEL EDWARD	7727 ST LAWRENCE AVE - PITTSBURGH PA 15218
16- 60	MCELWEE, LELAND STANFORD	D. FEBRUARY 8, 1957 UNION, ME.
42- 69	MCELYEA, FRANK	4908 CROSS CREEK CT,BDG 16 - EVANSVILLE IN 47715
74- 81	MCENANEY, WILLIAM HENRY	4051 NE 15TH AVENUE - OAKLAND PARK FL 33334
30- 50	MCEVOY, LOUIS ANTHONY	D. DECEMBER 16, 1953 WEBSTER GROVE, MO.
68- 61	MCFADDEN, LEON	15110 MARQUETTE #C - MOORPARK CA 92021
45- 67	MCFARLAND, HOWARD ALEXANDER	8321 WILLOWBROOK - WICHITA KS 67207
62- 85	MCFARLANE, ORLANDO DE JESUS	OLD ADD: 33 TAFT AVE - ASHEVILLE NC 28803
81- 82	MCGAFFIGAN, ANDREW JOSEPH	356 SWEET BRIAR LN - LAKELAND FL 33803
17- 46	MCGAFFIGAN, MARK ANDREW 'PATSY'	D. DECEMBER 22, 1940 CARLYLE, ILL.
46- 71	MCGAH, EDWARD JOSEPH	1070 GREEN ST #1900 - SAN FRANCISCO CA 94133
62- 86	MCGAHA, FRED MELVIN 'MEL'	P.O. BOX 273 - DISNEY OK 74340
12-122	MCGARR, JAMES VINCENT	D. JULY 21, 1981 MIAMI, FLA.
12-123	MCGARVEY, DANIEL FRANCIS	D. MARCH 7, 1947 PHILADELPHIA, PA.
34- 69	MCGEE, DANIEL ALOYSIUS	252 BUTTRICK AVE - BRONX NY 10465
25- 71	MCGEE, FRANCIS D. 'TUBBY'	D. JANUARY 30, 1934 COLUMBUS, O.
35- 68	MCGEE, WILLIAM HENRY	D. FEBRUARY 11, 1987 ST. LOUIS, MO.
82- 83	MCGEE, WILLIE DEAN	801 ORTON #3 - HERCULES CA 94547
11-114	MCGEEHAN, DANIEL DESALES	D. JULY 12, 1955 HAZELTON, PA.
12-124	MCGEHEE, PATRICK HENRY	D. DECEMBER 30, 1946 PADUCAH, KY.
50- 66	MCGHEE, WARREN EDWARD 'ED'	D. FEBRUARY 13, 1986 MEMPHIS, TENN.
44- 85	MCGHEE, WILLIAM MAC	MUSTANG ROAD - GULF BREEZE FL 32561
77- 90	MCGILBERRY, RANDALL KENT	4266 LAFITTE ROAD - SARALAND AL 36571
44- 86	MCGILLEN, JOHN JOSEPH	1214 5TH AVE - WOODLYN PA 19094
68- 62	MCGINN, DANIEL MICHAEL	1340 SOUTH 163RD ST - OMAHA NE 68120
72- 70	MCGLOTHEN, LYNN EVERATT	D. AUGUST 14, 1984 DUBACH, LA.
49- 51	MCGLOTHIN, EZRA MAC 'PAT'	2317 COREFIELD RD - KNOXVILLE TN 37919
65- 72	MCGLOTHLIN, JAMES MILTON	D. DECEMBER 23, 1975 UNION, KY.
22- 86	MCGOWAN, FRANK BERNARD 'BEAUTY'	D. MAY 6, 1982 HAMDEN, CONN.
48- 70	MCGOWAN, TULLIS EARL 'MICKEY'	618 SPRATT ST - WAYCROSS GA 31501
12-125	MCGRANER, HOWARD	D. OCTOBER 22, 1952 ZALESKI, O.
65- 73	MCGRAW, FRANK EDWIN "TUG"	COLESHILL ROSE VALLEY RD - MEDIA PA 19063
14-147	MCGRAW, JOHN	D. NOVEMBER 14, 1918 CLEVELAND, O.
17- 47	MCGRAW, ROBERT EMMETT	D. JUNE 2, 1978 BOISE, ID.
76- 61	MCGREGOR, SCOTT HOUSTON	641 WEST SYCAMORE - EL SEGUNDO CA 90245
22- 87	MCGREW, WALTER HOWARD 'SLIM'	D. AUGUST 21, 1967 PORT ARTHUR, TEX.
86- 97	MCGRIFF, FREDERICK STANLEY	2207 NORTH HAROLD AVENUE - TAMPA FL 33607
87- 94	MCGRIFF, TERENCE ROY	2905 LANGSTON DRIVE - FORT PIERCE FL 33450
62- 87	MCGUIRE, M C ADOLFUS 'MICKEY'	4326 DORSET DR - DAYTON OH 45405
14-148	MCGUIRE, THOMAS PATRICK	D. DECEMBER 8, 1959 PHOENIX, AZ.
86- 98	MCGWIRE, MARK DAVID	2329 SIENA COURT - CLAREMONT CA 91711
43- 87	MCHALE, JOHN JOSEPH	BOX 500 STATION M - MONTREAL QUEBEC H1V 3P2 CAN.
10- 99	MCHALE, MARTIN JOSEPH	D. MAY 7, 1979 HEMPSTEAD, N. Y.
18- 48	MCHENRY, AUSTIN BUSH	D. NOVEMBER 27, 1922 MT. OREB, O.
81- 83	MCHENRY, VANCE LOREN	2396 BROWN ST--DURHAM CA 95938
21- 59	MCILREE, VANCE ELMER	D. MAY 6, 1959 KANSAS CITY, MO.
57- 52	MCILWAIN, WILLIAM STOVER	D. JANUARY 15, 1966 BUFFALO, N. Y.
74- 82	MCINTOSH, JOSEPH ANTHONY	1002 PARKHILL - BILLINGS MT 59102
11-115	MCIVER, EDWARD OTTO	D. MAY 4, 1954 DALLAS, TEX.
37- 72	MCKAIN, ARCHIE RICHARD	D. MAY 21, 1985 SALINA, KAN.
27- 58	MCKAIN, HAROLD LEROY	D. JANUARY 24, 1970 SACRAMENTO, CAL.
75- 74	MCKAY, DAVID LAWRENCE	6102 EAST SURREY AVE - SCOTTSDALE AZ 85254
15-100	MCKAY, REEVE STEWART	D. JANUARY 18, 1946 DALLAS, TEX.
72- 71	MCKEE, JAMES MARION	OLD ADD: 31 S. HAMILTON - COLUMBUS OH 43213
13-117	MCKEE, RAY 'RED'	D. AUGUST 5, 1972 SAGINAW, MICH.
43- 88	MCKEE, ROGERS HORNSBY	409 FOREST HILL DRIVE - SHELBY NC 28150
32- 49	MCKEITHAN, EMMETT JAMES 'TIM'	D. AUGUST 20, 1969 FOREST CITY, N. C.
15-101	MCKENRY, FRANK GORDON 'LIMB'	D. NOVEMBER 1, 1956 FRESNO, CALIF.

86- 99 MCKEON, JOEL JACOB	1901 PIERCE STREET - HOLLYWOOD FL 33020
73- 83 MCKEON, JOHN ALOYSIUS 'JACK'	6525 DECANTURE ST - SAN DIEGO CA 92120
70- 88 MCKINNEY, CHARLES RICHARD 'RICH'	2393 EAST PETERSON - TROY OH 45373
60- 70 MCKNIGHT, JAMES ARTHUR	RR2 - BEE BRANCH AR 72013
63- 77 MCLAIN, DENNIS DALE	4933 COVENTRY PARKWAY - FORT WAYNE IN 46804
32- 50 MCLARNEY, ARTHUR JAMES	D. DECEMBER 20, 1984 SEATTLE, WASH.
12-126 MCLARRY, HOWARD ZELL 'POLLY'	D. NOVEMBER 4, 1971 BONHAM, TEX.
77- 91 MCLAUGHLIN, BYRON SCOTT	OLD ADD: 3464 SWEETWATER MESA - MALIBU CA 92154
14-149 MCLAUGHLIN, JAMES ANSON 'KID'	D. NOVEMBER 13, 1934 ALLEGANY, N.Y.
32- 51 MCLAUGHLIN, JAMES ROBERT	D. DECEMBER 18, 1968 MOUNT VERNON, ILL.
77- 92 MCLAUGHLIN, JOEY RICHARD	1611 SOUTH TROOST - TULSA OK 74120
31- 57 MCLAUGHLIN, JUSTIN THEODORE 'JUD'	D. SEPTEMBER 27, 1964 CAMBRIDGE, MASS.
76- 62 MCLAUGHLIN, MICHAEL DUANE 'BO'	3708 OAKWOOD - AMELIA OH 45102
37- 73 MCLAUGHLIN, PATRICK ELMER	1535 CHANTILLY LN - HOUSTON TX 77018
35- 69 MCLEAN, ALBERT ELDON	3005 HARNETT DRIVE - GREENSBORO NC 27407
51- 64 MCLELAND, WAYNE GAFFNEY	6622 BELDART - HOUSTON TX 77017
86-100 MCLEMORE, MARK TREMELL	1871 TINTAH DRIVE - DIAMOND BAR CA 91765
38- 61 MCLEOD, RALPH ALTON	30 ACTON ST - WOLLASTON MA 02170
30- 51 MCLEOD, SOULE JAMES 'JIM'	D. AUGUST 3, 1981 LITTLE ROCK, ARK.
44- 87 MCLISH, CALVIN COOLIDGE	700 TIMBER RIDGE RD - EDMOND OK 73034
56- 59 MCMAHAN, JACK WALLY	1717 TEREASA CIRCLE - BENTON AR 72015
57- 53 MCMAHON, DONALD JOHN	D. JULY 22, 1987 LOS ANGELES, CALIF.
60- 71 MCMANUS, JAMES MICHAEL	1244 BOYLSTON ST,%E.F. HUTTON - CHESTNUT HILL MA 02167
13-118 MCMANUS, JOAB LOGAN	D. DECEMBER 23, 1955 SKELTON, W. VA.
20- 81 MCMANUS, MARTIN JOSEPH	D. FEBRUARY 18, 1966 ST. LOUIS, MO.
68- 63 MCMATH, JIMMY LEE	3321 22ND ST - TUSCALOOSA AL 35401
22- 88 MCMILLAN, NORMAN ALEXIS	D. SEPTEMBER 28, 1969 LATTA, S. C
51- 65 MCMILLAN, ROY DAVID	1200 EAST 9TH ST - BONHAM TX 75418
77- 93 MCMILLAN, THOMAS ERWIN	3810 WEST COOPER LAKE DR - SMYRNA GA 30080
25- 72 MCMULLEN, HUGH RAPHAEL	D. MAY 23, 1986 WHITTIER, CALIF.
62- 88 MCMULLEN, KENNETH LEE	10 ESTABAN - CAMARILLO CA 93010
14-150 MCMULLIN, FREDERICK WILLIAM	D. NOVEMBER 21, 1952 LOS ANGELES, CALIF.
83- 96 MCMURTRY, JOE CRAIG	55 ROSE DRIVE - TROY TX 76579
45- 68 MCNABB, CARL MAC	BOX 203 - JASPER TN 37347
29- 71 MCNAIR, DONALD ERIC	D. MARCH 11, 1949 MERIDIAN, MISS.
62- 89 MCNALLY, DAVID ARTHUR	3305 RAMADA DR - BILLINGS MT 59102
15-102 MCNALLY, MICHAEL JOSEPH	D. MAY 29, 1965 BETHLEHEM, PA.
22- 89 MCNAMARA, GEORGE FRANCIS	10S652 HYACINTH DRIVE - HINSDALE IL 60521
69-114 MCNAMARA, JOHN FRANCIS	5 COUNTRYSIDE RD - NATICK MA 01760
27- 59 MCNAMARA, JOHN RAYMOND	D. DECEMBER 20, 1963 ARLINGTON, TEXAS
39- 78 MCNAMARA, ROBERT MAXEY	23810 BARONA MESA RD - RAMONA CA 92065
22- 90 MCNAMARA, THOMAS HENRY	D. MAY 5, 1974 DANVERS, MASS.
22- 91 MCNAMARA, TIMOTHY AUGUSTINE	21 SUMMIT AV - WOONSOCKET RI 02895
32- 52 MCNAUGHTON, GORDON JOSEPH	D. AUGUST 6, 1942 CHICAGO, ILL.
83- 97 MCNEALY, ROBERT LEE	3301 BOZEMAN STREET - SACRAMENTO CA 95838
24- 77 MCNEELY, GEORGE EARL	D. JULY 16, 1971 SACRAMENTO, CAL.
19- 57 MCNEIL, NORMAN FRANCIS	D. APRIL 11, 1942 BUFFALO, N. Y.
64- 71 MCNERTNEY, GERALD EDWARD	1719 GRAND AVENUE - AMES IA 50010
22- 92 MCNULTY, PATRICK HOWARD	D. MAY 4, 1963 HOLLYWOOD, CAL.
69-115 MCNULTY, WILLIAM FRANCIS	5408 TIBURON WAY - SACRAMENTO CA 95841
23- 89 MCQUAID, HERBERT GEORGE	D. APRIL 5, 1966 RICHMOND, CAL.
34- 70 MCQUAIG, GERALD JOSEPH	110 SCHOOL DR - BUFORD GA 30518
69-116 MCQUEEN, MICHAEL ROBERT	3206 CAMEO DR - HOUSTON TX 77055
18- 49 MCQUILLAN, HUGH A.	D. AUGUST 26, 1947 NEW YORK, N. Y.
38- 62 MCQUILLEN, GLENN RICHARD	4400 ANNTANA AVE - BALTIMORE MD 21206
36- 55 MCQUINN, GEORGE HARTLEY	D. DECEMBER 24, 1978 ALEXANDRIA, VA.
68- 64 MCRAE, HAROLD ABRAHAM	2531 LANDING CIRCLE - BRADENTON FL 33529
69-117 MCRAE, NORMAN	OLD ADD: 1009 LAURA ST - ELIZABETH NJ 07206
83- 98 MCREYNOLDS, WALTER KEVIN	CAMP ROBINSON - NORTH LITTLE ROCK AR 72118
11-116 MCTIGUE, WILLIAM PATRICK	D. MAY 11, 1920 NASHVILLE, TENN.
21- 60 MCWEENY, DOUGLAS LAWRENCE	D. JANUARY 1, 1953 MELROSE PARK, ILL.
78- 79 MCWILLIAMS, LARRY DEAN	736 HENSON DR - HURST TX 76053
31- 58 MCWILLIAMS, WILLIAM HENRY	1600 RICE ROAD - TYLER TX 75703
83- 99 MEACHAM, ROBERT ANDREW	15982 PLUMWOOD ST - WESTMINSTER CA 92683
43- 89 MEAD, CHARLES RICHARD	16350 FREMONTIA - HESPERIA CA 92345
20- 82 MEADOR, JOHN DAVIS	D. APRIL 11, 1970 WINSTON-SALEM, N. C.
15-103 MEADOWS, HENRY LEE	D. JANUARY 29, 1963 DAYTONA BEACH, FLA.
86-101 MEADOWS, MICHAEL RAY 'LOUIE'	20 HADLEY COLLINS ROAD - MAYSVILLE NC 28555
26- 55 MEADOWS, RUFUS RIVERS	D. MAY 10, 1970 WICHITA, KAN.
87- 95 MEADS, DAVID DONALD 'DON'	BOX 70, FEDERAL ROAD - ENGLISHTOWN NJ 07726
12-127 MEANEY, PATRICK	D. OCTOBER 20, 1922 PHILADELPHIA,PA.
14-151 MEARA, CHARLES EDWARD	D. FEBRUARY 8, 1962 KINGSBRIDGE, N. Y.
45- 69 MEDEIROS, RAY ANTON	313 SAN MIGUEL WAY - SAN MATEO CA 94403
72- 72 MEDICH, GEORGE FRANCIS 'DOC'	2332 LINDEN AVE - ALIQUIPPA PA 15001

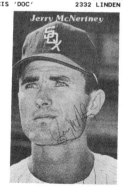

THE SPORT AMERICANA FOOTBALL, HOCKEY, BAS—
KETBALL & BOXING CARD PRICE IS THE AUTHORI—
TATIVE SOURCE FOR INFORMATION AND CURRENT
PRICES FOR CARDS OF THESE SPORTS.

49- 52	MEDLINGER, IRVING JOHN	D. SEPTEMBER 3, 1975 WHEELING, ILL.
32- 53	MEDWICK, JOSEPH MICHAEL	D. MARCH 21, 1975 ST. PETERSBURG, FLA.
10-100	MEE, THOMAS WILLIAM	D. MAY 16, 1981 CHICAGO, ILL.
15-104	MEEHAN, WILLIAM THOMAS	D. OCTOBER 8, 1982 DOUGLAS, WYO.
23- 90	MEEKER, CHARLES ROY	D. MARCH 25, 1929 ORLANDO, FLA.
48- 71	MEEKS, SAMUEL MACK	4963 HELENE - MEMPHIS TN 38117
72- 73	MEELER, CHARLES PHILLIP 'PHIL'	OLD ADD: 108 HAWTHORNE LN - LENOIR NC 28645
41- 71	MEERS, RUSSELL HARLAN	56 HICKORY TRAIL - KITTY HAWK NC 27949
84- 75	MEIER, DAVID KEITH	523 WEST STUART - FRESNO CA 93704
22- 93	MEINE, HENRY WILLIAM 'HEINIE'	D. MARCH 18, 1968 ST. LOUIS, MO.
13-119	MEINERT, WALTER HENRY	D. NOVEMBER 9, 1958 DECATUR, ILL.
10-101	MEINKE, ROBERT BERNARD	D. DECEMBER 29, 1952 CHICAGO, ILL.
13-120	MEISTER, KARL DANIEL	D. AUGUST 15, 1967 MARIETTA, O.
12-128	MEIXELL, MERTON MERRILL 'MOXIE'	D. AUGUST 17, 1982 LOS ANGELES, CALIF.
55- 81	MEJIAS, ROMAN GEORGE	3242 WEST 59TH ST - LOS ANGELES CA 90043
76- 63	MEJIAS, SAMUEL ELIAS	AVE ENRIQUILLO 31 - SANTIAGO DOMINICAN REP.
37- 74	MELE, ALBERT ERNEST 'DUTCH'	D. FEBRUARY 12, 1975 HOLLYWOOD, FLA.
47- 63	MELE, SABATH ANTHONY 'SAM'	340 ADAMS ST - QUINCY MA 02169
84- 76	MELENDEZ, FRANCISCO	OLD ADD: RR 3 BOX 590 - RIO PIEDRAS PR 00928
70- 89	MELENDEZ, LUIS ANTONIO	EXT. SAN JOSE D-2 - AIBONITO PR 00609
26- 56	MELILLO, OSCAR DONALD	D. NOVEMBER 14, 1963 CHICAGO, ILL.
27- 60	MELLANA, JOSEPH PETER	D. NOVEMBER 1, 1969 SAN RAFAEL, CALIF.
10-102	MELOAN, PAUL	D. FEBRUARY 11, 1950 TAFT, CALIF.
37- 75	MELTON, CLIFFORD GEORGE	D. JULY 28, 1986 BALTIMORE, MD.
56- 60	MELTON, DAVID OLIN	10253 RICHWOOD DR - CUPERTINO CA 95014
41- 72	MELTON, REUBEN FRANKLIN	D. SEPTEMBER 11, 1971 GREER, S. C.
68- 65	MELTON, WILLIAM EDWIN	4141 MACARTHUR #101 - NEWPORT BEACH CA 92660
85- 76	MELVIN, ROBERT PAUL	350 LINFIELD DR - MENLO PARK CA 94025
70- 90	MENDOZA, CRISTOBAL RIGOBERTO 'MINNIE'	4110 BROADVIEW DR - CHARLOTTE NC 28210
74- 83	MENDOZA, MARIO	LATERAL DE PACUAL OROZEO #1123 - CHIHUAHUA CHI. MEX.
79- 75	MENDOZA, MICHAEL JOSEPH	12812 ELMFIELD LN - POWAY CA 92064
62- 90	MENKE, DENIS JOHN	780 MAPLE RIDGE RD - PALM HARBOR FL 33563
14-152	MENOSKY, MICHAEL WILLIAM	D. APRIL 11, 1983 DETROIT, MICH.
12-129	MENSOR, EDWARD	D. APRIL 20, 1970 SALEM, ORE.
18- 50	MENZE, THEODORE CHARLES	D. DECEMBER 23, 1969 ST. LOUIS, MO.
33- 43	MEOLA, EMILE MICHAEL 'MIKE'	D. SEPTEMBER 1, 1976 FAIR LAWN, N. J.
71- 69	MEOLI, RUDOLPH BARTHOLOMEW	3233 EAST GREENLEAF DR - BREA CA 92621
82- 84	MERCADO, ORLANDO (RODRIGUEZ)	BOX 6145 - ARECIBO PR 00613
10-103	MERCER, JOHN	
12-224	MERCER, JOHN LOCKE	D. DECEMBER 22, 1982 SHREVEPORT, LA, 71106
81- 84	MERCER, MARK KENNETH	OLD ADD: 1465 THIRD ST - MINNEAPOLIS MN 55440
75- 75	MERCHANT, JAMES ANDERSON	716 EUCLID AVE - MOBILE AL 36601
34- 71	MERENA, JOHN JOSEPH	D. MARCH 9, 1977 BRIDGEPORT, CONN.
22- 94	MEREWETHER, ARTHUR FRANCIS	37-02 222ND ST - BAYSIDE NY 11361
84- 77	MERIDITH, RONALD KNOX	501 SYDNOR - RIDGECREST CA 93555
49- 53	MERRIMAN, LLOYD ARCHER	6691 NORTH DEWOLF - CLOVIS CA 93612
21- 61	MERRITT, HERMAN G.	D. MAY 26, 1927 KANSAS CITY, MO.
65- 74	MERRITT, JAMES JOSEPH	5924 THELMA AVE - LAPALMA CA 90623
13-121	MERRITT, JOHN HOWARD	D. NOVEMBER 3, 1955 TUPELO, MISS.
57- 54	MERRITT, LLOYD WESLEY	206 MARY AVE - PITTSBURGH PA 15209
51- 66	MERSON, JOHN WARREN	6264 OLD WASHINGTON RD - ELK RIDGE MD 21227
43- 90	MERTZ, JAMES VERLIN	5116 EMORY CIR - JACKSONVILLE FL 32207
41- 73	MERULLO, LEONARD RICHARD	159 SUMMER AVE - READING MA 01867
87- 96	MESA, JOSE RAMON	PROY. ISURA CALLERIO TAVARA #2 - AZUA DOMINICAN REP.
38- 63	MESNER, STEPHEN MATHIAS	D. APRIL 6, 1981 SAN DIEGO, CALIF.
24- 78	MESSENGER, ANDREW WARREN 'BUD'	D. NOVEMBER 4, 1971 LANSING, MICH.
68- 66	MESSERSMITH, JOHN ALEXANDER 'ANDY'	200 LAGUNITA DR. - SOQUEL CA 95073
63- 78	METCALF, THOMAS JOHN	1390 WISCONSIN RIVER DR-PORT EDWARDS WI 54469
40- 62	METHA, FRANK JOSEPH 'SCAT'	D. MARCH 2, 1975 FOUNTAIN VALLEY, CALIF.
43- 91	METHENY, ARTHUR BEAUREGARD 'BUD'	2424 NORTH SANDPIPER RD - VIRGINIA BEACH VA 23456
22- 95	METIVIER, GEORGE DEWEY	D. MARCH 2, 1947 CAMBRIDGE, MASS.
43- 92	METKOVICH, GEORGE MICHAEL 'CATFISH'	18191 DEVONWOOD CIR-FOUNTAIN VALLEY CA 92708
43- 93	METRO, CHARLES	7890 INDIANA ST-GOLDEN CO 80401
23- 91	METZ, LEONARD RAYMOND	D. FEBRUARY 24, 1953 DENVER, COLO.
74- 84	METZGER, CLARENCE EDWARD 'BUTCH'	132 BLUE WATER CIRCLE - SACRAMENTO CA 95831
70- 91	METZGER, ROGER HENRY	OLD ADD: 202 WESTMORELAND - SAN ANTONIO TX
44- 88	METZIG, WILLIAM ANDREW	2129 57TH ST - LUBBOCK TX 79412
25- 73	METZLER, ALEXANDER	D. NOVEMBER 30, 1973 FRESNO, CAL.
14-154	MEUSEL, EMIL FREDERICK 'IRISH'	D. MARCH 1, 1963 LONG BEACH, CALIF.
20- 83	MEUSEL, ROBERT WILLIAM	D. NOVEMBER 28, 1977 DOWNEY, CALIF.
13-122	MEYER, BENJAMIN	D. FEBRUARY 6, 1974 FESTUS, MO.
74- 85	MEYER, DANIEL THOMAS	222 REMINGTON LOOP - DANVILLE CA 94526
38- 64	MEYER, GEORGE FRANCIS	537 SOUTH WARREN - PALATINE IL 60067
55- 82	MEYER, JOHN ROBERT	D. MARCH 9, 1967 PHILADELPHIA, PA.

37- 76	MEYER, LAMBERT DALTON 'DUTCH'	2205 PARK HILL DR - FORT WORTH TX 76101
64- 72	MEYER, ROBERT BERNARD	24721 TARZANA - MISSION VIEJO CA 92690
46- 72	MEYER, RUSSELL CHARLES	334 ELM ST - OGLESBY IL 61348
78- 80	MEYER, SCOTT WILLIAM	OLD ADD: 15243 SOUTH HAMLIN AVE - MIDLOTHIAN IL
13-123	MEYER, WILLIAM ADAM	D. MARCH 31, 1957 KNOXVILLE, TENN.
54- 66	MICELOTTA, ROBERT PETER	295 SAVILLE RD - MINEOLA NY 11501
66- 59	MICHAEL, EUGENE RICHARD	147 GROVE STREET - BERGENFIELD NJ 07621
43- 94	MICHAELS, CASIMIR EUGENE	D. NOVEMBER 12, 1982 GROSSE POINTE, MICH.
32- 54	MICHAELS, JOHN JOSEPH	1825 NICARAGUA WAY - WINTER HAVEN FL 33881
24- 79	MICHAELS, RALPH JOSEPH	BOX 837,TRUST OFFICER 2021 - PITTSBURGH PA 15230
21- 62	MICHAELSON, JOHN AUGUST	D. APRIL 16, 1968 WOODRUFF, WIS.
50- 67	MICKELSON, EDWARD ALLEN	12620 FEE FEE RD - CREVE COUER MO 63141
53- 56	MICKENS, GLENN ROGER	7241 WHITE OAK AVE BOX 583 - RESEDA CA 91335
17- 48	MIDDLETON, JAMES BLAINE	D. JANUARY 12, 1974 ARGOS, IND.
22- 96	MIDDLETON, JOHN WAYNE	D. NOVEMBER 3, 1986 AMARILLO, TEXAS
12-223	MIDKIFF, EZRA MILLINGTON	D. MARCH 21, 1957 HUNTINGTON, W. VA.
38- 65	MIDKIFF, RICHARD JAMES	D. OCTOBER 30, 1956 TEMPLE, TEX.
87- 97	MIELKE, GARY ROGER	1300 POHL ROAD #404 - MANKATO MN 56001
45- 70	MIERKOWICZ, EDWARD FRANK	7530 MACOMB #1-A - GROSSE ILE MI 48138
48- 72	MIGGINS, LAWRENCE EDWARD	2405 KINGSTON DR - HOUSTON TX 77019
35- 70	MIHALIC, JOHN MICHAEL	D. APRIL 24, 1987 FORT OGLETHORPE, GA.
64- 73	MIKKELSEN, PETER JAMES	RR 1 BOX 1667 - PROSSER WA 99350
44- 89	MIKLOS, JOHN JOSEPH	19701 SOUTH 115TH AVE - MOKENA IL 60448
44- 90	MIKSIS, EDWARD THOMAS	3906 WHITMAN RD - HUNTINGDON VALLEY PA 19006
15-106	MILAN, HORACE ROBERT	D. JUNE 29, 1955 TEXARKANA, TEX.
74- 86	MILBOURNE, LAWRENCE WILLIAM	11228 83RD PL NE - KIRKLAND WA 98033
40- 63	MILES, CARL THOMAS	806 AUSTIN RD - HORSESHOE BEND AR 72512
58- 62	MILES, DONALD RAY	184 SOUTH DEERFOOT CIRCLE - WOODLANDS TX 77380
68- 67	MILES, JAMES CHARLIE	RR2 - BATESVILLE MS 38606
35- 71	MILES, WILSON DANIEL 'DEE'	D. NOVEMBER 2, 1976 BIRMINGHAM, ALA.
75- 76	MILEY, MICHAEL WILFRED	D. JANUARY 6, 1977 BATON ROUGE, LA.
15-107	MILJUS, JOHN KENNETH	D. FEBRUARY 11, 1976 POLSON, MONT.
66- 60	MILLAN, FELIX BERNARDO	CALLE 13R-14, EL CONQUISTADOR - TRUJILLO ALTO PR 00760
73- 84	MILLER, CHARLES BRUCE	2126 PARKLAND DR - FORT WAYNE IN 46825
12-130	MILLER, CHARLES ELMER	D. APRIL 23, 1972 WARRENSBURG, MO.
15-108	MILLER, CHARLES HESS	D. JANUARY 13, 1951 MILLERSVILLE, PA.
13-124	MILLER, CHARLES MARION	D. JUNE 16, 1961 HOUSTON, TEX.
84- 78	MILLER, DARRELL KEITH	6246 PROMONTORY LN - RIVERSIDE CA 92506
75- 77	MILLER, DYAR K	R 9 BOX 334 - GREENSBURG IN 47240
21- 63	MILLER, EDMUND JOHN 'BING'	D. MAY 7, 1966 PHILADELPHIA, PA.
77- 94	MILLER, EDWARD LEE	5014 HARTNETT - RICHMOND CA 94804
36- 56	MILLER, EDWARD ROBERT	204 CYPRESS DRIVE - LAKE WORTH FL 33461
12-131	MILLER, EDWIN	D. APRIL 17, 1980 LEBANON, PA.
12-132	MILLER, ELMER	D. NOVEMBER 28, 1944 BELOIT, WIS.
29- 72	MILLER, ELMER LEROY	153 MONTEREY CIR - MIRA LOMA CA 91752
13-125	MILLER, FRANK LEE	D. FEBRUARY 19, 1974 ALLEGAN, MICH.
10-104	MILLER, FREDERICK HOLMAN	D. MAY 2, 1953 BROOKVILLE, IND.
11-117	MILLER, HUGH STANLEY	D. DECEMBER 24, 1945 JEFFERSON BARRACKS, MO.
22- 97	MILLER, JACOB GEORGE	D. AUGUST 24, 1974 TOWSON, MD.
44- 91	MILLER, JAMES ELDRIDGE 'HACK'	D. NOVEMBER 21, 1966 DALLAS, TEX
66- 61	MILLER, JOHN ALLEN	20 SWIFT COURT - NEWPORT BEACH CA 92663
43- 95	MILLER, JOHN ANTHONY 'OX'	STAR RT - GEORGE WEST TX 78022
62- 91	MILLER, JOHN ERNEST	1216 REDCLIFFE RD - BALTIMORE MD 21228
87- 98	MILLER, KEITH ALAN	5432 MEADOWBROOK - BAY CITY MI 48706
44- 92	MILLER, KENNETH ALBERT	9344 RAMBLER DR - AFFTON MO 63123
64- 74	MILLER, LARRY DON	9226 NORTH BROADWAY - PHOENIX AZ 85028
16- 61	MILLER, LAWRENCE H. 'HACK'	D. SEPTEMBER 17, 1971 OAKLAND, CAL.
84- 79	MILLER, LEMMIE EARL	620 WEST GUTIERREZ #38 - SANTA BARBARA CA 93101
23- 92	MILLER, LEO ALPHONSO 'RED'	D. OCTOBER 20, 1973 ORLANDO, FL.
10-105	MILLER, LOWELL OTTO	D. MARCH 29, 1962 BROOKLYN, N.Y.
65- 75	MILLER, NORMAN CALVIN	P.O. BOX 288 - HOUSTON TX 77001
27- 61	MILLER, OTIS LOUIS 'OTTO'	D. JULY 26, 1959 BELLEVILLE, ILL.
21- 64	MILLER, RALPH HENRY	D. FEBRUARY 18, 1967 WHITE BEAR LAKE, MINN.
20- 84	MILLER, RALPH JOSEPH	D. MARCH 18, 1939 FORT WAYNE, IND.
77- 95	MILLER, RANDALL SCOTT	2502 PLANTERS HOUSE LANE - KATY TX 77449
17- 49	MILLER, RAYMOND PETER	D. APRIL 7, 1927 PITTSBURGH, PA.
85- 77	MILLER, RAYMOND ROGER	P. O. BOX 41 - NEW ATHENS OH 43981
71- 70	MILLER, RICHARD ALAN	130 DRAPER RD - WAYLAND MA 01778
53- 57	MILLER, ROBERT GERALD	104 LAKEWOOD CIR - BURR RIDGE IL 60521
49- 54	MILLER, ROBERT JOHN	17397 GLENMORE - DETROIT MI 48240
57- 55	MILLER, ROBERT LANE	7215 LINDEN TERR - CARLSBAD CA 92008
57- 56	MILLER, RODNEY CARTER	9162 WARFIELD DRIVE - HUNTINGTON BEACH CA 92646
74- 87	MILLER, ROGER WESLEY	RR 1 BOX 130 - MILL RUN PA 15464
41- 74	MILLER, ROLLAND ARTHUR 'RONNIE'	7511 LILA - HAZELWOOD MO 63042
10-106	MILLER, ROY OSCAR 'DOC'	D. JULY 31, 1938 JERSEY CITY, N. J.
29- 73	MILLER, RUDEL CHARLES	2246 TIPPERARY RD - KALAMAZOO MI 49001
27- 62	MILLER, RUSSELL LEWIS	D. AUGUST 30, 1962 BUCYRUS, O.
52- 74	MILLER, STUART LEONARD	252 DEVONSHIRE BLVD - SAN CARLOS CA 94070
18- 51	MILLER, THOMAS ROYALL	D. AUGUST 13, 1980 RICHMOND, VA.
24- 80	MILLER, WALTER JACOB 'JAKE'	D. AUGUST 20, 1975 VENICE, FLA.
11-118	MILLER, WALTER W.	D. MARCH 1, 1956 MARION, IND.
37- 77	MILLER, WILLIAM FRANCIS	D. FEBRUARY 26, 1982 HANNIBAL, MO.
52- 75	MILLER, WILLIAM PAUL	501 EXTON RD - HATBORO PA 19040
34- 72	MILLIES, WALTER LOUIS	5312 WEST 96TH ST - OAK LAWN IL 60453
28- 66	MILLIGAN, JLHN ALEXANDER	D. MAY 15, 1972 FORT PIERCE, FLA.
87- 99	MILLIGAN, RANDY ANDRE	2911 L STREET - SAN DIEGO CA 92102
53- 58	MILLIKEN, ROBERT FOGLE	1875 SOUTHWOOD LN - CLEARWATER FL 33516
11-119	MILLS, ABBOTT PAIGE 'JACK'	D. JUNE 3, 1973 WASHINGTON, D.C.
27- 63	MILLS, ARTHUR GRANT	D. JULY 23, 1975 UTICA, N. Y.
34- 73	MILLS, COLONEL BUSTER	BOX 13081 - ARLINGTON TX 76016
14-155	MILLS, FRANK LEMOYNE	D. AUGUST 31, 1983 YOUNGSTOWN, O.
34- 74	MILLS, HOWARD ROBINSON 'LEFTY'	D. SEPTEMBER 23, 1982 RIVERSIDE, CALIF.
80- 89	MILLS, JAMES BRADLEY 'BRAD'	BOX 54 - LEMONCOVE CA 93244
70- 92	MILLS, RICHARD ALAN	OLD ADD: 44 WOOD AVE - SCITUATE MA 02060
15-109	MILLS, RUPERT FRANK	D. JULY 20, 1929 LAKE HOPATCONG, N. J.
44- 93	MILLS, WILLIAM HENRY	BOX 43 - EL CAJON FL 33927
36- 57	MILNAR, ALBERT JOSEPH	19520 SHAWNEE AVE-CLEVELAND OH 44119
48- 73	MILNE, WILLIAM JAMES 'PETE'	BOX 160566 - MOBILE AL 36616
78- 81	MILNER, BRIAN TATE	1401 CAIRN CIR - FORT WORTH TX 76134

80- 90 MILNER, EDDIE JAMES	1815 ELDORA DRIVE EAST - COLUMBUS OH 43207
71- 71 MILNER, JOHN DAVID	1351 HOLCOMB AVE - EAST POINT GA 30344
44- 94 MILOSEVICH, MICHAEL	D. FEBRUARY 3, 1966 EAST CHICAGO, IND.
24- 81 MILSTEAD, GEORGE EARL	D. AUGUST 9, 1977 CLEBURNE, TEX.
55- 83 MINARCIN, RUDY ANTHONY	37 NORTH FIRST ST - NORTH VANDERGRIFT PA 15690
60- 72 MINCHER, DONALD RAY	BOX 120 - MERIDIANVILLE AL 35759
21- 65 MINER, RAYMOND THEADORE	D. SEPTEMBER 15, 1963 GLENRIDGE SAN., N. Y.
78- 82 MINETTO, CRAIG STEPHEN	1809 LAKESHURE DRIVE - LODI CA 95240
70- 93 MINGORI, STEPHEN BERNARD	11705 EAST 78TH TERRACE - RAYTOWN MO 64138
46- 73 MINNER, PAUL EDISON	115 GREEN LANE DR - CAMP HILL PA 17011
57- 57 MINNICK, DONALD ATHEY	FRANKLIN HGTS - ROCKY MOUNT VA 24151
49- 55 MINOSO, SATURNINO ORESTES 'MINNIE'	4250 MARIN DR - CHICAGO IL 60613
74- 88 MINSHALL, JAMES EDWARD	4207 3RD AVE NE - BRADENTON FL 33508
75- 78 MINTON, GREGORY BRIAN	256 PULIDO ROAD - DANVILLE CA 94526
78- 83 MIRABELLA, PAUL THOMAS	550 KNOLL RD - BOONTON MANOR NJ 07005
51- 67 MIRANDA, GUILLERMO PEREZ 'WILLIE'	5502 WHITWOOD RD - BALTIMORE MD 21206
14-156 MISSE, JOHN BEVERLY	D. MARCH 18, 1970 ST. JOSEPH, MO.
10-107 MITCHELL, ALBERT ROY	D. SEPTEMBER 8, 1959 TEMPLE, TEX.
84- 80 MITCHELL, CHARLES ROSS	5017 HASTY DR - NASHVILLE TN 37211
11-120 MITCHELL, CLARENCE ELMER	D. NOVEMBER 6, 1963 GRAND ISLAND, NEB.
75- 79 MITCHELL, CRAIG SETON	BOX 174 - ELK CA 95432
21- 66 MITCHELL, JOHN FRANKLIN	D. NOVEMBER 4, 1965 OAKLAND CO., MICH.
86-102 MITCHELL, JOHN KYLE	5017 HASTY DR - NASHVILLE TN 37211
84- 81 MITCHELL, KEVIN DARRELL	4812 LOGAN AVE - SAN DIEGO CA 92113
46- 74 MITCHELL, LOREN DALE	D. JANUARY 5, 1987 TULSA, OKLA.
23- 93 MITCHELL, MONROE BARR	D. SEPTEMBER 4, 1976 VALDOSTA, GA.
75- 80 MITCHELL, PAUL MICHAEL	7 WABASH AVE - WORCESTER MA O160J
70- 94 MITCHELL, ROBERT VANCE	38 EAST ELM ST - NORRISTOWN PA 19401
80- 91 MITCHELL, ROBERT VAN	25691 LUPITA DR - VALENCIA CA 91355
16- 62 MITTERLING, RALPH	D. JANUARY 22, 1956 PITTSBURGH, PA.
66- 62 MITTERWALD, GEORGE EUGENE	1721 MURDOCK BLVD - ORLANDO FL 32807
36- 58 MIZE, JOHN ROBERT	BOX 112 - DEMOREST GA 30535
52- 76 MIZELL, WILMER DAVID 'VINEGAR BEND'	RR 5 BOX 333 - WINSTON SALEM NC 27107
83-100 MIZEROCK, JOHN JOSEPH	RR 1 BOX 140 - ROCHESTER MILLS PA 15771
23- 94 MIZEUR, WILLIAM FRANCIS	D. AUGUST 27, 1976 DANVILLE, ILL.
74- 89 MOATES, DAVID ALLAN	6401 35TH AVE NW - BRADENTON FL 33529
45- 71 MODAK, MICHAEL JOSEPH ALOYSIUS	P.O. BOX 6041 - NALCREST FL 33856
62- 92 MOELLER, JOSEPH DOUGLAS	2512 OCEAN DR - MANHATTAN BEACH CA 90266
56- 61 MOELLER, RONALD RALPH	3560 GAILYNN DR - CINCINNATI OH 45211
72- 74 MOFFITT, RANDALL JAMES	110 LAKEOVER DRIVE - ATHENS GA 30606
55- 84 MOFORD, HERBERT	P.O. BOX 12 - MINERVA KY 41062
11-121 MOGRIDGE, GEORGE ANTHONY	D. MARCH 4, 1962 ROCHESTER, N.Y.
22- 98 MOHARDT, JOHN HENRY	D. NOVEMBER 24, 1961 SAN DIEGO, CAL.
20- 85 MOHART, GEORGE BENJAMIN	D. OCTOBER 2, 1970 SILVER CREEK, N.Y.
86-103 MOHORCIC, DALE ROBERT	15501 ROCKSIDE ROAD - MAPLE HEIGHTS OH 44137
53- 59 MOISAN, WILLIAM JOSEPH	BOX 41 - NEWTON NH 03858
21- 67 MOKAN, JOHN LEE	D. FEBRUARY 10, 1985 BUFFALO, N. Y.
49- 56 MOLE, FENTON LEROY	349 ALOHA DR - SAN LEANDRO CA 94578
75- 81 MOLINARO, ROBERT JOSEPH	50 WEST LINSLEY RD - CEDAR GROVE NJ 07009
78- 84 MOLITOR, PAUL LEO	OLD ADD: 924 EAST JUNEAU - MILWAUKEE WI 53202
14-157 MOLLENKAMP, FREDERICK HENRY	D. NOVEMBER 1, 1948 CINCINNATI, O.
13-126 MOLLWITZ, FREDERICK AUGUST 'FRITZ'	D. OCTOBER 3, 1967 BRADENTON, FLA.
70- 95 MOLONEY, RICHARD HENRY	125 MALLARD WAY - WALTHAM MA 02154
17- 50 MOLYNEAUX, VINCENT LEO	D. MAY 4, 1950 STAMFORD, CONN.
37- 78 MONACO, BLAS	410 FROST DR - SAN ANTONIO TX 78201
53- 60 MONAHAN, EDWARD FRANCIS	165 83RD ST - BROOKLYN NY 11209
58- 63 MONBOUQUETTE, WILLIAM CHARLES	271 CLARK HILL RD - NEW BOSTON NH 03070
28- 67 MONCEWICZ, FRED ALFRED	D. APRIL 23, 1969 BROCKTON, MASS.
40- 64 MONCHAK, ALEX	7414 8TH AVENUE WEST - BRADENTON FL 34209
66- 63 MONDAY, ROBERT JAMES 'RICK'	1056 RASHFORD DR - PLACENTIA CA 92670
68- 68 MONEY, DONALD WAYNE	282 OLD FOREST RD - VINELAND NJ 08360
75- 82 MONGE, ISIDRO PEDROZA 'SID'	9722 AVIARY DR - SAN DIEGO CA 92131
17- 51 MONROE, EDWARD OLIVER	D. APRIL 29, 1969 LOUISVILLE, KY.
21- 68 MONROE, JOHN ALLEN	D. JUNE 19, 1956 CONROE, TEX.
76- 64 MONROE, LAWRENCE JAMES	1916 JAMES COURT - SCHAUMBURG IL 60194
58- 64 MONROE, ZACHARY CHARLES	10 SANDALWOOD LN - BARTONVILLE IL 61607
28- 68 MONTAGUE, EDWARD FRANCIS	D. JUNE 17, 1988 DALY CITY, CALIF.
73- 85 MONTAGUE, JOHN EVANS	3313A FOUNTAIN LN - MONTGOMERY AL 36116
86-104 MONTALVO, RAFAEL EDGARDO	CALLE 12 S.O. #1783 LAS LOMES - RIO PIEDRAS PR 00921
66- 64 MONTANEZ, GUILLERMO NARANJO 'WILLIE'	ZONA RURAL 142 BUZON 36# - CAGUAS PR 00625
63- 79 MONTEAGUDO, AURELIO FAUNTINI	CALLE 27 NO. 16-26 - BARQUISIMETO, LARA VENEZUELA S.A.
38- 66 MONTEAGUDO, RENE MIRANDA	D. SEPTEMBER 14, 1973 HIALEAH, FL.
74- 90 MONTEFUSCO, JOHN JOSEPH	24 DOWNING HILL LN - COLTS NECK NJ 07722
61- 75 MONTEJO, MANUEL	CALLE 28 #4415 MUNICIPIO PLAYA - HAVANA CUBA
87-100 MONTELEONE, RICHARD	2515 WEST FERN STREET - TAMPA FL 33614

GUILLERMO MIRANDA (WILLY)

DALE MITCHELL

JOE MOELLER

RICK MONDAY

53- 61 MONTEMAYOR, FELIPE ANGEL	TORREON #308, MITRAS CENTRO - MONTERREY NUEVO LEON MEX.
41- 75 MONTGOMERY, ALVIN ATLAS	D. APRIL 26, 1942 WAVERLY, VA.
87-101 MONTGOMERY, JEFFREY THOMAS	OAK RIDGE ADDISON - WELLSTON OH 45692
71- 72 MONTGOMERY, MONTY BRYSON	BOX 1314 - ALBEMARLE NC 28001
70- 96 MONTGOMERY, ROBERT EDWARD	2 PARKWAY DR - SAUGUS MA 01906
72- 75 MONTREUIL, ALLAN ARTHUR	2016 LAUREL ST - GRETNA LA 70053
54- 67 MONZANT, RAMON SEGUNDO	CALLE 87 NRO 2A-33 - MARACAIBO EDO ZULIA VENEZ
72- 76 MONZON, DANIEL FRANCISCO	912 OLMSTEAD AVE - BRONX NY 10473
67- 73 MOOCK, JOSEPH GEOFFREY	12432 PECOS AVE - GREENWELL LA 70739
32- 55 MOON, LEO	D. AUGUST 25, 1970 NEW ORLEANS, LA.
54- 68 MOON, WALLACE WADE	1415 ANGELINA CIRCLE - COLLEGE STATION TX 77840
31- 59 MOONEY, JAMES IRVING	D. APRIL 27, 1979 JOHNSON CITY, TENN.
86-105 MOONEYHAM, WILLIAM CRAIG	9470 WEST OLIVE AVENUE - WINTON CA 95388
25- 74 MOORE, ALBERT JAMES	D. NOVEMBER 29, 1974 ATLANTIC OCEAN
76- 65 MOORE, ALVIN EARL 'JUNIOR'	3728 WALL AVE - RICHMOND CA 94804
46- 75 MOORE, ANSELM WINN	245 MARILYN DR - JACKSON MS 39208
64- 75 MOORE, ARCHIE FRANCIS	69 TOWNSEND DR - FLORHAM PARK NJ 07932
70- 97 MOORE, BALOR LILBON	OLD ADD: 3317 BOND - PASADENA TX 77503
30- 52 MOORE, CARLOS WHITMAN	D. JULY 2, 1958 NEW ORLEANS, LA.
12-133 MOORE, CHARLES WESLEY	D. JULY 29, 1970 PORTLAND, ORE.
73- 86 MOORE, CHARLES WILLIAM	5932 DAWSON COURT - GREENDALE WI 53129
36- 59 MOORE, D C 'DEE'	2600 UNIVERSITY - WILLISTON ND 58801
75- 83 MOORE, DONNIE RAY	4610 CERRO VISTA DRIVE - ANAHEIM CA 92807
34- 75 MOORE, EUEL WALTON	307 EAST 20TH - TISHOMINGO OK 73460
31- 60 MOORE, EUGENE JR.	D. MARCH 12, 1978 JACKSON, MISS.
14-158 MOORE, FERDINAND DEPAGE	D. MAY 6, 1947 ATLANTIC CITY, N.J.
70- 98 MOORE, GARY DOUGLAS	OLD ADD: 5018 AIRLINE - DALLAS TX 75205
23- 95 MOORE, GRAHAM EDWARD 'EDDIE'	D. FEBRUARY 10, 1976 FORT MYERS, FLA.
65- 76 MOORE, JACKIE SPENCER	509 CHAFFEE - ARLINGTON TX 76010
28- 69 MOORE, JAMES STANFORD	D. MAY 19, 1973 SEATTLE, WASH.
30- 53 MOORE, JAMES WILLIAM	D. MAY 7, 1986 MEMPHIS, TENN.
28- 70 MOORE, JOHN FRANCIS	4-A SWAN LAKE VLG - BRADENTON FL 33507
30- 54 MOORE, JOSEPH GREGG	BOX 65 - GAUSE TX 77857
81- 85 MOORE, KELVIN ORLANDO	RR 1 BOX 132 - LEROY AL 36548
36- 60 MOORE, LLOYD ALBERT 'WHITEY'	D. DECEMBER 10, 1987 CANTON, O.
82- 85 MOORE, MICHAEL WAYNE	2020 RIDGEWAY - WEATHERFORD OK 73096
27- 64 MOORE, RANDOLPH EDWARD	BOX 757 - OMAHA TX 75571
52- 77 MOORE, RAYMOND LEROY	6801 DOWER HOUSE ROAD - UPPER MARLBORO MD 20772
65- 77 MOORE, ROBERT BARRY	RR1 BOX 174 - CLEVELAND NC 27013
85- 78 MOORE, ROBERT DEVELL	1068 TEMPLE STREET #7 - LONG BEACH CA 90804
20- 86 MOORE, ROY DANIEL	D. APRIL 5, 1951 SEATTLE, WASH.
35- 72 MOORE, TERRY BLUFORD	501 RIDGEMONT DR - COLLINSVILLE IL 62234
72- 77 MOORE, TOMMY JOE	OLD ADD: RR 1 - DEKALB TX 75559
17- 52 MOORE, WILLIAM ALLEN 'SCRAPPY'	D. OCTOBER 13, 1964 LITTLE ROCK, ARK.
29- 74 MOORE, WILLIAM AUSTIN 'CY'	D. MARCH 28, 1972 AUGUSTA, GA.
25- 75 MOORE, WILLIAM CHRISTOPHER	D. JANUARY 24, 1984 CORNING, N. Y.
26- 57 MOORE, WILLIAM HENRY	D. MAY 24, 1972 KANSAS CITY, MO.
86-106 MOORE, WILLIAM ROSS	419 NORTH ASTELL AVENUE - WEST COVINA CA 91790
27- 65 MOORE, WILLIAM WILCY	D. MARCH 29, 1963 HOLLIS, OKLA.
62- 93 MOORHEAD, CHARLES ROBERT 'BOB'	D. DECEMBER 3, 1986 LEMOYNE, PA.
67- 74 MOOSE, ROBERT RALPH	D. OCTOBER 9, 1976 MARTINS FERRY, O.
36- 61 MOOTY, J. T. 'JAKE'	D. APRIL 20, 1970 FORT WORTH, TEX.
76- 66 MORA, ANDRES (IBARRA)	GALEANO 567,PTE. - LOS MOCHIS SINALOA MEX.
73- 87 MORALES, JOSE MANUEL	10435 LEHMAN - ORLANDO FL 32817
69-118 MORALES, JULIO RUBEN 'JERRY'	VILLA NUEVA CALLE 16-C5 - CAGUAS PR 00625
67- 75 MORALES, RICHARD ANGELO	1650 ROSITA RD - PACIFICA CA 94044
38- 67 MORAN, ALBERT THOMAS	88 CONGRESS ST #109 - SARATOGA SPRINGS NY 12866
74- 91 MORAN, CARL WILLIAM 'BILL'	200 SHORE DRIVE - PORTSMOUTH VA 23701
12-134 MORAN, HARRY EDWIN	D. NOVEMBER 28, 1962 BECKLEY, WEST VA
63- 80 MORAN, RICHARD ALAN 'AL'	34134 BAMBURY - FARMINGTON HILLS MI 48018
12-135 MORAN, ROY ELLIS	D. JULY 18, 1966 ATLANTA, GA.

58- 65 MORAN, WILLIAM NELSON	8245 GLEDSTONE WAY - FAIRBURN GA 30213
24- 82 MOREHART, RAYMOND ANDERSON	5939 VANDERBILT - DALLAS TX 75206
63- 81 MOREHEAD, DAVID MICHAEL	1342 TIKI CIR - TUSTIN CA 92680
57- 58 MOREHEAD, SETH MARVIN	8675 GROVER PLACE - SHREVEPORT LA 71115
58- 66 MOREJON, DANIEL TORRES	OLD ADD: 4401 SW 117TH AVE - MIAMI FL 33165
78- 85 MORELAND, BOBBY KEITH	1815 MONTGOMERY CT - DEERFIELD IL 60015
81- 86 MORENO, ANGEL	GOMEZ FARIAZ #604 - AGUASCALIENTES AGUAS. MEX.
80- 92 MORENO, JOSE DE LOS SANTOS	CORREA Y CIDRON 9 - SANTO DOMINGO DOM. REP.
50- 68 MORENO, JULIO GONZALES	D. JANUARY 2, 1987 MIAMI, FLA.
75- 84 MORENO, OMAR RENAN	APTD. #5 BALBOA, NCON - PANAMA CITY PAN.
70- 99 MORET, ROGELIO 'ROGER'	RR 1 #6742 - GUAYAMA PR 00654
13-127 MOREY, DAVID BEALE	D. JANUARY 4, 1986 OAK BLUFF, MASS.
35- 73 MORGAN, CHESTER COLLINS	602 ORIOLE LA-PASADENA TX 77502

21- 69	MORGAN, CYRIL ARLON	D. SEPTEMBER 11, 1946 LAKEVILLE, MASS.
28- 71	MORGAN, EDWARD CARRE	D. APRIL 9, 1980 NEW ORLEANS, LA.
36- 62	MORGAN, EDWIN WILLIS	D. JUNE 27, 1982 LAKEWOOD, O.
63- 82	MORGAN, JOSEPH LEONARD	5588 FERNHOFF ROAD - OAKLAND CA 94619
59- 59	MORGAN, JOSEPH MICHAEL	15 OAK HILL DRIVE - WALPOLE MA 02081
78- 86	MORGAN, MICHAEL THOMAS	2008 JANSEN ST - LAS VEGAS NV 89101
11-122	MORGAN, RAYMOND CARYLL	D. FEBRUARY 15, 1940 BALTIMORE, MD.
50- 69	MORGAN, ROBERT NORRIS	2212 BARCLAY RD - OKLAHOMA CITY OK 73120
51- 68	MORGAN, TOM STEPHEN	D. JANUARY 13, 1987 ANAHEIM, CALIF.
54- 69	MORGAN, VERNON THOMAS	D. NOVEMBER 8, 1975 MINNEAPOLIS, MINN.
61- 76	MORHARDT, MEREDITH GOODWIN 'MOE'	182 WILLIAMS AVE - WINSTED CT 06098
35- 74	MORIARTY, EDWARD JEROME	485 SOUTH ST #322 - HOLYOKE MA 01040
73- 88	MORLAN, JOHN GLEN	2348 SALEM AVE - GROVE CITY OH 43123
13-128	MORLEY, (WILLIAM MORLEY JENNINGS)	D. MAY 14, 1985 LUBBOCK, TEXAS
86-107	MORMAN, RUSSELL LEE	17704 CHEYENNE DRIVE - INDEPENDENCE MO 64056
83-101	MOROGIELLO, DANIEL JOSEPH	2365 EAST 72ND ST - BROOKLYN NY 11234
84- 82	MORONKO, JEFFREY ROBERT	OLD ADD: 3637 S. SHAVER #309 - PASADENA TX 77504
26- 58	MORRELL, WILLARD BLACKMER	D. AUGUST 5, 1975 BIRMINGHAM, ALA.
68- 69	MORRIS, DANNY WALKE	216 WILSON ST - GREENVILLE KY 42345
37- 79	MORRIS, DOYT THEODORE	D. JULY 4, 1984 GASTONIA, N. C.
86-108	MORRIS, JOHN DANIEL	2645 ELM DRIVE - NORTH BELLMORE NY 11710
77- 96	MORRIS, JOHN SCOTT 'JACK'	4705 OLD ORCHARD TRAIL - ORCHARD LAKE MI 48033
66- 65	MORRIS, JOHN WALLACE	5538 E. PARADISE LN - SCOTTSDALE AZ 85254
22-100	MORRIS, WALTER EDWARD	D. MARCH 3, 1932 CENTURY, FLA.
15-110	MORRISETTE, WILLIAM LEE	D. MARCH 25, 1966 VIRGINIA BEACH, VA.
77- 97	MORRISON, JAMES FOREST	11202 VERANDA COURT - BRADENTON FL 33529
20- 87	MORRISON, JOHN DEWEY	D. MARCH 20, 1966 LEXINGTON, KY.
21- 70	MORRISON, PHILIP MELVIN	D. JANUARY 18, 1955 LEXINGTON, KY.
27- 66	MORRISON, WALTER GUY	D. AUGUST 14, 1934 GRAND RAPIDS, MICH.
32- 56	MORRISSEY, JOSEPH ANSELM 'JO-JO'	D. MAY 2, 1950 WORCESTER, MASS.
29- 75	MORSE, NEWELL OBEDIAH 'BUD'	D. APRIL 6, 1987 SPARKS, NEV.
11-123	MORSE, PETER RAYMOND 'HAP'	D. JUNE 19, 1974 ST. PAUL, MINN.
69-119	MORTON, CARL WENDLE	D. APRIL 12, 1983 TULSA, OKLA.
54- 70	MORTON, GUY JR.	969 BLACHLEYVILLE ROAD - WOOSTER OH 44691
14-159	MORTON, GUY SR.	D. OCTOBER 18, 1934 SHEFFIELD, ALA.
61- 77	MORTON, WYCLIFFE NATHAN 'BUBBA'	7429 TIMBERACK ROAD - FALLS CHURCH VA 22043
54- 71	MORYN, WALTER JOSEPH	545 CHARLES ST - GLENDALE HEIGHTS IL 60137
65- 78	MOSCHITTO, ROSAIRO ALLEN 'ROSS'	32 MORTON ST - GARNERSVILLE NY 10923
80- 93	MOSEBY, LLOYD ANTHONY	3400 KINGMONT DR - LOOMIS CA 95650
13-129	MOSELEY, EARL VICTOR	D. JULY 1, 1963 ALLIANCE, O.
37- 80	MOSER, ARNOLD ROBERT	7714 ANTOINE - HOUSTON TX 77088
65- 79	MOSES, GERALD BRAHEEN	111 WALDEMAR AVE - SOUTH BOSTON MA 02128
82- 86	MOSES, JOHN WILLIAM	5343 EAST LAFAYETTE - PHOENIX AZ 85018
35- 75	MOSES, WALLACE	777 W. GERMANTOWN PIKE - PLYMOUTH MEETING PA 19462
77- 98	MOSKAU, PAUL RICHARD	4152 EAST SECOND ST - TUCSON AZ 85711
10-108	MOSKIMAN, WILLIAM BANKHEAD 'DOC'	D. JANUARY 11, 1953 SAN LEANDRO, CALIF.
29- 76	MOSOLF, JAMES FREDERICK	D. DECEMBER 28, 1979 DALLAS, ORE.
34- 76	MOSS, CHARLES CROSBY	2400 40TH AVE - MERIDIAN MS 39304
30- 55	MOSS, CHARLES MALCOLM 'MAL'	D. FEBRUARY 5, 1983 SAVANNAH, GA.
42- 70	MOSS, HOWARD GLENN	3805 KIMBLE RD-BALTIMORE MD 21218
46- 76	MOSS, JOHN LESTER 'LES'	420 TULLIS AVE - LONGWOOD FL 32750
26- 59	MOSS, RAYMOND EARL	3734 KINGS RD - CHATTANOOGA TN 37416
54- 72	MOSSI, DONALD LOUIS	1340 SANFORD RANCH RD - UKIAH CA 95482
51- 69	MOSSOR, EARL DALTON	3088 S.R. 222 - BETHEL OH 45106
18- 52	MOSTIL, JOHN ANTHONY	D. DECEMBER 10, 1970 MIDLOTHIAN, ILL.
62- 94	MOTA, MANUEL RAFAEL	3926 LOS OLIVOS LN - LA CRESCENTA CA 91214
81- 87	MOTLEY, DARRYL DEWAYNE	1324 NORTH RESSIT - PORTLAND OR 97201
45- 72	MOTT, ELISHA MATTHEW 'BITSY'	P.O. BOX 294 - BLUE RIDGE GA 30513
67- 76	MOTTON, CURTELL HOWARD	1522 25TH AVE - OAKLAND CA 94601
46- 77	MOULDER, GLEN HUBERT	2946 LAVISTA CT - DECATUR GA 30083
11-124	MOULTON, ALBERT THEODORE 'OLLIE'	D. JULY 10, 1968 PEABODY, MASS.
13-130	MOWE, RAYMOND BENJAMIN	D. AUGUST 14, 1968 SARASOTA, FLA.
33- 44	MOWRY, JOSEPH ALOYSIUS	6321 BANCROFT - ST LOUIS MO 63109
10-109	MOYER, CHARLES EDWARD	D. NOVEMBER 18, 1962 JACKSONVILLE, FLA.
86-109	MOYER, JAMIE	409 NORTH FOURTH STREET - SOUDERTON PA 18964
54- 73	MROZINSKI, RONALD FRANK	WASH. ARMS BLDG 100 #D2 - WASHINGTON NJ 07882
63- 83	MUDROCK, PHILIP RAY	2548 EAST 6600 SOUTH-SALT LAKE CITY UT 84121
20- 88	MUELLER, CLARENCE FRANCIS 'HEINIE'	D. JANUARY 23, 1975 DESOTO, MO.
48- 74	MUELLER, DONALD FREDERICK	11224 MUELLER LN - MARYLAND HEIGHTS MO 63042
38- 68	MUELLER, EMMETT JEROME 'HEINIE'	D. OCTOBER 3, 1986 ORLANDO, FLA.
50- 70	MUELLER, JOSEPH GORDON 'GORDY'	1404 CHESAPEAKE AVE - MIDDLE RIVER MD 21220
41- 76	MUELLER, LESLIE CLYDE	RR 2 BOX 294 - MILLSTADT IL 62260
35- 76	MUELLER, RAY COLEMAN	2433 NORTH 4TH STREET - HARRISBURG PA 17110
22-101	MUELLER, WALTER JOHN	D. AUGUST 16, 1971 ST. LOUIS, MO.

```
78- 87 MUELLER, WILLARD LAWRENCE 'WILLIE'   1246 WALLACE LAKE - WEST BEND WI 53095
42- 71 MUELLER, WILLIAM LAWRENCE            1615 WHITEHALL COURT - WHEELING IL 60090
57- 59 MUFFETT, BILLY ARNOLD                706 BAYOU SHORE DRIVE - MONROE LA 71203
24- 83 MUICH, IGNATIUS ANDREW 'JOE'         9244 LODGE POLE LN - ST LOUIS MO 63126
51- 70 MUIR, JOSEPH ALLEN                   D. JUNE 25, 1980 BALTIMORE, MD.
35- 77 MULCAHY, HUGH NOYES                  175 WAYNE ST - BEAVER PA 15009
86-110 MULHOLLAND, TERENCE JOHN             339 DERRICK AVENUE - UNIONTOWN PA 15401
30- 56 MULLEAVY, GREGORY THOMAS             D. FEBRUARY 1, 1980 ARCADIA, CALIF.
10-110 MULLEN, CHARLES GEORGE               D. JUNE 6, 1963 SEATTLE, WASH.
44- 95 MULLEN, FORD PARKER                  7127 MULLEN RD SE - OLYMPIA WA 98503
20- 89 MULLEN, WILLIAM JOHN                 D. MAY 4, 1971 ST. LOUIS, MO.
33- 45 MULLER, FREDERICK WILLIAM            D. OCTOBER 20, 1976 DAVIS, CALIF.
15-111 MULLIGAN, EDWARD JOSEPH              D. MARCH 15, 1982 SAN RAFAEL, CALIF.
34- 77 MULLIGAN, JOSEPH IGNATIUS            D. JUNE 5, 1986 WEST ROXBURY, MASS.
41- 77 MULLIGAN, RICHARD CHARLES            1205 EAST WALNUT AVENUE - VICTORIA TX 77901
40- 65 MULLIN, PATRICK JOSEPH               320 CHURCH ST - BROWNSVILLE PA 15417
77- 99 MULLINIKS, STEVEN RANCE              707 TEPIC - EL PASO TX 79912
80- 94 MULLINS, FRANCIS JOSEPH              6180 BROADWAY TER - OAKLAND CA 94618
21- 71 MULRENAN, DOMINICK JOSEPH            D. JULY 27, 1964 MELROSE, MASS.
30- 57 MULRONEY, FRANCIS JOSEPH             D.
74- 92 MUMPHREY, JERRY WAYNE                3913 SILVERWOOD - TYLER TX 75701
18- 53 MUNCH, JACOB FERDINAND               D. JUNE 8, 1966 LANSDOWNE, PA.
37- 81 MUNCRIEF, ROBERT CLEVELAND           731 RIDGE CREST - DUNCANVILLE TX 75116
13-131 MUNDY, WILLIAM EDWARD                D. SEPTEMBER 23, 1958 KALAMAZOO, MICH.
43- 96 MUNGER, GEORGE DAVID 'RED'           10121 WINDMILL LAKES BLVD #1407 - HOUSTON TX 77075
31- 61 MUNGO, VAN LINGLE                    D. FEBRUARY 12, 1985 PAGELAND, S. C.
71- 73 MUNIZ, MANUEL                        CALLE 23-R-12 VILLA NUEVA - CAGUAS PR 00626
80- 95 MUNNINGHOFF, SCOTT ANDREW            3418 SAYBROOK AVE - CINCINNATI OH 45208
34- 78 MUNNS, LESLIE ERNEST                 236 EAST 5TH - WAHOO NE 68066
25- 76 MUNSON, JOSEPH MARTIN NAPOLEON       7274 LAMPORT RD - UPPER DARBY PA 19082
69-120 MUNSON, THURMAN LEE                  D. AUGUST 2, 1979 AKRON-CANTON AIRPORT, O.
78- 88 MURA, STEPHEN ANDREW                 37 CHRISTAMON SOUTH - IRVINE CA 92720
64- 76 MURAKAMI, MASANORI                   1-4-15-1506,NISHO OHI SHINAGAWA - TOKYO JAPAN
65- 80 MURCER, BOBBY RAY                    3244 WHIPPOORWILL ROAD - OKLAHOMA CITY OK 73120
17- 53 MURCHISON, THOMAS MALCOM 'TIM'       D. OCTOBER 20, 1962 LIBERTY, N. C.
56- 62 MURFF, JOHN ROBERT "RED"             1005 LAWNDALE - BRENHAM TX 77833
76- 67 MURPHY, DALE BRIAN                   12055 HOUZE ROAD - ROSWELL GA 30076
60- 73 MURPHY, DANIEL FRANCIS               56 LOTHROP ST #5 - BEVERLY MA 01915
78- 89 MURPHY, DWAYNE KEITH                 1132 "W" AVENUE #H6 - LANCASTER CA 93534
42- 72 MURPHY, EDWARD JOSEPH                1319 JEFFERSON STREET - JOLIET IL 60435
14-160 MURPHY, HERBERT COURTLAND 'DUMMY'    D. AUGUST 10, 1962 TALLAHASSEE, FLA.
12-136 MURPHY, JOHN EDWARD                  D. FEBRUARY 20, 1969 DUNMORE, PA.
32- 57 MURPHY, JOHN JOSEPH                  D. JANUARY 14, 1970 NEW YORK, N. Y.
15-112 MURPHY, LEO JOSEPH                   D. AUGUST 12, 1960 RACINE, WIS.
12-137 MURPHY, MICHAEL JEROME               D. OCTOBER 26, 1952 JOHNSON CITY, N.Y.
54- 74 MURPHY, RICHARD LEE                  7114 MIAMI HILLS DR - CINCINNATI OH 45243
85- 79 MURPHY, ROBERT ALBERT                7820 SW 54TH AVENUE - MIAMI FL 33143
18- 54 MURPHY, ROBERT R. 'BUZZ'             D. MAY 11, 1938 DENVER, COLO.
68- 70 MURPHY, THOMAS ANDREW                26566 CALLE LORENZO - SAN JUAN CAPISTRANO CA 92675
31- 62 MURPHY, WALTER JOSEPH                16123 AMBERWOOD - DALLAS TX 75248
66- 66 MURPHY, WILLIAM EUGENE               10214 88TH AVE SW - TACOMA WA 98498
36- 63 MURRAY, AMBROSE JOSEPH               8297 SE COCONUT ST - HOBO SOUND FL 33455
23- 96 MURRAY, ANTHONY JOHN                 D. MARCH 19, 1974 CHICAGO, ILL.
74- 93 MURRAY, DALE ALBERT                  RR 2 BOX 1850 - YORKTOWN TX 78164
77-100 MURRAY, EDDIE CLARENCE               13401 BLYTHENIA ROAD - PHOENIX MD 21131
17- 54 MURRAY, EDWARD FRANCIS               D. NOVEMBER 8, 1970 CHEYENNE, WYO.
22-102 MURRAY, GEORGE KING                  D. OCTOBER 18, 1955 MEMPHIS, TENN.
22-103 MURRAY, JAMES FRANCIS                D. JULY 15, 1973 NEW YORK , N. Y.
50- 71 MURRAY, JOSEPH AMBROSE               2719 VIA SANTA TOMAS - SAN CLEMEMTE CA 92672
74- 94 MURRAY, LARRY                        OLD ADD: 3544 SOUTH CALUMET AVE - CHICAGO IL 60653
19- 58 MURRAY, PATRICK JOSEPH               D. NOVEMBER 5, 1983 ROCHESTER, N. Y.
48- 75 MURRAY, RAYMOND LEE                  BOX 453 - KENNEDALE TX 76060
80- 96 MURRAY, RICHARD DALE                 435 EAST 108TH ST - LOS ANGELES CA 90061
23- 97 MURRAY, ROBERT HAYES                 D. JANUARY 4, 1979 NASHUA, N. H.
17- 55 MURRAY, WILLIAM ALLENWOOD            D. SEPTEMBER 14, 1943 BOSTON, MASS.
63- 84 MURRELL, IVAN AUGUSTE                279 OCEAN AVE #1C - BROOKLYN NY 11226
41- 78 MURTAUGH, DANIEL EDWARD              D. DECEMBER 2, 1976 CHESTER PA.
69-121 MUSER, ANTHONY JOSEPH                11222 MARTHA ANN DR - LOS ALAMITOS CA 90720
65- 81 MUSGRAVES, DENNIS EUGENE             RR FOUR - CENTRALLIA MO 65240
41- 79 MUSIAL, STANLEY FRANK                85 TRENT DR - LADUE MO 63124
86-111 MUSSELMAN, JEFFREY JOSEPH            105 BRICK AVENUE - LANOKA HARBOR NJ 08734
82- 87 MUSSELMAN, RALPH RICHARD             5313 AUTUMN DR - WILMINGTON NC 28401
12-138 MUSSER, PAUL                         D. JULY 7, 1973 STATE COLLEGE, PA.
32- 58 MUSSER, WILLIAM DANIEL 'DANNY'       1062 HOMEWOOD CT - DECATUR GA 30033
44- 96 MUSSILL, BERNARD JAMES 'BARNEY'      912 MOORLAND DR -GROSSE POINTE WOODS MI 48236
40- 66 MUSTAIKIS, ALEXANDER DOMINICK        D. JANUARY 17, 1970 SCRANTON, PA.
38- 69 MYATT, GEORGE EDWARD                 1623 CANTON AVE-ORLANDO FL 32803
20- 90 MYATT, GLENN CALVIN                  D. AUGUST 9, 1969 HOUSTON, TEX.
25- 77 MYER, CHARLES SOLOMON 'BUDDY'        D. OCTOBER 31, 1974 BATON ROUGE, LA.
15-113 MYERS, ELMER GLENN                   D. JULY 29, 1976 COLLINGSWOOD, N. J.
87-102 MYERS, GREGORY RICHARD               2815 SHENANDOAH ROAD - RIVERSIDE CA 92506
38- 70 MYERS, LINNWOOD LINCOLN              1111 YVERDON DR #C1 - CAMP HILL PA 17011
10-111 MYERS, RALPH EDWARD 'HAP'            D. JUNE 30, 1967 SAN FRANCISCO, CALIF.
85- 80 MYERS, RANDALL KIRK                  P.O. BOX 9900 SUITE 155 - VANCOUVER WA 98668
56- 63 MYERS, RICHARD                       5400 SAMPSON BLVD - SACRAMENTO CA 95820
35- 78 MYERS, WILLIAM HARRISON              204 SALT RD-ENOLA PA 17025
76- 68 MYRICK, ROBERT HOWARD                3112K HONEYWOOD LANE - ROANOKE VA 24014
15-114 NABORS, HERMAN JOHN 'JACK'           D. OCTOBER 29, 1923 WILTON, ALA.
39- 79 NAGEL, WILLIAM TAYLOR                D. OCTOBER 8, 1981 FREEHOLD, N. J.
12-139 NAGELSON, LOUIS MARCELLUS            D. OCTOBER 22, 1965 FORT WAYNE, IND.
68- 71 NAGELSON, RUSSELL CHARLES            ONE POWDERDHORN CT - LITTLE ROCK AR 72212
11-125 NAGLE, WALTER HAROLD 'JUDGE'         D. MAY 27, 1971 SANTA ROSA, CALIF.
69-122 NAGY, MICHAEL TIMOTHY                8 INDIAN TRAIL - BRONX NY 10465
47- 64 NAGY, STEPHEN                        3435 63RD AVE SW - SEATTLE WA 98116
38- 71 NAHEM, SAMUEL RALPH                  624 VINCENTE - BERKELEY CA 94704
76- 69 NAHORODNY, WILLIAM GERARD            204 SOUTH COMET - CLEARWATER FL 33515
36- 64 NAKTENIS, PETER ERNEST               125 ADELAIDE RD - MANCHESTER CT 06041
24- 84 NALEWAY, FRANK                       D. JANUARY 28, 1949 CHICAGO, ILL.
12-140 NAPIER, SKELTON LEROY 'BUDDY'        D. MARCH 29, 1968 DALLAS, TEX.
```

101

49- 57 NAPLES, ALOYSIUS FRANCIS — 52 RODGER CT - WYCKOFF NJ 07481
65- 82 NAPOLEON, DANIEL — OLD ADD: 116 OLIVE AVE - TRENTON NJ
51- 71 NARAGON, HAROLD RICHARD — 1521 HAGEY DR - BARBERTON OH 44203
56- 64 NARANJO, LAZARO RAMON GONZALO — D #270, 10 Y 11 - LAWTON, HAVANA CUBA
54- 75 NARLESKI, RAYMOND EDMOND — 1183 CHEWS LANDING RD-LAUREL SPRINGS NJ 08021
29- 77 NARLESKI, WILLIAM EDWARD — D. JULY 22, 1964 LAUREL SPRINGS, N. J.
79- 76 NARRON, JERRY AUSTIN — 232 HILLCREST DR - GOLDSBORO NC 27530
35- 79 NARRON, SAMUEL — RR 1 BOX 125 - MIDDLESEX NC 27557
63- 85 NARUM, LESLIE FERDINAND 'BUSTER' — 324 SOUTH GLENWOOD AVE - CLEARWATER FL 33515
67- 77 NASH, CHARLES FRANCIS 'COTTON' — 600 SUMMERSHADE CIR - LEXINGTON KY 40502
66- 67 NASH, JAMES EDWIN — 37 REGINA DR NE - MARIETTA GA 30067
12-141 NASH, KENNETH LELAND — D. FEBRUARY 16, 1977 EPSOM, N. H.
78- 90 NASTU, PHILIP — 119 AUSTIN ST - BRIDGEPORT CT 06604
53- 62 NATON, PETER ALPHONSUS — 4136 SPLIT ROCK RD - CAMILLUS NY 13031
62- 95 NAVARRO, JULIO VENTURA — CALLE 3, BLOQUE 10, #32 - SANTA ROSA, BAYAMON PR 00619
42- 73 NAYLOR, EARL EUGENE — RR BOX 155-18 - CLEAR LAKE MN 55319
17- 56 NAYLOR, ROLEINE CECIL — D. JUNE 18, 1966 FORT WORTH, TEX.
39- 80 NAYMICK, MICHAEL JOHN — 8334 BERWICK WAY - STOCKTON CA 95210
56- 65 NEAL, CHARLES LENARD — 7251 BAYBERRY LANE - DALLAS TX 75249
16- 64 NEALE, ALFRED EARLE 'GREASY' — D. NOVEMBER 2, 1973 LAKE WORTH, FL.
52- 78 NECCIAI, RONALD ANDREW — 201 ROSEWOOD DR - MONONGAHELA PA 15063
57- 60 NEEMAN, CALVIN AMANDUS — 93 CHAMPAGNE - LAKE ST. LOUIS MO 63367
14-161 NEFF, DOUGLAS WILLIAM — 587 WEST NIMISLIA RD - AKRON OH 44319
52- 79 NEGRAY, RONALD ALVIN — D. NOVEMBER 11, 1951 BUFFALO, N.Y.
12-142 NEHER, JAMES GILMORE

15-115 NEHF, ARTHUR NEUKOM — D. DECEMBER 18, 1960 PHOENIX, ARIZ.
69-123 NEIBAUER, GARY WAYNE — 7110 VAN DORN #89 - LINCOLN NE 68506
60- 74 NEIGER, ALVIN EDWARD — 213 PINEHURST RD - WILMINTON DE 19803
39- 81 NEIGHBORS, ROBERT OTIS — D. AUGUST 8, 1952 NORTH KOREA
46- 78 NEILL, THOMAS WHITE — OLD ADD: 1526 HIDDEN HILL - HOUSTON TX 77064
20- 91 NEIS, BERNARD EDMUND — D. NOVEMBER 29, 1972 INVERNESS, FLA.
29- 78 NEKOLA, FRANCIS JOSEPH 'BOTS' — D. MARCH 11, 1987 ROCKVILLE CENTRE, N. Y.
10-112 NELSON, ALBERT FRANCIS 'RED' — D. OCTOBER 26, 1956 ST PETERSBURG, FLA.
68- 72 NELSON, DAVID EARL — 9355 NORTH 91ST #129 - SCOTTSDALE AZ 85258
35- 80 NELSON, GEORGE EMMETT — D. AUGUST 25, 1967 SIOUX FALLS, S. D.
49- 58 NELSON, GLENN RICHARD 'ROCKY' — BOX 35 - PORTSMOUTH OH 45662
70-100 NELSON, JAMES LORIN — 8648 LODESTONE CIR - ELK GROVE CA 95624
83-102 NELSON, JAMES VICTOR — OLD ADD: 16901 SIMS - HUNTINGTON BEACH CA 92649
19- 59 NELSON, LUTHER MARTIN 'LUKE' — BOX 14 - MATHERVILLE ILL 61263
30- 58 NELSON, LYNN BERNARD — D. FEBRUARY 15, 1955 KANSAS CITY, MO.
60- 75 NELSON, MELVIN FREDERICK — 27420 FISHER ST - HIGHLAND CA 92346
83-103 NELSON, RICKY LEE — 7250 SOUTH 46TH ST - PHOENIX AZ 85040
86-112 NELSON, ROBERT AUGUSTUS — 312 ALTA VISTA AVENUE - SOUTH PASADENA CA 91030
55- 85 NELSON, ROBERT SIDNEY — 10830 WALLBROOK - DALLAS TX 75238
67- 78 NELSON, ROGER EUGENE — OLD ADD: 533 WINDSOR - ARCADIA CA 91006
45- 73 NELSON, TOM COUSINEAU — D. SEPTEMBER 24, 1973 SAN DIEGO, CAL.
81- 88 NELSON, WAYLAND EUGENE 'GENE' — BOX 458 - LACOOCHIE FL 33537
63- 86 NEN, RICHARD LEROY — 7122 ORANGETHORPE - BUENA PARK CA 90621
11-126 NESS, JOHN CHARLES — D. DECEMBER 3, 1957 DELAND, FLA.
67- 79 NETTLES, GRAIG — 13 NORTH LANE - DEL MAR CA 92014
70-101 NETTLES, JAMES WILLIAM — 4632 DARIEN DR - TACOMA WA 98407
74- 95 NETTLES, MORRIS — 551 1/2 SAN JUAN - VENICE CA 90291
17- 58 NEU, OTTO ADAM — D. SEPTEMBER 19, 1932 KENTON, O.
25- 78 NEUBAUER, HAROLD CHARLES — D. SEPTEMBER 9, 1949 PROVIDENCE, R. I.
72- 78 NEUMEIER, DANIEL GEORGE — N2635 CITY HIGHWAY U - LODI WI 53555
25- 79 NEUN, JOHN HENRY — 3501 ST PAUL ST #118 - BALTIMORE MD 21218
50- 72 NEVEL, ERNIE WYRE — 615 MADDUX ST - BRANSON MO 65616
26- 60 NEVERS, ERNEST ALONZO — D. MAY 3, 1976 SAN RAFAEL, CALIF.
49- 59 NEWCOMBE, DONALD — 22507 PEALE DR - WOODLAND HILLS CA 91364
87-103 NEWELL, THOMAS DEAN — 1001 TILLMAN LANE - GARDNERVILLE NV 89410
72- 79 NEWHAUSER, DONALD LOUIS — 321 SHERYL DR - DELTONA FL 32738
39- 82 NEWHOUSER, HAROLD — 2584 MARCY-BLOOMFIELD HILLS MI 48013
34- 79 NEWKIRK, FLOYD ELMO — D. APRIL 15, 1976 CLAYTON, MO.
19- 60 NEWKIRK, JOEL IVAN — D. JANUARY 22, 1966 ELDORADO, ILL.
40- 67 NEWLIN, MAURICE MILTON — D. AUGUST 14, 1978 HOUSTON, TEXAS
85- 81 NEWMAN, ALBERT DWAYNE — 1044 LARODA - ONTARIO CA 91761
62- 96 NEWMAN, FREDERICK WILLIAM — D. JUNE 24, 1987 FRAMINGHAM, MASS.
76- 70 NEWMAN, JEFFREY LYNN — 537 QUIVIRA CT - DANVILLE CA 94526
71- 74 NEWMAN, RAYMOND FRANCIS — 1361 HOWARD - MUSKEGON MI 49442
10-113 NEWNAM, PATRICK HENRY — D. JUNE 20, 1938 SAN ANTONIO, TEX.
29- 79 NEWSOM, NORMAN LOUIS 'BOBO' — D. DECEMBER 7, 1962 ORLANDO, FLA.
41- 80 NEWSOME, HEBER HAMPTON 'DICK' — D. DECEMBER 15, 1965 AHOSKIE, N. C.
35- 81 NEWSOME, LAMAR ASHBY 'SKEETER' — 1626 17TH AVE-COLUMBUS GA 31901
46- 79 NIARHOS, CONSTANTINE GREGORY 'GUS' — 244 MONUMENT AVE - HARRISONBURG VA 22801

52- 80 NICHOLAS, DONALD LEIGH	12311 CHASE - GARDEN GROVE CA 92645
86-113 NICHOLS, CARL EDWARD	2603 BILLINGS STREET - COMPTON CA 90220
51- 72 NICHOLS, CHESTER RAYMOND JR	18 COLONIAL DR - LINCOLN RI 02865
26- 61 NICHOLS, CHESTER RAYMOND SR.	D. JULY 11, 1982 PAWTUCKET, R. I.
58- 67 NICHOLS, DOLAN LEVON	OLD ADD: 1351 OLD HICKORY RD - MEMPHIS TN
44- 97 NICHOLS, ROY	104 ARIAS WAY - HOT SPRINGS VILLAGE AR 71901
80- 97 NICHOLS, THOMAS REID	501 MARSHALL AVE - BIRMINGHAM AL 35215
60- 76 NICHOLSON, DAVID LAWRENCE	527 SPRINGINGSGUTH - ROSELLE IL 60172
12-143 NICHOLSON, FRANK COLLINS	D. NOVEMBER 11, 1972 JERSEY SHORE, PA.
17- 57 NICHOLSON, FREDERICK	D. JANUARY 23, 1972 KILGORE, TEXAS
12-144 NICHOLSON, OVID EDWARD	D. MARCH 24, 1968 SALEM, IND.
36- 65 NICHOLSON, WILLIAM BECK	RR 3 - CHESTERTOWN MD 21620
78- 91 NICOSIA, STEVEN RICHARD	8520 HW FIFTH STREET - PEMBROKE PINES FL 33024
21- 73 NIEBERGALL, CHARLES ARTHUR 'NIG'	D. AUGUST 29, 1982 HOLIDAY, FLA.
81- 89 NIEDENFUER, THOMAS EDWARD	9849 DENBIGH DRIVE - BEVERLY HILLS CA 90210
25- 80 NIEHAUS, ALBERT BERNARD	D. OCTOBER 14, 1931 CINCINNATI, O. .
13-132 NIEHAUS, RICHARD J.	D. MARCH 12, 1957 ATLANTA, GA.
13-133 NIEHOFF, JOHN ALBERT	D. DECEMBER 8, 1974 INGLEWOOD, CALIF.
67- 80 NIEKRO, JOSEPH FRANKLIN	214 ASH LN - LAKELAND FL 33801
64- 77 NIEKRO, PHILIP HENRY	4781 CASTLEWOOD DR - LILBURN GA 30247
86-114 NIELSEN, JEFFREY SCOTT	11910 28TH AVENUE EAST - TACOMA WA 98445
49- 60 NIELSON, MILTON ROBERT	824 MCGILL - ST PETER MN 56082
43- 97 NIEMAN, ELMER LEROY 'BUTCH'	1324 BOSWELL AVE-TOPEKA KS 66604
51- 73 NIEMAN, ROBERT CHARLES	D. MARCH 10, 1985 CORONA, CALIF.
79- 77 NIEMANN, RANDAL HAROLD	233 VALLEY AVENUE - FORTUNA CA 95540
43- 98 NIEMES, JACOB LELAND 'JACK'	D. MARCH 4, 1966 HAMILTON, O.

34- 80 NIEMIEC, ALFRED JOSEPH	BOX 467 - KIRKLAND WA 98033
64- 78 NIESON, CHARLES BASSETT	3209 WEST HIGHLAND DR - BURNSVILLE MN 55374
84- 83 NIETO, THOMAS ANDREW	18002 HORST AVE - ARTESIA CA 90701
21- 72 NIETZKE, ERNEST FREDRICH	D. APRIL 27, 1977 SYLVANIA, O.
86-115 NIEVES, JUAN MANUEL	500 OLD FARMS ROAD - AVON CT 06001
38- 72 NIGGELING, JOHN ARNOLD	D. SEPTEMBER 16, 1963 LEMARS, IA.
83-104 NIPPER, ALBERT SAMUEL	5105 VILLE MARIA LANE - HAZELWOOD MO 63042
62- 97 NIPPERT, MERLIN LEE	1015 NORTH MICHIGAN ST - MANGUM OK 73554
61- 78 NISCHWITZ, RONALD LEE	6790 GARBER RD - DAYTON OH 45415
45- 74 NITCHOLAS, OTHO JAMES	1500 ERWIN - MCKINNEY TX 75069
15-116 NIXON, ALBERT RICHARD	D. NOVEMBER 9, 1960 OPELOUSAS, LA.
83-105 NIXON, OTIS JUNIOR	BOX 23 HIGHWAY 74 - EVERGREEN NC 28438
87-104 NIXON, ROBERT DONELL	P.O. BOX 23, OLD HWY 74 - EVERGREEN NC 28438
57- 61 NIXON, RUSSELL EUGENE	BOX 1446 - COVINGTON GA 30209
50- 73 NIXON, WILLARD LEE	BOX 204 - LINDALE GA 30147
51- 74 NOBLE, RAFAEL MIGUEL 'RAY'	698 CHAUNCEY ST - BROOKLYN NY 11207
84- 84 NOBOA, MILCIADES ARTURO 'JUNIOR'	OLD ADD: EVA MARIA PELLERANO,CASTRO #1-SANTO DOMINGO DR
87-105 NOCE, PAUL DAVID	3362 BRITTAN AVENUE #2 - SAN CARLOS CA 94070
85- 82 NOKES, MATTHEW DODGE	13011 AVENIDA LA VALENCIA - POWAY CA 92064
67- 81 NOLAN, GARY LYNN	5825 WEST ROCHELLE #204 - LAS VEGAS NV 89103
72- 80 NOLAN, JOSEPH WILLIAM	9515 ALIX DR - MEHLVILLE MO 63123
67- 82 NOLD, RICHARD LOUIS	121 PARK PLAZA DR #6 - DALY CITY CA 94015
79- 78 NOLES, DICKIE RAY	708 BUNKER HILL - ARLINGTON TX 76011
87-106 NOLTE, ERIC CARL	682 SEVILLE DRIVE - HEMET CA 92343
33- 46 NONNENKAMP, LEO WILLIAM 'RED'	1 OAKWOOD RD - LITTLE ROCK AR 72202
74- 96 NORDBROOK, TIMOTHY CHARLES	OLD ADD: 302 LORI DRIVE #L - GLEN BURNIE MD 21061
76- 71 NORDHAGEN, WAYNE OREN	25896 RAMILLO WAY - VALENCIA CA 91355
50- 74 NOREN, IRVING ARNOLD	3215 VALLEY GLEN ROAD - OCEANSIDE CA 92056
69-124 NORIEGA, JOHN ALAN	2 EAST 900 SOUTH - KAYSVILLE UT 84037
77-101 NORMAN, DANIEL EDMUND	1336 MESA DR - BARSTOW CA 92311
62- 98 NORMAN, FREDIE ROBERT	6560 BAYWOOD LN - CINCINNATI OH 45224
31- 63 NORMAN, HENRY WILLIS PATRICK 'BILL'	D. APRIL 21, 1962 MILWAUKEE, WIS.
78- 92 NORMAN, NELSON AUGUSTO	EMILIO MOREL #54 - SAN PEDRO DE MACORIS DOM. REP.
77-102 NORRIS, JAMES FRANCIS	5524 MANSFIELD RD - ARLINGTON TX 76017
36- 66 NORRIS, LEO JOHN	ZACHARY HOME, DRAWER C - ZACHARY LA 70791
75- 85 NORRIS, MICHAEL KELVIN	1003 IMPERIAL DR - HAYWARD CA 94541
13-134 NORTH, LOUIS ALEXANDER	D. MAY 16, 1974 SHELTON, CONN.
71- 75 NORTH, WILLIAM ALEX	OLD ADD: 3303 E. MADISON - SEATTLE WA 98102
10-114 NORTHEN, HUBBARD ELWIN	D. OCTOBER 1, 1947 SHREVEPORT, LA.
42- 74 NORTHEY, RONALD JAMES	D. APRIL 16, 1971 PITTSBURGH, PA.
69-125 NORTHEY, SCOTT RICHARD	OLD ADD: 481 RIVIERA BLVD WEST - NAPLES FL
18- 55 NORTHROP, GEORGE HOWARD 'JAKE'	D. NOVEMBER 16, 1945 MONROETON, PA.
64- 79 NORTHRUP, JAMES THOMAS	1326 OTTER DR - PONTIAC MI 48054
72- 81 NORTON, THOMAS JOHN	4900 SOUTHWOOD - SHEFFIELD LAKES OH 44054
77-103 NORWOOD, WILLIE	17721 NORWALK BLVD #50 - ARTESIA CA 90701
64- 80 NOSSEK, JOSEPH RUDOLPH	437 TERRA LN - AMHERST OH 44001
60- 77 NOTTEBART, DONALD EDWARD	5442 LYMBAR - HOUSTON TX 77096
41- 81 NOVIKOFF, LOUIE ALEXANDER	D. SEPTEMBER 30, 1970 SOUTH GATE, CAL.
49- 61 NOVOTNEY, RALPH JOSEPH 'RUBE'	2311 WEST 165TH ST - TORRANCE CA 90504

```
13-135 NOYES, WINFIELD CHARLES            D. APRIL 8, 1969 CASHMERE, WASH.
11-127 NUNAMAKER, LESLIE GRANT            D. NOVEMBER 14, 1938 HASTINGS, NEB.
82- 88 NUNEZ, EDWIN (MARTINEZ)            BO. RIO ABAJO, BUZON 2762 - HUMACAO PR 00661
87-107 NUNEZ, JOSE                        MAURICIO BAEZ #40 VILLA JUANA - SANTO DOMINGO DOM. REP.
59- 60 NUNN, HOWARD RALPH                 RR1 - WESTFIELD NC 27053
19- 61 NUTTER, EVERETT CLARENCE 'DIZZY'   D. JULY 25, 1958 BATTLE CREEK, MICH.
44- 98 NUXHALL, JOSEPH HENRY              5706 LINDENWOOD LN - FAIRFIELD OH 45014
66- 68 NYE, RICHARD RAYMOND               1923 S. MANNHEIM RD - WESTCHESTER IL 60153
82- 89 NYMAN, CHRISTOPHER CURTIS          719 FLORENCE STREET - NOKOMIS FL 33555
68- 73 NYMAN, GERALD SMITH                2627 N. 16TH E. - LOGAN UT 84321
74- 97 NYMAN, NYLS WALLACE REX            300 KEOKUK - LINCOLN IL 62656
34- 81 OANA, HENRY KAUHANE 'PRINCE'       D. JUNE 19, 1976 AUSTIN, TEX.
70-102 OATES, JOHNNY LANE                 1704 LAKE AVE - WILMETTE IL 60091
77-104 OBERKFELL, KENNETH RAY             305 SOUTH DONK ST - MARYVILLE IL 62062
79- 79 OBERRY, PRESTON MICHAEL 'MIKE'     1100 DEARING DOWNS DR - HELENA AL 35017
78- 93 OBRADOVICH, JAMES THOMAS           1212 MAIN AVE #V - NITRO WV 25143
85- 83 OBRIEN, CHARLES HUGH               4932 EAST 38TH PLACE - TULSA OK 74135
78- 94 OBRIEN, DANIEL JOGUES              8104 VALLEY GLEN DR #2022 - DALLAS TX 75228
53- 63 OBRIEN, EDWARD JOSEPH              3414 108TH PL NE #1 - BELLEVUE WA 98004
```

When Lefty O'Doul was a Giant

```
23- 98 OBRIEN, FRANK ALOYSIUS 'MICKEY'       D. NOVEMBER 4, 1971 MONTEREY PARK, CAL.
15-117 OBRIEN, GEORGE JOSEPH                 D. MARCH 24, 1966 COLUMBUS, O.
53- 64 OBRIEN, JOHN THOMAS                   938 21ST ST EAST - SEATTLE WA 98112
82- 90 OBRIEN, PETER MICHAEL                 BOX 1037 - PEBBLE BEACH CA 93953
16- 65 OBRIEN, RAYMOND JOSEPH                D. MARCH 31, 1942 ST. LOUIS, MO.
71- 76 OBRIEN, ROBERT ALLEN                  3628 NORTH SHIRLEY - FRESNO CA 93727
69-126 OBRIEN, SYDNEY LLOYD                  OLD ADD: 4576 EVEREST CIRCLE - CYPRESS CA 90630
43- 99 OBRIEN, THOMAS EDWARD                 D. NOVEMBER 5, 1978 ANNISTON. ALA.
11-128 OBRIEN, THOMAS JOSEPH 'BUCK'          D. JULY 25, 1959 BOSTON, MASS.
35- 82 OCK, HAROLD DAVID 'WHITEY'            D. MARCH 18, 1975 MOUNT KISCO, N. Y.
44- 99 OCKEY, WALTER ANDREW                  D. DECEMBER 4, 1971 STATEN ISLAND, N.Y.
50- 75 OCONNELL, DANIEL FRANCIS              D. OCTOBER 2, 1969 CLIFTON, N. J.
23- 99 OCONNELL, JAMES JOSEPH                D. NOVEMBER 11, 1976 BAKERSFIELD, CALIF.
28- 72 OCONNELL, JOHN CHARLES                1611 19TH ST NE - CANTON OH 44714
81- 90 OCONNOR, JACK WILLIAM                 BOX 430 - YUCCA VALLEY CA 92284
16- 66 OCONNOR, JOHN CHARLES                 D. MAY 30, 1982 BONNER SPRINGS, KAN.
35- 83 ODEA, JAMES KENNETH 'KEN'             D. DECEMBER 17, 1985 LIMA, N. Y.
44-100 ODEA, PAUL                            D. DECEMBER 11, 1978 CLEVELAND, O.
54- 76 ODELL, WILLIAM OLIVER                 RR 1 BOX 60 - NEWBERRY SC 29108
21- 74 ODENWALD, THEODORE JOSEPH             D. OCTOBER 23, 1965 SHAKOPEE, MINN.
43-100 ODOM, DAVID EVERETT                   BOX 7564 DUNES STA. - MYRTLE BEACH SC 29577
25- 81 ODOM, HERMAN BOYD 'HEINIE'            D. AUGUST 31, 1970 RUSK, TEXAS
64- 81 ODOM, JOHN LEE 'BLUE MOON'            10337 SLATER AVE #206 - FOUNTAIN VALLEY CA 92708
54- 77 ODONNELL, GEORGE DANA                 121 HIGH STREET - WINCHESTER IL 62694
27- 67 ODONNELL, HARRY HERMAN                D. JANUARY 31, 1958 PHILADELPHIA, PA.
63- 87 ODONOGHUE, JOHN EUGENE                500 SOUTH CEDAR - INDEPENDENCE MO 64053
19- 62 ODOUL, FRANCIS JOSEPH 'LEFTY'         D. DECEMBER 7, 1969 SAN FRANCISCO, CAL.
12-145 ODOWD (JOHN LEO DOWD)                 D. JANUARY 31, 1981 FORT LAUDERDALE, FLA.
83-106 OELKERS, BRYAN ALOIS                  2700 LINK - OVERLAND MO 63114
58- 68 OERTEL, CHARLES FRANK                 BOX 90 - PONTIAC MI 48055
14-162 OESCHGER, JOSEPH CARL                 D. JULY 28, 1986 ROHNERT PARK, CALIF.
78- 95 OESTER, RONALD JOHN                   3780 NINEMILE ROAD - CINCINNATI OH 45255
15-118 OFARRELL, ROBERT ARTHUR               D. FEBRUARY 20, 1988 WAUKEGAN, ILL.
72- 82 OFFICE, ROWLAND JOHNNIE               4200 21ST STREET - SACRAMENTO CA 95822
18- 56 OGDEN, JOHN MAHLON                    D. NOVEMBER 9, 1977 PHILADELPHIA, PA.
22-104 OGDEN, WARREN HARVEY 'CURLY'          D. AUGUST 6, 1964 CHESTER, PA.
36- 67 OGLESBY, JAMES DORN                   D. SEPTEMBER 1, 1955 TULSA, OKLA.
71- 77 OGLIVIE, BENJAMIN AMBROSIO            917 BODARK LANE - AUSTIN TX 78745
36- 68 OGRODOWSKI, AMBROSE FRANCIS 'BRUSIE'  D. MARCH 5, 1956 SAN FRANCISCO, CAL.
25- 82 OGRODOWSKI, JOSEPH ANTHONY            D. JUNE 24, 1959 ELMIRA, N. Y.
80- 98 OJEDA, ROBERT MICHAEL                 14884 ROAD 312 - VISALIA CA 93277
20- 92 OKRIE, FRANK ANTHONY                  D. OCTOBER 16, 1959 DETROIT, MICH.
48- 76 OKRIE, LEONARD JOSEPH                 4603 STRATHMORE - FAYETTEVILLE NC 28304
14-163 OLDHAM, JOHN CYRUS 'RED'              D. JANUARY 28,1961 COSTA MESA, CALIF.
56- 66 OLDHAM, JOHN HARDIN                   1845 ANNE WAY - SAN JOSE CA 95124
53- 65 OLDIS, ROBERT CARL                    306 VIRGINIA DR - IOWA CITY IA 52240
62- 99 OLIVA, PEDRO 'TONY'                   212 SPRING VALLEY DR - BLOOMINGTON MN 55420
60- 78 OLIVARES, EDWARD BALZAC               HC02 BOX 12887 - SAN GERMAN PR 00753
68- 74 OLIVER, ALBERT                        2022 NORTH ST. ANDREWS COURT - ARLINGTON TX 76011
77-105 OLIVER, DAVID JACOB                   3604 NEWTON RD - STOCKTON CA 95205
59- 61 OLIVER, EUGENE GEORGE                 2805 35TH ST - ROCK ISLAND IL 61201
63- 88 OLIVER, NATHANIEL                     1320 104TH AVE - OAKLAND CA 94603
65- 83 OLIVER, ROBERT LEE                    4329 EIGHTH AVE - SACRAMENTO CA 95817
30- 59 OLIVER, THOMAS NOBLE                  D. FEBRUARY 26, 1988 MONTGOMERY, ALA.
60- 79 OLIVO, DIOMEDES ANTONIO               D. FEBRUARY 15, 1977 SANTO DOMINGO, DOM. REP.
```

```
61- 79  OLIVO, FEDERICO EMILIO 'CHI-CHI'      D. FEBRUARY 3, 1977 GUAYUBIN, DOMINICAN REP.
66- 69  OLLOM, JAMES DONALD                   8601 NINTH AVENUE - EVERETT WA 98204
43-101  OLMO, LUIS FRANCISCO RODRIGUEZ        620 FIGUEROA ST - SANTURCE PR 00907
80- 99  OLMSTED, ALAN RAY                     RR 4 BOX 233 - TROY MO 63379
22-105  OLSEN, ARTHUR 'OLE'                   D. SEPTEMBER 12, 1980 NORWALK, CONN.
41- 82  OLSEN, BERNARD CHARLES                D. MARCH 30, 1977 EVERETT, MASS.
39- 83  OLSEN, VERN JARL                      1916 BRISTOL AVE-WESTCHESTER IL 60153
11-129  OLSON, IVAN MASSIE 'IVY'              D. SEPTEMBER 1, 1965 INGLEWOOD, CALIF.
51- 75  OLSON, KARL ARTHUR                    P.O. BOX 1897 - ZEPHYR COVE NV 89448
31- 64  OLSON, MARVIN CLEMENT                 BOX 95 - GAYVILLE SD 57031
36- 69  OLSON, THEODORE OTTO                  D. DECEMBER 9, 1980 WEYMOUTH, MASS.
86-116  OLWINE, EDWARD R                      1100 HOWARD DRIVE - GREENVILLE OH 45331
82- 91  OMALLEY, THOMAS PATRICK               1120 LOCUST ST - MONTOURSVILLE PA 17754
12-146  OMARA, OLIVER EDWARD                  1550 SOUTH MARCH AVE - RENO NV 89502
25- 83  ONEAL, ORAN HERBERT 'SKINNY'          D. JUNE 2, 1981 SPRINGFIELD, MO.
84- 85  ONEAL, RANDALL JEFFREY                524 E. RAMBLING DR - WEST PALM BEACH FL 33411
19- 63  ONEIL, GEORGE MICHAEL 'MICKEY'        D. APRIL 8, 1964 ST. LOUIS, MO.
46- 80  ONEIL, JOHN FRANCIS                   ROBERSON ROAD - OKEECHOBEE FL 34974
39- 84  ONEILL, HARRY MINK                    D. MARCH 8, 1945 IWO JIMA, MARIANAS IS.
20- 93  ONEILL, JAMES LEO                     D. SEPTEMBER 5, 1976 CHAMBERSBURG, PA.
22-106  ONEILL, JOSEPH HENRY 'HARRY'          D. SEPTEMBER 5, 1969 RIDGETOWN, ONT.
85- 84  ONEILL, PAUL ANDREW                   1163 EAST COOKE ROAD - COLUMBUS OH 43224
43-103  ONEILL, ROBERT EMMETT                 748 RANCHO VISTA - SPARKS NV 89431
11-130  ONEILL, STEPHEN FRANCIS               D. JANUARY 26, 1962 CLEVELAND, O.
35- 84  ONIS, MANUEL DOMINGUEZ 'CURLY'        1515 RIVER LA-TAMPA FL 33603
12-147  ONSLOW, EDWARD JOSEPH                 D. MAY 8, 1981 DENNISON, O.
12-148  ONSLOW, JOHN JAMES                    D. DECEMBER 22, 1960 WEST ACTON, MASS.
85- 85  ONTIVEROS, STEVEN                     10195 EAST WOOD DRIVE - SCOTTSDALE AZ 85261
73- 89  ONTIVEROS, STEVEN ROBERT              20 LIGGET - BAKERSFIELD CA 93307
83-107  OQUENDO, JOSE MANUEL                  CALLE M-1M R.B. HILLSED - RIO PIEDRAS PR 00926
55- 86  ORAVETZ, ERNEST EUGENE                4417 PAUL AVE - TAMPA FL 33611
43-104  ORDENANA, ANTONIO RODRIGUEZ           NAZAVENO 157 - GUANABACOA CUBA
39- 85  ORENGO, JOSEPH CHARLES                866 FAXON AVE-SAN FRANCISCO CA 94112
69-127  ORILEY, DONALD LEE                    915 PACIFIC - KANSAS CITY MO 64106
20- 94  ORME, GEORGE WILLIAM                  D. MARCH 16, 1962 INDIANAPOLIS, IND.
79- 80  OROSCO, JESSE                         1359 TOMOL DR - CARPINTERIA CA 93013
12-149  OROURKE, JAMES FRANCIS                D. MAY 14, 1986 CHATHAM, N. J.
59- 62  OROURKE, JAMES PATRICK                N 15612 LITTLE SPOKANE DR - SPOKANE WA 99208
29- 80  OROURKE, JOSEPH LEO                   3151 ARAMINGO AVE - PHILADELPHIA PA 19134
13-136  ORR, WILLIAM JOHN                     D. MARCH 10, 1967 ST. HELENA, CALIF.
43-105  ORRELL, FORREST GORDON 'JOE'          420 PARKWAY - CHULA VISTA CA 92010
27- 68  ORSATTI, ERNEST RALPH                 D. SEPTEMBER 4, 1968 CANOGA PARK, CAL.
61- 80  ORSINO, JOHN JOSEPH                   11501 INDIAN SPRING TRAIL - BOYNTON BEACH FL 33437
83-108  ORSULAK, JOSEPH MICHAEL               29 KEANSBURG RD - PARSIPPANY NJ 07054
72- 83  ORTA, JORGE                           SAL CREEL 165,LOS MARGARITAS-TORREON COAHUILA MEX.
60- 80  ORTEGA, FILOMENO CORONADO 'PHIL'      OLD ADD: 4242 SPRING ST - LA MESA CA 92041
73- 90  ORTENZIO, FRANK JOSEPH                723 WEST GETTYSBURG - FRESNO CA 93705
82- 92  ORTIZ, ADALBERTO (COLON) 'JUNIOR'     CANDELARO ARRIBA,BUZON 590-HUMACAO PR 00661
69-128  ORTIZ, JOSE LUIS                      CALLE 14 HH-57,VILLA DEL CARMEN - PLAYA PONCE PR 00731
44-101  ORTIZ, OLIVRIO NUNEZ 'BABY'           D. MARCH 27, 1984 CENTRAL SENADO, CAMAGUEY, CUBA
41- 83  ORTIZ, ROBERTO GONZALO NUNEZ          D. SEPTEMBER 15, 1971 MIAMI, FLA.
28- 73  ORWOLL, OSWALD CHRISTIAN              D. MAY 8, 1967 DECORAH, IA.
75- 86  OSBORN, DANNY LEON                    7620 KNOX CT - WESTMINSTER CO 80030
25- 84  OSBORN, ROBERT                        D. APRIL 19, 1960 PARIS, ARK.
22-107  OSBORNE, ERNEST PRESTON 'TINY'        D. JANUARY 5, 1969 ATLANTA, GA.
57- 62  OSBORNE, LAWRENCE SIDNEY              1969 SEABOARD PLACE NW - ATLANTA GA 30318
```

COACH REGGIE OTERO
Cincinnati Reds

```
35- 85  OSBORNE, WAYNE HAROLD                 D. MARCH 13, 1987 VANCOUVER, WASH.
74- 98  OSBURN, LARRY PAT                     RR 2 BOX 308 - BRADENTON FL 33508
44-102  OSGOOD, CHARLES BENJAMIN              3 SOUTH MEADOW VLG #22 - CARVER MA 02330
62-100  OSINSKI, DANIEL                       3735 WEST 215TH STREET - MATTESON IL 60443
57- 63  OSTEEN, CLAUDE WILSON                 RR 3 BOX 453 - ANNVILLE PA 17003
65- 84  OSTEEN, MILTON DARRELL                1213 LAS POSAS - SAN CLEMENTE CA 92672
14-164  OSTENDORF, FREDERICK                  D. MARCH 9, 1965 HAMPTON, VA.
54- 78  OSTER, WILLIAM CHARLES                9 HARBOR HEIGHTS - CENTERPORT NY 11721
21- 75  OSTERGARD, ROY LUND 'RED'             D. JANUARY 13, 1977 HEMET, CALIF.
34- 82  OSTERMUELLER, FREDERICK RAYMOND       D. DECEMBER 17, 1957 QUINCY, ILL.
73- 91  OSTROSSER, BRIAN LEONARD              OLD ADD: 21 LAKE AVENUE SOUTH-STONEY CREEK ONTARIO CAN.
43-106  OSTROWSKI, JOHN THADDEUS              4943 SOUTH KOMENSKY AVE-CHICAGO IL 60632
48- 77  OSTROWSKI, JOSEPH PAUL                441 TRIPP ST - WEST WYOMING PA 18644
45- 75  OTERO, REGINO JOSE                    4675 WEST EIGHTH AVENUE - HIALEAH FL 33010
67- 83  OTIS, AMOS JOSEPH                     1327 FAIRWAY CIR - BLUE SPRINGS MO 64015
12-150  OTIS, PAUL FRANKLIN 'BILL'            2310 EAST THIRD ST - DULUTH MN 55817
69-129  OTOOLE, DENNIS JOSEPH                 3453 RIDGEWOOD DR - ERLANGER KY 41018
58- 69  OTOOLE, JAMES JEROME                  1010 LANETTE DR - CINCINNATI OH 45230
```

26- 62 OTT, MELVIN THOMAS	D. NOVEMBER 21, 1958 NEW ORLEANS, LA.
74- 99 OTT, NATHAN EDWARD 'ED'	RR 2 BOX 62AA - COUDERSPORT PA 16915
62-101 OTT, WILLIAM JOSEPH	OLD ADD: 25 DONGAN PL - NEW YORK NY 10040
74-100 OTTEN, JAMES EDWARD	BOX 242 - KALISPELL MT 59901
87-108 OTTO, DAVID ALAN	239 TANGLEWOOD DRIVE - ELK GROVE IL 60007
86-117 OUELLETTE, PHILIP ROLAND	2402 CHARFORD STREET - GLENDORA CA 91740
33- 47 OULLIBER, JOHN ANDREW	D. DECEMBER 26, 1980 NEW ORLEANS, LA.
33- 48 OUTEN, WILLIAM AUSTIN 'CHICK'	D. SEPTEMBER 11, 1961 DURHAM, N. C.
37- 82 OUTLAW, JAMES PAULUS	118 JAMES ST - JACKSON AL 36545
43-107 OVERMIRE, FRANK 'STBBY'	D. MARCH 3, 1977 LAKELAND, FLA.
76- 72 OVERY, HARRY MICHAEL	101 FAIRVIEW PL - CLINTON IL 61727
11-131 OVITZ, ERNEST GAYHART	D. SEPTEMBER 11, 1980 GREEN BAY, WISC.
76- 73 OWCHINKO, ROBERT DENNIS	8355 EAST RAINTREE #110 - SCOTTSDALE AZ 85260
37- 83 OWEN, ARNOLD MALCOLM 'MICKEY'	2731 E.LOMBARD - SPRINGFIELD MO 65802
83-109 OWEN, DAVE	RURAL ROUTE 5 BOX 281 - CLEBURNE TX 76031
81- 91 OWEN, LAWRENCE THOMAS	804 WHITE PINE ST - NEW CARLISLE OH 45344
31- 65 OWEN, MARVIN JAMES	42 HAWTHORNE WAY - SAN JOSE CA 95110
83-110 OWEN, SPIKE DEE	RURAL ROUTE 5 BOX 281 - CLEBURNE TX 76031
35- 86 OWENS, FURMAN LEE 'JACK'	D. NOVEMBER 14, 1958 GREENVILLE, S. C.
55- 87 OWENS, JAMES PHILIP	1761 CROTON DR - VENICE FL 33595
72- 84 OWENS, PAUL FRANCIS	RR 2 BOX 689 - MULLICA HILL NJ 08062
82- 93 OWNBEY, RICHARD WAYNE	2752 WEST STOCKTON AVE - ANAHEIM CA 92801
65- 85 OYLER, RAYMOND FRANCIS	D. JANUARY 26, 1981 REDMOND, WASH.
73- 92 OZARK, DANIEL LEONARD	BOX 6666 - VERO BEACH FL 32960
23-100 OZMER, HORACE ROBERT 'DOC'	D. DECEMBER 28, 1970 ATLANTA, GA.
77-106 PACELLA, JOHN LEWIS	6586 SUNBURY RD - WESTERVILLE OH 43081
87-109 PACILLO, PATRICK MICHAEL	15 ADDISON AVENUE - RUTHERFORD NJ 07070
87-110 PACIOREK, JAMES JOSEPH	13432 MOENART - DETROIT MI 48212
63- 89 PACIOREK, JOHN FRANCIS	8400 HUNTINGTON DR - SAN GABRIEL CA 91775
70-103 PACIOREK, THOMAS MARIAN	2389 BROAD CREEK DRIVE - STONE MOUNTAIN GA 30087
49- 62 PACK, FRANKIE	BOX 1623 - HENDERSONVILLE NC 28739
12-151 PACKARD, EUGENE MILO	D. MAY 19, 1959 RIVERSIDE, CALIF.
75- 87 PACTWA, JOSEPH MARTIN	232 154TH PL - CALUMET CITY IL 60409
32- 59 PADDEN, THOMAS FRANCIS	D. JUNE 11, 1973 MANCHESTER, N. H.
12-152 PADDOCK, DELMAR HAROLD	D. FEBRUARY 6, 1952 REMER, MINN.
37- 84 PADGETT, DON WILSON	D. DECEMBER 9, 1980 HIGH POINT, N. C.
23-101 PADGETT, ERNEST KITCHEN	D. APRIL 15, 1957 EAST ORANGE, N. J.
69-130 PAEPKE, DENNIS RAY	DRAWER #CE - CRESTLINE CA 92325
43-108 PAFKO, ANDREW	1420 BLACKHAWK DR - MOUNT PROSPECT IL 60056
73- 93 PAGAN, DAVID PERCY	BOX 1819 - NIPAWIN SASK. SOE 1EO CAN.
59- 63 PAGAN, JOSE ANTONIO	CALLE JASPE #15 - CAGUAS PR 00625
44-103 PAGE, JOSEPH FRANCIS	D. APRIL 21, 1980 LATROBE, PA.
68- 75 PAGE, MICHAEL RANDY	BOX 334 - WOODRUFF SC 29388
77-107 PAGE, MITCHELL OTIS	OLD ADD: 125 EAST 93RD STREET - LOS ANGELES CA 90003
28- 74 PAGE, PHILIPPE RAUSAC	D. JUNE 27, 1958 SPRINGFIELD, MASS.
39- 86 PAGE, SAMUEL WALTER	BOX 204-WOODRUFF SC 29388
38- 73 PAGE, VANCE LINWOOD	D. JULY 14, 1951 WILSON, N. C.
78- 96 PAGEL, KARL DOUGLAS	812 WEST OBISPO - MESA AZ 85202
55- 88 PAGLIARONI, JAMES VINCENT	10388 PARTRIDGE DR - GRASS VALLEY CA 95945
84- 86 PAGLIARULO, MICHAEL TIMOTHY	164 WEST WYOMING AVENUE - MELROSE MA 02176
87-111 PAGNOZZI, THOMAS ALAN	6046 EAST 16TH - TUCSON AZ 85711
11-132 PAIGE, GEORGE LYNN 'PAT'	D. JUNE 8, 1939 BERLIN, WIS.
48- 78 PAIGE, LEROY "SATCHEL"	D. JUNE 8, 1982 KANSAS CITY, MO.
51- 76 PAINE, PHILLIPS STEERE	D. FEBRUARY 19, 1978 LEBANON, PA.
87-112 PALACIOS, VICENTE	DOMICILIO CONOCIDO - MATALOMA VERACRUZ MEX.
39- 87 PALAGYI, MICHAEL RAYMOND	167 14TH ST-CONNEAUT OH 44030
45- 76 PALICA, ERVIN MARTIN	D. MAY 29, 1982 HUNTINGTON BEACH, CALIF.
48- 79 PALM, RICHARD PAUL 'MIKE'	63 NICHOLS RD - COHASSET MA 02025
86-118 PALMEIRO, RAFAEL CORRALES	223 NORTHWEST 32ND STREET - MIAMI FL 33127
78- 97 PALMER, DAVID WILLIAM	1395 EASTGATE DRIVE - STONE MOUNTAIN GA 30087
17- 59 PALMER, EDWIN HENRY	D. JANUARY 9, 1983 MARLOW, OKLA.
65- 86 PALMER, JAMES ALVIN	BOX 145 - BROOKLANDVILLE MD 21022
69-131 PALMER, LOWELL RAYMOND	P.O. BOX 1704 - ORANGEVALE CA 95662
15-119 PALMERO, EMILIO ANTONIO	D. JULY 15, 1970 TOLEDO, O.
31- 66 PALMISANO, JOSEPH	D. NOVEMBER 5, 1971 ALBUQUERQUE, N. M.
60- 81 PALMQUIST, EDWIN LEE	128 W.MARIPOSA ST - SAN CLEMENTE CA 92672
53- 66 PALYS, STANLEY FRANCIS	RR ONE - MOSCOW PA 18444
84- 87 PANKOVITS, JAMES FRANKLIN	9419 BONNIE DALE RD - RICHMOND VA 23229
71- 78 PANTHER, JAMES EDWARD	1125 SHARI LN - LIBERTYVILLE IL 60048
61- 81 PAPA, JOHN PAUL	29 PHILLIPS DR - SHELTON CT 06484
48- 80 PAPAI, ALFRED THOMAS	2553 SOUTH 7TH ST - SPRINGFIELD IL 62703
76- 74 PAPE, KENNETH WAYNE	2714 OAK FIRE - SAN ANTONIO TX 78217
74-101 PAPI, STANLEY GERARD	1111 WEST SIERRA MADRE - FRESNO CA 93705
45- 77 PAPISH, FRANK RICHARD	D. AUGUST 30, 1965 PUEBLO, COLO.

MILT PAPPAS
Cincinnati Reds

57- 64	PAPPAS, MILTON STEPHEN	205 THOMPSON DR - WHEATON ILL 60187
85- 86	PARDO, ALBERTO JUDAS	614 WEST BUFFALO AVE - TAMPA FL 33603
86-119	PARENT, MARK ALAN	P.O. BOX 591 - COTTONWOOD CA 96022
82- 94	PARIS, KELLY JAY	OLD ADD: 19961 SANTA RITA ST - WOODLAND HILLS CA 91364
43-109	PARISSE, LOUIS PETER	D. JUNE 2, 1956 PHILADELPHIA, PA.
15-120	PARK, JAMES	D. DECEMBER 17, 1970 LEXINGTON, KY.
37- 85	PARKER, CLARENCE MCKAY 'ACE'	210 SNEAD'S FAIRWAY-PORTSMOUTH VA 23701
15-121	PARKER, CLARENCE PERKINS 'PAT'	D. MARCH 21, 1967 CLAREMONT, N.H.
73- 94	PARKER, DAVID GENE	7864 RIDGE ROAD - CINCINNATI OH 45237
23-102	PARKER, DOUGLAS WOOLLEY 'DIXIE'	D. MAY 15, 1972 GREEN POND, ALA.
36- 70	PARKER, FRANCIS JAMES 'SALTY'	9201 CLAREWOOD #121 - HOUSTON TX 77036
70-104	PARKER, HARRY WILLIAM	3324 SOUTH ASH PLACE - BROKEN ARROW OK 74012
87-113	PARKER, JAMES CLAYTON 'CLAY'	RURAL ROUTE 1 BOX 37 - GRAYSON LA 71435
64- 82	PARKER, MAURICE WESLEY 'WES'	P.O. BOX 550 - SANTA MONICA CA 90406
19- 64	PARKER, ROY W.	B. 1897
71- 79	PARKER, WILLIAM DAVID	OLD ADD: 1975 EL PARQUE DRIVE - TEMPE AZ 85282
21- 76	PARKINSON, FRANK JOSEPH	D. JULY 4, 1960 TRENTON, N.J.
37- 86	PARKS, ARTIE WILLIAM	127 SOUTH HARVEY-GREENVILLE MS 38701
21- 77	PARKS, VERNON HENRY 'SLICKER'	D. FEBRUARY 21, 1978 ROYAL OAK, MICH.
29- 81	PARMELEE, LEROY EARL	D. AUGUST 31, 1981 MONROE, MICH.
47- 65	PARNELL, MELVIN LLOYD	700 TURQUOISE ST - NEW ORLEANS LA 70124
16- 67	PARNHAM, JAMES ARTHUR 'RUBE'	D. NOVEMBER 25, 1963 MCKEESPORT, PA.
86-120	PARRETT, JEFFREY DALE	722 SEATTLE DRIVE - LEXINGTON KY 40503
70-105	PARRILLA, SAMUEL	33 WYCKOFF ST - BROOKLYN NY 11201
77-108	PARRISH, LANCE MICHAEL	22370 STARWOOD DRIVE - YORBA LINDA CA 92686
74-102	PARRISH, LARRY ALTON	4989 EAST STATE RD #544 - HAINES CITY FL 33844
77-109	PARROTT, MICHAEL EVERETT ARCH	2784 MAGNOLIA ST - CAMARILLO CA 93010
10-115	PARSON, WILLIAM EDWIN 'JIGGS'	D. MAY 19, 1967 INGLEWOOD, CALIF.
81- 92	PARSONS, CASEY ROBERT	EAST 12124 25TH - SPOKANE WA 99206
39- 88	PARSONS, EDWARD DIXON 'DIXIE'	4723 WEST MARSHALL ST - LONGVIEW TX 75601
63- 90	PARSONS, THOMAS ANTHONY	LINCOLN CITY ROAD - LAKEVILLE CT 06039
71- 80	PARSONS, WILLIAM RAYMOND	2725 SOUTH AZALEA - TEMPE AZ 85281
43-110	PARTEE, ROY ROBERT	DRAWER 730 - TRINIDAD CA 95570
13-137	PARTENHEIMER, HAROLD PHILIP 'STEVE'	D. JUNE 16, 1971 MANSFIELD, O.
44-104	PARTENHEIMER, STANWOOD WENDELL	2501 LANCASTER ROAD - WILSON NC 27893
27- 69	PARTRIDGE, JAMES BUGG 'JAY'	D. JANUARY 4, 1974 NASHVILLE, TENN.
15-122	PASCHAL, BENJAMIN EDWIN	D. NOVEMBER 10, 1974 CHARLOTTE, N. C.
78- 98	PASCHALL, WILLIAM HERBERT	OLD ADD: 4557 PRINCESS ANNE RD - VIRGINIA BEACH VA 2346
54- 79	PASCUAL, CAMILO ALBERTO	7741 SW 32ND ST - MIAMI FL 33155
50- 76	PASCUAL, CARLOS ALBERTO	2540 SW 92ND COURT - MIAMI FL 33165
33- 49	PASEK, JOHN PAUL	D. MARCH 13, 1976 NIAGARA FALLS, N. Y.
82- 95	PASHNICK, LARRY JOHN	9625 BLACKBURN - LIVONIA MI 48150
74-103	PASLEY, KEVIN PATRICK	2701 LANCASTER DRIVE - SUN CITY CENTER FL 33570
85- 87	PASQUA, DANIEL ANTHONY	46 GAIL DRIVE - NEW CITY NY 10956
19- 65	PASQUELLA, MICHAEL JOHN	D. APRIL 5, 1965 BRIDGEPORT, CONN.
35- 87	PASSEAU, CLAUDE WILLIAM	113 LONDON ST - LUCEDALE MS 39452
79- 81	PASTORE, FRANK ENRICO	1542 NORTH FRAMIS WAY - UPLAND CA 91786
83-111	PASTORNICKY, CLIFFORD SCOT	15078 SE 44TH TERRACE - BELLEVUE WA 98006
26- 63	PATE, JOSEPH WILLIAM	D. DECEMBER 26, 1948 FORT WORTH, TEX.
80-100	PATE, ROBERT WAYNE	12330 OSBORNE STREET #30 - PACOIMA CA 91331
68- 76	PATEK, FREDERICK JOSEPH	GRANDY'S, 14440 E. 42ND ST #136 - INDEPENDENCE MO 64055
41- 84	PATRICK, ROBERT LEE	107 NORTH 18TH-FORT SMITH AR 72901
68- 77	PATTERSON, DARYL ALAN	20145 TOLLHOUSE RD - CLOVIS CA 93612
79- 82	PATTERSON, DAVID GLENN	OLD ADD: 25481 CLASSIC DRIVE - MISSION CA 95050
77-110	PATTERSON, GILBERT THOMAS	8185 NW 8 MANOR - PLANT FL 33324
32- 60	PATTERSON, HENRY JOSEPH	D. SEPTEMBER 30, 1970 PANORAMA CITY, CAL.
81- 93	PATTERSON, MICHAEL LEE	2419 RIDGELEY DR #9 - LOS ANGELES CA 90016
81- 94	PATTERSON, REGINALD ALLEN	2900 ARLINGTON AVE - BESSEMER AL 35020
85- 88	PATTERSON, ROBERT CHANDLER	201 CHEROKEE DRIVE - GREENVILLE SC 29615
21- 78	PATTERSON, WILLIAM JENNINGS BRYAN	D. OCTOBER 1, 1977 ST. LOUIS, MO.
68- 78	PATTIN, MARTIN WILLIAM	1520 ALVAMAR DR - LAWRENCE KS 66044
29- 82	PATTISON, JAMES WELLS	883 VANCE CIRCLE NE - PALM BAY FL 32905
44-105	PATTON, GENE TUNNEY	60 SOUTH 17TH AVE - COATESVILLE PA 19320
35- 88	PATTON, GEORGE WILLIAM	D. MARCH 15, 1986 PHILADELPHIA, PA.
10-116	PATTON, HARRY CLAUDE	D. JUNE 9, 1930 ST. LOUIS, MO.
57- 65	PATTON, THOMAS ALLEN	RR 4 BOX 335 - HONEY BROOK PA 19344
68- 79	PAUL, MICHAEL GEORGE	5121 CIRCULO SOBRIO - TUCSON AZ 85718
54- 80	PAULA, CARLOS (CONNILL)	D. APRIL 25, 1983 MIAMI, FLA.
11-133	PAULETTE, EUGENE EDWARD	D. FEBRUARY 8, 1966 LITTLE ROCK, ARK.
25- 85	PAULSON, PAUL GUILFORD	5502 109TH AVE EAST - PUYALLUP WA 98371
57- 66	PAVLETICH, DONALD STEPHEN	13645 ADELAIDE LANE - BROOKFIELD WI 53005
46- 81	PAWELEK,.THEODORE JOHN	D. FEBRUARY 12, 1964 CHICAGO HEIGHTS, ILL.
55- 89	PAWLOSKI, STANLEY WALTER	1013 GORMAN ST - PHILADELPHIA PA 19116
87-114	PAWLOWSKI, JOHN	9 LINDA DRIVE - BINGHAMTON NY 13905
77-111	PAXTON, MICHAEL DEWAYNE	OLD ADD: 345 LINCOLN #10 - BOSTON MA 02111

LARRY PARRISH

```
20- 95 PAYNE, GEORGE WASHINGTON          D. JANUARY 24, 1959 BELLFLOWER, CALIF.
84- 88 PAYNE, MICHAEL EARL              BOX 712 - WILLISTON FL 32696
75- 88 PAZIK, MICHAEL JOSEPH            9205 KIRKDALE - BETHESDA MD 20817
37- 87 PEACOCK, JOHN GASTON             D. OCTOBER 17, 1981 WILSON, N. C.
33- 50 PEARCE, FRANKLIN THOMAS          D. SEPTEMBER 3, 1950 VAN BUREN, N. Y.
12-153 PEARCE, GEORGE THOMAS            D. OCTOBER 11, 1935 ·JOLIET, ILL.
17- 60 PEARCE, HARRY JAMES              D. JANUARY 8, 1942 PHILADELPHIA, PA.
49- 63 PEARCE, JAMES MADISON            RR 5 BOX 404 - ZEBULON NC 27597
58- 70 PEARSON, ALBERT GREGORY          BOX 8995 - PALM SPRINGS CA 92263
39- 89 PEARSON, ISSAC OVERTON           D. MARCH 17, 1985 SARASOTA, FLA.
32- 61 PEARSON, MONTGOMERY MARCELLUS    D. JANUARY 27, 1978 FRESNO, CALIF.
10-117 PEASLEY, MARVIN WARREN           D. DECEMBER 27, 1948 SAN FRANCISCO, CALIF.
15-123 PECHOUS, CHARLES EDWARD          D. SEPTEMBER 13, 1980 KENOSHA, WIS.
43-111 PECK, HAROLD ARTHUR              1037 WEST SHAW COURT #3 - WHITEWATER WI 53190
10-118 PECKINPAUGH, ROGER THORPE        D. NOVEMBER 17, 1977 CLEVELAND, O.
86-121 PECOTA, WILLIAM JOSEPH           471 LIQUID AMBER WAY - SUNNYVALE CA 94086
53- 67 PEDEN, LESLIE EARL               17437 ELSINORE DRIVE - JACKSONVILLE FL 32226
85- 89 PEDERSON, STUART RUSSELL         24848 SKYLAND - LOS GATOS CA 95030
87-115 PEDRIQUE, ALFREDO JOSE           EL PARQ LAETAPA #16 CD. ALIANZA-GUACARA CARABOBO VENEZ
41- 85 PEEK, STEPHEN GEORGE             204 WEST HAMILTON AVE-SHERRILL NY 13461
27- 70 PEEL, HOMER HEFNER               3757 GREENWAY - SHREVEPORT LA 71105
35- 89 PEERSON, JACK CHILES             D. OCTOBER 23, 1966 FT. WALTON BEACH, FLA.
27- 71 PEERY, GEORGE A. 'RED'           D. MAY 6, 1985 SALT LAKE CITY, UTAH
56- 67 PEETE, CHARLES                   D. NOVEMBER 27, 1956 CARACAS, VENEZ.
46- 82 PELLAGRINI, EDWARD CHARLES       103 WEBB ST - WEYMOUTH MA 02188
74-104 PEMBERTON, BROCK                 1012 SOUTH FLORENCE - TULSA OK 74104
81- 95 PENA, ADALBERTO                  19-2-0-5, BAIROA MIRABEL-CAGUAS PR 00625
81- 96 PENA, ALEJANDRO                  1713 GERMAIN DR - MONTEBELLO CA 90640
80-101 PENA, ANTONIO FRANCISCO          COMP HAB 30 DEMARZO,MAN #1 ED 14-SANTIAGO DOM. REP.
86-122 PENA, HIPOLITO (CONCEPCION)      PEREZ RODRIGUEZ #13 - SANTO DOMINGO DOMINICAN REP.
69-132 PENA, JOSE                       A.FLORES #1116 NTE,C.JIQUILPAN-LOS MOCHIS SINOLOA MEX.
58- 71 PENA, ORLANDO                    P.O. BOX 553 - KEY BISCAYNE FL 33149
65- 87 PENA, ROBERT CESAR               D. JULY 23, 1982 SANTIAGO DOMINICAN REPUBLIC
22-108 PENCE, ELMER CLAIR               D. SEPTEMBER 17, 1968 SAN FRANCISCO, CAL.
21- 79 PENCE, RUSSELL WILLIAM           D. AUGUST 11, 1971 HOT SPRINGS, ARK.
53- 68 PENDLETON, JAMES EDWARD          6622 HARTWICK - HOUSTON TX 77016
84- 89 PENDLETON, TERRY LEE             512 N. VENTURA RD - PORT HUENEME CA 93041
16- 68 PENNER, KENNETH WILLIAM          D. MAY 28, 1959 SACRAMENTO, CAL.
17- 61 PENNINGTON, GEORGE LOUIS 'KEWPIE' D. MAY 5, 1953 NEWARK, N. J.
12-154 PENNOCK, HERBERT JEFFERIS        D. JANUARY 30, 1948 NEW YORK, N.Y.
54- 81 PENSON, PAUL EUGENE              711 LAKE OF THE FOREST-BONNER SPGS KS 66012
75- 89 PENTZ, EUGENE DAVID              919 PARSON ST - JOHNSTOWN PA 15902
62-102 PEPITONE, JOSEPH ANTHONY         OLD ADD: LIGHTHOUSE RD - SAUGERTIES NY 12477
29- 83 PEPLOSKI, HENRY STEPHEN          D. JANUARY 28, 1982 DOVER, N. J.
13-139 PEPLOSKI, JOSEPH ANTHONY 'PEPPER' D. 1946 OR 1947
66- 70 PEPPER, DONALD HOYTE             RR2 - GANSEVOORT NY 12831
54- 82 PEPPER, HUGH MCLAURIN 'LAURIN'   123 HOLCOMB BLVD - OCEAN SPRINGS MS 39564
32- 62 PEPPER, RAYMOND WATSON           BOX 40 - MOORESVILLE AL 35649
15-124 PEPPER, ROBERT ERNEST            D. APRIL 8, 1968 FORD CLIFF, PA.
69-133 PERAZA, LUIS                     CALLE 6 C.F. 13 RES. BAIROA-CAGUAS PR 00625
80-102 PERCONTE, JOHN PATRICK           6197 HINTERLONG COURT - LISLE IL 60532
11-134 PERDUE, HERBERT ROSCOE 'HUB'     D. OCTOBER 31, 1968 GALLATIN, TENN.
64- 83 PEREZ, ATANASIO RIGAL 'TONY'     LOS FLORES 113 - SANTURCE PR 00911
58- 72 PEREZ, GEORGE THOMAS             39646 87TH WEST - LEONA VALLEY CA 93550
69-134 PEREZ, MARTIN ROMAN              30 WILLOWICK DR - DECATUR GA 30034
87-116 PEREZ, MELIDO GROSS              NIGUA KM 21 1/2 - SANTO DOMINGO DOMINICAN REP.
80-103 PEREZ, PASCUAL (GROSS)           SALVADOR, CUCURULO #105 - SANTIAGO DOMINICAN REP.
78- 99 PERKINS, BRODERICK PHILLIP       2110 BURTON AVE - PITTSBURG CA 94565
67- 84 PERKINS, CECIL BOYCE             RR 1 BOX 100-P - MARTINSBURG WV 25401
30- 60 PERKINS, CHARLES SULLIVAN        D. MAY 25, 1988 SALEM, ORE.
15-125 PERKINS, RALPH FOSTER 'CY'       D. OCTOBER 2, 1963 PHILADELPHIA, PA.
50- 77 PERKOVICH, JOHN JOSEPH           16 ATHENA CT - LITTLE ROCK AR 72207
47- 66 PERKOWSKI, HAROLD WALTER         211 MCGINNIS - BECKLEY WV 25801
85- 90 PERLMAN, JONATHAN SAMUEL         1019 FORREST LANE - CARTHAGE TX 75633
77-112 PERLOZZO, SAMUEL BENEDICT        42 SCOTT COURT - CUMBERLAND MD 21502
42- 75 PERME, LEONARD JOSEPH            3350 D ST - HAYWARD CA 94541
10-119 PERNOLL, HENRY HUBBARD           D. FEBRUARY 18, 1944 GRANTS PASS, ORE.
61- 82 PERRANOSKI, RONALD PETER         18731 MARTHA STREET - TARAZANA CA 91356
21- 80 PERRIN, JOHN STEPHENSON          D. JUNE 24, 1969 DETROIT, MICH.
34- 83 PERRIN, WILLIAM JOSEPH           D. JUNE 30, 1974 NEW ORLEANS, LA.
12-155 PERRITT, WILLIAM DAYTON 'POL'    D. OCTOBER 15, 1947 SHREVEPORT, LA.
41- 86 PERRY, BOYD GLENN                RR 1 - SNOW CAMP NC 27349
62-103 PERRY, GAYLORD JACKSON           320 EAST JEFFERIES STREET - GAFFNEY SC 29342
```

108

83-112 PERRY, GERALD JUNE	BOX 1403 - HILTON HEAD SC 29928
15-126 PERRY, HERBERT SCOTT	D. OCTOBER 27, 1959 KANSAS CITY, MO.
59- 64 PERRY, JAMES EVAN	5720 DUNCAN LANE - MINNEAPOLIS MN 55436
63- 91 PERRY, MELVIN GAY "BOB"	621 HOLIDAY CITY - NEW BERN NC 28562
12-156 PERRY, WILLIAM HENRY 'HANK'	D. JULY 18, 1956 PONTIAC, MICH.
85- 91 PERRY, WILLIAM PATRICK 'PAT'	1115 WEST FRANKLIN - TAYLORVILLE IL 62568
15-127 PERRYMAN, EMMETT KEY 'PARSON'	D. SEPTEMBER 12, 1966 STARKE, FLA.
18- 57 PERTICA, WILLIAM ANDREW	D. DECEMBER 28, 1967 LOS ANGELES, CAL.
71- 81 PERZANOWSKI, STANLEY	3250 173RD ST - HAMMOND IN 46323
42- 76 PESKY, JOHN MICHAEL	25 PARSONS DR-SWAMPSCOTT MA 01907
42- 77 PETERMAN, WILLIAM DAVID	9823 WISTERIA ST - PHILADELPHIA PA 19115
59- 65 PETERS, GARY CHARLES	2626 ESPANOLA AVE - SARASOTA FL 33580
15-128 PETERS, JOHN WILLIAM	D. FEBRUARY 21, 1932 KANSAS CITY, MO.
12-157 PETERS, OSCAR C. 'RUBE'	B. MARCH 15, 1886 GRAND FORK, ILL.
70-106 PETERS, RAYMOND JAMES	1317 NORTH BARKLEY STREET - MESA AZ 85203
79- 83 PETERS, RICHARD DEVIN 'RICKY'	12601 SOUTH HALO DRIVE - COMPTON CA 90221
36- 71 PETERS, RUSSELL DIXON 'RUSTY'	BOX 751 - BEDFORD VA 24523
87-117 PETERS, STEVEN BRADLEY	RURAL ROUTE 11 BOX 531A - OKLAHOMA CITY OK 73170
87-118 PETERSON, ADAM CHARLES	6401 NE 144TH STREET - VANCOUVER WA 98686
55- 90 PETERSON, CARL FRANCIS 'BUDDY'	8665 FLORIN RD #101 - SACRAMENTO CA 95828
62-104 PETERSON, CHARLES ANDREW 'CAP'	D. MAY 16, 1980 TACOMA WA
66- 71 PETERSON, FRED INGELS 'FRITZ'	P.O. BOX 31206 - PALM BEACH GARDENS FL 33410
55- 91 PETERSON, HARDING WILLIAM 'PETE'	348 ORCHARD DR - PITTSBURGH PA 15228
31- 67 PETERSON, JAMES NIELS	D. APRIL 8, 1975 PALM BEACH, FLA.
44-106 PETERSON, KENT FRANKLIN	P.O. BOX 164 - PROVO UT 84603
43-112 PETERSON, SIDNEY HERBERT	4604 UNIVERSITY AVENUE - WICHITA FALLS TX 76308
34- 84 PETOSKEY, FREDERICK LEE 'TED'	RR 4 BOX 109 - HOPKINS SC 29061
82- 96 PETRALLI, EUGENE JAMES	2605 LAUREL VALLEY LANE - ARLINGTON TX 76006
63- 92 PETROCELLI, AMERICO PETER 'RICO'	19 TOWNSEND RD - LYNNFIELD MA 01940
79- 84 PETRY, DANIEL JOSEPH	1808 CARTLEN DRIVE - PLACENTIA CA 92670
83-113 PETTIBONE, HARRY JONATHAN 'JAM'	1261 WEST CATALPA - ANAHEIM CA 92801
14-165 PETTIGREW, JIM NED	D. AUGUST 20, 1952 DUNCAN, OKLA.
80-104 PETTINI, JOSEPH PAUL	BOX 37 - WINDSOR HEIGHTS WV 26075
82- 97 PETTIS, GARY GEORGE	927 BLENHEIM ST - OAKLAND CA 94603
51- 77 PETTIT, GEORGE WILLIAM PAUL	25313 WOODWARD - LOMITA CA 90717
35- 90 PETTIT, LEON ARTHUR	D. NOVEMBER 21, 1974 COLUMBIA, TENN.
21- 81 PETTY, JESSE LEE	D. OCTOBER 23, 1971 ST. PAUL, MINN.
14-166 PEZOLD, LORENZ JOHANNES 'LARRY'	D. OCTOBER 22, 1957 BATON ROUGE, LA.
35- 91 PEZZULLO, JOHN 'PRETZELS'	3127 WEST LEDBETTER-DALLAS TX 75233
11-135 PFEFFER, EDWARD JOSEPH 'JEFF'	D. AUGUST 15, 1972 CHICAGO, ILL.
13-138 PFEFFER, MONTE	D. SEPTEMBER 27, 1941 NEW YORK, N. Y.
69-135 PFEIL, ROBERT RAYMOND	840 BENJAMIN HALT DR - STOCKTON CA 95207
61- 83 PFISTER, DANIEL ALBIN	3600 NW 91ST AVE - WEST HOLLYWOOD FL 33024
41- 87 PFISTER, GEORGE EDWARD	215 JOHN ST - BOUND BROOK NJ 08805
45- 78 PFUND, LEROY HERBERT 'LEE'	1028 HOWARD STREET - WHEATON IL 60187
36- 72 PHEBUS, RAYMOND WILLIAM 'BILL'	930 LAKEVIEW AVE-BARTOW FL 33830
10-120 PHELAN, ARTHUR THOMAS	D. DECEMBER 27, 1964 FORT WORTH, TEX.
31- 68 PHELPS, ERNEST GORDON 'BABE'	1417 HALE ST - ODENTON MD 21113
80-105 PHELPS, KENNETH ALLEN	7531 EAST TURQUOISE AVE - SCOTTSDALE AZ 85258
30- 61 PHELPS, RAYMOND CLIFFORD	D. JULY 7, 1971 FT. PIERCE, FLA.
41- 88 PHILLEY, DAVID EARL	1336 EAST POLK ST-PARIS TX 75460
64- 84 PHILLIPS, ADOLFO EMILIO	APARTADO 6109 CHORILLA - PANAMA CITY PAN.
30- 62 PHILLIPS, ALBERT ABERNATHY 'BUZZ'	D. NOVEMBER 6, 1964 BALTIMORE, MD.
34- 85 PHILLIPS, CLARENCE LEMUEL 'RED'	2111 SOUTH ESTELLE - WICHITA KS 67211
42- 78 PHILLIPS, DAMON RUSSELL	BOX 805 - HENDERSON TX 75652
24- 85 PHILLIPS, EDWARD DAVID	D. JANUARY 26, 1968 BUFFALO, N.Y.
69-136 PHILLIPS, HAROLD ROSS 'LEFTY'	D. JUNE 12, 1972 FULLERTON, CAL.
53- 69 PHILLIPS, HOWARD EDWARD 'ED'	WEST ELY - HANNIBAL MO 63401
47- 67 PHILLIPS, JACK DORN	MAY RD #2 - POTSDAM NY 13676
45- 79 PHILLIPS, JOHN	D. JUNE 16, 1958 ST. LOUIS, MO.
55- 92 PHILLIPS, JOHN MELVIN 'BUBBA'	2704 MIMOSA LN - HATTIESBURG MS 39401
82- 98 PHILLIPS, KEITH ANTHONY 'TONY'	P.O. BOX 602 - ROSWELL GA 30075
73- 95 PHILLIPS, MICHAEL DWAINE	3322 RIDGEFIELD - IRVING TX 75060
70-107 PHILLIPS, NORMAN EDWIN 'EDDIE'	2207 EDGEHILL RD - LOUISVILLE KY 40205
62-105 PHILLIPS, RICHARD EUGENE	6280 MARLBOROUGH #302 - BURNABY BRIT. COL. V5H 3L8 CAN.
15-129 PHILLIPS, THOMAS GERALD	D. APRIL 12, 1929 PHILIPSBURG, PA.
56- 68 PHILLIPS, WILLIAM TAYLOR	BOX 13 - AUSTELL GA 30001
66- 72 PHOEBUS, THOMAS HAROLD	207 46TH ST NW - BRADENTON FL 33505
77-102 PICCIOLO, ROBERT MICHAEL 'ROB'	6421 FIREBRAND ST - LOS ANGELES CA 90045
45- 80 PICCIUTO, NICHOLAS THOMAS	261 ELMWOOD AVE - MAPLEWOOD NJ 07040
60- 82 PICHE, RONALD JACQUES	100 RUE DE GASPE #1208 - VERDUN QUEBEC H3E 1E5 CAN.
16- 69 PICINICH, VALENTINE JOHN	D. DECEMBER 5, 1942 NOBLEBORO, ME.
14-167 PICK, CHARLES THOMAS	D. JUNE 26, 1954 LYNCHBURG, VA.
23-103 PICK, EDGAR EVERETT	D. MAY 13, 1967 WEST LOS ANGELES, CAL.
31- 69 PICKERING, URBANE HENRY 'DICK'	D. MAY 13, 1970 MODESTO, CALIF.
10-121 PICKETT, CHARLES ALBERT	D. MAY 20, 1969 SPRINGFIELD, O.
33- 51 PICKREL, CLARENCE DOUGLAS	D. NOVEMBER 4, 1983 ROCKY MOUNT, VA.
18- 58 PICKUP, CLARENCE WILLIAM 'TY'	D. AUGUST 2, 1974 PHILADELPHIA, PA.
47- 68 PICONE, MARIO HENRY	8876 BAY 16 - BROOKLYN NY 11214
40- 68 PIECHOTA, ALOYSIUS EDWARD	1656 NORTH MAYFIELD AVE-CHICAGO IL 60639
13-140 PIEH, EDWIN JOHN 'CY'	D. SEPTEMBER 12, 1945 JACKSONVILLE, FLA.
73- 96 PIERCE, LAVERN JACK	314 SALAMANCA-COL INDUSTRIAL - LEON GUANAJUANTO MEX.
24- 86 PIERCE, RAYMOND LESTER	D. MAY 4, 1963 DENVER, COLO.
67- 85 PIERCE, TONY MICHAEL	5002 WILLOWBROOK DR - COLUMBUS GA 31909
45- 81 PIERCE, WALTER WILLIAM 'BILLY'	9000 SOUTH FRANCISCO - EVERGREEN PARK IL60642
17- 62 PIERCY, WILLIAM BENTON	D. AUGUST 28, 1951 LONG BEACH, CAL.
45- 82 PIERETTI, MARINO PAUL	D. JANUARY 30, 1981 SAN FRANCISCO, CALIF.
20- 96 PIEROTTI, ALBERT FELIX	D. FEBRUARY 12, 1964 EVERETT, MASS.
50- 78 PIERRO, WILLIAM LEONARD	1751 74TH ST - BROOKLYN NY 11204
50- 79 PIERSALL, JAMES ANTHONY	1105 OAKVIEW DR - WHEATON IL 60187
18- 59 PIERSON, WILLIAM MORRIS	D. FEBRUARY 21, 1959 ATLANTIC CITY, N. J.
31- 70 PIET, ANTHONY FRANCIS	D. DECEMBER 1, 1981 HINSDALE, ILL.
14-168 PIEZ, CHARLES WILLIAM 'SANDY'	D. DECEMBER 29, 1930 ATLANTIC CITY, N.J.
57- 67 PIGNATANO, JOSEPH BENJAMIN	150 78TH ST - BROOKLYN NY 11209
46- 83 PIKE, JAMES WILLARD	D. MARCH 28, 1984 SAN DIEGO, CALIF.
56- 69 PIKTUZIS, GEORGE RICHARD	12051 PARAMOUNT BLVD #9 - DOWNEY CA 90242
56- 70 PILARCIK, ALFRED JAMES	BOX 185 - ST JOHN IN 46373
49- 64 PILLETTE, DUANE XAVIER	165 BLOSSOM HILL RD #404 - SAN JOSE CA 95123
17- 63 PILLETTE, HERMAN POLYCARP	D. APRIL 30, 1960 SACRAMENTO, CAL.

15-130 PILLION, CECIL RANDOLPH 'SQUIZ'
36- 73 PILNEY, ANDREW JAMES
68- 80 PINA, HORACIO GARCIA
18- 60 PINELLI, RALPH ARTHUR 'BABE'
64- 85 PINIELLA, LOUIS VICTOR
58- 73 PINSON, VADA EDWARD
22-109 PINTO, WILLIAM LERTON
32- 63 PIPGRAS, EDWARD JOHN
23-104 PIPGRAS, GEORGE WILLIAM
13-141 PIPP, WALTER CHARLES
36- 74 PIPPEN, HENRY HAROLD 'COTTON'
78-100 PIRTLE, GERALD EUGENE
53- 70 PISONI, JAMES PETE
38- 74 PITKO, ALEXANDER
17- 64 PITLER, JACOB ALBERT
70-108 PITLOCK, LEE PATRICK THOMAS 'SKIP'
85- 92 PITTARO, CHRISTOPHER FRANCIS
21- 82 PITTENGER, CLARKE ALONZO 'PINKY'
81- 97 PITTMAN, JOSEPH WAYNE
74-105 PITTS, GAYLEN RICHARD
57- 68 PITULA, STANLEY
57- 69 PIZARRO, JUAN CORDOVA
79- 85 PLADSON, GORDON CECIL
31- 71 PLANETA, EMIL JOSEPH
78-101 PLANK, EDWARD ARTHUR
55- 93 PLARSKI, DONALD JOSEPH
62-106 PLASKETT, ELMO ALEXANDER
42- 79 PLATT, MIZELL GEORGE 'WHITEY'
13-142 PLATTE, ALFRED FREDERICK JOSEPH
61- 84 PLEIS, WILLIAM
86-123 PLESAC, DANIEL THOMAS
56- 71 PLESS, RANCE
56- 72 PLEWS, HERBERT EUGENE
18- 61 PLITT, NORMAN WILLIAM
72- 85 PLODINEC, TIMOTHY ALFRED
68- 81 PLUMMER, WILLIAM FRANCIS
86-124 PLUNK, ERIC VAUGHN
42- 80 POAT, RAYMOND WILLIAM
75- 90 POCOROBA, BIFF BENEDICT
49- 65 PODBIELAN, CLARENCE ANTHONY 'BUD'
40- 69 PODGAJNY, JOHN SIGMUND
53- 71 PODRES, JOHN JOSEPH
75- 91 POEPPING, MICHAEL HAROLD
26- 64 POETZ, JOSEPH FRANK
40- 70 POFAHL, JAMES WILLARD
79- 86 POFF, JOHN WILLIAM
37- 88 POFFENBERGER, CLETUS ELWOOD 'BOOTS'
50- 80 POHOLSKY, THOMAS GEORGE
36- 75 POINDEXTER, CHESTER JENNINGS 'JINKS'
63- 93 POINTER, AARON ELTON
43-113 POLAND, HUGH REID
73- 97 POLE, RICHARD HENRY

D. SEPTEMBER 30, 1962 PITTSBURGH, PA.
3309 RIDGEWAY DR-METAIRIE LA 70002
OLD ADD: VENUSTIANA CARRANZA 207-COAHUILA MEX
D. OCTOBER 22, 1984 DALY CITY, CALIF.
103 MACINTYRE LN - ALLENDALE NJ 07401
710 31ST ST - OAKLAND CA 94609
D. MAY 13, 1983 OXNARD, CALIF.
D. APRIL 13, 1964 CURRIE, MINN.
D. OCTOBER 19, 1986 GAINESVILLE, FLA.
D. JANUARY 11, 1965 GRAND RAPIDS, MICH.
D. FEBRUARY 15, 1981 WILLIAMS, CALIF.
9403 SOUTH 236TH EAST AVE - BROKEN ARROW OK 74012
10832 MUELLER RD - ST. LOUIS MO 63123
8001 E. BROADWAY #6512 - MESA AZ 85208
D. FEBRUARY 3, 1968 BINGHAMTON, N. Y.
3506 IONIA - OLYMPIA FIELDS IL 60461
42 PINTINALLI DRIVE - TRENTON NJ 08619
D. NOVEMBER 4, 1977 FORT LAUDERDALE, FLA.
809 MCKINNON DR - COLUMBUS GA 31907
2082 SOUTH HELENA STREET #C - AURORA CO 80013
D. AUGUST 16, 1965 HACKENSACK, N. J.
278 DEL RIO - SANTURCE PR 00912
OLD ADD: 11375 84TH AVE - DELTA BC
D. FEBRUARY 2, 1963 ROCKY HILL, CONN.
1468 WEST JUANITA - MESA AZ 85202
D. DECEMBER 29, 1981 ST. LOUIS, MO.
BOX 1764 - FREDERIKSTED VI 00840
D. JULY 27, 1970 WEST PALM BEACH, FLA.
D. AUGUST 29, 1976 GRAND RAPIDS, MICH.
6844 COUNTRY LAKES CIRCLE - SARASOTA FL 34243
717 PETTIBONE STREET - CROWN POINT IN 46307
RR 4 BOX 210 - GREENEVILLE TN 37743
1460 NORTHWESTERN RD - LONGMONT CO 80501
D. FEBRUARY 1, 1954 NEW YORK, N. Y.
2201 MCMINN - ALIQUIPPA PA 15001
3582 RHONDA ROAD - COTTONWOOD CA 96022
14725 BRUCE AVENUE - BELLFLOWER CA 90706
4833 WEST 109TH ST - OAK LAWN IL 60453
7002 DESHON RIDGE DRIVE - LITHONIA GA 30058
D. OCTOBER 26, 1982 SYRACUSE, N. Y.
D. MARCH 2, 1971 CHESTER, PA.
1 COLONIAL COURT - GLENS FALLS NY 12801
RR 2 - PIERZ MN 56364
D. FEBRUARY 7, 1942 ST. LOUIS, MO.
D. SEPTEMBER 14, 1984 OWATONNA, MINN.
78 BROWNS LN - FAIRFIELD CT 06430
13 1/2 NORTH CONOCOCHEAGUE-WILLIAMSPORT MD 21795
177 HORSESHOE DR - KIRKWOOD MO 63122
D. MARCH 3, 1983 NORMAN, OKLA.
4406 ARBORDALE AVE WEST - TACOMA WA 98466
D. MARCH 30, 1984 GUTHRIE, KY.
21012 WHITLOCK DRIVE - DEARBORN HEIGHTS MI 48127

ALFRED JAMES PILARCIK
(AL)

85- 93 POLIDOR, GUSTAVO ADOLFO
47- 69 POLIVKA, KENNETH LYLE
41- 89 POLLET, HOWARD JOSEPH
32- 64 POLLI, LOUIS AMERICO
37- 89 POLLY, NICHOLAS JOSEPH
77-114 POLONI, JOHN PAUL
87-119 POLONIA, LUIS ANDREW
34- 86 POMORSKI, JOHN LEON
85- 94 PONCE, CARLOS ANTONIO
10-122 POND, RALPH BENJAMIN
17- 65 PONDER, CHARLES ELMER
34- 87 POOL, HARLIN WELTY
25- 86 POOLE, JAMES RALPH
41- 90 POOLE, RAYMOND HERMAN
52- 81 POPE, DAVID
64- 86 POPOVICH, PAUL EDWARD
69-137 POPOWSKI, EDWARD JOSEPH
73- 98 POQUETTE, THOMAS ARTHUR
14-169 PORRAY, EDMUND JOSEPH
81- 98 PORTER, CHARLES WILLIAM

LA AV.DE PRO-PATRIA BLOQ.3 PATRIA B#9-CARACAS VENEZ
1532 SUNNYBROOK DR - NAPERVILLE IL 60540
D. AUGUST 8, 1974 HOUSTON, TEX.
BOX 45 - GRANITEVILLE VT 05654
2331 NORTH LEAVITT AVE-CHICAGO IL 60647
3205 ELLIS - CHANDLER AZ 85224
TURIDEPORTES SA EDCIO HACHETER PISO-LADO ESTE DOM. REP.
D. DECEMBER 6, 1977 BRAMPTON, ONTARIO
51-15 44TH ST,VILLA CAROLINA - CAROLINA PR 00630
D. SEPTEMBER 8, 1947 CLEVELAND, O.
D. APRIL 20, 1974 ALBUQUERQUE, N. M.
D. FEBRUARY 15, 1963 RODEO, CAL.
D. JANUARY 2, 1975 HICKORY, N. C.
RR 10 BOX 655-SALISBURY NC 28144
9020 PARMELEE AVE - CLEVELAND OH 44108
2501 PARTRIDGE - NORTHBROOK IL 60062
P.O. BOX 45 - SAYREVILLE NJ 08872
4624 WOODRIDGE DRIVE - EAU CLAIRE WI 54701
D. JULY 13, 1954 LACKAWAXEN, PA.
9321 SNYDER LN - PERRY HALL MD 21128

51- 78	PORTER, DANIEL EDWARD	7360 COWLES MT BLVD - SAN DIEGO CA 92119
71- 82	PORTER, DARRELL RAY	OLD ADD: 3833 WEST 73RD ST - MILWAUKEE WI 53216
14-170	PORTER, IRVING MARBLE	D. FEBRUARY 20, 1971 LYNN, MASS.
52- 82	PORTER, J. W. 'JAY'	9677 HEATHER CIR W-PALM BCH GARDENS FL 33410
26- 65	PORTER, NED SWINDELL	D. JUNE 30, 1968 GAINESVILLE, FLA.
29- 84	PORTER, RICHARD TWILLEY	D. SEPTEMBER 24, 1974 PHILADELPHIA, PA.
81- 99	PORTER, ROBERT LEE	4 EDITH COURT PARK BLVD - NAPA CA 94558
48- 81	PORTERFIELD, ERWIN COOLIDGE 'BOB'	D. APRIL 28, 1980 CHARLOTTE, N. C.
48- 82	PORTO, ALFRED	40943 13TH STREET WEST - PALMDALE CA 93551
54- 83	PORTOCARRERO, ARNOLD MARIO	D. JUNE 21, 1986 KANSAS CITY, KAN.
85- 95	PORTUGAL, MARK STEVEN	14008 CROSSDALE - NORWALK CA 90650
60- 83	POSADA, LEOPOLDO JESUS	8200 GRAND CANAL - MIAMI FL 33126
38- 75	POSEDEL, WILLIAM JOHN	179 HAUS AVE - SAN LEANDRO CA 94577
32- 65	POSER, JOHN FALK 'BOB'	551 WEST SCHOOL - COLUMBUS WI 53925
46- 84	POSSEHL, LOUIS THOMAS	715 EL CENTRO - LONGBOAT KEY FL 34228
22-110	POST, SAMUEL GILBERT	D. MARCH 31, 1971 PORTSMOUTH, VA.
49- 66	POST, WALTER CHARLES	D. JANUARY 6, 1982 SAINT HENRY, O.
22-111	POTT, NELSON ADOLPH	D. DECEMBER 3, 1963 MACK, O.
38- 75	POTTER, MARYLAND DYKES	3024 WEST MUDDY BRANCH ROAD - ASHLAND KY 41101
76- 75	POTTER, MICHAEL GARY	21582 ARCHER CIR - HUNTINGTON BEACH CA 92646
36- 78	POTTER, NELSON THOMAS	408 SOUTH MCKENDRIE AVE #110 - MOUNT MORRIS IL 61054
23-105	POTTER, SQUIRE	D. JANUARY 27, 1983 ASHLAND, KY.
14-171	POTTS, JOHN FREDERICK	D. SEPTEMBER 5, 1962 CLEVELAND, O.
67- 86	POULSEN, KEN STERLING	684 EAST WEAVER - SIMI VALLEY CA 93065
87-120	POWELL, ALONZO SIDNEY	620 GARFIELD STREET - SAN FRANCISCO CA 94132
30- 63	POWELL, ALVIN JACOB 'JAKE'	D. NOVEMBER 4, 1948 WASHINGTON. D. C.
85- 96	POWELL, DENNIS CLAY	P. O. BOX 133 - NORMAN PARK GA 31771
63- 94	POWELL, GROVER DAVID	D. MAY 21, 1985 RALEIGH, N. C.
78-102	POWELL, HOSKEN	115 MEMORY LANE - PENSACOLA FL 32503
61- 85	POWELL, JOHN WESLEY 'BOOG'	U. S. ANGLERS MARINE - KEY WEST FL 33040
71- 83	POWELL, PAUL RAY	810 NORTH MYERS - ELOY AZ 85231
13-143	POWELL, RAYMOND REATH	D. OCTOBER 16, 1962 CHILLICOTHE, O .
13-144	POWELL, REGINALD BERTRAND 'JACK'	D. MARCH 12, 1930 MEMPHIS, TENN.
55- 94	POWELL, ROBERT LEROY	5366 STAMPA ST - LAS VEGAS NV 89102
81-100	POWER, TED HENRY	P.O. BOX 419969 - KANSAS CITY MO 64141
54- 84	POWER, VICTOR PELLOT	CONDOMINEO TORRE,MOLINOS 703-GUAYNABO PR00657
32- 66	POWERS, ELLIS FOREE 'MIKE'	D. DECEMBER 2, 1983 LOUISVILLE, KY.
55- 95	POWERS, JOHN CALVIN	6727 FIRST AVE SOUTH - BIRMINGHAM AL 35206
27- 72	POWERS, JOHN LLOYD 'IKE'	D. DECEMBER 22, 1968 HANCOCK, MD.
38- 77	POWERS, LESLIE EDWIN	D. NOVEMBER 13, 1978 SANTA MONICA, CALIF.
57- 70	POWIS, CARL EDGAR	OLD ADD: 8502 EASTON COMMONS #104 - HOUSTON TX 77095
75- 92	PRALL, WILFRED ANTHONY 'WILLIE'	351 TERHUNE AVE - PASSAIC NJ 07055
49- 67	PRAMESA, JOHN STEVEN	111 INLET OAKS VILLAGE - MURRELLS INLET SC 29576
12-158	PRATT, DERRILL BURNHAM 'DEL'	D. SEPTEMBER 30, 1977 TEXAS CITY, TEX.
21- 83	PRATT, FRANCIS BRUCE	D. APRIL 8, 1974 CENTREVILLE, ALA.
14-172	PRATT, LESTER JOHN 'LARRY'	D. JANUARY 8, 1969 PEORIA, ILL.
63- 95	PREGENZER, JOHN ARTHUR	6314 104TH ST EAST - PUYALLUP WA 98373
40- 71	PREIBISCH, MELVIN ADOLPHUS	D. APRIL 12, 1980 SEALY, TEXAS
48- 83	PRENDERGAST, JAMES BARTHOLOMEW	330 FAIRFIELD AVE - BUFFALO NY 14223
14-173	PRENDERGAST, MICHAEL THOMAS	D. NOVEMBER 18, 1967 OMAHA, NEB.
61- 86	PRESCOTT, GEORGE BERTRAND 'BOBBY'	ESTAFETA PARQUE LEFEVRE ENTREGA GENERAL-PANAMA 10, PAN.
51- 79	PRESKO, JOSEPH EDWARD	1612 NE 77TH TER - KANSAS CITY MO 64118
84- 90	PRESLEY, JAMES ARTHUR	1108 HUNTSMAN CIRCLE - PENSACOLA FL 32514
38- 78	PRESSNELL, FOREST CHARLES 'TOT'	329 EAST LIMA ST-FINDLAY OH 45840
67- 87	PRICE, JIMMIE WILLIAM	1160 WELCH ROAD - WALLED LAKE MI 48088
46- 85	PRICE, JOHN THOMAS REID 'JACKIE'	D. OCTOBER 2, 1967 SAN FRANCISCO, CAL.
28- 75	PRICE, JOSEPH PRESTON	D. JANUARY 15, 1961 WASHINGTON. D. C.
80-106	PRICE, JOSEPH WALTER	BOX 1696 - LAKESIDE CA 92040
39- 90	PRICHARD, ROBERT ALEXANDER	523 SUNSET DRIVE - STAMFORD TX 79553
41- 91	PRIDDY, GERALD EDWARD	D. MARCH 3, 1980 NORTH HOLLYWOOD, CALIF.
62-107	PRIDDY, ROBERT SIMPSON	OLD ADD: 519 NORTH CASCADE TER-SUNNYVALE CA94087
11-136	PRIEST, JOHN GOODING	D. NOVEMBER 4, 1979 WASHINGTON. D. C.
33- 52	PRIM, RAYMOND LEE	19120 D STREET - MONTE RIO CA 95462
62-108	PRINCE, DONALD MARK	5 BAHAMA DR - WRIGHTSVILLE BEACH NC 28480
87-121	PRINCE, THOMAS ALBERT	277 NORTH DOUGLAS - BRADLEY IL 60915
57- 71	PRITCHARD, HAROLD WILLIAM 'BUDDY'	507 EAST SUNNY HILL RD - FULLERTON CA 92635
59- 66	PROCTOR, JAMES ARTHUR	609 COUNT FLEET CT - NAPERVILLE IL 60540
23-106	PROCTOR, NOAH RICHARD 'RED'	D. DECEMBER 17, 1954 RICHMOND, VA.
76- 76	PROLY, MICHAEL JAMES	2585 FRISCO DR - CLEARWATER FL 33519
23-107	PROPST, WILLIAM JACOB 'JAKE'	D. FEBRUARY 24, 1967 COLUMBUS, MISS.
20- 97	PROTHRO, JAMES THOMPSON 'DOC'	D. OCTOBER 14, 1971 MEMPHIS, TENN.
12-160	PROUGH, HERSCHEL CLINTON 'BILL'	D. NOVEMBER 29, 1936 RICHMOND, IND.
29- 85	PRUDHOMME, JOHN OLGUS	5935 FAIRFIELD AVE - SHREVEPORT LA 71106
20- 98	PRUESS, EARL HENRY 'GIBBY'	D. AUGUST 28, 1979 BRANSON, MO.

Wally Post—Cincinnati Redlegs

  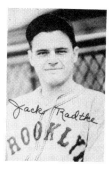 

```
22-112 PRUETT, HUBERT SHELBY            D. JANUARY 28, 1982 LADUE, MO.
44-107 PRUETT, JAMES CALVIN             1906 MADERA ST - WAUKESHA WI 53186
75- 93 PRUITT, RONALD RALPH             909 JOHNSON AVENUE - FLINT MI 48504
76- 77 PRYOR, GRDGORY RUSSELL           1135 GULF OF MEXICO #602-LONGBOAT KEY FL33548
30- 64 PUCCINELLI, GEORGE LAWRENCE      D. APRIL 16, 1956 SAN FRANCISCO, CAL.
84- 91 PUCKETT, KIRBY                   8924 ASHLEY TERRACE - BROOKLYN PARK MN 55443
11-137 PUCKETT, TROY LEVI               D. APRIL 13, 1971 WINCHESTER, IND.
70-109 PUENTE, MIGUEL ANTONIO           COBRE 106,COL MORALES-SAN LUIS POTOSI SAN LUIS POT MEX.
77-115 PUHL, TERRENCE STEPHEN           3523 GOLDEN TEE LN - MISSOURI CITY TX 77459
74-106 PUIG, RICHARD GERALD             16708 FOOTHILL DR - TAMPA FL 33624
77-116 PUJOLS, LUIS BIENVENIDO          NICOLAS HEREDIA - BANI DOMINICAN REP.
81-101 PULEO, CHARLES MICHAEL           8208 CORTELAND DRIVE - KNOXVILLE TN 37909
83-114 PULIDO, ALFONSO                  H.RICARDO MERCADO,CASILLAS 26-27-TIERRA BLANCA VER MEX.
25- 87 PUMPELLY, SPENCER ARMSTRONG      D. DECEMBER 5, 1973 SAYRE, PA.
64- 87 PURDIN, JOHN NOLAN               4748 GEORGE AVE - SARASOTA FL 33583
26- 66 PURDY, EVERETT VIRGIL 'PID'      D. JANUARY 16, 1951 BEATRICE, NEB.
54- 85 PURKEY, ROBERT THOMAS            5767 KING SCHOOL RD - BETHEL PARK PA 15102
76- 78 PUTMAN, EDDY WILLIAM             4 CAMPANA DRIVE - IRVINE CA 92720
77-117 PUTNAM, PATRICK EDWARD           309 MORSE PLAZA - TICE FL 33905
55- 96 PYBURN, JAMES EDWARD             RR 13 BOX 265 - JASPER AL 35501
54- 86 PYECHA, JOHN NICHOLAS            7015 FALCONBRIDGE RD - CHAPEL HILL NC 27514
39- 91 PYLE, EWALD                      538 HALLIDAY AVENUE - DUQUOIN IL 62832
28- 76 PYLE, HARLAN ALBERT              BOX 307 - LIBERTY NE 68381
32- 67 PYTLAK, FRANK ANTHONY            D. MAY 8, 1977 BUFFALO, N. Y.
86-125 PYZNARSKI, TIMOTHY MATTHEW       10716 SOUTH AUSTIN - CHICAGO RIDGE IL 60415
69-138 QUALLS, JAMES ROBERT             OLD ADD: RR 4 BOX 710 - LODI CA 95240
53- 72 QUALTERS, THOMAS FRANCIS         RR 2 BOX 39 - SOMERSET PA 15501
64- 88 QUEEN, MELVIN DOUGLAS            2130 NORTH MAIN - MORRO BAY CA 93442
42- 81 QUEEN, MELVIN JOSEPH             D. APRIL 4, 1982 FORT SMITH, ARK.
54- 87 QUEEN, WILLIAM EDDLEMAN          1616 EAST PERRY STREET - GASTONIA NC 28052
31- 72 QUELLICH, GEORGE WILLIAM         D. AUGUST 31, 1958 JOHNSVILLE, CALIF.
39- 92 QUICK, JAMES HAROLD              D. MARCH 9, 1974 SWANSEA, ILL.
65- 88 QUILICI, FRANK RALPH             BOX 3017 - NORTHBROOK IL 60062
13-145 QUINLAN, THOMAS ALOYSIUS 'FINNERS' D. FEBRUARY 17, 1966 SCRANTON, PA.
49- 68 QUINN, FRANK WILLIAM             OLD ADD: 530 SW 27TH WAY - BOYNTON BEACH FL 33435
11-138 QUINN, JOHN EDWARD PICK          D. APRIL 9, 1956 MARLBORO, MASS.
41- 92 QUINN, WELLINGTON HUNT 'WIMPY'   D. SEPTEMBER 1, 1954 LOS ANGELES, CAL.
83-115 QUINONES, LUIS RAUL              URB STA TERESITA CALLE 1 AE11-PONCE PR 00731
86-126 QUINONES, REY FRANCISCO          CLE RONDA 216 VILLA ANADALUCIA - RIO PIEDRAS PR 00926
74-107 QUINTANA, LUIS JOAQUIN           CASCRIO CATONI ED. 11 #70 - VEGA BAJA PR 00763
62-109 QUIRK, ARTHUR LINCOLN            27 PIPPIN DR - GLASTONBURY CT 06033
75- 94 QUIRK, JAMES PATRICK             8412 WEST 113TH TERRACE - OVERLAND PARK KS 66210
79- 87 QUISENBERRY, DANIEL RAYMOND      12208 BUENA VISTA - LEAWOOD KS 66209
82- 99 RABB, JOHN ANDREW                1321 WEST 106TH ST - LOS ANGELES CA 90014
22-113 RABBITT, JOSEPH PATRICK          D. DECEMBER 5, 1969 NORWALK, CONN.
57- 72 RABE, CHARLES HENRY              7725 LINDEN AVE - DARIEN IL 60559
40- 72 RACHUNOK, STEPHEN-STEPANOVICH    2660 WEST BALL ROAD #3 - ANAHEIM CA 92804
47- 70 RACKLEY, MARVIN EUGENE           3314 COVINGTON DR - DECATUR GA 30030
62-110 RADATZ, RICHARD RAYMOND          P.O. BOX 348,ATL. CONTAINER - BRAINTREE MA 02184
34- 88 RADCLIFF, RAYMOND ALLEN 'RIP'    D. MAY 23, 1962 ENID, OKLA.
11-139 RADEBAUGH, ROY                   D. JANUARY 17, 1945 CEDAR RAPIDS, IA.
71- 84 RADER, DAVID MARTIN              2114 OAKWOOD DR - BAKERSFIELD CA 93304
13-146 RADER, DONALD RUSSELL            D. JUNE 26, 1983 WALLA WALLA, WASH.
67- 88 RADER, DOUGLAS LEE               112-7 CEDAR POINT - STUART FL 33494
21- 84 RADER, DREW LEON                 D. JUNE 5, 1975 CATSKILL, N. Y.
36- 77 RADTKE, JACK WILLIAM             289 SOUTH LOCUST - TWIN FALLS ID 83301
54- 88 RAETHER, HAROLD HERMAN           5920 MEROLD DR - EDINA MN 55436
39- 93 RAFFENSBERGER, KENNETH DAVID     418 CLOVER DRIVE, RR 7 - YORK PA 17402
69-139 RAFFO, ALBERT MARTIN             BOX 866 - JASPER TN 37347
32- 68 RAGLAND, FRANK ROLAND            D. JULY 28, 1959 PARIS, MISS.
71- 85 RAGLAND, THOMAS                  20201 GREENLAWN ST - DETROIT MI 48224
75- 95 RAICH, ERIC JAMES                OLD ADD: 1625 WOODRUFF #45 - BELL CA 90201
57- 73 RAINES, LAWRENCE GLENN HOPE      D. JANUARY 28, 1978 LANSING, MICH.
79- 88 RAINES, TIMOTHY                  2316 AIRPORT BLVD - SANFORD FL 32771
79- 89 RAINEY, CHARLES DAVID            13340 GRANDVIA POINT - SAN DIEGO CA 92130
78-103 RAJSICH, DAVID CHRISTOPHER       5324 NORTH SIXTH ST - PHOENIX AZ 85012
82-100 RAJSICH, GARY LOUIS              5324 NORTH 6TH ST - PHOENIX AZ 85012
60- 84 RAKOW, EDWARD CHARLES            12259 HILLMAN CIR - LAKE PARK FL 33403
10-123 RALSTON, SAMUEL BERYL 'DOC'      D. AUGUST 29, 1950 LANCASTER, PA.
46- 86 RAMAZOTTI, ROBERT LOUIS          1111 SOUTH 26TH ST - ALTOONA PA 16602
39- 94 RAMBERT, ELMER DONALD 'PEP'      D. NOVEMBER 16, 1974 WEST PALM BEACH, FLA.
26- 67 RAMBO, WARREN DAWSON 'PETE'      CROWN POINT RD - THOROFARE NJ 08086
83-116 RAMIREZ, DANIEL ALLAN            2806 ERWIN - VICTORIA TX 77901
80-107 RAMIREZ, MARIO (TORRES)          RR 2 BOX 7 - YAUCO PR 00768
```

70-110 RAMIREZ, MILTON	7 TULIO LARRINAGA ST - MAYAGUEZ PR 00708
74-108 RAMIREZ, ORLANDO	TORICES PASO ABADIO #1325-CARTAGENA COLOMBIA S.A.
80-108 RAMIREZ, RAFAEL EMILIO	M.P. GAZETT #8,ENS. PRIMAVERA-SAN PEDRO DE MACORIS D.R.
78-104 RAMOS, DOMINGO ANTONIO	CARR DUARTE KM 8 1/2,LICEY AL MEDIO-SANTIAGO DOM. REP.
44-108 RAMOS, JESUS MANUEL GARCIA 'CHUCHO'	AVE SANTANDER, LAPINTA #4 - EL PARAISO VENEZ
55- 97 RAMOS, PEDRO	9367 FONTAINEBLEAU BLVD #G119 - MIAMI FL 33172
78-105 RAMOS, ROBERTO	3202 SW FIRST AVE - MIAMI FL 33129
47- 71 RAMSDELL, JAMES WILLARD 'WILLIE'	D. OCTOBER 8, 1969 WICHITA, KAN.
87-122 RAMSEY, MICHAEL JAMES	STAR ROUTE BOX 36F - HARLEM GA 30814
78-106 RAMSEY, MICHAEL JEFFREY	OLD ADD: 2900 CEDAR KNOLL DR - ROSWELL GA 30076
45- 83 RAMSEY, WILLIAM THRACE	769 ROSEBANK RD - MEMPHIS TN 38116
53- 73 RAND, RICHARD HILTON	18518 JEFFREY AVE - CERRITOS CA 90701
76- 79 RANDALL, ROBERT LEE	308 OPAL CIR - AMES IA 50010
71- 86 RANDLE, LEONARD SHENOFF	5101 LALUNA DRIVE - LAPALMA CA 90623
75- 96 RANDOLPH, WILLIE LARRY	648 JUNIPER PLACE - FRANKLIN LAKES NJ 07417
62-111 RANEW, MERRITT THOMAS	11339 HIGHWAY 326 - OCALA FL 32675
49- 69 RANEY, FRANK ROBERT DONALD 'RIBS'	11242 CHARLES DR - WARREN MI 48093
81-102 RANSOM, JEFFERY DEAN	2131 CURTIS ST - BERKELEY CA 94702
49- 70 RAPP, EARL WELLINGTON	301A SECOND STREET - SWEDESBORO NJ 08085
21- 85 RAPP, JOSEPH ALOYSIUS 'GOLDIE'	D. JULY 1, 1966 LAMESA, CALIF.
77-118 RAPP, VERNON FRED	14800 N. LOWELL BLVD - BLOOMFIELD CO 80020
46- 87 RASCHI, VICTOR JOHN ANGELO	1255 WEST WESTLAKE RD - CONESUS NY 14435
83-117 RASMUSSEN, DENNIS LEE	16210 WRIGHT CIRCLE - OMAHA NE 68130
75- 97 RASMUSSEN, ERIC RALPH	8829 NORTHWEST AVE - RACINE WI 53406
15-131 RASMUSSEN, HENRY FLORIAN	D. JANUARY 1, 1949 CHICAGO, ILL.
68- 82 RATH, FRED HELSHER	OLD ADD: 200 N. MIDLAND - LITTLE ROCK AR 72202
65- 89 RATLIFF, KELLY EUGENE 'GENE'	3403 MILLERFIELD RD - MACON GA 31201
63- 96 RATLIFF, PAUL HAWTHORNE	234 NORTH KENWOOD #304 - GLENDALE CA 91206
80-109 RATZER, STEVEN WAYNE	%C.EILERT,5310 HOLDER AVE-BALTIMORE MD 21214
72- 86 RAU, DOUGLAS JAMES	RR 1 BOX 154-A - COLUMBUS TX 78934
72- 87 RAUCH, ROBERT JOHN	OLD ADD: 1149 OLIVE RD - VIRGINIA BEACH VA 23462
66- 73 RAUDMAN, ROBERT JOYCE 'SHORTY'	OLD ADD: 17529 CHATSWORTH - GRANADA HILLS CA 91344

SHANE RAWLEY

77-119 RAUTZHAN, CLARENCE GEORGE 'LANCE'	RR 4 BOX 4454 - POTTSVILLE PA 17901
78-107 RAWLEY, SHANE WILLIAM	6315 APPROACH ROAD - SARASOTA FL 33583
14-174 RAWLINGS, JOHN WILLIAM	D. OCTOBER 16, 1972 INGLEWOOD, CALIF.
15-132 RAY, CARL GRADY	D. APRIL 3, 1970 WALNUT COVE, N.C.
65- 90 RAY, JAMES FRANCIS	OLD ADD: 7530 PROMPTON - HOUSTON TX 77025
81-103 RAY, JOHN CORNELIAS	RR 1 BOX 64 - CHAUTEAU OK 74337
82-101 RAY, LARRY DOYLE	OLD ADD: RR 3 - VEVAY IN 47043
10-124 RAY, ROBERT HENRY 'FARMER'	D. MARCH 11, 1963 ELECTRA, TEX.
58- 74 RAYDON, CURTIS LOWELL	1515 SOUTH BUNN ST - BLOOMINTON IL 61701
80-110 RAYFORD, FLOYD KINNARD	2518 HUDSPETH ST - INGLEWOOD CA 90303
59- 67 RAYMOND, JOSEPH CLAUDE	3 DE LA CITIERE, B.P. 911 - ST. LUC QUEBEC JOJ 2A0 CAN.
19- 66 RAYMOND, LOUIS ANTHONY	D. MAY 2, 1979 ROCHESTER, N. Y.
73- 99 RAZIANO, BARRY JOHN	1315 4TH ST - KENNER LA 70062
83-118 READY, RANDY MAX	4050 NORTH HIDDEN COVE PLACE - TUCSON AZ 85749
69-140 REAMS, LEROY	1638 85TH AVE - OAKLAND CA 94621
79- 90 REARDON, JEFFREY JAMES	4 MARLWOOD LN - PALM BEACH GARDENS FL 33410
38- 79 REBEL, ARTHUR ANTHONY	1726 WEST FORE DR-TAMPA FL 33610
68- 83 REBERGER, FRANK BEALL	1790 HILL ROAD - BOISE ID 83702
12-161 REDDING, PHILIP HAYDEN	D. MARCH 30, 1929 GREENWOOD, MISS.
32- 69 REDER, JOHN ANTHONY	BOX 1892 - FALL RIVER MA 02722
28- 77 REDFERN, GEORGE HOWARD 'BUCK'	D. SEPTEMBER 8, 1964 ASHEVILLE, N. C.
76- 80 REDFERN, PETER IRVINE	15131 PADDOCK - SYLMAR CA 91342
74-109 REDMON, GLENN VINCENT	BETHESDA BAPTIST CHURCH - BROWNSBURG IN 46112
65- 91 REDMOND, HOWARD WAYNE	OLD ADD: 16557 HEYDEN - DETROIT MI 48235
35- 92 REDMOND, JACKSON MCKITTRICK	D. JULY 28, 1968 GARLAND, TEX.
82-102 REDUS, GARY EUGENE	BOX 202 - TANNER AL 35671
78-108 REECE, ROBERT SCOTT	1906 WEST 23RD ST - LOVELAND CO 80537
58- 75 REED, HOWARD DEAN	D. DECEMBER 7, 1984 CORPUS CHRISTI, TEX.
84- 92 REED, JEFF SCOTT	RR 7 BOX 3570 - ELIZABETHTON TN 37643
81-104 REED, JERRY MAXWELL	21 GRANDVIEW RD - ASHEVILLE NC 28806
87-123 REED, JODY ERIC	2319 MERRILY CIRCLE NORTH - SEFFNER FL 33584
61- 87 REED, JOHN BURWELL	BOX 97 - SILVER CITY MS 39166
11-140 REED, MILTON D.	D. JULY 27, 1938 ATLANTA, GA.
15-133 REED, RALPH EDWIN 'TED'	D. FEBRUARY 16, 1959 BEAVER, PA.
69-141 REED, ROBERT EDWARD	108 ESSEX DRIVE - LONGWOOD FL 32750
66- 74 REED, RONALD LEE	2613 CLIFFVIEW DR - LILBURN GA 30247
52- 83 REED, WILLIAM JOSEPH	11807 MARRS - HOUSTON TX 77065
49- 71 REEDER, WILLIAM EDGAR	BOX 812 - WHITNEY TX 76692
18- 62 REES, STANLEY MILTON	D. AUGUST 29, 1937 LEXINGTON, KY.
27- 73 REESE, ANDREW JACKSON	D. JANUARY 10, 1966 TUPELO, MISS.
40- 73 REESE, HAROLD HENRY 'PEE WEE'	3211 BEALS BRANCH RD-LOUISVILLE KY 40206
30- 65 REESE, JAMES HERMAN	10797 ASHTON AVE - LOS ANGELES CA 90024

64- 89	REESE, RICHARD BENJAMIN	1709 SHAWNEE TRAIL - NORTHBROOK IL 60062
26- 68	REEVES, ROBERT EDWIN	702 BELVOIR AVE - CHATTANOOGA TN 37412
54- 89	REGALADO, RUDOLPH VALENTINO	5122 LOS ALTOS COURT - SAN DIEGO CA 92109
17- 66	REGAN, MICHAEL JOHN	D. MAY 23, 1961 ALBANY, N. Y.
60- 85	REGAN, PHILIP RAYMOND	1375 108TH ST - BYRON CENTER MI 49315
26- 69	REGAN, WILLIAM WRIGHT	D. JUNE 11, 1968 PITTSBURGH, PA.
24- 87	REGO, ANTONE	D. JANUARY 6, 1978 TULSA, OKLA.
12-162	REHG, WALTER PHILLIP	D. AUGUST 5, 1946 BURBANK, CALIF.
33- 53	REIBER, FRANK BERNARD	BOX 6284 - SARASOTA FL 33578
49- 72	REICH, HERMAN CHARLES	3779 PALA MESA DR - FALLBROOK CA 92028
64- 90	REICHARDT, FREDERIC CARL 'RICK'	2605 NW 90TH TER - GAINESVILLE FL 32606
22-114	REICHLE, RICHARD WENDELL	D. JUNE 13, 1967 ST. LOUIS, MO.
46- 88	REID, EARL PERCY	D. MAY 11, 1984 CULLMAN, ALA.
87-124	REID, JESSIE THOMAS	3614 CEDAR AVENUE - LYNWOOD CA 90262
69-142	REID, SCOTT DONALD	3611 EAST NAMBE COURT - PHOENIX AZ 85044
17- 67	REILLY, ARCHER EDWIN	D. NOVEMBER 29, 1963 COLUMBUS, O.
19- 67	REILLY, HAROLD J.	
74-110	REINBACH, MICHAEL WAYNE	% CREAMER, 9459 SLOPE ST - SANTEE CA 92071
19- 68	REINHART, ARTHUR CONRAD	D. NOVEMBER 11, 1946 HOUSTON, TEX.
28- 78	REINHOLZ, ARTHUR AUGUST	D. DECEMBER 29, 1980 NEWPORT RICHEY, FLA.
15-134	REINICKER, WALTER JOSEPH	D. APRIL 18, 1957 PITTSBURGH, PA.
11-141	REIS, HARRIE CRANE 'JACK'	D. JULY 20, 1939 CINCINNATI, O.
31- 73	REIS, ROBERT JOSEPH THOMAS	D. MAY 1, 1973 ST. PAUL, MINN.
38- 80	REIS, THOMAS EDWARD	41 HOLLY LN - FORT THOMAS KY 41075
40- 74	REISER, HAROLD PATRICK 'PETE'	D. OCTOBER 25, 1981 PALM SPRINGS, CALIF.
11-142	REISIGL, JACOB 'BUGGS'	D. FEBRUARY 24, 1957 AMSTERDAM, N.Y.
32- 70	REISS, ALBERT ALLEN	10 BLOSSOM LANE EAST - MIDDLETOWN NJ 07748
72- 88	REITZ, KENNETH JOHN	7541 WARNER - SAINT LOUIS MO 63117
79- 91	REMMERSWAAL, WILHELMUS ABRAHAM	DOKTOR VAN PRAAG ST 16 - WASSENAAR HOLLAND EUROP
12-163	REMNEAS, ALEXANDER NORMAN	D. AUGUST 27, 1975 PHOENIX, ARIZ.
75- 98	REMY, GERALD PETER	5 DENNIS DR - WESTPORT MA 02790
13-147	RENFER, ERWIN ARTHUR	D. OCTOBER 26, 1957 SYCAMORE, ILL.
59- 68	RENFROE, MARSHALL DALTON	D. DECEMBER 10, 1970 PENSACOLA, FLA.
68- 84	RENICK, WARREN RICHARD 'RICK'	4374 MEADOWLAND CIR - SARASOTA FL 33583
61- 88	RENIFF, HAROLD EUGENE	424 STAFFORD - SCRANTON PA 18505
38- 81	RENINGER, JAMES DAVID	BOX 9051 - SHAWNEE MISSION KS 66201
69-143	RENKO, STEVEN	10347 ALHAMBRA - OVERLAND PARK KS 66207
53- 74	RENNA, WILLIAM BENEDITTO	1476 LESHER CT - SAN JOSE CA 95125
30- 66	RENSA, GEORGE ANTHONY 'TONY'	D. JANUARY 4, 1987 WILKES-BARRE, PA.
86-127	RENTERIA, RICHARD AVINA	2645 NEBRASKA AVENUE - SOUTH GATE CA 90280
39- 95	REPASS, ROBERT WILLIS	169 BRIMFIELD RD-WETHERSFIELD CT 06109
78-109	REPLOGLE, ANDREW DAVID	1115 YELLOWWOOD CIR - NOBLESVILLE IN 46060
64- 91	REPOZ, ROGER ALLEN	1106 IRVING ST - BELLINGHAM WA 98225
53- 75	REPULSKI, ELDON JOHN 'RIP'	1541 8TH AVE NORTH - ST CLOUD MN 56301
43-114	RESCIGNO, XAVIER FREDERICK	163E FALMOUTH COURT - RIDGE NY 11961
49- 73	RESTELLI, DINO PAUL	1860 SAN CARLOS AVE - SAN CARLOS CA 94070
68- 85	RETTENMUND, MERVIN WELDON	16670 ESPOLA RD - POWAY CA 92064
22-115	RETTIG, ADOLPH JOHN 'OTTO'	D. JUNE 16, 1977 STUART, FLA.
61- 89	RETZER, KENNETH LEO	137 HICKORY STREET - WOOD RIVER IL 62095
75- 99	REUSCHEL, PAUL RICHARD	RR 1 BOX 76 - CAMP POINT IL 62320
72- 89	REUSCHEL, RICK EUGENE	618 EAST MAUDE - ARLINGTON HEIGHTS IL 60004
69-144	REUSS, JERRY	324 WEST 35TH STREET - CHICAGO IL 60616
78-110	REVERING, DAVID ALVIN	9050 EAST PARADISE DRIVE - SCOTTSDALE AZ 85260
83-119	REYES, GILBERTO ROLANDO	CALLE 2DA. #7 LOS MAMEYES - SANTO DOMINGO DOM. REP.
43-115	REYES, NAPOLEON AGUILERA	2203 NW 33RD ST - MIAMI FL 33142
42- 82	REYNOLDS, ALLIE PIERCE	2525 CASHION PL-OKLAHOMA CITY OK 73112
68- 86	REYNOLDS, ARCHIE EDWARD	601 PHEASANT RUN - BURLESON TX 76028
27- 74	REYNOLDS, CARL NETTLES	D. MAY 29, 1978 HOUSTON, TEX.
45- 84	REYNOLDS, DANIEL VANCE	BOX 55 - SCOTTS NC 28699
78-111	REYNOLDS, DONALD EDWARD	2605 SOUTHEAST RYAN - CORVALLIS OR 97330
75-100	REYNOLDS, GORDON CRAIG	5906 PARADISE VALLEY COURT - HOUSTON TX 77069
83-120	REYNOLDS, HAROLD CRAIG	2605 SE RYAN ST - CORVALLIS OR 97330
70-111	REYNOLDS, KENNETH LEE	182 GREENWOOD - MARLBOROUGH MA 01752
69-145	REYNOLDS, ROBERT ALLEN	32304 FOURTH PL #R12 - FEDERAL WAY WA 98003
83-121	REYNOLDS, ROBERT JAMES	7076 EL SORENO CIR - SACRAMENTO CA 95831
82-103	REYNOLDS, RONN DWAYNE	133 LONGWOOD AVENUE - AUSTIN TX 78748
14-175	REYNOLDS, ROSS ERNEST	D. JUNE 23, 1970 ADA, OKLA.
63- 97	REYNOLDS, THOMAS D	1577 SAN ALTOS - LEMON GROVE CA 92045
13-148	REYNOLDS, WILLIAM DEE	D. JUNE 5, 1924 CARNEGIE, OKLA.
47- 72	RHAWN, ROBERT JOHN	D. JUNE 9, 1984 DANVILLE, PA.
14-176	RHEAM, KENNETH JOHNSTON 'CY'	D. OCTOBER 23, 1947 PITTSBURGH, PA.
24- 88	RHEM, CHARLES FLINT	D. JULY 30, 1969 COLUMBIA, S. C.
29- 86	RHIEL, WILLIAM JOSEPH	D. AUGUST 16, 1946 YOUNGSTOWN, O.
74-111	RHODEN, RICHARD ALAN	235 SW 12TH AVENUE - BOYNTON BEACH FL 33435

52- 84 RHODES, JAMES LAMAR "DUSTY"   245 DIXON AVE - STATEN ISLAND NY 10303
29- 87 RHODES, JOHN GORDON   D. MARCH 22, 1960 LONG BEACH, CAL.
82-104 RHOMBERG, KEVIN JAY   5786 BEACH DR - MENTOR ON THE LAKE OH 44060
26- 70 RHYNE, HAROLD J.   D. JANUARY 7, 1971 ORANGEVALE, CAL.
64- 92 RIBANT, DENNIS JOSEPH   18201 VON KARMAN AVE #900 - IRVINE CA 92715
76- 81 RICCELLI, FRANK JOSEPH   P.O. BOX 6774 - SYRACUSE NY 13203
45- 85 RICE, DELBERT W   D. JANUARY 26, 1983 BUENA PARK, CALIF.
15-135 RICE, EDGAR CHARLES 'SAM'   D. OCTOBER 13, 1974 ROSSMOR, MD.
48- 84 RICE, HAROLD HOUSTON   %RON RICE,1008 W. HAINES AVE-MUNCIE IN 47303
23-108 RICE, HARRY FRANCIS 'SAM'   D. JANUARY 1, 1971 PORTLAND, ORE.
74-112 RICE, JAMES EDWARD   135 WODEN WAY - WINTER HAVEN FL 33880
44-109 RICE, LEONARD OLIVER   BOX 54 - ARNOLD CA 95223
26- 71 RICE, ROBERT TURNBULL   D. FEBRUARY 20, 1986 ELIZABETHTOWN, PA.
39- 96 RICH, WOODROW EARL   D. APRIL 18, 1983 MORGANTON, N.C.
71- 87 RICHARD, JAMES RODNEY   10235 SAGEDALE - HOUSTON TX 77089
71- 88 RICHARD, LEE EDWARD 'BEE BEE'   1621 EAST 14TH ST - PORT ARTHUR TX 77640
60- 86 RICHARDS, DUANE LEE   BOX 54 - PALESTINE OH 45352
77-120 RICHARDS, EUGENE   2 WOODSPRING CT - COLUMBIA SC 29210
51- 80 RICHARDS, FRED CHARLES   1760 DODGE NW - WARREN OH 44485
32- 71 RICHARDS, PAUL RAPIER   D. MAY 5, 1986 WAXAHACHIE, TEXAS
29- 88 RICHARDSON, CLIFFORD NOLEN   D. SEPTEMBER 25, 1951 ATHENS, GA.
64- 93 RICHARDSON, GORDON CLARK   RR 3 BOX 217 - COLQUITT GA 31737

15-136 RICHARDSON, JOHN WILLIAM   D. JANUARY 18, 1970 MARION, ILL.
42- 83 RICHARDSON, KENNETH FRANKLIN   4722 ASHBURY AVE,%SUSAN GRAY - CYPRESS CA 90630
55- 98 RICHARDSON, ROBERT CLINTON   47 ADAMS - SUMTER SC 29150
17- 68 RICHARDSON, THOMAS MITCHELL   D. NOVEMBER 15, 1939 ONAWA, IA.
80-111 RICHARDT, MICHAEL ANTHONY   3555 WEST BULLARD - FRESNO CA 93711
21- 86 RICHBOURG, LANCE CLAYTON   D. SEPTEMBER 10, 1975 CRESTVIEW, FLA.
62-112 RICHERT, PETER GERARD   5932 PARADISE PLAZA - PALM SPRINGS CA 92264
33- 54 RICHMOND, BERYL JUSTICE   D. APRIL 24, 1980 CAMERON, W. VA.
41- 93 RICHMOND, DONALD LESTER   D. MAY 24, 1981 ELMIRA, N. Y.
20- 99 RICHMOND, RAYMOND SINCLAIR   D. OCTOBER 21, 1969 DESOTO, MO.
51- 81 RICHTER, ALLEN GORDON   BOX 4 - VIRGINIA BEACH VA 23458
11-143 RICHTER, EMIL HENRY 'REGGIE'   D. AUGUST 3, 1934 CHICAGO, ILL.
42- 84 RICKERT, MARVIN AUGUST   D. JUNE 3, 1978 OAKVILLE, WASH.
63- 98 RICKETTS, DAVID WILLIAM   717 SEWARD ST - ROCHESTER NY 14611
59- 69 RICKETTS, RICHARD JAMES   D. MARCH 6, 1988 ROCHESTER, N.Y.
69-146 RICO, ALFREDO CRUZ 'FRED'   5207 TEESDALE - NORTH HOLLYWOOD CA 91607
16- 70 RICO, ARTHUR RAYMOND   D. JANUARY 3, 1919 BOSTON, MASS.
23-109 RICONDA, HARRY PAUL   D. NOVEMBER 15, 1958 MAHOPAC, N. Y.
39- 97 RIDDLE, ELMER RAY   D. MAY 14, 1984 COLUMBUS, GA.
30- 67 RIDDLE, JOHN LUDY   5445 FALLWOOD DRIVE #104 - INDIANAPOLIS IN 46220
70-112 RIDDLEBERGER, DENNIS MICHAEL   5001 NORTH REESE DRIVE - PORTSMOUTH VA 23703
14-177 RIDGWAY, JACOB A. 'JOHN'   D. FEBRUARY 23, 1928 PHILADELPHIA, PA.
50- 81 RIDZIK, STEPHEN GEORGE   910 TROPICAL DRIVE - BRADENTON FL 33508
42- 85 RIEBE, HARVEY DONALD 'HANK'   28031 LAKE SHORE BLVD-CLEVELAND OH 44132
10-125 RIEGER, ELMER JAY   D. OCTOBER 21, 1944 LOS ANGELES, CALIF.
11-144 RIGGERT, JOSEPH ALOYSIUS   D. DECEMBER 10, 1973 KANSAS CITY, MO.
34- 89 RIGGS, LEWIS SIDNEY   D. AUGUST 12, 1975 DURHAM, N. C.
79- 92 RIGHETTI, DAVID ALLAN   1574 KOCH LN - SAN JOSE CA 95125
22-116 RIGNEY, EMORY ELMO 'TOPPER'   D. JUNE 6, 1972 SAN ANTONIO, TEX.
37- 90 RIGNEY, JOHN DUNGAN   D. OCTOBER 21, 1984 LOMBARD, ILL.
46- 89 RIGNEY, WILLIAM JOSEPH   3136 ROUND HILL RD - ALAMO CA 94507
84- 93 RIJO, JOSE ANTONIO   CENTRAL CABRAL #66 - SAN CRISTOBAL DOMINICAN REP.
41- 94 RIKARD, CULLEY   50 HWY 304 - OLIVE BRANCH MS 38654
85- 97 RILES, ERNEST   RR 1 BOX 38 - WHIGHAM GA 31797
79- 93 RILEY, GEORGE MICHAEL   2900 OLLEY TURNPIKE RD - READING PA 19606
10-126 RILEY, JAMES JOSEPH   D. MARCH 25, 1949 BUFFALO, N.Y.
21- 87 RILEY, JAMES NORMAN   D. MAY 25, 1969 SEQUIN, TEXAS
44-110 RILEY, LEON FRANCIS   D. SEPTEMBER 13, 1970 SCHENECTADY, N. Y.
80-112 RINCON, ANDREW JOHN   5425 LOS TOROS - PICO RIVERA CA 90660
79- 94 RINEER, JEFFREY ALAN   RR 1 BOX 81A - PEQUEA PA 17565
17- 69 RING, JAMES JOSEPH   D. JULY 2, 1965 NEW YORK, N. Y.
50- 82 RINKER, ROBERT JOHN   10 NORTH MADISON - MCADOO PA 18237
69-147 RIOS, JUAN ONOFRE VELEZ   OLD ADD: 95 TANCA STREET - SAN SEBASTIAN PR 00755
85- 98 RIPKEN, CALVIN EDWIN, SR.   410 CLOVER ST - ABERDEEN MD 21001
81-105 RIPKEN, CALVIN EDWIN JR.   410 CLOVER ST - ABERDEEN MD 21001
87-125 RIPKEN, WILLIAM OLIVER   322 LIMESTONE VALLEY DR #H - COCKEYSVILLE MD 21030
78-112 RIPLEY, ALLEN STEVENS   BOX 349 %A. COOPER - NORTH ATTLEBORO MA 02760
35- 93 RIPLEY, WALTER FRANKLIN   55 WEST ST - NORTH ATTLEBORO MA 02760
62-113 RIPPELMEYER, RAYMOND ROY   RR 2 BOX 34 - VALMEYER IL 62295
44-111 RIPPLE, CHARLES DAWSON   D. MAY 6, 1979 WILMINGTON, N. C.
36- 78 RIPPLE, JAMES ALBERT   D. JULY 16, 1959 GREENSBURG, PA.
17- 70 RISBERG, CHARLES AUGUST 'SWEDE'   D. OCTOBER 13, 1975 RED BLUFF, CAL.

```
64- 94  RITCHIE, JAY SEAY                        1108 TERRACE DR - SALISBURY NC 28144
87-126  RITCHIE, WALLACE REID                    341 WONDERVIEW DRIVE - GLENDALE CA 91202
86-128  RITTER, REGGIE BLAKE                     RURAL ROUTE 1 BOX 297 - DONALDSON AR 71941
12-164  RITTER, WILLIAM HERBERT 'HANK'           D. SEPTEMBER 3, 1964 AKRON, O.
70-113  RITTWAGE, JAMES MICHAEL                  23931 COLUMBUS RD - BEDFORD HEIGHTS OH 44146
83-122  RIVERA, GERMAN (DIAZ)                    VIA LETICIA #4E-S4,V.FONTANA - CAROLINA PR 00630
75-101  RIVERA, JESUS MANUEL 'BOMBO'             G#2 AMALIA MARIN - PONCE PR 00732
86-129  RIVERA, LUIS ANTONIO                     LAZARO RAMOS #16 - CIDRA PR 00639
52- 85  RIVERA, MANUEL JOSEPH 'JIM'              RR 5 BOX 90 - ANGOLA IN 46703
70-114  RIVERS, JOHN MILTON 'MICKEY'             350 NW 48TH ST - MIAMI FL 33127
21- 88  RIVIERE, ARTHUR BERNARD 'TINK'           D. SEPTEMBER 27, 1965 LIBERTY, TEX.
12-165  RIXEY, EPPA                              D. FEBRUARY 28, 1963 TERRACE PARK, O.
38- 82  RIZZO, JOHN COSTA                        D. DECEMBER 4, 1977 HOUSTON, TEX.
```

```
41- 95  RIZZUTO, PHILIP FRANCIS                  912 WESTMINSTER AVE-HILLSIDE NJ 07205
53- 76  ROACH, MELVIN EARL                       106 WEST 30TH ST - RICHMOND VA 23225
10-127  ROACH, WILBUR CHARLES 'ROXY'             D. DECEMBER 26, 1947 BAY CITY, MICH.
61- 90  ROARKE, MICHAEL THOMAS                   11 ROSEVIEW DR - CRANSTON RI 02910
79- 95  ROBBINS, BRUCE DUANE                     3518 HIGHFIELD CT #B - INDIANAPOLIS IN 46222
33- 55  ROBELLO, THOMAS VARDASCO 'TONY'          3504 WESLEY AV - FORT WORTH TX 76111
79- 96  ROBERGE, BERTRAND ROLAND                 267 SUNDERLAND DRIVE - AUBURN ME 04210
41- 96  ROBERGE, JOSEPH ALBERT ARMAND 'SKIPPY'   173 CRAWFORD - LOWELL MA 01854
43-116  ROBERTS, CHARLES EMORY                   4705 WEST HIGHWAY 166 - CARROLLTON GA 30117
13-149  ROBERTS, CLARENCE ASHLEY 'SKIPPER'       D. DECEMBER 24, 1963 LONG BEACH, CALIF.
54- 90  ROBERTS, CURTIS BENJAMIN                 D. NOVEMBER 14, 1969 OAKLAND, CALIF
67- 89  ROBERTS, DALE                            206 BERRY AVE - VERSAILLES KY 40383
69-148  ROBERTS, DAVID ARTHUR                    OLD ADD: 6629 MAYARD - HOUSTON TX 77041
62-114  ROBERTS, DAVID LEONARD                   17510 MAYALL ST - NORTHRIDGE CA 91324
72- 90  ROBERTS, DAVID WAYNE                     2663 NW BLUEBELL - CORVALLIS OR 97330
24- 89  ROBERTS, JAMES NEWSOM                    D. JUNE 24, 1984 COLUMBUS, MISS.
86-130  ROBERTS, LEON JOSEPH 'BIP'               7706 TWIN HILLS - HOUSTON TX 77071
74-113  ROBERTS, LEON KAUFFMAN                   3200 TRANQUILITY - ARLINGTON TX 76016
19- 69  ROBERTS, RAYMOND                         D. JANUARY 30, 1962 CRUGER, MISS.
48- 85  ROBERTS, ROBIN EVAN                      504 TERRACE HILL DR - TEMPLE TERRACE FL 33617
54- 91  ROBERTSON, ALFRED JAMES 'JIM'            3342 AYITA CIR - LAS VEGAS NV 89109
81-106  ROBERTSON, ANDRE LEVETT                  2229 CROSS LN ST - ORANGE TX 77360
19- 70  ROBERTSON, CHARLES CULBERTSON            D. AUGUST 23, 1984 FORT WORTH, TEX.
62-115  ROBERTSON, DARYL BERDINE                 755 PRINCTON DR - MIDVALE UT 84047
12-166  ROBERTSON, DAVIS AYDELOTRE               D. NOVEMBER 5, 1970 VIRGINIA BEACH, VA.
54- 92  ROBERTSON, DONALD ALEXANDER              422 DOGWOOD ST - PARK FOREST IL 60466
19- 99  ROBERTSON, EUGENE EDWARD                 D. OCTOBER 21, 1981 FALLON, NEV.
69-149  ROBERTSON, JERRY LEE                     3251 PLASS - TOPEKA KS 66611
13-150  ROBERTSON, PRESTON                       D. OCTOBER 2, 1944 NEW ORLEANS, LA.
66- 75  ROBERTSON, RICHARD PAUL                  5823 RANDLESWOOD COURT - SAN JOSE CA 95129
67- 90  ROBERTSON, ROBERT EUGENE                 RR 1 SHINNAMON DR - LAVALE MD 21502
40- 75  ROBERTSON, SHERRARD ALEXANDER            D. OCTOBER 23, 1970 HOUGHTON, S. D.
85- 99  ROBIDOUX, WILLIAM JOSEPH 'BILLY JOE'     RR BOX 148 - WARE MA 01082
43-117  ROBINSON, AARON ANDREW                   D. MARCH 9, 1966 LANCASTER,O.
55- 99  ROBINSON, BROOKS CALBERT                 1506 SHERBROOK RD - LUTHERVILLE MD 21093
78-113  ROBINSON, BRUCE PHILLIP                  3968 SAN AUGUSTINE WAY - SAN DIEGO CA 92130
72- 91  ROBINSON, CRAIG GEORGE                   P.O. BOX 814 - PULASKI VA 24301
70-115  ROBINSON, DAVID TANNER                   6140 CAMINO DEL RIO - SAN DIEGO CA 92120
79- 97  ROBINSON, DEWEY EVERETT                  1733 WEST ARTHUR AVE - CHICAGO IL 60626
78-114  ROBINSON, DON ALLEN                      2012 POPLAR ST - KENOVA WV 25530
58- 76  ROBINSON, EARL JOHN                      6895 OAKWOOD DRIVE - OAKLAND CA 94611
60- 87  ROBINSON, FLOYD ANDREW                   5837 MARKET - SAN DIEGO CA 92114
56- 73  ROBINSON, FRANK                          15557 AQUA VERDE DR - LOS ANGELES CA 90077
55-100  ROBINSON, HUMBERTO VALENTINO             1695 BROOKLYN AVE - BROOKLYN NY 11210
47- 73  ROBINSON, JACK ROOSEVELT                 D. OCTOBER 24, 1972 STAMFORD, CONN.
84- 94  ROBINSON, JEFFREY DANIEL                 28821 GREENACRES - MISSION VIEJO CA 92692
87-127  ROBINSON, JEFFREY MARK                   1579 SAXON PLACE - EL CAJON CA 92021
```

49- 74	ROBINSON, JOHN EDWARD	210 FLORIDA SHORE BLVD - DAYTONE BEACH SHORE FL 32018
11-145	ROBINSON, JOHN HENRY 'HANK'	D. JULY 3, 1965 NORTH LITTLE ROCK, ARK.
84- 95	ROBINSON, RONALD DEAN	473 PINE ST - WOODLAKE CA 93286
42- 86	ROBINSON, WILLIAM EDWARD 'EDDIE'	6104 CHOLLA DR - FORT WORTH TX 76102
66- 76	ROBINSON, WILLIAM HENRY	RR 3 BOX 179A - SEWELL NJ 08080
69-150	ROBLES, RAFAEL RADAMES	INGENIO QUISQUEYA-SAN PEDRO DE MACORIS DOM. REP.
72- 92	ROBLES, SERGIO	ESCOBEDO #402 - MAGDALENA SONORA MEX.
74-114	ROBSON, THOMAS JAMES	611 EAST ALAMEDA DR - TEMPE AZ 85282
43-118	ROCCO, MICHAEL DOMINICK 'MICKEY'	868 WEST IOWA AVE - ST PAUL MN 55117
45- 86	ROCHE, ARMANDO BAEZ	OLD ADD: AVE LOS PINOS - HAVANA CUBA
14-178	ROCHE, JOHN JOSEPH	D. MARCH 31, 1983 PEORIA, ARIZ.
14-179	ROCHEFORT, BENNETT HAROLD	D. APRIL 2, 1981 RED BANK, N. J.
44-112	ROCHELLI, LOUIS JOSEPH	501 RATTON - VICTORIA TX 77901
36- 79	ROCK, LESTER HENRY	1027 OLIVE DR #6 - DAVIS CA 95616
76- 82	ROCKETT, PATRICK EDWARD	1335 VIEWRIDGE - SAN ANTONIO TX 78213
83-123	RODAS, RICHARD MARTIN	4945 STAMAS LANE #5 - FAIR OAKS CA 95628
57- 74	RODGERS, KENNETH ANDRE IAN	BOX N386 - NASSAU BAHAMAS W.I.
61- 91	RODGERS, ROBERT LEROY	5181 WEST KNOLL DR - YORBA LINDA CA 92686
15-137	RODGERS, WILBUR KINCAID	D. DECEMBER 24, 1978 GOLIAD, TEX.
44-113	RODGERS, WILLIAM SHERMAN	1433 NAUDAIN - HARRISBURG PA 17104
54- 93	RODIN, ERIC CHAPMAN	947 GARFIELD AVE - BRIDGEWATER TOWNSHIP NJ 08807
67- 91	RODRIGUEZ, AURELIO ITUARTE	BAHIA DE TOPOLOBAMPO,#197 SUR - LOS MOCHIS SONORA MEX.
73-100	RODRIGUEZ, EDUARDO	URB. CATALINA CALLE 4 #E34 - BARCELONETA PR 00617
82-105	RODRIGUEZ, EDWIN (MORALES)	JARDINES CARIBE 28 ST #Z-3 - PONCE PR 00731
68- 87	RODRIGUEZ, ELISEO C.'ELLIE'	LAGO VISTA #2 BLDG 29 #C - LEVITTOWN LAKES PR 00619
58- 77	RODRIGUEZ, FERNANDO PEDRO 'FREDDY'	OLD ADD: 555 MAYIA RODRIGUEZ - HAVANA CUBA
52- 86	RODRIGUEZ, HECTOR ANTONIO	OLD ADD: %A.CANIZARES,CERT. 99-A COL. POSTAL-MEXICO DF
16- 71	RODRIGUEZ, JOSE	D. MARCH 23, 1948 HAVANA, CUBA
86-131	RODRIGUEZ, RICARDO	5014 PROCTOR ROAD - CASTRO VALLEY CA 94546
67- 92	RODRIGUEZ, ROBERTO MUNOZ	CORTIJITO DESARRIAS,8 CJN RECOBE 30 - CARACAS VENEZ
86-132	RODRIGUEZ, RUBEN DARIO	10 #17 ENSANCHE LUPERON - SANTO DOMINGO DOMINICAN REP.
84- 96	RODRIGUEZ, VICTOR MANUEL	APTO. 464K., BO MAIZALES - NAGUABO PR 00718
38- 83	ROE, ELWIN CHARLES 'PREACHER'	204 WILDWOOD TER - WEST PLAINS MO 65775
23-110	ROE, JAMES CLAY	D. APRIL 3, 1956 CLEVELAND, MISS.
55-101	ROEBUCK, EDWARD JACK	3434 WARWOOD RD - LAKEWOOD CA 90712
76- 83	ROENICKE, GARY STEVEN	10800 MILL SPRINGS DRIVE - NEVADA CITY CA 95959
81-107	ROENICKE, RONALD JON	829 MANCHESTER COURT - CLAREMONT CA 91711
23-111	ROETTGER, OSCAR FREDERICK LOUIS	D. JULY 4, 1986 ST. LOUIS, MO.
27- 75	ROETTGER, WALTER HENRY	D. SEPTEMBER 14, 1951 CHAMPAIGN, ILL.
29- 89	ROETZ, EDWARD BERNARD	D. MARCH 16, 1965 PHILADELPHIA, PA.
38- 84	ROGALSKI, JOSEPH ANTHONY	D. NOVEMBER 20, 1951 ASHLAND, WIS.
25- 88	ROGELL, WILLIAM GEORGE	1700 GARNET DRIVE #206 - NEWPORT RICHEY FL 34652
14-180	ROGERS, JAY LOUIS	D. JULY 18, 1964 CARLISLE, PA.
38- 85	ROGERS, LEE OTIS	4920 HAWTHORNE RD-LITTLE ROCK AR 72207
35- 94	ROGERS, ORLIN WOODROW 'BUCK'	RR ONE BOX 222 - BLAIRS VA 24527
38- 86	ROGERS, STANLEY FRANK 'PACKY'	964 WALNUT ST-ELMIRA NY 14901
73-101	ROGERS, STEPHEN DOUGLAS	2718 SOUTH UTICA - TULSA OK 74114
17- 71	ROGERS, THOMAS ANDREW	D. MARCH 7, 1936 NASHVILLE, TENN.
15-138	ROGGE, FRANCIS CLINTON	D. JANUARY 6, 1969 MOUNT CLEMENS, MICH.
63- 99	ROGGENBURK, GARRY EARL	18828 CANYON ROAD - CLEVELAND OH 44126
73-102	ROGODZINSKI, MICHAEL GEORGE	1 EMLYN COURT - LAUREL SPRINGS NJ 08021
49- 75	ROGOVIN, SAUL WALTER	420 WEST 24TH DR - NEW YORK NY 10011
83-124	ROHN, DANIEL JAY	9247 WEST LONG LAKE RD - ALPENA MI 49707
67- 93	ROHR, LESLIE NORVIN	1340 WICKS LANE - BILLINGS MT 59105
67- 94	ROHR, WILLIAM JOSEPH	24 VIA CANDELARIA - COTO DE CAZA CA 92679
21- 89	ROHWER, RAY	D. JANUARY, 1988
53- 77	ROIG, ANTON AMBROSE	23310 INLET DR #12 - LIBERTY LAKE WA 99019
66- 77	ROJAS, MINERVINO ALEJANDRO 'MINNIE'	7101A PLASKA - HUNTINGTON PARK CA 90255
62-116	ROJAS, OCTAVIO 'COOKIE'	240 SHERYL LANE #L15 - NEW LLANO LA 71461
42- 87	ROJEK, STANLEY ANDREW	895 PAYNE AVE - NORTH TONAWANDA NY 14120
62-117	ROLAND, JAMES IVAN	5000 COUNTRY LANE - HIGH POINT NC 27263
31- 74	ROLFE, ROBERT ABIAL 'RED'	D. JULY 8, 1969 GILFORD, N. H.
12-167	ROLLINGS, RAYMOND COPELAND	D. AUGUST 25, 1966 ST.PAUL, MINN.
27- 76	ROLLINGS, WILLIAM RUSSELL 'RED'	D. DECEMBER 31, 1964 MOBILE, ALA.
61- 92	ROLLINS, RICHARD JOHN	2751 EAST WALLINGS RD - BROADVIEW HGTS OH 44147
84- 97	ROMAN, JOSE RAFAEL	VISTA ALEGRE #10 SANCHES LUPERON-PUERTO PLATA DOM. REP.
64- 95	ROMAN, WILLIAM ANTHONY	IBM,TOWER 3,FL-9,1701 GOLF RD-ROLLING MEADOWS IL 60008
84- 98	ROMANICK, RONALD JAMES	4221 135TH PL SE - BELLEVUE WA 98006
50- 83	ROMANO, JAMES KING	233 BURLINGTON AVE - DEER PARK NY 11729
58- 78	ROMANO, JOHN ANTHONY	7 TANGLEWOOD HOLLOW - UPPER SADDLE RIVER NJ 07458
87-128	ROMANO, THOMAS MICHAEL	132 WASHINGTON SQUARE - SYRACUSE NY 13208
54- 94	ROMBERGER, ALLEN IRVING	D. MAY 26, 1983 WEIKERT, PA.
77-121	ROMERO, EDGARDO	1380 WOOD ROW WAY - WEST PALM BEACH FL 33414
84- 99	ROMERO, ROMAN	CLE ULISES ESPAILLOT #60-SAN PEDRO DE MACORIS DOM. REP.

85-100 ROMINE, KEVIN ANDREW   8750 ROGUE RIVER AVE - FOUNTAIN VALLEY CA 92708
20-100 ROMMEL, EDWIN AMERICUS   D. AUGUST 26, 1970 BALTIMORE, MD.
77-122 ROMO, ENRIQUE   AVENIDA SOUTH NORTH CARLOS #923 - TORREON COAHUILA MEX.
68- 88 ROMO, VICENTE   CALLE 32 AVENIDA 17 #45 - GUAYMAS SONORA MEX.
53- 78 ROMONOSKY, JOHN   5090 BIXBY ROAD - GROVEPORT OH 43125
13-151 RONDEAU, HENRI JOSEPH   D. MAY 28, 1943 WOONSOCKET , R.I.
76- 84 RONDON, GILBERT   1836 WATSON AVE #3E - BRONX NY 10472
81-108 ROOF, EUGENE LAWRENCE   4571 WESTCHESTER LANE - PADUCAH KY 42001
61- 93 ROOF, PHILLIP ANTHONY   RR 1 BOX 402 - BOAZ KY 42027
68- 89 ROOKER, JAMES PHILIP   1684 CITATION DR - LIBRARY PA 15129
14-181 ROONEY, FRANK   D. APRIL 6, 1977 BESSEMER, MICH.
81-109 ROONEY, PATRICK EUGENE   925 SOUTH WALNUT - ARLINGTON HEIGHTS IL 60005
23-112 ROOT, CHARLES HENRY   D. NOVEMBER 5, 1970 HOLLISTER, CAL.
70-116 ROQUE, JORGE   BO SAN ANTON #135 - PONCE PR 00731
77-123 ROSADO, LUIS (ROBLES)   CALLE 508 B-213 #13 5TH-CAROLINA PR 00630
39- 98 ROSAR, WARREN VINCENT 'BUDDY'   733 EGGERT RD-BUFFALO NY 14215
71- 89 ROSARIO, ANGEL RAMON   CALLE 1 #421 HERNANDES DAVILA-BAYAMON PR00619
65- 92 ROSARIO, SANTIAGO   OLD ADD: VILLA GRILLASCA D.5B - PONCE PR
71- 90 ROSE, DONALD GARY   1133 HUNTINGDON - SAN JOSE CA 95129
63-100 ROSE, PETER EDWARD   100 RIVERFRONT STADIUM - CINCINNATI OH 45202
57- 75 ROSEBORO, JOHN JUNIOR   1703 VIRGINIA RD - LOS ANGELES CA 90019
55-102 ROSELLI, ROBERT EDWARD   1548 HEMLOCK AVE - SAN MATEO CA 94401
72- 93 ROSELLO, DAVID   PAZ 160 - BO PARIS - MAYAGUEZ PR 00708
47- 74 ROSEN, ALBERT LEONARD   BOX 24308 - SAN FRANCISCO CA 94124
37- 91 ROSEN, GOODWIN GEORGE   120 SHELBURNE AVE #1205 - TORONTO ONTARIO M6B 2M7 CAN.
30- 68 ROSENBERG, HARRY   23 MEADOWBROOK DR - SAN FRANCISCO CA 94127
23-113 ROSENBERG, LOUIS C   320 ALEMANY BLVD - SAN FRANCISCO CA 94110
31- 75 ROSENFELD, MAX   D. MARCH 10, 1969 MIAMI, FLA.
36- 80 ROSENTHAL, LAWRENCE JOHN   1335 WHITE BEAR AVE - ST. PAUL MN 55106
25- 89 ROSENTHAL, SIMON   D. APRIL 7, 1969 BOSTON, MASS.
44-114 ROSER, EMERSON COREY 'STEVE'   CAMP ROAD, CEDAR LAKE - CLAYVILLE NY 13322
22-118 ROSER, JOHN JOSEPH 'BUNNY'   D. MAY 6, 1979 ROCKY HILL, CONN.
24- 90 ROSS, CHESTER FRANKLIN 'BUSTER'   D. APRIL 24, 1982 MAYFIELD, KY.
39- 99 ROSS, CHESTER JAMES   %NORMAN ROSS,15 N. COVINGTON - BUFFALO NY 14220
54- 95 ROSS, CLIFFORD DAVID   2581 ROSEWOOD - ROSLYN PA 19001

38- 87 ROSS, DONALD RAYMOND   416 SOUTH OLD RANCH RD-ARCADIA CA 91006
50- 84 ROSS, FLOYD ROBERT 'BOB'   2245 EAST VERMONT - ANAHEIM CA 92806
68- 90 ROSS, GARY DOUGLAS   OLD ADD: 7985 LABRUSCA WAY - CARLSBAD CA 92008
18- 63 ROSS, GEORGE SIDNEY   D. APRIL 22, 1935 AMITYVILLE, N. Y.
36- 81 ROSS, LEE RAVON 'BUCK'   D. NOVEMBER 23, 1978 CHARLOTTE, NORTH . C.
82-106 ROSS, MARK JOSEPH   7951 GLENHEATH - HOUSTON TX 77061
52- 87 ROSSI, JOSEPH ANTHONY   934 STANNAGE AVE - ALBANY CA 94706
44-115 ROSSO, FRANCIS JAMES   D. JANUARY 26, 1980 SPRINGFIELD, MASS.
48- 86 ROTBLATT, MARVIN   584 NE RIVER ROAD - DES PLAINES IL 60018
14-182 ROTH, ROBERT FRANK 'BRAGGO'   D. SEPTEMBER 11, 1936 CHICAGO, ILL.
45- 87 ROTHEL, ROBERT BURTON   D. MAY 21, 1984 HURON, O.
25- 90 ROTHROCK JOHN HOUSTON   D. FEBRUARY 2, 1980 SAN BERNARDINO, CALIF.
81-110 ROTHSCHILD, LAWRENCE LEE   1136 BREABURN ST - FLOSSMOR IL 60422
70-117 ROUNSAVILLE, VIRL GENE   2901 LONE TREE WAY #A - ANTIOCH CA 94509
13-152 ROUSH, EDD J   D. MARCH 21, 1988 BRADENTON, FLA.
11-146 ROWAN, DAVID   D. JULY 30, 1955 TORONTO, ONT.
84-100 ROWDON, WADE LEE   OLD ADD: 12929 SW 64TH CT - MIAMI FL 33156
63-101 ROWE, DONALD HOWARD   19791 SCENIC BAY LN-HUNTINGTON BEACH CA 92648
16- 72 ROWE, HARLAND STIMSON   D. MAY 26, 1969 SPRINGVALE, ME.
63-102 ROWE, KENNETH DARRELL   4894 TWIN LAKES TRAIL - DORAVILLE GA 30360
33- 56 ROWE, LYNWOOD THOMAS 'SCHOOLBOY'   D. JANUARY 8, 1961 EL DORADO, ARK.
39-100 ROWELL, CARVEL WILLIAM 'BAMA'   RR 1 BOX 456 - CITRONELLE AL 36522
23-114 ROWLAND, CHARLIE LELAND   HIGHWAY 64 RR 2 - WENDELL NC 27591
15-139 ROWLAND, CLARENCE HENRY 'PANTS'   D. MAY 17, 1969 CHICAGO, ILL.
80-113 ROWLAND, MICHAEL EVAN   OLD ADD: 6425 EAST VIRGINIA - SCOTTSDALE AZ 85257
33- 57 ROY, EMILE ARTHUR   146 SOUTH COUNTRY CLUB ROAD - CRYSTAL RIVER FL 32629
46- 90 ROY, JEAN PIERRE   8969 VERVILLE - MONTREAL QUEBEC CAN.
24- 91 ROY, LUTHER FRANKLIN   D. JULY 24, 1963 GRAND RAPIDS, MICH.
50- 85 ROY, NORMAN BROOKS   53 CENTRAL ST - WEST CONCORD MA 01781
73-103 ROYSTER, JERON KENNIS   18858 BERNARDO TRAILS DR - SAN DIEGO CA 92128
81-111 ROYSTER, WILLIE ARTHUR   229 55TH NE - WASHINGTON DC 20019
50- 86 ROZEK, RICHARD LOUIS   BOX 249 - CEDAR RAPIDS IA 52406
77-124 ROZEMA, DAVID SCOTT   4434 OREGON ROAD - LAPEER MI 48446
64- 96 ROZNOVSKY, VICTOR JOSEPH   1686 WEST BULLARD - FRESNO CA 93711
40- 76 RUBELING, ALBERT WILLIAM   D. JANUARY 28, 1988 BALTIMORE, MD.
69-151 RUBERTO, JOHN EDWARD 'SONNY'   7354 WHITE HALL COLONIAL LN - ST. LOUIS MO 63119
66- 78 RUBIO, JORGE JESUS   1001 LERDO AVE - MEXICALI BAJA CALIF. MEX.
27- 77 RUBLE, WILLIAM ARTHUR   D. NOVEMBER 1, 1983 MARYVILLE, TENN.
81-112 RUCKER, DAVID MICHAEL   P.O. BOX 559 - PINION HILLS CA 92372
40- 77 RUCKER, JOHN JOEL   D. AUGUST 7, 1985 MOULTRIE, GA.

1940 PLAY BALL REPRINTS
SERIES 5 — The High Numbers
$ 7.00 plus postage & handling

The fifth and final series of the 1940 Play Ball reprints contains the last 60 cards in the set, traditionally known as "the high numbers". In this grouping are such notables as Joe Jackson, John McGraw, Wee Willie Keeler, Frank Chance, Hughie Jennings, Pie Traynor and a host of other Hall of Famers. All cards are marked "Reprint".

1940 PLAY BALL REPRINTS
SERIES 4
$ 5.00 plus postage & handling

This fourth series of the reprints of the 1940 Play ball set includes cards numbered 136 to 180. Among the more famous players in this series are Travis Jackson, Frankie Frisch, Honus Wagner and a subset of 12 former Major League stars featuring Speaker, Lajoie, Mathewson, Heilmann, Baker, Cochrane, Evers and others.

1940 PLAY BALL REPRINTS
SERIES 3
$ 5.00 plus postage & handling

This third of the reprint series features card numbers 91 to 135 of the 1940 Play Ball set. In this grouping are Chuck Klein, Big & Little Poisons Waner, Alexander, Mack, Foxx, Walter Johnson Joe Cronin and many more. Anyone who has any either the first two set in this reprint series will definitely want this third set.

1940 PLAY BALL REPRINTS
SERIES 1
$ 5.00 plus postage & handling

This 45-card set is a reprint of the first 45 cards of what has been called the finest black & white set ever made. Included in this first series are Joe DiMaggio, Lefty Gomez, Bill Dickey, Ted Williams, Hank Greenberg, Charlie Gehringer and 39 other players of the period. All cards are marked "Reprint", and will fit in Style 9PB plastic sheet.

1940 PLAY BALL REPRINTS
SERIES 2
$ 5.00 plus postage & handling

The second 45-card set of Play Ball reprints contains card numbers 46 to 90. Included in this group are Mel Ott, Carl Hubbell, Earl Averill, Cookie Lavagetto, Van Mungo and 40 more players of this era. As with other 1940 Play Ball reprints, all cards fit in Style 9PB plastic sheet, and all cards are clearly marked "Reprint".

67- 95 RUDI, JOSEPH ODEN	RR 1 BOX 66 - BAKER OR 97814
45- 88 RUDOLPH, ERNEST WILLIAM	RR 2 BOX 14A - BLACK RIVER FALLS WI 54615
57- 76 RUDOLPH, FREDERICK DONALD 'DON'	D. SEPTEMBER 12, 1968 ENCINO, CAL.
69-152 RUDOLPH, KENNETH VICTOR	2604 SOUTH SANTA BARBARA - MESA AZ 85202
10-128 RUDOLPH, RICHARD	D. OCTOBER 20, 1949 BRONX, N.Y.
15-140 RUEL, HEROLD DOMINIC 'MUDDY'	D. NOVEMBER 13, 1963 PALO ALTO, CALIF.
17- 72 RUETHER, WALTER HENRY 'DUTCH'	D. MAY 16, 1970 PHOENIX, ARIZ.
49- 76 RUFER, RUDOLPH JOSEPH	649 CORNWELL AVE - MALVERNE NY 11565
86-133 RUFFIN, BRUCE WAYNE	15610 FERN BASIN - HOUSTON TX 77084
24- 92 RUFFING, CHARLES HERBERT 'RED'	D. FEBRUARY 17, 1986 MAYFIELD HEIGHTS, O.
74-115 RUHLE, VERNON GERALD	%MEKULEN,1802 BEDFORD LN #A19 - SUN CITY FL 33570
64- 97 RUIZ, HIRALDO SABLON 'CHICO'	D. FEBRUARY 9, 1972 SAN DIEGO, CALIF.
78-115 RUIZ, MANUEL 'CHICO'	TAPIA 267 - SANTURCE PR 00912
43-119 RULLO, JOSEPH VINCENT	D. OCTOBER 28, 1969 PHILADELPHIA, PA.
14-183 RUMLER, WILLIAM GEORGE	D. MAY 26, 1966 LINCOLN, NEB.
81-113 RUNGE, PAUL WILLIAM	646 DELAWARE AVE - KINGSTON NY 12401
85-101 RUNNELLS, THOMAS WILLIAM	1017 29TH AVENUE COURT - GREELEY CO 80631
51- 82 RUNNELS, JAMES EDWARD 'PETE'	1106 WILMA-LOIS ST - PASADENA TX 77502
25- 91 RUSH, JESS HOWARD 'ANDY'	D. MARCH 16, 1969 FRESNO, CAL.
48- 87 RUSH, ROBERT RANSOM	1358 EAST 1ST PLACE - MESA AZ 85201
15-141 RUSSELL, ALLAN E.	D. OCTOBER 20, 1972 BALTIMORE, MD.
10-129 RUSSELL, CLARENCE DICKSON 'LEFTY'	D. JANUARY 22, 1962 BALTIMORE, MD.
13-153 RUSSELL, EWELL ALBERT 'REB'	D. SEPTEMBER 30, 1973 INDIANAPOLIS, IND.
39-101 RUSSELL, GLEN DAVID 'RIP'	D. SEPTEMBER 26, 1976 LOS ANGELES CAL.
14-184 RUSSELL, HARVEY HOLMES	D. JANUARY 8, 1980 ALEXANDRIA, VA.
26- 72 RUSSELL, JACK ERWIN	BOX 748 - CLEARWATER FL 33515

42- 88 RUSSELL, JAMES WILLIAM	D. NOVEMBER 24, 1987 PITTSBURGH, PA.
83-125 RUSSELL, JEFFREY LEE	28 BRANDYWINE DR - CINCINNATI OH 45246
17- 73 RUSSELL, JOHN ALBERT	D. NOVEMBER 19, 1930 ELY, NEV.
84-101 RUSSELL, JOHN WILLIAM	412 FOREMAN AVE - NORMAN OK 73069
38- 88 RUSSELL, LOYD OPAL	D. MAY 24, 1968 WACO, TEX.
69-153 RUSSELL, WILLIAM ELLIS	6037 E. 106TH ST - TULSA OK 74137
39-102 RUSSO, MARIUS UGO	27 NORFOLK DR - ELMONT NY 11003
66- 79 RUSTECK, RICHARD FRANK	OLD ADD: 6315 SW PEYTON RD-PORTLAND OR 97219
44-116 RUSZKOWSKI, HENRY ALEXANDER	8815 HARVARD AVE - CLEVELAND OH 44105
14-185 RUTH, GEORGE HERMAN 'BABE'	D. AUGUST 16, 1948 NEW YORK, N.Y.
10-130 RUTHERFORD, JAMES HOLLIS	D. SEPTEMBER 18, 1956 LAKEWOOD, O.
52- 88 RUTHERFORD, JOHN WILLIAM	911 HENRIETTA - BIRMINGHAM MI 48009
73-104 RUTHVEN, RICHARD DAVID	39779 BENEVENTE AVE - FREMONT CA 94538
47- 75 RUTNER, MILTON MICKEY	14 SHOTGUN LN - LEVITTOWN NY 11756
82-107 RYAL, MARK DWAYNE	BOX 291 - DEWAR OK 74431
42- 89 RYAN, CORNELIUS JOSEPH	626 NORTH BEAUCHENE DRIVE - MANDEVILLE LA 70448
12-168 RYAN, JOHN BUDD	D. JULY 9, 1956 SACRAMENTO, CALIF.
30- 69 RYAN, JOHN COLLINS 'BLONDY'	D. NOVEMBER 28, 1959 SWAMPSCOTT, MASS.
29- 90 RYAN, JOHN FRANCIS	D. SEPTEMBER 2, 1967 ROCHESTER, MINN.
66- 80 RYAN, LYNN NOLAN	719 DEZZO DR - ALVIN TX 77511
64- 98 RYAN, MICHAEL JAMES	126 NORTH MAIN ST - PLAISTOW NH 03865
19- 71 RYAN, WILFRED PATRICK DOLAN 'ROSY'	D. DECEMBER 10, 1980 PHOENIX, ARIZ.
35- 95 RYBA, DOMINIC JOSEPH 'MIKE'	D. DECEMBER 13, 1971 SPRINGFIELD, MO.
31- 76 RYE, EUGENE RUDOLPH	D. JANUARY 21, 1980 PARK RIDGE, ILL.
72- 94 RYERSON, GARY LAWRENCE	1059 TERRACE CREST - EL CAJON CA 92020

84-102 SABERHAGEN, BRET WILLIAM
36- 82 SABO, ALEXANDER
51- 83 SACKA, FRANK
60- 88 SADECKI, RAYMOND MICHAEL
73-105 SADEK, MICHAEL GEORGE
60- 89 SADOWSKI, EDWARD ROMAN
74-116 SADOWSKI, JAMES MICHAEL
63-103 SADOWSKI, ROBERT F.
60- 90 SADOWSKI, ROBERT FRANK
60- 91 SADOWSKI, THEODORE
49- 77 SAFFELL, THOMAS JUDSON
11-147 SAIER, VICTOR SYLVESTER
42- 90 SAIN, JOHN FRANKLIN
51- 84 SAINTCLAIRE, EDWARD JOSEPH 'EBBA'
84-103 SAINTCLAIRE, RANDY ANTHONY

19229 ARMINTA ST - RESEDA CA 91335
816 ANCHOR DR - FORKED RIVER NJ 08731
968 SYCAMORE ST - WYANDOTTE MI 48192
7710 EVERETT - KANSAS CITY KS 66112
6632 SPRUCE LANE - DUBLIN CA 94568
11181 CLARISSA ST - GARDEN GROVE CA 92640
914 HANSEN - PITTSBURGH PA 15209
4053 ASHENTREE DR - CHAMBLEE GA 30341
1465 CREEKSIDE DRIVE - HIGH RIDGE MO 63049
196 ALMA ST - PITTSBURGH PA 15223
11 SUNSET DR #501 - SARASOTA FL 33577
D. MAY 14, 1967 EAST LANSING, MICH.
2 SOUTH 707 AVENUE LATOUR - OAKBROOK IL 60521
D. AUGUST 22, 1982 WHITEHALL, N. Y.
174 COOPER STREET - LAKE GEORGE NY 12845

77-125 SAKATA, LENN HARUKI
84-104 SALAS, MARK BRUCE
83-126 SALAZAR, ARGENIS ANTONIO
80-114 SALAZAR, LUIS ERNESTO
24- 93 SALE, FREDERICK LINK
45- 89 SALKELD, WILLIAM FRANKLIN
12-169 SALMON, ROGER ELLIOTT
64- 99 SALMON, RUTHERFORD EDUARDO 'CHICO'
32- 72 SALTZGAVER, OTTO HAMLIN 'JACK'
33- 58 SALVESON, JOHN THEODORE
39-103 SALVO, MANUEL
76- 85 SAMBITO, JOSEPH CHARLES
51- 85 SAMCOFF, EDWARD WILLIAM
54- 96 SAMFORD, RONALD EDWARD
78-116 SAMPLE, WILLIAM AMOS
62-118 SAMUEL, AMADO RUPERTO
83-127 SAMUEL, JUAN MILTON
30- 70 SAMUELS, JOHN JONES
23-115 SANBERG, GUSTAVE E.
82-108 SANCHEZ, ALEJANDRO
72- 95 SANCHEZ, CELERINO
81-114 SANCHEZ, LUIS MERCEDES
81-115 SANCHEZ, ORLANDO
52- 89 SANCHEZ, RAUL GUADALUPE
23-116 SAND, JOHN HENRY 'HEINIE'
81-116 SANDBERG, RYNE DEE
45- 90 SANDERS, DEE WILMA
65- 93 SANDERS, JOHN FRANK
64-100 SANDERS, KENNETH GEORGE
42- 91 SANDERS, RAYMOND FLOYD
74-117 SANDERS, REGINALD JEROME
17- 74 SANDERS, ROY GARVIN
18- 64 SANDERS, ROY L.
78-117 SANDERSON, SCOTT DOUGLAS
42- 92 SANDLOCK, MICHAEL JOSEPH
67- 96 SANDS, CHARLES DUANE
75-102 SANDT, THOMAS JAMES
40- 78 SANFORD, JOHN DOWARD
43-120 SANFORD, JOHN FREDERICK 'FRED'
56- 74 SANFORD, JOHN STANLEY 'JACK'
67- 97 SANGUILLEN, MANUEL DE JESUS
49- 78 SANICKI, EDWARD ROBERT
29- 91 SANKEY, BENJAMIN TURNER
83-128 SANTANA, RAFAEL FRANCISCO
86-134 SANTIAGO, BENITO
54- 97 SANTIAGO, JOSE GUILLERMO
63-104 SANTIAGO, JOSE RAFAEL
60- 92 SANTO, RONALD EDWARD
79- 98 SANTODOMINGO, RAFAEL
68- 91 SANTORINI, ALAN JOEL
87-129 SANTOVENIA, NELSON GIL
21- 90 SARGENT, JOSEPH ALEXANDER
76- 86 SARMIENTO, MANUEL EDUARDO
51- 86 SARNI, WILLIAM FLORINE
87-130 SASSER, MACK DANIEL
61- 94 SATRIANO, THOMAS VICTOR
51- 87 SAUCIER, FRANCIS FIELD
78-118 SAUCIER, KEVIN ANDREW

467 HALEMAUMAU STREET - HONOLUL HI 96821
330 BARCA AVE - LAPUENTE CA 91744
RODRIGUEZ DOMINGUES MANZANA G#7-VARINA VENEZ
PRINC. DE HUACARAPA 34-HUARENAS MIRANDA VENEZ
D. MAY 27, 1956 HERMOSA BEACH, CAL.
D. APRIL 22, 1967 LOS ANGELES, CAL.
D. JUNE 17, 1974 BELFAST, ME.
ALMIRANTE, BOCAS DEL TORO - PANAMA PANAMA C.A.
D. FEBRUARY 2, 1978 KEOKUK, IA.
D. DECEMBER 28, 1974 NORWALK, CALIF.
3541 WOODBROOK DR - NAPA CA 94558
9041 BAYWOOD PARK DR - SEMINOLE FL 33543
8153 MADEIRA PORT LN - FAIR OAKS CA 95628
1325 WEST CANTERBURY CT - DALLAS TX 75208
10 PASCACK ROAD - WESTWOOD NJ 07675
1931 YALE DR - LOUISVILLE KY 40205
CALLE I #22 RESTAURACION-SAN PEDRO DE MACORIS DOM. REP.
9 HOWELL - BATH NY 14810
D. FEBRUARY 3, 1930 LOS ANGELES, CAL.
BOCA CHICA GATEY GAUTIR-SANTO DOMINGO DOMINICAN REP.
MUTUALISMO #222-A - CELAYA GUANAJUATO MEX.
CALLE SAN FELIPE 11-CARIACO,EST. SUCRE VENEZ
BOX SAN ISODRO P-52 - CANOVANAS PR 00629
17821 NW 56TH AVE - CORAL CITY FL 33054
D. NOVEMBER 3, 1958 SAN FRANCISCO, CAL.
1953 EAST MYRNA LANE #1 - TEMPE AZ 85284
1312 COUNTRY CLUB RD - MCALESTER OK 74501
6112 SOUTH 25TH ST - LINCOLN NE 68512
12141 PARKVIEW LN - HALES CORNERS WI 53130
D. OCTOBER 28, 1983 WASHINGTON, MO.
5281 NEWPORT - DETROIT MI 48213
D. JANUARY 17, 1950 KANSAS CITY, MO.
OLD ADD: 525 SOUTH THIRD ST - LOUISVILLE KY 40202
OLD ADD: 1271 WENDY DR - NORTHBROOK IL 60062
18 ROCK LAND PL-OLD GREENWICH CT 06870
2250 LONI CERA WAY - CHARLOTTESVILLE VA 22906
25 ORIOLE LANE - LAKE OSWEGO OR 97034
1001 KINON ST-WILSON NC 27893
1046 WEST 600 NORTH - SALT LAKE CITY UT 84116
2300 PRESIDENTIAL WAY - WEST PALM BEACH FL 33401
1200 FEDERAL HWY #204 - BOCA RATON FL 33432
12 BARTON RD - OLD BRIDGE NJ 08857
RR 3 BOX 603B - WASHINGTON GA 30673
VILLA PEREYRA CALLE IRA #99 - LAROMANA DOMINICAN REP.
URB. VILLA JAUCA #B21 - SANTA ISABEL PR 00757
56-SE-NO. 1167 - RIO PIEDRAS PR 00921
YOGRAMO 2-12,ARECIBO HEIGHTS - CAROLINA PR 00630
1303 SOMERSET - GLENVIEW IL 60025
BOX 277 - OROCOVIS PR 00720
RR 2, ARTHUR RD - BELLE MEADE NJ 08502
12340 SOUTHWEST 185TH STREET - MIAMI FL 33177
D. JULY 5, 1950 ROCHESTER, N. Y.
AVE DIAZ MORENO #90-13-VALENCIA CARABOBO VENEZUELA S.A.
D. APRIL 15, 1983 CREVE COEUR, MO.
4D WELLINGTON PLACE APTS - MIDLAND AL 36350
4816 LOS FELIZ BLVD - LOS ANGELES CA 90027
1615 BRYAN PL #9 - AMARILLO TX 79102
4170 ROMMITCH LANE - PENSACOLA FL 32504

43-121	SAUER, EDWARD	D. JULY, 1988
41- 97	SAUER, HENRY JOHN	207 VALLEJO CT - MILLBRAE CA 94030
70-118	SAUNDERS, DENNIS JAMES	OLD ADD: 19971 AVE DEL REY-ROWLAND HEIGHTS CA
27- 78	SAUNDERS, RUSSELL COLLIER 'RUSTY'	D. NOVEMBER 24, 1967 DOVER TWP.,OCEAN CO,N.J.
86-135	SAUVEUR, RICHARD DANIEL	7937 FREEHOLLOW DRIVE - FALLS CHURCH VA 22042
44-117	SAVAGE, DONALD ANTHONY	D. DECEMBER 25, 1961 MONTCLAIR, N. J.
12-170	SAVAGE, JAMES HAROLD	D. JUNE 26, 1940 NEW CASTLE, PA.
87-131	SAVAGE, JOHN JOSEPH	4402 LANDSIDE COURT - LOUISVILLE KY 40220
42- 93	SAVAGE, JOHN ROBERT 'BOB'	296 HOWARD ST - BERLIN NH 03570
62-119	SAVAGE, THEODORE EPHESIAN	4311 DRYDEN COURT - ST. LOUIS MO 63115
59- 70	SAVERINE, ROBERT PAUL	228 SLICE DR - STAMFORD CT 06907
29- 92	SAVIDGE, DONALD SNYDER	D. MARCH 22, 1983 SANTA BARBARA, CALIF.
54- 98	SAVRANSKY, MORRIS 'MOE'	2178 CEDARVIEW DR - CLEVELAND OH 44121
48- 88	SAWATSKI, CARL ERNEST	10201 MARKHAM ST WEST #214 - LITTLE ROCK AR 72205
15-142	SAWYER, CARL EVERETT	D. JANUARY 17, 1957 LOS ANGELES, CALIF.
48- 89	SAWYER, EDWIN MILBY	BOX 296 - VALLEY FORGE PA 19481
74-118	SAWYER, RICHARD CLYDE	3100 CREST DRIVE - BAKERSFIELD CA 93306
82-109	SAX, DAVID JOHN	2980 SAGEMILL WAY - SACRAMENTO CA 95833
28- 79	SAX, ERIK OLIVER 'OLLIE'	D. MARCH 21, 1982 NEWARK, N. J.
81-117	SAX, STEPHEN LOUIS	11 WESTPORT - MANHATTAN BEACH CA 90266
39-104	SAYLES, WILLIAM NISBETH	2830 NE LAKE DR - LINCOLN CITY OR 97367
48- 90	SCALA, GERARD DANIEL	19 BERNADOTTE CT - PERRY HALL MD 21128
39-105	SCALZI, FRANK JOSEPH	D. AUGUST 25, 1984 PITTSBURGH, PA.
31- 77	SCALZI, JOHN ANTHONY	D. SEPTEMBER 27, 1962 PORT CHESTER, N. Y.
74-119	SCANLON, JAMES PATRICK 'PAT'	7400 PORTLAND AVE SOUTH - RICHFIELD MN 55423
56- 75	SCANTLEBURY, PATRICIO ATHELSTAN	47 WOODLAND AVE - MONTCLAIR NJ 07042
79- 99	SCARBERY, RANDY JAMES	5010 EAST LEWIS - FRESNO CA 93727
42- 94	SCARBOROUGH, RAY WILSON	D. JULY 1, 1982 MOUNT OLIVE NC
72- 96	SCARCE, GUERRANT MCCURDY 'MAC'	1708 BROADMOOR DR - RICHMOND VA 23221
29- 93	SCARRITT, RUSSELL MALLORY	429 POU STATION RD - PENSACOLA FL 32507
35- 96	SCARSELLA, LESLIE GEORGE	D. DECEMBER 16, 1958 SAN FRANCISCO, CAL.
64-101	SCHAAL, PAUL	10545 REDWING CIR - LENEXA KS 66220
19- 72	SCHACHT, ALEXANDER	D. JULY 14, 1984 WATERBURY, CONN.
50- 87	SCHACHT, SIDNEY	783 NW 30TH AVE - DELRAY BEACH FL 33445
45- 91	SCHACKER, HAROLD	4609 NORTH MATANZAS AVE - TAMPA FL 33614
52- 90	SCHAEFFER, HARRY EDWARD	412 WHEATLAND AVE - SHILLINGTON PA 19607
72- 97	SCHAEFFER, MARK PHILIP	18261 PARTHENIA ST - NORTHRIDGE CA 91324
61- 95	SCHAFFER, JIMMIE RONALD	655 BIRCH TER - COOPERSBURG PA 18036
59- 71	SCHAFFERNOTH, JOSEPH ARTHUR	20 MARIAN AVE - BERKLEY HEIGHTS NJ 07922
58- 79	SCHAIVE, JOHN EDWARD	RR 2 BOX 55 - DAWSON IL 62520
32- 73	SCHALK, LEROY JOHN	1100 LAWRENCE #21 - GAINESVILLE TX 76240
12-171	SCHALK, RAYMOND WILLIAM	D. MAY 19, 1970 CHICAGO, ILL.
11-148	SCHALLER, WALTER 'BIFF'	D. OCTOBER 9, 1939 EMERYVILLE, CALIF.
51- 88	SCHALLOCK, ARTHUR LAWRENCE	155 CREST RD - NOVATO CA 94947
14-186	SCHANG, ROBERT MARTIN	D. AUGUST 29, 1966 SACRAMENTO, CALIF.
13-154	SCHANG, WALTER HENRY	D. MARCH 6, 1965 ST. LOUIS, MO.
44-118	SCHANZ, CHARLEY MURRELL	2217 MEER WAY - SACRAMENTO CA 95822
11-149	SCHARDT, WILBURT	D. JULY 20, 1964 VERMILION, O.
32- 74	SCHAREIN, ARTHUR OTTO	D. JULY 3, 1969 SAN ANTONIO, TEX.
37- 92	SCHAREIN, GEORGE ALBERT	D. DECEMBER 22, 1981 DECATUR, ILL.
81-118	SCHATTINGER, JEFFERY CHARLES	1322 WEST SAN MADELE - FRESNO CA 93711

77-126	SCHATZEDER, DANIEL ERNEST	33 EAST MADISON ST - VILLA PARK IL 60181
13-155	SCHAUER, ALEXANDER JOHN 'RUBE'	D. APRIL 15, 1957 MINNEAPOLIS, MINN.
13-156	SCHEER, ALLAN G.	D. MAY 6, 1959 LOGANSPORT, IND.
22-119	SCHEER, HENRY 'HEINIE'	D. MARCH 21, 1976 NEW HAVEN, CONN.
14-187	SCHEEREN, FREDERICK 'FRITZ'	D. JUNE 17, 1973 OIL CITY, PA.
43-122	SCHEETZ, OWEN FRANKLIN	275 ROBIN LN - REYNOLDSBURG OH 43068
41- 98	SCHEFFING, ROBERT BODEN	D. OCTOBER 26, 1985 PHOENIX, ARIZ.
12-172	SCHEGG, (GILBERT EUGENE PRICE) 'LEFTY'	D. FEBRUARY 27, 1963 NILES, O.
43-123	SCHEIB, CARL ALVIN	2922 OLD RANCH RD - SAN ANTONIO TX 78217
65- 94	SCHEINBLUM, RICHARD ALAN 'RICHIE'	10141 OLD RANCH CIR - VILLA PARK CA 92667
54- 99	SCHELL, CLYDE DANIEL 'DANNY'	D. MAY 11, 1972 MAYVILLE, MICH.
39-106	SCHELLE, GERARD ANTHONY 'JIM'	115 E. MELROSE AVE, LONG GREEN - BALTIMORE MD 21212
23-117	SCHEMANSKE, FREDERICK GEORGE	D. FEBRUARY 18, 1960 DETROIT, MICH.
45- 92	SCHEMER, MICHAEL "LEFTY"	D. APRIL 22, 1983 MIAMI, FLA.
13-157	SCHENEBERG, JOHN BLUFORD	D. SEPTEMBER 7, 1950 HUNTINGTON, W. VA.
46- 91	SCHENZ, HENRY LEONARD	4055 LANSDOWNE AVE - CINCINNATI OH 45236
19- 73	SCHEPNER, JOSEPH MARTIN	D. JULY 25, 1959 MOBILE, ALA.
50- 88	SCHERBARTH, ROBERT ELMER	4858 NORTH 61ST ST - MILWAUKEE WI 53218
69-154	SCHERMAN, FREDERICK JOHN	11546 STECK RD RT#1 - BROOKVILLE OH 45309
82-110	SCHERRER, WILLIAM JOSEPH	7166 CASCADE ST - SPRING HILL FL 33526
31- 78	SCHESLER, CHARLES 'DUTCH'	D. NOVEMBER 19, 1953 HARRISBURG, PA.
10-131	SCHETTLER, LOUIS MARTIN	D. MAY 1, 1960 YOUNGSTOWN, O.
17- 75	SCHICK, MAURICE FRANCIS	D. OCTOBER 25, 1979 HAZEL CREST, ILL.
61- 96	SCHILLING, CHARLES THOMAS	5 CARLISLE ROAD - MILLER PLACE NY 11764
22-120	SCHILLINGS, ELBERT ISAIAH 'RED'	D. JANUARY 7, 1954 OKLAHOMA CITY, OKLA.
20-101	SCHINDLER, WILLIAM GIBBONS	D. FEBRUARY 6, 1979 PERRYVILLE, MO.
84-105	SCHIRALDI, CALVIN DREW	2102 SAN JUAN - AUSTIN TX 78746
14-188	SCHIRICK, HARRY ERNEST 'DUTCH'	D. NOVEMBER 12, 1968 KINGSTON, N.Y.
65- 95	SCHLESINGER, WILLIAM CORDES	5708 ABELIA COURT - CINCINNATI OH 45213
23-118	SCHLIEBNER, FREDERICK PAUL 'DUTCH'	D. APRIL 15, 1975 TOLEDO, O.
71- 91	SCHLUETER, JAYD	5203 E. SAHUARO DRIVE - SCOTTSDALE AZ 85254
38- 89	SCHLUETER, NORMAN JOHN	4211 GULL COVE - NEW SMYRNA BEACH FL 32069
15-143	SCHMANDT, RAYMOND HENRY	D. FEBRUARY 1, 1969 ST. LOUIS, MO.
52- 91	SCHMEES, GEORGE EDWARD	2803 MONTE CRESTA WAY - SAN JOSE CA 95132
67- 98	SCHMELZ, ALAN GEORGE	4638 EAST DESERT COVE - PHOENIX AZ 85028
81-119	SCHMIDT, DAVID FREDERICK	26636 PORTALES - MISSION VIEJO CA 92675
81-120	SCHMIDT, DAVID JOSEPH	11 SOUTHWORK BRIDGE WAY - LUTHERVILLE MD 21093
44-119	SCHMIDT, FREDERICK ALBERT	1940 WINFIELD ST - EMMAUS PA 18049
13-158	SCHMIDT, HERMAN FREDERICK 'PETE'	D. NOVEMBER 11, 1973 PEMBROKE, ONT.
72- 98	SCHMIDT, MICHAEL JACK	24 LAKEWOOD DR - MEDIA PA 19063
58- 80	SCHMIDT, ROBERT BENJAMIN	9 HARDWOOD ST - ST CHARLES MO 63301
16- 73	SCHMIDT, WALTER JOSEPH	D. JULY 4, 1973 CERES, CALIF.
52- 92	SCHMIDT, WILLARD RAYMOND	1242 LOMA DRIVE - NORMAN OK 73069
41- 99	SCHMITZ, JOHN ALBERT	526 EAST UNION AVE-WAUSAU WI 54401
43-124	SCHMULBACH, HENRY ALRIVES	29 DALE ALLEN DR - BELLEVILLE IL 62223
14-189	SCHMUTZ, CHARLES OTTO	D. JUNE 27, 1962 SEATTLE, WASH.
72- 99	SCHNECK, DAVID LEE	3891 LEHIGH DR - NORTHAMPTON PA 18067
10-132	SCHNEIBERG, FRANK FREDERICK	D. MAY 18, 1948 MILWAUKEE, WIS.
63-105	SCHNEIDER, DANIEL LOUIS	11315 EAST MICHELLE LN - TUCSON AZ 85715
81-121	SCHNEIDER, JEFFERY THEODORE	2340 41ST - ROCK ISLAND IL 61201
14-190	SCHNEIDER, PETER JOSEPH	D. JUNE 1, 1957 LOS ANGELES, CALIF.
22-121	SCHNELL, KARL OTTO	130 MELVILLE AVE - PALO ALTO CA 94301
68- 92	SCHOEN, GERALD THOMAS	OLD ADD: 8588 DE INDIAN SCHOOL-SCOTTSDALE AZ
45- 93	SCHOENDIENST, ALBERT FRED 'RED'	331 LADUE WOODS CT - CREVE COEUR MO 63141
53- 79	SCHOFIELD, JOHN RICHARD 'DICK'	138 CIRCLE DR - SPRINGFIELD IL 62703
83-129	SCHOFIELD, RICHARD CRAIG	138 CIRCLE DRIVE - SPRINGFIELD IL 62703
55-103	SCHOONMAKER, JERALD LEE	8343 SCHREIDER AVE - MUNSTER IN 46321
15-144	SCHORR, EDWARD WALTER	D. SEPTEMBER 12, 1969 ATLANTIC CITY, N.J.
35- 97	SCHOTT, ARTHUR EUGENE 'GENE'	703 WARD CIRCLE - VALLEY CITY CENTER FL 33570
53- 80	SCHRAMKA, PAUL EDWARD	13111 WEST LUCILLE LANE - BUTLER WI 53007
11-150	SCHREIBER, DAVID HENRY 'BARNEY'	D. OCTOBER 6, 1964 CHILLICOTHE, O.
14-191	SCHREIBER, HENRY WALTER	D. FEBRUARY 23, 1968 INDIANAPOLIS, IND.
22-122	SCHREIBER, PAUL FREDERICK	D. JANUARY 28, 1982 SARASOTA, FLA.
63-106	SCHREIBER, THEODORE HENRY	144 JEROME ROAD - STATEN ISLAND NY 10305
65- 96	SCHRODER, ROBERT JAMES	4 DELOND PL - HATTIESBURG MS 39401
83-130	SCHROEDER, ALFRED WILLIAM 'BILL'	116 EXTONVILLE ROAD - TRENTON NJ 08620
58- 81	SCHROLL, ALBERT BRINGHURST	1504 EVARIST - ALEXANDRIA LA 71301
80-115	SCHROM, KENNETH MARVIN	713 ROSINANTE - EL PASO TX 79922
84-106	SCHU, RICHARD SPENCER	4607 CHARLESTON DR - CARMICHAEL CA 95608
27- 79	SCHUBLE, HENRY GEORGE 'HEINIE'	1802 FLORIDA ST - BAYTOWN TX 77520
72-100	SCHUELER, RONALD RICHARD	646 SWEET COURT - LAFAYETTE CA 94549
79-100	SCHULER, DAVID PAUL	12656 HOLMES STREET - OMAHA NE 68137
31- 79	SCHULMERICH, EDWARD WESLEY 'WES'	D. JUNE 26, 1985 CORVALLIS, ORE.
53- 81	SCHULT, ARTHUR WILLIAM	231 EAST LANTANA RD - LANTANA FL 33462
27- 80	SCHULTE, FRED WILLIAM	D. MAY 20, 1983 BELVIDERE, ILL.
40- 79	SCHULTE, HERMAN JOSEPH	1655 SOUTH RIVER RD-SAINT CHARLES MO 63301

JOHN ALBERT SCHMITZ
(JOHNNY)

23-119 SCHULTE, JOHN CLEMENT	D. JUNE 28, 1978 ST. LOUIS, MO.
44-120 SCHULTE, LEONWARD WILLIAM	D. MAY 6, 1986 ORLANDO, FLA.
75-103 SCHULTZ, CHARLES BUDD	4919 E.PARADISE DR - SCOTTSDALE AZ 85254
55-104 SCHULTZ, GEORGE WARREN 'BARNEY'	790 WOODLANE RD - BEVERLY NJ 08010
43-125 SCHULTZ, HOWARD HENRY	741 NORTH LEXINGTON - ST PAUL MN 55104
39-107 SCHULTZ, JOSEPH CHARLES	838 COALPORT - ST LOUIS MO 63141
12-173 SCHULTZ, JOSEPH CHARLES SR	D. APRIL 13, 1941 COLUMBIA, S.C.
51- 89 SCHULTZ, ROBERT DUFFY	D. MARCH 31, 1979 NASHVILLE, TENN.
24- 94 SCHULTZ, WEBB CARL	D. JULY 26, 1986 DELAVAN, WISC.
47- 76 SCHULTZ, WILLIAM MICHAEL 'MIKE'	502 ROBY AVE - EAST SYRACUSE NY 13057
12-174 SCHULZ, ALBERT CHRISTOPHER	D. DECEMBER 13, 1931 TOLEDO, O.
20-102 SCHULZ, WALTER FREDERICK	D. FEBRUARY 27, 1928 PRESCOTT, ARIZ.
83-131 SCHULZE, DONALD ARTHUR	313 EAST PINE - ROSELLE IL 60172
31- 80 SCHUMACHER, HAROLD HENRY	90 SOUTH MAIN ST - DOLGEVILLE NY 13329
13-159 SCHUPP, FERDINAND MAURICE	D. DECEMBER 16, 1971 LOS ANGELES, CALIF.
64-102 SCHURR, WAYNE ALLEN	RR ONE - HUDSON IN 46747
37- 93 SCHUSTER, WILLIAM CHARLES	D. JUNE 28, 1987 EL MONTE, CALIF.
61- 97 SCHWALL, DONALD BERNARD	2000 LAKE MARSHALL DR - GIBSONIA PA 15044
48- 91 SCHWAMB, RALPH RICHARD 'BLACKIE'	1974 ADD: 1348 PINE AVE - LONG BEACH CA 90813
65- 97 SCHWARTZ, DOUGLAS RANDALL 'RANDY'	757 EL RANCHO DR - EL CAJON CA 92021
14-192 SCHWARZ, WILLIAM DEWITT	D. JUNE 24, 1949 JACKSONVILLE BEACH, FLA.
13-160 SCHWENK, HAROLD EDWARD	D. SEPTEMBER 3, 1955 KANSAS CITY, MO.
14-193 SCHWERT, PIUS LOUIS	D. MARCH 11, 1941 WASHINGTON, D.C.
12-175 SCHWIND, ARTHUR EDWIN	D. JANUARY 13, 1968 SULLIVAN ,ILL.
55-105 SCHYPINSKI, GERALD ALBERT	10830 BALFOR AVE - DETROIT MI 48224
80-116 SCIOSCIA, MICHAEL LORRI	3447 NORTH YANKTON AVENUE - CLAREMONT CA 91711
36- 83 SCOFFIC, LOUIS	600 WEST 5TH ST-JOHNSTON CITY IL 62951
13-161 SCOGGINS, JAMES LYNN	D. AUGUST 16, 1923 COLUMBIA, S.C.
81-122 SCONIERS, DARYL ANTHONY	15918 TORREY AVENUE - FONTANA CA 92335
55-106 SCORE, HERBERT JUDE	RADIO STATION WWWE - CLEVELAND OH 44101
73-106 SCOTT, ANTHONY	1526 DIXMONT AVE - CINCINNATI OH 45207
83-132 SCOTT, DONALD MALCOLM	OLD ADD: 705 W. HENRY - TAMPA FL 33604
26- 73 SCOTT, FLOYD JOHN 'PETE'	D. MAY 3, 1953 DALY CITY, CAL.
66- 81 SCOTT, GEORGE	1316 GOODRICH ST - GREENVILLE MS 38701
20-103 SCOTT, GEORGE WILLIAM	OLD ADD: CORSICANA TX 75110
14-194 SCOTT, JAMES WALTER	D. MAY 12, 1972 SOUTH PASADENA, FLA.
74-120 SCOTT, JOHN HENRY	1766 EAST 111TH PLACE - LOS ANGELES CA 90059
16- 74 SCOTT, JOHN WILLIAM	D. NOVEMBER 30 1959 DURHAM, N. C.
39-108 SCOTT, LEGRANT EDWARD	RR 1 BOX 2168 - SHELBY AL 35143
14-195 SCOTT, LEWIS EVERETT	D. NOVEMBER 2, 1960 FORT WAYNE, IND.
45- 94 SCOTT, MARSHALL 'LEFTY'	D. MARCH 3, 1964 HOUSTON, TEX.
79-101 SCOTT, MICHAEL WARREN	5417 WEST 134TH PLACE - HAWTHORNE CA 90250
72-101 SCOTT, RALPH ROBERT 'MICKEY'	1134 VESTAL AVE - BINGHAMTON NY 13903
63-107 SCOTT, RICHARD LEWIS	124 SHORTLEAF PL - THOMASVILLE GA 31792
75-104 SCOTT, RODNEY DARRELL	4206 PRISCILLA - INDIANAPOLIS IN 46226
84-107 SCRANTON, JAMES DEAN	27500 HAMMACK AVE - PERRIS CA 92370
75-105 SCRIVENER, WAYNE ALLISON	23673 S. VILLAGE HOUSE #3A - SOUTHFIELD MI 48034
80-117 SCURRY, RODNEY GRANT	300 GREENBRAE DRIVE - SPARKS NV 89431
64-103 SEALE, JOHNNIE RAY	1941 COUNTY RD 207 - DURANGO CO 81301
79-102 SEAMAN, KIM MICHAEL	4212 KREOLE AVE - MOSS POINT MS 39563
81-123 SEARAGE, RAYMOND MARK	24472 VERDANT DRIVE - FARMINGTON HILLS MI 48018
43-126 SEARS, KENNETH EUGENE	D. JULY 17, 1968 BRIDGEPORT, TEX.
12-176 SEATON, THOMAS GORDON	D. APRIL 10, 1940 ELPASO, TEX.
40- 80 SEATS, THOMAS EDWARD	9829 DEL MAR DRIVE - SAN RAMON CA 94583
67- 99 SEAVER, GEORGE THOMAS 'TOM'	LARKSPUR LN - GREENWICH CT 06830
85-102 SEBRA, ROBERT BUSH	OLD ADD: 60 MANHASSET TRAIL - MEDFORD LAKES NJ 08055
40- 81 SECORY, FRANK EDWARD	3026 MILITARY ST - PORT HURON MI 48060
69-155 SECRIST, DONALD LAVERN	104 NORTH LEONARD - DUQUOIN IL 62832
21- 91 SEDGEWICK, HENRY KENNETH 'DUKE'	D. DECEMBER 4, 1982 CLEARWATER, FLA.
19- 74 SEE, CHARLES HENRY	D. JULY 19, 1948 BRIDGEPORT, CONN.
86-136 SEE, RALPH LAURENCE 'LARRY'	13312 CROSSDALE AVENUE - NORWALK CA 90650
30- 71 SEEDS, ROBERT IRA	STAR RT BOX 152-A - GRAFORD TX 76045
71- 92 SEELBACH, CHARLES FREDERICK	20715 BEACHCLIFF BLVD - ROCKY RIVER OH 44116
43-127 SEEREY, JAMES PATRICK 'PAT'	D. APRIL 28, 1986 JENNINGS, MO.
82-111 SEGELKE, HERMAN NEILS	384 HEATHER WAY - SOUTH SAN FRANCISCO CA 94080
52- 93 SEGRIST, KAL HILL	3813 55TH ST - LUBBOCK TX 79413
62-120 SEGUI, DIEGO PABLO	13421 LEAVENWORTH RD - KANSAS CITY KS 66109
79-103 SEIBERT, KURT ELLIOTT	6518 ALLVIEW DRIVE - COLUMBIA MD 21046
15-145 SEIBOLD, HARRY 'SOCKS'	D. SEPTEMBER 21, 1965 PHILADELPHIA, PA.
80-118 SEILHEIMER, RICKY ALLEN	2400 STONEHOLLOW #510 - BRENHAM TX 77833
86-137 SEITZER, KEVIN LEE	1306 NICHOLSON ROAD - LINCOLN IL 62656
34- 90 SELKIRK, GEORGE ALEXANDER	D. JANUARY 19, 1987 FORT LAUDERDALE, FLA.
22-123 SELL, ELWOOD LESTER 'EPP'	D. FEBRUARY 20, 1961 READING, PA.
85-103 SELLERS, JEFFREY DOYLE	1506 E. POINSETTIA ST - LONG BEACH CA 90805

10-133 SELLERS, OLIVER 'RUBE'	D. JANUARY 14, 1952 PITTSBURGH, PA.
72-102 SELLS, DAVID WAYNE	3233 EAST GREENLEAF - BREA CA 92621
65- 98 SELMA, RICHARD JAY	1493 N. DELMAR AVE - FRESNO CA 93726
29- 94 SELPH, CAREY ISOM	D. FEBRUARY 24, 1976 HOUSTON, TEX.
77-128 SEMBER, MICHAEL DAVID	6N041 LINDEN AVE - MEDINAH IL 60157
65- 99 SEMBERA, CARROLL WILLIAM	BOX 1103 - SHINER TX 77984
43-128 SEMINICK, ANDREW WASIL	1920 SOUTH PARK AVE - MELBOURNE FL 32901
58- 82 SEMPROCH, ROMAN ANTHONY 'RAY'	4220 BUECHNER AVE - CLEVELAND OH 44109
52- 94 SENERCHIA, EMANUEL ROBERT 'SONNY'	805 SHORE ROAD - SPRING LAKE HEIGHTS NJ 07762
82-112 SENTENEY, STEVE LEONARD	5452 HILLSDALE BLVD - SACRAMENTO CA 95842
77-127 SEOANE, MANUEL MODESTO	4703 NORTH ROME AVE - TAMPA FL 33603
42- 95 SEPKOWSKI, THEODORE WALTER	128 INVERNESS RD - SEVERNA PARK MD 21146
49- 79 SERENA, WILLIAM ROBERT	26777 CALAROGA AVE - HAYWARD CA 94541
81-124 SERNA, PAUL DAVID	777 PICO #24 - EL CENTRO CA 92243
77-129 SERUM, GARY WAYNE	13996 WELLINGTON DRIVE - EDEN PRAIRIE MN 55344
41-100 SESSI, WALTER ANTHONY	351 WEST ST - MOBILE AL 36604
28- 80 SETTLEMIRE, EDGAR MERLE	D. JUNE 12, 1988 RUSSELL POINT, O.
65-100 SEVCIK, JOHN JOSEPH	201 OAKWOOD ROAD - HOPKINS MN 55343
11-151 SEVERAID, HENRY LEVAI	D. DECEMBER 17, 1968 SAN ANTONIO, TEX.
69-156 SEVERINSEN, ALBERT HENRY	1032 ARCHER PL - BALDWIN NY 11510
70-119 SEVERSON, RICHARD ALLEN	15218 LINCOLN CIR - OMAHA NE 68131
43-129 SEWARD, FRANK MARTIN	117 LARCHMONT RD - ELMIRA NY 14905
21- 92 SEWELL, JAMES LUTHER 'LUKE'	D. MAY 14, 1987 AKRON, O.
20-104 SEWELL, JOSEPH WHEELER	1618 DEARING PL - TUSCALOOSA AL 35401
27- 81 SEWELL, THOMAS WESLEY	D. JULY 30, 1956 MONTGOMERY, ALA.
32- 75 SEWELL, TRUETT BANKS 'RIP'	827 RUSSELL DR - PLANT CITY FL 33566
48- 92 SEXAUER, ELMER GEORGE	8008 VALLEY FARMS CT - INDIANAPOLIS IN 46214
77-130 SEXTON, JIMMY DALE	RR 2 BOX 187-B - WILMER AL 36587
63-108 SEYFRIED, GORDON CLAY	832 STANLEY AVE - LONG BEACH CA 90804
14-196 SHAFER, RALPH NEWTON	D. FEBRUARY 5, 1950 AKRON, O.
65-101 SHAMSKY, ARTHUR LEWIS	WNEW-TV, 205 EAST 67TH ST - NEW YORK NY 10021
73-107 SHANAHAN, PAUL GREGORY 'GREG'	240 WEST HAWTHORNE ST - EUREKA CA 95501
23-120 SHANER, WALTER DEDAKER	5472 LONDONDERRY - LAS VEGAS NV 89119
70-120 SHANK, HARVEY TILLMAN	10001 N. SEVENTH ST #118 - PHOENIX AZ 85012
12-177 SHANKS, HOWARD SAMUEL	D. JULY 30, 1941 MONACA, PA.
12-178 SHANLEY, HENRY ROOT 'DOC'	D. DECEMBER 14, 1934 ST. PETERSBURG, FLA.
20-105 SHANNER, WILFRED WILLIAM 'BILL'	D. DECEMBER 18, 1986 EVANSVILLE, IND.
15-146 SHANNON, JOSEPH ALOYSIUS	D. JULY 28, 1955 JERSEY CITY, N.J.
15-147 SHANNON, MAURICE JOSEPH 'RED'	D. APRIL 12, 1970 JERSEY CITY, N.J.
62-121 SHANNON, THOMAS MICHAEL 'MIKE'	3104 SOUTHWICK DRIVE - ST. LOUIS MO 63128
59- 72 SHANNON, WALTER CHARLES	416 THUN CREEK RD - CREVE COEUR MO 63141
49- 80 SHANTZ, ROBERT CLAYTON	152 MOUNT PLEASANT AVE - AMBLER PA 19002
54-100 SHANTZ, WILMER EBERT 'BILLY'	3430 NW 40TH CT - FORT LAUDERDALE FL 33309
17- 76 SHARMAN, RALPH EDWARD	D. MAY 24, 1918 CAMP SHERIDAN, ALA.
73-108 SHARON, RICHARD LOUIS	P.O. BOX 709 - DILLON MT 59725
73-109 SHARP, WILLIAM HOWARD	2244 THORNWOOD - WILMETTE IL 60091
87-132 SHARPERSON, MICHAEL TYRONE	111 DORCHESTER AVENUE - ORANGEBURG SC 29115
22-124 SHAUTE, JOSEPH BENJAMIN	D. FEBRUARY 21, 1970 SCRANTON, PA.
17- 77 SHAW, BENJAMIN NATHANIEL	D. MARCH 16, 1959 AURORA, O.
67-100 SHAW, DONALD WELLINGTON	12228 POGGEMOELLER - ST. LOUIS MO 63138
13-162 SHAW, JAMES ALOYSIUS	D. JANUARY 27, 1962 WASHINGTON, D.C.
57- 77 SHAW, ROBERT JOHN	31 SADDLE BACK RD - JUPITER FL 33458
13-163 SHAWKEY, JAMES ROBERT 'BOB'	D. DECEMBER 31, 1980 SYRACUSE, N.Y.
16- 75 SHAY, ARTHUR JOSEPH 'MARTY'	D. FEBRUARY 20, 1951 WORCESTER, MASS.
47- 77 SHEA, FRANCIS JOSEPH 'SPEC'	72 JOHNSON - NAUGATUCK CT 06770
28- 81 SHEA, JOHN MICHAEL JOSEPH	D. NOVEMBER 30, 1956 MALDEN, MASS.
27- 82 SHEA, MERVYN DAVID JOHN	D. JANUARY 27, 1953 SACRAMENTO, CAL.
18- 65 SHEA, PATRICK HENRY	D. NOVEMBER 17, 1981 STAFFORD, CONN.
68- 93 SHEA, STEVEN FRANCIS	OLD ADD: RR 1, JUNIPER DR - AMHERST NH
87-133 SHEAFFER, DANNY TODD	779 FISHING CREEK ROAD - NEW CUMBERLAND PA 17070
28- 82 SHEALY, ALBERT BERLEY	D. MARCH 7, 1967 HAGERSTOWN, MD.
57- 78 SHEARER, RAY SOLOMON	D. FEBRUARY 21, 1982 YORK, PA.

12-179 SHEARS, GEORGE PENFIELD	D. NOVEMBER 12, 1978 LOVELAND, COLO.
36- 84 SHEEHAN, JAMES THOMAS	107 ROBERT DR - EAST HAVEN CT 06512
20-106 SHEEHAN, JOHN THOMAS	D. MAY 29, 1987 WEST PALM BEACH, FLA.
15-148 SHEEHAN, THOMAS CLANCY	D. OCTOBER 29, 1982 CHILLICOTHE, O.
21- 93 SHEELY, EARL HOMER	D. SEPTEMBER 16, 1952 SEATTLE, WASH.
51- 90 SHEELY, HOLLIS KIMBALL 'BUD'	D. OCTOBER 17, 1985 SACRAMENTO, CALIF.
36- 85 SHEERIN, CHARLES JOSEPH	D. SEPTEMBER 27, 1986 VALLEY STREAM, N. Y.
84-108 SHEETS, LARRY KENT	BOX 277 - POCONOKE MD 21851
81-125 SHELBY, JOHN T	711 HEADLEY AVE - LEXINGTON KY 40508
74-121 SHELDON, BOB MITCHELL	BOX 4993 - CANYON LAKE CA 92380
61- 98 SHELDON, ROLAND FRANK	614 NE CORONADO - LEES SUMMIT MO 64063
18- 66 SHELLENBACK, FRANK VICTOR	D. AUGUST 17, 1969 NEWTON, MASS.

66- 82 SHELLENBACK, JAMES PHILIP	BOX 614 - BAKER OR 97814
35- 98 SHELLEY, HUBERT LENEIRRE 'HUGH'	D. JUNE 16, 1978 BEAUMONT, TEX.
15-149 SHELTON, ANDREW KEMPER 'SKEETER'	D. JANUARY 9, 1954 HUNTINGTON, W. VA.
44-121 SHEMO, STEPHEN MICHAEL 'STAN'	RR 1 BOX 290A - MADISON NC 27025
53- 82 SHEPARD, JACK LEROY	2450 EL CAMINO RD #108 - PALO ALTO CA 94306
68- 94 SHEPARD, LAWRENCE WILLIAM	1716 PINEDALE - LINCOLN NE 68520
45- 95 SHEPARD, ROBERT EARL 'BERT'	8014 BANGOR AVE - HESPERIA CA 92345
24- 95 SHEPHARDSON, RAYMOND FRANCIS	D. NOVEMBER 8, 1975 LITTLE FALLS, N. Y.
84-109 SHEPHERD, RONALD WAYNE	RR 2 BOX 53X - KILGORE TX 75662
18- 67 SHERDEL, WILLIAM HENRY	D. NOVEMBER 14, 1968 MCSHERRYSTOWN, PA.
29- 95 SHERID, ROYDEN RICHARD	D. FEBRUARY 28, 1982 PARKER FORD, PA.
18- 68 SHERIDAN, EUGENE ANTHONY 'RED'	D. NOVEMBER 25, 1975 QUEENS VILLAGE, N. Y.
48- 93 SHERIDAN, NEILL RAWLINS	150 CHAUCER DR - PLEASANT HILL CA 94523
81-126 SHERIDAN, PATRICK ARTHUR	31654 TAFT- WAYNE MI 48184
24- 96 SHERLING, EDWARD CREECH	D. NOVEMBER 16, 1965 ENTERPRISE, ALA.
30- 72 SHERLOCK, JOHN CLINTON 'MONK'	D. NOVEMBER 26, 1985 BUFFALO, N. Y.
35- 99 SHERLOCK, VINCENT THOMAS	237 SUMMIT AVE-BUFFALO NY 14214
15-150 SHERMAN, JOEL POWERS	5318 MALALUKA CT - CAPE CORAL FL 33904
14-197 SHERMAN, LESTER DANIEL 'BABE'	D. SEPTEMBER 16, 1955 HIGHLAND PARK, MICH.
78-119 SHERRILL, DENNIS LEE	OLD ADD: 240 SW 63RD CT - MIAMI FL 33144
11-152 SHERRY, FRED PETER	D. JULY 27, 1975 HONESDALE, PA.
58- 83 SHERRY, LAWRENCE	27181 ARENA LN - MISSION VIEJO CA 92675
59- 73 SHERRY, NORMAN BURT	4383-89 NOBEL DRIVE - SAN DIEGO CA 92122
59- 74 SHETRONE, BARRY STEVAN	2170 SPRINGDALE RD - PASADENA MD 21122
30- 73 SHEVLIN, JAMES CORNELIUS	D. OCTOBER 30, 1974 FORT LAUDERDALE, FLA.
24- 97 SHIELDS, BENJAMIN COWAN	D. JANUARY 24, 1982 WOODRUFF, S. C.
15-151 SHIELDS, FRANCIS LEROY 'PETE'	D. FEBRUARY 11, 1961 JACKSON, MISS.
85-104 SHIELDS, STEPHEN MACK	LYNDA AVE, RR 11 - GADSDEN AL 35903
24- 98 SHIELDS, VINCENT WILLIAM	D. NOVEMBER 24, 1952 PLASTER ROCK, NEB.
57- 79 SHIFFLETT, GARLAND JESSIE	1095 CODY - LAKEWOOD CO 80215
39-109 SHILLING, JAMES ROBERT	D. SEPTEMBER 12, 1986 TULSA, OKLA.
21- 94 SHINAULT, ENOCH ERSKINE 'GINGER'	D. DECEMBER 29, 1930 DENVER, COLO.
83-133 SHINES, ANTHONY RAYMOND 'RAZOR'	7119 MARINERS WAY #C - INDIANAPOLIS IN 46224
22-125 SHINNERS, RALPH PETER	D. JULY 23, 1962 MILWAUKEE, WIS.
85-105 SHIPANOFF, DAVID NOEL	3 SALINA DRIVE - SAINT ALBERT, ALBERTA CAN.
86-138 SHIPLEY, CRAIG BARRY	52 BEAMISH ROAD - NORTHMEAD, N.S.W. AUSTRALIA 2152
58- 84 SHIPLEY, JOSEPH CLARK	OLD ADD: 29 HONEY LOCUST #7 - ST CHARLES MO
28- 83 SHIRES, CHARLES ARTHUR 'ART'	D. JULY 13, 1967 ITALY, TEX.
20-107 SHIREY, CLAIR LEE 'DUKE'	D. SEPTEMBER 1, 1962 HAGERSTOWN, MD.
41-101 SHIRLEY, ALVIS NEWMAN 'TEX'	416 LOWRENCE ROAD - RED OAK TX 75154
64-104 SHIRLEY, BARTON ARVIN	4602D CEDAR PASS - CORPUS CHRISTI TX 78413
24- 99 SHIRLEY, ERNEST RAEFORD 'MULE'	D. AUGUST 3, 1955 GOLDSBORO, N. C.
77-131 SHIRLEY, ROBERT CHARLES	3838 CAMINO DEL RIO NORTH #252-SAN DIEGO CA 92108
82-113 SHIRLEY, STEVEN BRIAN	9200 JAMES PLACE NE - ALBUQUERQUE NM 87111
31- 81 SHIVER, IVEY MERWIN	D. AUGUST 31, 1972 SAVANNAH, GA.
16- 76 SHOCKER, URBAN JAMES	D. SEPTEMBER 9, 1928 DENVER, COLO.
64-105 SHOCKLEY, JOHN COSTEN	405 WALTER ST - GEORGETOWN DE 19947
61- 99 SHOEMAKER, CHARLES LANDIS	2310 FAIRVIEW AVE - MOUNT PENN PA 19606
29- 96 SHOFFNER, MILBURN JAMES 'MILT'	D. JANUARY 19, 1978 MADISON, O.
47- 78 SHOFNER, FRANK STRICKLAND 'STRICK'	816 MAJESTIC - HEWITT TX 76643
41-102 SHOKES, EDWARD CHRISTOPHER	222 SPRING STREET - WINCHESTER VA 22601
16- 77 SHOOK, RAYMAND CURTIS	D. SEPTEMBER 16, 1970 SOUTH BEND, IND.
59- 75 SHOOP, RONALD LEE	BOX 92 - RURAL VALLEY PA 16249
67-101 SHOPAY, THOMAS MICHAEL	17923 SW 77TH CT - MIAMI FL 33157
12-180 SHORE, ERNEST GRADY	D. SEPTEMBER 24, 1980 WINSTON-SALEM, N.C.
46- 92 SHORE, RAYMOND EVERETT	675 SILVER LEDGE LN - CINCINNATI OH 45231
28- 84 SHORES, WILLIAM DAVID	D. FEBRUARY 19, 1984 PURCELL, OKLA.
59- 76 SHORT, CHRISTOPHER JOSEPH	1609 BARNABY ST - NEWARK DE 19702
40- 82 SHORT, DAVID ORVIS	D. NOVEMBER 22, 1983 SHREVEPORT, LA.
60- 93 SHORT, WILLIAM ROSS	2975 57TH ST - SARASOTA FL 33580
15-152 SHORTEN, CHARLES HENRY 'CHICK'	D. OCTOBER 23, 1965 SCRANTON, PA.
35-100 SHOUN, CLYDE MITCHELL	D. MARCH 20, 1968 MOUNTAIN HOME, TENN.
11-153 SHOVLIN, JOHN JOSEPH	D. FEBRUARY 16, 1976 BETHESDA, MD.
81-127 SHOW, ERIC VAUGHN	P.O. BOX 29009 - SAN DIEGO CA 92124
22-126 SHRIVER, HARRY GRAYDON	D. JANUARY 21, 1970 MORGANTOWN, W. VA.
48- 94 SHUBA, GEORGE THOMAS	3421 BENT WILLOW LN - YOUNGSTOWN OH 44511
11-154 SHULTZ, WALLACE LUTHER 'TOOTS'	D. JANUARY 30, 1959 MCKEESPORT, PA.
42- 96 SHUMAN, HARRY	7402 MALVERN AVE - PHILADELPHIA PA 19151
45- 96 SHUPE, VINCENT WILLIAM	D. APRIL 5, 1962 CANTON, O.
16- 78 SICKING, EDWARD JOSEPH	D. AUGUST 30, 1938 CINCINNATI, O.
56- 76 SIEBERN, NORMAN LEROY	4951 N. TAMIAMI TR #6 - NAPLES FL 33940
74-122 SIEBERT, PAUL EDWARD	4804 WEST 70TH ST - EDINA MN 55135
32- 76 SIEBERT, RICHARD WALTHER	D. DECEMBER 9, 1978 MINNEAPOLIS, MINN.

BOB SHIRLEY

TOMMY SHOPAY

64-106 SIEBERT, WILFRED CHARLES 'SONNY'   2583 BRUSH CREEK - ST LOUIS MO 63129
63-109 SIEBLER, DWIGHT LEROY   231 SOUTH WESGAYE - GRETNA NE 68028
25- 92 SIEMER, OSCAR SYLVESTER   D. DECEMBER 5, 1959 ST. LOUIS, MO.
86-139 SIERRA, RUBEN ANGEL   EDIF. 25 #2501, JARDINES SELLES - RIO PIEDRAS PR 00924
49- 81 SIEVERS, ROY EDWARD   11505 BELLEFONTAINE RD-SPANISH LAKE MO 63138
26- 74 SIGAFOOS, FRANCIS LEONARD   D. APRIL 12, 1968 INDIANAPOLIS, IND.
14-198 SIGLIN, WESLEY PETER 'PADDY'   D. AUGUST 5, 1956 OAKLAND, CALIF.
29- 97 SIGMAN, WESLEY TRIPLETT 'TRIPP'   D. MARCH 8, 1971 AUGUSTA, GA.
43-130 SIGNER, WALTER DONALD ALOYSIUS   D. JULY 23, 1974 GREENWICH, CONN.
37- 94 SILBER, EDWARD JAMES   D. OCTOBER 26, 1976 DUNEDIN, FLA.
19- 75 SILVA, DANIEL JAMES   D. APRIL 4, 1974 HYANNIS, MASS.
55-107 SILVERA, AARON ALBERT 'AL'   723 NORTH SIERRA DR - BEVERLY HILLS CA 90210
48- 95 SILVERA, CHARLES ANTHONY RYAN   1240 MANZANITA DR - MILLBRAE CA 94030
78-120 SILVERIO, LUIS PASCUAL   CLE NUMA SILVERIO#7 VIL GONZALEZ-STO DOMINGO DOM. REP.
70-121 SILVERIO, TOMAS ROBERTO   CALLE 9#14 COLINAS - SANTO DOMINGO DOMINICAN REP.
39-110 SILVESTRI, KENNETH JOSEPH   3328 WEST LAKE SHORE DR - TALLAHASSEE FL 32303
50- 89 SIMA, ALBERT   813 CENTER ST - BRANDON FL 33511
24-100 SIMMONS, ALOYSIUS HARRY   D. MAY 26, 1956 MILWAUKEE, WIS.
47- 79 SIMMONS, CURTIS THOMAS   200 PARK RD - PROSPECTVILLE PA 19002
10-134 SIMMONS, GEORGE WASHINGTON 'HACK'   D. APRIL 26, 1942 ARVERNE, N.Y.
49- 82 SIMMONS, JOHN EARL   9 LEE DR - FARMINGDALE NY 11735
84-110 SIMMONS, NELSON BERNARD   209 CEDARIDGE DR - SAN DIEGO CA 92114
28- 85 SIMMONS, PATRICK CLEMENT   D. JULY 3, 1968 ALBANY, N.Y.
68- 95 SIMMONS, TED LYLE   P.O. BOX 26 - CHESTERFIELD MO 63006
23-121 SIMON, SYLVESTER ADAM   D. FEBRUARY 28, 1973 CHANDLER, IND.
31- 82 SIMONS, MELBERN ELLIS   D. OCTOBER 11, 1974 PADUCAH, KY.
51- 91 SIMPSON, HARRY LEON   D. APRIL 3, 1979 AKRON, O.
75-106 SIMPSON, JOE ALLEN   704 CEDARBROOK - NORMAN OK 73072
62-122 SIMPSON, RICHARD CHARLES   696 SAN JUAN AVE - VENICE CA 90291
72-103 SIMPSON, STEVEN EDWARD   5031 SW 26TH TER - TOPEKA KS 66614
53- 83 SIMPSON, THOMAS LEO   22640 JAMESON DR - WOODLAND HILLS CA 91364
70-122 SIMPSON, WAYNE KIRBY   330 COLLAMER DR - CARSON CA 90744
15-153 SIMS, CLARENCE 'PETE'   D. DECEMBER 2, 1968 DALLAS, TEX.
64-107 SIMS, DUANE B. 'DUKE'   6 GALLOPING HILL ROAD - BROOKFIELD CENTER CT 06805
66- 83 SIMS, GREGORY EMMETT   6700 RANCHO PICO WAY - SACRAMENTO CA 95828
81-128 SINATRO, MATTHEW STEPHEN   68 MONTRE SQUARE NW - ATLANTA GA 30327
64-108 SINGER, WILLIAM ROBERT   1410 WEST BAY AVE - NEWPORT BEACH CA 92663
45- 97 SINGLETON, BERT ELMER   P.O. BOX 972 - OGDEN UT 84402
22-127 SINGLETON, JOHN EDWARD   D. OCTOBER 23, 1937 DAYTON, O.
70-123 SINGLETON, KENNETH WAYNE   5 TREMBLANT CT - LUTHERVILLE MD 21093
34- 91 SINGTON, FREDERIC WILLIAM   2017 5TH AVE NORTH - BIRMINGHAM AL 35203
45- 98 SIPEK, RICHARD FRANCIS   1611 JACKSON ST - QUINCY IL 62301
69-157 SIPIN, JOHN WHITE   328 HERMAN AVE - WATSONVILLE CA 95076
82-114 SISK, DOUGLAS RANDALL   1408 BENCH DR NE - TACOMA WA 98422
62-123 SISK, TOMMIE WAYNE   4325 FALCON AVENUE - LONG BEACH CA 90807
56- 77 SISLER, DAVID MICHAEL   11 HACIENDA DR - ST LOUIS MO 63124
15-154 SISLER, GEORGE HAROLD   D. MARCH 26, 1973 ST. LOUIS, MO.
46- 93 SISLER, RICHARD ALLEN   2315 ABBOTT MARTIN RD - NASHVILLE TN 37212
39-111 SISTI, SEBASTIAN DANIEL 'SIBBY'   39 CLIFFORD HEIGHTS - AMHERST NY 14226
36- 86 SIVESS, PETER   RR 1 BOX 555 - ST. MICHAELS MD 21663
82-115 SIWY, JAMES GERARD   103 DARLING ST - CENTRAL FALLS RI 02863
69-158 SIZEMORE, TED CRAWFORD   OLD ADD: 1059 FRUIT TREE LN - CREVE COEUR MO 63141
35-101 SKAFF, FRANCIS MICHAEL   D. APRIL 12, 1988 TOWSON, MD.
77-132 SKAGGS, DAVID LINDSEY   911 DAUGHERTY RD - NORCO CA 91760
57- 80 SKAUGSTAD, DAVID WENDALL   1113 N. MAR-LES DR - SANTA ANA CA 92706
10-135 SKEELS, DAVID   D. DECEMBER 2, 1926 SPOKANE, WASH.
42- 97 SKETCHLEY, HARRY CLEMENT 'BUD'   D. DECEMBER 19, 1979 LOS ANGELES, CALIF.
70-124 SKIDMORE, ROBERT ROE   815 SOUTH STONE - DECATUR IL 62521
21- 95 SKIFF, WILLIAM FRANKLIN   D. DECEMBER 25, 1976 BRONXVILLE, N.Y.
22-128 SKINNER, ELISHA HARRISON 'CAMP'   D. AUGUST 4, 1944 DOUGLASVILLE, GA.
83-134 SKINNER, JOEL PATRICK   9 FOXRUN DRIVE - INGLEWOOD NJ 07631
54-101 SKINNER, ROBERT RALPH   1576 DIAMOND ST - SAN DIEGO CA 92109
56- 78 SKIZAS, LOUIS PETER   2101 WEST WHITE - CHAMPAIGN IL 61821
73-110 SKOK, CRAIG RICHARD   105 ARBOUR RUN - SUWANEE GA 30174
54-102 SKOWRON, WILLIAM JOSEPH 'MOOSE'   1118 BEACHCOMBER DR - SCHAUMBURG IL 60193
82-116 SKUBF, ROBERT JACOB   3569 GREENVILLE DR - SIMI VALLEY CA 93063
30- 74 SLADE, GORDON LEIGH   D. JANUARY 2, 1974 LONG BEACH, CALIF.
79-104 SLAGLE, ROGER LEE   536 WEST THIRD ST - LARNED KS 67550
10-136 SLAGLE, WALTER JENNINGS   D. JUNE 17, 1974 SAN GABRIEL, CALIF.
11-155 SLAPNICKA, CYRIL CHARLES   D. OCTOBER 20, 1979 CEDAR RAPIDS, IA.
20-108 SLAPPEY, JOHN HENRY   D. JUNE 10, 1957 MARIETTA, GA.
71- 93 SLATON, JAMES MICHAEL   43515 28TH WEST - LANCASTER CA 93534
15-155 SLATTERY, PHILIP RYAN   D. MARCH 2, 1968 LONG BEACH, CAL9F.
82-117 SLAUGHT, DONALD MARTIN   5420 MEADOWDALE LN - RANCHO PALOS VD CA 90274

1945

DAVE SKAGGS

10-137	SLAUGHTER, BYRON ATKINS 'BARNEY'	D. MAY 17, 1961 PHILADELPHIA PA.
38- 90	SLAUGHTER, ENOS BRADSHER	RR 2-ROXBORO NC 27573
64-109	SLAUGHTER, STERLING FEORE	2530 S. EVERGREEN RD - TEMPE AZ 85282
26- 75	SLAYBACK, ELBERT 'SCOTTIE'	D. NOVEMBER 30, 1979 CINCINNATI, O.
72-104	SLAYBACK, WILLIAM GROVER	4918 CECILVILLE - LACRESCENTA CA 91214
28- 86	SLAYTON, FOSTER HERBERT 'STEVE'	D. DECEMBER 20, 1984 MANCHESTER, N. H.
50- 90	SLEATER, LOUIS MORTIMER	515 BROOK RD - TOWSON MD 21204
44-122	SLOAN, BRUCE ADAMS	D. SEPTEMBER 24, 1973 OKLAHOMA CITY, OKLA.
13-164	SLOAN, YALE YEASTMAN 'TOD'	D. SEPTEMBER 12, 1956 AKRON, O.
48- 96	SLOAT, DWAIN CLIFFORD	2101 EAST 5TH ST - ST PAUL MN 55119
69-159	SLOCUM, RONALD REECE	OLD ADD: 5715 BALTIMORE DR #82 - LAMESA CA 92041
30- 75	SMALL, CHARLES ALBERT	D. JANUARY 14, 1953 LEWISTON, ME.
78-121	SMALL, GEORGE HENRY 'HANK'	P.O. BOX 763 - MOUNT PLEASANT SC 29464
55-108	SMALL, JAMES ARTHUR	9420 TAYLORS TURN - STANWOOD MI 49346
48- 97	SMALLEY, ROY FREDERICK JR	534 WEST ARBOR VITAE - INGLEWOOD CA 90301
75-107	SMALLEY, ROY FREDERICK III	5739 LONG BRAKE CIRCLE - MINNEAPOLIS MN 55435
17- 78	SMALLWOOD, WALTER CLAYTON	D. APRIL 29, 1967
46- 94	SMAZA, JOSEPH PAUL	D. MAY 30, 1979 ROYAL OAK, MICH.
86-140	SMILEY, JOHN PATRICK	208 WEST THIRD AVENUE - TRAPPE PA 19426
34- 92	SMITH, ALFRED JOHN	D. APRIL 28, 1977 BROWNSVILLE, TEX.
26- 76	SMITH, ALFRED KENDRICKS	23928 GREEN HAVEN - RAMONA CA 92065
53- 84	SMITH, ALPHONSE EUGENE	8440 INDIANA 3RD FLOOR - CHICAGO IL 60619
12-182	SMITH, ARMSTRONG FREDERICK 'KLONDIKE'	D. NOVEMBER 15, 1959 SPRINGFIELD, MASS.
32- 77	SMITH, ARTHUR LAIRD	73 OENOKE RIDGE #307 - NEW CANAAN CT 06840
75-108	SMITH, BILLY ED	OLD ADD: 5439 TIMBER POST - SAN ANTONIO TX 78250
81-129	SMITH, BILLY LAVERN	8407 NEFF - HOUSTON TX 77036
57- 81	SMITH, BOBBY GENE	11808 WOODBINE LANE SW - TACOMA WA 98499
87-134	SMITH, BRICK DUDLEY	4743 AMITY PLACE - CHARLOTTE NC 28212
81-130	SMITH, BRYN NELSON	812 EAST FELSER - SANTA MARIA CA 93454
70-125	SMITH, CALVIN BERNARD 'BERNIE'	BOX 513 - LUTCHER LA 70071
66- 84	SMITH, CARL REGINALD 'REGGIE'	11764 DORAL AVENUE - NORTHRIDGE CA 91326
60- 94	SMITH, CHARLES WILLIAM	3060 SPROUT WAY - SPARKS NV 89431
81-131	SMITH, CHRISTOPHER WILLIAM	4817 E. CHOLLA - SCOTTSDALE AZ 85254
13-165	SMITH, CLARENCE OSSIE	D. FEBRUARY 16, 1924 SWEETWATER, TEX.
38- 91	SMITH, CLAY JAMIESON	RR 1 BOX 9 - CAMBRIDGE KS 67023
38- 92	SMITH, DAVID MERWIN	BOX 671-WHITEVILLE NC 28472
80-119	SMITH, DAVID STANLEY	1225 RANCHO ENCINITAS DR - ENCINITAS CA 92024
84-111	SMITH, DAVID WAYNE	16330 JERSEY DR - HOUSTON TX 77040
12-183	SMITH, DOUGLASS WELDON	D. SEPTEMBER 18, 1973 GREENFIELD, MASS.
55-109	SMITH, EARL CALVIN	2764 NORTH LEONARD - FRESNO CA 93727
16- 79	SMITH, EARL LEONARD	D. MARCH 14, 1943 PORTSMOUTH, O.
19- 76	SMITH, EARL SUTTON	D. JUNE 8, 1963 LITTLE ROCK, ARK.
36- 87	SMITH, EDGAR	ROUTE 130 KINKORA - BORDENTOWN NJ 08505
45- 99	SMITH, EDWARD MAYO	D. NOVEMBER 24, 1977 BOYNTON BEACH, FLA.
14-199	SMITH, ELMER JOHN	D. AUGUST 3, 1984 COLUMBIA, KY.
26- 77	SMITH, ELWOOD HOPE 'MIKE'	D. MAY 31, 1981 CHESAPEAKE, VA.
23-122	SMITH, EMANUEL CARR	731 SHIRLEY AVENUE - NORFOLK VA 23517
30- 76	SMITH, ERNEST HENRY	D. APRIL 6, 1973 BROOKLYN, N. Y.
50- 91	SMITH, FRANK THOMAS	120 89TH AVE - ST PETERSBURG FL 33702
13-166	SMITH, FREDERICK VINCENT	D. MAY 28, 1961 CLEVELAND, O.
16- 80	SMITH, GEORGE ALLEN	D. JANUARY 7, 1965 GREENWICH, CONN.
63-110	SMITH, GEORGE CORNELIUS	D. JUNE 15, 1987 ST. PETERSBURG, FLA.
26- 78	SMITH, GEORGE SELBY	D. MAY 26, 1981 RICHMOND, VA.
32- 78	SMITH, HAROLD LAVERNE	5200 N. OCEAN BLVD #612 - FORT LAUDERDALE FL 33308
56- 79	SMITH, HAROLD RAYMOND	6602 WINKLEMAN - HOUSTON TX 77083
55-110	SMITH, HAROLD WAYNE	2322 MAPLE CREST DRIVE - MISSOURI CITY TX 77459
12-183	SMITH, HARRISON M	D. JULY 26, 1964 DUNBAR, NEB.
10-138	SMITH, HENRY JOSEPH 'HAP'	D. FEBRUARY 26, 1961 SAN JOSE, CALIF.
62-124	SMITH, JACK HATFIELD	BOX 23 - NORTH MATEWAN WV 25688
11-156	SMITH, JACOB G	B. DUBOIS, PA.
11-157	SMITH, JAMES CARLISLE 'RED'	D. OCTOBER 11, 1966 ATLANTA, GA.
14-200	SMITH, JAMES HARRY	D. APRIL 1, 1922 CHARLOTTE, N.C.
14-201	SMITH, JAMES LAWRENCE	D. JANUARY 1, 1974 PITTSBURGH, PA.
82-118	SMITH, JAMES LORNE	4452 MISTY WAY - YORBA LINDA CA 92686
15-156	SMITH, JOHN	D. MAY 2, 1972 WESTCHESTER, ILL.
31- 83	SMITH, JOHN MARSHALL	D. MAY 9, 1982 SILVER SPRING, MD.
13-167	SMITH, JOHN WILLIAM 'CHICK'	D. OCTOBER 11, 1935 DAYTON, KY.
77-133	SMITH, KEITH LAVARNE	OLD ADD: 522 11TH ST NORTH - PALMETTO FL 33561
81-132	SMITH, KENNETH EARL	100 LANSDOWNE BLVD - YOUNGSTOWN OH 44506
20-109	SMITH, LAWRENCE PATRICK 'PADDY'	P.O. BOX 775 - QUECHEE VT 05059
80-120	SMITH, LEE ARTHUR	OLD ADD: 4170 N. MARINE #4L - CHICAGO IL 60613
84-112	SMITH, LEROY PURDY 'ROY'	472 GRAMATON AVE - MOUNT VERNON NY 10552
78-122	SMITH, LONNIE	185 RIDGEWOOD DRIVE - SPARTANBURG SC 29303
83-135	SMITH, MARK CHRISTOPHER	OLD ADD: 711 SOUTH 19TH ST - ARLINGTON VA 22202

128

ID	Name	Address/Status
25- 93	SMITH, MARVIN HAROLD 'RED'	D. FEBRUARY 19, 1961 LOS ANGELES, CAL.
84-113	SMITH, MICHAEL ANTHONY	3226 LIVINGSTON RD - JACKSON MS 39213
55-111	SMITH, MILTON	3505 CADET SHERIDAN RD #A - WAHIAWA HI 96786
62-125	SMITH, NATHANIEL BEVERLY	OLD ADD: 5303 ENNIS ST - HOUSTON TX 77004
78-123	SMITH, OSBORNE EARL 'OZZIE'	9914 LITZSINGER ROAD - ST. LOUIS MO 63124
84-114	SMITH, PATRICK KEITH	19537 CHADWAY ST - CANYON COUNTRY CA 91351
53- 85	SMITH, PAUL LESLIE	27 RAVENSWORTH RD - CONROE TX 77301
16- 81	SMITH, PAUL STONER	D. JULY 3, 1958 DECATUR, ILL.
87-135	SMITH, PETER JOHN	OLD ADD: BURLINGTON MA
62-126	SMITH, PETER LUKE	52 FAIRVIEW AVENUE - NATICK MA 01760
81-133	SMITH, RAYMOND EDWARD	OLD ADD: 1063 OAK DR - VISTA CA 92083
63-111	SMITH, RICHARD ARTHUR	2252 TABLE ROCK ROAD #143 - MEDFORD OR 97501
51- 92	SMITH, RICHARD HARRISON	1926 NORWOOD LN - STATE COLLEGE PA 16801
69-160	SMITH, RICHARD KELLY	RR 7 BOX 200 - LINCOLNTON NC 28092
27- 83	SMITH, RICHARD PAUL 'RED'	D. MARCH 8, 1978 TOLEDO, O.
13-169	SMITH, ROBERT ASHLEY	1914 ADD: HARDWICK VT
23-123	SMITH, ROBERT ELDRIDGE	D. JULY 19, 1987 WAYCROSS, GA.
55-112	SMITH, ROBERT GILCHRIST	47 FERNWOOD - TEXARKANA TX 75503
58- 85	SMITH, ROBERT WALKAY 'RIVERBOAT'	RR 1 BOX 21 - CLARENCE MO 63437
27- 84	SMITH, RUFUS FRAZIER	D. AUGUST 21, 1984 AIKEN, S. C.
13-168	SMITH, SALVATORE GIUSEPPE 'JOE'	D. JANUARY 12, 1974 YONKERS, N. Y.
11-158	SMITH, SHEROD MALONE	D. SEPTEMBER 12, 1949 REIDSVILLE, GA.
73-111	SMITH, TOMMIE ALEXANDER	1299 EAST CANNON AVE - ALBEMARIE NC 28001
41-103	SMITH, VINCENT AMBROSE	D. DECEMBER 14, 1979 VIRGINIA BEACH, VA.
11-159	SMITH, WALLACE H.	D. JUNE 10, 1930 FLORENCE, ARIZ.
17- 79	SMITH, WILLARD JEHU 'RED'	D. JULY 17, 1972 NOBLESVILLE, IND
58- 86	SMITH, WILLIAM GARLAND	4265 BRANCH SE AVENUE - TEMPLE HILLS MD 20748
63-112	SMITH, WILLIE	607 BRADFORD ST - HOBSON CITY AL 36201
84-115	SMITH, ZANE WILLIAM	RR 4 BOX 138-C1 - NORTH PLATTE NE 69101
82-119	SMITHSON, BILLY MIKE	BOX 204 - CENTERVILLE TN 37033
40- 83	SMOLL, CLYDE HETRICK	D. AUGUST 31, 1985 QUAKERTOWN, PA.
12-184	SMOYER, HENRY NEITZ	D. FEBRUARY 28, 1958 DUBOIS, PA.
16- 82	SMYKAL, FRANK JOHN	D. AUGUST 11, 1950 CHICAGO, ILL.
44-123	SMYRES, CLARENCE MELVIN 'CLANCY'	11470 ORCAS AVE - SAN FERNANDO CA 91342
15-157	SMYTH, JAMES DANIEL 'RED'	D. APRIL 14, 1958 INGLEWOOD, CALIF.
29- 98	SMYTHE, WILLIAM HENRY 'HARRY'	D. AUGUST 28, 1980 AUGUSTA, GA.
12-185	SNELL, CHARLES ANTHONY	D. APRIL 4, 1988 READING, PA.
84-116	SNELL, NATHANIEL	RR 2 BOX 42 - HOLLY HILL SC 29059
13-170	SNELL, WALTER HENRY	D. JULY 23, 1980 PROVIDENCE, R. I.
47- 80	SNIDER, EDWIN DONALD 'DUKE'	3037 LAKEMONT DR - FALLBROOK CA 92028
23-124	SNIPES, WYATT EURE 'ROXY'	D. MAY 1, 1941 FAYETTEVILLE, N. C.
73-112	SNOOK, FRANK WALTER	OLD ADD: RR2 - WHITEHOUSE STATION NJ
19- 77	SNOVER, COLONEL LESTER	D. APRIL 30, 1969 ROCHESTER, N. Y.
35-102	SNYDER, BERNARD AUSTIN	2415 WAVERLY - PHILADELPHIA PA 19146
85-106	SNYDER, BRIAN ROBERT	14834 WOOD HOME ROAD - CENTERVILLE VA 22020
59- 77	SNYDER, EUGENE WALTER	1960 NORTH SHERMAN ST - YORK PA 17402
12-186	SNYDER, FRANK ELTON	D. JANUARY 5, 1962 SAN ANTONIO, TEX.
86-141	SNYDER, JAMES CORY	816 AILEEN STREET - CAMARILLO CA 93010
61-100	SNYDER, JAMES ROBERT	8613 BACKWOOD - TAMPA FL 33615
52- 95	SNYDER, JERRY GEORGE	2420 GULFCREST BLVD - PEARLAND TX 77581
14-202	SNYDER, JOHN WILLIAM	D. DECEMBER 13, 1981 REDSTONE TWP., PA.
59- 78	SNYDER, RUSSELL HENRY	BOX 114 - NELSON NE 68961
19- 78	SNYDER, WILLIAM NICHOLAS	D. OCTOBER 8, 1934 VICKSBURG, MICH.
37- 95	SODD, WILLIAM	3845 DIAMON LOCK WEST - FORT WORTH TX 76118
71- 94	SODERHOLM, ERIC THANE	10 SOUTH 360 HAMPSHIRE LN WEST - HINSDALE IL 60521
86-142	SOFF, RAYMOND JOHN	9015 RODESILER HIGHWAY - RIGA MI 49276
79-105	SOFIELD, RICHARD MICHAEL	BASEBALL OFFICE, JMH CENTER - SALT LAKE CITY UT 84114
68- 96	SOLAITA, TOLIA 'TONY'	317 ALTA VISTA DR-SOUTH SAN FRANCISCO CA94080
83-136	SOLANO, JULIO CESAR	VILLA ESPANA C.O. 31 - LAROMANA DOMINICAN REP.
58- 87	SOLIS, MARCELINO	OLD ADD: CALLE VIDREA 8370 - MONTEREY MEXICO
73-113	SOLOMON, EDDIE 'BUDDY'	D. JANUARY 12, 1986 MACON, GA.
23-125	SOLOMON, MOSES HIRSCH	D. JUNE 25, 1966 MIAMI, FLA.
34- 93	SOLTERS, JULIUS JOSEPH 'MOOSE'	D. SEPTEMBER 28, 1975 PITTSBURGH, PA.
10-139	SOMERLOTT, JOHN WESLEY 'JOCK'	D. APRIL 21, 1965 BUTLER, IND.
12-187	SOMMERS, RUDOLPH	D. MARCH 18, 1949 LOUISVILLE,KY.
50- 92	SOMMERS, WILLIAM DUNN	2550 SW BOBOLINK COURT - PALM CITY FL 34990
24-101	SONGER, DON	D. OCTOBER 3, 1962 KANSAS CITY, MO.
77-134	SORENSEN, LARY ALAN	9 CHICORY LANE - RIVERWOODS IL 60015
28- 87	SORRELL, VICTOR GARLAND	D. MAY 4, 1972 RALEIGH, N. C.
65-102	SORRELL, JOHN	%A.WINTON,16476 BERNARDO CTR DR - SAN DIEGO CA 92128
22-129	SORRELLS, RAYMOND EDWIN 'CHICK'	D. JULY 20, 1983 TERRELL, TEXAS
72-105	SOSA, ELIAS	8658 EAST IRISH HUNTER TRAIL - SCOTTSDALE AZ 85258
75-109	SOSA, JOSE YNOCENCIO	HAINA KM12 CARRETERA SANCHEZ - SANTO DOMINGO DOM. REP.
26- 79	SOTHERN, DENNIS ELWOOD	D. DECEMBER 7, 1977 DURHAM, N. C.
14-203	SOTHORON, ALLEN SUTTON	D. JUNE 17, 1939 ST. LOUIS, MO
77-135	SOTO, MARIO MELVIN	JOACHS LACHAUSTEGUI #42 SUR - BANI DOMINICAN REP.
46- 95	SOUCHOCK, STEPHEN	441 SOUTHWEST 55TH TERRACE - PLANTATION FL 33317
11-160	SOUTHWICK, CLYDE AUBRA	D. OCTOBER 14, 1961 FREEPORT, ILL.
64-110	SOUTHWORTH, WILLIAM FREDERICK	320 DOBBEN RD - WEBSTER GROVES MO 63119
13-171	SOUTHWORTH, WILLIAM HARRISON	D. NOVEMBER 15, 1969 COLUMBUS, O.
80-121	SOUZA, KENNETH MARK	2317 BRITTAN - SAN CARLOS CA 94070
42- 98	SPAHN, WARREN EDWARD	RR 2 - HARTSHORNE OK 74547
27- 85	SPALDING, CHARLES HARRY 'DICK'	D. FEBRUARY 3, 1950 PHILADELPHA, PA.
59- 79	SPANGLER, ALBERT DONALD	27202 AFTON WAY - HUFFMAN TX 77336
64-111	SPANSWICK, WILLIAM HENRY	10 ST THOMAS STREET - ENFIELD CT 06082
64-112	SPARMA, JOSEPH BLASE	D. MAY 14, 1986 COLUMBUS, O.
55-113	SPEAKE, ROBERT CHARLES	4742 SW URISH RD - TOPEKA KS 66604
86-143	SPECK, ROBERT CLIFFORD 'CLIFF'	7975 SOUTHWEST 83RD AVENUE - PORTLAND OR 97223
24-102	SPEECE, BYRON FRANKLIN	D. SEPTEMBER 29, 1974 ELGIN, ORE.
75-110	SPEED, HORACE ARTHUR	1301 BANKERS DRIVE - CARSON CA 90746
43-131	SPEER,VERNIE FLOYD	D. MARCH 22, 1969 LITTLE ROCK, ARK.
71- 95	SPEIER, CHRIS EDWARD	6114 EAST MONTECITO - SCOTTSDALE AZ 85251
69-161	SPENCE, JOHN ROBERT 'BOB'	2521 SAN MARCOS - SAN DIEGO CA 92104
40- 84	SPENCE, STANLEY ORVILLE	D. JANUARY 9, 1983 KINSTON, N. C.
52- 96	SPENCER, DARYL DEAN	2740 LARKIN AVE - WICHITA KS 67216
12-188	SPENCER, FRED CALVIN	D. FEBRUARY 5, 1969 ST. ANTHONY, MINN.
50- 93	SPENCER, GEORGE ELWELL	8160 HICKORY AVE - GALENA OH 43021
28- 88	SPENCER, GLENN EDWARD	D. DECEMBER 30, 1958 BINGHAMTON, N. Y.
78-124	SPENCER, HUBERT THOMAS 'TOM'	2021 EAST CONNER STRAV - TUCSON AZ 85716

68- 97 SPENCER, JAMES LLOYD	725A OLD BANFIELD RD - SEVERNA PARK MD 21146
13-172 SPENCER, LLOYD BENJAMIN	D. SEPTEMBER 1, 1970 FINKSBURG, MD.
25- 94 SPENCER, ROY HAMPTON	D. FEBRUARY 8, 1973 PORT CHARLETTE, FLA.
20-110 SPENCER, VERNON MURRAY	D. JUNE 3, 1971 WIXOM, MICH.
20-111 SPERAW, PAUL BACHMAN	D. FEBRUARY 22, 1962 CEDAR RAPIDS, IA.
24-103 SPERBER, EDWIN GEORGE	D. JANUARY 5, 1976 CINCINNATI, O.
74-123 SPERRING, ROBERT WALTER	4515 MEREDITH WOOD - SAN ANTONIO TX 78249
36- 88 SPERRY, STANLEY KENNETH	D. SEPTEMBER 27, 1962 EVANSVILLE,WIS.
55-114 SPICER, ROBERT OBERTON	423 MCPHEE DR - FAYETTEVILLE NC 28305
64-113 SPIEZIO, EDWARD WAYNE	5620 N. BARRINGTON RD - MORRIS IL 60450
72-106 SPIKES, LESLIE CHARLES 'CHARLIE'	10921 KINNEIL RD - NEW ORLEANS LA 70127
74-124 SPILLNER, DANIEL RAY	27535 SE 154TH - ISSAQUAH WA 98027
78-125 SPILMAN, WILLIAM HARRY	RURAL ROUTE 4 BOX 36 - DAWSON GA 31742
39-112 SPINDEL, HAROLD STEWART	12816 EL MORO AVE-LA MIRADA CA 90638
69-162 SPINKS, SCIPIO RONALD	34 NE 66TH - OKLAHOMA CITY OK 73105
70-126 SPLITTORFF, PAUL WILLIAM	4204 HICKORY LN - BLUE SPRING MO 64015
32- 79 SPOGNARDI, ANDREA ETTORE	4394 WASHINGTON ST - ROSLINDALE MA 02131
28- 89 SPOHRER, ALFRED RAY	D. JULY 21, 1972 CARMEL, N. Y.
54-103 SPOONER, KARL BENJAMIN	D. APRIL 10, 1984 VERO BEACH, FLA.
30- 77 SPOTTS, JAMES RUSSELL	D. JUNE 15, 1964 MEDFORD, N. J.
47- 81 SPRAGINS, HOMER FRANK	BOX 113 - MINTER CITY MS 38944
68- 98 SPRAGUE, EDWARD NELSON	2316 NORTH DAVID ROAD - LODI CA 95240
11-161 SPRATT, HENRY LEE 'JACK'	D. JULY 3, 1969 WASHINGTON, PA.
65-103 SPRIGGS, GEORGE HERMAN	336 WEST BAY FRONT ROAD - LOTHIAN MD 20820
55-115 SPRING, JACK RUSSELL	8506 EAST DALTON - SPOKANE WA 99206
25- 95 SPRINGER, BRADFORD LOUIS	D. JANUARY 4, 1970 BIRMINGHAM, MICH.
30- 78 SPRINZ, JOSEPH CONRAD	1359 33RD AVE - SAN FRANCISCO CA 94122
45-100 SPROULL, CHARLES WILLIAM	D. JANUARY 13, 1980 ROCKFORD, ILL.
61-101 SPROUT, ROBERT SAMUEL	2858 FLEETWOOD DR - LANCASTER PA 17601
78-126 SPROWL, ROBERT JOHN	114 EAST 144TH AVE - TAMPA FL 33612
24-104 SPURGEON, FRED	D. NOVEMBER 5, 1970 KALAMAZOO, MICH.
75-111 SQUIRES, MICHAEL LYNN	879 HONEY LANE - CRETE IL 60417
80-123 STABLEIN, GEORGE CHARLES	9839 LA AMAPOLA AVE - FOUNTAIN VLY CA 92708
10-140 STACK, WILLIAM EDWARD	D. AUGUST 28, 1958 CHICAGO, ILL.
64-114 STAEHLE, MARVIN GUSTAVE	570 CHECKER DR - BUFFALO GROVE IL 60090
60- 95 STAFFORD, BILL CHARLES	6108 COURTLAND - PLYMOUTH MI 48170
16- 83 STAFFORD, HENRY ALEXANDER 'HEINIE'	D. JANUARY 29, 1972 LAKE WORTH, FLA.
77-136 STAGGS, STEPHEN ROBERT	38 NEWTON - DENVER CO 80219
64-115 STAHL, LARRY FLOYD	314 S. JULIA ST (BOX 36) - SMITHTON IL 62285
75-112 STAIGER, ROY JOSEPH	8127 SOUTH 77TH EAST AVE #301 - TULSA OK 74133
34- 94 STAINBACK, GEORGE TUCKER 'TUCK'	1000 ELYSIAN AVE - LOS ANGELES CA 90012
25- 96 STALEY, GEORGE GAYLORD 'GALE'	1935 GOLDEN RAIN RD - WALNUT CREEK CA 94529
47- 82 STALEY, GERALD LEE	2600 NE 99TH ST - VANCOUVER WA 98665
60- 96 STALLARD, EVAN TRACY	HCO5 BOX 316 - COEBURN VA 24230
47- 83 STALLCUP, THOMAS VIRGIL	PLEASANTDALE CIRCLE, RR 6 - GREENVILLE SC 29607
43-132 STALLER, GEORGE WALBORN	321 NORTH 67TH ST - HARRISBURG PA 17111
41-104 STANCEU, CHARLES	D. APRIL 3, 1969 CANTON, O.
25- 97 STANDAEART, JEROME JOHN	D. AUGUST 4, 1964 CHICAGO, ILL.
11-162 STANDRIDGE, ALFRED PETER	D. AUGUST 2, 1963 SAN FRANCISCO, CALIF.
63-113 STANEK, AL	96 ALLYN ST - HOLYOKE MA 01070
79-106 STANFIELD, KEVIN BRUCE	7565 NEWCOMB ST - SAN BERNARDINO CA 92410
61-102 STANGE, ALBERT LEE	148 VISTA DEL PARQUE - REDONDO BEACH CA 90277
72-107 STANHOUSE, DONALD JOSEPH	4347 COCHRAN CHAPEL CR - DALLAS TX 75209
87-136 STANICEK, PETER LOUIS	118 CHESTNUT - PARK FOREST IL 60466
87-137 STANICEK, STEPHEN BLAIR	118 CHESTNUT - PARK FOREST IL 60466
59- 80 STANKA, JOE CONRAD	1109 CONRAD SAUER - HOUSTON TX 77043
43-133 STANKY, EDWARD RAYMOND	2100 SPRING HILL RD - MOBILE AL 36607
69-163 STANLEY, FREDRICK BLAIR	8711 E. PINNACLE PEAK RD - SCOTTSDALE AZ 85255
14-204 STANLEY, JAMES F.	B. 1889
11-163 STANLEY, JOHN LEONARD 'BUCK'	D. AUGUST 13, 1940 NORFOLK, VA.
64-116 STANLEY, MITCHELL JACK 'MICKEY'	53510 GRAND RIVER #11B - NEW HUDSON MI 48165
86-144 STANLEY, ROBERT MICHAEL	1108 NORTHEAST 10TH AVENUE - FORT LAUDERDALE FL 33304
77-137 STANLEY, ROBERT WILLIAM	WM. FAIRFIELD DR - WENHAM MA 01984
18- 69 STANSBURY, JOHN JAMES	D. DECEMBER 26, 1970 EASTON, PA.
31- 84 STANTON, GEORGE WASHINGTON 'BUCK'	401 WINDING WAY DR - SAN ANTONIO TX 78232
70-127 STANTON, LEROY BOBBY	1751 NORWOOD LN - FLORENCE SC 29501
75-113 STANTON, MICHAEL THOMAS	BOX 2573 - PHENIX CITY AL 36867
87-138 STAPLETON, DAVID EARL	702 COTTONWOOD STREET - CLAYPOOL AZ 85532
80-123 STAPLETON, DAVID LESLIE	RR 1 BOX 600 - LOXLEY AL 36551
62-127 STARGELL, WILVER DORNEL	113 ASHLEY PLACE - STONE MOUNTAIN GA 30083
87-139 STARK, MATTHEW SCOTT	11543 NEWTON STREET - HACIENDA HEIGHTS CA 91745
32- 80 STARR, RAYMOND FRANCIS	D. FEBRUARY 9, 1963 BAYLISS, ILL.
47- 84 STARR, RICHARD EUGENE	613 NORTH CRESCENT DR - KITTANNING PA 19201
35-103 STARR, WILLIAM 'CHICK'	666 UPAS ST #1801 - SAN DIEGO CA 92103

63-114	STARRETTE, HERMAN PAUL	208 HERMITAGE ROAD - STATESVILLE NC 28677
72-108	STATON, JOSEPH	P.O. BOX 28582 - SEATTLE WA 98118
19- 79	STATZ, ARNOLD JOHN 'JIGGER'	D. MARCH 16, 1988 CORONA DEL MAR, CALIF.
63-115	STAUB, DANIEL JOSEPH 'RUSTY'	1271 3RD AVE - NEW YORK NY 10021
23-126	STAUFFER, CHARLES EDWARD 'ED'	D. JULY 2, 1979 ST PETERSBURG, FLA.
74-125	STEARNS, JOHN HARDIN	7107 CEDARWOOD CIRCLE - BOULDER CO 80301
16- 84	STEELE, ROBERT WESLEY	D. JANUARY 27, 1962 OCALA, FLA.
10-141	STEELE, WILLIAM MITCHELL	D. OCTOBER 19, 1949 OVERLAND, MO.
87-140	STEELS, JAMES EARL	712 WEST POLK STREET - SANTA MARIA CA 93454
12-189	STEEN, WILLIAM JOHN	D. MARCH 13, 1979 SIGNAL HILL, CALIF.
24-105	STEENGRAFE, MILTON HENRY	D. JUNE 2, 1977 OKLAHOMA CITY, OKLA.
62-128	STEEVENS, MORRIS DALE 'MOE'	14465 CADILLAC DRIVE - SAN ANTONIO TX 78248
83-137	STEFERO, JOHN ROBERT	529 MICHELLE ROAD - ODENTON MD 21113
78-127	STEGMAN, DAVID WILLIAM	316 EAST OAK - LOMPOC CA 93436
32- 81	STEIN, IRVIN MICHAEL	D. JANUARY 7, 1981 COVINGTON, LA.
38- 93	STEIN, JUSTIN MARION	1915 GRAPE AVE - ST LOUIS MO 63136
72-109	STEIN, WILLIAM ALLEN	2433 LEGAY ST - COCOA FL 32922
78-128	STEIN, WILLIAM RANDOLPH	1540 PALMER ST - POMONA CA 91766
86-145	STEINBACH, TERRY LEE	306 SOUTH JEFFERSON - NEW ULM MN 56073
37- 96	STEINBACHER, HENRY JOHN	D. APRIL 3, 1977 SACRAMENTO, CALIF.
12-190	STEINBRENNER, WILLIAM GASS	D. APRIL 25, 1970 PITTSBURGH, PA.
31- 85	STEINECKE, WILLIAM ROBERT	D. JULY 20, 1986 SAINT AUGUSTINE, FLA.
23-127	STEINEDER, RAYMOND	D. AUGUST 25, 1982 VINELAND, N. J.
45-101	STEINER, BENJAMIN SAUNDERS	205 BLACKBURN RD - NOKOMIS FL 33555
45-102	STEINER, JAMES HARRY 'RED'	17700 SOUTH WESTERN AVE #93 - GARDENA CA 90248
82-120	STEIRER, RICKY FRANCIS	2646 DULANY - BALTIMORE MD 21223
16- 85	STELLBAUER, WILLIAM JENNINGS	D. FEBRUARY 16, 1974 HOUSTON, TEX.
71- 96	STELMASZEK, RICHARD FRANCIS	2734 EAST 97TH ST - CHICAGO IL 60617
80-124	STEMBER, JEFFREY ALAN	330 WEST JERSEY ST - ELIZABETH NJ 07202
12-191	STENGEL, CHARLES DILLON 'CASEY'	D. SEPTEMBER 29, 1975 GLENDALE, CAL.
62-129	STENHOUSE, DAVID ROTCHFORD	70 WOODBURY RD - CRANSTON RI 02905
82-121	STENHOUSE, MICHAEL S	70 WOODBURY RD - CRANSTON RI 02905
71- 97	STENNETT, RENALDO ANTONIO	OLD ADD: BOCA RATON FL 33432
68- 99	STEPHEN, LOUIS ROBERTS 'BUZZ'	308 NORTH PARKVIEW - PORTERVILLE CA 93257
47- 85	STEPHENS, BRYAN MARIS	10222 WESLEY CIR - HUNTINGTON BEACH CA 92646
52- 97	STEPHENS, GLEN EUGENE 'GENE'	5804 NORTH BILLEN ST - OKLAHOMA CITY OK 73112
41-105	STEPHENS, VERNON DECATUR	D. NOVEMBER 4, 1968 LONG BEACH, CAL.
71- 98	STEPHENSON, CHESTER EARL	RR 1 BOX 295D - ANGIER NC 27501
21- 96	STEPHENSON, JACKSON RIGGS	D. NOVEMBER 15, 1985 TUSCALOOSA, ALA.
63-116	STEPHENSON, JERRY JOSEPH	1425 MARELEN DR - FULLERTON CA 92635
64-117	STEPHENSON, JOHN HERMAN	105 BELLEWOOD - HAMMOND LA 70401
43-134	STEPHENSON, JOSEPH CHESTER	822 JADE WAY - ANAHEIM CA 92805
55-116	STEPHENSON, ROBERT LOYD	1518 BROOKHAVEN BLVD - NORMAN OK 73069

ROYLE STILLMAN

35-104	STEPHENSON, WALTER MCQUEEN	3160 REISOR RD - SHREVEPORT LA 71118
74-126	STERLING, RANDALL WAYNE	2516 LINDA AVE - KEY WEST FL 33040
12-192	STERRETT, CHARLES HURLBUT 'DUTCH'	D. DECEMBER 9, 1965 BALTIMORE, MD.
41-106	STEVENS, CHARLES AUGUSTUS	12062 VALLEY VIEW #211-GARDEN GROVE CA 92645
45-103	STEVENS, EDWARD LEE	6211 SOUTH BRAESWOOD - HOUSTON TX 77096
14-205	STEVENS, JAMES ARTHUR	D. SEPTEMBER 25, 1966 BALTIMORE, MD.
58- 88	STEVENS, R. C.	1405 MOUND ST - DAVENPORT IA 52803
31- 86	STEVENS, ROBERT JORDAN	803 ROXBORO RD - ROCKVILLE MD 20850
13-173	STEWART, CHARLES EUGENE 'TUFFY'	D. NOVEMBER 18, 1934 CHICAGO, ILL.
78-129	STEWART, DAVID KEITH	817 MANCHESTER COURT - CLAREMONT CA 91711
41-107	STEWART, EDWARD PERRY	5501 WEST 119TH ST-INGLEWOOD CA 90304
27- 86	STEWART, FRANK	RR 1 BOX 290 - SAINT JOSEPH WI 54082
40- 85	STEWART, GLEN WELDON	60 SOUTH ALICIA-MEMPHIS TN 38112
63-117	STEWART, JAMES FRANKLIN	RR 1 BOX 298 - LAFAYETTE AL 36862
16- 86	STEWART, JOHN FRANKLIN 'STUFFY'	D. DECEMBER 30, 1980 LAKE CITY, FLA.
13-174	STEWART, MARK	D. JANUARY 17, 1942 MEMPHIS, TENN.
78-130	STEWART, SAMUEL LEE	107 SCENIC VIEW DR - SWANNANOA NC 28778
52- 98	STEWART, VESTON GOFF 'BUNKY'	RAY MCCOTTER REALTY CO - NEW BERN NC28560
21- 97	STEWART, WALTER CLEVELAND 'LEFTY'	D. SEPTEMBER 26, 1974 KNOXVILLE, TENN.
40- 86	STEWART, WALTER NESBITT	5260 ROBERTS MILL RD, RR 5 - LONDON OH 43140
44-124	STEWART, WILLIAM MACKLIN 'MACK'	D. MARCH 21, 1960 MACON, GA.
55-117	STEWART, WILLIAM WAYNE	2484 PONTIAC DR - SYLVAN LAKE MI 48053
79-107	STIEB, DAVID ANDREW	160 SHEFFIELD CIR EAST - PALM HARBOR FL 33563
29- 99	STIELY, FRED WARREN	D. JANUARY 6, 1981 VALLEY VIEW, PA.
60- 97	STIGMAN, RICHARD LEWIS	12914 5TH AVE SOUTH - BURNSVILLE MN 55337
30- 79	STILES, ROLLAND MAYS	10161 SAKURA DR - ST. LOUIS MO 63128
75-114	STILLMAN, ROYLE ELDON	5201 HARTFORD WAY - WESTMINSTER CA 92683
86-146	STILLWELL, KURT ANDREW	1417 DOVER AVENUE - THOUSAND OAKS CA 91360
61-103	STILLWELL, RONALD ROY	1417 DOVER - THOUSAND OAKS CA 91360
80-125	STIMAC, CRAIG STEVEN	OLD ADD: 1603 ROBINHOOD LN - LAGRANGE IL 60525
23-128	STIMSON, CARL REMUS	D. NOVEMBER 9, 1936 OMAHA, NEB.

34- 95 STINE, LEE ELBERT	1939 CALLE PASITO - HEMET CA 92343
69-164 STINSON, GORRELL ROBERT 'BOB'	10663 NE 133RD PLACE - KIRKLAND WA 98033
43-135 STIRNWEISS, GEORGE HENRY 'SNUFFY'	D. SEPTEMBER 15, 1958 NEWARK, N. J.
47- 86 STOBBS, CHARLES KLEIN	5150 HONORE AVE - SARASOTA FL 33583
13-175 STOCK, MILTON JOSEPH	D. JULY 16, 1977 MONTROSE, ALA.
59- 81 STOCK, WESLEY GAY	5917 FRANCES AVE NE - TACOMA WA 98422
81-134 STODDARD, ROBERT LYLE	15760 SUNNYSIDE AVE - MORGAN HILL CA 95037
75-115 STODDARD, TIMOTHY PAUL	3928 EAST BUTTERNUT ST - EAST CHICAGO IN 46312
25- 98 STOKES, ALBERT JOHN	55 CAVALRY HILL RD - WILTON CT 06897
25- 99 STOKES, ARTHUR MELTON	D. JUNE 3, 1962 TITUSVILLE, PA.
45-104 STONE, CHARLES RICHARD 'DICK'	D. FEBRUARY 18, 1980 OKLAHOMA CITY, OKLA.
53- 86 STONE, DARRAH DEAN	1221 7TH AVE CT - SILVIS IL 61282
13-176 STONE, DWIGHT ELY	D. JULY 3, 1976 GLENDALE, CALIF.
23-129 STONE, EDWIN ARNOLD 'ARNIE'	D. JULY 29, 1948 HUDSON FALLS N. Y.
69-165 STONE, EUGENE DANIEL	800 O'SULLIVAN DAM ROAD - OTHELLO WA 99344
67-102 STONE, GEORGE HEARD	1206 EASTLAND AVE - RUSTON LA 71270
66- 85 STONE, HARRY RONALD 'RON'	FARMER'S INS.,3738 MAIN - SPRINGFIELD OR 97478
83-138 STONE, JEFFREY GLEN	RR 2 BOX 346 - PORTAGEVILLE MO 63873
28- 90 STONE, JOHN THOMAS	D. NOVEMBER 30, 1955 SHELBYVILLE, TENN.
43-136 STONE, JOHN VERNON 'VERN'	D. NOVEMBER 12, 1986 FOUNTAIN VALLEY, CALIF.
71- 99 STONE, STEVEN MICHAEL	OLD ADD: 4333 N. BROWN AVE - SCOTTSDALE AZ 85251
23-130 STONE, WILLIAM ARTHUR 'TIGE'	D. JANUARY 1, 1960 JACKSONVILLE, FLA.
33- 59 STONEHAM, JOHN ANDREW	7201 OAK HILL DR - HOUSTON TX 77017
67-103 STONEMAN, WILLIAM HAMBLY	P.O. BOX 500, STATION M - MONTREAL QUEBEC H1V 3P2 CAN.
22-130 STONER, ULYSSES SIMPSON GRANT 'LIL'	D. JUNE 26, 1966 ENID, OKLA.
31- 87 STORIE, HOWARD EDWARD	D. JULY 27, 1968 PITTSFIELD, MASS.
30- 80 STORTI, LINDO IVAN	D. JULY 24, 1982 ONTARIO, CALIF.
64-118 STOTTLEMYRE, MELVIN LEON	9 SOUTH THIRD STREET - YAKIMA WA 89801
31- 88 STOUT, ALLYN MCCLELLAND	D. DECEMBER 22, 1974 SIKESTON, MO.
38- 94 STOVIAK, RAYMOND THOMAS	2501 SOUTH OCEAN BLVD #208 - BACON RATON FL 33432
60- 98 STOWE, HAROLD RUDOLPH	RR 3 BOX 281 - GASTONIA NC 28052
70-128 STRAHLER, MICHAEL WAYNE	2501 38TH AVE - SACRAMENTO CA 95822
54-104 STRAHS, RICHARD BERNARD	OLD ADD: 3400 NORTH LAKE SHORE DR - CHICAGO IL 60657
79-108 STRAIN, JOSEPH ALLAN	8167 SOUTH PENNSYLVANIA CT - LINCOLN CO 80122
87-141 STRAKER, LESTER PAUL	AVE. REPUBLICA NO. 6 - ESTADO BOLIVAR VENEZ
72-110 STRAMPE, ROBERT EDWIN	BOX 672 - WASHTUCNA WA 99371
13-177 STRAND, PAUL EDWARD	D. JULY 2, 1974 SALT LAKE CITY, UT.
15-158 STRANDS, JOHN LAWRENCE	D. JANUARY 19, 1957 FOREST PARK, ILL.
34- 96 STRANGE, ALAN COCHRANE	8239 41ST AVE NE - SEATTLE WA 98115
34- 97 STRATTON, MONTY FRANKLIN PIERCE	D. SEPTEMBER 29, 1982 GREENVILLE, TEXAS
83-139 STRAWBERRY, DARRYL EUGENE	1419 RED BLUFF COURT - SAN DIMAS CA 91773
28- 91 STRELECKI, EDWARD HAROLD	D. JANUARY 9, 1968 NEWARK, N. J.
54-105 STREULI, WALTER HERBERT	1107 WESTMINSTER - GREENSBORO NC 27410
50- 94 STRICKLAND, GEORGE BEVAN	6328 CONSTANCE ST - NEW ORLEANS LA 70118
71-100 STRICKLAND, JAMES MICHAEL	179 PRYCE ST - SANTA CRUZ CA 95060
37- 97 STRICKLAND, WILLIAM GOSS	4444 US HWY 98 NORTH #532 - LAKELAND FL 33805
59- 82 STRIKER, WILBUR SCOTT 'JAKE'	120 SCHELL AVE - BUCYRUS OH 44820
40- 87 STRINCEVICH, NICHOLAS MIHAILOVICH	1308 CAMELOT MANOR - PORTAGE IN 46368
41-108 STRINGER, LOUIS BERNARD	207 CALLE FELICIDAD - SAN CLEMENTE CA 92672
28- 92 STRIPP, JOSEPH VALENTINE	1001 W. NEW HAMPSHIRE - ORLANDO FL 32804
70-129 STROHMAYER, JOHN EMERY	4120 BURSELL ST - CENTRAL VALLEY CA 96019
72-111 STROM, BRENT TERRY	1628 WHITSETT DR - EL CAJON CA 92020
39-113 STROMME, FLOYD MARVIN	3029 SHERIDAN - NORTH BEND OR 97459
29-100 STRONER, JAMES M.	D. NOVEMBER 16, 1971 CHICAGO, ILL.
66- 86 STROUD, EDWIN MARVIN	1696 OAK ST - WARREN OH 44485
10-142 STROUD, RALPH VIVIAN 'SAILOR'	D. APRIL 11, 1970 STOCKTON, CALIF.
82-122 STROUGHTER, STEPHEN LOUIS	323 NE 2ND - VISALIA CA 93277
34- 98 STRUSS, CLARENCE HERBERT 'STEAMBOAT'	D. SEPTEMBER 12, 1985 GRAND RAPIDS, MICH.
24-106 STRYKER, STERLING ALPA 'DUTCH'	D. NOVEMBER 5, 1964 RED BANK, N. J.
22-131 STUART, JOHN DAVIS	D. MAY 13, 1970 CHARLESTON, W. VA.
21- 98 STUART, LUTHER LANE 'LUKE'	D. JUNE 15, 1947 WINSTON-SALEM, N. C.
49- 83 STUART, MARLIN HENRY	RR 1 BOX 133 - PARAGOULD AR 72450
58- 89 STUART, RICHARD LEE	36 LAKEWOOD CIRCLE NORTH - GREENWICH CT 06832
84-117 STUBBS, FRANKLIN LEE	RR 1 BOX 521C - HAMLET NC 28345
67-104 STUBING, LAWRENCE GEORGE	10627 QUEZADA - EL PASO TX 79935
21- 99 STUELAND, GEORGE ANTON	D. SEPTEMBER 9, 1964 ONAWA, IA.
50- 95 STUFFEL, PAUL HARRINGTON	13136 VINE STREET NE - ALLIANCE OH 44601
57- 82 STUMP, JAMES GILBERT	939 WESTON - LANSING MI 48906
31- 89 STUMPF, GEORGE FREDERICK	222 STAFFORD AV - NEW ORLEANS LA 70124
12-193 STUMPF, WILLIAM FREDRICK	D. FEBRUARY 14, 1966 CROWNSVILLE, MD.
82-123 STUPER, JOHN ANTON	BUTLER COUNTY COMM. COLLEGE - BUTLER PA 16001
55-118 STURDIVANT, THOMAS VIRGIL	8901 SOUTH VICTORIA DRIVE - OKLAHOMA CITY OK 73159
27- 87 STURDY, GUY R.	D. MAY 4, 1965 MARSHALL, TEX.
40- 88 STURGEON, ROBERT HARWOOD	3903 LEWIS AVE-LONG BEACH CA 90807

14-206 STURGIS, DEAN DONNELL	D. JUNE 4, 1950 UNIONTOWN, PA.
41-109 STURM, JOHN PETER JOSEPH	3840 FRENCH CT-ST LOUIS MO 63116
26- 80 STUTZ, GEORGE	D. DECEMBER 29, 1930 PHILADELPHIA, PA.
19- 80 STYLES, WILLIAM GRAVES 'LENA'	D. MARCH 14, 1956 HUNTSVILLE, ALA.
66- 87 SUAREZ, KENNETH RAYMOND	1301 FINDLAY DR - ARLINGTON TX 76012
44-125 SUAREZ, LUIS ABELARDO	OLD ADD: AGUILA #4 - HAVANA CUBA
70-130 SUCH, RICHARD STANLEY	2100 LORD ASHLEY DR - SANFORD NC 27330
38- 95 SUCHE, CHARLES MORRIS	D. FEBRUARY 11, 1984 SAN ANTONIO, TEXAS
50- 96 SUCHECKI, JAMES JOSEPH	RR 2 - ZIMMERMAN MN 55398
68-100 SUDAKIS, WILLIAM PAUL	4352 PICKWICK CIR #204 - HUNTINGTON BEACH CA 92649
41-110 SUDER, PETER	903 ROOSEVELT AVE - ALIQUIPPA PA 15001
30- 81 SUHR, AUGUST RICHARD	341 HAZEL AVE - MILLBRAE CA 94030
26- 81 SUKEFORTH, CLYDE LEROY	RR 3 BOX 123 - WALDOBORO ME 04572
80-126 SULARZ, GUY PATRICK	19602 WATERBURY LN - HUNTINGTON BEACH CA 92646
36- 89 SULIK, ERNEST RICHARD	D. MAY 31, 1963 OAKLAND, CAL.
44-126 SULLIVAN, CARL MANUEL 'JACK'	%V.CROWDER,602 BARNES ST - MCKINNEY TX 75069
28- 93 SULLIVAN, CHARLES EDWARD	D. MAY 28, 1935 MAIDEN, N. C.
53- 87 SULLIVAN, FRANKLIN LEAL	BOX 1873 - LIHUE HI 96766
55-119 SULLIVAN, HAYWOOD COOPER	FENWAY PARK - BOSTON MA 02215
21-100 SULLIVAN, JAMES RICHARD	D. FEBRUARY 12, 1972 BURTONSVILLE, MD.
35-105 SULLIVAN, JOE	D. APRIL 8, 1985 SEQUIM, WASH.
19- 81 SULLIVAN, JOHN JEREMIAH	D. JULY 7, 1958 CHICAGO, ILL.
20-112 SULLIVAN, JOHN LAWRENCE	D. APRIL 1, 1966 UNION CO., PA.
42- 99 SULLIVAN, JOHN PETER	2301 183RD ST #403A - HOMEWOOD IL 60430
63-118 SULLIVAN, JOHN PETER	24 HIGHLAND ST - DANSVILLE NY 14437
82-124 SULLIVAN, MARC COOPER	134 SPRING LN - CANTON MA 02021
39-114 SULLIVAN, PAUL THOMAS 'LEFTY'	6602 NORTH 82ND WAY - SCOTTSDALE AZ 85253
51- 93 SULLIVAN, RUSSELL GUY H	1701 HILL-N-DALE DR - FREDERICKSBURG VA 22401
22-132 SULLIVAN, THOMAS AUGUSTIN	D. SEPTEMBER 23, 1962 BOSTON, MASS.
25-100 SULLIVAN, THOMAS BRANDON	D. AUGUST 16, 1944 SEATTLE, WASH.
31- 90 SULLIVAN, WILLIAM JOSEPH JR	7957 N. TAMIAMI TRAIL - SARASOTA FL 33580
20-113 SUMMA, HOMER WAYNE	D. JANUARY 29, 1966 LOS ANGELES, CAL.
74-127 SUMMERS, JOHN JUNIOR	2091 TREVINO - OCEANSIDE CA 92056
28- 94 SUMNER, CARL RINGDAHL	24 WINTERSET DRIVE - CHATHAM MA 02633
74-128 SUNDBERG, JAMES HOWARD	4610 RIVERFOREST DR - ARLINGTON TX 76017
56- 80 SUNDIN, GORDON VINCENT	505 WHISPERING PINE LN - NAPLES FL 33940
36- 90 SUNDRA, STEPHEN RICHARD	D. MARCH 23, 1952 CLEVELAND, O.
37- 98 SUNKEL, THOMAS JACOB	RR 1 BOX 194-A - PARIS IL 61944
85-107 SURHOFF, RICHARD CLIFFORD	239 PURCHASE ST - RYE NY 10580
87-142 SURHOFF, WILLIAM JAMES	131 PURCHASE STREET #42E - RYE NY 10580
49- 84 SURKONT, MATTHEW CONSTANTINE 'MAX'	D. OCTOBER 8, 1986 LARGO, FLA.
29-101 SUSCE, GEORGE CYRIL METHODIUS SR.	D. FEBRUARY 25, 1986 SARASOTA, FLA.
55-120 SUSCE, GEORGE DANIEL JR	12 JARVIS CIRCLE - NEEDHAM MA 02192
34- 99 SUSKO, PETER JONATHAN	D. MAY 22, 1978 JACKSONVILLE, FLA.
38- 96 SUTCLIFFE, CHARLES INIGO 'BUTCH'	33 MALVEY ST-FALL RIVER MA 02720
76- 87 SUTCLIFFE, RICHARD LEE 'RICK'	313 NW NORTH SHORE DR - PARKVILLE MO 64151
64-120 SUTHERLAND, DARRELL WAYNE	3445 LAS PALMAS AVE - GLENDALE CA 91208
66- 88 SUTHERLAND, GARY LYNN	338 NORTH OAK CLIFF - MONROVIA CA 91016
21-101 SUTHERLAND, HARVEY SCOTT 'SUDS'	D. MAY 11, 1972 PORTLAND, ORE.
49- 85 SUTHERLAND, HOWARD ALVIN 'DIZZY'	D. AUGUST 26, 1979 WASHINGTON, D. C.
80-127 SUTHERLAND, LEONARDO CANTIN	2237 S. OERTLEY DR - ANAHEIM CA 92802
76- 88 SUTTER, HOWARD BRUCE	1368 HAMILTON RD - KENNESAW GA 30144
66- 89 SUTTON, DONALD HOWARD	25442 GALLUP CIR - LAGUNA HILLS CA 92653

77-138 SUTTON, JOHNNY IKE	RR 1 BOX 857 - DESOTO TX 75115
86-147 SVEUM, DALE CURTIS	248 DON CASTER DRIVE - VALLEJO CA 94590
83-140 SWAGGERTY, WILLIAM DAVID	OLD ADD: 3542 TERRACE HILL #204 - RANDALLSTOWN MD 21133
73-114 SWAN, CRAIG STEVEN	72 ROCKWOOD LN - GREENWICH CT 06830
14-207 SWAN, HARRY GORDON 'DUCKY'	D. MAY 9, 1946 PITTSBURGH, PA.
55-121 SWANSON, ARTHUR LEONARD	15718 WENDY GLEN - HOUSTON TX 77095
29-102 SWANSON, ERNEST EVAR	D. JULY 17, 1973 GALESBURG, ILL.
28- 95 SWANSON, KARL EDWARD	212 HILLCREST DR - AVON PARK FL 33825
71-101 SWANSON, STANLEY LAWRENCE	235 ANTIGNE DRIVE - HAMILTON MT 59840
14-208 SWANSON, WILLIAM ANDREW	D. OCTOBER 14, 1954 NEW YORK, N.Y.
47- 87 SWARTZ, SHERWIN MERLE	1937 NORTH BEVERLY DR - BEVERLY HILLS CA 90210
20-114 SWARTZ, VERNON MONROE 'DAZZY'	D. JANUARY 13, 1980 GERMANTOWN, O.
14-209 SWEENEY, CHARLES FRANCIS	D. MARCH 13, 1955 PITTSBURGH, PA.
44-127 SWEENEY, HENRY LEON	D. MAY 6, 1980 COLUMBIA, TENN.
28- 96 SWEENEY, WILLIAM JOSEPH	D. APRIL 18, 1957 SAN DIEGO, CAL.
78-131 SWEET, RICHARD JOE 'RICK'	16127 SE 46TH WAY - BELLEVUE WA 98006

27- 88 SWEETLAND, LESTER LEO	D. MARCH 4, 1974 MELBOURNE, FL.
22-133 SWENTOR, AUGUST WILLIAM	D. NOVEMBER 10, 1969 WATERBURY, CONN.
29-103 SWETONIC, STEPHEN ALBERT	D. APRIL 22, 1974 CANONSBURG, PA.
40- 89 SWIFT, ROBERT VIRGIL	D. OCTOBER 17, 1966 DETROIT, MICH.
85-108 SWIFT, WILLIAM CHARLES	170 PICKETT ST - SOUTH PORTLAND ME 04106
32- 82 SWIFT, WILLIAM VINCENT	D. FEBRUARY 23, 1969 BARTOW, FLA.
39-115 SWIGART, OADIS VAUGHN	2917 SENECA BLVD - ST. JOSEPH MO 64507
17- 80 SWIGLER, ADAM WILLIAM	D. FEBRUARY 5, 1975 PHILADELPHIA, PA.
86-148 SWINDELL, FOREST GREGORY 'GREG'	7706 TWIN HILLS - HOUSTON TX 77071
11-164 SWINDELL, JOSHUA ERNEST	D. MARCH 19, 1969 FRUITA, COLO.
74-129 SWISHER, STEVEN EDWARD	RR 1 BOX 5A - MINERAL WELLS WV 26150
65-104 SWOBODA, RONALD ALAN	603 EAST LAMARCHE - PHOENIX AZ 85022
77-139 SYKES, ROBERT JOSEPH	509 WEST MAIN ST - CARMI IL 62821
53- 88 SZEKELY, JOSEPH	3260 ALLEN - PARIS TX 75460
70-131 SZOTKIEWICZ, KENNETH JOHN	1709 BEECH ST - WILMINGTON DE 19805
76- 89 TABB, JERRY LYNN	4502 RUIDOSO COURT - MIDLAND TX 79707
26- 82 TABER, EDWARD TIMOTHY 'LEFTY'	D. NOVEMBER 5, 1983 LINCOLN, NEB.
81-135 TABLER, PATRICK SEAN	11943 TIMBERLAKE DRIVE - CINCINNATI OH 45249
87-143 TABOR, GREGORY STEPHEN	21100 GARY DRIVE #306 - HAYWARD CA 94546
38- 97 TABOR, JAMES REUBIN	D. AUGUST 22, 1953 SACRAMENTO, CAL.
13-178 TAFF, JOHN GALLATIN	D. MAY 15, 1961 HOUSTON, TEX.
28- 97 TAITT, DOUGLAS JOHN	D. DECEMBER 12, 1970 PORTLAND, ORE.
63-119 TALBOT, FREDERICK LEALAND	770 LUNSEFORD LN - FALLS CHURCH VA 22043
53- 89 TALBOT, ROBERT DALE	608 WEST KAWEAH - VISALIA CA 93277
43-137 TALCOTT, LEROY EVERETT	5060 SW 82ND AVE - MIAMI BEACH FL 33143
66- 90 TALTON, MARION LEE 'TIM'	RR 2 BOX 255 - PIKEVILLE NC 27863
76- 90 TAMARGO, JOHN FELIX	7901 NORTH EDISON - TAMPA FL 33604
34-100 TAMULIS, VITAUTIS CASIMIRUS	D. MAY 5, 1974 NASHVILLE, TENN.
73-115 TANANA, FRANK DARYL	28492 SOUTH HARWICK - FARMINGTON HILLS MI 48018
25-101 TANKERSLEY, LAWRENCE WILLIAM 'LEO'	D. SEPTEMBER 18, 1980 DALLAS, TEXAS
85-109 TANNER, BRUCE MATTHEW	34 MAITLAND LANE EAST - NEW CASTLE PA 16101
55-122 TANNER, CHARLES WILLIAM	34 MAITLAND LN EAST - NEW CASTLE PA 16101
54-106 TAPPE, ELVIN WALTER	2424 SPRING ST - QUINCY IL 62301
50- 97 TAPPE, THEODORE NASH	203 MARR - WENATCHEE WA 98801
14-221 TAPPEN, WALTER VAN DORN	D. DECEMBER 19, 1967 LYNWOOD, CALIF.
27- 89 TARBERT, WILBER ARLINGTON 'ARLIE'	D. NOVEMBER 27, 1946 CLEVELAND, O.
84-118 TARTABULL, DANILO	9665 WILSHIRE BLVD #420 - BEVERLY HILLS CA 90212
62-130 TARTABULL, JOSE	4105 NW 185TH ST - CORAL CITY FL 33055
86-149 TARVER, LASCHELLE	60 WEST NINTH #D - CLOVIS CA 93612
58- 90 TASBY, WILLIE	1486 12TH ST - OAKLAND CA 94607
46- 96 TATE, ALVIN WALTER	739 WEST 3400 SOUTH - BOUNTIFUL UT 84010
24-107 TATE, HENRY BENNETT 'BENNIE'	D. OCTOBER 27, 1973 FRANKFORT, ILL.
58- 91 TATE, LEE WILLIE	6905 PRATT - OMAHA NE 68131
75-116 TATE, RANDALL LEE	RR 1 BOX 423 - KILLEN AL 35645
68-101 TATUM, JARVIS	727 SOUTH ARTHUR - FRESNO CA 93706
69-166 TATUM, KENNETH RAY	340 WOODWARD RD - BIRMINGHAM AL 35228
41-111 TATUM, THOMAS VEE TEE	4929 PATE AVE-OKLAHOMA CITY OK 73112
35-106 TAUBY, FRED JOSEPH	D. NOVEMBER 23, 1955 CONCORDIA, CAL.
28- 98 TAUSCHER, WALTER EDWARD	2600 WESTERN PARKWAY - ORLANDO FL 32803
58- 92 TAUSSIG, DONALD FRANKLIN	BOX 225 - LONG BEACH NY 11561
21-102 TAVENER, JOHN ADAM	D. SEPTEMBER 14, 1969 FT. WORTH, TEX.
76- 91 TAVERAS, ALEJANDRO ANTONIO 'ALEX'	A. MONSANTO 8 TAMBORIL - SANTIAGO DOMINICAN REP.

71-102 TAVERAS, FRANKLIN CRISOSTOMO	CALLE 31 #16 LOS COLINOS - SANTIAGO DOMINICAN REP.
58- 93 TAYLOR, ANTONIO	2772 MARSEILLE CIRCLE - BROUSSARD QUEBEC J4Y 1L1 CAN.
21-103 TAYLOR, ARLAS WALTER	D. SEPTEMBER 10, 1958 DADE CITY, FLA.
12-194 TAYLOR, BENJAMIN HARRISON	D. NOVEMBER 3, 1946 MARTIN COUNTY, IND.
77-140 TAYLOR, BRUCE BELL	8 HIGHLAND PARK RD - RUTLAND MA 01543
25-102 TAYLOR, C. L. 'CHINK'	D. JULY 7, 1980 TEMPLE, TEXAS
68-102 TAYLOR, CARL MEANS	OLD ADD: 530 SOUTH VENICE BY-PASS - VENICE FL
69-167 TAYLOR, CHARLES GILBERT	1619 GEORGETOWN LN - MURFREESBORO TN 37130
26- 83 TAYLOR, DANIEL TURNEY	D. OCTOBER 11, 1972 LATROBE, PA.
87-144 TAYLOR, DONALD CLYDE 'DORN'	1645 FRANKLIN AVENUE - WILLOW GROVE PA 19090
86-150 TAYLOR, DWIGHT BERNARD	1628 EAST SPEEDWAY BOULEVARD - TUCSON AZ 85719
26- 84 TAYLOR, EDWARD JAMES	BOX 2237 - CHULA VISTA CA 92012
51- 94 TAYLOR, EUGENE BENJAMIN 'BEN'	12677 COULSON - HOUSTON TX 77015
50- 98 TAYLOR, FREDERICK RANKIN	3144 DRRBY RD - COLUMBUS OH 43221
69-168 TAYLOR, GARY WILLIAM	OLD ADD: 827 N. MARTHA - DEARBORN MI 48128
57- 83 TAYLOR, HARRY EVANS	2125 COOKS LN - FORT WORTH TX 76112
32- 83 TAYLOR, HARRY WARREN	D. APRIL 27, 1969 TOLEDO, O.
46- 97 TAYLOR, JAMES HARRY	RR 13 BOX 111 - WEST TERRE HAUTE IN 47885
20-115 TAYLOR, JAMES WREN 'ZACK'	D. SEPTEMBER 19, 1974 ORLANDO, FLA.
54-107 TAYLOR, JOE CEPHUS	705 WATT LN - PITTSBURGH PA 15219
23-131 TAYLOR, LEO THOMAS	D. MAY 20, 1982 SEATTLE, WASH.

11-165 TAYLOR, PHILIP WILEY	D. JULY 9, 1954 TOPEKA, KAN.
57- 84 TAYLOR, ROBERT DALE 'HAWK'	RR 5 BOX 897 - MURRAY KY 42071
70-132 TAYLOR, ROBERT LEE	27 SUNNYBROOK RD - SPRINGFIELD MA 01109
62-131 TAYLOR, RONALD WESLEY	19 ALVIN AVE - TORONTO ONTARIO M4T 2A7 CAN.
58- 94 TAYLOR, SAMUEL DOUGLAS	BOX 152 - WOODRUFF SC 29388
24-108 TAYLOR, THOMAS LIVINGSTONE CARLTON	D. APRIL 5, 1956 GREENVILLE, MISS.
52- 99 TAYLOR, VERNON CHARLES 'PETE'	823 CEDARCROFT DR - MILLERSVILLE MD 21108
54-108 TAYLOR, WILLIAM MICHAEL	BOX 146 - ACTON CA 93510
30- 82 TEACHOUT, ARTHUR JOHN 'BUD'	D. MAY 11, 1985 LAGUNA BEACH, CALIF.
36- 91 TEBBETTS, GEORGE ROBERT 'BIRDIE'	229 OAK AVE-ANNA MARIA FL 33501
14-211 TEDROW, ALLEN SEYMOUR	D. JANUARY 23, 1958 WESTERVILLE, O.
53- 90 TEED, RICHARD LEROY	45 TAYLOR STREET - WINDSOR CT 06095
86-151 TEJADA, WILFREDO ARISTIDES	J.ALVAREZ ALEJO#8,VILLA CONSUELO-SANTO DOMINGO DOM REP.
74-130 TEKULVE, KENTON CHARLES	1531 SEQUOIA - PITTSBURGH PA 15241
79-109 TELLMANN, THOMAS JOHN	W160 S7131 DAISY DR - MUSKEGO WI 53150
52-100 TEMPLE, JOHN ELLIS	RR 2 BOX 293C - IRMO SC 29063
55-123 TEMPLETON, CHARLES SHERMAN	BOX 457 - WYOMING MN 55092
76- 92 TEMPLETON, GARRY LEWIS	13552 DEL PONENTE - POWAY CA 92064
69-169 TENACE, FURY GENE	15368 MARKER RD - POWAY CA 92064
29-104 TENNANT, JAMES MCDONNELL	D. APRIL 16, 1967 TRUMBULL, CONN.
12-195 TENNANT, THOMAS FRANCIS	D. FEBRUARY 16, 1955 SAN CARLOS, CALIF.
67-105 TEPEDINO, FRANK RONALD	95 DAVIS ST - HAUPPAUGE NY 11787
46- 98 TEPSIC, JOSEPH JOHN	RR3 BOX 164 - TYRONE PA 16686
72-112 TERLECKI, ROBERT JOSEPH	760 NORWAY AVE - TRENTON NJ 08629
75-117 TERLECKY, GREGORY JOHN	1042 EAST GROVECENTER ST - WEST COVINA CA 91790
74-131 TERPKO, JEFFREY MICHAEL	RR 1 BOX 156 - SAYRE PA 18840
82-125 TERRELL, CHARLES WALTER 'WALT'	630 WESTCHESTER - GROSSE POINTE PARK MI 48230
73-116 TERRELL, JERRY WAYNE	1301 SUNNY CREEK LN - BLUE SPRINGS MO 64015
40- 90 TERRY, LANCELOT YANK	D. NOVEMBER 4, 1979 BLOOMINGTON, IND.
56- 81 TERRY, RALPH WILLARD	801 PARK - LARNED KS 67550
86-152 TERRY, SCOTT DALE	123 RICE DRIVE - PORTLAND TX 78374
23-132 TERRY, WILLIAM HAROLD	5598 FAIR LANE DRIVE - JACKSONVILLE FL 32244
16- 87 TERRY, ZEBULON ALEXANDER	D. MARCH 14, 1988 LOS ANGELES, CALIF.
32- 84 TERWILLIGER, RICHARD MARTIN	D. JANUARY 21, 1969 GREENVILLE, MICH.
49- 86 TERWILLIGER, WILLARD WAYNE	6549 BARTLETT BLVD - MOUND MN 55364
15-160 TESCH, ALBERT JOHN	D. AUGUST 3, 1947 JERSEY CITY, N.J.
12-196 TESREAU, CHARLES MONROE 'JEFF'	D. SEPTEMBER 24, 1946 HANOVER, N.H.
58- 95 TESTA, NICHOLAS	2544 LURTING AVE - BRONX NY 10469
55-124 TETTELBACH, RICHARD MORLEY	7 BEACHWOOD RD - WOODRIDGE CT 06525
84-119 TETTLETON, MICKEY LEE	10405 LESTER LANE - OKLAHOMA CITY OK 73101
83-141 TEUFEL, TIMOTHY SHAWN	37 BYRAM TERRACE DR - GREENWICH CT 06830
86-153 TEWKSBURY, ROBERT ALAN	48 SUMNER STREET - PENACOOK NH 03301
14-212 TEXTOR, GEORGE	D. MARCH 11, 1954 MASSILLON, O.
58- 96 THACKER, MORRIS BENTON 'MOE'	10206 BLUFFSPRINGS TRACE - LOUISVILLE KY 40223
78-132 THAYER, GREGORY ALLEN	1000 3RD ST NORTH - SAUK RAPIDS MN 56379
20-116 THEIS, JOHN LOUIS	D. JULY 6, 1941 GEORGETOWN, O.
77-141 THEISS, DUANE CHARLES	276I RIDGEWOOD CT - MARIETTA OH 45750
71-103 THEOBALD, RONALD MERRILL	9 FLEUTI - MORAGA CA 94556
73-117 THEODORE, GEORGE BASIL	3254 ELGIN DRIVE - SALT LAKE CITY UT 84109
44-128 THESENGA, ARNOLD JOSEPH 'JUG'	3907 COUNTRYSIDE PLAZA - WICHITA KS 67218
24-109 THEVENOW, THOMAS JOSEPH	D. JULY 28, 1957 MADISON, IND.
52-101 THIEL, MAYNARD BERT	RR2 - MARION WI 54950
63-120 THIES, DAVID ROBERT	6140 ARCTIC WAY - MINNEAPOLIS MN 55436
54-109 THIES, VERNON ARTHUR 'JAKE'	4 CORNFLOWER COURT - FLORISSANT MO 63033
86-154 THIGPEN, ROBERT THOMAS	P.O. BOX 87 - MONTICELLO FL 32344
67-106 THOENEN, RICHARD CRISPIN	51 NORTH PEACH ST - MEDFORD OR 97501
26- 85 THOMAS, ALPHONSE THOMAS 'TOMMY'	D. APRIL 27, 1988 YORK COUNTY, PA.
85-110 THOMAS, ANDRES PERES	35 DUARTE #35 - BOCA CHICA DOMINICAN REP.
11-166 THOMAS, BLAINE M.	D. AUGUST 21, 1915 PAYSON, ARIZ.
60- 99 THOMAS, CARL LESLIE	5850 EAST ORANGE BLOSSOM LN - PHOENIX AZ 85018
12-197 THOMAS, CHESTER DAVID 'PINCH'	D. DECEMBER 24, 1953 MODESTO, CALIF.
25-103 THOMAS, CLARENCE FLETCHER 'LEFTY'	D. MARCH 21, 1952 CHARLOTTESVILLE, VA.
16- 88 THOMAS, CLAUDE ALFRED	D. MARCH 6, 1946 SULPHUR, OKLA.
76- 93 THOMAS, DANNY LEE	D. JUNE 12, 1980 MOBILE, ALA.
71-104 THOMAS, DERREL OSBON	236 W. 73RD ST - LOS ANGELES CA 90003
27- 90 THOMAS, FAY WESLEY	10526 ANDORA AVE - CHATSWORTH CA 91311
51- 95 THOMAS, FRANK JOSEPH	118 DORAY DR - PITTSBURGH PA 15237
18- 70 THOMAS, FREDERICK HARVEY	D. JANUARY 15, 1986 RICE LAKE, WISC.
57- 85 THOMAS, GEORGE EDWARD	12733 PORTLAND AVE SOUTH - BURNSVILLE MN 55337
24-110 THOMAS, HERBERT MARK	818 WEST PRATT ST - STARKE FL 32071
73-118 THOMAS, JAMES GORMAN	P.O. BOX 718 - ELK GROVE WI 53122
61-104 THOMAS, JAMES LEROY 'LEE'	50 EAST CARDIGAN ST - ST LOUIS MO 63135
51- 96 THOMAS, JOHN TILLMAN 'BUD'	2607 STEPHENSON ST - SEDALIA MO 65301
52-102 THOMAS, KEITH MARSHALL 'KITE'	112 N. CIRCLE DR #7275 - ROCKY MOUNT NC 27801
50- 99 THOMAS, LEO RAYMOND	2024 SANDCREEK WAY - ALAMEDA CA 94501
32- 85 THOMAS, LUTHER BAXTER 'BUD'	RR 1 BOX 400 - NORTH GARDEN VA 22959
26- 86 THOMAS, MYLES LEWIS	D. DECEMBER 12, 1963 TOLEDO, O.
38- 98 THOMAS, RAYMOND JOSEPH	607 WEST VANCE ST - WILSON NC 27893
21-104 THOMAS, ROBERT WILLIAM 'RED'	D. MARCH 29, 1962 FREMONT, O.
77-142 THOMAS, ROY JUSTIN	4055 HIDDEN VALLEY LN - SAN JOSE CA 95127
74-132 THOMAS, STANLEY BROWN	10827 159TH COURT NE - REDMOND WA 98052
57- 86 THOMAS, VALMY	BOX 9184 - SANTURCE PR 00908
10-143 THOMASEN, ARTHUR WILSON	D. MAY 2, 1944 KANSAS CITY, MO.
74-133 THOMASON, MELVIN ERSKINE	405 SOUTH BROAD ST - CLINTON SC 29325
72-113 THOMASSON, GARY LEAH	4515 EAST ONYX ST - PHOENIX AZ 85028
78-133 THOMASSON, BOBBY LARUE	OLD ADD: 3106 CAPITOL DR #2 - CHARLOTTE NC 28208
54-110 THOMPSON, CHARLES LEMOINE 'TIM'	536 SUMMIT DR - LEWISTOWN PA 17044
70-133 THOMPSON, DANNY LEON	D. DECEMBER 10, 1976 ROCHESTER, MINN.
48- 98 THOMPSON, DAVID FORREST	D. FEBRUARY 26, 1979 CHARLOTTE, N. C.
49- 87 THOMPSON, DONALD NEWLIN	87 EAST EUCLID PKWY - ASHEVILLE NC 28804
39-116 THOMPSON, EUGENE EARL	7934 E. CRESTWOOD WAY - SCOTTSDALE AZ 85253
20-117 THOMPSON, FRANK E.	D. JUNE 27, 1940 JASPER CO., MINERAL TWP., MO.
11-167 THOMPSON, FULLER WEIDNER	D. FEBRUARY 19, 1972 LOS ANGELES, CALIF.
19- 82 THOMPSON, HAROLD	D. FEBRUARY 14, 1951 RENO, NEV.
47- 88 THOMPSON, HENRY CURTIS	D. SEPTEMBER 30, 1969 FRESNO, CAL.
14-213 THOMPSON, JAMES ALFRED 'SHAG'	101 SECOND ST - BLACK MOUNTAIN NC 28711
76- 94 THOMPSON, JASON DOLPH	26351 SORRELL - LAGUNA HILLS CA 92653
21-105 THOMPSON, JOHN DUDLEY 'LEE'	D. FEBRUARY 17, 1965 SANTA BARBARA, CAL.
48- 99 THOMPSON, JOHN SAMUEL 'JOCKO'	10 BEL PRE CT - ROCKVILLE MD 20853

25-104	THOMPSON, LAFAYETTE FRESCO	D. NOVEMBER 20, 1968 FULLERTON, CAL.
71-105	THOMPSON, MICHAEL WAYNE	7565 TURNER DR - DENVER CO 80221
84-120	THOMPSON, MILTON BERNARD	RR 2 BOX 95 - NINETY SIX SC 29666
85-111	THOMPSON, RICHARD NEIL	7 CHAMBERS COURT - HUNTINGTON STATION NY 11746
86-155	THOMPSON, ROBERT RANDALL	4438 GUN CLUB ROAD - WEST PALM BEACH FL 33406
33- 60	THOMPSON, RUPERT LUCKHART 'TOMMY'	D. MAY 24, 1971 AUBURN, CAL.
12-198	THOMPSON, THOMAS CARL	D. JANUARY 16, 1963 LAJOLLA, CALIF.
12-199	THOMPSON, THOMAS HOMER	D. SEPTEMBER 19, 1957 ATLANTA, GA.
78-134	THOMPSON, VERNON SCOT	110 BEACON RD - RENFREW PA 16053
46- 99	THOMSON, ROBERT BROWN	122 SUNLIT DR - WATCHUNG NJ 07060
79-110	THON, RICHARD WILLIAM 'DICKIE'	HB-12 LOMBARDIA ST - RIO PIEDRAS PR 00924
17- 81	THORMAHLEN, HERBERT EHLER 'HANK'	D. FEBRUARY 6, 1955 LOS ANGELES, CALIF.
77-143	THORMODSGARD, PAUL GAYTON	6531 EAST CYPRESS - SCOTTSDALE AZ 85257
73-119	THORNTON, ANDRE	BOX 395 - CHAGRIN FALLS OH 44022
85-112	THORNTON, LOUIS	115 MCLEAN ROAD - HOPE HULL AL 36043
73-120	THORNTON, OTIS BENJAMIN	BOX 164 - DOCENA AL 35060
51- 97	THORPE, BENJAMIN ROBERT 'BOB'	BOX 46 - WAVELAND MS 39576
13-179	THORPE, JAMES FRANCIS	D. MARCH 28, 1953 LOMITA, CALIF.
55-125	THORPE, ROBERT JOSEPH	D. MARCH 17, 1960 SAN DIEGO, CAL.
16- 89	THRASHER, FRANK EDWARD 'BUCK'	D. JUNE 12, 1938 CLEVELAND, TENN.
55-126	THRONEBERRY, MARVIN EUGENE	12102 MACON RD - COLLIERVILLE TN 38017
52-103	THRONEBERRY, MAYNARD FAYE	12016 MACON RD - COLLIERVILLE TN 38017
75-118	THROOP, GEORGE LYNFORD	672 WEST HIGHLAND AVE - SIERRA MADRE CA 91024
39-117	THUMAN, LOUIS CHARLES FRANK	6117 EDLYNNE RD - BALTIMORE MD 21212
87-145	THURMAN, GARY MONTEZ	7222 RUE DE MARGOT - INDIANAPOLIS IN 46260
55-127	THURMAN, ROBERT BURNS	9316 BEDELL - WICHITA KS 67207
83-142	THURMOND, MARK ANTHONY	4706 MISTY SHADOWS DR - HOUSTON TX 77041
23-133	THURSTON, HOLLIS JOHN 'SLOPPY'	D. SEPTEMBER 14, 1973 LOS ANGELES, CAL.
64-121	TIANT, LUIS CLEMENTE	150 INDIAN LANE - CANTON MA 02021
84-121	TIBBS, JAY LINDSEY	216 REDSTONE WAY - BIRMINGHAM AL 35215
72-114	TIDROW, RICHARD WILLIAM	1601 VIA HELENA - SAN LORENZO CA 94580
52-104	TIEFENAUER, BOBBY GENE	300 SOUTH LINCOLN - DESLOGE MO 63603
62-132	TIEFENTHALER, VERLE MATHEW	1852 QUINT AVE - CARROLL IA 51401
20-118	TIERNEY, JAMES ARTHUR 'COTTON'	D. APRIL 18, 1953 KANSAS CITY, MO.
33- 61	TIETJE, LESLIE WILLIAM	RR 2 BOX 107 - KASSON MN 55944
57- 87	TIGHE, JOHN THOMAS	3201 NE 5TH COURT #4 - POMPANO BEACH FL 33062
15-161	TILLMAN, JOHN LAWRENCE	D. APRIL 7, 1964 HARRISBURG, PA.
62-133	TILLMAN, JOHN ROBERT 'BOB'	403 WADERBROOK DR - GALLATIN TN 37066
82-126	TILLMAN, KERRY JEROME 'RUSTY'	130 JACKSON RD - ATLANTIC BEACH FL 32233
67-107	TILLOTSON, THADDEUS ASA	870 DONNA DR - MERCED CA 95340
69-170	TIMBERLAKE, GARY DALE	HIGHWAY 11 - LACONIA IN 47135
69-171	TIMMERMANN, THOMAS HENRY	4900 COOLEY LAKE - MILFORD MI 48042
14-214	TINCUP, AUSTIN BEN	D. JULY 5, 1980 CLAREMORE, OK.
82-127	TINGLEY, RONALD IRVIN	OLD ADD: 1830 GREENBRAE - SPARKS NV 89431
32- 86	TINNING, LYLE FORREST 'BUD'	D. JANUARY 17, 1961 EVANSVILLE, IND.
15-162	TIPPLE, DANIEL E	D. MARCH 26, 1960 OMAHA, NEB.
39-118	TIPTON, ERIC GORDON	125 NINA LN - WILLIAMSBURG VA 23185
48-100	TIPTON, JOSEPH JOHN	1129 2ND AVE - PLEASANT GROVE AL 35127
69-172	TISCHINSKI, THOMAS ARTHUR	2607 NE 68TH TER - GLADSTONE MO 64119
36- 92	TISING, JOHNNIE JOSEPH	D. SEPTEMBER 5, 1967 LEADVILLE, COLO.
78-135	TOBIK, DAVID VANCE	4852 SOUTH SEDGEWICK RD - LYNDHURST OH 44124
37- 99	TOBIN, JAMES ANTHONY	D. MAY 19, 1969 OAKLAND, CAL.
32- 87	TOBIN, JOHN MARTIN	D. AUGUST 8, 1983 RHINEBECK, N. Y.
45-105	TOBIN, JOHN PATRICK	D. JANUARY 18, 1982 OAKLAND, CALIF.
14-215	TOBIN, JOHN THOMAS	D. DECEMBER 10, 1969 ST. LOUIS, MO.
41-112	TOBIN, MARION BROOKS 'PAT'	D. JANUARY 21, 1975 SHREVEPORT, LA.
32- 88	TODD, ALFRED CHESTER	D. MARCH 8, 1985 ELMIRA, N. Y.
77-144	TODD, JACKSON A	7129 SOUTH BRADEN - TULSA OK 74136
74-134	TODD, JAMES RICHARD JR.	8630 EAST PAWNEE DR - PARKER CO 80134
24-111	TODT, PHILIP JULIUS	D. NOVEMBER 15, 1973 ST. LOUIS, MO.
47- 89	TOENES, WILLIAM HARRELL 'HAL'	5119 BRANCH AVE - TAMPA FL 33603
65-105	TOLAN, ROBERT	6988 CAMINO AMERO - SAN DIEGO CA 92111
84-122	TOLIVER, FREDDIE LEE	27470 STRATFORD ST - HIGHLAND CA 92346
81-136	TOLLESON, JIMMY WAYNE	352 LANHAM CIRCLE - SPARTANBURG SC 29302
81-137	TOLMAN, TIMOTHY LEE	8601 E. FAIRMOUNT PLACE - TUCSON AZ 85715
25-105	TOLSON, CHESTER JULIUS 'CHICK'	D. APRIL 16, 1965 WASHINGTON, D. C.
53- 91	TOMANEK, RICHARD CARL	165 DUFF DR - AVON LAKE OH 44012
49- 88	TOMASIC, ANDREW JOHN	230 7TH ST - WHITEHALL PA 18052
13-180	TOMER, GEORGE CLARENCE	D. DECEMBER 15, 1984 PERRY, IOWA
72-115	TOMLIN, DAVID ALLEN	2020 CLAYTON ROAD - MANCHESTER OH 45144
12-200	TOMPKINS, CHARLES HERBERT	D. SEPTEMBER 20, 1975 PRESCOTT, ARK.
65-106	TOMPKINS, RONALD EVERETT	188 EAST "J" ST - CHULA VISTA CA 92010
75-119	TOMS, THOMAS HOWARD	GREENWOOD VA 22943
11-168	TONEY, FRED ALEXANDRA	D. MARCH 11, 1953 NASHVILLE, TENN.
11-169	TONNEMAN, CHARLES RICHARD 'TONY'	D. AUGUST 7, 1951 PRESCOTT, ARIZ.

11-170	TOOLEY, ALBERT	D. AUGUST 17, 1976 MARSHALL, MICH.
21-106	TOPORCER, GEORGE 'SPECS'	30 TEED ST - HUNTINGTON STATION NY 11747
62-134	TOPPIN, RUPERTO	OLD ADD: 601 CROWN ST - BROOKLYN NY 11213
64-122	TORBORG, JEFFREY ALLEN	1375 CHAPEL HILL - MOUNTAINSIDE NJ 07092
47- 90	TORGESON, CLIFFORD EARL	2121 RUCKER - EVERETT WA 98201
17- 82	TORKELSON, CHESTER LEROY 'RED'	D. SEPTEMBER 22, 1964 CHICAGO, ILL.
20-119	TORPHY, WALTER ANTHONY 'RED'	D. FEBRUARY 11, 1980 FALL RIVER, MASS.
56- 82	TORRE, FRANK JOSEPH	13100 GREENBOUGH DRIVE - ST.LOUIS MO 63341
60-100	TORRE, JOSEPH PAUL	3088 GREENFIELD DR - MARIETTA GA 30067
75-120	TORREALBA, PABLO ARNOLDO	AVE PTE.MEDINA,MARIO 50,PISO 19-CARACAS VENEZ
77-145	TORRES, ANGEL RAFAEL	CALLE 16 DE AGOSTO #19 - AZUA DOMINICAN REP.
40- 91	TORRES, DON GILBERTO NUNEZ 'GIL'	D. JANUARY 11, 1983 REGLA, HAVANA, CUBA
62-135	TORRES, FELIX	RR 3 BOX 105 - SANTA ISABEL PR 00757
68-103	TORRES, HECTOR EPITACIO	RR 3 BOX 950 - EFFINGHAM SC 29541
20-120	TORRES, RICARDO J.	D. HAVANA, CUBA
71-106	TORRES, ROSENDO 'RUSTY'	151-34 136TH AVE - JAMAICA NY 11434
67-108	TORREZ, MICHAEL AUGUSTINE	208 NORTH LAKE ST - TOPEKA KS 66616
42-100	TOST, LOUIS EUGENE	D. FEBRUARY 22,1967 SANTA CLARA, CAL.
62-136	TOTH, PAUL LOUIS	6538 SUDER - ERIE MI 48133
28- 99	TOUCHSTONE, CLAYLAND MAFFITT	D. APRIL 28, 1949 BEAUMONT, TEX.
65-107	TOVAR, CESAR LEONARDO	CALLE REAL PRADO MARIA #58 - CARACAS VENEZ
20-121	TOWNSEND, IRA DANCE	D. JULY 21, 1965 SCHULENBERG, TEX.
20-122	TOWNSEND, LEO ALPHONSE	D. DECEMBER 3, 1976 MOBILE, ALA.
84-123	TRABER, JAMES JOSEPH	10387 GREEN MOUNTAIN CIR - COLUMBIA MD 21044
62-137	TRACEWSKI, RICHARD JOHN	5 FLORA DR - PECKVILLE PA 18452
80-128	TRACY, JAMES EDWIN	4785 CELADON AVE - FAIRFIELD OH 45014
13-181	TRAGESSER, WALTER JOSEPH	D. DECEMBER 14, 1970 LAFAYETTE, IND.
40- 92	TRAMBACK, STEPHEN JOSEPH 'RED'	D. DECEMBER 28, 1979 BUFFALO, N. Y.
77-146	TRAMMELL, ALAN STUART	7346 SANDY CREEK LANE - BIRMINGHAM MI 48010
15-163	TRAUTMAN, FREDERICK ORLANDO	D. FEBRUARY 15, 1964 BUCYRUS, O.
12-201	TRAVERS, ALOYSIUS JOSEPH 'ALLAN'	D. APRIL 21, 1968 PHILADELPHIA, PA.
74-135	TRAVERS, WILLIAM EDWARD	10 SHORELINE DR - FOXBORO MA 02035
33- 62	TRAVIS, CECIL HOWELL	2260 HWY 138 - RIVERDALE GA 30296
20-123	TRAYNOR, HAROLD JOSEPH 'PIE'	D. MARCH 16, 1972 PITTSBURGH, PA.
30- 83	TREADAWAY, EDGAR RAYMOND 'RAY'	D. OCTOBER 12, 1935 CHATTANOOGA, TENN.
87-146	TREADWAY, HUGH JEFFERY 'JEFF'	1413 RAINBOW CIRCLE - GRIFFIN GA 30223
44-129	TREADWAY, THADFORD LEON 'RED'	190 ALPINE DRIVE - ROSWELL GA 30075
86-156	TREBELHORN, THOMAS JOHN	4344 SOUTHEAST 26TH AVENUE - PORTLAND OR 97202
37-100	TRECHOCK, FRANK ADAM	4600 29TH AVE S. - MINNEAPOLIS MN 55406
13-182	TREKELL, HARRY ROY	D. NOVEMBER 4, 1963 SPOKANE, WASH.
34-101	TREMARK, NICHOLAS JOSEPH	1906 LAUREL DR - HARLINGEN TX 78550
54-111	TREMEL, WILLIAM LEONARD	315 EAST 23RD AVE - ALTOONA PA 16601
27- 91	TREMPER, CARLTON OVERTON	15777 BOLESTA RD #143 - CLEARWATER FL 33520
38- 99	TRESH, MICHAEL	D. OCTOBER 1, 1966 DETROIT, MICH.
61-105	TRESH, THOMAS MICHAEL	4206 EAST WING RD, RR 6-MOUNT PLEASANT MI 48858
78-136	TREVINO, ALEJANDRO	ALONDRA #103,CUACHTEMOC-MONTERREY NUEVO LAREDO MEX.
68-104	TREVINO, CARLOS CASTRO 'BOBBY'	ALONDRA #102, CUAUHTEMOC - MONTERREY NUEVO LAREDO MEX.
53- 92	TRIANDOS, CONSTANTIN GUS	1207 WOODLAWN AVE - SAN JOSE CA 95128
53- 93	TRICE, ROBERT LEE	RR 2 BOX 25-R-9 - WEIRTON WV 26062
73-121	TRILLO, JESUS MANUEL 'MANNY'	CENTRO RES. HUMBOLDT #1B-PRADOS DEL ESTE CARACAS VENEZ
55-128	TRIMBLE, JOSEPH GERARD	71 ARBOR DR - PROVIDENCE RI 02903
43-138	TRINKLE, KENNETH WAYNE	D. MAY 10, 1976 PAOLI, ILL.
38-100	TRIPLETT, HERMAN COAKER	RR 1 BOX 72-C - BOONE NC 28607
73-122	TROEDSON, RICHARD LAMONTE	505 CHURCHILL PARK DR - SAN JOSE CA 95136
58- 97	TROSKY, HAROLD ARTHUR JR	1919 HAMILTON ST SW - CEDAR RAPIDS IA 52404
33- 63	TROSKY, HAROLD ARTHUR SR	D. JUNE 18, 1979 CEDAR RAPIDS, IOWA
37-101	TROTTER, WILLIAM FELIX	D. AUGUST 26, 1984 ARLINGTON, MASS.
52-105	TROUPPE, QUINCY THOMAS	P.O. BOX 1551 - HATTIESBURG MS 39401
39-119	TROUT, PAUL HOWARD 'DIZZY'	D. FEBRUARY 28, 1972 HARVEY, ILL.
78-137	TROUT, STEVEN RUSSELL	719 RIVERVIEW DR - SOUTH HOLLAND IL 60473
56- 83	TROWBRIDGE, ROBERT	D. APRIL 3, 1980 HUDSON, N. Y.
12-202	TROY, ROBERT 'BUN'	D. OCTOBER 7, 1918 MEUSE, FRANCE
41-113	TRUCKS, VIRGIL OLIVER 'FIRE'	2156 GRAYSON VALLEY DR - BIRMINGHAM AL 35235
10-144	TRUESDALE, FRANK DAY	D. AUGUST 27, 1943 ALBUQUERQUE, N. M.
85-113	TRUJILLO, MICHAEL ANDREW	2636 SOUTH STUART WAY - DENVER CO 80219
57- 88	TSITOURIS, JOHN PHILIP	5207 AUSTIN ROAD - MONROE NC 28110
27- 92	TUCKER, OSCAR DINWIDDIE	D. JULY 13, 1940 RADIANT, VA.
42-101	TUCKER, THURMAN LOWELL	2400 SOUTH MACARTHUR #11 - OKLAHOMA CITY OK 73128
79-111	TUDOR, JOHN THOMAS	14 FOREST ST - PEABODY MA 01960
18- 71	TUERO, OSCAR MONZON	D. OCTOBER 21, 1960 HOUSTON, TEXAS
81-138	TUFTS, ROBERT MALCOLM	27 WING RD - LYNNFIELD MA 01940
82-128	TUNNELL, BYRON LEE	5905 RISING HILLS DR - AUSTIN TX 78759
35-107	TURBEVILLE, GEORGE ELKINS	D. OCTOBER 5, 1983 SALISBURY, N. C.
43-139	TURCHIN, EDWARD LAWRENCE	D. FEBRUARY 8, 1982 BROOKHAVEN, N. Y.
23-134	TURGEON, EUGENE JOSEPH 'PETE'	D. JANUARY 24, 1977 WICHITA FALLS, TEX.
22-134	TURK, LUCAS NEWTON	RR 1 - HOMER GA 30547
51- 98	TURLEY, ROBERT LEE	P.O. BOX 786 - MARCO ISLAND FL 33937
48-101	TURNER, EARL EDWIN	OLD ADD: 7 SULLIVAN DR - LENOX MA
37-102	TURNER, JAMES RILEY	1004 WOODMONT BLVD-NASHVILLE TN 37204
74-136	TURNER, JOHN WEBBER 'JERRY'	807 CALIFORNIA - VENICE CA 90291
67-109	TURNER, KENNETH CHARLES	4913 NEBLINA DR - CARLSBAD CA 92008
77-162	TURNER, ROBERT EDWARD 'TED'	1018 PEACHTREE ST NW - ATLANTA GA 30309
20-124	TURNER, THEODORE HOLTOP	D. FEBRUARY 4, 1958 LEXINGTON, KY.
15-164	TURNER, THOMAS LOVATT 'TINK'	D. FEBRUARY 25, 1962 PHILADELPHIA, PA.
40- 93	TURNER, THOMAS RICHARD	D. MAY 14, 1986 KENNEWICK, WASH.
52-106	TUTTLE, WILLIAM ROBERT	115 HARLEM RD #155 - KANSAS CITY MO 64116
11-171	TUTWEILER, GUY ISBELL	D. AUGUST 15, 1930 ANNISTON, ALA.
28-100	TUTWILER, ELMER STRANGE	D. MAY 3, 1976 PENSACOLA, FLA.
16- 90	TWINING, HOWARD EARLE 'TWINK'	D. JUNE 14, 1973 LANSDALE, PA.
70-134	TWITCHELL, WAYNE LEE	7129 SW 33RD PL - PORTLAND OR 97219
80-129	TWITTY, JEFFREY DEAN	1734 C AVENUE - NORTH COLUMBIA SC 29169
20-125	TWOMBLY, CLARENCE EDWARD 'BABE'	D. NOVEMBER 23, 1974 SAN CLEMENTE, CALIF.
21-107	TWOMBLY, EDWIN PARKER 'CY'	D. DECEMBER 3, 1974 SAVANNAH, GA.
14-216	TWOMBLY, GEORGE FREDERICK	D. FEBRUARY 17, 1975 LEXINGTON, MASS.
43-140	TYACK, JAMES FRED	2901 MANOR AVE - BAKERSFIELD CA 93308
14-217	TYLER, FREDERICK FRANKLIN	D. OCTOBER 14, 1945 DERRY, N.H.
10-145	TYLER, GEORGE ALBERT 'LEFTY'	D. SEPTEMBER 29, 1953 LOWELL, MASS.
34-102	TYLER, JOHN ANTHONY	D. JULY 11, 1972 MOUNT PLEASANT, PA.
14-218	TYREE, EARL CARLTON	D. MAY 17, 1954 RUSHVILLE, ILL.

JIM UMBARGER

62-138	TYRIVER, DAVID BURTON	680 BOYD STREET - OSHKOSH WI 54901
72-116	TYRONE, JAMES VERNON	484 WEST MONTANA - PASADENA CA 91103
76- 95	TYRONE, OSCAR WAYNE	2301 NW 10TH AVE - MIAMI FL 33127
26- 87	TYSON, ALBERT THOMAS 'TY'	D. AUGUST 16, 1953 BUFFALO, N. Y.
44-130	TYSON, CECIL WASHINGTON 'TURKEY'	RR 1 BOX 202, TYSON LN - ELM CITY NC 27822
72-117	TYSON, MICHAEL RAY	479 THUNDERHEAD CANYON DR-BALDWIN MO 63011
26- 88	UCHRINSCKO, JAMES EMERSON	204 WATER STREET - WEST NEWTON PA 15089
62-139	UECKER, ROBERT GEORGE	N60W15734 HAWTHORNE DR - MENOMONEE FALLS WI 53051
34-103	UHALT, BERNARD BARTHOLOMEW 'FRENCHY'	231 CROSS RD - OAKLAND CA 94618
65-108	UHLAENDER, THEODORE OTTO	BOX 1355 - MCALLEN TX 78502
19- 83	UHLE, GEORGE ERNEST	D. FEBRUARY 26, 1985 LAKEWOOD, O.
38-101	UHLE, ROBERT ELLWOOD	8721 LANCASTER DR - ROHNERT PARK CA 94928
14-219	UHLER, MAURICE WILLIAM	D. MAY 4, 1918 BALTIMORE MD.
34-104	UHLIR, CHARLES	OLD ADD: 11 SOUTH LASALLE - CHICAGO IL
80-130	UJDUR, GERALD RAYMOND	3312 BERKELEY RD - DULUTH MN 55811
45-106	ULISNEY, MICHAEL EDWARD	OLD ADD: 1405 NW 4TH AVE - FT LAUDERDALE FL 33311
83-143	ULLGER, SCOTT MATTHEW	9 BETH LANE - PLAINVIEW NY 11803
44-131	ULLRICH, CARLOS SANTIAGO CASTELLO	3671 NW 15TH ST - MIAMI FL 33125
25-106	ULRICH, FRANK W. 'DUTCH'	D. FEBRUARY 11, 1929 BALTIMORE, MD.
64-123	UMBACH, ARNOLD WILLIAM	655 SOUTH DEAN RD - AUBURN AL 36830
75-121	UMBARGER, JAMES HAROLD	OLD ADD: 181 E.56TH AVE #200 - DENVER CO 80216
59- 83	UMBRICHT, JAMES	D. APRIL 8, 1964 HOUSTON, TEX.
53- 94	UMPHLETT, THOMAS MULLEN	RR 2 BOX 17C - AHOSKIE NC 27910
27- 93	UNDERHILL, WILLIE VERN	D. OCTOBER 26, 1970 BAY CITY, TEXAS
79-112	UNDERWOOD, PATRICK JOHN	1810 WEST JEFFERSON STREET - KOKOMO IN 46901
74-137	UNDERWOOD, THOMAS GERALD	4677 NW 89TH AVENUE - SUNRISE FL 33351
42-102	UNSER, ALBERT BERNARD	2096 NORTH UNION-DECATUR IL 62526
68-105	UNSER, DELBERT BERNARD	495 FERNWOOD DR - MORAGA CA 94556
35-108	UPCHURCH, JEFFERSON WOODROW 'WOODY'	D. OCTOBER 23, 1971 BUIES CREEK, N. C.
67-110	UPHAM, JOHN LESLIE	1100 HURON CHURCH RD - WINDSOR ONTARIO N9C 2K7 CAN.
15-165	UPHAM, WILLIAM LAWRENCE	D. SEPTEMBER 14, 1959 NEWARK, N.J.
53- 95	UPRIGHT, ROY T. 'DIXIE'	D. NOVEMBER 13, 1986 CONCORD, N. C.
66- 91	UPSHAW, CECIL LEE	709 BURNT CREEK DR - LILBURN GA 30247
78-138	UPSHAW, WILLIE CLAY	BOX 395 - BLANCO TX 78606
50-100	UPTON, THOMAS HERBERT	4638 LARWIN - CYPRESS CA 90630
54-112	UPTON, WILLIAM RAY	BOX 3441 - LAMESA CA 92041
57- 89	URBAN, JACK ELMER	8607 FOWLER - OMAHA NE 68134
27- 94	URBAN, LOUIS JOHN 'LUKE'	D. DECEMBER 7, 1980 SOMERSET, MASS.
31- 81	URBANSKI, WILLIAM MICHAEL	D. JULY 12, 1973 PERTH AMBOY, N. J.
84-124	URIBE, JOSE ALTAGRACIA	CLE D #9 SAB.GRANDF DE PALENQUE - JUAN DOMINICAN REP.
77-147	URREA, JOHN GODBY	12540 YOSEMITE - CERRITOS CA 90701
46-100	USHER, ROBERT ROYCE	1022 NORTH FIFTH ST - SAN JOSE CA 95112
25-107	USSAT, WILLIAM AUGUST 'DUTCH'	D. MAY 29, 1959 DAYTON, O.
25-108	VACHE, ERNEST LEWIS 'TEX'	D. JUNE 11, 1953 LOS ANGELES, CALIF.
75-122	VAIL, MICHAEL LEWIS	3253 HARVESTMOON DR - PALM HARBOR FL 33563
57- 90	VALDES, RENE GUTIERREZ	AVENIDA 7A,14511 ALTURAS-MANANA,HAVANA CUBA
44-132	VALDES, ROGELIO LAZARO 'ROY'	241 PONCE DE LEON BLVD - CORAL GABLES FL 33134
65-109	VALDESPINO, HILARIO 'SANDY'	17920 NW 43RD AVE - CAROL CITY FL 33055
80-131	VALDEZ, JULIO JULIAN CASTILLO	MAXIMO GAHEZ #4,NIZAO - BANI DOMINICAN REP.
86-157	VALDEZ, SERGIO SANCHEZ	CAL LA PAZ #14,HERRERA-SANTO DOMINGO DOMINICAN REP.
55-129	VALDIVIELSO, JOSE LOPEZ	14 RITA DR - MOUNT SINAI NY 11766
75-123	VALENTINE, ELLIS CLARENCE	5601 VALLEY GLEN WAY - LOS ANGELES CA 90043
59- 84	VALENTINE, FRED LEE	4838 BLAGDEN AVE NW - WASHINGTON DC 20011
54-113	VALENTINE, HAROLD LEWIS 'CORKY'	RR 1, OLD BIRMINGHAM RD - CANTON GA 30114
69-173	VALENTINE, ROBERT JOHN	2113 GRETA LANE - FORT WORTH TX 76112
54-114	VALENTINETTI, VITO JOHN	271 SUMMIT AVE - MOUNT VERNON NY 10552
58- 98	VALENZUELA, BENJAMIN BELTRAN	BAHIA SAN ESTEBAN #267 SUR - LOS MOCHIS SINOLOA MEX.
80-132	VALENZUELA, FERNANDO	3004 N. BEACHWOOD DR - HOLLYWOOD CA 90068
84-125	VALLE, DAVID	20947 34TH ROAD - FLUSHING NY 11361
65-110	VALLE, HECTOR JOSE	URB. CATONI #7 - VEGA BAJA PR 00763
40- 94	VALO, ELMER WILLIAM	571 COLUMBIA AVE-PALMERTON PA 18071
50-101	VAN CUYK, CHRISTIAN GERALD	14405 AMY LANE - HUDSON FL 33562
47- 91	VAN CUYK, JOHN HENRY	104 WEST FIRST ST - KIMBERLEY WI 54136
27- 95	VANALSTYNE, CLAYTON EMERY	D. JANUARY 5, 1960 HUDSON, N. Y.
33- 64	VANATTA, RUSSELL	D. OCTOBER 10, 1986 ANDOVER, N. J.
54-115	VANBRABANT, CAMILLE OSCAR 'OSSIE'	OLD ADD: 2330 N. WASHINGTON - ROYAL OAK MI 48073
28-101	VANCAMP, ALBERT JOSEPH	D. FEBRUARY 2, 1981 DAVENPORT, IOWA
15-166	VANCE, CLARENCE ARTHUR 'DAZZY'	D. FEBRUARY 16, 1961 HOMOSASSA SPRINGS, FLA.
70-135	VANCE, GENE COVINGTON 'SANDY'	953 FOYE DRIVE - LAFAYETTE CA 94549
35-109	VANCE, JOSEPH ALBERT	D. JULY 4, 1978 DEVINE, TEXAS
14-220	VANDAGRIFT, CARL WILLIAM	D. OCTOBER 9, 1920 FORT WAYNE, IND.
82-129	VANDEBERG, EDWARD JOHN	1331 CLOCK AVE - REDLANDS CA 92374
35-110	VANDENBURG, HAROLD HARRIS 'HY'	10143 THIRD AVE SOUTH - MINNEAPOLIS MN 55420

37-103 VANDERMEER, JOHN SAMUEL	4005 LEONA AVE-TAMPA FL 33606
55-130 VANDUSEN, FREDERICK WILLIAM	826 ROCKRIMMON RD - STAMFORD CT 06903
19- 84 VANGILDER, ELAM RUSSELL	D. APRIL 30, 1977 CAPE GIRARDEAU, MO.
82-130 VANGORDER, DAVID THOMAS	3906 SOUTH BIRCH ST - SANTA ANA CA 92707
13-183 VANN, JOHN SILAS	D. JUNE 10, 1958 SHREVEPORT, LA.
51- 99 VANNOY, JAY LOWELL	1092 NORTH 1700 EAST - LOGAN UT 84321
39-120 VANROBAYS, MAURICE RENE	D. MARCH 1, 1965 DETROIT, MICH.
83-144 VANSLYKE, ANDREW JAMES	24 HARTFORD TER - NEW HARTFORD NY 13413
50-102 VARGA, ANDREW WILLIAM	1964 ADD: 2429 M - BELLVILLE KS 66935
82-131 VARGAS, HEDIBERTO	BOX 1172 - GUANICA PR 00653
55-131 VARGAS, ROBERTO ENRIQUE	24 BRISAIDA ST,URB. L.M.RIVERA - GUAYNABO PR 00657
25-109 VARGUS, WILLIAM FAY	D. FEBRUARY 12, 1979 HYANNIS, MASS.
52-107 VARNER, GLEN GANN	1737 EAST VARNER RD - HIXSON TN 37343
73-123 VARNER, RICHARD FRED 'PETE'	14 JUNIPER RIDGE RD - ACTON MA 01720
79-113 VASQUEZ, RAFAEL (SANTIAGO)	CALLE JULIO A JARSIA #29 - LA ROMANA DOMINICAN REP.
40- 95 VAUGHAN, CECIL PORTER	2881 BRAIDWOOD RD-RICHMOND VA 23225
66- 92 VAUGHAN, CHARLES WAYNE	1802 FOREST LANE - WESLACO TX 78596
63-121 VAUGHAN, GLENN EDWARD	3050 POST OAK BLVD #300 - HOUSTON TX 77056
32- 89 VAUGHAN, JOSEPH FLOYD 'ARKY'	D. AUGUST 30, 1952 EAGLEVILLE, CAL.
34-105 VAUGHN, CLARENCE LEROY	D. MARCH 1, 1937 MARTINSVILLE, VA.
44-133 VAUGHN, FREDERICK THOMAS	D. MARCH 2, 1964 LAKE WALES, FLA.
35-111 VEACH, ALVIS LINDELL	620 CHURCH ST - SELMA AL 36701
12-203 VEACH, ROBERT HENRY	D. AUGUST 7, 1945 DETROIT, MICH.
58- 99 VEAL, ORVILLE INMAN 'COOT'	1258 TIMBERLANE - MACON GA 31204
62-140 VEALE, ROBERT ANDREW	1502 LOMB AVE WEST - BIRMINGHAM AL 35208
20-126 VEDDER, LOUIS EDWARD	1201 WEST CORNELL #57 - AVON PARK FL 33825
79-114 VEGA, JESUS ANTONIO	OLD ADD: MAGOLY CENTRAL NH22-LEVITTOWN PR
39-121 VEIGEL, ALLEN FRANCIS	1907 DOVER AVE-DOVER OH 44622
87-147 VELARDE, RANDY LEE	904 NORTH DALLAS STREET - MIDLAND TX 79701
73-124 VELAZQUEZ, CARLOS	OLD ADD: BO MEDINA ALTA - LUIZA ALDEA PR
69-174 VELAZQUEZ, FEDERICO ANTONIO	JOSE AMADO SOLER NO. 70 - SANTO DOMINGO DOMINICAN REP.
73-125 VELEZ, OTONIEL FRONCESCHI 'OTTO'	LOS CAOBOS CALLE #35 T-2 - PONCE PR 00731

26- 89 VELTMAN, ARTHUR PATRICK	D. OCTOBER 1, 1980 SAN ANTONIO, TEXAS
79-115 VENABLE, WILLIAM MCKINLEY 'MAX'	2528 LAS CASAS WAY - RANCHO CORDOVA CA 95670
45-107 VENTURA, VINCENT	23-54 29TH ST - ASTORIA NY 11102
44-134 VERBAN, EMIL MATTHEW	245 REGENT AVENUE - LINCOLN IL 62656
66- 93 VERBANIC, JOSEPH MICHAEL	85462 LORANE HWY - EUGENE OR 97405
51-100 VERBLE, GENE KERMIT	1091 OLD CHARLOTTE HWY - CONCORD NC 28025
44-135 VERDEL, ALBERT ALFRED	BOX 925 BORDENTOWN RD - BORDENTOWN NJ 08505
53- 96 VERDI, FRANK MICHAEL	10961 PEPPERTREE LANE - PORT RICHEY FL 34668
15-167 VEREKER, JOHN JAMES	D. APRIL 2, 1974 BALTIMORE, MD.
31- 92 VERGEZ, JOHN LOUIS	112 KRISTEE PLACE - OROVILLE CA 95966
76- 96 VERHOEVEN, JOHN C	1950 HORSESHOE CR - PLACENTIA CA 92670
39-122 VERNON, JAMES BARTON 'MICKEY'	100 EAST ROSE VALLEY RD - WALLINGFORD PA 19086
12-204 VERNON, JOSEPH HENRY	D. MARCH 13, 1955 PHILADELPHIA, PA.
59- 85 VERSALLES, ZOILO	8645 FREMONT SOUTH - BLOOMINGTON MN 55420
73-126 VERYZER, THOMAS MARTIN	41 UNION AVE - ISLIP NY 11751
80-133 VESELIC, ROBERT MICHAEL	1111 SOUTH BELBURY DR - WALNUT CA 91789
22-135 VICK, HENRY ARTHUR 'ERNIE'	D. JULY 16, 1980 ANN ARBOR, MICH.
17- 83 VICK, SAMUEL BRUCE	D. AUGUST 17, 1986 MEMPHIS, TENN.
48-102 VICO, GEORGE STEVE	219 PASEO DE LE DELICIAS - REDONDO BEACH CA 90278
66- 94 VIDAL, JOSE NICOLAS	1972 ADD: JUAN ERAZO 152 - SANTO DOMINGO D R
24-112 VINES, ROBERT EARL	D. OCTOBER 18, 1982 ORLANDO, FLA.
64-124 VINEYARD, DAVID KENT	RR 2 BOX 83B - LEFT HAND WV 25251
66- 95 VINSON, CHARLES ANTHONY	3821 WALTERS LN - FORESTVILLE MD 20747
82-132 VIOLA, FRANK JOHN	844 SWEETWATER ISLAND CIRCLE - LONGWOOD FL 32779
12-205 VIOX, JAMES HENRY	D. JANUARY 6, 1969 ERLANGER, KY.
55-132 VIRDON, WILLIAM CHARLES	1311 RIVER RD - SPRINGFIELD MO 65804
80-134 VIRGIL, OSVALDO JOSE JR. 'OZZIE'	4316 WEST MESCAL ST - GLENDALE AZ 85301
56- 84 VIRGIL, OSVALDO JOSE SR. 'OZZIE'	4316 WEST MESCAL ST - GLENDALE AZ 85301
44-136 VITELLI, ANTONIO JOSEPH 'JOE'	D. FEBRUARY 7, 1967 PITTSBURGH, PA.
12-206 VITT, OSCAR JOSEPH	D. JANUARY 31, 1963 OAKLAND, CALIF.
23-135 VOGEL, OTTO HENRY	D. JULY 19, 1969 IOWA CITY, IA.
24-113 VOIGT, OLEN EDWARD	D. APRIL 7, 1970
42-103 VOISELLE, WILLIAM SYMMES	RR 2 BOX 318 - NINETY SIX SC 29666
42-104 VOLLMER, CLYDE FREDERICK	P.O. BOX 3321 - CINCINNATI OH 45201
65-111 VONHOFF, BRUCE FREDERICK	423 RIVER HILLS DR - TEMPLE TERRACE FL 33617
14-222 VONKOLNITZ, ALFRED HOLMES 'FRITZ'	D. MARCH 18, 1948 MOUNT PLEASANT, S.C.
83-145 VONOHLEN, DAVID	OLD ADD: 11-06 128TH STREET - COLLEGE POINT NY 11356
86-158 VOSBERG, EDWARD JOHN	4542 EAST 14TH STREET - TUCSON AZ 85711
30- 84 VOSMIK, JOSEPH FRANKLIN	D. JANUARY 27, 1962 CLEVELAND, O.
65-112 VOSS, WILLIAM EDWARD	OLD ADD: 5882 SIERRA SIENA - IRVINE CA 92650
29-105 VOYLES, PHILIP VANCE	D. NOVEMBER 3, 1972 MARLBORO, MASS.
75-124 VUCKOVICH, PETER DENNIS	6080 SOUTH 118TH ST - HALES CORNER WI 53130

80-135 VUKOVICH, GEORGE STEPHEN — 421 NORTH HARVARD AVE - ARLINGTON HEIGHTS IL60005
70-136 VUKOVICH, JOHN CHRISTOPHER — 11 SHERI WAY - PINE HILL NJ 08021
17- 84 WACHTEL, PAUL HORINE — D. DECEMBER 15, 1964 SAN ANTONIO, TEX.
84-126 WADDELL, THOMAS DAVID — 47 FIFTH STREET - CLOSTER NJ 07624
31- 93 WADDEY, FRANK ORUM — 4505 HARDING ROAD #52E - NASHVILLE TN 37205
48-103 WADE, BENJAMIN STYRON — 1165 MEDFORD RD - PASADENA CA 91107
55-133 WADE, GALEARD LEE — RR 1 BOX 766 - NEBO NC 28761
36- 93 WADE, JACOB FIELDS — RR 2 BOX 558 - MOREHEAD CITY NC 28557
23-136 WADE, RICHARD FRANK 'RIP' — D. JUNE 15, 1957 SANDSTONE, MINN.
38-102 WAGNER, CHARLES THOMAS — 1523 LINDEN ST-READING PA 19604
65-113 WAGNER, GARY EDWARD — RR 4 BOX 480 - JACKSON NJ 08527
37-104 WAGNER, HAROLD EDWARD — D. AUGUST 7, 1979 RIVERSIDE NJ
15-168 WAGNER, JOSEPH BERNARD — D. NOVEMBER 15, 1948 BRONX, N.Y.
58-100 WAGNER, LEON LAMAR — 161 CRESTWOOD ST #11 - DALY CITY CA 94015
76- 97 WAGNER, MARK DUANE — 1616 WINTER HAVEN DR - ASHTABULA OH 44004
13-184 WAGNER, WILLIAM GEORGE 'BULL' — D. OCTOBER 2, 1967 MUSKEGON, MICH.
14-223 WAGNER, WILLIAM JOSEPH — D. JANUARY 11, 1951 WATERLOO, IA.
44-137 WAHL, KERMIT EMERSON — D. SEPTEMBER 16, 1987 TUCSON, ARIZ.
41-114 WAITKUS, EDWARD STEPHEN — D. SEPTEMBER 15, 1972 BOSTON, MASS.
73-127 WAITS, MICHAEL RICHARD 'RICK' — OLD ADD: 4750 N. CAMINO CORTO - TUCSON AZ 85718
41-115 WAKEFIELD, RICHARD CUMMINGS — D. AUGUST 26, 1985 REDFORD TWP., WAYNE CO., MICH.
64-125 WAKEFIELD, WILLIAM SUMNER — 2101 BAKER #4 - SAN FRANCISCO CA 94115
23-137 WALBERG, GEORGE ELVIN 'RUBE' — D. OCTOBER 27, 1978 TEMPE, ARIZ.
45-108 WALCZAK, EDWIN JOSEPH — 544 NEW LONDON - NORWICH CT 06360
17- 85 WALDBAUER, ALBERT CHARLES 'DOC' — D. JULY 16, 1969 YAKIMA, WASH.

Greetings from   vous salut!
TOM WALKER

12-207 WALDEN, THOMAS FRED' — D. SEPTEMBER 27, 1955 JEFFERSON BARRACKS, MO.
87-148 WALEWANDER, JAMES — 5133 NORTH OCTAVIA STREET - HARWOOD HEIGHTS IL 60656
80-136 WALK, ROBERT VERNON — %C.SHIELDS,BOX 954 - FRAZIER PARK CA 93225
48-104 WALKER, ALBERT BLUFORD 'RUBE' — 342 CUMBERLAND WAY - SMYRNA GA 30080
86-159 WALKER, ANTHONY BRUCE — 4024 PETERLYNN WAY - SAN DIEGO CA 92154
17- 86 WALKER, CHARLES FRANKLIN — D. SEPTEMBER 16, 1974 BRISTOL, TENN.
11-172 WALKER, CLARENCE WILLIAM 'TILLY' — D. SEPTEMBER 21, 1959 UNICOI, TENN.
80-137 WALKER, CLEOTHA 'CHICO' — 5344 SOUTH EMERALD AVENUE - CHICAGO IL 60609
82-133 WALKER, DUANE ALLEN — 3108 GRANT ST - PASADENA TX 77503
13-185 WALKER, ERNEST ROBERT — D. APRIL 1, 1965 PELL CITY, ALA.
31- 94 WALKER, FRED "DIXIE" — D. MAY 17, 1982 BIRMINGHAM, ALA.
10-146 WALKER, FREDERICK MITCHELL — D. FEBRUARY 1, 1958 OAK PARK, ILL.
31- 95 WALKER, GERALD HOLMES 'GEE' — D. MARCH 20, 1981 WHITFIELD, MISS.
82-134 WALKER, GREGORY LEE — 16 TOURNAMENT BLVD - PALM BEACH GARDENS FL 33418
40- 06 WALKER, HARRY WILLIAM — RR 2 BOX 145 - LEEDS AL 35094
31- 96 WALKER, HARVEY WILLOS 'HUB' — D. NOVEMBER 26, 1982 SAN JOSE, CALIF.
65-114 WALKER, JAMES LUKE — 316 LOMA LINDA - WAKE VILLAGE TX 75501
12-208 WALKER, JAMES ROY — D. FEBRUARY 10, 1962 NEW ORLEANS, LA.
57- 91 WALKER, JERRY ALLEN — 2015 COLLINS BLVD - ADA OK 74820
19- 85 WALKER, JOHN MILES — D. AUGUST 19, 1976 HOLLYWOOD, FLA.
23-138 WALKER, JOSEPH RICHARD — D. JUNE 20, 1959 WEST MIFFLIN, PA.
28-102 WALKER, MARTIN VAN BUREN — D. APRIL 24, 1978 PHILADELPHIA, PA.
72-118 WALKER, ROBERT THOMAS 'TOM' — 234 MONTCLAIR AVE - PITTSBURGH PA 15229
19- 86 WALKER, WILLIAM CURTIS 'CURT' — D. DECEMBER 9, 1955 BEEVILLE, TEX.
27- 96 WALKER, WILLIAM HENRY — D. JUNE 14, 1966 EAST ST. LOUIS, ILL.
34-106 WALKUP, JAMES ELTON — P.O. BOX 124 - HAVANA AR 72842
27- 97 WALKUP, JAMES HUEY — 1111 GRAND - DUNCAN OK 73533
50-103 WALL, MURRAY WESLEY — D. OCTOBER 8, 1971 LONE OAK, TEXAS
75-125 WALL, STANLEY ARTHUR — 9907 E. 80TH ST - RAYTOWN MO 64138
15-169 WALLACE, CLARENCE EUGENE 'JACK' — D. OCTOBER 15, 1960 WINNFIELD, LA.
73-128 WALLACE, DAVID WILLIAM — 63 STONEHEDGE LANE - ATTLEBORO MA 02703
67-111 WALLACE, DONALD ALLEN — 23 KRIS LN - MANITOU SPRINGS CO 80829
19- 87 WALLACE, FREDERICK RENSHAW 'DOC' — D. DECEMBER 31, 1964 HAVERFORD TWP., PA.
12-209 WALLACE, HARRY CLINTON 'HUCK' — D. JULY 9, 1951 CLEVELAND, O.
42-105 WALLACE, JAMES HAROLD 'LEFTY' — D. JULY 28, 1982 EVANSVILLE, IND.
73-129 WALLACE, MICHAEL SHERMAN — RR 1 BIX 176AA - MIDLAND VA 22728
80-138 WALLACH, TIMOTHY CHARLES — 14742 FEATHERHILL RD - TUSTIN CA 92680
40- 97 WALLAESA, JOHN — D. DECEMBER 27, 1986 EASTON, PA.
45-109 WALLEN, NORMAN EDWARD — 3429 NORTH WEIL - MILWAUKEE WI 53212
80-139 WALLER, ELLIOTT TYRONE 'TY' — 5146 LAPAZ DR - SAN DIEGO CA 92114
75-126 WALLING, DENNIS — BOX 1312 - WAYNESBORO VA 22980
75-127 WALLIS, HAROLD JOSEPH 'JOE' — RR 3 BOX 3552 - PIEDMONT MO 63957
52-108 WALLS, RAYMOND LEE — OLD ADD: 3002 N. 70TH ST - SCOTTSDALE AZ 85251
27- 98 WALSH, AUGUST SOTHLEY — D. NOVEMBER 12, 1985 SAN RAFAEL, CALIF.
14-224 WALSH, AUSTIN EDWARD — D. JANUARY 26, 1955 GLENDALE, CALIF.
28-103 WALSH, EDWARD ARTHUR — D. OCTOBER 31, 1937 MERIDEN, CONN.
12-210 WALSH, JAMES CHARLES — D. JULY 3, 1962 SYRACUSE, N.Y.
46-101 WALSH, JAMES GERALD — RR 1, LAYTON RD - OLYPHANT PA 18447
21-108 WALSH, JAMES THOMAS — D. MAY 13, 1967 BOSTON, MASS.

10-147 WALSH, JOSEPH FRANCIS
38-103 WALSH, JOSEPH PATRICK 'TWEET'
13-186 WALSH, LEO THOMAS 'DEE'
10-148 WALSH, MICHAEL TIMOTHY 'JIMMY'
20-127 WALSH, WALTER WILLIAM
85-114 WALTER, GENE WINSTON
30- 85 WALTER, JAMES BERNARD 'BERNIE'
15-170 WALTERS, ALFRED JOHN 'ROXY'
69-175 WALTERS, CHARLES LEONARD
45-110 WALTERS, JAMES FREDERICK 'FRED'
60-101 WALTERS, KENNETH ROGERS
83-146 WALTERS, MICHAEL CHARLES
31- 97 WALTERS, WILLIAM HENRY 'BUCKY'
68-106 WALTON, DANIEL JAMES
80-140 WALTON, REGINALD SHERARD
14-225 WAMBSGANSS, WILLIAM ADOLPH
27- 99 WANER, LLOYD JAMES
26- 90 WANER, PAUL GLEE
25-110 WANNINGER, PAUL LOUIS 'PEE WEE'
65-115 WANTZ, RICHARD CARTER
17- 87 WARD, AARON LEE
17- 88 WARD, CHARLES WILLIAM

D. JANUARY 6, 1967 BUFFALO, N.Y.
7 ST.LUKE'S RD - ALLSTON MA 02134
D. JULY 14, 1971 ST. LOUIS, MO.
D. JANUARY 21, 1947 BALTIMORE, MD.
D. JANUARY 15, 1966 NEPTUNE, N. J.
6042 SOUTH MONITOR - CHICAGO IL 60638
BOX 121 - DOVER TN 37058
D. JUNE 3, 1956 ALAMEDA, CALIF.
12387 PASEO VERANO - YUMA AZ 85365
D. FEBRUARY 1, 1980 LAUREL, MISS.
9545 BELLE MEADE DR - SAN RAMON CA 94583
OLD ADD: 80119 PALM CIRCLE DRIVE - INDIO CA 92201
515 FOX RD - GLENSIDE PA 19038
BOX 291 - CEDAR CREST NM 87008
1142 SOUTH CARSON AVE - LOS ANGELES CA 90019
D. DECEMBER 8, 1985 LAKEWOOD, O.
D. JULY 22, 1982 OKLAHOMA CITY, OKLA.
D. AUGUST 29, 1965 SARASOTA, FLA.
D. MAY 7, 1981 NORTH AUGUSTA, S. C.
D. MAY 13, 1965 INGLEWOOD, CAL.
D. JANUARY 30, 1961 NEW ORLEANS, LA.
D. APRIL 4, 1969 ST. PETERSBURG, FLA.

72-119 WARD, CHRIS GILBERT
85-115 WARD, COLIN NORVAL
79-116 WARD, GARY LAMELL
63-122 WARD, JOHN FRANCIS 'JAY'
12-211 WARD, JOSEPH NICHOLAS 'HAP'
62-141 WARD, PETER THOMAS
48-105 WARD, PRESTON MEYER
34-107 WARD, RICHARD OLE
86-160 WARD, ROY DUANE
68-107 WARDEN, JONATHAN EDGAR
84-127 WARDLE, CURTIS RAY
13-187 WARES, CLYDE ELLSWORTH 'BUZZY'
16- 91 WARMOTH, WALLACE WALTER 'CY'
30- 86 WARNEKE, LONNIE
12-212 WARNER, EDWARD EMORY
16- 92 WARNER, HOKE HAYDEN 'HOOKS'
62-142 WARNER, JACK DYER
25-111 WARNER, JOHN JOSEPH 'JACK'
66- 96 WARNER, JOHN JOSEPH
35-112 WARNOCK, HAROLD CHARLES
39-123 WARREN, BENNIE LOUIS
83-147 WARREN, MICHAEL BRUCE
44-138 WARREN, THOMAS GENTRY
14-226 WARREN, WILLIAM HACKNEY
30- 87 WARSTLER, HAROLD BURTON 'RABBIT'
75-128 WARTHEN, DANIEL DEAN
61-106 WARWICK, CARL WAYNE
21-109 WARWICK, FIRMAN NEWTON 'BILL'
37-105 WASDELL, JAMES CHARLES
37-106 WASEM, LINCOLN WILLIAM
41-116 WASHBURN, GEORGE EDWARD
69-176 WASHBURN, GREGORY JAMES
61-107 WASHBURN, RAY CLARK
74-138 WASHINGTON, CLAUDELL
74-139 WASHINGTON, HERBERT
78-139 WASHINGTON, LARUE
77-148 WASHINGTON, RONALD
35-113 WASHINGTON, SLOAN VERNON 'VERN'
77-149 WASHINGTON, U. L.
86-161 WASINGER, MARK THOMAS
67-112 WASLEWSKI, GARY LEE
76- 98 WATERBURY, STEVEN CRAIG
55-134 WATERS, FRED WARREN
76- 99 WATHAN, JOHN DAVID
69-177 WATKINS, DAVID ROGER
30- 88 WATKINS, GEORGE ARCHIBALD

17469 VIA LA JOLLA - SAN LORENZO CA 94580
356 VISTA BONITA ST - AZUSA CA 91702
318 WEST RAYMOND ST - COMPTON CA 90220
13 PINEBROOK PARK ROAD - SPARTANBURG SC 29302
D. SEPTEMBER 13, 1979 ELMER, N. J.
575 SOUTHWEST "G" - LAKE OSWEGO OR 97034
4371 DESILVA PLACE - LAS VEGAS NV 89109
D. JUNE 1, 1966 FREELAND, WASH.
209 WEST 24TH STREET - FARMINGTON NM 87401
9573 LOVELAND MADEIRA RD - LOVELAND OH 45140
30886 CURZULLA ROAD - WINCHESTER CA 92396
D. MAY 26, 1964 SOUTH BEND, IND.
D. JUNE 20, 1957 MOUNT CARMEL, ILL.
D. JUNE 23, 1976 HOT SPRINGS, ARK.
D. FEBRUARY 2, 1954 FITCHBURG, MASS.
D. FEBRUARY 19, 1947 SAN FRANCISCO, CAL.
239 EAST ST. JOHNS - PHOENIX AZ 85022
D. MARCH 13, 1986 MOUNT VERNON, ILL.
649 CRESTVIEW DRIVE - GLENDORA CA 91740
BOX 871 - TUCSON AZ 85702
3708 NW 18TH ST-OKLAHOMA CITY OK 73107
12342 BROWNING RD - GARDEN GROVE CA 92640
D. JANUARY 2, 1968 TULSA, OKLA.
D. JANUARY 28, 1960 WHITEVILLE, TENN.
D. MAY 31, 1964 NORTH CANTON, O.
6336 NORTH 38TH ST - OMAHA NE 68111
14102 BONNEY BRIER - HOUSTON TX 77069
D. DECEMBER 19, 1984 SAN ANTONIO, TEXAS
D. AUGUST 6, 1983 NEWPORT RICHEY, FLA.
D. MARCH 6, 1979 SOUTH LAGUNA, CALIF.
D. JANUARY 5, 1979 BATON ROUGE, LA.
1685 E. STELLON ST - COAL CITY IL 60416
16309 JUANITA WOODVILLE WAY NE - BOTHELL WA 98011
12 CHARLES HILL RD - ORINDA CA 94563
431 WEST MAIN STREET - ROCHESTER NY 14608
709 WEST PLUM ST - COMPTON CA 90222
1133 NORTH PRIEUR STREET - NEW ORLEANS LA 70116
D. FEBRUARY 17, 1985 LINDEN, TEXAS
BOX 164 - STRINGTOWN OK 74569
523 HOWZE STREET - FORT BLISS TX 79916
MCKENZIE DR - SOUTHINGTON CT 06489
710 N. GARFIELD - MARION IL 62958
1350 EAST AVERY - PENSACOLA FL 32503
1401 DEER RUN TRAIL - BLUE SPRINGS MO 64015
1502 ROOSEVELT RD - OWENSBORO KY 42301
D. JUNE 1, 1970 HOUSTON, TEX.

69-178 WATKINS, ROBERT CECIL	4417 WEST 58TH PLACE - LOS ANGELES CA 90043
53- 97 WATLINGTON, JULIUS NEAL	BOX 418 - YANCEYVILLE NC 27379
14-227 WATSON, ARTHUR STANHOPE	D. MAY 9, 1950 BUFFALO, N. Y.
13-188 WATSON, CHARLES JOHN 'DOC'	D. DECEMBER 30, 1949 SAN DIEGO, CALIF.
18- 72 WATSON, JOHN REEVES 'MULE'	D. AUGUST 25, 1949 SHREVEPORT, LA.
30- 89 WATSON, JOHN THOMAS	D. APRIL 29, 1965 HUNTINGTON, W. V.
16- 93 WATSON, MILTON WILSON	D. APRIL 10, 1962 PINE BLUFF, ARK.
66- 97 WATSON, ROBERT JOSE	6427 ASCOT DRIVE - OAKLAND CA 94611
20-128 WATT, ALBERT BAILEY	D. MARCH 15, 1968 NORFOLK, VA.
66- 98 WATT, EDDIE DEAN	BOX 7 - NORTH BEND NE 68649
31- 98 WATT, FRANK MARION	D. AUGUST 31, 1956 GLEN COVE, MD.
29-106 WATWOOD, JOHN CLIFFORD	D. MARCH 1, 1980 GOODWATER, ALA.
52-109 WAUGH, JAMES ELDEN	3109 OAKRIDGE - CORSICANA TX 75110
27-100 WAY, ROBERT CLINTON	D. JUNE 20, 1974 PITTSBURGH, PA.
24-114 WAYENBERG, FRANK	D. APRIL 16, 1975 ZANESVILLE, O.
36- 94 WEAFER, KENNETH ALBERT	66 RYCKMAN AVE - ALBANY NY 12208
36- 95 WEATHERLY, CYRIL ROY 'STORMY'	1175 DENTON DRIVE - BEAUMONT TX 77707
62-143 WEAVER, DAVID FLOYD	RR 1 BOX 579 - POWDERLY TX 75473
68-108 WEAVER, EARL SIDNEY	19016 WEST LAKE DR - HIALEAH FL 33015
12-213 WEAVER, GEORGE DANIEL 'BUCK'	D. JANUARY 31, 1956 CHICAGO, ILL.
15-171 WEAVER, HARRY ABRAHAM	D. MAY 30, 1983 ROCHESTER, N. Y.
67-113 WEAVER, JAMES BRIAN	276 RHODA DR - LANCASTER PA 17601
28-104 WEAVER, JAMES DEMENT	D. DECEMBER 12, 1983 LAKELAND, FLA.
85-116 WEAVER, JAMES FRANCIS	212 77TH STREET - HOLMES BEACH FL 33510
31- 99 WEAVER, MONTGOMERY MORTON	826 SOUTH LAKE ADAIR BLVD - ORLANDO FL 32804
10-149 WEAVER, ORLIE FOREST	D. NOVEMBER 28, 1970 NEW ORLEANS, LA.
80-141 WEAVER, ROGER EDWARD	BOX 15 - SAINT JOHNSVILLE NY 13452
10-150 WEBB, CLEON EARL 'LEFTY'	D. JANUARY 12, 1958 CIRCLEVILLE, O.
72-120 WEBB, HENRY GAYLON	38 HARBOR OAKS CIR - SAFETY HARBOR FL 33572
32- 90 WEBB, JAMES LEVERNE 'SKEETER'	D. JULY 8, 1986 MERIDIAN, MISS.
48-106 WEBB, SAMUEL HENRY 'RED'	5609 35TH PL - HYATTSVILLE MD 20782
25-112 WEBB, WILLIAM EARL	D. MAY 22, 1965 JAMESTOWN, TENN.
43-141 WEBB, WILLIAM FREDERICK	3758 SHARON DR - POWDER SPRINGS GA 30073
17- 89 WEBB, WILLIAM JOSEPH	D. JANUARY 12, 1943 CHICAGO, ILL.
42-106 WEBBER, LESTER ELMER	D. NOVEMBER 13, 1986 SANTA MARIA, CALIF.
83-148 WEBSTER, MITCHELL DEAN	4201 SANDPIPER LN - GREAT BEND KS 67530
67-114 WEBSTER, RAMON ALBERTO	BOX 1340 - COLON PANAMA C.A.
59- 86 WEBSTER, RAYMOND GEORGE	410 CENTER ST - YUBA CITY CA 95991
11-173 WEEDEN, CHARLES ALBERT	D. JANUARY 7, 1939 NORTHWOOD, N.H.
62-144 WEEKLY, JOHN	D. NOVEMBER 24, 1974 WALNUT CREEK, CAL.
69-179 WEGENER, MICHAEL DENIS	P.O. BOX 634 - BROOMFIELD CO 80020
85-117 WEGMAN, WILLIAM EDWARD	1720 CLIFTMONT CIRCLE - LAWRENCEBURG IN 47025
30- 90 WEHDE, WILBUR 'BIGGS'	D. SEPTEMBER 21, 1970 SIOUX FALLS,S.D.
45-111 WEHMEIER, HERMAN RALPH	D. MAY 21, 1973 DALLAS, TEX.
76-100 WEHRMEISTER, DAVID THOMAS	4216 DUBBE CT - CONCORD CA 94521
46-102 WEIGEL, RALPH RICHARD	1404 WHEATON RD - MEMPHIS TN 38117
48-107 WEIK, RICHARD HENRY	17532 70TH CT - TINLEY PARK IL 60477
40- 98 WEILAND, EDWIN NICHOLAS	D. JULY 12, 1972 CHICAGO, ILL.
28-105 WEILAND, ROBERT GEORGE	5518 W. MELROSE - CHICAGO ILL 60641
12-214 WEILMAN, CARL WOOLWORTH	D. MAY 25, 1924 HAMILTON, O.
19- 88 WEINERT, PHILLIP WALTER 'LEFTY'	D. APRIL 17, 1973 ROCKLEDGE, FLA.
45-112 WEINGARTNER, ELMER WILLIAM	13604 LORAIN - CLEVELAND OH 44111
33- 65 WEINTRAUB, PHILIP	D. JUNE 21, 1987 PALM SPRINGS, CALIF.
36- 96 WEIR, WILLIAM FRANKLIN 'ROY'	1521 WEST CRIS PLACE - ANAHEIM CA 92802
62-145 WEIS, ALBERT JOHN	902 SOUTH POPLAR - ELMHURST IL 60126
22-136 WEIS, ARTHUR JOHN 'BUTCH'	209 KINGSVILLE CT - WEBSTER GROVES MO 63119
15-172 WEISER, HARRY BUDSON 'BUD'	D. JULY 31, 1961 SHAMOKIN, PA.
80-142 WEISS, GARY LEE	RR 1 BOX 80 - BRENHAM TX 77833
15-173 WEISS, JOSEPH HAROLD	D. JULY 7, 1967 CEDAR RAPIDS, IA.
87-149 WEISS, WALTER WILLIAM	10 SYLVAN WAY - SUFFERN NY 10901
39-124 WELAJ, JOHN LUDWIG	1519 COLLEGE ST #103 - ARLINGTON TX 76010
14-228 WELCH, FLOYD JOHN	D. JANUARY 6, 1943 GREAT BEND, KAN.
19- 89 WELCH, FRANK TIGUER	D. JULY 25, 1957 BIRMINGHAM, ALA.
25-113 WELCH, HERBERT M.	D. APRIL 13, 1967 MEMPHIS, TENN.
26- 91 WELCH, JOHN VERNON	D. SEPTEMBER 2, 1940 ST. LOUIS, MO.
45-113 WELCH, MILTON EDWARD	2860 TAYLOR ST - EUGENE OR 97405
78-140 WELCH, ROBERT LYNN	4150 DELPHI CIR - HUNTINGTON BEACH CA 92649
82-135 WELCHEL, DONALD RAY	10327 GARWOOD DR - DALLAS TX 75238
11-174 WELCHONCE, HARRY MONROE	D. FEBRUARY 26, 1977 ARCADIA, CALIF.
16- 94 WELF, OLIVER HENRY	D. JUNE 25, 1967 CLEVELAND, O.
82-136 WELLMAN, BRAD EUGENE	18081 JOSEPH DR - CASTRO VALLEY CA 94546
48-108 WELLMAN, ROBERT JOSEPH	855 ROLLING WOOD DR - COVINGTON KY 41017
87-150 WELLS, DAVID LEE	4944 NEWPORT - SAN DIEGO CA 92107
23-139 WELLS, EDWIN LEE	D. MAY 1, 1986 BIRMINGHAM, ALA.

81-139 WELLS, GREGORY DEWAYNE 'BOOMER'	RR 1 BOX 98 - MCINTOSH AL 36553
44-139 WELLS, JOHN FREDERICK	3115 1/2 WEST STATE RD - OLEAN NY 14760
42-107 WELLS, LEO DONALD	1755 HIGHLAND PKWY - ST PAUL MN 55116
81-140 WELSH, CHRISTOPHER CHARLES	4112 PLUMOSA TER - BRADENTON FL 33507
25-114 WELSH, JAMES DANIEL	D. OCTOBER 30, 1970 OAKLAND, CAL.
48-109 WELTEROTH, RICHARD JOHN	122 ELDRED ST - WILLIAMSPORT PA 17701
26- 92 WELZER, ANTON FRANK	D. MARCH 18, 1971 MILWAUKEE, WIS.
15-174 WENDELL, LEWIS CHARLES	D. JULY 11, 1953 BRONX, N. Y.
43-142 WENSLOFF, CHARLES WILLIAM 'BUTCH'	8 RYAN AVE - MILL VALLEY CA 94941
45-114 WENTZEL, STANLEY AARON	2900 OLEY TURNPIKE RD #U8 - READING PA 19606
68-109 WENZ, FREDERICK CHARLES	1 CIRCLE DR - SOMERVILLE NJ 08876
27-101 WERA, JULIAN VALENTINE	D. DECEMBER 12, 1975 ROCHESTER, MINN.
30- 91 WERBER, WILLIAM MURRAY	350 NEPTUNES BIGHT - NAPLES FL 33940
64-126 WERHAS, JOHN CHARLES	7420 STONE CREEK LANE - ANAHEIM CA 92807
49- 89 WERLE, WILLIAM GEORGE	833 WEST 28TH AVE - SAN MATEO CA 94403
56- 85 WERLEY, GEORGE WILLIAM	16429 HORSESHOE RIDGE - CHESTERFIELD MO 63017
75-129 WERNER, DONALD PAUL	19 FAIRWAY CT - APPLETON WI 54915
63-123 WERT, DONALD RALPH	RR 1 BOX 288 - NEW PROVIDENCE PA 17560
79-117 WERTH, DENNIS DEAN	BOX 8 - MOUNT PULASKI IL 62548
14-229 WERTZ, DWIGHT LEWIS 'DEL'	B. 1891
26- 93 WERTZ, HENRY LEVI 'JOHNNY'	1704 NANCE ST - NEWBERRY SC 29108
47- 92 WERTZ, VICTOR WOODROW	D. JULY 7, 1983 DETROIT, MICH.
79-118 WESSINGER, JAMES MICHAEL	504 KINGSTON RD - UTICA NY 13502
38-104 WEST, MAX EDWARD	507 SIERRA KEYS DR-SIERRA MADRE CA 91024
38-105 WEST, RICHARD THOMAS	BOX 5095 - FORT WAYNE IN 46805
27-102 WEST, SAMUEL FILMORE	D. NOVEMBER 23, 1985 LUBBOCK, TEXAS
28-106 WEST, WALTER MAXWELL 'MAX'	D. APRIL 25, 1971 HOUSTON, TEX.
44-140 WEST, WELDON EDISON 'LEFTY'	D. JULY 23, 1979 HENDERSONVILLE, N. C.
55-135 WESTLAKE, JAMES PATRICK	909 SEAMAS AVE - SACRAMENTO CA 95801
47- 93 WESTLAKE, WALDON THOMAS	3800 61ST - SACRAMENTO CA 95820
29-107 WESTON, ALFRED JOHN	1 ALPINE TER - NEEDHAM MA 02192
47- 94 WESTRUM, WESLEY NOREEN	1235 NORTH SUNNYVALE #40 - MESA AZ 85205
27-103 WETZEL, CHARLES EDWARD 'BUZZ'	D. MARCH 7, 1941 GLOBE, ARIZ.
20-129 WETZEL, FRANKLIN BURTON 'BUZZ'	D. MARCH 5, 1942 BURBANK, CAL.
82-137 WEVER, STEFAN MATTHEW	2240 LOMBARD ST #202 - SAN FRANCISCO CA 94123
23-140 WHALEY, WILLIAM CARL	D. MARCH 3, 1943 INDIANAPOLIS, IND.
13-189 WHALING, ALBERT JAMES	D. JANUARY 21, 1965 LOS ANGELES, CALIF.
54-116 WHEAT, LEROY WILLIAM	6125 PINE TER - FORT LAUDERDALE FL 33317
15-175 WHEAT, MCKINLEY DAVIS 'MACK'	D. AUGUST 14, 1979 LOS BANOS, CALIF.
12-215 WHEATLEY, CHARLES	D. DECEMBER 10, 1982 TULSA, OKLA.
43-143 WHEATON, ELWOOD PIERCE	BOX 7091 - LANCASTER PA 17604
49- 90 WHEELER, DONALD WESLEY	8127 COLFAX AVE SOUTH - MINNEAPOLIS MN 55420
45-115 WHEELER, EDWARD RAYMOND	OLD ADD: 135 NORTH EUCALYPTUS ST - INGLEWOOD CA
21-110 WHEELER, FLOYD CLARK 'RIP'	D. SEPTEMBER 18, 1968 MARION, KY.
10-151 WHEELER, GEORGE HARRISON	D. JUNE 14, 1918 CLINTON, IND.
18- 73 WHEELER, RICHARD	D. FEBRUARY 12, 1962 LEXINGTON, MASS.
76-101 WHEELOCK, GARY RICHARD	1928E LAKE SAMMAMISH PKWY SE - ISSAQUAH WA 98027
13-190 WHELAN, JAMES FRANCIS	D. NOVEMBER 29, 1929 DAYTON, O.
20-130 WHELAN, THOMAS JOSEPH	D. JUNE 26, 1957 BOSTON, MASS.
71-107 WHILLOCK, JACK FRANKLIN	2007 EDGEBROOK CT - ARLINGTON TX 76015
52-110 WHISENANT, THOMAS PETER 'PETE'	218 WEST GRACE ST - PUNTA GORDA FL 33950
77-150 WHISENTON, LARRY	2507 SLATTERY ST - ST LOUIS MO 63106
77-151 WHITAKER, LOUIS RODMAN	803 PIPE - MARTINSVILLE VA 24112
66- 99 WHITAKER, STEVE EDWARD	OLD ADD: 2501 N. OCEAN DR - HOLLYWOOD BEACH FL 33019
64-127 WHITBY, WILLIAM EDWARD	RR 1 BOX 1060 - HUNTERSVILLE NC 28078
45-116 WHITCHER, ROBERT ARTHUR	156 GRAHAM RD - CUYAHOGA FALLS OH 44223
37-107 WHITE, ADEL 'ABE'	D. OCTOBER 1, 1978 ATLANTA, GA.
40- 99 WHITE, ALBERT EUGENE 'FUZZ'	RR 1 BOX 1049 - BRANSON MO 65616
54-117 WHITE, CHARLES ,	OLD ADD: 8167 HUDSON ST - VANCOUVER BC
85-118 WHITE, DEVON MARKES	474 WEST 158TH ST #42 - NEW YORK NY 10032
48-110 WHITE, DONALD WILLIAM	D. JUNE 15, 1987 CARLSBAD, CALIF.
55-136 WHITE, EDWARD PERRY	D. SEPTEMBER 28, 1962 LAKELAND, FLA.
62-146 WHITE, ELDER LAFAYETTE	919 COLONY AVE - AHOSKIE NC 27910
40-100 WHITE, ERNEST DANIEL	D. MAY 22, 1974 AUGUSTA, GA.
73-130 WHITE, FRANK	8925 LAMBERT DRIVE - LEE'S SUMMIT MO 64063
41-117 WHITE, HAROLD GEORGE	612 BIRD BAY DR #113C - VENICE FL 33595
74-140 WHITE, JEROME CARDELL	7 HAMILTON COURT - PACIFICA CA 94044
27-104 WHITE, JOHN PETER	D. JUNE 19, 1971 FLUSHING, N. Y.
32- 91 WHITE, JOYNER CLIFFORD 'JO-JO'	D. OCTOBER 9, 1986 TACOMA, WASH.
63-124 WHITE, JOYNER MICHAEL 'MIKE'	1820 284TH EAST - ROᵞ WA 98580
83-149 WHITE, LARRY DAVID	11240 DEHAVEN AVENUE - POLOMA CA 91331
78-141 WHITE, MYRON ALAN	3201 SOUTH DEEGAN DR - SANTA ANA CA 92704
65-116 WHITE, ROY HILTON	30 ASPEN WAY - UPPER SADDLE RIVER NJ 07458

51-101 WHITE, SAMUEL CHARLES	BOX 121 - HANALEI HI 96714
19- 90 WHITE, SAMUEL LAMBETH	D. NOVEMBER 11, 1929 PHILADELPHIA, PA.
12-216 WHITE, STEPHEN VINCENT	D. JANUARY 29, 1975 BRAINTREE, MASS.
45-117 WHITE, WILLIAM BARNEY	3721 DARRELL LN - TYLER TX 75701
56- 86 WHITE, WILLIAM DEKOVA	71 CALLOWHILL RD - CHALFONT PA 18914
33- 66 WHITEHEAD, BURGESS URQUHART	206 KING ST - WINDSOR NC 27983
35-114 WHITEHEAD, JOHN HENDERSON	D. OCTOBER 20, 1964 BONHAM, TEX.
23-141 WHITEHILL, EARL OLIVER	D. OCTOBER 22, 1954 OMAHA, NEB.
14-231 WHITEHOUSE, CHARLES EVIS	D. JULY 19, 1960 INDIANAPOLIS, IND.
12-217 WHITEHOUSE, GILBERT ARTHUR	D. FEBRUARY 14, 1926 BREWER, ME.
81-141 WHITEHOUSE, LEONARD JOSEPH	1874 NORTH AVE - BURLINGTON VT 05401
62-147 WHITFIELD, FRED DWIGHT	RR 1 BOX 91 - VANDIVER AL 35176
74-141 WHITFIELD, TERRY BERTLAND	2729 CARMAR DR - LOS ANGELES CA 90046
46-103 WHITMAN, DICK CORWIN	184 PETER DR - CAMPBELL CA 95008
46-104 WHITMAN, WALTER FRANKLIN 'FRANK'	44 BELLEVUE #5 - COLLINSVILLE IL 62234
80-143 WHITMER, DANIEL CHARLES	823 ROBINHOOD LN - REDLANDS CA 92373
28-107 WHITNEY, ARTHUR CARTER	D. SEPTEMBER 2, 1987 CENTER, TEXAS
77-152 WHITSON, EDDIE LEE	127 YELTON ST - ERWIN TN 37650
76-102 WHITT, ERNEST LEO	18330 13 MILE RD - ROSEVILLE MI 48066
16- 95 WHITTAKER, WALTER ELTON	D. AUGUST 7, 1965 PEMBROKE, MASS.
12-218 WHITTED, GEORGE BOSTIC 'POSSUM'	D. OCTOBER 16, 1962 WILMINGTON, N.C.
68-110 WICKER, FLOYD EULISS	RR 2 BOX 166A - SNOW CAMP NC 27349
36- 97 WICKER, KEMP CASWELL	D. JUNE 11, 1973 KERNERSVILLE, N. C.
60-102 WICKERSHAM, DAVID CLIFFORD	9118 WEST 104TH TER - OVERLAND PARK KS 66204
13-191 WICKLAND, ALBERT	D. MARCH 14, 1980 PORT WASHINGTON, WISC.
47- 95 WIDMAR, ALBERT JOSEPH	3919 SOUTH OSWEGO AV - TULSA OK 74135
58-101 WIEAND, FRANKLIN DELANO ROOS. 'TED'	216 WALNUT ST - SLATINGTON PA 18080
34-108 WIEDEMEYER, CHARLES JOHN	D. OCTOBER 27, 1979 LAKE GENEVA, FLA.
79-119 WIEDENBAUER, THOMAS JOHN	25 KNOLLWOOD ESTATES DR - ORMOND BEACH FL 32074
81-142 WIEGHAUS, THOMAS ROBERT	RR 1 BOX 169 - GRANT PARK IL 60940
21-111 WIENEKE, JOHN	D. MARCH 16, 1933 PLEASANT RIDGE, MICH.
51-102 WIESLER, ROBERT GEORGE	2325 INDIAN CUP DR - FLORISSANT MO 63031
39-125 WIETELMANN, WILLIAM FREDERICK 'WHITEY'	7712 GOLFCREST DR - SAN DIEGO CA 92119
81-143 WIGGINS, ALAN ANTHONY	125 EAST WOODBURY RD - ALTADENA CA 91001
46-105 WIGHT, WILLIAM ROBERT	6247 MEADOW VISTA DR - CARMICHAEL CA 95608
23-142 WIGINGTON, FREDERICK THOMAS	D. MAY 8, 1980 MESA, ARIZ.
79-120 WIHTOL, ALEXANDER AMES 'SANDY'	2120 SURREY PLACE - CAMPBELL CA 95008
46-106 WILBER, DELBERT QUENTIN	513 WOODLEAF CT - KIRKWOOD MO 63122
40-101 WILBORN, CLAUDE EDWARD	RR 1 BOX 167 - ROXBORO NC 27573
79-121 WILBORN, THADDEAUS IGLEHART	2722 26TH STREET #2 - SACRAMENTO CA 95818
70-137 WILCOX, MILTON EDWARD	OLD ADD: 6405 RAINTREE DR - CANTO MI 48187
77-153 WILES, RANDALL E	3600 RUE ANDREE - NEW ORLEANS LA 70114
75-130 WILEY, MARK EUGENE	720 RIO VISTA DRIVE - MIAMI SPRINGS FL 33166
77-154 WILFONG, ROBERT DONALD	16246 BENBOW - COVINA CA 91722
53- 98 WILHELM, CHARLES ERNEST 'SPIDER'	1490 SANDERLING DR - ENGLEWOOD FL 33533
52-111 WILHELM, JAMES HOYT	BOX 2217 - SARASOTA FL 33578
78-142 WILHELM, JAMES WEBSTER	BOX 99 - BELVEDERE CA 94920
16- 96 WILHOIT, JOSEPH WILLIAM	D. SEPTEMBER 25, 1930 SANTA BARBARA, CALIF.
11-175 WILIE, DENNEY EARNEST	D. JUNE 20, 1966 HAYWARD, CALIF.
27-105 WILKE, HARRY JOSEPH	1302 MILLVILLE AVE - HAMILTON OH 45013
83-150 WILKERSON, CURTIS VERNON	RR 1 BOX 191 - SUTHERLAND VA 23885
41-118 WILKIE, ALDON JAY	P.O. BOX 364, 902 W. 1ST ST - NEWBERG OR 97132
79-122 WILKINS, ERIC LAMOINE	2233 EAST MILLER - SEATTLE WA 98112
44-141 WILKINS, ROBERT LINWOOD	160 CHARLES - SHREVEPORT LA 71105
11-176 WILKINSON, EDWARD HENRY	D. APRIL 9, 1918 TUCSON, ARIZ.
18- 74 WILKINSON, ROY HAMILTON	D. JULY 2, 1956 LOUISVILLE, KY.
85-119 WILKINSON, WILLIAM CARL	7919 SOUTH POPLAR WAY - ENGLEWOOD CO 80112
44-142 WILKS, TEDDY	5531 MCCORMICK - HOUSTON TX 77023
57- 92 WILL, ROBERT LEE	410 NORTH MICHIGAN AVE - CHICAGO IL 60611
84-128 WILLARD, GERALD DUANE	806 THAYER LANE - PORT HUENEME CA 93041
58-102 WILLEY, CARLTON FRANCIS	BOX 64 - CHERRYFIELD ME 04622
63-125 WILLHITE, JON NICHOLAS 'NICK'	7325 EAST HINSDALE PLACE - ENGLEWOOD CO 80112
80-144 WILLIAMS, ALBERT HAMILTON	PEARL LAGOON, DEPOT ZELOYA - NICARAGUA NICARAGUA C.A.
37-108 WILLIAMS, ALMON EDWARD	D. JULY 19, 1969 GROVES, TEX.
11-177 WILLIAMS, ALVA MITCHEL 'RIP'	D. JULY 23, 1933 KEOKUK, IA.
11-178 WILLIAMS, AUGUST JOSEPH	D. APRIL 16, 1964 STERLING, ILL.
70-138 WILLIAMS, BERNARD	861 47TH ST - OAKLAND CA 94608
59- 87 WILLIAMS, BILLY LEO	586 PRINCE EDWARD RD - GLEN ELLYN IL 60137
71-108 WILLIAMS, CHARLES PROSEK	259-04 KENSINGTON PL - GREAT NECK NY 11021
13-192 WILLIAMS, CLAUD PRESTON 'LEFTY'	D. NOVEMBER 4, 1959 LAGUNA BEACH, CALIF.
81-144 WILLIAMS, DALLAS MCKINLEY	734 BERKLEY ROAD - INDIANAPOLIS IN 46208
49- 91 WILLIAMS, DAVID CARLOUS	4645 COUNTRY CREEK #1101 - DALLAS TX 75236
13-193 WILLIAMS, DAVID CARTER 'MUTT'	D. MARCH 30, 1962 FAYETTEVILLE, ARK.
44-143 WILLIAMS, DEWEY EDGAR	720 13TH STREET WEST - WILLISTON ND 58801

TERRY WHITFIELD

ERIC WILKINS   CLEVELAND INDIANS

58-103 WILLIAMS, DONALD FRED   11405 ROKEBY AVE - GARRETT PARK MD 20766
63-126 WILLIAMS, DONALD REID   5546 CHATEAU DR - SAN DIEGO CA 92117
28-108 WILLIAMS, EARL BAXTER   D. MARCH 10, 1958 KNOXVILLE, TENN.
70-139 WILLIAMS, EARL CRAIG   OLD ADD: 2900 CAMP CREEK PKWY - COLLEGE PARK GA
86-162 WILLIAMS, EDWARD LAQUAN   4393 MCCLINTOCK STREET - SAN DIEGO CA 92105
30- 92 WILLIAMS, EDWIN DIBRELL 'DIB' BOX 43 - GREENBRIER AR 72058
21-112 WILLIAMS, EVON DANIEL 'DENNY' D. MARCH 24, 1929 LOS ANGELES CO., CAL.
84-129 WILLIAMS, FRANK LEE   1121 THIRD STREET - LEWISTON ID 83501
45-118 WILLIAMS, FRED 'PAP'   1120 46TH AVE - MERIDIAN MS 39305

12-219 WILLIAMS, FREDERICK 'CY'   D. APRIL 23, 1974 EAGLE RIVER, WIS.
61-108 WILLIAMS, GEORGE   4267 TYLER ST - DETROIT MI 48238
13-194 WILLIAMS, HARRY PETER   D. DECEMBER 20, 1963 HAYWOOD, CALIF.
69-180 WILLIAMS, JAMES ALFRED   16350 HARBOR BLVD #2512 - SANTA ANA CA 92704
66-100 WILLIAMS, JAMES FRANCIS 'JIMY' 1630 HONEY BEAR LN - DUNEDIN FL 33528
14-232 WILLIAMS, JOHN BRODIE   D. SEPTEMBER 8, 1963 LONG BEACH, CALIF.
15-176 WILLIAMS, KENNETH ROY   D. JANUARY 22, 1959 GRANTS PASS, ORE.
86-163 WILLIAMS, KENNETH ROYAL   3255 SELVA DRIVE - SAN JOSE CA 95148
26- 94 WILLIAMS, LEON THEO   626 OLD IVY RD NE - ATLANTA GA 30305
77-155 WILLIAMS, MARK WESTLY   51 MAIN STREET - ROSENDALE NY 12472
16- 97 WILLIAMS, MARSHALL MCDIARMID D. FEBRUARY 22, 1935 TUCSON, ARIZ.
87-151 WILLIAMS, MATTHEW DERRICK   309 GARDEN GATE - CARSON CIY NV 89706
83-151 WILLIAMS, MATTHEW EVAN   243 MOORE STREET - CLUTE TX 77531
86-164 WILLIAMS, MITCHELL STEVEN   4355 RIVERVIEW #2 - WEST LINN OR 97068
14-233 WILLIAMS, REES GEPHARDT 'STEAMBOAT' D. JUNE 29, 1979 DEER RIVER, MINN.
85-120 WILLIAMS, REGINALD DEWAYNE   1490 SINGING TREES AVE - MEMPHIS TN 38116
78-143 WILLIAMS, RICHARD ALLEN   1217 WESSMITH - MADERA CA 93638
51-103 WILLIAMS, RICHARD HIRSCHFIELD 98 UNION #507 - SEATTLE WA 98101
14-234 WILLIAMS, RINALDO LEWIS   D. APRIL 24, 1966 COTTONWOOD, ARIZ.
11-179 WILLIAMS, ROBERT ELIAS   D. AUGUST 6, 1962 NELSONVILLE, O.
40-102 WILLIAMS, ROBERT FULTON 'ACE' OLD ADD: CROSS ST - MARSHFIELD MA 02050
58-104 WILLIAMS, STANLEY WILSON   4702 HAYTER AVE - LAKEWOOD CA 90712
39-126 WILLIAMS, THEODORE SAMUEL   P.O. BOX 5127 - CLEARWATER FL 34618
64-128 WILLIAMS, WALTER ALLEN   2417 MONTEREY DR - BROWNWOOD TX 76801
69-181 WILLIAMS, WILLIAM   3227 RANDOLPH AVE - OAKLAND CA 94602
38-106 WILLIAMS, WOODROW WILSON   PAMPLIN VA 23958
87-152 WILLIAMSON, MARK ALAN   1983 FAIRHAVEN STREET - LEMON GROVE CA 92045
28-109 WILLIAMSON, NATHANIEL HOWARD 'HOWIE' D. AUGUST 15, 1969 TEXARKANA, ARK.
28-110 WILLIAMSON, SILAS ALBERT   D. NOVEMBER 29, 1978 HOT SPRINGS, ARK.
30- 93 WILLINGHAM, THOMAS HUGH   D. JUNE 15, 1988 EL RENO, OKLA.
84-130 WILLIS, CARL BLAKE   RR 1 BOX 274 - YANCEYVILLE NC 27379
25-115 WILLIS, CHARLES WILLIAM 'LEFTY' D. MAY 10, 1962 BETHESDA, MD.
63-127 WILLIS, DALE JEROME   1110 ESTATEWOOD DR - BRANDON FL 33511
53- 99 WILLIS, JAMES GLADDEN   BOX 35 - BOYCE LA 71409
11-180 WILLIS, JOSEPH DENK   D. DECEMBER 3, 1966 IRONTON, O.
47- 96 WILLIS, LESTER EVANS   D. JANUARY 22, 1982 JASPER, TEXAS
77-156 WILLIS, MICHAEL HENRY   3081 OAKVIEW DR - PALM HARBOR FL 33563
66-101 WILLIS, RONALD EARL   D. NOVEMBER 21, 1977 MEMPHIS, TENN.
25-116 WILLOUGHBY, CLAUDE WILLIAM   D. AUGUST 14, 1973 MCPHERSON, KAN.
71-109 WILLOUGHBY, JAMES ARTHUR   205 BONITA AVENUE - MODESTO CA 95351
77-157 WILLS, ELLIOTT TAYLOR 'BUMP' 2409 MIGUEL LANE - ARLINGTON TX 76016
83-152 WILLS, FRANK LEE   733 GEN. PERSHING ST - NEW ORLEANS LA 70115
59- 88 WILLS, MAURICE MORNING   1723 STANFORD AVE - REDONDO BEACH CA 90278
59- 89 WILLS, THEODORE CARL   524 CLOVIS AVE - CLOVIS CA 93612
18- 75 WILLSON, FRANK HOXIE 'KID'   D. APRIL 17, 1964 UNION GAP, WASH.
34-109 WILSHERE, VERNON SPRAGUE 'WHITEY' D. MAY 23, 1985 COOPERSTOWN, N. Y.
73-131 WILSHUSEN, TERRY WAYNE   1207 EAST 222ND STREET - CARSON CA 90745
51-104 WILSON, ARCHIE CLIFTON   1620 WOODLAND ST SE - DECATUR AL 35601
51-105 WILSON, ARTHUR LEE   2226 NE 10TH AVE - PORTLAND OR 97212
31-100 WILSON, CHARLES WOODROW   D. DECEMBER 19, 1970 ROCHESTER, N. Y.
66-102 WILSON, DONALD EDWARD   D. JANUARY 5, 1975 HOUSTON, TEX.
58-105 WILSON, DUANE LEWIS   1522 COOLIDGE - WICHITA KS 67203
59- 90 WILSON, EARL LAWRENCE   BOX 662 - PONCHATOULA LA 70454
36- 98 WILSON, EDWARD FRANCIS   D. APRIL 11, 1979 HAMDEN, CONN.
14-235 WILSON, FINIS ELBERT   D. MARCH 9, 1959 CORAL GABLES, FLA.
24-115 WILSON, FRANCIS EDWARD   D. NOVEMBER 25, 1974 LEICESTER, MASS.
79-123 WILSON, GARY STEVEN   RURAL ROUTE 2 BOX 644 - CAMDEN AR 71701
11-181 WILSON, GEORGE FRANCIS 'SQUANTO' D. MARCH 26, 1967 WINTHROP, ME.
34-110 WILSON, GEORGE PEACOCK 'ICEHOUSE' D. OCTOBER 13, 1973 MORAGA, CAL.
52-112 WILSON, GEORGE WASHINGTON   D. OCTOBER 29, 1974 GASTONIA, N.C.
82-138 WILSON, GLENN DWIGHT   3303 PINE CHASE - MONTGOMERY TX 77356
24-116 WILSON, GOMER RUSSELL 'TEX' D. SEPTEMBER 15, 1946 SULPHUR SPRINGS, TEX.
48-111 WILSON, GRADY HERBERT   5512 ORCHARD DR - COLUMBUS GA 31904

23-143 WILSON, JAMES	D. JUNE 1, 1947 PALMETTO, FLA.
45-119 WILSON, JAMES ALGER	D. SEPTEMBER 2, 1986 NEWPORT BEACH, CALIF.
85-121 WILSON, JAMES GEORGE	202 SW 9TH - CORVALLIS OR 97333
34-111 WILSON, JOHN FRANCIS 'JACK'	4111 164TH ST SW #62 - LYNNWOOD WA 98037
13-195 WILSON, JOHN NICODEMUS	D. SEPTEMBER 23, 1954 ANNAPOLIS, MD.
27-106 WILSON, JOHN SAMUEL	D. AUGUST 27, 1980 CHATTANOOGA, TENN.
11-182 WILSON, LESTER WILBUR	D. APRIL 4, 1969 EDMONDS, WASH.
23-144 WILSON, LEWIS ROBERT 'HACK'	D. NOVEMBER 23, 1948 BALTIMORE, MD.
40-103 WILSON, MAX	D. JANUARY 2, 1977 GREENSBORO, N. C.
83-153 WILSON, MICHAEL "TACK"	1832 EAST 15TH STREET - OAKLAND CA 94606
58-106 WILSON, ROBERT	627 COVE HOLLOW DR - DALLAS TX 75224
51-106 WILSON, ROBERT JAMES 'RED'	806 CABOT LN - MADISON WI 53711
28-111 WILSON, ROY EDWARD	D. DECEMBER 3, 1969 CLARION, IA.
60-103 WILSON, SAMMY O'NEIL 'NEIL'	RR1 BOX 285 - LEXINGTON TN 38351
21-113 WILSON, SAMUEL MARSHALL 'MIKE'	D. MAY 16, 1978 BOYNTON BEACH, FLA.
14-236 WILSON, THOMAS C.	D. MARCH 7, 1953 SAN PEDRO, CALIF.
45-120 WILSON, WALTER WOOD	RR 1 BOX 676A - FRANKLIN GA 30217
20-131 WILSON, WILLIAM CLARENCE 'MUTT'	D. AUGUST 31, 1962 WILDWOOD, FLA.
50-104 WILSON, WILLIAM DONALD	11121 AGNES PL - CERRITOS CA 90701
69-182 WILSON, WILLIAM HARLAN	10108 S. 198TH EAST AVE - BROKEN ARROW OK 74012
80-145 WILSON, WILLIAM HAYWOOD 'MOOKIE'	OLD ADD: 150 HIGHLAND AVE - STATEN ISLAND NY 10301
76-103 WILSON, WILLIE JAMES	3905 WEST 110TH TERRACE - LEAWOOD KS 66211
26- 95 WILTSE, HAROLD JAMES	D. NOVEMBER 2, 1983 BUNKIE, LA.
56- 87 WINCENIAK, EDWARD JOSEPH	10828 SOUTH AVE "O" - CHICAGO IL 60617
59- 91 WINDHORN, GORDON RAY	145 BENT CREEK RD - DANVILLE VA 24540
28-112 WINDLE, WILLIS BREWER	D. DECEMBER 8, 1981 CORPUS CHRISTI TX.
86-165 WINE, ROBERT PAUL JR.	2614 WOODLAND AVENUE - NORRISTOWN PA 19403
60-104 WINE, ROBERT PAUL SR.	2612 WOODLAND AVE - NORRISTOWN PA 19401
29-108 WINEAPPLE, EDWARD	960 PARK AVE - NEW YORK NY 10028
30- 94 WINEGARNER, RALPH LEE	245 S. WICHITA ST - BENTON KS 67017
73-132 WINFIELD, DAVID MARK	367 W. FOREST - TEANECK NJ 07666
32- 92 WINFORD, JAMES HEAD	D. DECEMBER 16, 1970 MIAMI, OKLA.
24-117 WINGARD, ERNEST JAMES	D. JANUARY 17, 1977 PRATTVILLE, ALA.
23-145 WINGFIELD, FREDERICK DAVIS 'TED'	D. JULY 18, 1975 JOHNSON CITY, TENN.
19- 91 WINGO, ABSALOM HOLBROOK 'AL'	D. OCTOBER 9, 1954 DETROIT, MICH.
20-132 WINGO, EDMOND ARMAND	D. DECEMBER 5, 1964 LACHINE, QUE.
11-183 WINGO, IVEY BROWN	D. MARCH 1, 1941 NORCROSS, GA.
73-133 WINKLES, BOBBY BROOKS	P.O. BOX 1158 - LAQUINTA CA 92680
19- 92 WINN, GEORGE BENJAMIN	D. NOVEMBER 1, 1969 ROBERTA, GA.
83-154 WINN, JAMES FRANCIS	RURAL ROUTE 1 - CLEVER MO 65631
84-131 WINNINGHAM, HERMAN SON	1542 BELLEVILLE RD - ORANGEBURG SC 29115
30- 95 WINSETT, JOHN THOMAS 'TOM'	BOX 32183 - PALM BEACH GARDENS FL 33410
33- 67 WINSTON, HENRY RUDOLPH	D. FEBRUARY 7, 1974 JACKSONVILLE, FLA.
24-118 WINTERS, CLARENCE JOHN	D. JUNE 29, 1945 DETROIT, MICH.
19- 93 WINTERS, JESSE FRANKLIN 'BUCK'	D. JUNE 5, 1986 ABILENE, TEXAS
78-144 WIRTH, ALAN LEE	1012 WEST MOUNTAIN VIEW - MESA AZ 85201
21-114 WIRTS, ELWOOD VERNON 'KETTLE'	D. JULY 12, 1968 SACRAMENTO, CAL.
32- 93 WISE, ARCHIBALD EDWIN	D. FEBRUARY 2, 1978 WAXAHACHIE, TEX.
30- 96 WISE, HUGH EDWARD	D. JULY 21, 1987 PLANTATION, FLA.
57- 93 WISE, KENDALL COLE 'CASEY'	3631 RUM ROW - NAPLES FL 33940
64-129 WISE, RICHARD CHARLES 'RICK'	RR 2 BOX 307 - HILLSBORO OR 97123
64-119 WISE, RICHARD CHARLES	8235 SW 184TH STREET - BEAVERTON OR 97007
44-144 WISE, ROY OGDEN	11841 MELODY LN DR - GARDEN GROVE CA 92640
19- 94 WISNER, JOHN HENRY	D. DECEMBER 15, 1981 JACKSON, MICH.
64-130 WISSMAN, DAVID ALVIN	20 WELLINGTON ST - SHELBURNE FALLS MA 01370
34-112 WISTERT, FRANCIS MICHAEL 'WHITEY'	D. APRIL 23, 1985 PAINESVILLE, OHIO
14-230 WISTERZIL, GEORGE JOHN 'TEX'	D. JUNE 27, 1964 SAN ANTONIO, TEX.
40-104 WITEK, NICHOLAS JOSEPH 'MICKEY'	30 WEST RIDGE ST - SHAVERTOWN PA 18708
20-133 WITHROW, FRANK BLAINE	D. SEPTEMBER 5, 1966 OMAHA, NEB.
63-128 WITHROW, RAYMOND WALLACE 'CORKY'	1730 QUEENSWAY COURT - OWENSBORO KY 42301
57- 94 WITT, GEORGE ADRIAN	2209 CATALINA ST - LAGUNA BEACH CA 92651
16- 98 WITT, LAWTON WALTER 'WHITEY'	RR 1 BOX 522 - WOODSTOWN NJ 08098
81-145 WITT, MICHAEL ATWATER	8042 SAN LEON CIR DR - BUENA PARK CA 90620
86-166 WITT, ROBERT ANDREW	30 OAKDALE ROAD - CANTON MA 02021
46-107 WITTE, JEROME CHARLES	7515 OAK VISTA - HOUSTON TX 77087
38-107 WITTIG, JOHN CARL	163 STAFFORD STREET - BALTIMORE MD 21227
74-142 WOCKENFUSS, JOHN BILTON	428 NORTH STREET - ELKTON MD 21921
23-146 WOEHR, ANDREW EMIL	270 SCARLET WAY - EUSTIS FL 32726
72-121 WOHLFORD, JAMES EUGENE	P.O. BOX 6036 - ATASCADERO CA 93422
62-148 WOJCIK, JOHN JOSEPH	33 HAMILTON ST - BUFFALO NY 14207
54-118 WOJEY, PETER PAUL	2359 SOUTH BUENA DR - MOBILE AL 36605
85-122 WOJNA, EDWARD DAVID	48 WILLIAMSBURG DR - MONROE CT 06468
12-220 WOLF, ERNEST G	D. MAY 23, 1964 ATLANTIC HIGHLANDS, N.J.
27-107 WOLF, RAYMOND BERNARD	D. OCTOBER 6, 1979 FORT WORTH, TEXAS
69-183 WOLF, WALTER BECK	17711 TRAIL VIEW - YORBA LINDA CA 92686

21-115	WOLF, WALTER FRANCIS 'LEFTY'	D. SEPTEMBER 25, 1971 NEW ORLEANS, LA.
23-147	WOLFE, CHARLES HENRY	D. NOVEMBER 27, 1957 SCHELLSBURG, PA.
52-113	WOLFE, EDWARD ANTHONY	3070 BEAUFORT - STOCKTON CA 95209
17- 90	WOLFE, HAROLD	D. JULY 28, 1971 FORT WAYNE, IND.
77-158	WOLFE, LAURENCE MARCY	2616 SARDA WAY - RANCHO CORDOVA CA 95670
12-221	WOLFE, ROY CHAMBERLAIN 'POLLY'	D. NOVEMBER 21, 1938 MORRIS, ILL.
41-119	WOLFF, ROGER FRANCIS	1307 KNOTT-CHESTER IL 62233
14-237	WOLFGANG, MELDON JOHN	D. JUNE 30, 1947 ALBANY, N.Y.
66-103	WOMACK, HORACE GUY 'DOOLEY'	119 CENTURY DR - COLUMBIA SC 29210
26- 96	WOMACK, SIDNEY KIRK	D. AUGUST 8, 1958 JACKSON, MISS.
30- 97	WOOD, CHARLES ASHER 'SPADES'	D. MAY 18, 1986 WICHITA, KAN.
23-148	WOOD, CHARLES SPENCER 'DOC'	D. NOVEMBER 3, 1974 NEW ORLEANS, LA.
08	WOOD, HOWARD ELLSWORTH 'SMOKEY JOE'	D. JULY 27, 1985 WEST HAVEN, CONN.
61-109	WOOD, JACOB	851 MAGNOLIA AVE - ELIZABETH NJ 07201
44-145	WOOD, JOE FRANK	BOX 53 - CLINTON CT 06413
43-144	WOOD, JOSEPH PERRY	D. MARCH 25, 1985 HOUSTON, TEXAS
48-112	WOOD, KENNETH LANIER	6337 TERESA AVE - CHARLOTTE NC 28214
13-196	WOOD, ROY WINTON	D. APRIL 6, 1974 FAYETTEVILLE, ARK.
61-110	WOOD, WILBUR FORRESTER	8 WACHUSETT DR - LEXINGTON MA 02173
20-134	WOODALL, CHARLES LAWRENCE 'LARRY'	D. MAY 6, 1963 CAMBRIDGE, MASS.
78-145	WOODARD, DARRELL LEE	1227 EAST 69TH ST - LOS ANGELES CA 90001
85-123	WOODARD, MICHAEL CARY	P.O. BOX 35 - MAYWOOD IL 60153
11-184	WOODBURN, EUGENE STEWART	D. JANUARY 18, 1961 SANDUSKY, O.
44-146	WOODEND, GEORGE ANTHONY	D. FEBRUARY 6, 1980 HARTFORD, CONN.
56- 88	WOODESHICK, HAROLD JOSEPH	803 WYCLIFFE DR - HOUSTON TX 77079
43-145	WOODLING, EUGENE RICHARD	926 REMSEN RD - MEDINA OH 44256
14-239	WOODMAN, DANIEL COURTENAY	D. DECEMBER 14, 1962 TOPSFIELD, MASS.
77-159	WOODS, ALVIS	2518 60TH AVE - OAKLAND CA 94605
14-238	WOODS, CLARENCE COFIELD	D. JULY 2, 1969 RISING SUN, IND.
76-104	WOODS, GARY LEE	6701 E. 38TH - TUCSON AZ 85730
43-146	WOODS, GEORGE ROWLAND 'PINKY'	D. OCTOBER 30, 1982 LOS ANGELES, CALIF.
57- 95	WOODS, JAMES JEROME	151 ROSS WAY - SAN BRUNO CA 94066
24-119	WOODS, JOHN FULTON	D. OCTOBER 4, 1946 NORFOLK, VA.
69-184	WOODS, RONALD LAWRENCE	413 PLYMOUTH ST - INGLEWOOD CA 90302
69-185	WOODSON, RICHARD LEE	3416 LONESOME TRAIL - GEORGETOWN TX 78626
87-153	WOODSON, TRACY MICHAEL	6232 SHANNON ROAD - MECHANICSVILLE VA 23111
18- 76	WOODWARD, FRANK RUSSELL	D. JUNE 11, 1961 NEW HAVEN, CONN.
85-124	WOODWARD, ROBERT JOHN	15 PLEASANT ST - WEST LEBANON NH 03784
63-129	WOODWARD, WILLIAM FREDERICK 'WOODY'	13 LAMBERT DR - SPARTA NJ 07871
55-137	WOOLDRIDGE, FLOYD LEWIS	214 BARBER ST - GREENFIELD MO 65661
47- 97	WOOTEN, EARL HAZELL	702 WILLIAMS ST - WILLIAMSTON SC 29697
14-240	WORDEN, FRED B	D. NOVEMBER 9, 1941 ST. LOUIS, MO.
38-108	WORKMAN, CHARLES THOMAS	D. JANUARY 3, 1953 KANSAS CITY, MO.
24-120	WORKMAN, HARRY HALL 'HOGE'	D. MAY 20, 1972 FORT MYERS, FLA.
50-105	WORKMAN, HENRY KILGARIFF	307 19TH ST - SANTA MONICA CA 90402
85-125	WORRELL, TODD ROLAND	306 HARVARD DRIVE - ARCADIA CA 91006
78-146	WORTHAM, RICHARD COOPER	10302 TIMBERCREST LN - AUSTIN TX 78750
53-100	WORTHINGTON, ALLAN FULTON	LIBERTY BAPTIST COL - LYNCHBURG VA 24506
31-101	WORTHINGTON, ROBERT LEE 'RED'	D. DECEMBER 8, 1963 LOS ANGELES, CAL.
16- 99	WORTMAN, WILLIAM LEWIS 'CHUCK'	D. AUGUST 19, 1977 LAS VEGAS, NEV.
83-155	WOTUS, RONALD ALLAN	CRESTVIEW DRIVE - COLCHESTER CT 06415
33- 68	WRIGHT, ALBERT EDGAR	86 LINDA AVE - OAKLAND CA 94611
35-115	WRIGHT, ALBERT OWEN 'AB'	P.O. BOX 3 - MUSKOGEE OK 74401
16-100	WRIGHT, CEYLON	D. NOVEMBER 7, 1947 HINES, ILL.
66-104	WRIGHT, CLYDE	528 JEANINE AVE - ANAHEIM CA 92806
24-121	WRIGHT, FOREST GLENN	D. APRIL 6, 1984 OLATHE, KAN.
82-139	WRIGHT, GEORGE DEWITT	3704 PELICAN COURT - ARLINGTON TX 76016
45-121	WRIGHT, HENDERSON EDWARD 'ED'	827 LAKE ROAD - DYERSBURG TN 38024
27-108	WRIGHT, JAMES	D. APRIL 12, 1963 OAKLAND, CAL.
78-147	WRIGHT, JAMES CLIFTON	439 HARRISON ST - COOPERSVILLE MI 49404
81-146	WRIGHT, JAMES LEON	2822 SOUTH 29TH - ST. JOSEPH MO 64503
82-140	WRIGHT, JAMES RICHARD 'RICKY'	3605 WEST HOUSTON - PARIS TX 75460
70-140	WRIGHT, KENNETH WARREN	1416 WISTERIA AVE - PENSACOLA FL 32507
54-119	WRIGHT, MELVIN JAMES	D. MAY 16, 1983 HOUSTON, TEX.
15-177	WRIGHT, ROBERT CASSIUS	5757 CYPRESS AVE #207 - CARMICHAEL CA 95608
56- 89	WRIGHT, ROY EARL	331 PINEHURST CIR - CHICKAMAUGA GA 30707
38-109	WRIGHT, TAFT SHEDRON	D. OCTOBER 22, 1981 ORLANDO, FLA.
48-113	WRIGHT, THOMAS EVERETT	RR 2 BOX 45 - SHELBY NC 28150
17- 91	WRIGHT, WAYNE BROMLEY 'RASTY'	D. JUNE 12, 1948 COLUMBUS, O.
15-178	WRIGHT, WILLIAM JAMES 'DICK'	D. JANUARY 24, 1952 BETHLEHEM, PA.
20-135	WRIGHTSTONE, RUSSELL GUY	D. MARCH 1, 1969 HARRISBURG, PA.
29-109	WUESTLING, GEORGE 'YATS'	D. APRIL 26, 1970 ST. LOUIS, MO.
44-147	WURM, FRANK JAMES	P.O. BOX 573 - GLENS FALLS NY 12801
61-111	WYATT, JOHN	3439 BELLEFONTAINE - KANSAS CITY MO 64128

29-110 WYATT, JOHN WHITLOW 'WHIT'
24-122 WYATT, LORAL JOHN 'JOE'
13-197 WYCKOFF, JOHN WELDON
76-105 WYNEGAR, HAROLD DELANO 'BUTCH'
39-127 WYNN, EARLY
63-130 WYNN, JAMES SHERMAN
83-156 WYNNE, MARVELL
67-115 WYNNE, WILLIAM VERNON
42-108 WYROSTEK, JOHN BARNEY
42-109 WYSE, HENRY WASHINGTON
30- 98 WYSONG, HARLIN 'BIFF'
72-122 YANCY, HUGH
42-110 YANKOWSKI, GEORGE EDWARD
12-222 YANTZ, GEORGE WEBB
26- 97 YARNALL, WALDO WARD 'RUSTY'
22-137 YARRISON, BYRON WARDSWORTH 'RUBE'
21-116 YARYAN, CLARENCE EVERETT 'YAM'
61-112 YASTRZEMSKI, CARL MICHAEL
71-110 YATES, ALBERT ARTHUR
24-123 YDE, EMIL OGDEN
19- 95 YEABSLEY, ROBERT WATKINS 'BERT'
72-123 YEAGER, STEPHEN WAYNE
22-138 YEARGIN, JAMES ALMOND
17- 92 YELLE, ARCHIE JOSEPH
63-131 YELLEN, LAWRENCE ALAN
21-117 YELLOWHORSE, MOSES J. 'CHIEF'
27-109 YERKES, CHARLES CARROLL
85-126 YETT, RICHARD MARTIN
57- 96 YEWCIC, THOMAS
11-185 YINGLING, EARL HERSHEY
51-107 YOCHIM, LEONARD JOSEPH
48-114 YOCHIM, RAYMOND AUSTIN ALOYSIUS
19- 96 YORK, JAMES EDWARD 'LEFTY'
70-141 YORK, JAMES HARLAN
34-113 YORK, RUDOLPH PRESTON
44-148 YORK, TONY BATTEN
80-146 YOST, EDGAR FREDERICK 'NED'
44-149 YOST, EDWARD FRED JOSEPH
21-118 YOTER, ELMER ELLSWORTH
85-127 YOUMANS, FLOYD EVERETT
15-179 YOUNG, CHARLES
83-157 YOUNG, CURTIS ALLEN
37-109 YOUNG, DELMER EDWARD
65-117 YOUNG, DONALD WAYNE
13-198 YOUNG, GEORGE JOSEPH
87-154 YOUNG, GERALD ANTHONY
11-186 YOUNG, HERMAN JOHN
71-111 YOUNG, JOHN THOMAS
78-148 YOUNG, KIP LANE
33- 69 YOUNG, LEMUEL FLOYD 'PEP'
83-158 YOUNG, MATTHEW JOHN
82-141 YOUNG, MICHAEL DARREN
36- 99 YOUNG, NORMAN ROBERT 'BABE'
13-199 YOUNG, RALPH STUART
51-108 YOUNG, RICHARD ENNIS
48-115 YOUNG, ROBERT GEORGE
31-102 YOUNG, RUSSELL CHARLES
22-139 YOUNGBLOOD, ARTHUR CLYDE 'CHIEF'
76-106 YOUNGBLOOD, JOEL RANDOLPH
17- 93 YOUNGS, ROSS MIDDLEBROOK
37-110 YOUNT, FLOYD EDWIN 'EDDIE'
14-241 YOUNT, HERBERT MACON 'DUCKY'
71-112 YOUNT, LAWRENCE KING
74-143 YOUNT, ROBIN R

BUCHANAN GA 30113
D. DECEMBER 5, 1970 OBLONG, ILL.
D. MAY 8, 1961 SHEBOYGAN FALLS, WIS.
528 SPRING CREEK DR - LONGWOOD FL 32779
P.O. BOX 218 - NOKOMIS FL 34724
OLD ADD: 932 1/2 E. 41ST PL - LOS ANGELES CA 90053
8052 SOUTH CALUMET - CHICAGO IL 60619
3945 CHESTWOOD AVE - JACKSONVILLE FL 32211
D. DECEMBER 12, 1986 ST.LOUIS, MO.
1133 SE 14TH ST- PRYOR OK 74361
D. AUGUST 8, 1951 XENIA, O.
BOX 9064 - SARASOTA FL 33578
164 CHAPMAN ST-WATERTOWN MA 02172
D. FEBRUARY 26, 1967 LOUISVILLE, KY.
D. OCTOBER 9, 1985 LOWELL, MASS.
D. APRIL 22, 1977 WILLIAMSPORT, PA.
D. NOVEMBER 16, 1964 BIRMINGHAM, ALA.
4621 SOUTH OCEAN BLVD - HIGHLAND BEACH FL 33431
OLD ADD: 11613 WEST YUMA CT - NEW BERLIN WI
D. DECEMBER 4, 1968 LEESBURG, FLA.
D. FEBRUARY 8, 1961 PHILADELPHIA, PA.
5225 - 4 WHITE OAK - ENCINO CA 91316
D. MAY 8. 1937 GREENVILLE, S. C.
D. MAY 2, 1983 WOODLAND, CALIF.
OLD ADD: 67-30 CLYDE ST - FOREST HILLS NY 11375
D. APRIL 10, 1964 PAWNEE, OKLA.
D. DECEMBER 20, 1950 OAKLAND, CAL.
11860 BUTTERFIELD - CHINO CA 91710
31 CHEORKEE RD - ARLINTON MA 02174
D. OCTOBER 2, 1962 COLUMBUS, O.
316 NELSON DR - NEW ORLEANS LA 70123
3728 45TH ST - METAIRIE LA 70001
D. APRIL 9, 1961 YORK, PA.
10957 EAST HOLBECK AVE - NORWALK CA 90650
D. FEBRUARY 5, 1970 ROME, GA.
D. APRIL 18, 1970 HILLSBORO, TEXAS
110 GLEN IRIS - JACKSON MS 39204
48 OAKRIDGE ROAD - WELLESLEY MA 02181
D. JULY 26, 1966 CAMP HILL, PA.
591 LANCEWOOD - RIALTO CA 92376
D. MAY 12, 1952 RIVERSIDE, N. J.
13354 NORTH 100TH PLACE - SCOTTSDALE AZ 85260
D. DECEMBER 8, 1979 SAN FRANCISCO, CALIF.
OLD ADD: 1350 TRENTON ST - DENVER CO 80220
D. MARCH 13, 1950 BRIGHTWATERS, N.Y.
1618 WEST BROOK STREET - SANTA ANA CA 92703
D. DECEMBER 13, 1966 IPSWICH, MASS.
124 WEST 57TH ST - LOS ANGELES CA 90037
RR 2 BOX 113-C - WINCHESTER OH 45697
D. JANUARY 14, 1962 JAMESTOWN, N. C.
4248 COMMONWEALTH - LACANADA CA 91011
3250 SUNNYBROOK CT - HAYWARD CA 94541
D. DECEMBER 25, 1983 EVERETT, MASS.
D. JANUARY 24, 1965 PHILADELPHIA, PA.
OLD ADD: 6923 189TH - LYNNWOOD WA 98036
D. JANUARY 28, 1985 BALTIMORE, MD.
D. MAY 13, 1984 ROSEVILLE, CALIF.
D. JULY 6, 1968 AMARILLO, TEX.
8270 EAST WINDROSE - SCOTTSDALE AZ 85254
D. OCTOBER 22, 1927 SAN ANTONIO, TEX.
D. OCTOBER 26, 1973 NEWTON, N. C.
D. MAY 9, 1970 WINSTON-SALEM, N. C.
OLD ADD: 8101 EAST CLARENDON - SCOTTSDALE AZ 85251
5010 EAST SHEA BLVD #D200 - SCOTTSDALE AZ 85254

MATI YOUNG

Seattle Mariners

24-124 YOWELL, CARL COLUMBUS — D. JULY 27, 1985 JACKSONVILLE, TEXAS
52-114 YUHAS, JOHN EDWARD 'EDDIE — D. JULY 6, 1986 WINSTON-SALEM, N. C.
78-149 YURAK, JEFFREY LYNN — 424 SOUTH 188TH STREET - SEATTLE WA 98148
47- 98 YVARS, SALVADOR ANTHONY — 1 ALLEN ST - VALHALLA NY 10595
45-122 ZABALA, ADRIAN RODRIGUEZ — 11243 ANDREA DR - JACKSONVILLE FL 32218
13-200 ZABEL, GEORGE WASHINGTON 'ZIP' — D. MAY 31, 1970 BELOIT, WIS.
44-150 ZACHARY, ALBERT MYRON 'CHINK' — 426 LORRAINE AVE - UTICA NY 13502
18- 77 ZACHARY, JONATHAN THOMPSON WALTON — D. JANUARY 24, 1969 GRAHAM, N. C.
63-132 ZACHARY, WILLIAM CHRIS — P.O. BOX 5093 - KNOXVILLE TN 37928
10-152 ZACHER, ELMER HENRY — D. DECEMBER 20, 1944 BUFFALO, N.Y.
76-107 ZACHRY, PATRICK PAUL — 12003 WOODBRIAR CIRCLE - WACO TX 76710
11-187 ZACKERT, GEORGE CARL — D. FEBRUARY 18, 1977 BURLINGTON, IA.
73-134 ZAHN, GEOFFREY CLAYTON — 17931 RIVER CIRCLE #1 - CANYON COUNTRY CA 91351
23-149 ZAHNISER, PAUL VERNON — D. SEPTEMBER 26, 1964 KLAMATH FALLS, ORE.
44-151 ZAK, FRANK THOMAS — D. FEBRUARY 6, 1972 PASSAIC, N.J.
13-201 ZAMLOCH, CARL EUGENE — D. AUGUST 19, 1963 SANTA BARBARA, CALIF.
74-144 ZAMORA, OSCAR JOSE — OLD ADD: 2201 BRICKELL AVE #82 - MIAMI FL 33129
58-107 ZANNI, DOMINICK THOMAS — 7 SUSSEX AVE NORTH - MASSAPEQUA NY 11758
33- 70 ZAPUSTAS, JOSEPH JOHN — 16 VESEY RD - RANDOLPH MA 02368
45-123 ZARDON, JOSE ANTONIO SANCHEZ — 13721 SW 45TH TERRACE - MIAMI FL 33175
43-147 ZARILLA, ALLEN LEE 'ZEKE' — 431 NAHUA ST #705 - HONOLULU HI 96815
84-132 ZASKE, LLOYD JEFFREY 'JEFF' — 16731 68TH AVE WEST - LYNNWOOD WA 98037
51-109 ZAUCHIN, NORBERT HENRY 'NORM' — 818 NORTH MONTEZ DR - THOMAS ACRES AL 35020
77-160 ZDEB, JOSEPH EDWARD — 107 ARLINGTON DRIVE - BARRINGTON IL 60010
77-161 ZEBER, GEORGE WILLIAM — 9722 RAVENSCROFT RD - SANTA ANA CA 92705
10-153 ZEIDER, ROLLIE HUBERT — D. SEPTEMBER 12, 1967 AUBURN, IND.
14-242 ZEISER, MATTHEW J. — D. JUNE 10, 1942 NORWOOD PARK, ILL.
70-142 ZELLER, BARTON WALLACE — 5112 IMPERIAL DR - RICHTON PARK IL 60471
69-186 ZEPP, WILLIAM CLINTON — 35430 BROOKVIEW DR - LIVONIA MI 48152
49- 92 ZERNIAL, GUS EDWARD — 474 EAST ALLUVIAL #123 - FRESNO CA 93710
54-120 ZICK, ROBERT GEORGE — 14960 SOUTH PULASKI - MIDLOTHIAN IL 60445
87-155 ZIEM, STEVEN GRAELING — 663 SOUTH 22ND STREET - BANNING CA 92220
41-120 ZIENTARA, BENEDICT JOSEPH — D. APRIL 16, 1985 LAKE ELSINORE, CALIF.
54-121 ZIMMER, DONALD WILLIAM — 10124 YACHT CLUB DR - ST PETERSBURG FL 33706
61-113 ZIMMERMAN, GERALD ROBERT — 13650 FERNRIDGE - MILWAUKIE OR 97222
45-124 ZIMMERMAN, ROY FRANKLIN — 24 NORTH ST - TREMONT PA 17981
15-180 ZIMMERMAN, WILLIAM H. — D. OCTOBER 4, 1952 NEWARK, N.J.
21-119 ZINK, WALTER NOBLE — D. JUNE 12, 1964 QUINCY, MASS.
11-188 ZINN, GUY — D. OCTOBER 6, 1949 CLARKSBURG, W. VA.
19- 97 ZINN, JAMES EDWARD — 5614 APPLEWOOD DR - NORTH LITTLE ROCK AR72118
44-152 ZINSER, WILLIAM FREDERICK — 8834 ROYAL HEIGHTS DR - CINCINNATI OH 45239
61-114 ZIPFEL, MARION SYLVESTER 'BUD' — 57 WHITESIDE DR - BELLEVILLE IL 62221
71-113 ZISK, RICHARD WALTER — OLD ADD: 1411 MEADOWLARK DR - PITTSBURGH PA 15243
19- 98 ZITZMANN, WILLIAM ARTHUR — D. MAY 29, 1985 PASSAIC, N. J.
10-154 ZMICH, EDWARD ALBERT — D. AUGUST 20, 1950 CLEVELAND, O.
44-153 ZOLDAK, SAMUEL WALTER — D. AUGUST 25, 1966 MINEOLA, N. Y.
36-100 ZUBER, WILLIAM HENRY — D. NOVEMBER 2, 1982 CEDAR RAPIDS, IA.
57- 97 ZUPO, FRANK JOSEPH — 2824 MARIPOSA DR - BURLINGAME CA 94010
82-142 ZUVELLA, PAUL — 1396 LASSEN AVE - MILPITAS CA 95305
51-110 ZUVERINK, GEORGE — 1721 ELLIS DR - TEMPE AZ 85282
10-155 ZWILLING, EDWARD HARRISON 'DUTCH' — D. MARCH 27, 1978 LA CRESCENTA, CALIF.

DON ZIMMER
Cincinnati Reds

Bill Zuber's Dugout Restaurant Homestead, Iowa

149

UMPIRES DEBUTING FROM 1910 TO 1987

U14- 1 ANDERSON, OLIVER O	D. JULY 7, 1945 LOS ANGELES, CALIF.
U70- 1 ANTHONY, GEORGE MERLYN	OLD ADD: 2361 WILMPALA ST - MESA AZ 85203
U66- 1 ASHFORD, EMMETT LITTLETON	D. MARCH 1, 1980 MARINA DEL REY, CALIF.
U69- 1 AVANTS, NICK R	5805 WOODLAWN - LITTLE ROCK AR 72205
U36- 1 BALLANFANT, EDWARD LEE	D. JULY 15, 1987 DALLAS, TEXAS
U40- 1 BARLICK, ALBERT JOSEPH	RR 2 - RIVERTON IL 62561
U68- 1 BARNETT, LAWRENCE ROBERT	6464 HUGHES RD - PROSPECT OH 43342
U31- 1 BARR, GEORGE MCKINLEY	D. JULY 26, 1974 SULPHUR, OKLA.
U28- 1 BARRY, DANIEL	D.
U36- 2 BASIL, STEPHEN JOHN	D. JUNE 24, 1962 GILCHRIST, TEX.
U42- 1 BERRY, CHARLES FRANCIS	PLAYER DEBUT 1925
U76- 1 BETCHER, RALPH	153 PARKFEL AVE - PITTSBURGH PA 15237
U22- 4 BIERHALTER	
U70- 2 BLANDFORD, FRED	1123 CHARLES ST - ELMIRA NY 14904
U44- 1 BOGGESS, LYNTON ROSS 'DUSTY'	D. JULY 8, 1968 DALLAS, TEX.
U85- 1 BONIN, GREGORY	101 PROVIDENCE COURT - LAFAYETTE LA 70506
U44- 2 BOYER, JAMES MURRY	D. JULY 25, 1959 FINKSBURG, MD.
U17- 1 BRANSFIELD, WILLIAM EDWARD 'KITTY'	D. MAY 1, 1947 WORCESTER, MASS.
U74- 1 BREMIGAN, NICHOLAS GREGORY	1303 BUCKINGHAM ROAD - GARLAND TX 75040
U15- 1 BREWER,	
U73- 1 BRINKMAN, JOSEPH NORBERT	1021 INDIAN RIVER DRIVE - COCOA FL 32922
U79- 1 BROCKLANDER, FRED WILLIAM	123-40 83RD AVE #10J - KEW GARDENS NY 11415
U57- 1 BURKHART, WILLIAM KENNETH 'KEN'	PLAYER DEBUT 1945
U11- 1 BUSH, GARNET C.	D. DECEMBER 30, 1919 ST. LOUIS, MO.
U13- 1 BYRON, WILLIAM J. 'LORD'	D. DECEMBER 27, 1955 YPSILANTI, MICH.
U28- 2 CAMPBELL, WILLIAM M	OLD ADD: 676 SOUTH BELVEDERE - MEMPHIS TN
U61- 1 CARRIGAN, HERVE SAMUEL 'SAM'	OLD ADD: 651 MCKINSTRY AVE - CHICOPEE FALLS MA 01020
U14- 2 CHILL, OLIVER P. 'OLLIE'	OLD ADD: MAJESTIC HOTEL - KANSAS CITY MO
U54- 1 CHYLAK, NESTOR	D. FEBRUARY 17, 1982 DUNMORE, PA.
U76- 2 CLARK, ALAN MARSHALL	16 INDEPENDENCE PL - NEWTOWN PA 18940
U30- 1 CLARKE, ROBERT M	
U82- 1 COBLE, GEORGE DREW	RR 3 BOX 368 - GRAHAM NC 27253
U15- 2 COCKILL, GEORGE W	D. NOVEMBER 2, 1937 STEELTOWN, PA.
U76- 3 COHEN, ALFRED	1026 NORTH HIGHLAND AVE - PITTSBURGH PA 15206
U10- 1 COLLIFLOWER, JAMES HARRY	D. AUGUST 14, 1961 WASHINGTON, D. C.
U68- 2 COLOSI, NICHOLAS	68-17 54TH AVE - MASPETH NY 11378
U41- 1 CONLAN, JOHN BERTRAND 'JOCKO'	PLAYER DEBUT 1934
U75- 1 COONEY, TERRANCE JOSEPH	4860 N. WOODROW #101 - FRESNO CA 93726
U14- 3 CORCORAN, THOMAS WILLIAM	D. JUNE 25, 1960 PLAINFIELD, CONN.
U83- 1 COSTELLO, PERRY	901 WEST BARNES - LANSING MI 48910
U79- 2 COUSINS, DERRYL	702 4TH STREET - HERMOSA BEACH CA 90254
U76- 4 CRAWFORD, GERALD JOSEPH	1 PINZON AVE - HAVERTOWN PA 19083
U56- 1 CRAWFORD, HENRY CHARLES 'SHAG'	1530 VIRGINIA AVE - HAVERTOWN PA 19083
U14- 4 CROSS, MONTFORD MONTGOMERY	D. JUNE 21, 1934 PHILADELPHIA, PA.
U71- 1 DALE, JERRY PARKER	428 W. HUNTINGTON SR #4 - ARCADIA CA 91006
U86- 1 DARLING, GARY R	2003 EAST BALBOA - TEMPE AZ 85282
U48- 1 DASCOLI, FRANK	BOX 75 - DANIELSON CT 06239
U69- 2 DAVIDSON, DAVID LEROY 'SATCH'	2400 WESTHEIMER ST #209W - HOUSTON TX 77098
U82- 2 DAVIDSON, ROBERT ALLAN	2405 TRAILS END - ALTOONA IA 50009
U83- 2 DAVIS, GERALD	616 CAMELLIA LN - APPLETON WI 54915
U70- 3 DEEGAN, WILLIAM EDWARD JOHN	2745 SURREY LANE - ESCONDIDO CA 92025
U56- 2 DELMORE, VICTOR	D. JUNE 10, 1960 SCRANTON, PA.
U83- 3 DEMUTH, DANA ANDREW	8388 VIA AIROSA - RANCHO CUCAMONGA CA 91730
U69- 3 DENKINGER, DONALD ANTON	3322 DORAL DRIVE - WATERLOO IA 50701
U66- 2 DEZELAN, FRANK JOHN	1314 WOOD ST - PITTSBURGH PA 15221
U63- 1 DIMURO, LOUIS JOHN	D. JUNE 7, 1982 ARLINGTON, TEX.
U53- 1 DIXON, HAL HAYWORTH	D. JULY 28, 1966 CHURNEE, S.C.
U50- 1 DONATELLI, AUGUST JOSEPH	4681 FIRST ST NE - ST PETERSBURG FL 33703
U31- 2 DONNELLY, CHARLES H	D. DECEMBER 13, 1968 LAKE WORTH, FLA.
U30- 2 DONOHUE, MICHAEL R	D. AUGUST 7, 1968 ST. LOUIS, MO.
U11- 2 DOYLE, JOHN JOSEPH 'DIRTY JACK'	D. DECEMBER 31, 1958 HOLYOKE, MASS.
U63- 2 DOYLE, WALTER JAMES	OLD ADD: 3314 HENDERSON BLVD - TAMPA FL 33609
U60- 1 DRUMMOND, CALVIN TROY	D. MAY 2, 1970 DES MOINES, IOWA
U51- 1 DUFFY, JAMES FRANCIS	165 2ND ST - PAWTUCKET RI 02861
U39- 1 DUNN, THOMAS PATRICK	D. JANUARY 20, 1976 PRINCE GEORGES CO., MD.
U14- 5 ELDRIDGE, CLARENCE E	
U65- 1 ENGEL, ROBERT ALLEN	3500 HARMONY LN - BAKERSFILED CA 93306
U52- 1 ENGELN, WILLIAM RAYMOND	D. APRIL 17, 1968 PALO ALTO, CALIF.
U72- 1 EVANS, JAMES BREMOND	1801 ROGGE LANE - AUSTIN TX 78723
U13- 2 FERGUSON, CHARLES AUGUSTUS	D. MAY 17, 1931 SAULT SAINTE MARIE, MICH.
J79- 3 FIELDS, STEPHEN HAROLD	216 EAST GLENDALE #2 - ALEXANDRIA VA 22301
U11- 3 FINNERAN, WILLIAM F	D. JULY 30, 1961 ERIE, PA.
U79- 4 FITZPATRICK, MICHAEL	262 LODGE LANE - KALAMAZOO MI 49009
U53- 2 FLAHERTY, JOHN FRANCIS 'RED'	9 FOWLER LN - FALMOUTH MA 02540
U75- 2 FORD, ROBERT DALE	RR 7 BOX 222 - JONESBORO TN 37659
U61- 2 FORMAN, ALLEN SANFORD	61 WASHINGTON AVE - MORRISTOWN NJ 07960
U69- 4 FRANTZ, ARTHUR FRANK	OLD ADD: 276 LYCEUM ST - ROCHESTER NY
U11- 4 FRARY, RALPH	D. NOVEMBER 10, 1925 ABERDEEN, WASH.
U20- 1 FRIEL, WILLIAM EDWARD	D. DECEMBER 24, 1959 ST. LOUIS, MO.
U71- 2 FROEMMING, BRUCE NEAL	5045 ELK CT - MILWAUKEE WI 53223
U52- 2 FROESE, GROVER A	D. JULY 20, 1982 BAY SHORE NY
U15- 3 FYFE, LOUIS	
U75- 3 GARCIA, RICHARD RAUL	2633 FIRESTONE DR - CLEARWATER FL 33519
U25- 1 GEISEL, HARRY CHRISTIAN	D. FEBRUARY 20, 1966 INDIANAPOLIS, IND.
U14- 6 GOECKEL, E	
U36- 3 GOETZ, LAWRENCE JOHN	D. OCTOBER 31, 1962 CINCINNATI, O.
U68- 3 GOETZ, RUSSELL LOUIS	1010 VERMONT ST - GLASSPORT PA 15045
U46- 1 GORE, ARTHUR JOSEPH 'ARTIE'	D. SEPTEMBER 29, 1986 WOLFEBORO, N. H.
U51- 2 GORMAN, THOMAS DAVID	PLAYER DEBUT 1939
U77- 1 GREGG, ERIC EUGENE	2635 MIMI CIR - PHILADELPHIA PA 19131
U38- 1 GRIEVE, WILLIAM TURNER	D. AUGUST 17, 1979 YONKERS, N. Y.
U70- 4 GRIMSLEY, JOHN WILLIAM	204 RAVENWOOD DR - GREENVILLE NC 27834
U83- 4 GRINDER, SCOTT	128 NORTH VIEW DR - ZELIONOPLE PA 16063
U14- 7 GROOM, ROBERT	D. FEBRUARY 19, 1948 BELLEVILLE, ILL.
U70- 5 GRYGIEL, GEORGE R.	7620 EAST LINDEN STREET - TUCSON AZ 85715
U76- 5 GUCKERT, ELMER	590 CRANE AVE - PITTSBURGH PA 15216
U52- 3 GUGLIELMO, ANGELO AUGIE	183 JERSEY ST - WATERBURY CT 06706

U13- 3 GUTHRIE, WILLIAM J	D. MARCH 6, 1950 CHICAGO, ILL
U61- 3 HALLER, WILLIAM EDWARD	2013 SOUTH LAKE DR - VANDALIA IL 62471
U85- 2 HALLION, THOMAS FRANCIS	246 ST. MATTHEWS AVENUE - LOUISVILLE KY 40207
U79- 5 HARRIS, LANNY DEAN	3313 COLLEGE CORNER RD - RICHMOND IN 47374
U16- 1 HARRISON, PETER A	D. MARCH 9, 1921 SARANAC LAKE, N. Y.
U12- 1 HART, EUGENE F	D. MAY 10, 1937 LOWELL MASS.
U62- 1 HARVEY, HARVEY DOUGLAS	10231 VERA CRUZ CT - SAN DIEGO CA 92124
U77- 2 HENDRY, EUGENE 'TED'	2709 EAST SHAW BUTTE DR - PHOENIX AZ 85028
U45- 1 HENLINE, WALTER JOHN 'BUTCH'	PLAYER DEBUT 1921
U12- 2 HILDEBRAND, GEORGE ALBERT	D. MAY 30, 1960 WOODLAND HILLS, CALIF.
U83- 5 HIRSCHBECK, JOHN FRANCIS	8465 HILLTOP DR - POLAND OH 44514
U23- 1 HOLMES, HOWARD ELBERT 'DUCKY'	D. SEPTEMBER 18, 1945 DAYTON, O.
U49- 1 HONOCHICK, GEORGE JAMES 'JIM'	10 SOUTH OTT ST - ALLENTOWN PA 18104
U15- 4 HOWELL, HENRY 'HANDSOME HARRY'	D. MAY 22, 1956 SPOKANE, WASH.
U22- 5 HOWLEY	
U36- 4 HUBBARD, ROBERT CAL	D. OCTOBER 16, 1977 ST PETERSBURG, FLA.
U83- 6 HUMPHREY, RICHARD	1476 BROWNLEAF DR - RICHMOND VA 23225
U47- 1 HURLEY, EDWIN HENRY	D. NOVEMBER 12, 1969 BOSTON, MASS.
U12- 3 HYATT, ROBERT HAMILTON 'HAM'	D. SEPTEMBER 11, 1963 LIBERTY LAKE, WASH.
U52- 4 JACKOWSKI, WILLIAM ANTHONY	64 CHURCH ST - NORTH WALPOLE NH 03608
U14- 8 JOHNSON, HARRY S	D. FEBRUARY 20, 1951 MEMPHIS, TENN.
U84- 1 JOHNSON, MARK STEPHEN	666 PROSPECT ROAD - HONOLULU HI 96813
U36- 5 JOHNSTON, CHARLES EDWARD	D.
U44- 3 JONES, NICHOLAS ITTNER 'RED'	D. MARCH 19, 1987 MIAMI, FLA.
U27- 1 JORDA, LOUIS DE LAROND	D. MAY 27, 1964 LARGO, FLA.
U77- 3 KAISER, KENNETH JOHN	123 NORTHWOOD DR - ROCHESTER NY 14616
U10- 2 KECHER, W. H.	
U63- 3 KIBLER, JOHN WILLIAM	3046 SONIA CT - OCEANSIDE CA 92056
U60- 2 KINNAMON, WILLIAM ERVIN	8240 BRENTWOOD RD - LARGO FL 33543
U33- 1 KOLLS, LOUIS CHARLES	D. FEBRUARY 23, 1941 HOOPPOLE, ILL.
U76- 6 KOSC, GREGORY JOHN	3900 FERN ROAD - MEDINA OH 44256
U68- 4 KUNKEL, WILLIAM GUSTAVE JAMES	PLAYER DEBUT 1961
U55- 1 LANDES, STANLEY ALBERT	OLD ADD: BOX 9608 - PHOENIX AZ
U15- 5 LANGEVIN, JOSEPH	D. MARCH 18, 1953 BINGHAMTON, N. Y.
U79- 6 LAWSON, WILLIAM	7228 EAST EASTVIEW DR - TUCSON AZ 85710
U85- 3 LEPPERD, THOMAS	7713 OLTIS CIR - URBANDALE IA 50322
U14- 9 LINCOLN, FREDERICK H	
U61- 4 LINSALATA, JOSEPH N	4017 WASHINGTON ST - HOLLYWOOD FL 33021
U69- 5 LUCIANO, RONALD MICHAEL	105 BADGER AVE - ENDICOTT NY 13760
U28- 2 MAGEE, SHERWOOD ROBERT 'SHERRY'	D. MARCH 13, 1929 PHILADELPHIA, PA.
U29- 1 MAGERKURTH, GEORGE LEVI 'MAJOR'	D. OCTOBER 7, 1966 ROCK ISLAND, ILL.
U70- 6 MALONEY, GEORGE PATRICK	3745 NE 171ST ST #60 - NORTH MIAMI FL 33160
U35- 1 MARBERRY, FRED 'FIRPO'	PLAYER DEBUT 1923
U82- 3 MARSH, RANDALL GILBERT	3271 MADONNA DR - COVINGTON KY 41017
U14-10 MAXWELL, JAMES ALBERT 'BERT'	D. DECEMBER 10, 1961 BRADY, TEX.
U83- 7 MCCLELLAND, TIMOTHY REID	5405 WOODLAND AVENUE - WEST DES MOINES IA 50265
U14-11 MCCORMICK, WILLIAM J. 'BARRY'	D. JANUARY 28, 1956 CINCINNATI, O.
U71- 3 MCCOY, LARRY SANDERS	RR 1 - GREENWAY AR 72430
U10- 3 MCGINNIS,	
U25- 2 MCGOWAN, WILLIAM ALOYSIUS	D. DECEMBER 9, 1954 SILVER SPRING, MD.
U12- 4 MCGREEVY, EDWARD	
U30- 3 MCGREW, HARRY HANCOCK 'TED'	D. JUNE 29, 1969 BEDFORD, VA
U74- 2 MCKEAN, JAMES GILBERT	4601 DOVER ST NE - ST PETERSBURG FL 33703
U46- 2 MCKINLEY, WILLIAM FRANCIS	D. AUGUST 1, 1980 MOUNT PLEASANT, PA.
U29- 2 MCLAUGHLIN, EDWARD J	D. NOVEMBER 28, 1965 PHILADELPHIA, PA.
U24- 1 MCLAUGHLIN, PETER J	OLD ADD: 99 POPLAR ST - WATERTOWN MA
U71- 4 MCSHERRY, JOHN PATRICK	10933 GRAND FORK DR - SANTEE CA 92071
U77- 4 MERRILL, EDWIN DURWOOD	BOX 115 - HOOKS TX 75561
U76- 7 MONTAGUE, EDWARD MICHAEL	2047 KINGS LN - SAN MATEO CA 94402
U17- 2 MORAN, CHARLES BARTHEL	D. JUNE 13, 1949 HORSE CAVE, KY.
U70- 7 MORGENWECK, HENRY CHARLES	33 BOGERT ST - TEANECK NJ 07666
U17- 3 MORIARTY, GEORGE JOSEPH	D. APRIL 8, 1964 MIAMI, FLA.
U84- 2 MORRISON, DAN G.	9223 122ND WAY NORTH - SEMINOLE FL 33542
U15- 6 MULLANEY, DOMINIC J	D. AUGUST 21, 1964 JACKSONVILLE, FLA.
U14-12 MURRAY, J. A.	OLD ADD: 95 MALCOLM ST - MINNEAPOLIS MN
U15- 7 NALLIN, RICHARD F	D. SEPTEMBER 7, 1956 FREDERICK, MD.
U51- 3 NAPP, LARRY ALBERT	200 NW BEL AIR DR - FORT LAUDERDALE FL 33314
U79- 7 NELSON, RICHARD	RR 2 BOX 129E - PERRYVILLE AR 72126
U66- 3 NEUDECKER, JEROME A	700 BRIAN CIR - MARY ESTHER FL 32569
U22- 1 O'SULLIVAN, JOHN J	
U12- 5 OBRIEN, JOSEPH	D. NOVEMBER 5, 1925 TROY, N. Y.
U14-13 OCONNOR, ARTHUR	
U64- 1 ODOM, JAMES CECIL	304 KING ST - BENNETTSVILLE SC 29512
U68- 5 ODONNELL, JAMES MICHAEL	OLD ADD: 204 NORTH DIAMOND ST - CLIFTON HEIGHTS PA
U15- 8 OHARA,	
U68- 6 OLSEN, ANDREW HOLGER	451 93RD AVE NORTH - ST PETERSBURG FL 33702
U23- 2 ORMSBY, EMMETT T. 'RED'	D. OCTOBER 11, 1962 CHICAGO, ILL.
U77- 5 PALERMO, STEPHEN MICHAEL	10540 WASHINGTON STREET - KANSAS CITY MO 64114
U79- 8 PALLONE, DAVID MICHAEL	1265 YORK AVENUE #37L - NEW YORK NY 10021
U46- 3 PAPARELLA, JOSEPH JAMES	RR 1, CRYSTAL LAKE - CARBONDALE PA 18407
U36- 6 PARKER, GEORGE LAMBACH	OLD ADD: 18320 NE 20TH PL-NORTH MIAMI BEACH FL
U11- 5 PARKER, HARLEY P	
U79- 9 PARKS, DALLAS FINNEY	5540 SHADY CREEK CT #23 - LINCOLN NE 68516
U41- 2 PASSARELLA, ARTHUR MATTHEW	D. OCTOBER 12, 1981 HEMET, CALIF.
U60- 3 PELEKOUDAS, CHRISTOS GEORGE	D. NOVEMBER 30, 1984 SUNNYVALE, CALIF.
U22- 2 PFIRMAN, CHARLES H. 'CY'	D. MAY 16, 1937 NEW ORLEANS, LA.
U12- 6 PHELPS, EDWARD JAYKILL	D. JANUARY 31, 1942 EAST GREENBUSH, N. Y.
U71- 5 PHILLIPS, DAVID ROBERT	29 HOLLOWAY DRIVE - LAKE ST. LOUIS MO 63367
U35- 2 PINELLI, RALPH ARTHUR 'BABE'	PLAYER DEBUT 1918
U38- 2 PIPGRAS, GEORGE WILLIAM	PLAYER DEBUT 1923
U85- 4 PONCINO, LARRY L	242 CABRILLO #G - SAN CLEMENTE CA 92672
U23- 3 POWELL, CORNELIUS JOSEPH	D. JULY 25, 1971 LYNWOOD, CALIF.
U61- 5 PRYOR, JOHN PAUL	1088 45TH AVE NE - ST PETERSBURG FL 33703
U72- 2 PULLI, FRANK VICTOR	4898 CARDINAL TRAIL - PALM HARBOR FL 33563
U76- 8 PUSKARIC, JOSEPH	429 35TH AVE - MCKEESPORT PA 15132
U76- 9 QUICK, JAMES EDWARD	P.O. BOX 6538 - INCLINE VILLAGE NV 89450
U35- 3 QUINN, JOHN ALOYSIUS	D. JULY 4, 1968 PHILADELPHIA, PA.
U14-14 QUISSER, ARTHUR	
U26- 1 REARDON, JOHN EDWARD 'BEANS'	D. JULY 31, 1984 LONG BEACH, CALIF.

U79-10	REED, RICK ALAN	6190 BLUEHILL - DETROIT MI 48224
U77- 6	REILLY, MICHAEL EUGENE	44 LAKESIDE DR - BATTLE CREEK MI 49015
U73- 2	RENNERT, LAURENCE HENRY 'DUTCH'	306 NORTH LARK ST - OSHKOSH WI 54901
U55- 2	RICE, JOHN LA CLAIRE	2666 EAST 73RD ST #A12W - CHICAGO IL 60649
U83- 8	RIPPLEY, THOMAS STEVEN 'STEVE'	11505 7TH WAY NORTH #2308 - ST. PETERSBURG FL 33702
U47- 2	ROBB, DOUGLAS W. 'SCOTTY'	D. APRIL 10, 1969 MONTCLAIR, N.J.
U53- 3	ROBERTS, LEONARD WYATT	OLD ADD: 5505 SPRUCE VIEW - DALLAS TX 75232
U74- 3	RODRIGUEZ, ARMANDO HUMBERTO	OLD ADD: INDEPENCIA 1375 - VERACRUZ VERACRUZ MEXICO
U80- 1	ROE, JOHN 'ROCKY'	2846 TAMWOOD CT - MILFORD MI 48042
U38- 3	ROMMEL, EDWIN AMERICUS	PLAYER DEBUT 1920
U23- 4	ROWLAND, CLARENCE HENRY 'PANTS'	D. MAY 17, 1969 CHICAGO, ILL.
U38- 4	RUE, JOSEPH WILLIAM	D. DECEMBER 1, 1984 LAGUNA HILLS, CALIF.
U54- 2	RUNGE, EDWARD PAUL	4949 CRESITA DR - SAN DIEGO CA 92115
U72- 3	RUNGE, PAUL EDWARD	649 CALLE DE LA SIERRA - EL CAJON CA 92021
U62- 2	SALERNO, ALEX JOSEPH	1913 TILDEN AVE - NEW HARTFORD NY 13413
U70- 8	SATCHELL, DAROLD L	OLD ADD: 1613 NORTH DUKE ST - DURHAM NC 27701
U60- 4	SCHWARTS, HARRY CLARK	D. FEBRUARY 22, 1963 CLEVELAND, O.
U85- 5	SCOTT, DALE ALLAN	0542 SW CALIFORNIA - PORTLAND OR 97219
U30- 4	SCOTT, JAMES 'DEATH VALLEY JIM'	D. APRIL 7, 1957 PALM SPRINGS, CALIF.
U34- 1	SEARS, JOHN WILLIAM 'ZIGGY'	D. DECEMBER 16, 1956 HOUSTON, TEX.
U52- 5	SECORY, FRANK EDWARD	PLAYER DEBUT 1940
U14-15	SHANNON, WILLIAM PORTER 'SPIKE'	D. MAY 16, 1940 MINNEAPOLIS, MINN.
U79-11	SHULOCK, JOHN RICHARD	445 38TH SQUARE SW - VERO BEACH FL 32962
U57- 2	SMITH, VINCENT AMBROSE	PLAYER DEBUT 1941
U60- 5	SMITH, WILLIAM ALARIC 'AL'	609 DELHI ST - BOSSIER CITY LA 71111
U50- 2	SOAR, ALBERT HENRY 'HANK'	60 CONCH RD - NARRAGANSETT RI 02882
U77- 7	SPENN, FREDERICK CHARLES	81 VILLAGE BLVD - BRADENTON FL 33507
U66- 4	SPRINGSTEAD, MARTIN JOHN	5 BRUCE CT - SUFFERN NY 10901
U28- 3	STARK, ALBERT D. 'DOLLY'	D. AUGUST 24, 1968 NEW YORK, N.Y.
U61- 6	STEINER, MELVIN JAMES	1701 HARBOR WAY - SEAL BEACH CA 90740
U68- 7	STELLO, RICHARD JACK	D. NOVEMBER 18, 1987 LAKELAND, FLA.
U48- 2	STEVENS, JOHN WILLIAM	D. SEPTEMBER 9, 1981 PHILADELPHIA PA.
U41- 3	STEWART, ERNEST DRAPER	107 SAN MARCOS - DEL RIO TX 78840
U59- 1	STEWART, ROBERT WILLIAM	D. 1982 WOONSOCKET RI
U33- 2	STEWART, WILLIAM JOSEPH	D. FEBRUARY 18, 1964 JAMAICA PLAIN, MASS.
U15- 9	STOCKDALE, M. J.	OLD ADD: 314 WEST 42ND ST - NEW YORK NY
U57- 3	SUDOL, EDWARD LAWRENCE	415 REVILO BLVD - DAYTONA BEACH FL 32014
U33- 3	SUMMERS, WILLIAM REED	D. SEPTEMBER 12, 1966 UPTON, MASS.
U24- 2	SWEENEY, JAMES M	D. JANUARY 29, 1950 TYLER, TEX.
U56- 3	TABACCHI, FRANK TULE	D. OCTOBER 26, 1983 HOBOKEN, N. J.
U73- 3	TATA, TERRY ANTHONY	8 PROMONTORY DR - CHESHIRE CT 06410
U70- 9	TREMBLAY, RICHARD HENRY	RR 2 - WHITEFIELD NH 03598
U85- 6	TSCHIDA, TIMOTHY J.	2296 BENSON AVENUE - ST. PAUL MN 55116
U54- 3	UMONT, FRANK WILLIAM	2116 NE 63RD CT - FORT LAUDERDALE FL 33308
U63- 4	VALENTINE, WILLIAM TERRY	BOX 5599 - LITTLE ROCK AR 72215
U27- 2	VAN GRAFLAN, ROY	D. SEPTEMBER 4, 1953 ROCHESTER, N. Y.
U14-16	VAN SICKLE, CHARLES F	D. 1950
U60- 6	VARGO, EDWARD PAUL	101 FREEDOM RD - BUTLER PA 16001
U57- 4	VENZON, ANTHONY	D. SEPTEMBER 20, 1971 PITTSBURGH PA
U77- 8	VOLTAGGIO, VITO HENRY 'VIC'	646 BRENTWOOD DR - VINELAND NJ 08360
U22- 3	WALSH, EDWARD AUGUSTIN 'BIG ED'	D. MAY 26, 1959 POMPANO BEACH, FLA.
U61- 7	WALSH, FRANCIS D.	D. 1985 SAN ANTONIO, TEX.
U49- 2	WARNEKE, LONNIE	PLAYER DEBUT 1930
U43- 1	WEAFER, HAROLD LEON	7726 GRANITE HALL AVE - RICHMOND VA 23225
U83- 9	WELKE, TIMOTHY JAMES	5843 THUNDER BAY - KALAMAZOO MI 49002
U66- 5	WENDELSTEDT, HARRY HUNTER	88 SOUTH ST ANDREWS - ORMOND BEACH FL 32074
U76-10	WEST, JOSEPH HENRY	114 NORTH EASTERN ST - GREENVILLE NC 27834
U11- 6	WESTERVELT, FREDERICK E	D. MAY 4, 1955 DREXEL HILL, PA.
U61- 8	WEYER, LEE HOWARD	D. JULY 4, 1988 SAN MATEO, CALIF.
U63- 5	WILLIAMS WILLIAM GEORGE	RR 2 BOX 822 #O-29 - POMPANO BEACH FL 33067
U72- 4	WILLIAMS, ARTHUR	D. FEBRUARY 8, 1979 BAKERSFIELD, CALIF.
U78- 1	WILLIAMS, CHARLES HERMAN	5020 SOUTH LAKE DR #1715 - CHICAGO IL 60615
U21- 1	WILSON, FRANK	D. JUNE, 1928 BROOKLYN, N. Y.
U83-10	YOUNG, LARRY EUGENE	3538 SHADY BLUFF DRIVE - LARGO FL 33540

COACHES WITH NO MAJOR LEAGUE PLAYING OR MANAGERIAL EXPERIENCE DEBUTING FROM 1910 TO 1987

C67- 1	BERINGER, CARROLL JAMES 'C.B.'	4917 GRANITE SHOALS - FORT WORTH TX 76103
C64- 1	BLACKBURN, WAYNE CLARK	1414 OFFNERE ST - PORTSMOUTH OH 45662
C74- 1	BLOOMFIELD, GORDON LEIGH 'JACK'	1310 IRIS - MCALLEN TX 78501
C67- 2	BRAGAN, JAMES ALTON	1059 MARTINWOOD LN - BIRMINGHAM AL 35235
C86- 1	BREEDEN, HAROLD SCOTT	6619 BAYBROOKS CIR - TEMPLE TERRACE FL 33617
C69- 1	CAMACHO, JOSEPH GOMES	48 MASSASOIT AVE - FAIRHAVEN MA 02719
C70- 1	CARNEVALE, DANIEL JOSEPH	161 DORCHESTER RD - BUFFALO NY 14213
C59- 1	CARTER, RICHARD JOSEPH	D. SEPTEMBER 11, 1969 PHILADELPHIA, PA.
C77- 1	CLEAR, ELWOOD ROBERT 'BOB'	120 EAST 234TH ST - CARSON CA 90745
C79- 2	CLUCK, ROBERT	6065 MISSION GORGE RD #91 - SAN DIEGO CA 92120
C85- 1	CONNOR, MARK P.	524 CIMARRON TRAIL - KNOXVILLE TN 37919
C77- 2	CRESSE, MARK EMERY	3840 GOLDENROD ST - SEAL BEACH CA 90740
C79- 1	DEWS, ROBERT WALTER	423 AUDUBON - ALBANY GA 31707
C80- 1	DONNELLY, RICHARD FRANCIS	156 BROCKTON ROAD - STEUBENVILLE OH 43952
C61- 1	DOUGLAS, OTIS W	HAGUE VA 22469
C69- 2	DUNLOP, HARRY ALEXANDER	7470 29TH ST - SACRAMENTO CA 95820
C83- 1	DUSAN, EUGENE	61174 CONCHO ST - BEND OR 97701
C83- 2	EZELL, GLENN WAYNE	1504 LAUREL DR - ARLINGTON TX 76012
C47- 1	FITZGERALD, JOSEPH PATRICK	D. AUGUST 29, 1967 ORLANDO, FLA.
C53- 1	FITZPATRICK, JOHN ARTHUR	1728 EAST COMMONWEALTH #102-FULLERTON CA 92631
C85- 2	GALANTE, MATTHEW JOSEPH	177 CROSSFIELD AVE - STATEN ISLAND NY 10312
C82- 1	HARMON, THOMAS HAROLD	6101 BON TERRA DRIVE - AUSTIN TX 78731
C84- 1	HINES, BENJAMIN	2709 SECOND ST - LAVERNE CA 91750
C84- 2	HOLMQUIST, DOUGLAS LEONARD	D. FEBRUARY 27, 1988 ALTAMONTE SPRINGS, FLA.
C48- 1	HOLT, GOLDEN DESMOND 'GOLDIE'	4937 STERN AVE - SHERMAN OAKS CA 91423
C68- 1	HOSCHEIT, VERNARD ARTHUR	BOX 36 - PLAINVIEW NE 68769
C55- 1	KAHN, LOUIS	P.O. BOX 4066 - MESA AZ 85201
C30- 1	KELLY, BERNARD FRANCIS	D. OCTOBER 23, 1968 INDIANAPOLIS, IND.
C69- 3	KISSELL GEORGE MARSHALL	658 MOUNT OAK AVENUE NE - ST. PETERSBURG FL 33702

C71- 1	KITTLE, HUBERT MILTON 'HUB'	3801 RICHEY ROAD - YAKIMA WA 98902
C70- 2	KOENIG, FRED CARL	6721 EAST 51ST ST - TULSA OK 74145
C57- 1	LEVY, LEONARD HOWARD	%J.SNELSON,324 COLTART ST-PITTSBURGH PA 15213
C84- 3	LEYVA, NICHOLAS	4407 STONEWOOD COURT - ST.LOUIS MO 63128
C51- 1	LOBE, WILLIAM CHARLES	D. JANUARY 7, 1969 CLEVELAND, O.
C72- 1	LOWE, Q. V.	1118 NE 31ST ST - OCALA FL 32670
C85- 3	MAZZONE, LEO DAVID	RURAL ROUTE 3 BOX 278 - RAWLINGS MD 21557
C51- 2	MCDONNELL, ROBERT 'MAJE'	7423 REVERE ST - PHILADELPHIA PA 19152
C86- 2	MCLAREN, JOHN LOWELL	1518 SEATLES DRIVE - SUGARLAND TX 77478
C85- 4	MERRILL, CARL HARRISON 'STUMP'	18 MERRYMEETING ROAD - TOPSHAM ME 04086
C77- 3	MOZZALI, MAURICE JOSEPH 'MO'	D. MARCH 2, 1987 LAKELAND, FLA.
C85- 5	MULL, JACK	1041 WILSON AVENUE - CHAMBERSBURG PA 17201
C83- 3	NAPOLEON, EDWARD G	1312 73RD ST NW - BRADENTON FL 33529
C83- 4	NOTTLE, EDWARD WILLIAM	6612 PINEHURST DR - EVANSVILLE IN 47711
C58- 1	OCEAK, FRANK JOHN	D. MARCH 19, 1983 JOHNSTOWN, PA.
C62- 1	ONEIL, JOHN B. 'BUCK'	3049 EAST 32ND ST - KANSAS CITY MO 64128
C63- 1	OSBORN, DONALD EDWIN	D. MARCH 23, 1979 TORRANCE, CALIF.
C74- 2	PACHECO, ANTONIO ARISTIDES 'TONY'	D. 1987 MIAMI, FLA.
C61- 2	PAEPKE, JACK	P.O. DRAWER 3039 - CRESTLINE CA 92325
C85- 6	PAVLICK, GREGORY MICHAEL	10136 SEMINOLE ISLE DR - SEMINOLE FL 33343
C84- 4	PETERSON, ERIC HARDING 'RICK'	P.O. BOX 1359 - BRADENTON FL 33506
C69- 4	PLAZA, RONALD EDWARD	2050 68TH AVE SOUTH - ST PETERSBURG FL 33712
C66- 1	RESINGER, GROVER S.	D. JANUARY 11, 1986 ST. LOUIS, MO.
C81- 1	REYES, BENJAMIN 'CANANEA'	MATAMOROS Y CACATECAS - HERMOSILLO SONORA MEX.
C87- 1	RIDDOCH, GREGORY LEE	1711 GLEN MEADOWS DRIVE - GREELEY CO 80631
C66- 2	ROBINSON, WARREN GRANT 'SHERIFF'	OLD ADD: 305 OAKLEY ST - CAMBRIDGE MD
C73- 1	ROSENBAUM, GLEN OTIS	BOX 1 - UNION MILLS IN 46382
C72- 2	ROWE, RALPH EMANUEL	4224 FIRWOOD LANE - CHARLOTTE NC 28209
C76- 2	SAUL, JAMES ALLEN	2405 OSBORNE ST - BRISTOL VA 23201
C70- 3	SCHERGER, GEORGE RICHARD	701 ST JULIEN - CHARLOTTE NC 28205
C87- 2	SLIDER, RACHEL W. 'RAC'	RURAL ROUTE 1 - DEKALB TX 75559
C84- 5	SMITH, BILLLY FRANKLIN	109 POTTER DRIVE - JAMESTOWN NC 27282
C85- 7	SNITKER, BRIAN GERALD	672 PEPPERWOOD TRAIL - STONE MOUNTAIN GA 30087
C77- 4	SOMMERS, DENNIS JAMES	210 WEST BATH - HORTONVILLE WI 54944
C79- 3	SPARKS, JOSEPH EVERETT	3915 EAST CHOLLA ST - PHOENIX AZ 85028
C22- 1	THOMAS, RAY	
C81- 2	VAN ORNUM, JOHN CLAYTON	6624 NORTH HAZEL ST - FRESNO CA 93711
C43- 1	VINCENT, ALBERT LINDER	260 MANOR AVE - BEAUMONT TX 77706
C61- 3	WALKER, VERLON LEE 'RUBE'	D. MARCH 24, 1971 CHICAGO, ILL.
C73- 2	WALTON, JAMES ROBERT	BOX 787 - SHATTUCK OK 73858
C77- 5	WARNER, HARRY CLINTON	106 BELFAIR - REEDERS PA 18352
C77- 6	WILLIAMS, DONALD ELLIS	205 FOXFIRE - PARAGOULD AR 72450
C81- 3	WILLIAMS, JAMES BERNARD	4 OLD SOUND ROAD - JOPPATOWNE MD 21085
C32- 1	WOLGAMOT, CLIFTON EARL	D. APRIL 25, 1970 INDEPENDENCE, IA.

GLOSSARY

The definitions presented in this glossary are definitions as they are interpreted by autograph collectors. For example, PHOTO refers to an autographed photo and HOFer refers to the autograph of a HOFer. Some of the definitions may appear self-explanatory and hence unnecessary; however, they are included for completeness.

ALL STAR BALL—A ball autographed by most or all members of a particular baseball all star game.

AUTOPEN—A mechanical device used to affix a signature on a document, letter or other paper medium. Autopen autographs are not considered collectible.

BALL POINT—A type of pen through which the ink is delivered by means of a revolving ball tip.

BASEBALL COMMEMORATIVE ENVELOPE—A stamped envelope postmarked on the date of a significant event in baseball history. The envelope contains some graphic or illustrative identification of the event. These envelopes autographed by a participant of the event are quite attractive and popular with autograph collectors. These envelopes should not be confused with first day covers popular with stamp collectors, although a hybrid first day cover/baseball commemorative envelope does exist. (This envelope contains the 1969 commemorative stamp of baseball's first hundred years and is cacheted with many different baseball superstars.)

CARD—A card autographed by the player portrayed on the card. Cards are normally autographed on the front; however, cards autographed on the back still qualify under this definition.

CHECK—A cancelled check or bank note containing the autograph of a ball player. Checks are quite often obtained from the estate of deceased ball players. Official ball club checks in many cases contain more than one autograph.

CLUB ISSUED POSTCARDS—Postcard size pictures of ball players, the older ones normally being in black and white with modern postcards being predominantly in color. They are usually blank backed, sold at ballparks and make excellent autograph media. Many players send autographed copies of these postcards to fans requesting autographs.

CONTRACT—A legal document, for any purpose, including agreements concerning players and management, equipment or other product manufacturers, or personal agreements signed by the sports personality.

CUT—An autograph that has been "cut" from a larger piece of paper, photo, letter or other written or printed matter.

DATED—An autograph which contains both the signature and the date when the signature was written.

DEBUT YEAR—The year in which a player first appeared in a game in the big leagues. For a manager or coach with no player experience the debut year refers to the year he first appeared as a manager or coach.

DEBUT YEAR NUMBER—Within a particular debut year the number for a player obtained by placing in alphabetical order all players who debuted that particular year and placing a number on each, from 1 to "the total number of players debuting that year," based on this alphabetical order.

FACSIMILE—A copy of an original signature. Facsimile autographs are not considered collectible.

FELT TIP—A type of pen which has a felt tip and which provides a smooth unbroken signature.

HOFer—The autograph of a member of baseball's Hall of Fame.

LETTER—A typed or handwritten communication with a heading listing to whom the letter is written and a closing autographed by a sports personality.

ORIGINAL ART—A unique drawing, painting or other piece of artwork portraying a personality or an event and bearing the signature of a partici- pant of the event or the personality portrayed.

PENCIL—A signature in pencil by a sports personality. Pencil signatures predominated during the early parts of this century and are sometimes the only types of signatures available of certain sports personalities. Care should be taken with pencil signatures as they smear quite easily.

PLACQUE—Postcard pictures of the bronzed placques of Hall of Fame base- ball players in the Baseball Hall of Fame in Cooperstown, NY. Through the years there have been several different color placques issued by the Hall of Fame, including black and white types.

PERSONALIZED—An autograph which contains a reference to the person for whom the autograph was written.

PHOTO—A glossy picture, normally 5" X 7" or 8" X l0," which contains an autograph of the player portrayed on the photo.

SASE—Self-addressed stamped envelope. When requesting autographs, SASE's should be sent to insure that returned autographs will be sent to the proper place and to provide the autograph giver a convenient means of returning autographed material.

SHARPIE—A brand of ink pen very popular with autograph collectors because of its broad stroke and its rapid drying characteristics on almost any surface.

STAMP—A signature affixed by means of a rubber or wooden device which contains a facsimile of the sports personality's autograph. Stamped signatures are not considered collectible.

TEAM BALL—A ball autographed by most or all members of a particular team.

TEAM SHEET—A single sheet of paper containing the autographs of most or all members of a particular team during a particular year. Many team sheets are on club stationery.

3 X 5—An index card, either lined or unlined, which many collectors use for obtaining autographs. The 3 X 5 refers to the approximate dimensions of the card. 3 X 5's usually contain only one signature.

Your Address for Hobby Fun!

You can't collect everything. Choices must be made. Topical collecting affords many 'hot' options for collectors.

'I went to a spring game and got Joe Carter's autograph. He scribbled on the back of the card to see if the pen worked.'